The Encyclopedia of
ANGELS

The Encyclopedia of
ANGELS
Second Edition

Rosemary Ellen Guiley, Ph.D.

Foreword by
Lisa J. Schwebel, Ph.D.

Facts On File, Inc.

The Encyclopedia of Angels, Second Edition

Facts On File, Inc.
132 West 31st Street
New York NY 10001

Library of Congress Cataloging-in-Publication Data

Guiley, Rosemary.
The encyclopedia of angels / Rosemary Ellen Guiley; foreword by Lisa Schwebel.—2nd Ed.
p. cm.
Includes bibliographical references and index.
ISBN 0-8160-5023-6 (alk. paper)
1. Angels—Dictionaries. I. Title.
BL477.G87 2003
202'.15'03—dc22   2003060147

Facts On File books are available at special discounts when purchased in bulk quantities for businesses, associations, institutions, or sales promotions. Please call our Special Sales Department in New York at (212) 967-8800 or (800) 322–8755.

You can find Facts On File on the World Wide Web at http://www.factsonfile.com

Text design by Erika K. Arroyo
Cover design by Semadar Megged

Printed in the United States of America

VB FOF 10 9 8 7 6 5 4 3 2 1

This book is printed on acid-free paper.

For Lynne Hertsgaard

CONTENTS

ACKNOWLEDGMENTS

My deepest appreciation goes to Joanne P. Austin, who was instrumental in researching and compiling portions of the first edition of this book.

FOREWORD

A huge fan of encyclopedias, I only recently updated the one-volume encyclopedia I have used since childhood (there is no entry for "particle accelerator" in the 1950s edition). It saw me through grade school, high school, several colleges, graduate school in Scotland, and back home again to a career as a teacher and writer. It has attended more family dinners than some members of my family and any number of bets have been settled by "going to the encyclopedia." For a while, encyclopedias seemed to go out of fashion. I could not understand this. Of course, some encyclopedias tell you too much about a subject, or presume you know more than you do, and so are more obfuscating than illuminating, but this is certainly not true of all of them. A good encyclopedia is still the best first line of information on just about any topic, and I wouldn't think of beginning a research project without checking the relevant encyclopedias. When students come by for help in getting started on a topic, I direct them to the set of encyclopedias in our main office, telling them to come back to me if they don't find anything. Mostly, they don't come back. In fact, it was while doing research for my doctoral dissertation on mysticism that I came upon Rosemary Ellen Guiley through her excellent *Encyclopedia of Mystical and Paranormal Experience*. I became an instant fan and collector of her work.

Rosemary Guiley epitomizes the qualities one hopes for in an encyclopedist. She takes a historical and phenomenological approach to her subject matter, reporting—in a neutral and nonjudgmental manner—what folklore, myth, and religion have to say about angels, about their significance, and about developments in thinking about them over time. Suitable for teenagers as well as adults, experts and nonexperts, believers and nonbelievers, her specialized encyclopedias (on witches, saints, ghosts, and angels) provide solidly researched, comprehensive, detailed, cross-cultural information on what are complex and—for many people highly charged—topics. It is difficult to strike the right tone when dealing with such subjects, and Rosemary Guiley has perfect pitch. Nowhere is this more necessary, and more in evidence, than in her *Encyclopedia of Angels*. Here her low-key and respectful presentation is just what is needed to engage a wide audience.

As a resource, this is *the* go-to book on angels; the revisions add both breadth and depth to the original while maintaining its accessible style. This is a volume for looking up specific topics and for dipping into at random. As with all of her encyclopedias, I tend to do both: I start out needing to know about the angel Gabriel and end up also reading about Schemhamphorae. I frequently recommend the first edition of this encyclopedia, but always with the warning that it is not possible to read only one entry. The short bibliographies included after most entries are useful in directing the reader to supplemental reading. Last, the artwork is wonderful; Rosemary is to be commended for finding pieces—whether they are paintings, photos, or 19th-century sheet music covers—that not only illustrate an entry but also reveal new dimensions of it. I have found that the artwork constitutes a reference resource on its own.

My religious upbringing was such that I knew angels to be messengers or agents of God's will who appeared mysteriously and usually in disguise to mortal men and women. The angels I grew up reading about in the Bible were not particularly sweet, loving, or delightful; their appearance was not unambiguously good news. On the contrary, angels did serious and difficult work. The Hebrew Bible is full of the delicate missions entrusted to angels; missions that, according to the Bible, changed the course of human history. Angels tell Abraham that Sarah will bear him a son, and it is an angel who later stops Abraham from sacrificing Isaac. Angels are involved in the destruction of Sodom and Gomorrah, and though they lead Lot and his daughters to safety, the fate of Lot's wife (being turned into a pillar of salt) is a chilling lesson in what happens to those who do not listen to angels. Not two chapters later an angel of God attempts to comfort Hagar, Abraham's outcast mistress and the mother of his first-born son, Ishmael, with the promise that Ishmael will be "made into a great nation." The business of angels, it was clear to me as a child, was dark, dangerous, and demanding. One did not trifle with angels or get in their way; they dealt with important people and with the very very good and the very very bad. As a result I did not grow up thinking of angels as having much to do with ordinary people, let alone as being potential friends or advisers. In fact it seemed safer on the whole—the example of Lot's wife before me—to stay as far away from their notice as possible.

My view of the subject did not change much as an adult and as a Ph.D. student in religion. The appearance of angels was still an ambiguous blessing; whatever "good" news they brought was invariably tempered by pain and suffering. Reading the Annunciation, it seemed to me that the angel Gabriel should have warned Mary: "The good news is you will bear a son, the bad news is he will die a slow and horrible death." To be sure there was better news to come but, from the point of view of motherhood, what agony Mary must have known seeing those nails pounded into the flesh of her beloved child, standing helplessly by as hour after hour he slowly asphyxiated. On balance, I thought, it was best not to be the subject of an angel's attention.

However, as my research interests developed in the area of religious experience, especially in the area of visionary experience, I found myself surrounded by accounts of angel visitations. Despite—or perhaps because of—my previous conviction that angels were best avoided, I had now made them an "unavoidable" area of study. What were angels? How did they function in visionary experiences? What role did they play in the lives of religious people? The approach that made the most sense to me, that most fit in terms of

comprehensiveness, clarity, and consistency, was that angels are transpersonal figures of archetypal significance. That is, as messenger figures between God and human beings, as intermediaries who both deliver and effect the divine will in the world, angels symbolize the connection between the conscious mind and the unconscious, that vast, unbounded reservoir of psyche from and through which the great visionaries of all religions claim the divine makes itself known. Angels appear to "move the story along"; they "force the plot" in particular directions by shaking things up, disturbing the status quo. Understood as manifestations of consciousness, the appearance of an angel in one or another form is always a revelation of some unacknowledged, and generally difficult, truth (e.g., the appearance of the "angel of death" for one obvious example). Thus psychologically, angels are agents of change and growth. The range and variety of angels speaks to the depth and complexity of the psyche; and, transcultural and transhistorical similarities among angel figures suggest that consciousness has a collective or cosmic quality to it.

It seemed, though, that in all of this I had left out the most important questions about angels: Are angels supernatural beings? Do they have spatiotemporal existence? Can a manifestation of consciousness exist independently of consciousness? A student, responding to my suggestions about writing a paper on angels, had this to say: "though it would probably be easier [sic] to write about angels as archetypes, I think it would be much more interesting to focus on angels as created beings." The student's interest reflects the central concern people have today about angels—not "what are they?" but "where are they?" But even this betrays, it needs be pointed out, an archetypal character. The student adds: "I'm not sure how much text I will come across with regard to that, but I find *the concept of powerful beings with free will* a compelling track." Indeed.

Not satisfied by the psychic reality of angels, we seek their "material" reality, as if psyche and matter, or mind and body, are independent and separate realities and only the second half of each pair—matter and body—are "really" real. However, if we consider consciousness as a whole with many dimensions operating on and experienced in different levels, then at one and the same time, angels can be understood as separate supernatural beings and also as ultimately in and from the psyche. This is what Alexandra David-Neel, a religious adept in the yogic traditions and practices of Tibet, discovered when one of her mental projections developed a life of its own. Following certain visualization exercises David-Neel spent months creating the image of a monk in her mind. So well did she succeed in bringing the monk to life in her mind, that he sprang to life outside of her mind. He would appear without her having to think about him, and he performed activities on his own initiative. Once he was even seen by someone visiting her tent. David-Neel reports that it took six months and considerable mental effort for her to withdraw the projection and get rid of him.

Finally, I want to say that whether one thinks of angels as supernatural beings, as archetypal figures, or as some combination of both, Rosemary Ellen Guiley has written, and now revised, the one essential resource book on the subject.

—Lisa J. Schwebel, Ph.D.
Hunter College, City University of New York

Author's Introduction to the Second Edition

The second edition of *The Encyclopedia of Angels* is significantly changed from the first edition, published in 1996. Content is increased with the addition of several hundred new entries and more than 70 new illustrations. Nearly all major entries and numerous smaller ones have been revised, reorganized, and cross-referenced to make the book more valuable as a resource. I have included many more entries on individual angels, including fallen angels. If you use the "angels" and "angelology" entries as starting points, you will find your way to all of the principal entries in the book.

In particular, I have added significant depth and detail from apocryphal, mystical, and esoteric texts, which are rich sources of our angel beliefs and lore. Visionary recitals of journeys into the heavens written nearly two millennia ago retain their power today in their vivid portrayals of mighty beings called angels. The angels experienced then are different in many ways from the angels experienced today; the history of that evolution is a fascinating one. The angel of the prophets is fierce and enigmatic. Today's angel is more accessible, more personal, more like us. What remains unchanged, however, is the alluring mystery that surrounds angels.

I am indebted to the groundwork laid by Gustav Davidson's *Dictionary of Angels*, which I do not attempt to re-create. Readers who are familiar with that work will appreciate the longer treatments and discussions of topics related to angels made possible in this book by an encyclopedia format. The "further reading" recommendations at the ends of many entries are not intended to be exhaustive references but to direct readers to useful sources.

In the years since I completed the first edition of this encyclopedia, my views on angels have not changed in any profound ways, but they have in more subtle ways. I consider angels to exist in their own right, but also as part of us and all creation. To attempt to define them too precisely shatters their mystery. Angels exist in a realm that can be grasped only through intuitive knowing and visionary experience. Nonetheless, intellectual inquiry and study of angels is valuable, for consciousness is raised to a higher plane and made fertile for visionary understanding.

Readers will notice at times that the names of angels can be confusing. Even within a single text, the name of an angel may be spelled in different ways. The entries on individual angels give alternative spellings and names in parentheses. Sometimes variant names describe what appear to be different angels altogether, or perhaps aspects of an angel. For example, Sariel is the alternate name of Uriel, but Sariel is not always Uriel. An alternate name of Sariel is Saraqael, which is also an alternate name of Sarakiel. There are both overlaps and differences in identities and duties, depending on the texts in which the angels are mentioned. As noted in the entry NAMES, many early angel names were the products of trance recitations of prayers and incantations. Readers may wish to read the names entry as one of the first, along with ANGELOLOGY as an orientation to this book.

The literature on angels describes their many roles: messenger, protector, guardian, punisher, destroyer, administrator, minister, teacher, and servant and worshiper of God. These roles capture only pieces of their essence. Above all, angels are participants with us in the glory of creation. They sing the wonders of God and the cosmos. Their song is ours to sing too.

—Rosemary Ellen Guiley, Ph.D.

Author's Introduction to the First Edition

The angel is a mystery, one that we have attempted to explain for more than two thousand years. The study of angels is vast and complex. Contradictions abound concerning name spellings, functions, duties, and identities. In fact, one can become submerged in minutiae about angels that does little to shed light on their true essence.

In this *Encyclopedia of Angels,* significant angels are listed by name and by group. The characteristics, functions and nature of angels, and our beliefs about them and experiences with them, are covered under general subject headings and under biographical profiles of mystics, theologians, philosophers, and others. I also compare angels to some similar beings in non-Western religions. The collection of these entries provides what I hope will be for the reader a fascinating journey into the evolution of the angel in Western thought. This evolution has been shaped largely by visionary experience. What we know about angels comes through our otherworldly contact with them.

My own interest in angels was sparked in the mid-1980s (before angels became the darlings of the media), when I began having archetypal dreams that included a mysterious figure I identified as an angel. This figure served as a psychopomp into the reaches of inner space, leading me through a psychic transformation from one life-stage of consciousness to another, which unfolded over time. Earlier in life I had received no particular religious indoctrination about angels, and felt rather neutral about the question of their existence as portrayed in text and art. However, it seemed to me that I was nonetheless tapping into an archetypal form that exists in the collective unconscious regardless of my own personal views. This is an ancient archetype, shaped by countless experiences, which in turn shaped beliefs, which evolved to shape experience. And now this archetype was breaking through the *unus mundus,* the undifferentiated whole of the universe, in response to my own psychic need. I found that the more I accepted this angel, the more the archetype became energized in my life, expressing itself not only through dreams but through inspiration, creativity, intuition, and even visionary experience.

Do I believe in angels? The answer must of course be yes, although even after years of study on the subject, I remain open as to their exact nature. I do not believe there are easy answers. Do they exist in their own right, in celestial realms? Perhaps so. Or perhaps there is an energy, a vibration of love and light from the Godhead, which becomes an "angel" when it interacts with human consciousness, taking on a form that we can comprehend and integrate into our spiritual and cosmological outlooks. Perhaps it is our need for semi-divine messengers, for spiritual companions, protectors and guides, and for divine beauty in our own likeness, that draws to us what we call the angel. Our monotheistic God is imageless, abstract, and remote. The angel, upon whom we project a form that is an exalted image of ourselves, helps us to feel closer to the Source of All Being.

The world's mystical traditions teach oneness, that everything is part of everything else. Quantum physics tells us that there is no separation between object and observer, that we are inexorably bound up in what we think we merely observe. Consequently we and the angels are part of each other; the good angel can be seen as an expression of our higher self, and the demon or fallen angel as an expression of our lower nature. The dynamics between the two, high and low, are what psychic integration and spiritual growth are all about.

The angel is a profound mystery, as deep as the mystery of the soul, as limitless as the mystery of infinity and eternity. This is a puzzle we may never be able to solve, but our probing of the mystery yields endless permutations that deepen our insights into ourselves.

The experience of an angel—an angelophany—is just as powerful today as it was for the visionary prophets of the biblical era. The prophets were escorted to a state of consciousness called heaven and were given the word of God in the form of laws and moral codes. Today the epiphanies are more personal, but just as life-changing. Via the angel we glimpse the unknown, and we are encouraged to press on.

—Rosemary Ellen Guiley, Ph.D.

A

Abaddon (Apollyon)

ANGEL OF DEATH, destruction, and the netherworld. Abaddon is derived from the Hebrew term for "to destroy," and means "place of destruction." Apollyon is the Greek name.

Originally, Abaddon was a place and not an angel or being. In rabbinic writings and the Old Testament, Abaddon is primarily a place of destruction, and it is a name for one of the regions of Gehenna (HELL). The term occurs six times in the Old Testament. In Proverbs 15:11 and 27:20, it is named with SHEOL as a region of the underworld. In Psalm 88:11, Abaddon is associated with the grave and the underworld.

In Job 26:6, Abaddon is associated with Sheol. Later, Job 28:22 names Abaddon and Death together, implying personified beings.

In REVELATION 9:10, Abaddon is personified, and it is the king of the abyss, the bottomless pit of hell. Revelation also cites the Greek version of the name, Apollyon, probably a reference to Apollo, Greek god of pestilence and destruction.

In magic, Abaddon is often equated with Satan and Samael. His name is used in conjuring spells for malicious deeds. According to AGRIPPA, Abaddon is the prince who rules the seventh hierarchy of DEMONS, the Furies who govern powers of evil, discord, war, and devastation.

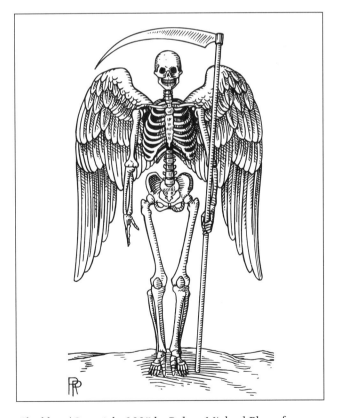

Abaddon (Copyright 1995 by Robert Michael Place, from *The Angels Tarot* by Rosemary Ellen Guiley and Robert Michael Place. Reprinted courtesy of HarperSanFrancisco)

FURTHER READING
Dictionary of Deities and Demons in the Bible. 2d ed. Karel van der Toorn, Bob Becking, and Pieter W. van der Horst, eds. Grand Rapids, Mich.: William B. Eerdmans, 1999.

Abasdarhon

In the LEMEGETON, the angel of the fifth hour of the night, called Sanayfar. Abasdarhon commands 101,550 dukes and other servants divided into 12 degrees of orders.

Abezethibou

One-winged demon who lives in the Red Sea, and who plots against every wind under the heavens and is the enemy of MOSES. In the Testament of SOLOMON, Abezethibou says he once sat in the first heaven named Amelouth. He was present when Moses was taken before the pharaoh of Egypt, and was summoned to the aid of the Egyptian magicians when they sought to discredit Moses. Abezethibou takes credit for turning the pharaoh against Egypt and for inciting the Egyptians to pursue the Israelites in their exodus. When the parted Red Sea falls in on the Egyptians, Abezethibou is trapped with the pillar of air until the DEMON Ephippas arrives to take him to King Solomon. Solomon binds Abezethibou and Ephippas to the pillar (perhaps a reference to the Milky Way) and commands that they hold it up in the air until the end of time.

Abigor   See ELIGOR.

Abraham

Patriarch of the Hebrews who was a frequent recipient of instructions and interventions from God and the ANGEL OF THE LORD. Abraham features prominently in Genesis and in apocryphal writings.

The text of Genesis often reads "Yahweh said;" Genesis 15:1 reads "it happened . . . that the word of Yahweh was spoken to Abram [his original name] in a vision."

By the time they are old, Abram and his wife Sarai are still childless. At Sarai's suggestion, Abram impregnates their slave, HAGAR. The girl's air of superiority angers Sarai, who expels her from the house. Yahweh then makes a covenant with Abraham, promising him the birth of a son—though he and his wife are both elderly—and also land. He instructs Abram to circumcise himself and all in his household. Abram's name from now on will be Abraham and Sarai's will be Sarah.

Three angels disguised as men come to visit Abraham and he feeds them beneath the oak tree at Mamre. One tells him Sarah will have a son in a year. Sarah is amused by this. Abraham shows the men the way to SODOM AND GOMORRAH, which are destroyed.

ISAAC is born, and God tests Abraham's obedience by ordering him to offer his son as a burnt sacrifice on Mount Moriah. Abraham complies, but he is stopped from slitting his son's throat at the last moment by the Angel of the Lord.

Theologians and philosophers have examined and debated the story of Abraham for centuries. Was his vision at Mamre a theophany (manifestation of God) or an ANGELOPHANY (manifestation of an angel)? Did the angels, whom Abraham initially assumed were mortal, really eat food or only appear to eat food? It was established early in the history of Christianity that his vision was an angelophany, and that the angels, being incorporeal, only gave the appearance of eating.

God or Angel?

Confusions remain over the distinction between God and the Angel of the Lord, however. The first confusion occurs with Hagar. After her expulsion, the angel of Yahweh meets her and speaks to her. The angel foretells Hagar's numerous descendants and tells her to name her son Ishmael. She calls the angel "El Roi," the

Three angels visiting Abraham (Gustave Doré)

God of Vision. The well where this meeting takes place is renamed Lahai Roi.

One midrash says that Isaac's birth is announced three days after Abraham's circumcision of his entire household, and that God commands Michael, Gabriel, and Raphael to comfort Abraham, who suffers great pain, as happens on the third day after circumcision. The archangels protest: "Would you send us to an unclean place, full of blood?" God answers: "By your lives, the odor of Abraham's sacrifice pleases me better than myrrh and frankincense! Must I go Myself?" The angels accompany God disguised as Arab wayfarers. Michael is to announce Isaac's birth; Raphael is to heal Abraham; and Gabriel is to destroy the evil city of Sodom.

The midrash ties in with the story that follows, the most frequently discussed angel episode in the Abraham story, Genesis 18 and 19. The text says, "Yahweh appeared to him at the Oak of Mamre while he was sitting by the entrance of his tent during the hottest part of the day. He looked up and there he saw three men standing near him. As soon as he saw them he ran from the entrance of the tent to meet them, and bowed to the ground." This was not a sign of adoration but a sign of respect.

At first Abraham sees his guests as human beings and welcomes them warmly. Their superhuman character is only gradually revealed. Abraham hurries to get a meal prepared and stands by them while they eat under the tree. They ask where Sarah is and Abraham says she is in the tent. Then one says he will come and visit in a year and Sarah will have a son. Sarah overhears and laughs. The guest asks why Sarah laughed; when is anything too wonderful for Yahweh?

"From there the men set out and arrived within sight of Sodom, with Abraham accompanying them to show them the way. Now Yahweh had wondered, 'Shall I conceal from Abraham what I am going to do?'" Yahweh is referring to his plans for Abraham's line to live in his righteous way. He says, "How great an outcry there is against Sodom and Gomorrah" and says he will go and investigate. "The men left there and went to Sodom, while Abraham remained standing before Yahweh" (18:22) and convinced Yahweh to spare the city if he finds 10 righteous men there. Genesis 19:1 reads, "when the two angels reached Sodom that evening." Then follows the account of the destruction of Sodom and Gomorrah, the escape of Lot and his daughters, and the changing of Lot's wife into a pillar of salt. Genesis 19:5 reads "when dawn broke the angels urged Lot. . . ."

Concerning the sacrifice of Isaac in Genesis 22, Abraham's first instruction to take Isaac to the land of Moriah and offer him as a burnt offering comes from God, yet it is the Angel of the Lord who intervenes at the last minute to prevent Abraham's knife from killing Isaac.

The rabbis writing the Sefer Hayashar add this to the story. As Abraham and Isaac are ascending Mount Moriah, the FALLEN ANGEL Samael comes in the shape of a humble greybeard, and says: "Can a command to kill the son of your old age proceed from a God of mercy and justice? You have been deceived!" Abraham sees through the disguise and drives him away; but he reappears in the shape of a handsome youth to Isaac, whispering, "Wretched son of a wretched mother! Was it for this she awaited your birth so long and patiently? Why should your besotted father slaughter you without reason? Fell, while there is yet time!" Isaac repeats these words to Abraham, who curses Samael and sends him away.

Different explanations have been advanced to explain the seeming interchangeability of God and his angels. According to MAIMONIDES, angels are references to prophetic vision or to a dream in which either God or an angel may be perceived or heard. Or, Old Testament angel messengers may have been remnants of stories of visitations and encounters with desert holy men who were using their dramatic and occult arts to intervene in the spiritual development of the Hebrew nomads. This might also explain how Sarah was impregnated.

Abraham in the Apocryphal Texts

JUBILEES

JUBILEES, written circa 160–140 B.C.E. and attributed to a narration to MOSES by an ANGEL OF THE PRESENCE, focuses on the promise of progeny and land. It does not mention the theophany (manifestation of God), nor the angels' eating of food. The angels, who are not specified by number, are involved in Sarah's pregnancy. Angels appear to Abraham on the "new moon of the fourth month" at the oak at Mamre and inform him that Sarah will bear a son. When Sarah gets this news, she laughs. The angels reproach her, and she denies laughing. They tell her she will bear a son and will name him Isaac.

It is not God's idea to test Abraham, but a plot by Mastema, the accuser. Word comes into heaven that Abraham loves the Lord and is faithful in all ways. Mastema, in the role of a satan, goes to God and tells him to instruct Abraham to offer his son Isaac as a sacrifice, in order to test him further. God does so. When Abraham is about to slay Isaac, the angel of the presence who narrates Jubilees comes to stand before him and Prince Mastema. God tells the angel to instruct Abraham not to harm his son. Abraham obeys and sacrifices a ram instead. Prince Mastema is shamed.

THE APOCALYPSE OF ABRAHAM

The Apocalypse of Abraham is a pseudepigraphon written sometime during the first or second centuries C.E., and after the destruction of Jerusalem in 70. Its original language probably was Hebrew, but it survives only in a Slavonic version. The text concerns Israel's election and its covenant with God, and presents a rich angelology, demonology, and cosmology. There is a final judgment with redemption and punishment, but no resurrection, perhaps due to the influence of the Bogomils, who did not believe in resurrection of the body. The work also is influenced by the biblical books of Genesis and EZEKIEL, and the apocryphal work of 1 ENOCH. The restoration of the Temple of Jerusalem is important in its end.

The first part of the apocalypse concerns Abraham's early life, and the second part concerns his visionary journey to HEAVEN. In his youth, Abraham becomes aware of the wrongs of idolatry, and argues about this with his father, Terah. He pledges to seek the one true God, the God of gods. The voice of the true God comes down from heaven and orders him out of his father's house. As soon as Abraham departs, thunder comes from heaven and the house is burned to the ground, killing Terah and all who are in it.

God, who refers to himself as "Before-the-World and Mighty, the God who created previously, before the light of the age" (9:1–2), then instructs Abraham to purify himself for 40 days and make a sacrifice on a high mountain (Mt. Horeb). God promises to reveal the nature of creation.

Abraham falls trembling to the ground. God sends his angel, Iaoel, in the form of a man to consecrate and strengthen him. Iaoel's appearance is brilliant like jewels and the rainbow. He introduces himself and describes his powers—which include the quelling of all reptiles and the loosening of Hades—and acknowledges that he is the one who burned down the house of Terah.

Iaoel keeps company with Abraham during his fast and purification; Abraham calls his ability to see the angel as his food and his conversation with him his drink. After 40 days they go to Mt. Horeb to make the sacrifice of birds and animals. Iaoel gives specific instructions for how it is to be done, after which he will take Abraham on a journey to see "the fullness of the universe."

Abraham follows the instructions, and an unclean bird comes to the carcasses of the sacrificed animals. It speaks to Abraham and urges him to flee from Iaoel or risk being destroyed in the heavens. Iaoel identifies it as Azazel, the angel of disgrace, lies, wrath, and trials of the impious, whose domain is the earth. He is the lord of HELL. Iaoel orders Abraham to send Azazel away and not to answer him if he speaks again.

The visionary journey then begins at sunset. Iaoel places Abraham on the right wing of the sacrificed pigeon and himself on the left wing of the sacrificed turtledove, and they ascend up into a fiery Gehenna filled with the forms of men running, changing shape, prostrating themselves, and crying aloud. The Eternal One approaches in fire and with a voice like the roaring sea, and the angel and Abraham bow to worship in song.

The fire rises and Abraham sees a throne of fire upon the flames and "many-eyed ones" around it worshiping with the same song. Under the throne are four fiery living creatures similar to those described by EZEKIEL. Each creature has four heads with four faces each, of a man, an ox, an eagle, and a lion, so that each creature has 16 faces total. They have six wings, two at the shoulder, two halfway down the body, and two at the loins that extend to cover the feet. They fly erect with the two middle wings. After singing, they threaten each other. It is Iaoel's job to turn their faces to stop the threatening. Behind the fiery creatures is a chariot with fiery wheels full of eyes. The throne is above the chariot, covered with fire and encircled by fire and an "indescribable light."

The voice of God emanates from the fire. Abraham is shown the seventh firmament, upon which he stands, and the expanses of heaven. He sees multitudes of incorporeal angels who carry out the orders of fiery angels who are on the eighth firmament. The angels of the seventh firmament command those on the sixth firmament. The fifth firmament contains the stars and the elements.

Looking down, Abraham sees the earth and its men and creatures, and the impiety in the souls of men. He sees Leviathan in the watery depths.

He sees the Garden of Eden, and a multitude of people, half on the right and half on the left. God says that the ones on the left are the people of Azazel, and the ones on the right have been prepared for judgment; and so the entire world is divided into two parts, one good and one corrupt.

Abraham also sees the huge forms of ADAM AND EVE entwined in front of a tree, and Azazel standing behind it, in the form of a dragon with 12 wings and human hands and feet. Abraham is shown the corruption of all humanity. Azazel does not have control over the righteous of the world, and he will not be able to reveal the secrets of heaven, lest he be banished to the desert forever.

God tells Abraham the future. There will be 12 periods of tribulations, after which will come the final judgment and then the redemption of the righteous. During the 12 periods, God will send 10 plagues: sorrow from great need; fiery conflagrations in the cities; destruction of cattle by pestilence; famine; earthquakes and wars; hail and snow; devouring wild beasts; pestilence and hunger; execution by sword and flight into distress; and thunder, voices, and destroying earthquakes. God then will send his "chosen one" who will help him gather up all the people and punish the heathen. Apostates will burn in the fire of Azazel, and the Temple (of Jerusalem) and its sacrifices will be restored.

FURTHER READING

Charlesworth, James H., ed. *The Old Testament Pseudepigrapha.* Vols. 1 and 2. New York: Doubleday, 1983, 1985.

Field, M. J. *Angels and Ministers of Grace.* New York: Hill and Wang, 1971.

Graves, Robert, and Raphael Patai. *Hebrew Myths.* New York: Doubleday Anchor Books, 1964.

Maimonides. *Guide of the Perplexed.* Abridged. Introduction by Julius Guttmann. London: East and West Library, 1952.

Abraxas (Abrasax, Abraxis)

An ancient name attributed to a god, a sun, an angel, and a DEMON. Abraxas was the name of a sun mounting an ouroborus (a snake biting its tail) held by the highest Egyptian god Isis, the creator of the sun and mistress of all the gods. Isis mythology found its way deeply into GNOSTICISM, in which Abraxas is the name of the ruler of the 365th (highest and final) AEON, or sphere ascending to the unknowable God. Abraxas thus became the Gnostic demigod or Aeon of the High Heaven. Abraxas is mentioned frequently in Gnostic literature as one of the great aeons—along with Gamaliel and Sablo—who brings the elect into HEAVEN.

Abraxas also was associated with the Mithraic mystery religion of Persian origin, the chief rival of Christianity in Rome in its first 400 years. Like Gnosticism, Mithraism featured a complex astrology and numerology. Numerical values of Mithra's and Abraxas's names each total 365.

Abraxas was assimilated into the Gnostic "Lord of the World," the Old Testament God (really a creation/son of Sophia, a high Aeon) who created the material world and had demonic qualities. Orthodox Christians came to view Abraxas as a demon. In turn, Abraxas became a favorite deity of heretical sects of the Middle Ages.

Abraxas appears in the works of CARL G. JUNG, who had Gnostic interests. The father of depth psychology wrote a vast amount of material on his personal visionary experiences, little of which has been released by his heirs. One such document, reported by Jung to have been composed on three nights between December 15,

1916, and February 16, 1917, entitled *Seven Sermons to the Dead,* purports to be written by the Gnostic teacher Basilides in Alexandria; several of the sermons feature Abraxas.

In contrast to Helios, the god of light, and the devil, god of darkness, Abraxas appears as the supreme power of being in whom light and darkness are both united and transcended. He is also defined as the principle of irresistible activity and is a close approximation of an active manifestation of the Pleroma. Gnostic talismans bearing the figure of Abraxas were saved because they were carved into valuable stones, usually oval. They show a figure with a human body, the head of a rooster (or more seldom of a hawk), and legs fashioned like serpents. The god's hands hold a shield and a whip, the shield usually inscribed with the name IAO, reminiscent of the Jewish four-letter name of God. He is often mounted on a chariot drawn by four white horses, with both sun and moon, gold and silver, masculine and feminine overhead.

The symbolism is usually explained as follows: the rooster represents wakefulness and is related to the

Abraxas (Copyright 1995 by Robert Michael Place, from *The Angels Tarot* by Rosemary Ellen Guiley and Robert Michael Place. Reprinted courtesy of HarperSanFrancisco)

human heart and the universal heart, the sun, invoked by chanticleer; the human torso embodies the principle of logos, or articulated thought; the snake legs indicate prudence whereby the dynamic rulership of universal being governs its own all-powerful energies; the shield is symbolic of wisdom, the great protector of divine warriors, while the whip denotes the relentless driving power of life, the four horses the tetramorphic forces of the universal libido or psychic energy (four elements, Jung's four functions). The number 365 appears again, for in both Greek and Hebrew the seven letters of the name Abraxas yield 365 in numerology, and the seven letters correspond to the seven rays of the planetary spheres, according to Gnostic principles.

Jung calls Abraxas the truly terrible one because of his ability to generate truth and falsehood, good and evil, light and darkness with the same word and in the same deed. In Jungian psychology there is no easy way out of psychic conflict; one must not only fight on the side of the angels, but occasionally join the host of the fallen angels. According to Jung, fear of Abraxas is the beginning of wisdom, and liberation, or gnosis, is achieved by not resisting.

FURTHER READING

Charlesworth, James H., ed. *The Old Testament Pseudepigrapha.* Vols. 1 and 2. New York: Doubleday, 1983, 1985.

Hoeller, Stephan A. *The Gnostic Jung and the Seven Sermons to the Dead.* Wheaton, Ill.: Quest Books, 1982.

acclamations

One of three primary hierarchies of angels designated by the alchemist Robert Fludd. The other two are APPARITIONS and VOICES.

Adam and Eve

According to the Bible, the first man and first woman.

Genesis 2:7–9 tells how God creates Adam ("man") in his own likeness from dust and plants in the garden of Eden. In Genesis 2:21–22, God decides man should not be alone and takes a rib from Adam while he sleeps, fashioning it into Eve ("the mother of all things").

Their paradisal life ends, however, in Genesis 3 when Eve is tempted by a serpent to eat the forbidden fruit of the tree of life in the center of the garden. She does so and gives fruit to Adam to eat. As a result they fall from grace. God, angry, curses the serpent to crawl on its belly, curses Eve to be submissive to her husband and to have pain in childbirth, and curses Adam to sweat and toil and suffer pain and death. The two are

sent out of Eden. God places CHERUBIM with a turning flaming sword at the east gate of Eden to guard access to the Tree of Life.

In some texts Adam is an angel. He is the "bright angel" in The Book of Adam and Eve and is the "second angel" in 2 ENOCH. He is sometimes associated with the sixth sephira of the Kabbalistic TREE OF LIFE, Tipareth ("Beauty"). The Tree of Life itself represents ADAM KADMON, the archetypal man.

According to the lore of Lilith, the queen of DEMONS and night terrors, Lilith was the first woman to have sex with Adam. The union spawned demons, including Asmodeus.

The Life of Adam and Eve

The Life of Adam and Eve, written in the latter part of the first century, provides more details of angelic involvement in the story of Adam and Eve. The Vita text is written in Slavonic (Latin) and the Apocalypse text in Greek. A third version, the Apocalypse of MOSES, dates to late medieval times and is derived from earlier Hebrew and Aramaic sources.

The Vita begins with the expulsion of Adam and Eve from Eden. Adam says that in order to repent, he will fast for 40 days in the Jordan River. He instructs Eve to go into the Tigris River up to her neck and stand there silently for 37 days. Eve obeys. After 18 days, Satan transforms himself into a bright angel and seeks to lure Eve out of the water with a promise of food. Fooled, she does so, and Satan takes her to Adam. Both Adam and Eve are distressed at Eve's seduction again.

Satan blames his own fall on Adam. He tells them that when Adam was created, the angel Michael brought him into heaven and made the angels worship him as the image of the Lord. Satan and the angels under him refused to do so. This angered God and he cast them out of HEAVEN. Jealous of Adam and Eve in Paradise, Satan plotted to get them cast out in return. Hearing this, Adam cries out to God to be delivered from Satan, and the devil disappears.

When Eve gives birth to Cain, she is attended by 12 angels and two EXCELLENCIES, or VIRTUES. Michael stands to her right and touches her from her head to her breast and blesses her and pledges the help of the angels. After the birth of the child, God sends Michael to give Adam seeds and teach him how to become a farmer.

After the birth of Seth, Adam tells Seth about a vision he had. He says that after he and Eve were driven out of Paradise, they prayed and Michael came to them. Adam saw a chariot like the wind with wheels of fire. It carried him into the Paradise of righteousness, where he saw the Lord in the appearance of unbearable flaming fire. Thousands of angels were to the left and right of the chariot.

Filled with fear, Adam worshiped God, but he is told he will die because he listened to Eve instead of God. Adam begged for mercy, and so God says he will permit descendants from Adam who will serve him. Michael immediately took Adam by the hand and ejected him from the "Paradise of visitation" (evidently a special receiving area). The angel then took a rod and touched the waters around Paradise, freezing them. Michael returned Adam to the place where his vision had begun.

At age 930, Adam falls into his final illness. He gathers all his 30 sons around him and relates the story of the Fall. He asks Seth and Eve to go to the gates of Paradise and beg for the oil from the tree of mercy to ease his pain.

In Paradise, a wild beast (Satan) attacks Seth and bites him, infecting future generations with transgression and sin. Seth and Eve continue on. They encounter Michael, who tells them the oil cannot be taken until the "last days," a reference to the future redemptive power of Christ. Michael says that Adam will die in six days, and, at the moment he does, Seth and Eve will see a great vision of heavenly wonders.

Adam dies in six days, and for seven days the sun, moon, and stars are darkened. While Seth mourns, Michael appears to him and says he will show him what the merciful God has in store for Adam. As angels sound trumpets and praise God for showing pity, God hands Adam to Michael to stay in his custody until the day of judgment, at which time Adam shall have the throne that once belonged to Satan before his fall.

God instructs Michael and Uriel to place three linen cloths over Adam and his son Abel, and bury them. The angels proceed, and instructions are given that burials must be done in this fashion.

Six days after Adam dies, Eve announces her impending death and gathers her 30 sons and 30 daughters. She instructs them to write the story of Adam and Eve on clay and stone tablets, one of which will survive no matter how the Lord will judge humanity: The stone tablets will survive judgment by water and the clay will survive judgment by fire. Eve dies and is buried.

Seth writes the tablets in an automatic script: An angel holds his hand and he knows not what he writes. He places the tablets in Adam's oratory where Adam once prayed.

After the Flood, the tablets are seen by many but not read, until SOLOMON finds them. The angel who held Seth's hand tells Solomon to build a temple upon the place where Adam and Eve had once prayed.

Cherub driving Adam and Eve out of the Garden of Eden (Gustave Doré)

Solomon completes the temple. He finds on the stones the prophecy made by ENOCH before the Flood, namely, that the Lord will come to judge the impious. So ends the Vita.

The Greek Apocalypse text states that it is the narrative and life of Adam and Eve as revealed by God to Moses when he received the tablets of law. The story line is similar. When Adam falls ill, it is Eve, however, who tells their children the story of Paradise and the Fall.

When Adam dies, Eve beholds a chariot of light coming down from heaven. It is preceded by angels and is pulled by four radiant eagles whose glory and faces cannot be seen by the living. The chariot comes to Adam and SERAPHIM stand between it and his body. Angels bring bowls of incense to the altar and breathe on them, causing the sky to be hidden behind the fumes. The angels fall down and beg God to forgive Adam.

The sun, moon, and stars darken. An angel sounds a trumpet, and the angels who had fallen on their faces rise and declare God has forgiven Adam. A seraph carries Adam off to the Lake of Acheron—waters over which the souls of the dead are transported to the underworld—and washes him three times in the presence of God. Adam lies for three hours, and then God hands him to Michael to take into the third heaven, where he is to be left until "that great and fearful day which I am about to establish for the world" (37:6).

Michael asks God how Adam's remains shall be treated. God sends angels to take Adam's body to Paradise, and he instructs Michael, Gabriel, Uriel, and Raphael to go to the third heaven and etch three cloths of linen and silk and oil from the oil of fragrance. With these they are to prepare the bodies of both Adam and Abel. Abel's body, which had been rejected by the earth, had been taken by an angel to a rock where it awaited his father's death. Adam and Abel are buried in Paradise where God first took the dust to form Adam. God promises resurrection to Adam and his descendants on the last day. He places a triangular seal upon the tomb.

Knowing her own impending death, Eve begs God to be buried with Adam. Michael attends her death, and he and three other angels take her body to be buried with Abel. Michael instructs Seth that all people are to be buried in this way, with cloths and oils, until the day of resurrection. Mourning is to last no more than six days, and the seventh day is for rejoicing, for on that day God and the angels rejoice in the migration from the earth of the righteous soul. Michael ascends to heaven, praising God. So ends the Apocalypse text.

The Apocalypse of Adam

The Apocalypse of Adam is a Gnostic text written between the first and fourth centuries, and it forms part of the pseudepigrapha. It comprises a secret revelation given by Adam to Seth immediately before Adam's death. It is intended to be passed on down through Seth's line. As is characteristic of Gnostic literature, it presents two Gods, the creator God who is the Demiurge and the supreme God who is remote. The creator God rules the AEONS and POWERS, and becomes hostile toward the "eternal God." The Apocalypse of Adam stands out from most other Gnostic texts in its use of the name "God" for both deities. The followers or the creator God are doomed, whereas the followers of Seth hold the secret knowledge of the higher God, and will have salvation in imperishability.

Adam begins his revelation by telling Seth that he and Eve once had the glory of the aeon from which they had come. Eve teaches him a word knowledge of the eternal God, and they are "like great eternal angels," loftier than God. But upon the fall they become two aeons and their glory returns to a higher level. Their knowledge passes into humanity through

Seth. But the knowledge of God leaves them, and their world is dark and full of "dead things, like men."

Three men—possibly angels, similar to the "men" who appeared to ABRAHAM—come to Adam and give him a revelation. He predicts the Flood, the division of the earth by NOAH, and the establishment of the 12 kingdoms. Three great aeons—Abraxas, Gamaliel, and Sablo—will carry off the elite into heaven. The *Photor,* or ILLUMINATOR of knowledge, will come to redeem souls, and those who accept his truth will live forever.

The Testament of Adam

The Testament of Adam is a short pseudepigraphon written between the second and fifth centuries C.E. It is rich in ANGELOLOGY and shares some common ground with the Life of Adam and Eve. It is divided into three sections: the Horarium, about the hours of the night and day; the Prophecy, in which Adam gives a revelation to Seth about creation, the Fall, the Flood, the coming of Christ, and the end of the world; and the Hierarchy, which describes the nine levels of the angelic kingdom.

The text presents God as the creation of everything good and evil; there is no dualism, and everything has its proper place in the scheme of things. Adam intended to become a god, but he made the mistake that resulted in the Fall.

The Horarium describes the various aspects of all the hours of the night and day, their purposes and events that take place at those times. The hours are:

First hour of the night: The praise of demons; they do not injure or harm anyone.

Second hour of the night: The praise of doves.

Third hour of the night: The praise of fish, all the lower depths, and fire.

Fourth hour of the night: The "holy, holy, holy" praise of the seraphim. Adam comments that once he heard the beat of their wings to the sound of their triple praise, but after his fall, heard them no more.

Fifth hour of the night: Praise of the waters that are above heaven. Adam once heard the sound of these waves, which prompted the angels to sing hymns of praise to God.

Sixth hour of the night: The construction of the clouds and the "great fear" that comes in the middle of the night.

Seventh hour of the night: The viewing of powers while the waters are asleep. Priests can mix the waters with consecrated oil and anoint those who are afflicted, so that they rest.

Eighth hour of the night: The sprouting of grass upon the earth while dew descends from heaven.

Ninth hour of the night: The praise of the CHERUBIM.

Tenth hour of the night: The praise of human beings. The gate of heaven opens and the prayers of all living things enter; they worship and leave. Whatever a person asks shall be given in this hour, when the seraphim and the roosters beat their wings (dawn).

Eleventh hour of the night: Joy on earth as the sun rises from Paradise and shines on all creation.

Twelfth hour of the night: The waiting for incense. Silence is imposed on all the ranks of fire and wind until the priests burn incense to his divinity. All heavenly powers are dismissed.

First hour of the day: The petition of the heavenly ones.

Second hour of the day: The prayer of the angels.

Third hour of the day: The praise of the birds.

Fourth hour of the day: The praise of the beasts.

Fifth hour of the day: The praise which is above heaven.

Sixth hour of the day: The praise of the cherubim who plead against the wickedness of human nature.

Seventh hour of the day: The entry and exit from the presence of God, when the prayers of all living things enter, worship, and leave.

Eighth hour of the day: The praise of the fire and the waters.

Ninth hour of the day: The petition to those angels who stand before the throne of God.

Tenth hour of the day: The visitation of the waters when the spirit (Lord) descends and "broods upon the waters and upon the fountains." If the Lord does not do this, the demons will injure everyone they see. The waters are taken up by priests, mixed with consecrated oil, and administered to the afflicted, so that they have rest and are healed.

Eleventh hour of the day: The exultation and joy of the righteous.

Twelfth hour of the day: The petitioning of God for his gracious will.

In the Prophecy, Adam foretells the birth of Christ into a human body, and his miraculous powers. He tells Seth that after he ate of the forbidden fruit—a fig—God spoke to him. God said he knew Adam wanted to be a god, and he would make him one, but not for a long time because he had listened to the serpent. Thus, Adam was consigned to death but would not waste away in SHEOL. For the sake of Adam, God would be born into flesh through the Virgin Mary, and God would establish a new heaven for the seed of Adam. God said that after three days from his death, he

would rise from the tomb, set Adam at his right hand, and restore to him and his posterity "the justice of heaven."

Adam also predicts the Flood because of the sins of Eve and the daughters of Cain. After the Flood, there would be a period of 6,000 years, and then the world would end.

Seth then writes that after Adam died, he was buried at the east of Paradise opposite the first city built on Earth, which was named after Enoch. Adam was taken to his grave by angels and the POWERS. For seven days, the sun and moon were dark. The testament was placed in the "cave of treasures," along with the gold, myrrh, and frankincense that Adam had taken from Paradise. These gifts would be taken by the magi to the infant Jesus.

The Hierarchy describes the duties of the levels of angels and how they are involved in service to the world. The orders, from lowest to highest are:

Angels: One angel is assigned to every person to accompany that individual everywhere.

Archangels: They direct everything in creation according to the plan of God.

Archons: They govern the elements and the weather.

Authorities: They govern the celestial lights of the sun, moon, and stars.

Powers: They prevent the demons from destroying the world.

Dominions: They rule over earthly kingdoms and decide the outcome of wars. In biblical battle descriptions, they are angels riding on red horses.

Thrones: They stand before God and guard the gate of the holy of holies. They glorify God every hour with hymns of "holy, holy, holy." (See QEDUSSAH.)

Cherubim: They stand before God and reverence his throne and keep the seals. They sing the hourly "holy, holy, holy."

Seraphim: They stand before God and serve his inner chamber. They sing the hourly "holy, holy, holy."

FURTHER READING

Charlesworth, James H., ed. *The Old Testament Pseudepigrapha.* Vols. 1 and 2. New York: Doubleday, 1983, 1985.

Hurtak, J. J. *The Scrolls of Adam and Eve: A Study of Prophetic Regenesis.* Los Gatos, Calif.: The Academy for Future Science, 1989.

Adam Kadmon

The Celestial Man, the heavenly body of light of the primordial, archetypal form of the Adamic race. The

Adam as the angel Adamel (Copyright 1995 by Robert M. Place; from *The Angels Tarot* by Rosemary Ellen Guiley and Robert M. Place)

Fall nearly separates ADAM AND EVE from their Adam Kadmon, or perfected state. The Adam Kadmon has a divine GEMATRIA. In the Pistis Sophia, JESUS refers to 12 emanations of light, which are the radiance of the universe and which are multiplied into orders and suborders from two to 144,000.

See ARCHETYPES.

Adimus

One of the seven REPROBATED ANGELS in a church council trial in 745 in Rome.

adityas

In Vedic lore, the 12 descendants or "shining ones" of Aditi, the goddess who is the mother of the world, and, according to some texts, the mother of Vishnu, the preserver god and second in importance after the creator god Brahma, and Indra, the weather and storm god. The 12 adityas correspond to the months of the year.

Adnachiel (Advachiel, Adernahael)

Angel who rules November and the sign of Sagittarius. Adnachiel also shares rulership of the order of angels with Phaleg.

Adonael

In the Testament of SOLOMON, one of seven ARCHANGELS, and the angel who has the power to thwart the demons Methathiax and Bobel, who cause diseases.

See DECANS OF THE ZODIAC.

Adonai (Adonay)

Name that refers to an angel or is also another name for God. In Phoenician mythology, Adonai is one of the seven ELOHIM or ANGELS OF THE PRESENCE who create the universe. In GNOSTICISM, he is one of the 12 powers created by Ialdabaoth. In MAGIC, Adonai is conjured in many rituals and in exorcisms of fire.

aeons

In GNOSTICISM, celestial planes and the rulers or powers of the planes. Aeon (aion in Greek) means "eternity" or "eternal realm."

The Gnostics conceived of the HEAVENS as a series of concentric spheres called aeons. Basilides enumerated 365 aeons, though others counted far fewer, up to 30.

The chiefs of the aeons are called aeons themselves. They are emanations of God, the first created beings, and compare to SERAPHIM in closeness to the Godhead. Abraxas is chief among aeons. Sophia rules the 30th aeon, the highest level of the Pleroma, which are the 30 aeons closest to earth and which form earth's celestial heavens. Before the angelic hierarchy of PSEUDO-DIONYSIUS became established, aeons were included in hierarchies of angels as a 10th order.

The Greek term "aion" is used in the Bible to describe "eternity" or "world." In Greek lore, Aion is the proper name of a divine being born of Kore, the daughter of Persephone, who marks the coming of a new age.

Aeshma

In Persian lore, one of the AMARAHSPANDS or ARCHANGELS. The DEMON name Asmodeus is derived from Aeshma.

Af

Angel of anger and destruction and one of the ANGELS OF PUNISHMENT. Af means "anger." Af governs the death of mortals. He is 500 PARASANGS tall and is made of chains of black and red fire, and he lives in the seventh HEAVEN.

In the Zohar, Af is one of three angels in Gehenna (HELL)—along with Mashit and Hemah—who punish those who sin by idolatry, incest, and murder. Af helps Hemah to swallow MOSES.

Agares

Formerly a member of the order of VIRTUES and now one of the FALLEN ANGELS. Agares is the first duke of the power of the east, and rules over 30 legions. According to the LEMEGETON, he appears as a handsome man riding a crocodile and carrying a goshawk. He makes those who run stand still and can bring back runaways. He teaches all languages, causes earthquakes, and destroys spiritual and temporal dignities. Agares is one of the 72 spirits of SOLOMON.

Agla

Angel invoked in MAGIC; also a name of God. The name Agla comes from the first letters of the Hebrew words for "Thou art mighty forever, O Lord," a common sentiment expressed in the Old Testament.

Agla is invoked in various magical rites. The LEMEGETON (see GRIMOIRES) refers to Agla as a "great and mighty" name of God. According to the English occultist A. E. Waite, Agla is an important protection invoked in the magical preparation of ritual instruments. The name is inscribed on the blade of the magician's sword. It also is inscribed (with a male goose quill) on the blade of the white-handled knife, which is used for magical purposes except for the casting of the magical circle, done with a black-handled knife.

Agrat bat Mahlat See ANGELS OF PROSTITUTION; SAMAEL.

Agrippa, Henry Cornelius (1486–1535)

One of the most important occult philosophers of the 16th century. Henry Cornelius Agrippa—also known as Henry Cornelius Agrippa of Nettesheim—wrote extensively on Neoplatonic and Kabbalistic MAGIC and the occult. His detailed accounts of the magical functions of angels, DEMONS, INTELLIGENCES, spirits, planetary and celestial forces, numbers, gems, stones, and other topics influenced generations of thinkers who followed. Far ahead of his time and contemptuous of other intellectuals, he was not often understood by his contemporaries and often ran afoul of the authorities of the Catholic Church and the state.

Life

Agrippa was born on September 14, 1486, in Cologne, and was educated at the university there. Some biographers say he was born into a noble family, but the prevailing view is that he adopted the name "von Nettesheim," or "of Nettesheim," himself, after the founder of Cologne.

Agrippa entered the University of Cologne in 1499. A quick student, he learned eight languages and engaged in a deep study of alchemy, the Hermetic literature and the KABBALAH. His personal aim was to achieve a spiritual union with the Godhead.

His first job was an appointment as court secretary and then soldier to Maximilian I, king of Rome and emperor of Germany. He became involved in conspiratorial intrigues, an activity he would continue throughout his life.

He earned a doctorate of divinity and lectured on the Kabbalah at the University of Dole. He tried to win the patronage of Maximilian's daughter, Margaret of Ghent, with a flattering work, *The Nobility of Women,* but the local monks denounced him as a heretic, and he was forced to flee to England.

Agrippa spent years drifting around Europe, forming secret societies and working at various jobs. He was frequently at odds with the church, for he considered many monks to be ignorant and narrow-minded. He was unlucky in marriage: two wives died and the third ruined him emotionally and financially.

In Lyons, he was appointed physician to Louise of Savoy, the queen mother of the king of France. She was chiefly interested in having him tell her fortune by astrology, but he said he had more important work to do. She was slow to pay him, and kept him confined to Lyons, impoverished, from 1524 to 1526, until he was able to quit.

In 1519, he undertook the defense of a woman accused of witchcraft by the inquisitor of Metz. The chief evidence against the woman was that her mother had been burned as a witch. Agrippa destroyed the case against her—and the credibility of the inquisitor—with the theological argument that man could be separated from Christ only by his own sin, not by that of another. The humiliated inquisitor threatened to prosecute Agrippa for heresy. He left town and resumed his traveling around Europe, taking various jobs and securing the patronage of Margaret of Austria.

By 1529, he had accumulated enough money to spend his time studying alchemy. But when Margaret died his fortunes turned, and he found himself jailed for debt in 1531. His friends released him, but only a year later, his writings led to charges against him of impiety. The Dominicans attempt to block publication of some of his work. Emperor Charles V demanded that he recant many of his opinions. In 1535 the emperor condemned him to death as a heretic. Agrippa fled to France but was imprisoned. Sprung free by friends once again, he set out for Lyons but fell sick along the way and died.

During his life, Agrippa attracted many pupils. One of the most famous was JOHANN WEYER, who wrote extensively on demonology.

Works

By the time he was 23, Agrippa had collected a vast store of occult knowledge, and began making notes for what would become his most important work, the three-volume *Occult Philosophy,* a summation of all the magical and occult knowledge of the time. In 1510 he sent the manuscript to Abbot JOHANNES TRITHEMIUS at the monastery of St. James in Wurzburg for approval. The first published edition appeared in 1531 and the complete work was published in 1533.

Agrippa wrote numerous other works, which he collected together with his letters toward the end of his life and published as *Opera.*

In *Occult Philosophy,* Agrippa maintains that magic has nothing to do with the devil or sorcery, but it depends upon natural psychic gifts such as second sight. He believes in the ultimate power of will and imagination to effect magic, and understands the power the mind has over the body: a jilted lover can truly die of grief. Man achieves his highest potential by learning the harmonies of nature. The astral body is the "chariot of the soul" and can leave the physical body like a light escaping from a lantern. The greatest and highest wonder-working name is Jesus.

According to occult scholar Donald Tyson, Agrippa may have been the first to blend Neoplatonic and Kabbalist streams of thought. The result was the leading encyclopedic authority on practical magic of the day.

Dominican inquisitors successfully blocked publication of the entire work but only temporarily. A spurious fourth book appeared in 1567, but it was denounced by Weyer. An English translation of *Occult Philosophy,* published in 1651, was plagiarized by the occultist FRANCIS BARRETT, who published a truncated version of it as his own book *THE MAGUS* in 1801. The Hermetic Order of the Golden Dawn, the premier magical fraternity of Western occultism, which flourished in the late 19th and early 20th centuries, used *Occult Philosophy* as a key source for much of its material.

In book one, Agrippa covers natural magic in the elementary world, including stones, herbs, metals, and so forth. Book two covers the celestial or mathematical world and discusses the magical properties of celestial bodies and numbers. Book three covers the intellectual world of pagan gods and spirits—including angels and demons—and gives magical procedures for invoking and communicating with them, as well as with God. There are instructions for making sigils and AMULETS, working with angelic scripts, and working with sound and fumes. The Kabbalistic TREE OF LIFE is explained, including the angels and demons associated with each sephirot.

Agrippa says that angels can impart either virtues or suffering, and bestow certain occult powers upon those who follow the right path:

> All men therefore are governed by the ministry of divers angels, and are brought to any degree of virtue, deserts, and dignity, who behave themselves worthy of them; but they which carry themselves unworthy of them are deposed, and thrust down, as well by evil spirits, as good spirits, unto the lowest degree of misery, as their evil merits shall require: but they that are attributed to the sublimer angels, are preferred before other men, for angels having the care of them, exalt them, and subject others to them by a certain occult power, which although neither of them perceive, yet he that is subjected, feels a certain yoke of presidency, for which he cannot easily acquit himself, yea he fears and reverenceth that power, which the superior angels make to flow upon superiors, and with a certain terror bring the inferiors into a fear of presidency.

THE ANGELIC HIERARCHY

Agrippa equates angels to "intelligences" and "spirits," in that they all are nonphysical entities, are immortal, and wield great influences over things in creation. Angels are "knowing, understanding and wise." There are three kinds in the traditions of the magicians.

The first kind are the supercelestial angels, rather like intellectual spheres focused on worshiping the one and only God. So full of God and "overwhelmed with the divine nectar" are they that they cannot participate in the lower, inferior realms. The supercelestials infuse the lower orders with the light they receive from God, and instruct the orders in their duties.

The second kind are the celestial angels, or worldly angels, for they are concerned with the spheres of the world and for governing "every heaven and star." The celestials are divided into orders, as many as there are heavens and as there are stars in the heavens. The celestials also include the angels who govern planets, the signs, triplicities, decans, quinaries, degrees, and stara. There are 12 PRINCES who rule the signs of the zodiac, 36 who rule the DECANS OF THE ZODIAC, 72 who rule the quinaries, four who rule the triplicities and the elements, and seven governors of the whole world, according to the seven planets. All of these angels have NAMES and SEALS that are used in ceremonial magic operations.

The third kind of angels are the ministers, who are committed to the affairs of earth and people, including travel, business, wars, and daily affairs. The ministers, who are everywhere, can help procure success and happiness, and also inflict adversity. The orders of ministers fall into four categories aligned with the characteristics of the four elements, which govern different faculties of mind, reason, imagination, and action.

Agrippa also discusses the CELESTIAL HIERARCHIES of PSEUDO-DIONYSIUS, Iamblichus, Athanasius, and the Kabbalists.

There are more good angels than the human mind can comprehend, but the good angels have corresponding FALLEN ANGELS or demons.

THE DEMONIC HIERARCHY

There are nine orders of demons that correspond to the nine orders of the Pseudo-Dionysius hierarchy of angels. They are, from the most important to the least:

- False Gods, who are ruled by Beelzebub and who usurp the name of God and demand worship, sacrifices, and adoration;
- Spirits of Lies, who are ruled by Pytho and deceive oracles, diviners, and prophets;
- Vessels of Iniquity, also called Vessels of Wrath, who invent evil things and the "wicked arts" such as card games and gambling, and who are ruled by Belial;
- Revengers of Evil, who are ruled by Asmodeus and cause bad judgment;
- Deluders, who are ruled by Satan and imitate miracles, serve wicked conjurers and witches, and seduce people by their false miracles;
- Aerial Powers, who are ruled by Meririm and cause pestilence and terrible destroying storms, and who are personified by the Four Horsemen of the Apocalypse in the book of REVELATION;
- Furies, who are ruled by Abbadon (Apollyon) and wreak war, discord, devastation, and evil;
- Accusers, who are ruled by Astaroth and lie and slander;
- Tempters and Ensnarers, who are ruled by Mammon and inspire covetousness and "evil genius."

All these evil spirits wander up and down the earth, enraged and fomenting trouble, but they have the potential for redemption if they repent.

FURTHER READING

Morley, Henry. *The Life of Henry Cornelius Agrippa.* London: Chapman and Hall, 1856.

Three Books of Occult Philosophy Written by Henry Cornelius Agrippa of Nettesheim. Translated by James Freake. Edited and annotated by Donald Tyson. St. Paul, Minn.: Llewellyn Publications, 1995.

Ahriman

The evil god of ZOROASTRIANISM. Ahriman, originally called Angra Mainyu, is the source of all evil. He opposes the good god, Ohrmazd, in a cosmic battle for supremacy, but one that ultimately he will lose. He is aided by demonic forces, including six arch-demons who struggle against the six archangel AMARAHSPANDS or "Bounteous Immortals."

RUDOLF STEINER named Ahriman as the arch-fiend principle of the cosmos, comparable to the devil or Satan.

Ahura Mazda   See OHRMAZD; ZOROASTRIANISM.

Aini

One of the FALLEN ANGELS and 72 spirits of SOLOMON. In HELL Aini is a strong duke. He appears as a handsome man with three heads: a serpent, a man with two stars on his forehead, and a cat. He rides on a viper and carries a blazing firebrand, with which he spreads much destruction. He imparts cunning and gives true answers to questions about "private matters."

Aion   See AEONS.

aishim; ashim   See ISSIM.

Akatriel (Achtariel, Akat(h)riel Yah Yedhod Sebaoth, Aktriel, Kethriel, Yehadriel)

A crown PRINCE of judgment over other angels. Akatriel is often equated with the ANGEL OF THE LORD and is identified with Metatron. When ELIJAH ascends to HEAVEN, he sees Akatriel surrounded by 120 myriads of MINISTERING ANGELS.

Akatriel also is the name of the Godhead on the throne of Glory.

Akoman   See ZOROASTRIANISM.

Akriel

Angel of barrenness. In Jewish magical lore, Akriel's name is invoked in prayers for children by repeating Deuteronomy 7:12, which promises fruitfulness of body and materiality in reward for keeping God's laws. The invocation of the NAME enhances the supernatural forces inherent in the biblical verses.

al-Suhrawardi, Shihab al-Din Yaha (1154–1191)

Sufi mystic, philosopher, and founder of the *Ishraqi* (Illuminationist) school of philosophy.

Life

Shibab as-Din Yaha al-Suhrawardi was born in the village of Surhrawardi in what is now northwestern Iran. He studied in Maraghah and Isfahan, and he then went to Anatolia, where he associated with royalty. He went to Aleppo, where he taught and wrote and became close friends with the governor, Malik Zahir. In his youth he had a dream in which Aristotle appeared to him and discussed philosophy. He was inspired by this to reject the prevailing philosophy of IBN SINA and revive the philosophy of the "Ancients." He turned to Hermeticism, Plato, Aristotle, and Sufi mysticism, and developed his own Illuminationist school of philosophy in which the ancient Divine Wisdom passes from Hermes to Egypt to Persia.

Malik Zahir, the son of Saladin, the sultan of Egypt, filled his court with Sufis and scholars. Saladin became concerned at Suhrawardi's growing influence on his son and incited local opposition against Suhrawardi. The philosopher was charged with heresy and imprisoned. Saladin ordered his execution, and Malik was forced to comply.

In death Surhawardi became known as al-Maqtul ("he who was killed"), al-Shahid ("the martyr"), and Shaikh al-Ishraq ("Master of Illumination").

Works

Suhrawardi authored approximately 50 works in Arabic and Persian. His four major philosophical works are *Kitab al-talwihat (The Imitations)*, *Kitab al-muqawamat (The Oppositions)*, *Kitab al-mashari' wa-'l-mutarahat (The Paths and the Heavens)* and *Kitab hikmat al-ishraq (The Philosophy of Illumination)*.

Suhrawardi holds that because ibn Sina lacked knowledge of ZOROASTRIANISM his work is incomplete. Suhrawardi sees philosophy and mystical experience as inseparable: A philosophy that does not culminate in a metaphysic of ecstasy is vain speculation; a mystical experience that is not grounded on a sound philosophical education is in danger of degenerating and going astray.

Suhrawardi's physical world consists of bodies of varying mixtures of light and darkness, which pass different degrees of light. Above the physical world is a vertical array of lights similar to the scheme of ibn Sina; however, they number more than ibn Sina's 10. They are not infinite, but are as many as the number of stars fixed in the HEAVENS. The vertical lights interact with each other to produce a horizontal array of lights. The interaction of the vertical and horizontal lights produces the bodies of the lower world, which vary in their ability to receive and pass light.

Angels are divided into two orders: the *tuli,* who are the vertical, longitudinal order, and the *'ardi,* who are the horizontal, latitudinal order. Each of the *tuli* emanates a radiation of positive attributes (dominion, independence, active contemplation, and so on) that produces an angel below it, which forms a fructifying feminine world. The higher angel relates to the lower one through dominance, and the lower angel relates to the higher one through love. The angels form a *barzakh* or bridge from one to another, veiling the purer light from the higher order; the higher order is revealed only to the amount of light that is passed through. The *barzakh* functions like the *mundus imaginalis.*

The negative emanations of the *tuli* (dependence, passive illumination, love as intelligence) produce the heaven of the fixed stars.

The relationship of dominance and love among the levels of *tuli* creates the masculine *'ardi* order, which exists as an equal whole and does not engender one another. The *'ardi* are the approximation of Platonic Forms or ARCHETYPES; they also have characteristics of GUARDIAN ANGELS. Each one is lord of a species or class of being in the visible world that it governs and watches over. The *'ardi* also correspond to the sevenfold powers of Ohrmazd, the AMARAHSPANDS. The chiefs of the amarahspands are the ARCHANGELS, headed by Bahman, the Zoroastrian Vohu Manah, who is the greatest and closest to the absolute light of Deity.

The archangel Gabriel is the archetype of humanity and is its lordly light and revealer of knowledge. Every human being is a reflection of an angel. At birth, the soul (which preexists) separates from its angel, and spends its incarnation seeking to be reunited with its angelic self and to return to higher light. The soul's home or true abode is the "Oriental Source," the numinous orient of light beyond the stars, where it can find peace and bliss. The soul struggles against its prison of occidental darkness. The invocation of Gabriel enables one to discern light from darkness and also different levels of light, and thus begin the journey home.

Illumination—*ishraq*—is the soul's return to its home through reason and intuition. An intermediate world, the world of subsistent images (*'alam al-mithal*) or immaterial bodies, which Suhrawardi calls the cosmic "Intermediate Orient," is home to the imagination, where theophanies take place.

Suhrawardi's work includes a complete cycle of recitals to initiation in Persian, which are continuation of ibn Sina's recitals. "The Recital of the Occidental Exile" and "The Purple Archangel" are among those about the Quest, a progressive initiation into self-knowledge through illumination.

In *The Familiar of the Mystical Lovers* (*Mu'nis al-'Ushshaq*) Suhrawardi dramatizes three beings proceeding from the meditation of the First Archangel (Bahman, the Intelligence) bearing the names Joseph, Zulaykha, and Jacob, and representing respectively Beauty, Love, and Sadness reflecting upon his being. Sadness (Jacob) corresponds to the heaven whose subtle matter "materializes" the thought of a nonbeing; it measures the zone of shadow, the distance that always intrudes between Love and Beauty to which it aspires. At the same time, Sadness is the instrument that allows the Soul, by the roundabout way of a long pilgrimage, to approach Beauty.

Suhrawardi claims to have seen in a vision the primordial Flame which is the source of these epiphanies or "dawn splendors" that revealed to him the authentic "Oriental Source." This is the "Light of Glory," the eternal radiance of the Light of Lights, Bahman.

Suhrawardi's "theosophy of Light" did not pass into Christian Europe but rather endured as a lasting influence upon Islamic esoteric philosophy. It also had an impact upon Jewish philosophy, such as in the works of Isaac Luria and the Safed Kabbalists. Modern translations of his works have gained new attention in the West.

FURTHER READING

Corbin, Henry. *History of Islamic Philosophy.* Translated by Liadain Sherrard. London: Kegan Paul International, 1993.

Nosr, Seyyed Hossein. *An Introduction to Islamic Cosmological Doctrines.* Boulder, Colo.: Shambhala, 1978.

Nosr, Seyyed Hossein, and Oliver Leaman, eds. *History of Islamic Philosophy.* London: Routledge, 1996.

Allocen (Allocer)

One of the FALLEN ANGELS and 72 spirits of SOLOMON. A duke in HELL, Allocen appears as a soldier who rides a large horse. His lion face is very red, and he speaks in a loud and hoarse voice. He teaches astronomy and the liberal sciences, and makes a good familiar. He rules over 36 legions.

amarahspands (amesha spentas)

In ZOROASTRIANISM, six "bounteous immortals" or "holy immortal ones" who are created by the good god Ohrmazd for the purpose of assisting him with their creativity and organizing ability. The amarahspands are similar to ARCHANGELS and organize the material world. Each is responsible for a sphere of the world, and each embodies a virtue or quality. They are:

- Vahuman (Good Thought, Good Mind), Ohrmazd's first creation and his chief promoter, who welcomes the blessed souls, leads the founding prophet Zarasthustra to Ohrmazd, is invoked for peace, and has special charge over useful animals
- Artvahisht (Best Righteousness or Truth), who personifies divine law and order, and rules all fires
- Shahrevar (Choice Kingdom, Material Sovereignty), who personifies Ohrmazd's might, majesty, regal power, and triumph and presides over metals, his signs, and symbols
- Spandarmat (Bounteous Right-Mindedness, Wisdom in Piety), who is daughter of Ohrmazd and heaven, personifies religious harmony and piety and presides over the earth, which manifests her bounty
- Hurdat (Health, Wholeness, Salvation), a feminine principle almost always associated with Amurdat, and who personifies complete health and perfection, and who governs water
- Amurdat (Life or Immortality), a feminine principle who personifies immortality and governs plants, and who, with Hurdat, is the promised reward of the blessed after death in paradise

A seventh amarahspand sometimes named is S(a)raosha.

The amarahspands receive special worship in ritual, and are said to descend to the oblation on paths of gold.

The amarahspands are opposed by their evil counterparts, devas ruled by AHRIMAN, the Zoroastrian god of evil.

The amarahspands can be seen as forerunners of the sephirot of the TREE OF LIFE in the KABBALAH.

FURTHER READING

Dhalla, Maneckji Nusservanji. *History of Zoroastrianism.* New York: Oxford University Press, 1938. Reprint AMS Press, 1977.

Amduscias

One of the FALLEN ANGELS and 72 spirits of SOLOMON. Amduscias is a great duke of HELL who rules over 29 legions. He appears as a unicorn. He will take on human shape if commanded to do so, but this will cause musical instruments to be heard but not seen. The LEMEGETON says that he gives people the power to make trees fall, and he also gives excellent FAMILIARS.

Amitiel See ANGEL OF TRUTH.

amesha spentas See AMARAHSPANDS.

Amon (Aamon)

One of the FALLEN ANGELS and 72 spirits of SOLOMON. According to the LEMEGETON, Amon is a strong and powerful marquis who rules over 40 legions. He appears as a wolf with a serpent's head, vomiting flame. He appears as a human when ordered to do so, but has dog's teeth. He is invoked to see the past and the future, procure love, and reconcile people.

Amriel (Ambriel)

Angel of the month of May, prince of THRONES, and ruler of the zodiac sign of Gemini. Amriel's name is invoked to protect against evil. He can be conjured with the seventh SEAL of the planet Mars. In MAGIC, Amriel is chief officer of the 12th hour of the night.

amulets

Magical objects of healing and protection against harm, disease, and misfortune, which often invoke the help of God or gods, angels, DEMONS, or other supernatural powers. Amulet comes from either the Latin word *amuletum* or the Old Latin term *amoletum,* which means "means of defense."

The premise of amulets is that the powers of the cosmos can be accessed through special or magically charged objects to ward off trouble in the natural world. Amulets exist universally and were widely used in ancient Egypt, the classical world, and the Near East. Probably the first amulets were natural objects such as stones, animal parts, and herbs. The magical properties of such objects were presumed to be inherent.

Over time, amulets became more creative and diverse. Stones, gems, and other objects were used in the making of animal shapes, symbols, rings, seals, and plaques. They were ritually imbued with magical power with inscriptions, words, spells, little prayers (charms), and the NAMES of deities and supernatural beings.

Written amulets for healing and protection were especially popular among Jews during the Talmudic period and in the Middle Ages. Formulae for amulets are given in texts. In addition, magical texts called GRIMOIRES offer magical procedures for making amulets drawn from Neoplatonic philosophy and the KABBALAH. Astrological influences, tools, colors, fumes, and so forth are all important parts of the process.

Names especially are believed to access divine powers. One of the greatest and most powerful names is the Hebrew personal name of God, Yahweh (YHVH), called the Tetragrammaton. Many Christianized amulets use Jesus as the great name of power.

Amulets invoke the names of major angels such as Michael, Gabriel, and Raphael as well as the names of numerous angels (and demons) whose specific powers are appropriate for the purpose of the amulet. For example, if an amulet is to ward off a specific illness, the name of the demon responsible for that illness and his THWARTING ANGEL would be invoked. Amulet inscriptions sometimes are written in one of the ANGEL ALPHABETS and decorated with powerful symbols such as the Star of David or geometric shapes. Some amulets are magical squares of letters or numbers.

The Jewish historian Joshua Trachtenberg cites four elements that are included in almost all Jewish amulets: (1) the names of God or angels; (2) biblical expressions or phrases that describe God's attributes and power; (3) meticulous detailed functions of the amulet; and (4) the name of the person the amulet serves, and the name of his/her mother.

Some amulets can be long and complex, such as this multipurpose one:

> In the name of Shaddai, who created heaven and earth, and in the name of the angel Raphael, the *memuneh* in charge of this month, and by you, *Smmel, Hngel, Vngsursh, Kndors, Ndmh, Kmiel, S'ariel, Abrid, Gurid,* memunim of the summer equinox, and by your Price, *Or'anir,* by the angel of the hour and the star, in the name of the Lord, God of Israel, who rests upon the cherubs, the great, mighty, and awesome God, YHVH Zebaot is His name, and in thy name, God of mercy, and by thy name, Adiriron, trustworthy healing-God, in whose hand are the heavenly and earthly households, and by the name YHVH, save me by this writing and by this amulet, written in the name of _____ so of [mother's name]. Protect him in all his two hundred and forty-eight organs against imprisonment and against the two-edged sword. Help him, deliver him, save him, rescue him from evil men and evil speech, and from a harsh litigant, whether he be Jew or Gentile. Humble and bring low those who rise against him to do him evil by deed or by speech, by counsel or by thought. May all who seek his harm be overthrown, destroyed, humbled, afflicted, broken so that not a limb remains whole; may those who wish him ill be put to shame. Save him, deliver him from all sorcery, from all reverses, from poverty, from wicked men, from sudden death, from the evil effects of passion, from every sort of tribulation and disease. Grant him grace, and love, and mercy before the throne of God, and before all being who behold him. Let the fear of him rest on all creatures, as the mighty lion dreads the mightier *mafgi'a.* I conjure [name], son of [mother's name], in the name of Uriron and Adriron [sic]. Praised be the Lord forever. Amen and Amen.

Many amulets are much simpler and may not contain all four elements, such as the following for winning favor:

Hasdiel at my right, Haniel at my left, Rahmiel at my head, angels, let me find favor and grace before all men, great and small, and before all of whom I have need, in the name of Yah Yah Yah Yau Yau Yau Yah Zebaot. Amen Amen Amen Selah.

Amulets must be worn on the body in order to protect a person or animal. They also protect spaces by being placed in homes and buildings or buried under thresholds. Written amulets on pieces of parchment or animal skin can be placed in pouches, bottles, and boxes for wearing or placement.

See MAGIC; MEMUNIM; MEZUZAH; TALISMANS.

FURTHER READING

Budge, E. A. Wallis. *Amulets and Superstitions.* New York: Dover Publications, 1978. First published 1930.

Three Books of Occult Philosophy Written by Henry Cornelius Agrippa of Nettesheim. Translated by James Freake. Edited and annotated by Donald Tyson. St. Paul, Minn.: Llewellyn Publications, 1995.

Trachtenberg, Joshua. *Jewish Magic and Superstition: A Study in Folk Religion.* New York: Berhman's Jewish Book House, 1939.

Amurdat See AMARAHSPANDS.

Amy

One of the FALLEN ANGELS and 72 spirits of SOLOMON. Amy was once a member of the orders of ANGELS and POWERS. According to the LEMEGETON, he is a president in HELL, where he governs 36 legions. He possesses perfect knowledge of the liberal sciences and astrology. He rules over good FAMILIARS. He appears first as a huge flaming fire and then as a man. Amy reveals hidden treasures guarded by other spirits. In 1,200 years he hopes to be restored to the "seventh throne," that is, to the place before God reserved for the highest of angels. Demonologist JOHANN WEYER called this claim "not credible."

Anael (Anafiel, Aniel, Aniyel, Ariel, Aufiel, Hamiel, Haniel, and Onoel)

Angel who rules Venus and human sexuality; Friday angels; the second HEAVEN; and, in some references, the moon. Anael also is one of the seven ANGELS OF CREATION and is PRINCE of ARCHANGELS and chief of PRINCIPALITIES.

In the second heaven, Anael is in charge of prayers that ascend from the first heaven.

The Jewish historian Joshua Trachtenberg says that in the Middle Ages, the Jewish mezuzah, a parchment scroll in a holder placed on doorways to ward off evil, was to be written only on Sunday or on Thursday, in the fourth hour, presided over by Venus and the angel Anael. The name of Anael was included in the angel names inscribed on MEZUZOT.

In the LEMEGETON, Anael rules the second hour of the day, called Cevorym. He commands 70 chief dukes and 100 lesser dukes and their servants.

Anapiel YHVH (Anafiel, Anaphiel, Anpiel)

Angel associated with the prophet ENOCH and the angel METATRON. Anapiel means "branch of God."

In the MERKABAH, Anapiel is one of the eight great angels and is named as the PRINCE of water and the chief SEAL bearer. He keeps the keys of the seven palaces in Arabot, the seventh HEAVEN.

In 3 ENOCH, Anapiel YHVH is one of the angels identified as the one who carries Enoch to heaven. He is called "the honored, glorified, beloved, wonderful, terrible and dreadful Prince" (16:7). He is chosen by God to punish Metatron on one occasion with a flogging of 60 lashes. Metatron says that Anapiel is so named because his majesty, glory, crown, brilliance, and splendor overshadow all the chambers of Arabot in the same way that God's majesty veils the heavens and fills the Earth with his glory.

Anapiel bows down to Soterasiel.

Anahel

In 2 ENOCH, ruler of the third HEAVEN, and in the Sixth and Seventh Books of MOSES, a resident of the fourth heaven. Anahel also is described as a guardian of the Gate of the West Wind.

Ancient of Days

A NAME of Yahweh/God or the highest of holy ones. In the book of DANIEL, the prophet Daniel sees the Ancient of Days in his fiery, heavenly court in the first of four visions:

> As I looked, thrones were placed and one that was ancient of days took his seat; his raiment was white as snow, and the hair of his head like pure wool; his throne was fiery flames, its wheels were burning fire. A stream of fire issued and came forth from before him; a thousand thousands served him, and ten thousand times ten thousand stood before him; the court sat in judgment, and the books were opened. (7:9–10)

In the KABBALAH, Ancient of Days describes Keter (Crown), the first sephirah of the TREE OF LIFE, also called Macroprosopus, meaning "God of concealed form."

Andra See ZOROASTRIANISM.

Andras

One of the FALLEN ANGELS and 72 spirits of SOLOMON. Andras is a great marquis who rules over 30 legions, and he appears in the form of a raven-headed angel who rides a black wolf and carries a gleaming and sharp sword. According to the LEMEGETON, he creates discord and kills those who are not careful and wary, including the master, servants, and all assistants of any household.

Andrealphus

One of the FALLEN ANGELS and 72 spirits of SOLOMON. The LEMEGETON says that Andrealphus is a mighty marquis who rules 30 legions. He first appears as a noisy peacock and then as a human. He can transform people into birds. He teaches geometry, everything pertaining to measurements, and astronomy.

Andromalius

One of the FALLEN ANGELS and 72 spirits of SOLOMON. Andromalius is both a great duke and an earl. He appears as a man holding a serpent. He returns stolen goods, reveals thieves, discovers wicked deeds and underhanded dealings, and reveals hidden treasures.

angel alphabets

Secret written languages used in MAGIC and mysticism and conveyed by angels. Angel alphabets are used to invoke and communicate with angels and spirits, and to translate and encode prayers, charms, texts, AMULETS, and TALISMANS.

One of the most widely copied and used celestial alphabets comes from the SEFER RAZIEL and is of unknown origin. Various alphabets are attributed to individual angels, including Metatron, Michael, Gabriel, Raphael, and other angels.

In form, some angel alphabets resemble cuneiform; others are related to early Hebrew or Samaritan script. They are called "eye writing" in Kabbalistic literature because the letters are formed with straight and curved lines and circles resembling eyes. There is one character for each letter in the Hebrew alphabet. The scripts may be used in conjunction with SEALS, symbols, and magical squares of numbers.

Significant magical scripts are:

Celestial Writing. A type of eye writing related to the stars.
Malachim. A type of eye writing that takes its inspiration from the angelic order of MALACHIM ("kings") and from the book of Malachi, whose proper name is derived from the Hebrew term for "my messenger." Of special significance in Malachi is verse 3:16:

> Then those who feared the Lord spoke with one another; the Lord heeded and heard them, and a book of remembrance was written before him of those who feared the Lord and thought on his name.

The Greater Key of SOLOMON refers to Malachim as "the tongue of angels." According to occultist S.L. MacGregor-Mathers, Malachim is formed by the positions of stars. The characters are shaped by drawing imaginary lines from one star to another.

Passing of (through) the River. A type of eye writing, but with more embellishments than the previous two. Also known as the Talismanic Script of King Solomon, this script is so-named from the four rivers that flow through the garden of Eden: Pison, Euphrates, Gihon, and Hiddekel.
Theban. A script of curved symbols. Also known as the Honorian Script, this alphabet is related to lunar energies and affects the lower astral and etheric planes. It is equated to English.

See ANGEL LANGUAGES; GRIMOIRES.

Different angelic scripts, from The Magus *by Francis Barrett*

FURTHER READING

Goddard, David. *The Sacred Magic of Angels.* York Beach, Maine: Samuel Weiser, 1996.

James, Geoffrey. *Angel Magic: The Ancient Art of Summoning and Communicating with Angelic Beings.* St. Paul, Minn.: Llewellyn Publications, 1999.

Savedow, Steve. *Sepher Rezial Hemelach: The Book of the Angel Rezial.* York Beach, Maine: Samuel Weiser, 2000.

Three Books of Occult Philosophy Written by Henry Cornelius Agrippa of Nettesheim. Translated by James Freake. Edited and annotated by Donald Tyson. St. Paul, Minn.: Llewellyn Publications, 1995.

Trachtenberg, Joshua. *Jewish Magic and Superstition: A Study in Folk Religion.* New York: Berhman's Jewish Book House, 1939.

angel bread

Manna. The Hebrew term for manna is *lehem abbirim*, or "bread of powerful beings." According to the Zohar, angel bread, or manna—a flaky substance like thin cakes of honey—is a product of divine emanation that provides both physical and spiritual nourishment. The Zohar says that angels are nourished by it each according to his diet. The Talmud describes manna as "bread that the ministering angels eat."

Exodus 16 describes angel bread as bread from HEAVEN, given to the Israelites by Yahweh during their trip through the desert out of Egypt; it fell as dew during the evening, appearing in the morning like a coating of frost.

Manna sustained the Israelites during 40 years in the wilderness: "Then the Lord said to Moses, 'Behold I will rain bread from heaven for you'" (Exodus 16:4); "And the people of Israel ate the manna forty years," (Exodus 16:35).

There may be a real manna: a substance excreted by plant lice on tamarisk shrubs (found in the Sinai wilderness), which hardens in the dry desert air.

One must be of a certain purity to be able to eat angel bread, which emanates from a very high sphere

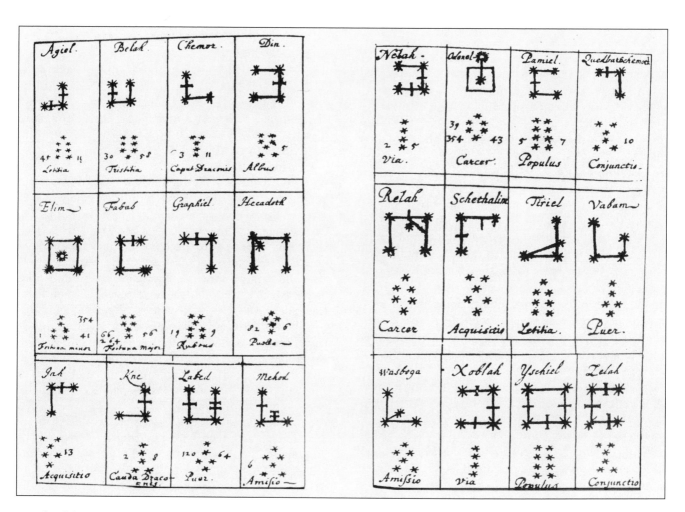

Angelic alphabet for magical purposes

of heaven and penetrates deep into the soul. The Zohar says that Comrades, those who study the Torah, receive the highest food of all, namely, WISDOM.

angel language

The language understood by all angels, for the purposes of communication, intercession, duties, petitions, and prayers. According to the Talmud, God understands all languages, but the official language of angels is Hebrew. Thus, angels might ignore petitions made in any other language.

The belief in Hebrew as the official angel language was prevalent among Jews through the Middle Ages. This principle apparently was fostered in order to discourage prayers in Aramaic, the popular tongue (but also held by some to be the "official" language of angels). Aramaic prayers were allowed for the sick, because it was believed that the SHEKINAH hovered over the head of the patient and received prayers directly without the intervention of angelic messengers. Other prayers composed in Aramaic may have been written expressly to avoid understanding by angels, perhaps due to the contents.

The importance of Hebrew as the official language of angels can be seen in the old custom for Jews to be given a Hebrew name in addition to a secular name, so that during religious rites the angels could recognize individuals. The Hebrew name was especially important for the passage of death and the ANGEL OF DEATH.

The importance of Hebrew also was evident in medieval Jewish magical texts. Procedures and instructions might be written in the vernacular, but the charms themselves, intended for the angels, were given in Hebrew. The belief that angels understood only Hebrew was oddly contradicted, however, by the Talmud itself, which states that angels know the thoughts hidden in the heart.

In other lore, angelic speech has nothing to do with sounds or words and is not impeded by time or distance. An angel speaks by directing its thought to another angel. Angels "speak" to God by consulting his divine will and contemplating him.

In various systems of MAGIC, different magical alphabets and symbols are used to communicate petitions and make charms intended to procure angelic intervention; many use Hebrew. The Renaissance alchemist JOHN DEE, working with Edward Kelly, composed an elaborate system of angelic keys, or calls, to communicate with the heavenly host.

Popular belief in contemporary times holds that angels, like God, understand any language.

EMMANUEL SWEDENBORG, who made visionary trips to HEAVEN and HELL, conversed with angels in a universal language that is instinctive and does not need to be learned. In *Heaven and Hell* (1758) Swedenborg says that angelic speech flows from their affection of thought, and unites the wisdom and love that is in their interiors. The angels express ideas and nuances beyond the comprehension of mortals, and they can convey in a single word what a mortal would say in 1,000 words.

See ANGEL ALPHABETS; MERKABAH; NAMES; SEALS.

FURTHER READING

Three Books of Occult Philosophy Written by Henry Cornelius Agrippa of Nettesheim. Translated by James Freake. Edited and annotated by Donald Tyson. St. Paul, Minn.: Llewellyn Publications, 1995.

Trachtenberg, Joshua. *Jewish Magic and Superstition: A Study in Folk Religion.* New York: Berhman's Jewish Book House, 1939.

angel names See NAMES.

Angel of Death

Angel charged with announcing death and taking the soul to either HEAVEN or HELL. The Angel of Death is known by various names. In his true form, the Angel of Death has a terrible countenance, but he is able to manifest in any pleasing form in order to trick or calm the living into giving up their souls to him.

Serving as the Angel of Death is one of the functions ascribed to the GUARDIAN ANGEL in Christian belief. According to ORIGEN, the "celestial escort" receives the soul at the moment it leaves the body.

Among the prominent Angels of Death are Michael, who leads souls of the dead to the afterlife (see PSYCHOPOMPOI), and who takes away the souls of ABRAHAM and MARY; Gabriel, a guardian of the underworld; Satan; Samael, who holds a sword over the mouths of the dying, from which falls a drop of poison; and Iblis. In rabbinic writings, other angels of death are Metatron, Azrael, Abbadon (Apollyon), Hemah, Kafziel, Kezef, Leviathan, Malach ha-Mavet, Mashit, Yehudiah, and Yetzer-hara. Azrael is prominent in Arabic lore; in ZOROASTRIANISM, it is Mairya. In folktales the Angel of Death often is not named.

The Testament of ABRAHAM relates the story of Abraham's encounter with the angel of death. The story begins when Abraham is 175 years old and at the end of his life. Both his wife Sarah and son ISAAC figure in the story, although according to Genesis Sarah's death preceded that of Abraham, and Isaac was married to Rebecca when his father died.

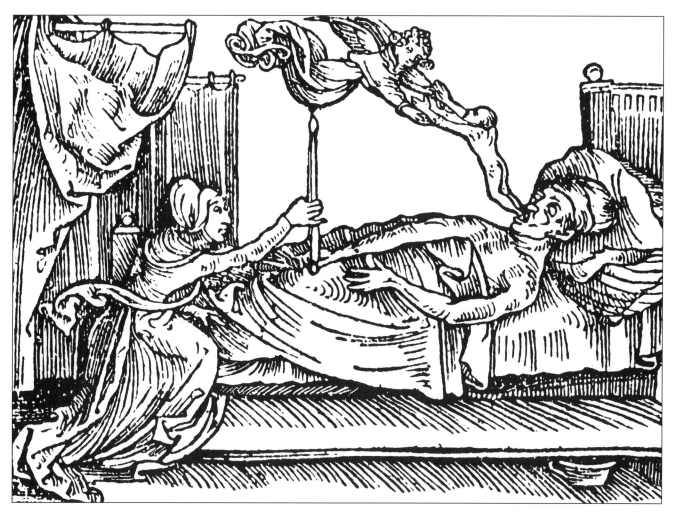

Angel of Death taking a soul, in the form of a child, from a dying man (Reiter, *Mortilogus,* 1508)

God sends Michael to Abraham to tell him it is time to die. Abraham still lives by the oak tree at Mamre, where he had earlier in his life served and fed three visitors who were angels in disguise. He sees Michael approach him, and though he looks like a splendid warrior, he does not recognize him as an angel. He invites Michael to come with him, and the two walk back to Abraham's house. Isaac, recognizing Michael as an angel, falls at the angel's feet. He tells Sarah that Michael is an angel.

Abraham has Isaac fetch water, which he uses to wash Michael's feet. He begins to weep, and sees that Michael weeps tears of precious stones. Abraham then orders Isaac to prepare a room for a banquet.

Michael excuses himself and goes immediately to heaven, where he has a conversation with God. Abraham is so righteous, he says, that he cannot pronounce death upon him. God decides to send a prophecy of

death in a dream to Isaac, which Michael can then interpret.

Michael also wonders how he will be able to eat food. God says he will send an all-devouring spirit to consume the food and protect Michael's identity. Michael goes back to Abraham and joins him in the meal. They pray together.

When Isaac goes to sleep, he dreams the death prophecy and awakens weeping. Michael also weeps. Sarah attends them, and realizes that Michael is one of the three mysterious visitors from before. She quietly lets Abraham know. Abraham hears Isaac's dream, and Michael interprets it.

Abraham persuades Michael to admit that he is an angel, and to reveal the purpose of his visit. He refuses to die. He discusses death with God, and Michael takes him on a tour of the cosmos. Still Abraham refuses to die.

Angels taking away souls of the dead (Author's collection)

God then sends the Angel of Death to Abraham at Mamre, and he reveals his true appearance: "The Death made his appearance dark and more fierce than any sort of beast . . . and he showed Abraham seven fiery heads of dragons, fourteen faces of the most flaming fire . . . and a gloomy viper's face. And the face of a terrible precipice, and the fiercer face of an asp, and the face of a fearsome lion . . . and he also showed him the face of fiery sword . . . and another face of a wild sea raging and a river rushing and a fearsome three-headed dragon and a mingled cup of poisons." Death prevails in the end, and Abraham dies.

The Angel of Death manifests in a much friendlier form in the 19th-century Hasidic folk tale of the esteemed Reb Pinhas. The angel appears as a visiting Hasid, and politely presents a petition of death to Reb Pinhas that reveals his true identity. The rabbi answers with his own petition: He will be happy to go wherever the Angel of Death wishes to take him, but if he could

have a choice, he wishes to go to Gehenna (hell), because he wishes to be of service to the souls there and work for their release.

This places the Angel of Death in a predicament, for he has been ordered not to deny Reb Pinhas any wish. Yet, he cannot bring himself to take the rabbi to hell. Like Michael, he goes back to heaven to ask God what to do. He is given an answer, whispered through a curtain.

The angel goes back to Reb Pinhas and presents him with a petition, to which has been appended a single word inscribed in black flames. The petition tells Reb Pinhas that he has been given a holy name that will take him either to Paradise or to Gehenna, depending on how the name is pronounced. The true pronunciation is so secret that only the angel Metatron knows it. Not even the Angel of Death can help.

Reb Pinhas, still intent on going to hell, studies the word but ultimately must guess at its pronunciation. He goes to heaven, illustrating that there is no escape from one's fate: One cannot go to hell if one deserves to go to heaven, and vice versa.

A rabbinic tale from Babylon in the fifth century also illustrates that there is no escaping the Angel of Death. One morning, King SOLOMON hears birds chirping, and, because he understands the language of birds, he learns that the Angel of Death plans to take two of his closest advisers. He tells them, and they beg him to help them escape their doom. He urges them to flee to the enchanted city of Luz, which the Angel of Death is forbidden to enter.

(Luz, according to the Talmud, is a secret city where everyone remains immortal as long as they do not venture outside the gates. Solomon, because of his magical powers, is able to know the location of it. Also, in Genesis 28:19 Luz is the place where JACOB had his dream of the ladder.)

But the Angel of Death knows all, and when the men arrive at the city gates, they find the angel waiting for them just outside, barring their way.

This and other tales about the Angel of Death show that mortals cannot escape fate, and that once God has decreed it, Death always has the last word. However, another rabbinic story tells that Rabbi Joshua ben Levi outfoxes the Angel of Death by talking the angel into letting him hold his sword. He refuses to give it back, and leaps straight into the Garden of Eden while he is still alive.

The Beit ha-Midrash tells the story that Moses wrote 13 Torahs on the day he was told he was going to die, as a means of preventing the Angel of Death from taking him. According to lore, one cannot die while one is studying the Torah. The 13 Torahs included one for each of the 12 tribes of Israel, plus a celestial Torah (the best of the lot) that was taken to heaven and used by the angels. (Gabriel gave this Torah to Rabbi Meir ben Baruch of Rothenburg, a leader of German Jewry in the 13th century who spent much time in prison, and who copied the Torah during his confinement. He put the copy in a casket and sailed it off down the Rhine, to be discovered by Jews.)

Still another Jewish story demonstrates how angels exert free will, and how God can change his mind and retrieve the Angel of Death. A mystical tale from Yemen in the 14th century tells about the fate of a bride and bridegroom. An old man, Reuben, sins once in his life by rebuking another man for sitting in his place at the synagogue. God decides to punish him by sending the Angel of Death to take away his son, who is about to be married. Reuben pleads with the angel to spare his son until he is married and has tasted the joy of life. Moved with pity, the angel agrees.

God rebukes the angel for disobeying him. Chastened, the angel decides to revenge himself by taking the son with the same tremendous anger shown him by God. The prophet Elijah tells the son that at his wedding, an old man in rags will appear, and it will be the Angel of Death.

The angel appears and Reuben offers himself as a surrogate. The angel displays his faces of cruelty, anger, wrath, and severity, and draws his sword to cut off Reuben's head. Reuben flees. Reuben's wife offers herself, and then she flees in terror.

Finally, the bride offers herself and does not flee. The Angel of Death sheds a tear of mercy. God, watching from heaven, has pity and orders the Angel of Death to retreat. He grants both bride and bridegroom 70 more years of life.

FURTHER READING
Schwartz, Howard. *Gabriel's Palace: Jewish Mystical Tales.* New York: Oxford University Press, 1993.

Angel of Glory
One of the titles of Sandalphon, along with ANGEL OF PRAYER and ANGEL OF TEARS.

Angel of Great Counsel
A title ascribed to the Messiah in the Greek rendition of the Old Testament. The Angel of Great Counsel was to be the ruler of Israel. The title may have consolidated the four titles in the Hebrew version, given in Isaiah 9:6: Wonderful Counselor, Mighty God, Everlasting Father, and Prince of Peace. Those four titles may eventually have been dispersed among the top four archangels, Michael, Gabriel, Raphael, and Uriel/Phanuel, aspects of the ANGEL OF THE LORD.

FURTHER READING
Barker, Margaret. *The Great Angel: A Study of Israel's Second God.* Louisville, Ky.: Westminster/John Knox Press, 1992.

Angel of Hostility
Name associated with the evil angel Mastema, prince of DEMONS. In the Dead Sea Scrolls (see QUMRAN TEXTS) and in JUBILEES, Israelites who obey the law of MOSES and are circumcised will not suffer at the hands of the Angel of Hostility.

See ANGELS OF MASTEMOTH.

Angel of Peace
According to Jewish lore, an unnamed angel who, with the ANGEL OF TRUTH, opposed the creation of man. God punished the angels and their host by burning them.

In 1 Enoch, the angel of peace accompanies ENOCH on his heavenly journeys, answers questions, and gives him the names of the four archangels of the presence: Michael, Raphael, Gabriel, and Phanuel (Uriel).

St. John Chrysostom referred to the GUARDIAN ANGEL as an "angel of peace" in terms of helping people to maintain their inner calm and equilibrium.

See ANGELS OF PEACE; PRINCE OF PEACE.

Angel of Prayer

Angel who carries prayers to God. Serving as a messenger of prayers is a duty ascribed to angels in general, but certain angels are especially identified with this task. The most often named angels of prayer are Sandalphon, Michael, Metatron, Gabriel, Raphael, and, in Persian lore, Sizouze. Some angels carry prayers only to a certain level of HEAVEN, where they are handed over to angels who will carry them to the next level. Sandalphon is one of the highest angels of prayer.

Tertullian, one of the Roman Catholic Church fathers, said the GUARDIAN ANGEL functions as the angel of prayer, assisting people in their most important spiritual task.

Angel of Punishment See ANGELS OF PUNISHMENT.

Angel of Repentance

Title given to various angels, including Michael, Penuel, Phanuel, Raphael, Salathiel, and Suriel. In The Shepherd of HERMAS, the Angel of Repentance is an otherwise unnamed angel who appears in the form of a glorious shepherd and interprets some of Hermas's visions. The angel stays permanently with Hermas, similar to one of the good DAIMONES or a GUARDIAN ANGEL.

Angel of Tears

A title ascribed to Sandalphon, who hears the prayers of the suffering, and sometimes to Cassiel. In Islamic lore, the Angel of Tears is not named but resides in the fourth HEAVEN.

Praying angel at cathedral in Coutances, France (Author's collection)

The Angel of Prayer (Reprinted courtesy of U.S. Library of Congress)

Angel of the Lord (Angel of Yahweh)

Angel identified with, and possibly the same as, God. While any angel sent to execute the commands of God might be called the Angel of the Lord—such as in 2 Samuel 24:16 and 1 Kings 19:5,7—frequent mention is made in Scripture of a particular angel who is distinguished from Yahweh, and yet is identified with him. Whether or not the angel represents a direct visitation or manifestation of God, God appearing through an angel, God giving an angel more direct power than usual, an angel taking the form of man, or some other phenomenon is still debated.

The Angel of the Lord reveals the face of God (Genesis 32:30) and is Yahweh's name (Exodus 23:21). The angel's presence is equivalent to Yahweh's presence (Exodus 32:34; 33:14; and Isaiah 63:9). The Angel of the Lord thus appears as a manifestation of Yahweh himself, one with Yahweh and yet different from him. Sometimes the angel of the Lord may be described as a floating conception, at one moment an angel, at another the Lord.

Examples of other references to Angel of the Lord in the Old Testament occur in:

- Genesis 16:7–14; 18:1–4, 13–14, 33; 21:17; 22:11–12, 15–16; 31:11, 13;
- Exodus 3:1–6; 23:20–24;
- Numbers 20:16; 22:21–35;
- Joshua 5:13–15; 6:2;
- Judges 2:1–5; 5:23; 6:11–24; 13:1–25;
- 1 Samuel 29:9;
- 1 Chronicles 21:15–30;
- Zechariah 1:10–13; 3:1–2.

In the New Testament, angelic voices and dream visions surround the birth and early lives of John the Baptist and JESUS. The Angel of the Lord who appears to Zechariah (Luke 1:11–20) says, "I am Gabriel, who stand in God's presence." The Angel of the Lord is a title applied to an unnamed angel throughout the Gospels, including those present at the tomb on Easter morning. But the Angel of the Lord came to be identified with Christ himself in early church writings. This controversy in Christian theology continues.

Justin Martyr (ca. 100–ca. 165 C.E.) was the first to advocate that the Angel of the Lord was a pre-incarnate appearance of Christ in the guise of an angel. Others attracted to this concept interpreted Old Testament references to "Angel of the Lord" as referring to Christ. It was Christ who wrestled with JACOB, according to St. Clement of Alexandria (ca. 150–ca. 220). St. Hilary of Poitiers (ca. 315–367) took Jesus's words in John 8:56 ("Abraham saw my day") to mean he was one of the three angels who visited ABRAHAM (Genesis 16:10). St.

Angel of the Lord destroying the army of King Sennacherib (Gustave Doré)

AUGUSTINE was aware of the dangers of embracing the idea that Christ had been corporeal prior to the Incarnation and opined that the Trinity was incorporeal in the Old Testament. Nevertheless, he broadened the idea of angel/messenger to include the Holy Spirit. Augustine's views prevailed for over a millennium. St. THOMAS AQUINAS did not pursue the issue.

During the PROTESTANT REFORMATION, John Calvin committed himself in the *Institutes* to a descent of the non-yet-incarnate Christ "in a mediatorial capacity, that he might approach the faithful with greater familiarity" (1.13.10; 14.5). The Lutherans deemed it heresy to deny that the Angel of the Lord was Christ. In his list of accusations against Servetus, Calvin indicted him for heresy for not holding that the angel was Christ (*Institutes,* 1.13.10). Eventually it was argued that every theophany in the Old Testament was a "Christophany" by the angel-Christ advocates, who said that because these angels were sometimes worshiped or that people who saw them believed they had seen God, they were indeed God. They held that the Old and New Testaments must be mediated by the same source in name, form, and substance; Christ was the Messiah and true God. Major 19th-century

Angel appearing to Zacharias

Christologists maintained the angel-Christ identification, as well as many since.

M. J. Field has argued that the earliest angel messengers, particularly in Genesis, are real men appearing to be angels. According to Field's thesis, the unschooled Hebraic nomads could have been guided and led to make decisions through the intervening powers of holy men of the deserts who were interested in drawing these people toward monotheism. Field spent many years in Africa witnessing the magical and persuasive powers of men and women hermits who exerted "spiritual oversight" over tribes. Field notes that these people are often adept in "special effects" such as fire, sparks and smoke, and ventriloquism, like the voice in the burning bush (Exodus 3:2). Their luminosity, dignity, powers, and charismatic presence would derive from years of spiritual practice. These individuals existed in the lands and especially the deserts of the Bible, and they created the beginnings of the Western monastic traditions.

Others, such as William G. MacDonald, argue against the wholesale interpretation of the Angel of the Lord as Christ mainly on the grounds that pre-incarnation appearances of Christ make it impossible theologically to reconcile the full deity of Christ with the full humanity of Christ. For example, *malak* means not only "messenger" but "agent." Servants had full authority to carry on their masters' business. It would make sense for an angel to represent itself as *malak Yahweh* ["Angel of the Lord"] or *malak Elohim* ["the angel of God"].

In *The Great Angel*, Margaret Barker makes a case for the Great Angel, or Angel of Yahweh, as originally a second and lesser God of the Hebrews. Yahweh was one of several sons of God (EL ELYON), the High God. Early, more polytheistic beliefs influenced by exposure to Babylon and Egypt were consolidated by the Deuteronomist reforms in the establishment of the Law. Yahweh also was one of the four angels around the throne in EZEKIEL; in Psalms 58 and 82 he is the judge of the heavenly court of law. Yahweh the Great Angel overlaps with, and eventually came to be represented by, four facets in the chief archangels, Michael, Gabriel, Raphael, and Uriel. Metatron and Melchizedek also have associations with the Great Angel.

FURTHER READING

Barker, Margaret. *The Great Angel: A Study of Israel's Second God.* Louisville, Ky.: Westminster/John Knox Press, 1992.

Field, M. J. *Angels and Ministers of Grace: An Ethno-Psychiatrist's Contribution to Biblical Criticism.* New York: Hill & Wang, 1971.

Heick, O. W. *A History of Christian Thought.* Philadelphia: Fortress Press, 1965.

MacDonald, William Graham. "Christology and 'The Angel of the Lord.'" In *Current Issues in Biblical Studies.* Edited by G. F. Hawthorne and Merrill Tenney. Grand Rapids, Mich.: Eerdman, 1975.

Angel of Truth

In Jewish lore, an unnamed angel who, with the ANGEL OF PEACE and the angels under them, opposes the creation of man. All the opposing angels are punished by God by being burned into cinders. Amitiel is sometimes identified as the Angel of Truth.

In Islamic lore, Gabriel, the angel who brings revelations to MUHAMMAD, is the Angel of Truth.

See PRINCE(S) OF LIGHT(S).

Angel of Yahweh   See ANGEL OF THE LORD.

angel wreath   (feather crown)

In the folklore of the Ozarks area of the United States, lumps of feathers formed into wreath shapes found inside bed pillows. An angel wreath found inside the pillow of someone who has just died is a lucky omen that the person is saintly and has gone to heaven. The wreath is a symbol of the golden crown the person will wear in heaven.

Angel wreaths vary in shape and size. Some are tightly bunched and others loosely formed. They resemble rings, buns, caps, and balls, and they are from two to six inches in diameter. Most likely the wreaths form naturally from pressure and handling of the pillow. The feathers become attached by the minute barbs on the quills.

Folkloric tradition holds that the feathers inside the pillow of a deceased person should be searched for signs of an angel wreath. If one is found, the family is relieved. Angel wreaths have been preserved in families as lucky charms.

In earlier times, the discovery of an angel wreath was worthy of mention in the town newspaper. Angel wreaths once were so highly prized that they were stolen or secreted into pillows. Sometimes people would ask to be buried with the angel wreaths of their deceased spouses or relatives. It was widely believed that the wreaths were not made by humans or by chance but were of divine origin.

Ozark superstition also holds that angel wreaths are not from heaven but from the devil, and they are a sign of witchcraft at work. Thus, feather pillows should be regularly searched, and any partially formed wreaths destroyed.

FURTHER READING
Randolph, Vance. *Ozark Magic and Folklore.* New York: Dover Publications, 1964. First published 1947.

angelic keys See ANGEL ALPHABETS; DEE, JOHN.

angel-man

In German folklore, an effigy representing the solar fire, traditionally burned at celebrations of the summer solstice. The burning of fires once was a widespread practice in honor of the solstice and to help the sun, at its peak power, change its course in the sky. Scriptures and other sacred writings describe angels as "burning" and "clothed in fire." An angel became an appropriate image in some seasonal fire festivals.

The German ritual was called "beheading the angel-man." It was performed on Midsummer Day, at least up through the early 20th century and perhaps later. The angel-man was an effigy made of a stump driven into the ground, wrapped in straw, and fashioned into a crude human figure with arms, head, and face. Wood was piled around the effigy. Boys armed with swords covered it with flowers. The wood was lit. When the angel-man burst into flames, the boys attacked it and cut the burning figure into small pieces. They then jumped backward and forward over the fire.

Straw effigies of humans—usually a man but sometimes a woman—commonly were burned as a part of summer solstice festivals.

FURTHER READING
Frazer, James G. *The Golden Bough.* New York: Avenel Books, 1981. First published in 1890.

angelology

The study of angels. The existence, nature, function, duties, and influences of heavenly forces called angels are important in the development of the monotheistic religions of Judaism, Christianity, and Islam. All three religions honor the texts of the Old Testament as divine revelation. They share roots in Middle Eastern history and Semitic languages; for example, the term for angel or messenger is *malak* in both Hebrew and Arabic.

Michael holding the cube of Metatron (Reprinted courtesy of Jayne M. Howard)

All three religions also share the belief in the presence of an evil force, a disobedient angel, an adversary of God—a *satan* in Hebrew—who wreaks havoc on the human plane. In both the Koran and the Bible, angels are sent to strengthen believers, succor them here and in eternity, undertake military assistance, punish disbelievers, intercede for humans, act as GUARDIAN ANGELS, and mete out God's judgment on the last day. Angels represent God, but are not to be worshiped for themselves.

Angels in Judaism

Judaic angelology acknowledges angels as both intermediary and intercessory. Angel lore was heavily influenced by ZOROASTRIANISM, to which part of the Jewish population was exposed during the Babylonian captivity in the seventh century B.C.E. In pre-exilic times angels belonged to popular rather than prophetic Judaic religion, but after the exile angels sprang into prominence and played crucial roles in visionary experiences such as those described in the Tanakh, the Old Testament, by ISAIAH, EZEKIEL, ELIJAH, ZECHARIAH, DANIEL, and in apocryphal works like the book of ENOCH. The Enochian writings in particular feature an elaborate scheme of heaven and the hierarchy of angels.

During the Babylonian captivity, a complete system of angels, both good and bad, was developed; it shares many parallels with Zoroastrian concepts. Heaven is composed of different levels, above which rests Yahweh on his throne. The heavens below him are filled with a great multitude of angels who do his bidding, and who have specific duties to keep the universe organized and functioning. Many angelic duties overlap or even conflict among angels, with different angels or order of angels performing the same tasks. In between angels and man are hosts of DEMONS.

Talmudic times saw the developments of angelology and demonology, both complex and both containing entities and beliefs inherited from cultures throughout the Mediterranean: Egyptian, Graeco-Roman, and Gnostic, in addition to Babylonian. Magical and mystical practices for dealing with these entities focused on the power of NAMES. Magical practices sought to borrow power from entities in order to protect against others or to effect some action in the world. Mystical practices, such as in the MERKABAH tradition and later the KABBALAH, also employed names of power to interact with angels and demons.

In Scripture the function of angels is to glorify God (such as in the visionary accounts mentioned above) and act out God's commands and will. Angels, appearing either as men (see ABRAHAM) or as an ANGEL OF THE LORD, reveal the presence and might of God in the world. Angels punish on God's command (see SODOM

Angel (Copyright 1995 by Robert Michael Place, from *The Angels Tarot* by Rosemary Ellen Guiley and Robert Michael Place. Reprinted courtesy of HarperSanFrancisco)

AND GOMORRAH) but they also protect (see DANIEL, GUARDIAN ANGELS). But angels—or those interpreted to be angels—are themselves punished by God if they displease him. (See LUCIFER; SONS OF GOD; WATCHERS.)

The references to angels in the Old Testament did not prevent the aristocratic Jewish intellectual Sadducees in ancient Israel from denying the existence of angels. However, the majority of Jews from post-exilic times onward had not only affirmed the existence of angels but also developed additional ideas about them as intermediaries who are accessible to humans and can be called upon for help. In Talmudic times, prayers to angels appealed to their intercessory abilities. As angelology developed along more magical lines, prayers were converted into magical incantations. (See MAGIC.)

In mysticism, the angels of the Merkabah—especially those closest to God—are powerful, remote beings often hostile to humans, many of whom stand as barriers between man and God. According to tradition, when God thinks about creating man, he first creates a company of angels and then asks their advice. The angels oppose the creation of man, and God destroys them by burning them. He creates a second company who also oppose the idea, and he destroys them as well. A third company of angels agree to the creation of man. But after mankind becomes so corrupted that God decides to destroy everything by sending the Flood, the angels remind him of the original advice and say, "Lord of the Universe, did not the first company of angels speak aright?" God replies that he has promised to carry and sustain man; thus NOAH repopulates the earth. Similarly, angels oppose the delivery of the Law to MOSES and the passing of the SEFER RAZIEL book of cosmic secrets to ADAM, but they are unsuccessful on both accounts. In 3 ENOCH, they object unsuccessfully to Rabbi Ishmael (the purported author of the text) entering the heights of heaven and participating in the angels' devotional rights.

Myriads of angels infinite in number attend everything in creation. (See MEMUNIM.) Numerous individual angels are recognized, including seven archangels who can be compared to the six Bounteous Immortals—AMARAHSPANDS—of Zoroastrianism. In the KABBALAH, there are 10 orders of angels assigned to the 10 sephiroth of the TREE OF LIFE, the system set forth in the primary Kabbalistic work, the Sefer Yetzirah. Guardian angels assigned to every person from birth to death are derived in part from the Persian FRAVASHIS, beings who also are guardians of place, similar to the GENII.

The identities of the individual angels often blur with different names given for the same being. Long lists of angels are given in literature; works such as 3 Enoch and the Sefer Raziel contain detailed descriptions of cosmic workings, the angels assigned to them, and—in the case of the Sefer Raziel—procedures for invoking those angels.

See MAIMONIDES; PHILO; QUMRAN TEXTS.

Angels in Christianity

In the New Testament, the roles of intermediary and intercessor of God are taken over by JESUS; angels play supporting roles. Gabriel announces to Mary her impending pregnancy. Angels proclaim the birth of Jesus to shepherds. Joseph is visited by an angel in his dreams: to be instructed to marry Mary despite her pregnancy; to take his family to Egypt after the birth of

Diptych of Gabriel's annunciation to Mary, from St. Cozia Monastery, Romania (Author's collection)

Jesus to avoid the persecutions of Herod; and to return to Israel from Egypt when it was safe to do so.

After Jesus begins his ministry, angels recede in importance. They are not the channels of miracles, for he has taken over that role as well. Jesus mentions angels but does not emphasize them in his preaching. He states that not even the angels will know when the tribulation will come; when the Son of man returns he will be surrounded by angels.

Angels are involved as secondary figures in some of Jesus' key experiences. After Jesus rejects Satan during his temptation in the desert, angels come and minister to him. One or two angels are at his tomb ("Why do you seek the living among the dead?"—Luke 24:5).

Forty days after Jesus' crucifixion, during which he appears and speaks numerous times to his apostles, Jesus ascends to heaven; two angels disguised as men speak to his awestruck apostles:

> And when he [Jesus] had said this, as they were looking on, he was lifted up, and a cloud took him out of their sight. And while they were gazing into heaven as he went, behold, two men stood by them in white robes,

and said, "Men of Galilee, why do you stand looking into heaven? This Jesus, who was taken up from you into heaven, will come in the same way as you saw him go into heaven." (Acts 1:9–11)

Angels figure in the subsequent acts and lives of the apostles. For example, when Peter and other apostles are imprisoned by the Sadducees, an Angel of the Lord appears at night and opens the prison doors and leads them out.

In his epistles, St. PAUL writes about angels and devils, giving emphasis to the superiority of Jesus over angels, and the role of devils (demons) as enemies of the faithful.

The early church fathers accepted angels but opposed anything that might encourage idolatry. St. AUGUSTINE said that while Christ did not die for the angels, his redemption nonetheless benefited them, helping to repair the damage of their ruin (a reference to the WATCHERS). In 325, the Council of Nicaea incorporated angels into the dogma of the Christian Church, stimulating art and theological and philosophical commentaries on them for centuries to come.

Angels figure prominently in the lore of the saints. Legends and hagiographies of the early saints and martyrs include references to angels. They appear in DREAMS AND VISIONS; act as guides; dictate messages, instructions, and revelations; and serve as support in times of trial. Their presence symbolizes the saints' holiness. In many cases of hagiographies, angels may have been more a literary device to explain inspired thought or a means by which to inspire the faithful. Many saints, however, had genuine visionary experiences of angels. (See St. TERESA OF AVILA.)

The Christian monastic tradition—the withdrawal from the world in order to dedicate one's life to God—developed in the early centuries after the death of Jesus. St. Pachomius was a fourth-century Egyptian Copt who, after his conversion to Christianity while in the Roman army, spent years in retreat with another hermit. He was praying alone in the desert of Tabenna when an angelic figure spoke to him and told him to found a monastery according to the rule the angel would give. His companion helped him to build what would become the first Christian cloister. A wall surrounded the humble structure as a symbol of the monk's separation from the world, and no stranger was allowed beyond a certain point, leaving "the inner sanctum" unsullied. Pachomius's "Angelic Rule," one

Angel at the tomb of the resurrected Christ (Gustave Doré)

Angel delivering St. Peter from prison (Gustave Doré)

of the major monuments of early Christian literature, was innovative in one major fact: It was a binding commandment, akin to a law. After living as a novice for a number of years, each monk accepted the rule as an unalterable canon of life.

Christian monasticism was most profoundly influenced by St. Augustine, whose teachings on angels coincided with monastic spirituality. According to Augustine, monks are a group chosen for the heavenly city. The terrestrial church has only a partial vision of God, whereas the celestial church enjoys the full vision of God. As the counterparts of the angels, monks occupy a special place at the heart of the church universal. They bear witness to the bliss that awaits the pure of heart; their penances and ascetic practices prepare them for the incorporeal life of angels.

Early monks frequently defined their vocation as the angelic life, insofar as they were detached, pure, and devotional. Poverty, chastity, and obedience were rooted in angelic reality, as angels had no bodily needs and served God unceasingly. Indeed, in accordance with Christ's words (Matthew 22:30; Mark 12:25; Luke 20:35–36) that the blessed will be "like the angels in heaven."

Celibacy is especially important in the process of sanctification, or becoming angel-like. In his tract *Holy Virginity,* Augustine praises virginity as *vita angelica,* the angelic life, "a sharing in the life of the angels and a striving for endless immortality here in this perishable flesh." Practicing continence dedicated to God means "reflecting on the life of heaven and of the angels amid this earthly mortality." Thus, whoever has taken a vow of celibate chastity, whether a man or woman, must "live on earth the life of the angels," and begin to be on this side of the grave what other Christians "will be only after the resurrection." Augustine saw further resemblances to the angelic life in the way the celibate direct their senses and their efforts to "what is eternal and immutable," and in their zeal for performing works of virtue, "so that they show to earth how life is lived in heaven." Following from this, Augustine developed the theme of the "heavenly life," *vita caelestis,* a psychology of living on earth with one's eyes turned upward. The contemplation (*vita contemplativa*) of God practiced in the monastery would in time proceed to freedom from passion; the monks like angels would be immersed in happiness derived from divine truth and beauty while still in this world.

This striving toward the angelic was emphasized by many who followed Augustine. In the ninth century, the works of PSEUDO-DIONYSIUS were translated, and the hierarchy of angels became a model for the ascent of the soul.

The monastic literature of angelology and contemplation reached its apex in the 12th century with St.

Bernard of Clairvaux. The waning of monastic culture after 1200 (with the rise of new orders like the Franciscans and Dominicans, who were not cloistered) brought a lessening of interest in Augustinian angelology.

The great medieval scholar St. THOMAS AQUINAS, who favored Aristotlean philosophy, wrote extensively on angels, defining their nature and activities, confirming the existence of guardian angels, and commenting on the Dionsyian hierarchy. Others, however, such as the Rhineland mystic Meister Eckhardt, saw angels less as role models and more as messengers.

The PROTESTANT REFORMATION that began in the 16th century dramatically changed and split Christian angelology. The Protestants accepted the existence of angels as helpers and messengers, but they increasingly emphasized the demonic: Satan and his legions were a terrible threat. John Calvin expressed great skepticism that guardian angels existed, and dismissed the Pseudo-Dionysius writings as "babble." Calvinist thought has wielded considerable influence on Protestant philosophy into contemporary times.

Angels have retained a stronger place in Catholicism, although the church officially recognizes only three angels by name: Michael, Gabriel, and Raphael. The general presence of angels in spiritual life is more readily acknowledged than in Protestantism. Modern popes have talked of angels. (See PIUS XI, PIUS XII, and JOHN XXIII.) Saints such as Padre Pio have underscored the importance of enlisting the help of one's guardian angel. Various DEVOTIONAL CULTS put angels in the proper context of spiritual living.

A renaissance of popular interest in angels began in the late 20th century and spawned a popular angelology. This view portrays angels as more than messengers and administrators of God's will, but as personal companions, healers, and helpers. The modern angel is a being who is always good and benevolent, in contrast to the biblical angel who metes out punishment and justice when God so commands. Popular angelology has brought angels down to earth: They have personal names, beautiful humanlike appearances and characteristics, and they have personal conversations with their human charges. In many respects, the modern angel is like an idealized human being. While it is likely that intuition, inspiration, and imagination have taken on angel faces, extraordinary visionary experiences also occur, including dream encounters that parallel many accounts of earlier times.

See ANGELOPHANY; ANGELS; GNOSTICISM; IMAGES OF ANGELS.

Angels in Islam

The Koran establishes angels as the second of five articles of faith, along with divine unity, messengers (prophets), revealed books, and the day of resurrection. Surah 35.1 describes angels as having subtle and luminous bodies with two, three, four, or more wings. They can assume various forms; they are endowed with perfect knowledge and have power over their acts. Their ministry is to glorify God; they manifest themselves to the prophets and their spiritual heirs (*wasi*) to signify a divine communication to them. Attempting to explain any more about angels strays from the proper road. Scholars and holy men who applied angelology to metaphysics, psychology, cosmology, and mystical practice often provoked alarm, incomprehension, and even open hostility from the legalists. Nonetheless, a rich angelology emerged from the prophets, mystics, and philosophers outside of Islamic orthodoxy, and among Shiites and some sects of Sufism.

General beliefs hold that angels are created of light and are endowed with life, speech, and reason. They are sanctified from carnal desire and the disturbance of anger. They do not disobey God, and do whatever he commands of them. They are distinctly different from DJINN and genii. They are inferior to human prophets because all the angels were commanded to prostrate themselves before Adam (Surah 2.32).

According to Sufi teacher Abdul Karim Jili, the highest angel is identified with the Spirit mentioned in the Koran. He is made from God's light—the Muhammadan light—and "from him God created the world and made him His organ of vision in the world." He is the divine command, chief of the kerubim (CHERUBIM), the axis of creation. He has eight major forms, great angels who bear the throne of God. All other angels are created from him "like drops from the ocean." He is also the eternal "prophetic light" from which all prophets derive their inner being; the breath or spirit sent to Mary to conceive Jesus; and MUHAMMAD in his perfect manifestation.

The archangels and angels created from the highest angel preside over the principles of the universe. Four archangels, or kerubim, are named in the Koran. From the great angel's heart comes Israfil, the mightiest of the angels who will sound the trumpet at the last day; from his intelligence comes Gabriel (Jibril), treasurer of divine knowledge and revelations, who dictated the Koran to Muhammad; from his judgment comes Azrael (Azrail or Izrail), the ANGEL OF DEATH, and from his *himma* (spiritual aspiration) comes Michael, who metes out the fate of all things. From his thoughts come all the celestial and terrestrial angels who are "the souls of the spheres and of mankind." From his imagination comes the very stuff of the universe itself, which is "Imagination within Imagination within

Imagination." From his soul or ego comes both the sublime and contemplative angels and the Satan and his hosts.

Two other angels (though not Koranic) are known by name, Munkar and Nakir, who visit the graves of the newly buried as soon as the funeral party departs. They are charged with examining the dead person with regard to belief.

Other angels who have special functions are Ridwan, the angel in charge of heaven, sometimes called the "treasurer of the Garden," even the "door-keeper of the Garden," which may connect in some way to the cherubim in Genesis keeping the way of the tree of life with a flaming sword.

A main duty of angels is to praise the Lord and intercede for humans, asking God to forgive them: "the angels celebrate the praise of their Lord, and ask forgiveness for the dwellers on earth" (Surah 42.3). In addition, a guardian angel looks after each person all through life, with duties of giving assistance against unbelievers, and having the ability to intercede if necessary: "Each hath a succession of angels before him, who watch over him by God's behest" (Surah 13.12) and "He is the supreme guard over his servants, and sendeth forth guardians who watch over you, until, when death overtaketh any one of you, our messengers receive him and fail not" (Surah 6.61). When God so orders, angels are sent as military warriors to aid in battle.

Every believer is attended by two RECORDING ANGELS, called the *kiramu'l katibin*. One has its station on the right, the one who contemplates and dictates; the other has its station on the left, the one who records. Like the angels of Jacob's vision, sometimes the recording angels come down to humans. The Koran adds: "it is said that among their number are those to whom the human being is entrusted and whom the Holy Book calls 'Guardians and Noble Scribes'" (82.10–11). The recording angels are acknowledged daily in the Muslim prayer ritual, the *salat*.

Both Satan and Devil are named in the Koran. Satan originally was a good angel, but declined to share in the worship of Adam and so was expelled from Paradise. He is often mentioned with the adjective "the Stoned," which may refer to the *jamrah*, the throwing of stones at three *shayatin* (djinn) during the pilgrimage rites.

On the day of Resurrection the four bearers of God's throne—similar to the four living creatures in Isaiah—will be raised to eight. They shall "bear the Throne and those round about it, proclaim the praises of their Lord, and believe in Him" (Surah 40.7); "Upon the day when the Spirit and the angels stand in ranks" . . .

"thou shalt see angels encircling about the throne" (Surah 68.77).

The death of Muhammad in 632 officially brought an end to prophecy, for no other prophets can follow Muhammad. However, traditions of esoteric prophecy continued in Shia and Sunni philosophies, centered around imams, teachers or holy guides. There are four types of prophets. One is the *nabi* or prophet who has revelations only for himself and is not obliged to proclaim what is received. Another is the *nabi* who hears the voice of the angel while dreaming, but does not see the angel in a waking state and also is not obliged to proclaim his vision to anyone. Third is the *nabimursal,* the prophet-messenger who has the vision or perception of an angel in both sleeping and waking states. This prophet may be sent to bring light to others. Fourth are the seven great *nabimursal* messengers— Adam, Noah, Abraham, Moses, David, Jesus, and Muhammad—whose mission (*risalah*) is to proclaim a *shari'ah,* a new divine law. The Shiites hold that only the *shari'ah* or legislative kind of prophecy ended with Muhammad's death, whereas the esoteric prophecy continues.

The prophet/messenger's waking visions of angels differ from sense perception; they take the form of an inner vision called *wahy,* or divine communication in which the angel/intelligence imparts a knowing to the human intellect. The angel-intelligence is identified with the Angel of Revelation, the Holy Spirit or the angel Gabriel, and also is called the Pen (*qalam*) because it is the intermediary between God and humankind that actualizes knowledge in the heart, as the pen mediates between writer and paper. Knowledge through God is only actualized through the angels, according to Surah 42.50–51: "It is not vouchsafed to any mortal that God should speak to him save by communication from behind a veil, or by sending a messenger."

The visionary experience also can be likened to a veil that lifts between two mirrors, the divine mirror and the mirror of the heart. The veil is lifted by hand, as the philosophers try to do, or by blowing wind or by an angel through divine grace. The mirror is a metaphor for the imagination, upon which angels can impress symbols that help further the ascent of the soul to the Origin.

See AL-SUHRAWARDI; IBN SINA.

FURTHER READING

Bishop, Eric F. F. "Angelology in Judaism, Islam and Christianity," *Anglican Theological Review.* Vol. 46 (January 1964).

Carter, George William. *Zoroastrianism and Judaism.* New York: AMS Press, 1970.

Corbin, Henry. *History of Islamic Philosophy.* Translated by Liadain Sherrard. London: Kegan Paul International, 1993.

Giudici, Maria Pia. *The Angels: Spiritual and Exegetical Notes.* New York: Alba House, 1993.

Lang, Judith. *The Angels of God: Understanding the Bible.* Hyde Park, N.Y.: New City Press, 1997.

Nasr, Seyyed Hossein. *An Introduction to Islamic Cosmological Doctrines.* Boulder, Colo.: Shambhala, 1978.

Nigg, Walter. *Warriors of God: The Great Religious Orders and Their Founders.* Translated by Mary Ilford. New York: Alfred Knopf, 1959.

Scholem, Gershom. *Kabbalah.* New York: Dorset Press, 1987. First published 1974.

Trachtenberg, Joshua. *Jewish Magic and Superstition: A Study in Folk Religion.* New York: Berhman's Jewish Book House, 1939.

Zumkeller, Adolar. *Augustine's Ideal of the Religious Life.* Translated by Edmund Colledge. New York: Fordham University Press, 1986.

angelophany

The experience of perceiving an angel with one or more of the five senses. The characteristics of angelophanies differ, probably in accordance to cultural conditioning, expectations, and acceptance or rejection of such experiences. Since angels have no corporeal form, the exact nature of their appearances has been the subject of debate and controversy. (See IMAGES OF ANGELS.)

Ancient angelophanies found in the Bible, apocryphal texts, rabbinic literature, and other lore often occur within the context of DREAMS AND VISIONS. The great prophets, such as EZEKIEL, MOSES, ISAIAH, and ENOCH had grand visions of angels and transport to heavenly realms. They saw angels, were guided by them, beheld the throne of God, and were anointed as holy messengers to return to their people and disseminate the word of God through warnings and moral and ethical codes. They heard the voices of angels and the voice of God. Such visions involved common elements of brilliant light, fire and lightning, and sounds of thunder and earthquakes. The angels were described as having the forms of men, but being clothed in brilliant light or garments. Sometimes they were said to have wings; other times wings are not specified.

The dramatic nature of such visions may have been necessary to gain the attention of people; the angelophanies—and theophanies, or experiences of God—certified the prophets as official agents of the Lord. Such visions also were central to MERKABAH mysticism in which one rode to the heavens via prayer and meditation to attain access to the "throne-chariot" of God.

Portrait of St. Francis Xavier (Bartolomé Esteban Murillo, c. 1670; reprinted courtesy of the Ella Gallup Sumner and Mary Catlin Sumner Collection Fund, Wadsworth Atheneum, Hartford, Conn.)

On some occasions in early writings, angels pass for mortals, and seem to have the ability to disguise their heavenly light. In Genesis, ABRAHAM is so fooled when three men visit him on the plains of Mamre and partake of a feast he offers them in hospitality. They converse with him. Similarly, the archangel Raphael appears as a mortal man in the book of TOBIT and acts as a guide on the journey of Tobias.

In Catholicism, angels are considered to be pure spirits who have the ability to take the form of men and women. They intervene to help people in their spiritual and temporal needs. Angels appear often in hagiographies, the legends and lives of the saints, and figure in many of their miracle stories. Typically, they do not have names (Michael is the most often named of those who do). They may be accompanied by fire, or displays of elements, or fragrant smells. They play roles in healing, mystical experience, miracles, protection, and guidance. Their

presence—probably fictional and symbolic in many cases—serves to demonstrate the presence of God, or a saint's closeness to God.

St. Simeon Stylites reportedly spent the last 37 years of his life confined by his own accord atop a 60-foot-high pillar. His disciples gave him food and removed his waste with buckets and ropes. Even this deprivation was not enough for him, and so he had himself bound to the platform so tightly that the ropes cut into his flesh, and maggots began eating at the wounds. It was documented that he was often and visibly visited by his guardian angel, who devoted many hours to teaching him the mysteries of God. The angel also foretold his death. St. Theodosius claimed that an angel enabled him to endure his torture by refreshing his burning wounds. When the torture ended, the angel went away, which made Theodosius unhappy. A story concerning St. Agnes holds that when a Roman judge ordered her to be punished by rape in a house of prostitution, an angel struck blind the man who attempted to do so. The man's companion begged for her mercy; she prayed for him, and his sight was restored. St. Agnes eventually underwent severe torture and was executed. St. FRANCIS OF ASSISI beheld an angel who played the violin for him, filling him with such joy that he thought his soul would leave his body. A seraph also gave him his stigmata. St. FRANCES OF ROME was able to see and hear a guiding angel for the last 28 years of her life. (See also St. GEMMA GALGANI; St. TERESA OF AVILA.)

Modern angelophanies differ significantly from those described in the past. In the modern West, the culture does not support grand prophetic visions in the style of the Old Testament prophets; however, the NEAR-DEATH EXPERIENCE incorporates many of the same elements (guiding beings of light, visions of heaven, prophetic visions of the future, warnings about the present course of humanity).

Few in the contemporary Western secular world report constant communication with angels. An angelophany is likely to be a once-in-a-lifetime event, usually in response to a crisis or severe psychological need. For example, an angelophany bolsters spiritual faith or jolts one on to a spiritual path. Angels are most likely to appear as mortals, either adult or child (see MYSTERIOUS STRANGER), probably due to cultural conditioning. Other visual perceptions are of balls, clouds, and pillars of light. (See ANGEL OF THE LORD.) If angels manifest as a being of light, they invariably have a beautiful human form and countenance, and occasionally wings. Many people believe that angels have appeared to them in the form of animals, such as animals to the rescue. Some people have experiences that could be classed as angelophanies, though they do not identify any presences as "angels" (see

CHARLES LINDBERGH). This may be due to cultural conditioning in which individuals do not believe in "real" angels or in the possibility of encountering angels.

Many angelophanies take place entirely on the inner planes. People who attempt to cultivate communication with angels do so in meditation and prayer; many feel they receive spiritual guidance in return.

A trend in Western popular culture has been to identify and name one's GUARDIAN ANGEL.

FURTHER READING

Adler, Mortimer J. *The Angels and Us.* New York: Collier Books/Macmillan, 1982.

Guiley, Rosemary Ellen. *Angels of Mercy.* New York: Pocket Books, 1994.

Parente, Fr. Pascal P. *The Angels: The Catholic Teaching on the Angels.* Rockford, Ill.: Tan Books and Publishers, 1973. First published 1961.

Parisen, Maria, comp. *Angels & Their Co-creative Power.* Wheaton, Ill.: Quest Books, 1990.

angels

Incorporeal beings who mediate between God and mortals. Angels, created by God, minister over all living things and the natural world, and also all things in the cosmos. In CELESTIAL HIERARCHIES, angels are one of various classes of angels in general; they are those closest to the material world, the GUARDIAN ANGELS of souls and the couriers of the HEAVENS who deliver prayers to God and God's answers and inspirations to humans.

The term angel comes from the Greek *angelos,* which means "messenger." Similarly, the Persian term *angaros* means "courier." In Hebrew, the term is *malak,* which also means "messenger." Serving as messenger refers to one of the angel's primary duties, to shuttle back and forth between earth and heavenly realms. Angels also mete out the will of God, whether it be to aid or to punish humans. Angels are specific to Judaism, Christianity, and Islam; however, they derive from concepts of helping and tutelary spirits that exist in mythologies the world over.

Angels (Gustave Doré)

The Western concept of the angel evolved primarily from the mythologies of Babylonia and Persia. ZOROASTRIANISM developed a complex angelology that influenced the Jews, who spent time exiled in Babylonia. The angel also absorbed characteristics from Sumerian, Egyptian, and Greek beings. Syncretic Jewish, Hellenistic, and Gnostic angel beliefs were absorbed into Christianity and then into Islam. (See ANGELOLOGY.)

The Bible presents angels as representatives of God. The term ANGEL OF THE LORD appears frequently and may refer to an angel or to God himself. Angels exist in a celestial realm. They are incorporeal, but have the ability to assume form and pass as mortals. They also appear as beings of fire, lightning, and brilliant light, sometimes with wings and sometimes without. (See IMAGES OF ANGELS.) Various classes of angels are mentioned in the Bible and apocryphal texts; they are organized into different hierarchies.

Angel (From *The Hierarchie of the Blessed Angells* by Thomas Heywood [1635])

In the Bible, angels play roles in the working out of humanity's relationship to the Divine. Except for Michael, Gabriel, and Raphael, they are not referred to with proper names. However, numerous angels are mentioned by name in APOCRYPHA AND PSEUDEPIGRAPHA TEXTS. By the Middle Ages, midrashim, kabbalistic writings, and other sources had cited thousands of angels by name. (See KABBALAH; MERKABAH; NAMES.)

The ranks of heavenly angels have evil counterparts in the FALLEN ANGELS cast out of heaven because they angered God. (See LUCIFER; SATAN; WATCHERS.) As DEMONS, they tempt humankind into sin and steal souls into hell. The fallen angels also include the demonized gods of pagan cultures.

The early church fathers of Christianity gave extensive consideration to the duties, nature, numbers, abilities, and functions of angels. This theological interest peaked by the Middle Ages and began to decline in the Renaissance. The scientific revolution diminished the stature and importance of angels, though DEVOTIONAL CULTS kept their interest alive in Christianity. Angels renewed in popular interest in the late 20th century, due in part to a widespread spiritual hunger for personal relationships with the Divine and in part for the comfort of ready supernatural assistance and guidance. Popular culture portrays angels as anthropomorphized "best friends," which is in stark contrast to the awesome, impartial, unknowable beings of Jewish angelology and early Christian lore.

Numbers of Angels

Early writings refer only to numberless numbers of angels—their ranks are so vast as to be beyond calculation. The stars and all heavenly bodies are angels or angelic INTELLIGENCES. The biblical prophet DANIEL had a vision of heaven in which at least 100 million angels appeared: "a thousand thousands served him and ten thousand times ten thousand stood before him." The prophet ENOCH, in his travels to heaven, observed "angels innumerable, thousands of thousands, and myriads and myriads." Enoch's description is echoed in the New Testament book of REVELATION, authored by John of Patmos.

In the Kabbalah, the Zohar states that 600 million angels were created on the second day of creation, but adds that other angels were created on other days for other purposes. In the third century, the Jewish scholar Simon ben Lakish related angels to the seven heavens of Enoch and the signs of the Zodiac. There were a total of 1.06434 quintillion angels, he said, organized into hosts, camps, legions, cohorts, and myriads.

In Islam, the Koran states only that "numerous angels are in heaven." However, an Islamic tradition about the archangel Michael holds that he is responsible for creating 700 quadrillion CHERUBIM alone. Michael is covered with saffron hairs, each of which has a million faces, and each face has a million eyes, from each of which fall 700,000 tears, each of which becomes a cherub.

ORIGEN, a church father, said that angels "multiply like flies." But the Roman Catholic Church declared that the numbers of angels were fixed at the time of creation.

By the Middle Ages, speculation on the numbers of angels reached a peak. St. THOMAS AQUINAS said that every person on earth has a guardian angel, but that the total ranks of angels are much greater. St. Albert the Great, a Dominican monk who was a teacher to Aquinas, said that each of the nine ranks of angels has 66,666 legions, each of which has 6,666 angels, for a total of nearly 4 billion angels. Other medieval scholars placed the total number of heavenly host at 301,655,722, of which 133,306,668 are fallen.

In contemporary popular culture, the question of the numbers of angels is moot: There are as many angels in the universe as are necessary. Even in the 17th century, the folly of angel counting was recognized. Said Thomas Heywood, an English playwright who authored *The Hierarchy of the Blessed Angels*, counting angels would "grow from ignorance to error." The modern rhetorical question, "How many angels can dance on the head of a pin?" points to the futility of trying to calculate the numbers of the heavenly host.

Do Angels Eat?

Angels are incorporeal, so therefore they cannot eat food in the same manner as mortals. How, then, to explain texts in which angels eat food with mortals? The accepted answer is that angels only appear to eat, which is sometimes necessary to protect their disguise as humans.

In Genesis 18, ABRAHAM is visited by three angels, whom he mistakes for men. They partake of a feast of food and drink he prepares for them. In the book of Tobit, Raphael, in the guise of a man, eats food with his mortal companion and charge, Tobias (see TOBIT). In The Testament of Abraham, Michael arrives as the ANGEL OF DEATH to fetch the soul of Abraham and is offered a feast.

In the latter work, Michael in a quick visit to God protests that he will not be able to eat; God says he will send an all-devouring spirit to enable Michael to give the appearance of eating. Similarly, theologians explain that the angels of Genesis (thought to be Michael, Gabriel, and Raphael) only appear to eat. In Tobit, Raphael explains that visions are created to give the appearance of eating; the angels actually consume manna, a special food of heaven. (See ANGEL BREAD.)

Sometimes angels turn away food. In Judges 6:21 GIDEON presents food to the ANGEL OF THE LORD, who burns it up; this is a sign that the angel is who he says he is, and his instructions to Gideon must be followed. In Judges 13:15–16, an angel declines a kid offered by Manoah: "If you detain me, I will not eat of your food; but if you make ready a burnt offering, then offer it to the Lord."

Modern-day accounts of angelophanies sometimes involve eating by angels.

FURTHER READING

Adler, Mortimer J. *The Angels and Us*. New York: Collier Books/Macmillan, 1982.

Giudici, Maria Pia. *The Angels: Spiritual and Exegetical Notes*. New York: Alba House, 1993.

Guiley, Rosemary Ellen. *Angels of Mercy*. New York: Pocket Books, 1994.

Godwin, Malcolm. *Angels: An Endangered Species*. New York: Simon & Schuster, 1990.

Lang, Judith. *The Angels of God: Understanding the Bible*. Hyde Park, N.Y.: New City Press, 1997.

Parisen, Maria, comp. *Angels & Their Co-creative Power*. Wheaton, Ill.: Quest Books, 1990.

angels of destruction

Angels who function as the "sword of God" and who are dispatched to mete out punishment to humans. Punishment can be in the form of illness, plagues, pestilence, misfortune, or death. Accounts of destroying angels often do not give names of the angels. Numbers of angels of destruction vary in the literature, ranging from 40,000 total to 90,000 in hell alone.

In the MERKABAH tradition, angels of destruction try to confound the mystic on his attempts to ascend through the HEAVENS. Angels of destruction are mentioned frequently in rabbinic texts, where they have two primary tasks: to punish the wicked and to torture and purify souls in HELL. In 3 ENOCH, they are present at the heavenly court of law when people are called to judgment. When God sits on the judgment throne, the angels of destruction stand facing him. The ANGELS OF MERCY stand on his right and the ANGELS OF PEACE stand on his left. There are two scribes and a host of higher angels, the SERAPHIM and OPHANIM. The judgment book is made half of fire and half of flame. When God opens it, the angels of destruction immediately go out to execute his punishment with his unsheathed sword. Two of them, Za'afiel (ZAAPIEL) and Simkiel, take the souls of the wicked to SHEOL. The souls who are "intermediate"—that is, they have some redeeming qualities—are purified there by Simkiel. The condemned are taken by Za'afiel on down to Gehenna (hell) where they are punished with rods of burning coals.

Angels of destruction who are cited by name are Uriel, Harbonah, Azrael, Simkiel, Za'afiel, Af, Kolazonta, Hermah, and Kemuel. Kemuel or Simkiel are most often named as the chief of the group. Other angels not specifically "angels of destruction" also carry out God's orders of punishment. The archangel Gabriel is sometimes cited as the angel dispatched to destroy the wicked SODOM AND GOMORRAH.

Incidents of angelic punishment are cited in Scripture and other religious tracts. The Zohar observes that there is no act of annihilation or punishment that does not involve a destroying angel. Besides the destruction of Sodom and Gomorrah, biblical accounts of punishing angels include a number of episodes.

In 2 Kings 19, King Hezekiah battles the Assyrians and is assured by God that not a single Assyrian arrow will be shot into Jerusalem. A lone destroying angel visits the Assyrian soldiers one night, and the next morning all 185,000 of the troops are found dead.

However, God is not so pleased with Jerusalem because King David has displeased him (1 Chronicles 21). Satan incites David to number Israel against God's orders. God gives David a choice of punishments (1 Chronicles 21:11–12): "Take what you will: either three years of famine; or three months of devastation by your foes, while the sword of your enemies overtakes you; or else three days of the sword of the Lord, pestilence upon the land, and the ANGEL OF THE LORD destroying throughout all the territory of Israel." David opts not to be punished by his mortal enemies. God sends the pestilence and the destroying angel. David sees the angel, stretched between heaven and earth, ready to smite Jerusalem with his sword, and begs for mercy. The angel instructs him to set up an altar. David

The Destroying Angel (Reprinted courtesy of U.S. Library of Congress)

does and offers a sacrifice to God. The Lord accepts and orders the angel to stay his hand.

One of the best-known accounts is that of the destroying angel who slaughters the firstborn of Egypt in the Passover, recounted in Exodus 12:18–30. God warns the Israelites held captive in Egypt that he will pass judgment on the land. The faithful are told to smear blood on their lintels and doorposts as a sign. At midnight on the appointed night, the destroying angel sweeps over Egypt and kills the firstborn of man and beast in every household except those marked by blood.

In Job 2, Satan again functions as an angel of destruction when God, seeking to test Job's faith as a righteous man, delivers Job into Satan's hands. Satan smites Job with "loathsome sores" (boils) all over his body, but Job only curses the day of his birth, and not God. Eventually, God restores Job to favor and rewards him with prosperity.

Punishing angels appear in the New Testament as well. In Matthew 13, Jesus goes out into a boat and addresses a large crowd on shore, speaking in parables. In 13:47–50, he describes the kingdom of heaven as like a net thrown into the sea, which gathers every kind of fish. Fishermen must sort out the good from the bad. "So it will be at the close of the age," he explains. "The angels will come out and separate the evil from the righteous and throw them into the furnace of fire; there men will weep and gnash their teeth."

Acts 12 tells of the punishment of King Herod. Herod is angry with the people of Tyre and Sidon. A group of them come to him and ask him for peace, because their people depend on his country for food. Herod dons his royal robes, ascends his throne, and delivers an oration to them. They cry out, "The voice of a god, and not of man!" (Acts 20–22). Acts 20:23: "Immediately an angel of the Lord smote him, because he did not give God the glory; and he was eaten by worms and died."

The book of REVELATION, a vision of the end times, is filled with angels of destruction who obliterate sinners. Revelation 8 describes seven angels who blow their trumpets, raining down upon the earth hail and fire mixed with blood, turning part of the sea into blood, dimming the sun, moon, and stars, and wreaking tremendous havoc. A host of angels unleashes pestilence, plagues, searing fires, and earthquakes upon the earth. The angels promise to torture with fire and sulphur anyone who worships "the beast" (the devil). The author of Revelation is assured that Jesus has sent his angel to reveal the prophecies, and to remind people that he is "coming soon, bringing my recompense, to repay everyone for what he has done. I am the Alpha and the Omega, the first and the last, the beginning and the end," (Revelation 22:12–13).

The concept of angels of destruction conflicts with modern popular ideas about angels as solely beings of goodness, protection, and beneficence. The body of early lore on angels presents them as neither intrinsically "good" nor "bad," but as capable of acting out in either "good" or "bad" ways as seen from the perspective of the human recipient. Angels are charged with carrying out the instructions of God, whether those instructions call for reward or punishment.

See ANGELS OF PUNISHMENT; EZRA.

FURTHER READING
Charlesworth, James H., ed. *The Old Testament Pseudepigrapha*. Vols. 1 and 2. New York: Doubleday, 1983, 1985.
Graham, Billy. *Angels: God's Secret Agents*. New York: Doubleday & Co., 1975.
Scholem, Gershom. *Kabbalah*. New York: Dorset Press, 1987. First published 1974.

angels of glory

High-level group of angels often equated with the ANGELS OF SANCTIFICATION. According to 3 ENOCH and the SEFER RAZIEL, angels of glory live in Arabot, the highest HEAVEN, and are 660,000 myriads in number. They "stand over against the throne of Glory and the divisions of flaming fire."

angels of hell See ANGELS OF DESTRUCTION; ANGELS OF PUNISHMENT; EZRA.

Angels of Mastemoth

In the Dead Sea Scrolls, a name for the WATCHERS, FALLEN ANGELS who cohabited with women and begat giants. The Angels of Mastemoth are "Enemy Angels" and "Angels of Darkness." The Qumran text 4Q390 refers to sinners being delivered into the power of the Angels of Mastemoth who will rule them.

See ENOCH; MASTEMA; QUMRAN TEXTS.

angels of mercy

Angels who stand at the right side of God in the heavenly court of law in the seventh HEAVEN. The angels are present when people are called to judgment. Most angels of mercy are not named. Among those who are named are Uzziel, acting under Metatron; Rhamiel, the angelic name of ST. FRANCIS OF ASSISI; Rachmiel; Gabriel; Michael; Zadkiel; and Zehanpuryu.

angels of Mons See MONS, ANGELS OF.

angels of peace

In 3 ENOCH, angels who stand at the left side of God during sessions of the heavenly court. The Zohar refers to seven angels of peace. In other lore, angels of peace traditionally visit Jewish homes at the start of the Sabbath.

angels of prostitution

Four angels who rule whoredom and prostitution. Three of them—Lilith, Agrat bat Mahlat, and Naamah—are also partners or brides of Samael. The fourth angel of prostitution is Eisheth Zenunim.

angels of punishment

Angels who carry out the discipline and punishments of sinning humans and other angels. In the Shepherd of Hermas, the visionary HERMAS has a permanent Angel of Punishment who looks like a mean, whip-wielding shepherd, and who keeps Hermas morally in line. In 2 ENOCH and the Testament of the Twelve Patriarchs, the angels of punishment—presumably also evil—reside in the third HEAVEN.

Some angels in charge of punishment are named. In the Pistis Sophia, Ariel is the chief; in other Coptic Gnostic writings, Asmodeus holds the position. The Midrash Tehillim lists five angels of punishment encountered by MOSES in heaven: Af, the angel of anger; Kezef, the angel of wrath; Hemah, the angel of fury; Hasmed, the angel of annihilation; and Mashit, the angel of destruction. The Maseket Gan Eden and Gehinnon lists seven angels of punishment: Lahatiel, the flaming one; Shoftiel, the judge of God; Makatiel, the plague of God; Hutriel, the rod of God; Puriel/Pusiel, the fire of God; and Rogziel, the wrath of God.

See ANGELS OF DESTRUCTION; EZRA.

angels of sanctification

A high-level order of angels, who according to the book of JUBILEES, were created on the first day already circumcised so that they could join God in observing the sabbath in heaven and on earth. Jubilees says that the angels of sanctification are one of two high orders, along with the ANGELS OF THE PRESENCE. They also are sometimes equated with the ANGELS OF GLORY. Principal angels of sanctification are Phanuel, Michael, Metatron, Zagzagael, and Suriel.

angels of the days of the week

Angels who govern the days of the week in magical lore. Their names are to be invoked in rituals.

In addition to days, the angels also have other associations: the seven major planets of the ancient world, the air, the directions of the wind and different levels of heaven. Within each level of heaven are four directions, each associated with angels. Each day is ideal for different activities. Duplication among angels occurs.

The associations, drawn from *The Magus* by occultist Francis Barrett (1801) are as follows:

SUNDAY
Chief angel: Michael
Other angels: Dardiel, Huratapel
Angels of the air: Varcan, king, and his ministers Tus, Andus, and Cynabal
Wind: North
Heaven: Fourth
Angels of the east: Samael, Baciel, Abel, Gabriel, Vionatraba
Angels of the west: Anael, Pabel, Ustael, Burchat, Suceratos, Capabili
Angels of the north: Aiel, Ariel, Aquiel, Masgrabiel, Saphiel, Matuyel
Angels of the south: Haluliel, Machasiel, Charsiel, Uriel, Naromiel
Planet: Sun

Angels punishing Heliodorus (Gustave Doré)

Favorable activities: acquiring gold and gems (wealth), seeking favor and honors, dissolving ill will, eliminating infirmities

MONDAY
Chief angel: Gabriel
Other angels: Michael, Samael
Angels of the air: Arcan, king, and his ministers Bilet, Missabu, Abuhaza
Wind: West
Heaven: First
Angels of the east: Gabriel, Madiel, Deamiel, Janak
Angels of the west: Sachiel, Zaniel, Habiel, Bachanae, Corobael
Angels of the north: Mael, Uvael, Valmuum, Baliel, Balay, Humastraw
Angels of the south: Curaniel, Dabriel, Hanun, Vetuel
Planet: Moon
Favorable activities: procuring silver, conveying things from place to place, disclosing secrets of people both present and future, making horses swift

TUESDAY
Chief angel: Samael
Other angels: Satael, Amabiel
Angels of the air: Samax, king, and his ministers Carmax, Ismoli, Paffran
Wind: East
Heaven: Fifth
Angels of the east: Friagne, Guel, Damael, Calzas, Arragon
Angels of the west: Lama, Astagna, Lobquin, Soneas, Jazel, Isael, Irel
Angels of the north: Rhaumel, Hyniel, Rayel, Seraphiel, Fraciel, Mathiel
Angels of the south: Sacriel, Janiel, Galdel, Osael, Vianuel, Zaliel
Planet: Mars
Favorable activities: bringing or causing war, death, infirmity, and combustions (fire)

WEDNESDAY
Chief angel: Raphael
Other angels: Meil, Seraphiel
Angels of the air: Mediat, king, and his ministers Suquinos, Sallales
Wind: Southwest
Heaven: Second
Angels of the east: Mathlai, Tarmiel, Baraborat
Angels of the west: Jerusque, Merattron
Angels of the north: Thiel, Rael, Harihael, Venahel, Velel, Abuiori, Ucirmiel

Angels of the south: Milliel, Nelapa, Calvel, Laquel
Planet: Mercury
Favorable activities: procuring all sorts of metals, revealing all earthly things past, present, and future, pacifying judges, giving victory in war, teaching experiments and sciences, changing things alchemically, procuring health, raising the poor and casting down the rich, binding or loosing spirits, opening locks and bolts

THURSDAY
Chief angel: Sachiel
Other angels: Cassiel, Asasiel
Angels of the air: Suth, king, and his ministers Maguth, Gutrix
Wind: South
Heaven: None, because there are no angels of the air above the fifth heaven (instead of prayers to angels, prayers are directed to the four directions)
Planet: Jupiter
Favorable activities: procuring the love of women, causing merriment and joy, pacifying strife, appeasing enemies, healing the diseased, procuring things lost

FRIDAY
Chief angel: Anael
Other angels: Rachiel, Sachiel
Angels of the air: Sarabotes, king, and his ministers Amahiel, Aba, Abalidoth, Blaef
Wind: West
Heaven: Third
Angels of the east: Setchiel, Chedusitaniel, Corat, Tamuel, Tenaciel
Angels of the west: Turiel, Coniel, Babiel, Kadie, Maltiel, Huphaltiel
Angels of the south: Porosa, Sachiel, Chermiel, Samael, Santanael, Famiel
Planet: Venus
Favorable activities: procuring silver and luxuries, causing marriages, alluring men to love women, causing or removing infirmities, and doing all things which have motion

SATURDAY
Chief angel: Cassiel
Other angels: Machatan, Uriel
Angels of the air: Maymon, king, and his ministers Abumalith, Assabibi, Balidet
Wind: South
Heaven: None; same as Thursday

Hours Day.	Angels and Planets ruling SUNDAY.	Angels and Planets ruling MONDAY.	Angels and Planets ruling TUESDAY.	Angels and Planets ruling WEDNESDAY.	Angels and Planets ruling THURSDAY.	Angels and Planets ruling FRIDAY.	Angels and Planets ruling SATURDAY.
	Day.	*Day.*	*Day.*	*Day.*	*Day.*	*Day.*	*Day.*
1	☉ Michael	☽ Gabriel	♂ Samael	☿ Raphael	♃ Sachiel	♀ Anael	♄ Cassiel
2	♀ Anael	♄ Cassiel	☉ Michael	☽ Gabriel	♂ Samael	☿ Raphael	♃ Sachiel
3	☿ Raphael	♃ Sachiel	♀ Anael	♄ Cassiel	☉ Michael	☽ Gabriel	♂ Samael
4	☽ Gabriel	♁ Samael	☿ Raphael	♃ Sachiel	♀ Anael	♄ Cassiel	☉ Michael
5	♄ Cassiel	☉ Michael	☽ Gabriel	♂ Samael	☿ Raphael	♃ Sachiel	♀ Anael
6	♃ Sachiel	♀ Anael	♄ Cassiel	☉ Michael	☽ Gabriel	♂ Samael	☿ Raphael
7	♂ Samael	☿ Raphael	♃ Sachiel	♀ Anael	♄ Cassiel	☉ Michael	☽ Gabriel
8	☉ Michael	☽ Gabriel	♁ Samael	☿ Raphael	♃ Sachiel	♀ Anael	♄ Cassiel
9	♀ Anael	♄ Cassiel	☉ Michael	☽ Gabriel	♂ Samael	☿ Raphael	♃ Sachiel
10	☿ Raphael	♃ Sachiel	♀ Anael	♄ Cassiel	O Michael	☽ Gabriel	♂ Samael
11	☽ Gabriel	♂ Samael	☿ Raphael	♃ Sachael	♀ Anael	♄ Cassiel	☉ Michael
12	♄ Cassiel	☉ Michael	☽ Gabriel	♂ Samael	☿ Raphael	♃ Sachiel	♀ Anael
Hours Night	*Night.*	*Night.*	*Night.*	*Night.*	*Night.*	*Night.*	*Night.*
1	♃ Sachael	♀ Anael	♄ Cassiel	☉ Michael	☽ Gabriel	♂ Samael	☿ Raphael
2	♂ Samiel	☿ Raphael	♃ Sachiel	♀ Anael	♄ Cassiel	☉ Michael	☽ Gabriel
3	☉ Michael	☽ Gabriel	♂ Samael	☿ Raphael	♃ Sachiel	♀ Anael	♄ Cassiel
4	♀ Anael	♄ Cassiel	☉ Michael	☽ Gabriel	♂ Samael	☿ Raphael	♃ Sachiel
5	☿ Raphael	♃ Sachiel	♀ Anael	♄ Cassiel	☉ Michael	☽ Gabriel	♂ Samael
6	☽ Gabriel	♂ Samael	☿ Raphael	♃ Sachiel	♀ Anael	♄ Cassiel	☉ Michael
7	♄ Cassiel	☉ Michael	☽ Gabriel	♂ Samael	☿ Raphael	♃ Sachiel	♀ Anael
8	♃ Sachiel	♀ Anael	♄ Cassiel	☉ Michael	☽ Gabriel	♂ Samael	☿ Raphael
9	♂ Samael	☿ Raphael	♃ Sachiel	♀ Anael	♄ Cassiel	☉ Michael	☽ Gabriel
10	☉ Michael	☽ Gabriel	♂ Samael	☿ Raphael	♃ Sachiel	♀ Anael	♄ Cassiel
11	♀ Anael	♄ Cassiel	☉ Michael	☽ Gabriel	♂ Samael	☿ Raphael	♃ Sachiel
12	☿ Raphael	♃ Sachiel	♀ Anael	♄ Cassiel	☉ Michael	☽ Gabriel	♂ Samael

Angels and planets that rule the days of the week and the hours of the day and night (From *The Magus* by Francis Barrett)

Planet: Saturn
Favorable activities: sowing of discord, hate, evil thoughts and irritations, maiming and murdering

FURTHER READING

Barrett, Francis. *The Magus.* Secaucus, N.J.: The Citadel Press, 1967. First published 1801.

angels of the earth

Seven angels who watch over the planet. The angels are Azriel, Admael, Arkiel (also Archas), Arciciah, Ariel, Harabael or Aragael, Saragael, and Yabbashael. Other angels also given this title are Haldiel, Tebliel, Phorlakh, Raguel, and Samuil. Thomas Heywood gives four angels of the earth, each of whom is in charge of one of the four winds: Gabriel in the north, Uriel in the south, Michael in the east, and Raphael in the west.

angels of the elements See ELEMENTALS.

angels of the end of the world See ANGELS OVER THE CONSUMMATION; EZRA.

angels of the hours

Angels assigned to govern each hour-long period of the day and night. Thus, at any given moment a particular angel can be called upon for service or favor. In MAGIC, an angel of the hour may be summoned during ritual.

In Greek magical lore, the angels of the hours of the night work under the aegis of Selene, one of the principal lunar goddesses, and the goddess of dreams. The angels of the hours are summoned to send dream messages to another person. The *Papyri Graecae Magicae* states that the practitioner first invokes Selene to:

> give a sacred angel or a holy assistant who serves this very night, in this very hour . . . and order the angel to go off to her, NN ("so-and-so"), to draw her by her hair, by her feet; may she, in fear, see phantoms, sleepless because of her passion for me and her love for me, NN, come to my consecrated bedroom.

Trithemius of Spanheim's *Book of Secret Things,* translated in FRANCIS BARRETT's *The Magus,* assigns the seven PLANETARY ANGELS to repeating duty as angels of the hours. The day and night are divided into equal parts of 12 hours each. Every hour of every day of the week is governed by one of the seven (see accompanying table).

The Lemegeton, a magical GRIMOIRE, gives another list of the names of the angels of the hours of every day and night:

Day

1 Samuel
2 Anael
3 Vequaniel
4 Vahrmiel
5 Sasquiel
6 Saniel
7 Barquiel
8 Osmadiel
9 Quabriel
10 Oriel
11 Bariel
12 Beratiel

Night

1 Sabrathan
2 Tartys
3 Serguanich
4 Jesfischa
5 Abasdarhon
6 Zaazenach
7 Mendrion
8 Narcoriel
9 Pamyel
10 Lssuarim
11 Dardariel
12 Sarandiel

See ADAM AND EVE.

Time-keeping angel at Chartres Cathedral, France (Author's collection)

FURTHER READING
Barrett, Francis. *The Magus.* Secaucus, N.J.: Citadel Press, 1967. First published 1801.
Henson, Michael, ed. *Lemegeton: The Complete Lesser Key of Solomon.* Jacksonville, Fla.: Metatron Books, 1999.

angels of the Lord of the Spirits

Multitudes of angels who stand before the glory of the Lord of the Spirits, witnessed by the prophet ENOCH. 1 Enoch 40:1–10 describes their numbers as "a hundred thousand times a hundred thousand, ten million times ten million, an innumerable and uncountable (multitude)." The angels stand on the four wings of the Lord of the Spirits.

Enoch sees among the multitudes four faces, and hears four voices sing praises before the Lord of Glory.

The ANGEL OF PEACE, who is Enoch's guide, identifies the four as: Michael, the merciful and forbearing; Raphael, who is set over all disease and every wound of the children of the people; Gabriel, who is set over all exercise of strength; and Phanuel, who is set over all actions of repentance unto the hope of those who would inherit eternal life.

After hearing the identities revealed, Enoch learns "all the secrets in HEAVEN."

angels of the months

Angels assigned to the months of the year. In some cases where angels are equated with other angels, more than one angel may govern a month. Angels of the months are invoked in magical rituals.

The following list is derived from Kabbalistic lore. Alternate spellings of names are given in parentheses.

January: Gabriel; Cambiel
February: Barakiel (Barchiel; Barkiel)
March: Malchidiel
April: Asmodel
May: Amriel (Ambiel; Ambriel)
June: Muriel
July: Verchiel
August: Hamaliel
September: Uriel; Zuriel
October: Barbiel
November: Adnachiel (Advachiel, Adernahael)
December: Hanael; Anael

In Persian lore the angels of the months are:

January: Bahman
February: Isfandarmend
March: Farvardin
April: Ardibehist
May: Khurdad
June: Tir
July: Murdad
August: Shahrivar
September: Mhr (Miher)
October: Aban
November: Azar
December: Dai

angels of the planets

Archangels assigned to govern each of the seven planetary bodies of the ancient world and the distribution of their astrological influences. In Jewish lore, these seven archangels play an important role in the order of the universe.

Different sources give different and often conflicting associations as well as variations in the spellings of the angel names. Various angels may be named to more than one planet. The use of these associations in astrology and ritual magic depends on which system one follows.

The angels of the planets are called the "seven governors of the world" and always stand before the face of God.

Historian Joshua Trachtenberg collated five lists, including those given in the SEFER RAZIEL and in Ginzburg's *Legends of the Jews*, to produce the following. Variations of name spellings are in parentheses:

Sun: Raphael; Michael
Moon: Gabriel; Aniel (Anael)
Mercury: Michael; Zadkiel; Barkiel; Hasdiel; Raphael
Venus: Aniel; Hasdiel
Mars: Samael; Gabriel
Jupiter: Zadkiel; Barkiel
Saturn: Kafziel; Michael

AGRIPPA makes the following associations:

Sun: Semeliel (Semeschia)
Moon: Jareahel
Mercury: Cochabiah (Cochabiel)
Venus: Nogahel
Mars: Madimiel
Jupiter: Zedekiel
Saturn: Sabathiel

FRANCIS BARRETT gives two lists:

Sun: Michael	Sun: Raphael
Moon: Gabriel	Moon: Gabriel
Mercury: Raphael	Mercury: Michael
Venus: Anael	Venus: Haniel
Mars: Zamael	Mars: Camael
Jupiter: Zachariel	Jupiter: Zadkiel
Saturn: Oriphael	Saturn: Zaphiel

The Muslim philosopher Averroës gives the following associations:

Sun: Michael
Moon: Gabriel
Mercury: Raphael
Venus: Anael
Mars: Samael
Jupiter: Sachiel (Zadkiel)
Saturn: Cassiel (Kafziel)

See ANGELS OF THE ZODIAC; GEMATRIA.

FURTHER READING

Savedow, Steve. *Sepher Rezial Hemelach: The Book of the Angel Rezial.* York Beach, Maine: Samuel Weiser, 2000.

Three Books of Occult Philosophy Written by Henry Cornelius Agrippa of Nettesheim. Translated by James Freake. Edited and annotated by Donald Tyson. St. Paul, Minn.: Llewellyn Publications, 1995.

Trachtenberg, Joshua. *Jewish Magic and Superstition: A Study in Folk Religion.* New York: Behrmaris Jewish Book House, 1939.

angels of the presence

High-level angels also known as "angels of the face." According to the book of JUBILEES, angels of the presence and ANGELS OF SANCTIFICATION are the two highest orders of angels. They are created on the first day already circumcised so that they can participate in the keeping of the sabbath with God in heaven and on earth. God instructs one of these angels (thought to be Michael), to write the history of creation for MOSES. The angel takes the tablets of history and law, and in a long revelation, recites them to Moses with instructions to write them down.

Other angels usually identified as angels of the presence are Metatron, Suriel, Sandalphon, Astanphaeus, Sarakiel, Phanuel, Jehoel, Zagzagael, Uriel, Yefefiah, Sabaoth, and Akatriel. The angels of the presence also are equated with the ANGELS OF GLORY.

In rabbinic tradition, there are 70 tutelary angels called the angels of the presence. According to the Zohar, the angels of the presence revealed the "mystery" (purpose) of God to people, and thus were expelled from the divine presence.

In the Testaments of the Twelve Patriarchs, Judah, one of the 12 sons of JACOB and Leah, testifies that he was blessed by an angel of the presence.

In Phoenician mythology, the angels of the presence are the creators of the universe.

See ADONAI.

FURTHER READING

Charlesworth, James H., ed. *The Old Testament Pseud-epigrapha.* Vols. 1 and 2. New York: Doubleday, 1983, 1985.

angels of the seasons

Angels who have jurisdiction over the seasons of the year. Their names are invoked at appropriate times for magical purposes. Different systems assign different angels to the seasons.

FRANCIS BARRETT gives the following associations:

Spring
Governing angel: Spugliguel
Angels: Amatiel, Caracasa, Commissoros, Core

Summer
Governing angel: Tubiel
Angels: Gargatel, Gaviel, Tariel

Autumn
Governing angel: Torquaret
Angels: Guabarel, Tarquarn

Winter
Governing angel: Attarib
Angels: Amabael, Cetarari (Ctarai)

RUDOLF STEINER ascribes the seasonal and angelic qualities to stages of spiritual growth in humankind. He begins with autumn; his associations are:

Autumn: Michael
Winter: Gabriel
Spring: Raphael
Summer: Uriel

The SEFER RAZIEL gives long lists of angels who govern numerous activities to be undertaken in every season. The ANGELS OF THE PLANETS and the ANGELS OF THE ZODIAC also have attending angels that change by season.

FURTHER READING

Barrett, Francis. *The Magus.* Secaucus, N.J.: Citadel Press, 1967.

Savedow, Steve. *Sepher Rezial Hemelach: The Book of the Angel Rezial.* York Beach, Maine: Samuel Weiser, 2000.

Steiner, Rudolph. *The Four Seasons and the Archangels.* Bristol, England: Rudolf Steiner Press, 1992.

angels of the winds   See NATURE SPIRITS.

angels of the zodiac

Angels assigned to rule over the 12 houses of the zodiac, and to govern and disperse their astrological influences. Different systems assign different angels to the signs and also different spellings of angel names.

Some of the seven major archangels who are ANGELS OF THE PLANETS also are angels of the zodiac. According to historian Joshua Trachtenberg, other angels were either borrowed from ancient sources, such as the lore of the Chaldeans and Babylonians, or even invented in order to fill out the list.

According to the SEFER RAZIEL, the associations are:

Aries the Ram: Ovavorial
Taurus the Bull: Lehetial
Gemini the Twins: Pheniel

Gemini, the Twins, depicted as angels (Hyginus, *Poeticon Astronomicon*, 1504)

Cancer the Crab: Zorial
Leo the Lion: Bereqiel
Virgo the Virgin: Cheial
Libra the Scales: Tzorial
Scorpio the Scorpion: Gabrial
Sagittarius the Archer: Medonial
Capricorn the Goat: Shenial
Aquarius the Water-Carrier: Gabrial
Pisces the Fishes: Romial

AGRIPPA gives the following:

Aries: Teletiel
Taurus: Suriel
Gemini: Tomimiel
Cancer: Sattamiel
Leo: Ariel
Virgo: Betuliel
Libra: Masniel
Scorpio: Acrabiel
Sagittarius: Chesetiel
Capricorn: Gediel
Aquarius: Deliel
Pisces: Dagymiel

According to occultist Donald Tyson, two of these angel names may be incorrect. Based upon Hebrew, the angel of Cancer probably should be Sartaniel, and the angel of Libra probably should be Maznimiel.

In *The Book of Secret Things,* written in the late Middle Ages by JOHANNES TRITHEMIUS, the signs and their respective governing angels are set forth as:

Aries: Malahidael; Machidiel
Taurus: Asmodel
Gemini: Ambriel
Cancer: Muriel
Leo: Verchiel
Virgo: Hamaliel
Libra: Uriel; Zuriel
Scorpio: Barbiel
Sagittarius: Advachiel; Adnachiel
Capricorn: Hanael
Aquarius: Cambiel; Gabriel
Pisces: Barchiel

FRANCIS BARRETT drew a connection between the angels of the zodiac and the 12 angels mentioned in REVELATION. In John of Patmos's vision of the holy city of New Jerusalem, descending from the heavens, there is a high wall with 12 gates, each of which is guarded by an unnamed angel.

In MAGIC, the names of zodiac angels are invoked in rituals pertaining to astrological influences. The angels are petitioned for help in effecting spells and enchantments.

FURTHER READING
Barrett, Francis. *The Magus.* Secaucus, N.J.: Citadel Press, 1967. First published 1801.
Savedow, Steve. *Sepher Rezial Hemelach: The Book of the Angel Rezial.* York Beach, Maine: Samuel Weiser, 2000.
Three Books of Occult Philosophy Written by Henry Cornelius Agrippa of Nettesheim. Translated by James Freake. Edited and annotated by Donald Tyson. St. Paul, Minn.: Llewellyn Publications, 1995.
Trachtenberg, Joshua. *Jewish Magic and Superstition: A Study in Folk Religion.* New York: Behrman's Jewish Book House, 1939.

angels over the consummation
Nine angels in the Greek Apocalypse of EZRA who will rule or judge at "the consummation," or the end of the world. The angels are Michael, Gabriel, Uriel, Raphael, Gabuthelon, Aker, Arphugitonos, Beburos, and Zebuleon. Their names are revealed (6:1–2) to Ezra by God during Ezra's journey to HEAVEN and Tartarus (HELL).

Angra Mainyu See AHRIMAN.

animistics (animastics; dii animalie)

An order of beings who are half human and half angel or god. Animistics are nobles, lords, and princes who are inferior to the angelic hierarchies but above the earth. They are heroes and demigods, the "Strong and Mighty" who have done good deeds for humans and have certain divine powers. The name "animistics" means "the animated." They are sometimes called ISSIM.

Among Agrippa's examples of animistics are Merlin, the Arthurian wizard; Priapus, the son of Dionysius and Aphrodite; Hippo, the daughter of Oceanus and Theys; and Vertumnus, an Etruscan diety carried to Rome. The 12 apostles of Christ are the chief animistics, followed by the 70 or 72 disciples of Christ appointed by him to go ahead of him (Luke 10:1). After them come a multitude of saints.

According to AGRIPPA, the animistics, when prayed to and supplicated, respond with greater gifts, benefits, and graces than do the angelic powers.

Animistics are associated with the 10th sephiroth of Malkuth (Kingdom). Agrippa states that they "have their influence on the sons of men, and give knowledge and the wonderful understanding of things, also industry and prophecy," and are ruled by Metatron. An animistic is the GUARDIAN ANGEL of MOSES.

Anpiel

In kabbalistic lore, the angel who protects birds. Anpiel resides in the sixth HEAVEN. He wears 70 crowns, crowns all prayers sent up from earth and sends them up to the seventh heaven. In *The Legends of the Jews*, Anpiel is credited with taking ENOCH to heaven.

Ansiel

Angel known as "the constrainer." Ansiel is invoked in MAGIC against forgetting and stupidity.

Apocalypse   See REVELATION.

Apocrypha and pseudepigrapha texts

Ex-canonical Jewish and Christian texts, many of which contain detailed ANGELOLOGIES, celestial organizations, and mystical visionary recitals. Most angel lore is in works outside of the Old and New Testaments.

Traditional Apocrypha

The term *apocrypha* means "that which is hidden." All Bibles contain the same 27 books of the New Testament and the 39 books of the Old Testament that are part of the Hebrew canon. In addition, there traditionally are 15 books or portions of books considered to be the Apocrypha, and were written between about 200 B.C.E. and 200 C.E. These books were either deliberately hidden from all but initiates because of their profound esoteric lore or were "hidden" because they were heretical.

The traditional 15 Apocrypha texts are:

1 Esdras (Ezra)
2 Esdras (Ezra)
Tobit
Judith
Additions to the Book of Esther
The Wisdom of Solomon
Sirach (Ecclesiasticus)
Baruch
The Letter of Jeremiah
The Prayer of Azariah and the Song of the Three Young Men
Susanna
Bel and the Dragon
The Prayer of Manasseh
1 Maccabees
2 Maccabees

Eastern Orthodoxy also considers 3 Maccabees, 4 Maccabees, and Psalm 151 as part of the Apocrypha (4 Maccabees is placed in an appendix).

Acceptance or rejection of the Apocrypha has changed over the centuries. Though they are not part of the Hebrew canon, many of the Old Testament books refer to the Apocrypha. The Septuagint, the Greek version of the Old Testament, includes the Apocrypha. Most of the early fathers of the Christian Church accepted the Apocrypha as Scripture. In the fourth century, the great biblical scholar St. Jerome was commissioned by Pope Damascus to prepare a standard Latin version of the Bible. Jerome's version, known as the Latin Vulgate, included the Apocrypha, but noted that it belonged in a separate category from the Old Testament. This distinction was a fine one to many, and the Apocrypha were generally considered part of the Scriptures up through the Middle Ages.

The first English version of the Bible, translated from the Latin Vulgate near the end of the 14th century, includes all of the Apocrypha but 2 Esdras, but makes a distinction between the Apocrypha and other Scriptures.

The PROTESTANT REFORMATION saw numerous disputes over doctrine. English Protestants eventually rejected the apocryphal books as sources of doctrine and excluded them from the Revised Standard Version of the Bible.

In response in part to the Reformation, the Apocrypha were officially declared part of the Christian canon in 1546 by the Council of Trent; anyone who did not accept them was anathema. However, the books are given a lesser status than the rest of the Scriptures.

In angelology, the most important apocryphal work is TOBIT, which tells the story of the blind man Tobit, his son Tobias, and the archangel Raphael. It is considered to be a historically based novel, the purpose of which is to impart lessons on righteousness and morality, and to teach occult lore concerning healing and exorcism.

Despite its troubled standing in doctrine, the Apocrypha nonetheless have had a tremendous influence upon the arts, especially poetry, drama, music, literature, sculpture, and painting. Shakespeare may have been familiar with the Apocrypha, though that is debated by scholars. The composer Handel was influenced.

Other Apocryphal and Pseudepigrapha Texts

In additional to the traditional Apocrypha, there are numerous other texts also excluded from the canon. Many of these are pseudepigrapha, inspired Jewish and Jewish-Christian works written by anonymous authors but attributed to important prophets and patriarchs. These texts are also rich sources of angelologies, angel MAGIC, visionary recitals of HEAVEN and HELL guided by angels, and MERKABAH ascents. Many are apocalyptic in nature, dealing with the end of time, the final judgment and resurrection, and the fate of souls after death. Included in this general category are the QUMRAN TEXTS.

Most pseudepigrapha were written primarily between 200 B.C.E. and 200 C.E., though some were written or added to much later. They were composed in Hebrew, Aramaic, and Greek and later translated, often into Latin, Slavonic, Ethiopic, or Armenian. Some were not translated into English until the Middle Ages or much later.

The book of ENOCH is the most detailed and significant pseudepigrapha in terms of angels. Its importance was dismissed by some influential fathers of the church—for example, Ss. Jerome and AUGUSTINE—who considered it to be too old and full of errors to be of value. Also significant for its angel content is the book of JUBILEES.

See ADAM AND EVE; BARUCH; EZRA; DREAMS AND VISIONS; GNOSTICISM; HERMAS; ISAIAH; JACOB; LEVI; SOLOMON; ZEPHANIAH.

FURTHER READING
Charlesworth, James H., ed. *The Old Testament Pseudepigrapha.* Vols. 1 and 2. New York: Doubleday, 1983; 1985.

May, Herbert G., and Bruce M. Metzger, eds. *The New Oxford Annotated Bible with the Apocrypha.* New York: Oxford University Press, 1977.

Apollyon See ABADDON.

apparitions

One of three primary hierarchies of angels designated by the alchemist Robert Fludd. The other two are ACCLAMATIONS and VOICES.

Arael (Ariel)

In Jewish lore, angel who is PRINCE over the people of the birds. In the Testament of SOLOMON, the name may be a variation of Uriel.

See DECANS OF THE ZODIAC.

aralim, arelim See ERELIM.

Arapiel YHVH (Araphiel, Nirpiel)

In 3 ENOCH, one of the PRINCES who guards the seventh HEAVEN. Arapiel means "neck of God." Arapiel bows down to Asroilu.

Araqiel (Araquiel, Arakiel, Araciel, Arqael, Saraquael, Arkiel, Arkas)

Angel who has dominion over the earth. Araqiel is identified as both a good and a bad angel. In 1 ENOCH he is one of 200 FALLEN ANGELS and teaches the signs of the earth to people. In the Sibylline Oracles he is good, and he is one of five angels—with Ramiel, Aziel, Uriel, and Samiel—who leads souls to judgment.

Araton (Arathron)

One of the seven ruling angels of the 196 Olympic provinces of HEAVEN, according to the Arbatel of Magic. As the first angel, Arathron rules 49 provinces, 49 kings, 42 princes, 35 satraps, 28 dukes, 21 servants, 14 councillors, 7 enjoys, and 36,000 legions of spirits, each legion having 490 beings. Arathron has great magical ability and knowledge. He can make a person invisible, a barren woman fertile, change animals and vegetables into stones, and transmute metals. He teaches medicine, alchemy, and MAGIC.

archai

A class of angels who rule and govern, and who have the ability to influence the destiny of humanity. The name "archai" is Greek for "sphere of authority or power," and its Latin equivalent is "principia." The term was used in Judaism and early Christianity and was adopted by the Gnostics. Archai can be compared or equated to AUTHORITIES (EXOUSIAI), POWERS (potestates), and PRINCIPALITIES; the name is sometimes used interchangeably with ARCHONS. Archai are referred to as both benevolent and hostile supernatural forces. In Christian writings they are often named as the first of three celestial powers, along with exousiai and dynameis (powers). St. PAUL uses the term archai in his famous passage of Romans 8:38–39, often translated as "angels."

archangels

In the Pseudo-Dionysian hierarchy, the second highest rank of angels. The name "archangels" comes from the Greek term "archangelos," meaning "chief messenger" or "eminent messenger." Archangels, also known as "Holy Ones," are liaisons between God and mortals;

Michael the archangel (From *The Hierarchie of the Blessed Angells* by Thomas Heywood [1635])

they are in charge of heaven's armies in the battle against HELL; and they are the supervisors of the GUARDIAN ANGELS. They also serve as guardian angels to great people, such as heads of religions and states. They carry the divine decrees of God. Archangels are sometimes equated with the BENE ELOHIM.

The figures of archangels appear in the Old Testament, but the term "archangel" is not used in Greek versions. "Archangel" does appear in Greek versions of pseudepigrapha texts such as the Enochian writings, which give classes of angels, and it appears twice in the New Testament. Jude 1:9 refers to Michael as an archangel, and 1 Thessalonians 4:16 refers to a nameless archangel who heralds the second coming and the resurrection of the dead: "For the Lord himself will descend from heaven with a cry of command, with the archangel's call, and with the sound of the trumpet of God." Archangels also appear in Judeo-Christian magical texts.

Joshua 5:13–15 describes a forerunner of the archangel in the form of a man whom Joshua sees in a vision, and who identifies himself as "commander of the army of the Lord." Daniel names two high-level angels, Michael and Gabriel, but he does not call them archangels.

Angels who have a special place before God are often interpreted as archangels. Groups of four, six, and seven are mentioned in various texts. For example, REVELATION 8:2 speaks of "seven angels who stand before God;" EZEKIEL 9:2 describes seven punishing angels (six who wield swords and a seventh who carries a writing case); and TOBIT 12:15 has Raphael identifying himself as one of seven angels who transmit prayers of the holy, or who stand in the presence of the Lord.

In the Enochian writings, 1 ENOCH 9 lists Michael, Sariel, and Gabriel (and in some versions also Raphael) as significant angels who watch from the sky. 1 Enoch 20:1–7 lists the six "holy angels who watch" by name: Sariel (Suruel) or Uriel, Raphael, Raguel, Michael, Gabriel, and Saraqael, and 1 Enoch 40:1–10 describes Michale, Gabriel, Sariel, and Phanuel as the four angels who "stand before the glory of the Lord of the Spirits."

Among other angels described as archangels are Oriphiel, Zadkiel, Anael, Jehudiel, Sealtiel, and Barachiel.

The Roman Catholic Church elevated the archangels Michael, Gabriel, and Raphael to sainthood. Michael is by far the most significant of the three. He is the ruling prince of the order, who defends the church against the forces of darkness. Michael is the only angel named in the Bible who is specifically called an archangel (Jude 1:9). In Daniel (10:13, 21), he is called "one of the chief princes" and "your prince," but in Revelation 12:7 he is only an angel.

Gabriel is often identified as the angel who visits Elizabeth and MARY to announce the forthcoming births of John the Baptist and JESUS, respectively.

Raphael, identified as the prince of archangels, is a central figure in the book of Tobit, part of the Catholic canon but otherwise considered apocryphal.

In Islam, the Koran acknowledges the existence of four archangels but names only two: Jibril (Gabriel), the angel of revelation, and Michael, the warrior angel. The other two are likely Azrael, the ANGEL OF DEATH and Israfil, the angel of MUSIC.

See DEVOTIONAL CULTS; ENOCH.

FURTHER READING

Charlesworth, James H., ed. *The Old Testament Pseud-epigrapha*. Vols. 1 and 2 New York: Doubleday, 1983, 1985.

van der Toorn, Karl, Bob Becking, and Pieter W. van der Horst, eds. *Dictionary of Deities and Demons in the Bible*. 2d ed. Grand Rapids, Mich.: William B. Eerdmans, 1999.

archetypes

Universal primordial images and instincts that reside in the collective unconscious, and are expressed in behavior and experience. Archetypes have existed since the dawn of humanity. Mythologies, religions, sacred rites, and folktales are especially rich in archetypal themes and characters (for example, the hero, the trickster, forces of nature, the elements are all archetypal representations). Angels are representations of archetypes.

Carl G. JUNG developed, but did not originate, the concept of archetypes. Heraclitus was the first to view the psyche as the archetypal first principle. Plato articulated the idea of archetypes in his Theory of Forms, which holds that the essence of a thing or concept is its underlying form or idea. The term "archetype" occurs in the writing of PHILO, Irenaeus, and PSEUDO-DIONYSIUS. The concept, but not the term, is found in the writings of St. AUGUSTINE.

Jung first wrote of primordial images in the unconscious of his patients in 1912. He first used the term "archetype" in 1919, in order to distinguish between the archetype itself and the archetypal image which is perceived on a conscious level. Archetypes are without end, created by the repetition of situations and experiences engraved upon the psychic constitution. They are forms without content—they wait to be realized in the personality, and are recognizable in outer behaviors.

Archetypes are a means through which the *unus mundus*, the unitary world or undifferentiated whole, can express itself in our conscious reality. The *unus mundus* is found in all spiritual traditions and is lawfully ordered by a transcendent plan that links everything together. This order is of such a sublime nature that it is beyond sensory perception but can be grasped through expressions of archetypes. The expressions themselves are not archetypes but representations of archetypes. All psychic imagery, such as is found in dreams and sacred art and ritual, is archetypal to some extent.

Historian Mircea Eliade observes that human history is governed by archetypes, and is a reflection of celestial archetypes; thus, myths and symbols share similarities among diverse cultures. Cities, temples, and houses represent the sacred center, for example, and the cross of Christianity represents the Cosmic Tree.

In this context angels are representations of the positive-negative polarity, the yin and yang, the light and dark, the good and evil. They also represent the ability of the human soul to ascend to heaven or descend to the underworld, as well as the immortality and inherent divine nature of the soul. The functions and characteristics ascribed to individual angels all express archetypes.

Angels gazing toward the world of archetypes, with correspondences in Sphere of Nature below (Malachias Geiger, *Microcosmus Hypochondriacus*, 1652)

The stronger and more active is the belief in archetypal representations, the stronger they become in the collective unconscious and the more they express themselves by impinging on the outer world through such things as synchronistic events (in the case of angels, these would be an array of angelic interventions). The pagan deities of the classical world have lost strength due to neglect over ensuing centuries; meanwhile, the archetypal forces serving newer religions, such as Christianity, have gained strength. Angels reached a peak of popularity in the Middle Ages and then declined as a force active in the psyche. As of the late 20th century, the angel archetypal force has been reactivated in Western consciousness.

FURTHER READING

Eliade, Mircea. *The Myth of the Eternal Return.* Princeton, N.J.: Princeton University Press, 1971. First published 1954.

————. *Images and Symbols.* Princeton University Press, 1991. First published 1952.

Jung, Carl G. *The Archetypes and the Collective Unconscious.* 2d ed. Bollingen Series XX. Princeton, N.J.: Princeton University Press, 1968.

Archistrategos

Title of "commander in chief of an army," usually given to Michael. (See HERMAS.) In the Greek Apocalypse of EZRA, the Archistrategos is Raphael, who assists Ezra in his vision.

archons (archontes)

Ruling angels of the HEAVENS and underworld, and also of nations. Archons are sometimes equated with AEONS, ARCHANGELS, PRINCES, DEMONS, Satan, and planetary deities. The term "archon" (singular) is Greek and means "high official" or "chief magistrate" and was used by the early Greeks as a designation for high human officials. The term appears as a designation for supernatural beings in the writings of the early Jews and early Christians, and also in Neoplatonism and GNOSTICISM. Archons can be either good or evil, but more often the term is used for beings who are hostile or evil.

Iamblichus, in his hierarchy of beings between God and the soul, places archons below archangels, angels, and demons but ahead of heroes. He says there are two kinds of archons, cosmic ones (*kosmokratores*) and hylic ones (*tes hyles parestekotes*).

In the Septuagint, "archons" is used to translate 36 different Hebrew terms relating to positions of leadership and authority in military, political, and priestly ranks. In Jewish and Christian writings, archon refers to the chief evil being, known variously as Satan, Mastema, Belial, and the devil. In the synoptic gospels, Satan is called the *archon ton daimonion,* or "prince of demons." (See DAIMONES.)

As a name of good angels, "archon" appears in DANIEL as a translation of the Aramaic term *sar,* or prince. Daniel 10 refers to the archons or princes of nations, implying the existence of celestial governors assigned to nations on earth. St. Ignatius of Antioch, one of the early fathers of the church, uses "archons" (translated as princes) as a designation for a type of angel.

The Enochian writings equate archons both with angelic princes and with Semyaza, the chief of the WATCHERS.

In Gnosticism, Sophia's son Ialdabaoth creates archons to rule over all the hierarchies, but he gives them lesser powers, so that he can rule over all of them. The principal archons rule the seven planets and impede the upward progress of the soul. The earliest author to name the seven, St. Irenaeus, lists Ialdabaoth as the chief archon, followed by Iao, Sabaoth, Adoneus, Eloeus, Oreus, and Astanphaeus.

ORIGEN, in his description of Orphic mythology in *Contra Celsum,* names the principal seven as Ialdabaoth, Iao, Sabaoth, Adonaios, Astaphaios, Eloaios, and Horaios. Origen also gives specific rituals for the soul to get past the archontes.

In the Apocryphon of John 48:10–17, seven archons create ADAM.

The Hypostasis of the Archons ("The Reality of the Rulers") is an anonymous Gnostic work that gives an esoteric interpretation of Genesis 1–6. Its date of origin is unknown, but it was originally written in Greek, probably in Egypt. The document declares that archons are not imaginary but are real. The archons generally exhibit arrogance, cruelty, and base behavior; they are called the Rulers of Darkness and Rulers of Unrighteousness.

Norea, the daughter of Eve, cries out to God to be rescued from the clutches of the Rulers of Unrighteousness, and is immediately visited by Eleleth, the Great Angel who stands in the presence of the Holy Spirit. He says he is one of the Four Light-givers. None of the Rulers has true power over her, he tells Norea, because they cannot prevail against the Root of Truth. He tells her the story of how the androgynous Ialdabaoth came into being, and how he created the archons, seven in number and all androgynous like himself. He proclaims himself "God of the entirety," which angers Zoe, the daughter of Sophia. She breathes fire into his face, and the fire becomes an angel and casts Ialdabaoth into the underworld (Tartaros).

His offspring Sabaoth repents and condemns his father and his mother (Matter), and Sophia and Zoe lift him up to the seventh heaven, where he rules in splendor. Ialdabaoth becomes jealous, and this is the origin of Envy. Envy engenders Death, and Death creates the offspring of Chaos (similar to the fallen angels). The lesson of the story is that when humanity discovers the Spirit of Truth, they will exist deathless. When Death is conquered, the archons (authorities) will come to an end as well, and angels will weep over their destruction. Humanity will become the Children of Light.

A Gnostic sect called the Archontici took its name from the archons.

See PRONOIA.

FURTHER READING

Barnstone, Willis. *The Other Bible*. San Francisco: HarperSanFrancisco, 1984.

van der Toorn, Karel, Bob Becking, and Pieter W. van der Horst, eds. *Dictionary of Deities and Demons in the Bible*. 2d ed. Grand Rapids, Mich.: William B. Eerdmans, 1999.

Ariel (Arael, Ariael)

Angel whose name means "lion of God." Ariel appears in biblical, apocryphal, Gnostic, Coptic, and occult literature in a variety of guises, both angel and demon.

In 4 EZRA Ariel is an angel. In the Old Testament, the book of ISAIAH refers to Ariel as an altar, man, and city. This was echoed by the Renaissance occultist, AGRIPPA, who referred to Ariel as a demon, angel, or city. In Jewish lore, Ariel is a name for Jerusalem, and in Kabbalistic lore it is the name of a VIRTUE. Ariel is ranked among the seven PRINCES by Thomas Heywood in *The Hierarchy of the Blessed Angels*. In the Coptic Pistis Sophia, Ariel rules the lower world, and in GNOSTICISM he is associated with the creator god Ialdabaoth. In magical texts, Ariel is described as a lion-headed angel. In the Testament of SOLOMON, he controls demons.

Shakespeare named a fairy Ariel in *The Tempest*. Ariel also figures in Gaelic prayers of protection for the home and hearth.

Ariel also is one of the 72 angels of the SCHEMHAMPHORAE.

Aristotle See INTELLIGENCES.

Ark of the Covenant

Gilded wooden chest made to contain the tablets of God's covenant with Israel—the Ten Commandments—and a pot of MANNA and the rod or Aaron. The chest is protected by two CHERUBIM, the twins Jael and Zarall. When King SOLOMON built the first Temple of Jerusalem, the Ark was placed in the innermost chamber, the Holy of Holies. When transported, it was covered with a veil of badgers' skins and a blue cloth, which kept it from being seen.

God's instructions to MOSES for constructing the Ark are given in Exodus 18:10–22. God specifies that it be made of shittim (acacia wood) and measure two-and-a-half cubits long by one-and-a-half cubits wide. The chest is gilded inside and out and crowned with gold. Four golden rings are at the corners for staves used to carry the ark. The mercy seat of God sits atop the Ark, from which God addresses Israel. Two gilded wood cherubs are at the ends of the Ark, stretching their wings across it.

The Ark served as an important source of prophecy. In Exodus 25:22, God tells Moses that he will speak from above the ark-cover and between the two cherubim. The two cherubim perhaps served as the focal point for intense spiritual energy and meditation, and thus they were the primary channels of prophecy for Moses and other prophets. When the First Temple was destroyed, this vein of prophecy ceased to exist.

The Zohar says that the two cherubim represent the 10 sephirot of the TREE OF LIFE divided into a masculine and feminine array (five commandments on each tablet correspond to five sephirot on the Tree). This masculine-feminine tension enabled the spiritual force of prophecy to manifest.

FURTHER READING

Kaplan, Aryeh. *Sefer Yetzirah: The Book of Creation*. Rev. ed. York Beach, Maine: Samuel Weiser, 1997.

Armaros (Abaros, Ardearos, Armers, Pharmaros)

In 1 ENOCH, a FALLEN ANGEL who teaches "the resolving of enchantments."

Armisael

Angel of the womb invoked to aid pregnancies and childbirth. The Talmud gives a prescription for difficult pregnancies that instructs the recitation of Psalm 20 nine times in the presence of the pregnant woman. The psalm is repeated another nine times if there is no relief. If there is still no relief, Armisael is invoked in this prayer: "I conjure you, Armisael, angel who governs the womb, that you help this woman and the child in her body to life and peace. Amen, Amen, Amen."

See CHILDBIRTH ANGELS; MAGIC.

Armogen See HARAHEL.

Moses with the Ark of the Covenant, from a 19th-century Bible (Author's collection)

Artyahisht See AMARAHSPANDS.

Asariel
Angel who is one of the 28 rulers of the MANSIONS OF THE MOON. Asariel means "whom God has bound," specifically, by oath.

Asmoday (Ashmeday, Asmodius, Hasmoday, Sydonay)
One of the FALLEN ANGELS and 72 spirits of SOLOMON. The LEMEGETON describes Asmoday as a strong and powerful king who had three heads: a bull, a man, and a ram. He also has a serpent's tail and webbed goose feet, and he vomits fire. Asmoday rides a dragon and carries a lance and pennon. He bestows the ring of virtues, teaches arithmetic, geomancy and all handicrafts, answers all questions, makes people invisible, and guards hidden treasures but reveals them. He rules 72 legions of spirits. A magician must invoke him bareheaded, otherwise he will lie.

As Hasmoday, he rules the moon.

Asmodeus (Ashmedai)
One of the most prominent and evil of FALLEN ANGELS. Asmodeus is an "archdemon" who rules lechery, jealousy, anger, and revenge. His goals are to prevent intercourse between husband and wife, wreck new marriages, and force husbands to commit adultery. He is frequently blamed in cases of demonic possession.

Asmodeus has three heads: that of an ogre, a ram, and a bull, all sexually licentious creatures. He also has the feet of a cock, another sexually aggressive creature. He has ugly wings, rides on a dragon (a Christian symbol of Satan and evil), and breathes fire.

Asmodeus has his roots in ancient Persian mythology, in which he is identified with Aeshma, one of seven ARCHANGELS. The Jews absorbed him into their mythology, where he attained the highest status and most power of his legends. According to Jewish lore, he is the son of Naamah and Shamdon. He is part of the SERAPHIM, the highest order of angels, but fell from grace when Lucifer was cast from HEAVEN. He also is either associated with, or is the husband of, Lilith, the demon queen of lust. He is also said to be the offspring of Lilith and ADAM.

According to the Testament of SOLOMON, Asmodeus lives in the constellation of the Great Bear (Ursa Major). He spreads the wickedness of men, plots against newlyweds, spreads madness about women through the stars, ruins the beauty of virgins, and commits murders. He is thwarted by Raphael and the smoking liver and gall of a fish, especially the sheatfish, which lives in Assyrian rivers. He has knowledge of the future.

Asmodeus is brought to the presence of King SOLOMON by the Prince of Demons, Beelzebub. Sullen and defiant, he tells the king he was born of a human mother and an angel father. Solomon will have only a temporary hold over the DEMONS; his kingdom eventually will be divided, and demons will go out again among men and will be worshiped as gods because humans will not know the names of the angels who thwart the demons. He admits that he is afraid of water.

Solomon binds Asmodeus with care, puts him in chains, and surrounds him with jars full of water, which makes the demon complain bitterly. Asmodeus is forced to make clay vessels for the temple. Solomon also burns the liver and gall of a fish beneath the demon, which quells his nasty tongue.

A rabbinic tale relates how Asmodeus is captured by King Solomon and then steals his magical ring. In order to cut stone for his Temple of Jerusalem, Solomon requires a *shamir,* a stone-cutting worm. Asmodeus knows where the worm is, for he comes to earth to watch debates in the house of learning and to take a drink of water from a stone-capped mountain well. Solomon sends his chief man, Benaiah ben Jehoiadah, to the well with a chain engraved with the divine name, a ring engraved with the divine name, a bundle of wool, and a skein of wine. Benaiah drills a hole and drains the well and stuffs the hole with the wool. He fills the well with the wine. Asmodeus comes and drinks the wine and falls asleep. Benaiah chains him about the neck and traps him with the seal of the ring. Asmodeus and other demons are forced to build Solomon's temple.

After completion of the temple, Solomon tells Asmodeus that he cannot understand why demons are so powerful when their leader could be so easily chained. Asmodeus says he will prove his greatness if Solomon will remove his chains and lend him the magical ring. Solomon does so, only to be hurled far away from Jerusalem. Asmodeus steals the ring, forces Solomon into exile, and becomes king himself. He throws the ring into the sea. But Solomon's lover, the Ammonite Namah, finds the ring in a fish belly, and the king regains his power. He is immediately trans-

Asmodeus (Francis Barrett, *The Magus,* 1805)

ported to Jerusalem when he puts on the ring. As punishment, he puts Asmodeus in a jar.

In the apocryphal book of TOBIT, Asmodeus plagues a young woman named Sarah by killing her husbands on their wedding nights in the bridal chamber before the marriages can be consummated. Sarah loses seven husbands before being rescued by Tobias, a young man who is aided by the archangel Raphael, disguised as a man. Raphael instructs Tobias to take the liver, heart, and gall of a fish and burn them to make a foul incense that will drive away Asmodeus. Tobias is dubious, but Raphael assures him the trick will work, and Tobias will be able to claim Sarah as his wife. Tobias becomes betrothed to Sarah, and, on their wedding night, prepares the foul smoke to repel Asmodeus. The demon is driven out and flees to Egypt, where he is bound up by another angel.

Asmodeus appears in Christian demonology as one of Satan's leading agents of provocation. Witches in the Middle Ages were said to worship him, and magicians and sorcerers attempted to conjure him to strike out at enemies. The medieval GRIMOIRES of magical instruction sternly admonish anyone seeking an audience with Asmodeus to summon him bareheaded out of respect. According to JOHANN WEYER, a 16th-century physician and demonologist, Asmodeus also ruled the gambling houses.

Asmodeus was one of the infernal agents blamed for the obscene sexual possession of a convent of nuns in 17th-century France, during the height of the witch scare that ran through Europe. The incident occurred at a convent in Louviers in 1647, and involved 18 nuns who allegedly were possessed through the bewitchments of the nunnery's director and the vicar of Louviers. According to confessions—most extracted under torture—the possessed nuns committed unspeakable sexual acts with the devil and demons; attended witches' sabbats, where they ate babies; and uttered obscenities and spoke in tongues. The nuns were subject to public exorcisms. The vicar, Father Thomas Boullé, was burned alive. The body of the nunnery director, Mathurin Picard, who died before sentencing was passed, was exhumed and burned. A nun who broke the story to authorities, Sister Madeleine Bavent, was sentenced to the dungeon.

FURTHER READING

Charlesworth, James H., ed. *The Old Testament Pseudepigrapha*. Vols. 1 and 2. New York: Doubleday, 1983, 1985.

Guiley, Rosemary Ellen. *The Encyclopedia of Witches and Witchcraft*. 2d ed. New York: Facts On File, 1999.

Asroilu YHVH

In 3 ENOCH, one of the PRINCES who guards the seventh HEAVEN and is the head of every season in the heavenly academy. Asroilu bows down to Gallisur.

Assiah See KABBALAH.

Astanphaeus (Astaphaeus, Astaphai, Astaphaios)

Important angel in GNOSTICISM. According to ORIGEN, the name Astanphaeus is derived from the art of

Holy Face of Christ displayed by two angels (Albrecht Dürer, 1513)

MAGIC. Astanphaeus is one of seven ARCHONS whom Ialdabaoth makes in his own image, and he is also one of seven ANGELS OF THE PRESENCE. As an archon, he guards the third gate of the aeon of the archons.

Astanphaeus also is identified as one of the seven sons of Melchizedek, and as an angel who rules the planet Mercury.

Astaroth

One of the FALLEN ANGELS and 72 spirits of SOLOMON. Of Syrian origin (according to Voltaire), Astaroth is a demonized version of the goddess Astarte. In Jewish lore, Astaroth was one of the SERAPHIM and a PRINCE of THRONES prior to his fall. In HELL, according to demonologist JOHANN WEYER, he reigns as a "grand-duke." He commands 40 legions of demons and serves as great treasurer. According to the LEMEGE-TON, he appears either as a "foul angel" or a "beautiful angel" who rides a dragon and holds a viper in his right hand. His breath stinks so badly that a magician must use his magic ring to defend his face. Astaroth will give true answers to questions about the past, present, and future. He discovers secrets and is skilled in liberal sciences. He encourages slothfulness and laziness. Astaroth believes he was punished unjustly by God, and that someday he will be restored to his rightful place in heaven.

Asteraoth

In the Testament of SOLOMON, the angel who can thwart Power, one of the seven demonic HEAVENLY BODIES, who feeds men's greed for power and control. Asteraoth is one of the PLANETARY RULERS.

asuras   See HINDUISM.

Atrugiel (Atarguniel, Atarniel, Atrigiel, Atruggiel, Tagriel)

In 3 ENOCH, a great PRINCE in the seventh HEAVEN who bows down to Naaririel. Atrugiel also is one of the many names of Metatron.

Atziluth   See KABBALAH.

Augustine, St. (354–430)

One of the most influential of the early church fathers. Augustine is remarkable among Catholic saints for having been in his youth a reckless sinner who wrote a detailed account of his conversion: the *Confessions,* addressed to God. At about age 72, Augustine sat down to review his writings and put them in chronological order, and was astounded at the quantity. His complete works, written in Latin, are about the size of an encyclopedia. Thomas Merton termed his monumental *The City of God* "the autobiography of the Catholic Church."

Augustine devotes much attention to angels: how they were created, how they differ from demons, and how they operate in expediting the progress of the human soul to holiness.

Life and Works

Augustine was born November 13, 354, in Tagaste, North Africa. His mother Monica was a Christian and his father Patricius a pagan, whom Monica eventually converted by her patience and good example. He was not baptized as an infant, but his mother enrolled him as a catechumen in the Catholic Church. He studied Latin and Greek grammar and literature in his boyhood, complaining about rough treatment by his schoolmasters.

After his father died in 370, Augustine went to Carthage to study rhetoric to prepare for a public life. There he met a young woman at a church service, began to live with her, and fathered a son named Adeodatus ("God's gift"). He confides to God in *Confessions,* "both love and lust boiled within me, and swept my youthful immaturity over the precipice of evil desires to leave me half drowned in a whirlpool of abominable sins. . . . my soul was sick, and broke out in sores, whose itch I agonized to scratch with the rub of carnal things," including stage plays, "with the mirror they held up to my own miseries and the fuel they poured on my flame."

In 373 Augustine joined the Manichees, who taught that there are two supreme gods, one good and one evil, and similarly two competing souls within the human person. For nine years he maintained interest in this cult. After his move to Rome in 383 to teach a better class of rhetoric students, he was the guest of a Manichee and socialized with many prominent members of the sect.

In 384 he was appointed professor of rhetoric in Milan. Within two years he abandoned Manicheism and gradually came under the influence of his Christian mentors: St. Ambrose, the influential local bishop, and Simplicianus, a wise elderly former bishop. At the same time, he wanted to advance himself in position and possessions, so marriage seemed the next step. His mother had joined him and helped him to arrange a marriage to a girl who was not yet 12; he agreed to wait two years. Augustine's mistress of many years had to leave him as part of this marriage plan, which threw Augustine into emotional turmoil. "My heart which had held her very dear was broken and wounded and shed blood," he wrote. "She went back to Africa, swearing that she would never know another man, and left with me the natural son I had of her. . . . I was simply a slave of lust. So I took another woman, not of course as a wife; and thus my soul's disease was kept alive as vigorously as ever." He was tormented by both the loss of his former lover and the hopelessness for him of a life of continence, which ran in circles alongside his growing seriousness in reexamining Christianity.

Then one day while in a garden, he experienced a striking conversion in which his self-doubt was expelled. His mother was exultant. Augustine decided to give up his teaching position and was baptized along with his son Adeodatus and another close friend on Easter 387. About a year later the group was at the port of Ostia on their way home to Africa when Monica died. She and Augustine had shared an ecstatic experience five days previously, after which she had told him that all her prayers had been answered in superabundance and she no longer hoped for anything in this world.

When Augustine finally returned in 388 to Tagaste in North Africa, he set up a sort of monastery on his family land with his close friends. His beloved son Adeodatus died within a year at age 16. Augustine soon gave away his possessions, and for the rest of his life lived simply as a monk in community with men.

In 391 he was ordained a priest in Hippo by Bishop Valerius, who permitted Augustine to preach almost immediately. Upon Valerius's death in 396, Augustine became bishop of Hippo, a post he held for 35 years. He composed the *Rule* for the Augustinian Order. In the 390s he started a convent for women following the *Rule*. He preached almost daily and wrote incessantly: theological treatises, letters, polemics against heresies, the *Confessions* (finished in 400), and *The City of God,* written in installments between 413 and 426. He died on August 28, 430, during a siege by the Vandals.

Angelology in The City of God

When Rome was sacked by the Goths under Alaric in 410, many intellectuals made accusations that Christianity had debilitated the empire and made it vulnerable. *The City of God* is Augustine's response. His defense of Christian doctrine was informed by politics and history, full of direct references to pagan philosophers from Plato to his contemporaries.

The fall of the earthly city of Rome was the inevitable result of the sinful wills of its rulers and citizens; at the same time the rise of the city of God (the Catholic Church) was a process that had begun before time and was infused with grace, personified by Jesus Christ. Augustine summarizes the concept of the two cities: "Two loves have built two cities: the love of self, which reaches even to contempt for God, the earthly City; and the love of God, which reaches even to contempt for self, the heavenly City. One glories in itself, the other in the Lord. One seeks its own glory amongst men; the greatest glory of the other is God, witness of its conscience. One, swollen with pride, uplifts its haughty head; the other cries out to God with the Psalmist: 'Thou are my glory, it is Thou who dost lift up my head.'"

Duality is intrinsic to human souls (and by extension to angelic spirits) who dwell on a middle ground between God's eternal immutable perfection and the lowest level of bodily mutable mortality. Humans can look upward to God and the eternal truths (the *conversio ad Deum*) or downward to mutable creatures (the *pervasio animae*). The upward gaze of the soul contains the workings of the *ratio superior;* in the downward glance, the *ratio inferior.* These are not two faculties of the soul, but are two dispositions of one and the same mind. The soul is not divided, but the being is. It is on the same basis that the two "loves" are distinguished, and so two societies of intellectual creatures. Augustine makes a similar distinction of time and eternity, a topic dear to him.

In Books XI and XII Augustine shows how the good and bad angels had inaugurated the two cities on the basis of the two loves. Though there is no explicit verse in Genesis saying how and when the angels were created, Augustine concludes that in "Let there be light, and there was light" "we are justified in understanding in this light the creation of the angels." He says, "They were created partakers of the eternal light which is the unchangeable Wisdom of God." Whereas "the true Light, which lighteth every man that cometh into the world" (John 1:9) "lighteth also every pure angel, that he may be light not in himself but in God," . . . "if an angel turn away, he becomes impure, as are all those who are called unclean spirits, and are no longer light in the Lord, but darkness in themselves, being deprived of the light eternal. For evil has no positive nature; but the loss of good has received the name 'evil.'"

In Books XIII and XIV, Augustine explains how this error was repeated by ADAM AND EVE. This brought humanity into a state of original sin, which Augustine calls a fortunate fall, because humanity is then redeemed by the intervention of Christ. From God, our first parents received a free will capable of loving Him. But they, like the FALLEN ANGELS, preferred to love themselves and to live according to a law of their own, thereby establishing themselves in pride and falsehood.

The angels who remained blessed enjoyed uninterrupted and unchangeable connection with God; the others "of their own will did fall from the light of goodness." Augustine considers whether the fallen angels may have enjoyed something on this level before their fall, and says it is possible but not accompanied with foresight of their eternal felicity that the good angels had. "If it is hard to believe that they were not all from the beginning on an equal footing . . . it is harder to consider that some good angels are now uncertain of their eternal felicity. . . . For what catholic Christian does not know that no new devil will ever arise among the good angels, as he knows that this present devil will never again return into the fellowship of the good?"

Augustine does not talk about the leader of the fallen angels per se, but he cites several words of Christ as clues to understanding how and when this sin of the angels occurred: "He was a murderer from the beginning, and abode not in the truth" (Matthew 25:46). Augustine interprets "beginning" as "from the beginning of the human race, when man, whom he could kill by his deceit was made." He refutes the interpretation that this passage indicates that the devil was flawed from his very creation, as the Manichees posited. On this same ground he refutes the interpretation of the Apostle John's comment "the devil sinneth from the beginning" (1 John 3:8), citing "prophetic proof:" "How art thou fallen, O Lucifer, son of the morning" (Isaiah 14:12) and "Thou hast been in Eden, the garden of God; every precious stone was thy covering" (Ezekiel 33:13), which Augustine says, "it is meant that he was some time without sin."

Augustine considers how a good God could create beings whom he knew would become evil, and says that God "makes good use of evil wills." He causes the devil to be cast down from his high position and to become the mockery of his angels.

In Book XII, Augustine returns to the subject and offers this conclusion: the bad angels "either received less of the grace of the divine love than those who persevered in the same; or if both were created equally good, then while the one fell by their evil will the others were more abundantly assisted, and attained to that pitch of blessedness at which they became certain they would never fall from it. . . . We must therefore acknowledge, with the praise due the Creator, that not only of holy men, but also of holy angels, 'the love of God is shed abroad in their hearts by the Holy Ghost' . . . [and] not only of men, but primarily and principally of angels it is true, as it is written, 'it is good to draw near to God.' And those who have this good in common, have, both with Him to whom they draw near, and with one another, a holy fellowship, and form one city of God—His living sacrifice, and His living temple."

Augustine also works with a two-tiered elaboration of the two cities idea. There is an imperfect city of God on earth and an imperfect city of God in HEAVEN flawed by the defection of the bad angels; the present earthly city has no connection with God. Wicked angels are stirring up persecutions of Christians, constantly seducing those in power over nations, and otherwise setting struggles in motion on political, spiritual, and psychological levels. But the church can raise the earthly city up, an ascent through the ministry of angels and aspiring humans.

A just man seeking to accomplish this is therefore much higher than a reprobate angel. "All who understand or believe them to be worse than unbelieving men are well aware that they are called 'darkness' . . . we understand these two societies of angels—the one enjoying God, the other swelling with pride; the one to whom it is said 'Praise ye Him, all His angels,' the other whose prince [Satan] says [to Jesus, Matthew 4:9] "all these things will I give Thee if Thou wilt fall down and worship me;' the one blazing with the holy love of God, the other reeking with the unclean lust of self advancement."

Another way to look at this is that there are only two cities, each containing angels and men; the city of God contains good men and angels while the city of man contains both kinds of reprobate creatures, man and angels. Augustine says the nature of the good angels ("the holy angels who maintain their allegiance to God, who never were, nor ever shall be apostate, between whom and those who forsook light eternal and became darkness, God . . . made at the first a separation") determines the nature of the subsequent city of God by providing the earthly city with a prototype. All Christians must try to be like good angels.

Those who succeed will actually become angels. The angels form the link between the two manifestations of the *civitatis Dei,* the earthly and the heavenly. Together the angels and the elect comprise the one city of God. The fall of the reprobate angels left gaps in the celestial court. God desires to fill these openings with his elect. The city of God in heaven will remain imperfect and unfulfilled until the temporal city of God reaches heaven after the Parousia (the Second Coming of Christ). Man's plight here below is temporary, since his goal is to resume his place in heaven. Aspiring humans are obligated to yearn to return to the voids reserved exclusively for them. Here on earth they are expected to behave in a manner befitting angels—a key inspiration in Augustinian monasticism. The angels assist the elect in their pilgrimage to the perfect homeland above.

However, Augustine warns in Book XIX that devils can imitate angels. "As Satan, as we read [2 Corinthians 11:14] sometimes transforms himself into an angel of light, to tempt those whom it is necessary to discipline, or just to deceive, there is great need of God's mercy to preserve us from making friends with demons in disguise, while we fancy we have good angels as friends; for the astuteness and deceitfulness of these wicked spirits is equaled by their hurtfulness." This is part of human misery, and the saints themselves are often tempted in this manner.

Men and angels are joined symbiotically, each dependent on the other. The angels need humans to fill their depleted ranks. Humans long to rise to the occasion. Angels assist them both in practical terms and by offering their example. The office of assistance by the good angels pertains only to the earthly elect, not to the reprobate men who also reside in the church universal.

The earlier books of *The City of God* are devoted primarily to refuting the arguments of pagan philosophers. Augustine is well aware that many pagans consider DAIMONES the mediators between gods (immortals) and mortals. In Book IV he explains how Christ alone is the mediator between God and man. There is "a wicked mediator [the evil angels or Satan] who separates friends, and a good Mediator [Christ] who reconciles enemies. And those who separate are numerous. . . . The evil angels being deprived, they are wretched, and interpose to hinder rather than to help this blessedness, and by their very number prevent us from reaching that one beatific good." By becoming mortal Christ showed us that "in order to obtain that blessed and beatific good, we need to seek mediators to lead us through the successive steps of this attainment, but . . . having Himself become a partaker of our humanity, has afforded us ready access to the participation of His divinity. For in delivering us from our mortality and misery, He does not lead us to the immortal and blessed angels . . . but he leads us straight to that Trinity, by participating in which the angels themselves are blessed. Therefore, when He chose to be in the form of a servant, and lower than the angels, that He might be our Mediator, He remained higher than the angels, in the form of God—Himself at once the way of life on earth and life itself in heaven."

In Book X Augustine argues against the invocation of DEMONS in many magical practices. He states that miracles in the Bible were wrought "for the purpose of commending the worship of the one true God, and prohibiting the worship of a multitude of false gods." They were "wrought by simple faith and godly confidence," not by "a criminal tampering with the unseen world." There is no distinction between theurgy (practiced by honorable people) and necromancy (practiced by magicians "addicted to the illicit arts") because

"both classes are the slaves of the deceitful rites of the demons whom they invoke under the names of angels."

Good angels minister to perform miracles and the place and time of miracles are dependent on God's unchangeable will. Angels will never demand sacrifices or worship for themselves but instead inspire us to worship and serve God.

Angels in Other Works
Several of Augustine's other works discuss angels in detail.

On Genesis Against the Manichees states that the ultimate destiny of humankind is a "renewal," and a "liberation," which he terms a "change into angelic form." This constitutes a restoration to our original status lost by sin.

In *De Quantitae Animae,* a dialogue with his friend Evodius, Augustine agrees with Evodius's firm conviction that he is "soul," but adds "our souls are not *in* bodies." He tells his friend that the soul is by its nature "equal of the angel," and any inferiority is a consequence of its sin.

In *Literal Commentary on Genesis,* written before *The City of God,* Augustine says much on angels' involvement with creation and the administration of it. He states that every being is first made in the eternal uttering of its idea in the Word of God ("Let there be . . ."). According to the phrase "and so it was made," the angels receive knowledge of the things, still to be created, in its idea within the Word. With the phrase "and so God made," the thing take its finite actuality. This does not mean that the angels are the mediators of creation; God is the sole creator, the one who makes things in their separate existence. No creatures beneath the angels were created without their knowledge.

Creation does not take place in six days, but it is completed in the first moment of time. Augustine draws a parallel between two kinds of knowledge and evening and daylight, and he postulates this might be what "day" means in Genesis. When things are known directly in themselves as parts of creation they are known dimly, as if seen in the partial darkness of the evening. When the same things are known in their eternal principles (*rationes aeternae*), as they are in the Word of God, they are known clearly, in the full light of day. Thus, there is in the spiritual order a very real succession of night and day. The ordinary mode of knowledge which the angels enjoy, for instance, is that of spiritual daylight; they see the *rationes* of things in the Word of God.

Since the angels have direct knowledge (though inferior to God's) of creation subsequent to themselves, the six days could be thought of as a recapitulation of

Angel keeping demons at bay (Author's collection)

the process by which this happened. The evening which concludes each day is the angels' looking in turn at each realm (first themselves, then the firmament, and so on) as it is completed and stands forth in its own being, the outcome of God's creative intention, yet inferior to what it remains in the *rationes aeternae*. The morning which follows is the referring of these various creatures to the praise of their Creator; and the new day reaches its full brightness in their looking to the divine ideas to see what next is to be created. The angels are connected to God without interruption, therefore their knowledge is "day." But they also know created things as they are in themselves, and this looking downward is "evening." If they should turn away from "day" knowledge (as Lucifer did), then their knowledge turns into that of the "evening."

In the treatise *De Trinitatae*, devoted to distinguishing the Father, Son, and Holy Spirit, Augustine discusses the question of divine theophanies—the appearances of God on earth. Except for the theophanies pertaining to Christ, all the other appearances of God to man may have been affected through the intervention of angels, including the tongues of fire at the

Pentecost. Angels never lose connection with the infinite, eternal God, and they refer all things toward their source.

FURTHER READING

Augustine. *The City of God.* Translated by Marcus Dods, George Wilson, and J. J. Smith. Introduction by Thomas Merton. New York: Modern Library, 1950.

———. *Confessions.* Translated by F. J. Sheed. New York: Sheed and Ward, 1943, 1970.

Battenhouse, Roy W., ed. *A Companion to the Study of St. Augustine.* New York: Oxford University Press, 1955.

Bourke, Vernon J. *Wisdom from St. Augustine.* St. Thomas, Tex.: Center for Thomistic Studies, 1984.

Brown, Peter. *Augustine of Hippo.* Berkeley: University of California Press, 1967.

authorities (exousiai)

Celestial forces or entities, or an order of angels, who are the bearers of authority. "Authorities" is sometimes used as an alternate for POWERS and VIRTUES. PSEUDO-DIONYSIUS gives them equal order with the DOMINIONS and powers. St. John of Damascus names authorities as sixth in rank, one level below the powers.

References to authorities in the New Testament imply that they were celestial forces that became evil and had to be defeated by Christ. Ephesians 1:20–21 states that when Christ was raised from the dead, he sat at the right hand of God "far above all rule and authority and power and dominion." Similarly, 1 Corinthians 15:24 says, "Then comes the end, when he delivers the kingdom to God the Father after destroying every rule and every power and every authority." Such references are taken to mean celestial forces as well as earthly ones.

Authorities are mentioned frequently in Gnostic, apocryphal, and apocalyptic texts. ENOCH sees them in the seventh HEAVEN, along with the CHERUBIM, SERAPHIM, ORIGINS, THRONES, ARCHANGELS, and "the incorporeal forces" (2 Enoch 20:1). The Testament of ADAM places authorities sixth in rank, behind powers, and says they govern the celestial lights of the sun, moon, and stars. The Testament of SOLOMON opens with a declaration that the text describes how King Solomon subdued all the spirits and tells "what their authorities are against men, and by what angels these demons are thwarted," implying the evil nature of authorities. The Testament of LEVI places authorities in the fourth heaven, along with the thrones.

Authorities also appear in the apocryphal Acts of the Apostles, especially the acts of Andrew, John, Philip, and Thomas.

See ST. PAUL.

FURTHER READING

van der Toorn, Karel, Bob Becking, and Pieter W. van der Horst, eds. *Dictionary of Deities and Demons in the Bible.* 2d ed. Grand Rapids, Mich.: William B. Eerdmans, 1999.

avatars

In Hinduism, human incarnations of the divine who function as mediators between men and God, thus serving in an angel-like capacity. The term "avatar" is Sanskrit for "descent." Avatars incarnate of their own free will in order to help the spiritual progress of other incarnated souls. Like angels, avatars can bestow divine knowledge upon people, usually by touch, a glance, or even silence.

Avatars appear in the *Ramayana* and *Mahabharata* (the latter of which includes the *Bhagavad-Gita*) but not in the *Vedas* or the *Upanishads*. Avatars in the *Ramayana* and *Mahabharata* are Rama and Krishna, incarnations of Vishnu, the sky god and protector of the universe. Vishnu is said to have had anywhere from 10 to 39 incarnations, all of whom appear to save the world in times of crisis. Rama and Krishna are the most beloved and worshiped; Krishna is considered the most perfect expression of the divine.

The potential number of avatars is countless. Vishnu's final avatar will be Kalki, who will appear at the end of Kali-Yuga, the present era, and destroy the wicked and usher in the new era of Maha-Yuga.

Gautama Buddha is considered an avatar. Various living holy men, such as Sai Baba of India, also are called avatars.

Avicenna   See IBN SINA.

Ayil

Angel who governs the zodiac sign of Sagittarius.

Azael   (Assiel, Azazel, Azzael, Azzazel)

One of the principal evil angels who cohabited with mortal women. Azael means "who God strengthens." According to lore, Azael slept with Naamah and spawned Assyrian guardian spirits known as SEDIM, invoked in the exorcism of evil spirits. As punishment, Azael is chained in a desert until Judgment Day. In magical lore, he guards hidden treasure and teaches witchcraft that enables men to make the sun, moon, and stars come down from the sky.

In 3 ENOCH, Azael is named as one of three primary MINISTERING ANGELS with Azza and Uzza, who live in the seventh (highest) HEAVEN. In later lore, he is fallen and is punished by having his nose pierced.

Azael is sometimes synonymous with Azza. In Akkadian lore, he is one of the MASKIM, a prince of HELL.

See WATCHERS.

Azazel   (Azael, Azazael, Hazazel)

Name or epithet of a god or DEMON. The name Azazel means "God strengthens." He originally may have been a Semitic god of the flocks who became demonized.

Azazel is associated with the ritual of scapegoating as an expiation of sin, as described in Leviticus 16. In verse nine, God instructs MOSES that his brother Aaron shall take two goats and sacrifice one to the Lord for sin. The second goat is for Azazel, and it is to be presented live to the Lord for atonement and then sent into the wilderness to Azazel. This reference to the wilderness has led to beliefs that Azazel was a demon of the desert.

Apocalyptic writings emphasize the evil nature of Azazel. He is one of the chief SONS OF GOD who comes to earth and is corrupted by cohabitation. (See WATCHERS.) In 1 ENOCH, he is described as one of 21 chiefs of 200 FALLEN ANGELS. He has seven serpent heads, 14 faces, and 12 wings. He brings aggression by teaching men metalworking and how to make swords and shields, and vanity by teaching women how to use jewelry and cosmetics. He teaches oppression, leads men and women into adultery, and reveals divine secrets. Azazel's instruction of metals and metalworking was taken by Hellenistic alchemists as evidence of the angelic origins of alchemy.

In the Apocalypse of ABRAHAM, Azazel is the angel of disgrace, lies, evil, wrath, and trials and the lord of HELL, who is confined to earth by God because he became enamored with it. He appears to ABRAHAM first in the form of an unclean bird and then as a dragon with 12 wings and human hands and feet.

In Jewish lore, Azazel figures prominently in folktales, along with another fallen angel, Semyaza (Semyaz, Shemhazai). Azazel refuses to bow to Adam when he is presented to God and the heavenly hierarchies.

Islamic lore also tells of Azazel refusing to bow down to Adam, and so God casts him out of heaven and changes him into Iblis (Eblis).

FURTHER READING

van der Toorn, Karel, Bob Becking, and Pieter W. van der Horst, eds. *Dictionary of Deities and Demons in the Bible.* 2d ed. Grand Rapids, Mich.: William B. Eerdmans, 1999.

Azbogah YHVH   (Azbuga)

In the MERKABAH, one of eight great angelic PRINCES of the throne of judgment who rank higher than Metatron. Azbogah means "strength," and it also is a secret name of God, one of the NAMES of Divine Glory and a name of power.

Azbogah is significant in GEMATRIA because it has three groups of letters that each add up to eight. The eightfold name reflects the concept in GNOSTICISM of the Ogdoad, the eight firmament in which dwells Divine Wisdom, and which is over the seven firmaments of creation.

In 3 ENOCH, Azbogah YHVH is an angelic prince, a glorious and dreaded angel who knows the secrets of the throne of Glory—that is, he is privileged to serve within the curtain that hides God. He is called Azbogah because his principal duty is to clothe the worthy with righteousness when they arrive in heaven. He bows down to Soperiel.

Azbogah is invoked as an angel of healing against all illness, all hurt, and all evil.

See YHVH.

Azrael (Ashriel, Azrail, Azriel, Gabriel)

In Jewish and Islamic angelologies, the ANGEL OF DEATH. The name Azrael means "whom God helps." With other angels charged with the same task, Azrael's hands are stretched out to receive the souls of evildoers in the agonies of dying.

Azrael is one of the greatest of the angels, with his shape pleasing to the believer in order to facilitate the release from life. According to Sufi teacher Abdul Karim Jili, Azrael appears to the soul in a form provided by its most powerful metaphors. He may even manifest invisibly, "so that a man may die of a rose in aromatic pain"—or of a rotting stench. When the soul sees Azrael it "falls in love," and its gaze is thus withdrawn from the body as if by seduction. Great prophets and saints may be invited politely by Azrael in corporeal form, as he did to MOSES and MUHAMMAD.

When the Sufi poet Rumi lay on his deathbed, Azrael appeared as a beautiful youth: "I am come by divine command to inquire what commission the Master may have to entrust to me." Rumi's human companions almost fainted with fear, but the Sufi master replied: "Come in, come in, thou messenger of my King. Do that which thou art bidden, and God willing thou shalt find me one of the patient."

Islamic angelology holds that Azrael is another form of Raphael, and possess 70,000 feet and 40,000 wings. He has as many eyes and tongues as there are people. Arabic mythology tells that Azrael constantly writes and erases in a large book. The writing brings birth and the erasing brings death.

A story regarding the creation of ADAM has Azrael fulfilling a crucial task. The angels Michael, Gabriel, and Israfil do not produce seven handfuls of earth necessary to make Adam; Azrael does. Thus, he is endowed with the power to separate the soul from the body.

See DEATHBED APPARITIONS.

FURTHER READING

Barnstone, Willis, ed. *The Other Bible*. San Francisco: HarperSanFrancisco, 1984.

Klein, F. A. *The Religion of Islam*. London: 1906. Reprint 1971.

Azriel (Mahniel)

One of the chief ANGELS OF DESTRUCTION. Azriel is invoked to ward off evil. His name is one of seven or 10 angel names inscribed on some MEZUZOT.

Azriel is known as "Azriel the Ancient." His name Mahniel means "mighty camp." He resides on the north side of HEAVEN, where he commands 60 myriads of legions of angels, and he also receives prayers.

Azza (Semyaza)

FALLEN ANGEL. Azza means "the strong." In rabbinic lore, Azza cohabited with women (see WATCHERS) and was punished to fall eternally from HEAVEN with one eye shut and the other open in order to see and suffer more.

In 3 Enoch, Azza is named as one of three primary MINISTERING ANGELS with Azael and Uzza, who live in the seventh (highest) heaven. The three object to the elevation of the prophet ENOCH into the great angel Metatron. Azza heads a group of angels of justice.

In the Talmud, Azza and Azael begot the SEDIM, Assyrian guardian spirits, by having sexual relations with Naamah, angel of prostitution, prior to the fall.

In other lore, Azza is the angel who bestows knowledge upon King SOLOMON.

In Akkadian lore, he is one of the MASKIM, a prince of HELL.

ba

In Egyptian mythology, the *ba* is the soul, represented in art as a human-headed bird. As the winged, eternal part of a person, it provided an early inspiration for the image of the winged angel.

The Egyptians associated the *ba* with the *ka,* or the person's double, and the *ib,* or heart. The *ba* is invisible and does not permanently leave the body upon death, but remains with it in the tomb, sometimes coming out at night with a lamp to roam a bit and then returning to the tomb. The body must remain intact in order for the *ba* to return to it (hence the need to preserve the corpse by embalming). The *ba* is fed cakes and is cared for by the sycamore tree goddess.

The Egyptians left small openings in the pyramids so that the *ba* would have easy access. Small ledges inside were built for the *ba* to stand upon.

The ancient Egyptians believed that the stars were *ba*, lit by their tomb lamps.

See WINGS.

Baal (Bael, Baell)

One of the FALLEN ANGELS and 72 spirits of SOLOMON. Many small deities of ancient Syria and Persia carry this name, which means "the lord," but the greatest Baal was an agricultural and fertility deity of Canaan.

The son of EL, the high god of Canaan, Baal was the lord of life, and ruled the death-rebirth cycle. He engaged in a battle with Mot ("death") and was slain and sent to the underworld. The crops withered, until Baal's sister, Anath, the maiden goddess of love, found his body and gave it proper burial. The Canaanites worshiped Baal by sacrificing children by burning. According to the Zohar, Baal is equal in rank to the archangel Raphael.

According to the LEMEGETON, Baal is a king ruling in the East and governs 66 legions. Baal has three heads: a toad, a man, and a cat. He speaks with a hoarse voice. Bael is invoked to impart invisibility and wisdom.

Balam (Balan)

A former member of the order of DOMINIONS and now one of the FALLEN ANGELS with 40 legions under his command. Balam also is one of the 72 spirits of SOLOMON. He is a terrible and powerful king with the heads of a bull, man, and ram; the tail of a serpent; and eyes of flaming fire. He rides on an angry bear (in some depictions he is naked) and carries a goshawk on his wrist. He speaks hoarsely and gives true answers concerning the past, present, and future. He also can render men invisible, and he makes them have wit.

Angel appearing to Balam (Gustave Doré)

Balberith (Baalberith, Berith, Beal, Elberith)
FALLEN ANGEL and former PRINCE of the order of
CHERUBIM. As a DEMON, Balberith serves as a master of
ceremonies and grand pontiff in HELL. He notarizes
pacts with the devil. Balberith was named as a key
demon in the famous possession of nuns at Aix-en-
Provence, France, in 1611. He appears wearing a
crown and riding a horse.

Balthioul (Balthial, Bathiel)
In the Testament of SOLOMON, angel who has the
power to thwart Distress, one of the seven demonic
HEAVENLY BODIES who creates jealousy. Balthioul is one
of the PLANETARY RULERS.

Baradiel
In 3 ENOCH, PRINCE of the third HEAVEN and angel of hail.
See NURIEL.

Barakiel (Barachiel, Baraqiel, Barchiel, Barkiel, Barquiel
and Barbiel)
Angel who is the "lightning of God" and thus rules
lightning. Barakiel is one of the seven ARCHANGELS and
planetary angels and rules Jupiter and the month of
February. He is one of the four chief SERAPHIM, ruler of
the CONFESSORS, and PRINCE of the second and third
HEAVEN. Barakiel is cited as the ruler of the zodiac sign
of Scorpio and also Pisces. He is invoked for luck in
gambling.

As Barkiel he is one of the guards of the gates of the
East Wind. As Barbiel he is one of the angels ruling the
28 MANSIONS OF THE MOON.

Barakiel (Copyright 1995 Robert M. Place; from *The Angels
Tarot* by Rosemary Ellen Guiley and Robert M. Place)

Baraqijal

FALLEN ANGEL who teaches astrology. Baraqijal (possibly a variant of Barakiel) is named in 1 ENOCH as a "chief of 10" leader of troops of fallen angels. In JUBILEES he is identified as one of the WATCHERS.

Barattiel (Ataphiel, Atapiel, Atatiel)

In 3 ENOCH, angel PRINCE who supports Arabot, the seventh HEAVEN, on the tops of his three fingers.

Barbas See MORBAS.

Barbatos

One of the FALLEN ANGELS and 72 spirits of SOLOMON. Formerly one of the VIRTUES, Barbatos is a great count, earl, and duke of HELL, where he rules 30 legions. When the sun is in Sagittarius, he appears with four kings and three companies of troops. He understands the languages of all animals, especially the singing of birds, the barking of dogs, and the lowings of bullocks. Barbatos can reveal treasures hidden by MAGIC, and he can reconcile friends and people in power. He teaches all sciences, and knows all things in the past and of the future.

Barbiel (Barakiel, Barbuel, Baruel)

Angel who is both good and bad. As a good angel, Barbiel is ruler of October and, when equated with Barakiel, also February. He is one of the angels of the 28 MANSIONS OF THE MOON. As a FALLEN ANGEL, he is ex-prince of the orders of VIRTUES and ANGELS. In HELL, Barbiel serves under Zaphiel as one of the seven Electors.

Bariel

In the LEMEGETON, the ruling angel of the 11th hour of the day, called Maneloym. Bariel commands thousands of dukes and their thousands of servants.

Barman (Bahman, Bahrman)

Important angel in ZOROASTRIANISM. Barman is the first of the AMARAHSPANDS, the INTELLIGENCE from whom all other angels proceed. He rules the animals of earth and is chief of the ANGELS OF THE MONTHS.

In Islamic lore, Barman is equated with Gabriel, the mightiest of angels. He rules January and the second day of the month.

Barman is portrayed in human form wearing a red crown.

Barquiel

In the LEMEGETON, the ruling angel of the seventh hour of the day, called Hamarym. Barquiel commands 10 chief dukes and 100 lesser dukes.

Barrett, Francis (19th century)

English magician and occultist. Little is known about Francis Barrett beyond his authorship of *The Magus*, a compendium of occult information, including the lore of angels and DEMONS and how to work in MAGIC with them, published in London in 1801.

Barrett billed himself as a Rosicrucian and a teacher of chemistry, metaphysics, and natural occult philosophy. He gave lessons in the magical arts from his apartment in Marlebourne. Most of his occult knowledge probably came from books.

The Magus stimulated a revival of interest in occultism; the great occultist Eliphas Levi was influenced by it. However, there is very little original material in the book. Barrett lifted material from the works of AGRIPPA, Peter of Albano, Jean Baptiste von Helmont, and other experts on alchemy and occultism. Barrett did contribute some new illustrations: portraits of various demons, which he may have seen while scrying.

The English historian Montague Summers credited Barrett with turning Cambridge into a center of magic, though this probably exaggerates his influence.

FURTHER READING

Barrett, Francis. *The Magus*. Secaucus, N.J.: The Citadel Press, 1967. First published 1801.

Melton, J. Gordon, ed. *Encyclopedia of Occultism & Parapsychology*. 5th ed. Detroit: Gale Group, 2001.

Baruch

Secretary to the Old Testament prophet Jeremiah credited with authorship of apocalyptic works. Baruch is briefly mentioned twice in Jeremiah (32:14 and 36:4). The apocalypses feature encounters with angels.

2 Baruch

2 Baruch, also known as the Syriac Apocalypse of Baruch, was written after the fall of Jerusalem (70 C.E.), probably sometime in the early second century. It describes how Baruch is desolate after the fall of Jerusalem, fasts, and then sends up lamentations and prayers to God. He warns the people of the final judgment, which will be preceded by 12 disasters. He has a vision. (See DREAMS AND VISIONS.)

Early in the text, as enemies are coming to destroy Jerusalem, Baruch is lifted up by a spirit and carried above the wall of Jerusalem. He sees four angels standing at the four corners of the city, each holding a burning torch. A fifth angel descends from HEAVEN and instructs them to hold the torches and not light them until told to do so, for he is commanded to come and first speak to the earth.

The angel then enters the temple, into the Holy of Holies, and takes away all the holy objects and clothing. He announces these will be guarded so that they will not be taken by strangers, and they eventually will be restored to Jerusalem. The items are swallowed up by the earth.

The angel commands the four angels with torches to destroy the walls down to their foundations so that the enemies cannot boast of doing so. The angels comply and the city walls come down. Baruch leaves. Later the Chaldean army arrives and seizes the city.

In his lamentations, Baruch wonders whether there is anything to be gained by being righteous. God says that man must not fall into corruption. He tells Baruch of the coming 12 tribulations, followed by the salvation of the coming of the Messiah. The tribulations are: commotions; the slaughtering of the great; the death of many; fighting and war; famine and drought; earthquakes and terrors; a multitude of ghosts and the appearance of demons; the fall of fire; rape and much violence; injustice and unchastity; and disorder and a mixture of everything that has come before.

Baruch warns the people. He has a vision that God interprets for him, concerning the destruction of the destroyer of Jerusalem and the establishment of the dominion of the "Anointed One." Baruch has another vision of 12 clouds pouring black water upon the earth, bringing destruction. There is lightning, and then 12 rivers come from the sea and surround the lightning, becoming subject to it.

Baruch ponders his vision and prays. The angel Ramael (Ramiel), who governs true visions, comes to him and asks why he is troubled by what he has seen. Ramael explains the vision of the clouds of water: Each cloud represents a stage in history, beginning with the corruption of angels who came to earth and cohabited with women, and ending with the coming of "the word," the rebuilding of a New Jerusalem, and the routing of all evils.

Ramael tells Baruch he will depart the world in 40 days, but he will not die but will be kept until the end of times. Before he leaves, he must instruct people so that they will not die, but live in the last times. Baruch writes a long letter to the people, ties it to the neck of an eagle, and lets it go.

3 Baruch
3 Baruch was written between the first and third centuries C.E. and exists in both Greek and Slavonic, the

The last judgment (Gustave Doré)

latter of which is a translation of a lost Greek original. Angels and the heavenly realms are described in detail in this text. The central figures are Michael, the holder of the keys of heaven, and Phanuel (Phamael), who serves as the heavenly guide.

After the destruction of Jerusalem, Baruch weeps bitterly. God sends Phanuel, an archangel, ANGEL OF THE LORD, and the angel of hosts, to tell him his prayers have been heard, not to be concerned about the salvation of Jerusalem, and to stop irritating God with his lamentations. The angel says he will take him into heaven to reveal the mysteries of God. Baruch is shown five heavens. According to the Greek manuscript, the descriptions are:

FIRST HEAVEN
After crossing a river and passing through a large door "like the passing of 30 days," Baruch sees a plain with men who have the faces of cattle, the horns of deer, the feet of goats, and the loins of rams. These are men who built a tower of war against God, and they have been thrown out.

SECOND HEAVEN

Baruch and Phanuel pass through another large door, "flying about the distance of 60 days," to a great prison holding creatures with the faces of dogs and the feet of deer. These are the ones who planned the building of the tower and who enslaved men and women in its construction. They attempted to bore into heaven to see if it was made of copper or iron. God struck them blind and confused their tongues and changed them into strange beasts.

THIRD HEAVEN

Baruch and Phanuel go on a journey of about 185 days to a plain with a serpent who appears to be stone. The serpent eats the bodies of those who live their lives badly, and his belly is Hades. Baruch is shown Hades, which is "gloomy and unclean."

Baruch asks to be shown the tree which caused the fall of ADAM. Phanuel says it was planted by Samael and thus was forbidden by God, but Samael tricked Adam. Because of the resulting evil, God sent the Flood that destroyed all flesh and 409,000 giants, and all vegetation in Paradise. A sprig of the tree was uprooted and removed. Noah found the sprig and the angel Sarasael was sent to tell him to replant the tree, whose fruit will become the blood of God.

Baruch is then shown where the sun goes forth, a chariot on top of fire drawn by four horses and 40 angels and driven by a man with a fiery crown. The chariot is preceded by a bird, PHOENIX, as big as nine mountains, who is the guardian of the world. It absorbs the rays of the sun so that men can stand the intensity and live on earth. The Phoenix excretes a worm, which is made into cinnamon.

A thunderclap announces the opening of the 365 gates of heaven by the angels—the separation of light from darkness. Baruch sees the crowned Phoenix carried by angels. He is frightened by the splendor and hides in the wings of Phanuel.

Phanuel takes him to the west to the end of the day, where he sees four angels take the crown from a tired Phoenix and remove it to heaven for renewal. Phanuel says that the sun is defiled by the sin, corruption, and lawlessness of men.

Baruch is then shown the mysteries of the moon, drawn in a chariot driven by a woman and preceded by oxen, lambs, and many angels. Phanuel says that when Adam fell, the moon woman gave light to Samael when he took the serpent as a garment. Angry, God diminished her and shortened her days, which is why the moon waxes and wanes.

FOURTH HEAVEN

At the next level, Baruch sees a plain with a lake in the middle, and birds unlike those on earth, who continu-ously praise God. This is where the souls of the right-eous assemble "living together choir by choir." It is the source of the "dew of heaven."

FIFTH HEAVEN

The gate of this heaven is closed and can be opened only by Michael, the "commander in chief" who holds the keys. Michael descends in a noise like thunder and the gates open in more thunderous sounds. Phanuel makes obeisance to him and says, "Hail, commander in chief of all our regiment." Michael responds, "Hail thou also, our brother, interpreter of revelations to those who pass through life rightly" (11:6–7). Michael holds a large bowl whose depth reaches from heaven to earth, in which he carries the good works and virtues of the righteous to God.

Then angels of power and angels of principalities arrive with flower-filled baskets, which they give to Michael for his bowl. The flowers are the virtues of the righteous. Other angels come with baskets less than full, and they are frightened to approach Michael. Michael tells them to bring what they have, but he and Phanuel are distressed because the bowl is not filled.

Other angels come bearing nothing, crying because they have been handed over to evil men and begging to be released from them. Michael declines, saying they cannot go in order that the enemy will not win in the end. The angels still beg to be transferred. Michael tells them to wait until God tells him what to do. In a noise like thunder, he takes the bowl of virtues to God, and the doors to the fifth heaven close.

After a time Michael reappears bringing oil. It is the oil of mercy or the oil of God's glory. For the angels who brought baskets of flowers, he fills their baskets with oil according to the measure of what they brought, and tells them to give it as a reward to the righteous. To the angels who brought nothing, he instructs them to torment and punish the evil men to whom they are assigned, for their deeds have angered him. They are to provoke anger, bitterness, and jeal-ousy; bring plagues of caterpillars, locusts, rust, and grasshoppers with hail, lightning, and fury; torment their children with demons and punish them with sword and death.

The door closes while Michael is speaking, and Baruch and Phanuel withdraw. Phanuel returns the scribe to earth, where he praises God for the revela-tions. The story ends.

The Slavonic manuscript of 3 Baruch mentions other angels in addition to Michael, Phanuel, and Sarasael. Samael is referred to as Satanael, Satan's name before the fall. The Garden of Eden is planted by 200,003 angels, each of whom plants a different thing. Michael plants the olive, Gabriel the apple, Uriel the nut, Raphael the melon, and Satanael the vine or the tree.

FURTHER READING

Charlesworth, James H., ed. *The Old Testament Pseudepigrapha*. Vols. 1 and 2. New York: Doubleday, 1983, 1985.

Baruchiel (Baruchiachel)

In the Testament of SOLOMON, angel who has the power to thwart Strife, one of the seven demonic HEAVENLY BODIES. In 3 ENOCH, Baruchiel is one of seven PLANETARY RULERS.

Bat(h) Qol (Bath Kol)

In Kabbalistic lore, a female angel associated with divine prophecy, whose name means "daughter of the voice" or "heavenly voice." Bath Qol appears in the form of a dove, perhaps a parallel to the dove of the Holy Spirit or Holy Ghost of Christianity. She is the angel said to visit Rabbi Simeon (Shim'on) ben Yohai, the reputed author of the Zohar in the second century, who spent 12 years in seclusion in a cave in Israel.

Bathin (Mathim)

One of the FALLEN ANGELS and 72 spirits of SOLOMON. Bathin is a strong and great duke of HELL with 30 legions under his command. He appears as a man with a serpent's tail astride a pale horse. He understands the lore of herbs and precious stones. He can transport people from country to country instantly.

Bazazath (Bazazarath)

Archangel of the second HEAVEN. According to the Testament of SOLOMON, Bazazath is the angel who has the power to thwart the demon WINGED DRAGON.

Beelzebub (Beelzeboul)

Syrian god who became demonized as a FALLEN ANGEL in Jewish and Christian lore. According to the KABBALAH, Beelzebub was the prince of DEMONS who governed the nine evil hierarchies of the underworld. In Christian demonology, he is second to Satan among the fallen angels, the prince of devils and chief of demons.

Also known as Baal-zebub, "the lord of the flies," the name is a distortion of Baal-zebul, the chief Canaanite or Phoenician god meaning "lord of the divine abode" or "lord of the heavens." Beelzebub has always been considered a demon of great power, and sorcerers have conjured him at great risk. Most depictions show him as an enormous fly.

Pharisees tried to cast doubt on Jesus' power to cast out demons by accusing him of being possessed by Beelzebub. The incident is recounted in Matthew (12:24–29), Mark (3:22–27), and Luke (11:14–22):

> And the scribes which came down from Jerusalem said, he hath Beelzebub, and by the prince of devils casteth he out devils. And he called them unto him, and said unto them in parables, How can Satan cast out Satan? And if a kingdom be divided against itself, that house cannot stand. And if Satan rise up against himself, and be divided, he cannot stand but hath an end. No man can enter into a strong man's house, and spoil his goods, except he will first bind the strong man; and then he will spoil his house. (Mark 3: 22–27)

This incident also presents the idea of binding (adjuring) Satan to the will of God before he can be thrown out of the "house," or the body of the possessed victim.

During the time of ELIJAH, the god Baal was the main rival to the Israelite god Yahweh (Jehovah). King Ahab was not constant in his faith and had allowed his wife Jezebel to introduce the worship of the Canaanite Baals into Israel. In 1 Kings 18:20–40, Elijah challenges the 450 prophets of Baal to a contest to see which god is greater. The prophets prepare a sacrificial bull and place it on a pyre but do not light the fire. Elijah does the same. The prophets of Baal call on their god all day, but to no avail. Elijah taunts the prophets, suggesting that Baal had gone on a journey, or perhaps is asleep or tending to bodily functions.

Elijah takes 12 stones representing the 12 tribes of Israel and places them near the bull and altar. He digs a small trench around the altar and fills it with water, drenching the pyre as well. Water is added a second time. Elijah calls on the Lord to show Himself as God. The pyre and all the stones and water are consumed by flame. Elijah captures the 450 prophets of Baal and assassinates them.

In the Testament of Solomon, Beelzebub (Beelzeboul) is the Prince of Demons, and he is summoned and subdued by King SOLOMON with the help of his magical ring. Solomon commands Beelzebub to explain the manifestation of demons, and he promises to bring to the king all unclean spirits bound. He tells Solomon that he lives in the Evening Star (Venus). He alone is the Prince of Demons because he was the highest-ranking angel in heaven, and he is the only one left of the heavenly angels who fell. He was accompanied by another fallen angel (Abezethibou), who was cast into the Red Sea.

Beelzebub says he destroys tyrants, causes men to worship demons, and arouses sexual desire in holy men and "select priests." He also causes wars, instigates murders, and arouses jealousy. He is thwarted by "the Almighty God" and will disappear if anyone uses the oath "the Elo-i" ("my God," which JESUS later cried on the cross).

Solomon sets Beelzebub to cutting blocks of Theban marble for his temple. All the other demons cry out. Solomon tells the demon that if he wishes to obtain his release, he will tell the king about other "heavenly things." Beelzebub says that Solomon can strengthen his house by doing the following: burn oil of myrrh, frankincense, sea bulbs, spikenard, and saffron, and light seven lamps during an earthquake. Lighting the seven lamps at dawn will reveal the heavenly dragons pulling the chariot of the sun. Solomon does not believe him, and he orders the demon to continue cutting marble and producing other demons for interrogation.

During the Inquisition, Beelzebub was regarded as one of the chief demons over witches. At sabbats, witches supposedly denied Christ in his name, and chanted it as they danced. Numerous accounts attest to him copulating with witches in wild orgies.

Beelzebub also was among the demons blamed for the demonic possession cases. In 1566, he tormented a young girl named Nicole Obry in Laon, France. Her daily exorcisms before huge crowds were used by the Catholic Church, embroiled in religious struggles with the French Huguenots, as examples of the church's power over the devil. Through Obry, Beelzebub claimed the Huguenots as his own people, gleefully noting that their supposed heresies made them even more precious to him. The demon was exorcised through repeated administration of holy wafers.

Beelzebub also was blamed for the bewitchment of nuns at Loudon, Louviers, and Aix-en-Provence in the late 16th and early 17th centuries, leading to the fiery deaths of his accused lieutenants, Father Louis Gaufridi and Father Urbain Grandier.

One of the demon's most notorious appearances in the 20th century was as the possessing devil of Anna Ecklund. He entered the young woman at the behest of her father Jacob, angry that Anna would not engage in incestuous sex with him. The demon left on December 23, 1928, in a terrible roar of "Beelzebub, Judas, Jacob, Mina (Anna's aunt and Jacob's mistress)" followed by "hell, hell, hell" and a terrible stench.

FURTHER READING

Charlesworth, James H., ed. *The Old Testament Pseud-epigrapha.* Vols. 1 and 2. New York: Doubleday, 1983, 1985.

Elledge, Scott, ed. *John Milton: Paradise Lost, An Authoritative Text.* New York: W. W. Norton, 1975.

Guiley, Rosemary Ellen. *The Encyclopedia of Witches and Witchcraft.* 2d ed. New York: Facts On File, 1999.

Behemoth

The male counterpart to Leviathan, one of the FALLEN ANGELS and a DEMON of the deep. Like Leviathan, Behemoth is associated with Rahab and the sea, and is personified variously as a whale, crocodile, and hippopotamus. He is also associated with the ANGEL OF DEATH.

The book of ENOCH says that Behemoth and Leviathan were separated by God at the creation, with Leviathan being sent to the sea and Behemoth being sent to an immeasurable desert named Dendain. In the Bible, Job 40:15–24 describes Behemoth as a mighty beast, "the first of the works of God" (40:19). Rabbinic lore holds that on the Day of Judgment, he will slay and be slain by Leviathan. His fate is to furnish meat for the Messiah's feast, and his flesh will be distributed to the faithful. Another rabbinic legend says that God destroyed Leviathan on the day he created both monsters, but placed Behemoth, in the form of a giant ox, on enchanted mountains to fatten him up. There he eats the grass of 1,000 mountains each day; the grass grows back each night. Behemoth is doomed to remain there alone until the end of time, because God realized that such a monster could not be loosed upon the world.

In Christian lore, Behemoth is considered one of the prime representations of evil. The demonologist JOHANN WEYER, who catalogued the ranks of HELL, did not include Behemoth in his list, but he did include him in another work, *Praestigiorum Daemonum,* in which he said that Behemoth represents Satan himself. Other demonologists of medieval times did include Behemoth in their rankings.

Behemoth is sometimes described as being overweight and stupid; thus he encourages gluttony and the pleasures of the belly. His shape shifts to various animal forms, and often he is depicted as an elephant with a huge stomach.

FURTHER READING

Hyatt, Victoria, and Joseph W. Charles. *The Book of Demons.* New York: Fireside Press, 1974.

Beleth (Bileth, Bilet, Byleth)

One of the FALLEN ANGELS and 72 spirits of SOLOMON. The LEMEGETON, a GRIMOIRE, says that Beleth is a terrible and mighty king who rules over 85 legions. He arrives on a pale horse, preceded by many musicians. He is very angry when first summoned, and must be sent at once to a magical triangle by a magician pointing a hazel wand to the southeast. He must be treated with great courtesy, but if the magician shows fear, Beleth will forever lose respect for him. The magician must protect himself by wearing a silver ring on the middle finger of the left hand and holding it up to the face. If Beleth refuses to cooperate, the magician must proceed with his commands. JOHANN WEYER writes that a bottle of wine helps to mellow Beleth into cooperation.

Belial (Beliar)

One of the FALLEN ANGELS. Belial ranks as one of Satan's most important and evil DEMONS, who is deceptively beautiful in appearance and soft in voice, but full of treachery, recklessness, and lies. He is dedicated to creating wickedness and guilt in mankind, especially in the form of sexual perversions, fornication, and lust.

Belial's name probably comes from the Hebrew term *beli ya'al*, which means "without worth." In Jewish lore, Belial was the next angel created after Lucifer. He was evil from the start, being one of the first to revolt against God. After his fall from HEAVEN, he became the personification of evil. St. PAUL considered him to be chief of demons. According to lore, Belial danced before King SOLOMON, and was among the demons who worked under the king's command, ruled by Solomon's magical ring.

In HELL Belial commands 80 legions of demons and served as infernal ambassador to Turkey. The LEMEGETON describes him as appearing in the deceptive form of a beautiful angel seated in a chariot of fire and speaking in a pleasant voice.

Belial distributes preferences for senatorships, favors to friends and foes, and gives excellent FAMILIARS. Because of his power, sacrifices and offerings are necessary to invoke him. Belial sometimes break his promises, but those who gain his true favor are handsomely rewarded.

Belial's name is sometimes a synonym for Satan or the Antichrist, the epitome of evil. In the Old Testament, the "sons of Belial" refers to people of worthlessness and recklessness.

Belial is among the 72 spirits of Solomon. Prior to his fall, he was in the order of the VIRTUES.

In a QUMRAN TEXT called the Testament of Amran (Q543, 545–548), Belial is identified as one of the WATCHERS whose three titles are Belial, Prince of Darkness, and King of Evil. He is empowered over all darkness and his every way and every work are darkness.

FURTHER READING

Charlesworth, James H., ed. *The Old Testament Pseudepigrapha*. Vols. 1 and 2. New York: Doubleday, 1983, 1985.

Eisenman, Robert, and Michael Wise. *The Dead Sea Scrolls Uncovered*. London: Element Books, 1992.

Guiley, Rosemary Ellen. *The Encyclopedia of Witches and Witchcraft*. 2d ed. New York: Facts On File, 1999.

Belphegor (Baal-Peor, Belfagor)

Moabite god of licentiousness and both good and FALLEN ANGEL. Belphegor means "lord of opening" or "lord Baal of Mt. Phegor." According to Kabbalistic lore, Belphegor was an angel in the order of PRINCIPALITIES prior to his fall. In HELL he rules inventions and discoveries, and he serves as infernal ambassador to France.

benad hasche

In Arabic lore, female angels. The benad hasche are common—and traditionally were the objects of veneration.

bene elohim (ben elohim, beni elohim, bene elim, b'ne elohim)

An order of angels or archangels whose name means "sons of god," sometimes translated as "sons of man" because of the sexual activities of the SONS OF GOD.

The bene elohim are a subdivision of the THRONES, though they sometimes are equated with thrones and also the ISSIM and ARCHANGELS. The main duty of the bene elohim is to ceaselessly sing the praises of God. According to the Zohar, they rank ninth in the CELESTIAL HIERARCHY, and their ruling chief is Hofniel. Azazel is also given as their chief. The Maseket Azilut also places them ninth, MAIMONIDES eighth, and the Berith Menucha ranks them third in importance.

Berith (Beal, Bofi, Belfry)

One of the FALLEN ANGELS and the 72 spirits of SOLOMON.

Bernael

Angel of darkness and evil equated with Belial. Bernael sometimes is equated with Haziel, who is otherwise a cherub and good angel.

Bethor

One of the seven ruling angels of the 196 Olympic provinces of HEAVEN, according to the Arbatel of Magic. Bethor is the second angel, ruling over 42 provinces, 42 kings, 35 princes, 28 dukes, 21 councillors, 14 servants, seven envoys, and 29,000 legions of spirits, each legion having 490 beings. Bethor possesses the powers and attributes of the planet Jupiter. The SEAL of Bethor is used in Kabbalistic MAGIC.

Bifrons

One of the FALLEN ANGELS and 72 spirits of SOLOMON. The earl Bifrons has a monstrous appearance but will take on human shape when ordered to do so. He teaches astronomy, geometry, other mathematical arts, and the knowledge of herbs, precious stones, and woods. He removes dead bodies from their graves and leaves them in other places, and he lights phantom candles on the grave.

Binah See TREE OF LIFE.

black angels

In Islamic lore, angels who are black in appearance. Two blue-eyed black angels are named Monker and Nakir; a third mentioned has no name but has the appearance of a rakasha ("destroyer"), an evil spirit. Rakashas are flesh-eating, shape-shifting ghouls who are black with yellow or flaming hair.

Blake, William (1757–1827)

English poet, artist, engraver, mystic, and iconoclast. William Blake received little appreciation for his work during his lifetime but fascinates a modern audience. He often depicted angels in his engravings and poems, finding them representations of authority, power, and divinity.

Life

Born in London on November 28, 1757, Blake had little formal schooling until his father sent him as a teenager to the Royal Academy to study art. He had read extensively as a young man and was well versed in literature, philosophy, and religion. From an early age, Blake experienced extraordinary visions of angels and other religious figures. He claimed to have talked to Gabriel, EZEKIEL, the Virgin Mary, and others. At age eight, Blake saw a tree filled with angels whose bright wings covered the tree boughs like stars.

In 1772 he became apprenticed to an engraver and began earning a living in the trade at age 22. He developed a technique called "Illumined Printing" in 1788 whereby illustrations and print could be engraved simultaneously, but it was so costly that he did not reap the financial rewards that he expected. Blake continued to use the technique for his own work, however.

With the exception of his first book, *Poetical Sketches,* published conventionally in 1783, Blake pub-lished all of his own writings and illustrations. He invented his own mythology. His ideas were beyond the comprehension of most of his contemporaries or audience, and he died in 1827 unappreciated and in poverty.

Works

Heavily influenced by the more spiritual movements of his day, such as Swedenborgianism, Blake rebelled against the 18th-century emphasis on reason versus the "natural" pull of feeling and emotion. He especially detested Newtonian physics as an example of life following orderly precepts. Nearly all his poems and engravings depict his mistrust and disdain of Reason, finding it responsible for poverty, racism, denigration of women, sexual repression, and any and all ills of the period.

Christ in the sepulchre, guarded by angels (William Blake; reprinted courtesy of Victoria and Albert Museum, London)

Although Blake communicated with angels, he depicts them in his early works as servants of the enemy Reason. They represent absolutism, political empire, and the exercise of pure power. Even so-called good angels are not so; the angels who clothe ADAM AND EVE in Blake's engraving "The Angel of the Divine Presence Clothing Adam and Eve with Coats of Skins" represent cold reason and repression against divine Innocence.

In his poem "I Asked a Thief" (1795), Blake sarcastically describes an angel as an 18th-century version of a modern corporate baron, one who can have it all:

> I asked a thief to steal me a peach,
> He turned up his eyes;
> I ask'd a lithe lady to lie her down,
> Holy & meek she cries.
>
> As soon as I went
> An angel came.
> He wink'd at the thief
> And smild at the dame—
>
> And without one word said
> Had a peach from the tree
> And still as a maid
> Enjoy'd the lady.

Blake particularly chafed at his society's conventions against women and sexual freedom and often portrayed his men and women in graphic sexual poses.

Later in life Blake's philosophy changed, and he came to rely on the supremacy of imagination over anything in nature. Additionally, he believed that when man begins to imitate divine images in his life and art, represented by angels, he can begin to realize his own divinity.

By the early 19th century, Blake had honed his engraving into the style of romantic classicism. He saw such art as the ultimate example of beautiful, specific detail, enabling any practitioner to achieve a divine vision of Innocence. Blake maintained that the human form must be carefully drawn and delineated in art, emphasizing every particularity, in order to sanctify every inch, limb, and part of the divine whole.

Blake's great epic poem, "Jerusalem," sums up his final philosophy: that orthodox Christianity has perverted Christ's forgiving love into a system that vengefully punishes sin and rejects sexual pleasure and love. He depicts this evil as a cowering cherub, the same description of Lucifer before his fall from heaven. He is the Antichrist incarnate: a hermaphroditic, hypocritical, egotistical entity that incorporates all the Pharisees, scribes, and Sadducees of ancient Jerusalem. He has a contracted and constricted body that portrays an outward show of pomp and ceremony but in reality serves the Whore of Babylon. The figure is a grotesque rendering of the human form divine.

Blake illustrated the works of JOHN MILTON and the Book of Job as well as his own writings.

See LITERATURE AND ANGELS.

FURTHER READING
Mellor, Anne Kostelanetz. *Blake's Human Form Divine.* Berkeley: University of California Press, 1974.

Blavatsky, Helena Petrovna See DEVAS.

Boehme, Jakob (1575–1624)
Bohemian shoemaker and mystic. Jakob Boehme gained an eminent following in his lifetime and in generations to come. His admirers include Isaac Newton, the English theologian William Law, German philosopher Friedrich W. J. von Schelling, and poets WILLIAM BLAKE, JOHANN WOLFGANG VON GOETHE, and Samuel Taylor Coleridge.

Life
Boehme was born in Altsteidenberg, Upper Lusatia, to a peasant family. In childhood he tended his family's sheep and briefly attended school. At age 13 he went to Gorlitz, where he learned the shoemaking trade and became a master by 1599. He married Katharina Kantzschmann, the daughter of a butcher.

Boehme began to write philosophical and theological works after becoming a master shoemaker. His first work, a philosophical treatise titled *Aurora, oder die morgenrote in Aufgang,* was immediately popular and was passed among scholars. Threatened by his writings, the Lutheran Church charged him with heresy and publicly denounced him. The town council seized the original manuscript and forbade him to write.

Boehme could not be censored for long, however, and he resumed writing by 1618. Some of his shorter pieces were published in book form. He was denounced by the church again and decided to leave town for Dresden to meet with a group of his supporters. While there he fell fatally ill with fever and was carried back home, where he died.

Works
Boehme's principal works concern the study of God; the structure of the world and man; and theological speculations. His best-known work is *Von der Chadenwahl: Mysterium magnum.*

Boehme was influenced by the alchemical works of Paracelsus and the Protestant mystic Kaspar Schwenfeld. He did not claim to communicate with angels, spirits, or saints or to perform miracles that were attributed to him.

CARL G. JUNG considered Boehme a modern Christian Gnostic. He noted that Boehme's life-cycle, which moves through seven "Forms" or "properties" of Nature, creates a Gnostic mandala holding threefold "hellish" or dark elements (attraction, expulsion, and the wheel of anguish) and "heavenly" or light elements (light or love, intelligible sound, and the all-embracing Reality) in balance with lightning sparking between them, much like the Gnostic figure Abraxas.

In Boehme's visionary scheme, all seven Forms are found within all things, even in God's name. The same forces operating above in the celestial world also operate below, in stones, earth, and plants. The shapes of individual beings are ruled by the angels, who repre-

Of Divine Revelation (Jakob Boehme)

sent the formed powers of God's Word and his Thoughts. Originally angels existed in two forms only, and were created from the first principle, being of Light's matrix. Boehme states: "They are the essence of both the inner internal fires. Their powers are from the great emanating names of God. All have sprung from the Yes and been led into the No, in order that powers might become manifest."

Angels help God rule the world; they are his instruments by and through which he reveals his powers, numbering a thousand times 10,000, unequal in rank, ranged in three realms and seven dominions, according to the seven Forms of Nature, with each having a Throne with seven princely hierarchies. Each angelic realm is ruled by a PRINCE: Michael, Lucifer, and Uriel. Lucifer, ruler of the second kingdom, is the most beautiful of all heavenly creatures.

Angels are free and have the possibility of falling. Before Lucifer's fall they were able to imagine themselves into the world of matter. Rather than fall, angels humble themselves before God's great majesty so that the eternal No may not secure dominion over them. The ensemble of stars represents the totality of divine forces. The stars also "mean" the angels.

Within each angelic creature, the divine forces are incessantly exciting one another, harkening to the music of eternity, receiving impulses from without and rising up to sing. In each angelic body the seven spirits forge the five senses and coordinate the consensual and expressive faculties. Embodying pure force and pure sensory awareness, the angels are wholly alive, unlike the human "half-dead angel" that has fallen from grace.

The great mystery to Boehme is the human creature. He believed angels are brethren to human beings in looks because they too were created in the image of God, with hands, feet, mouth, nose; they eat paradisiacal fruit of the divine power of God's Word. Matter, like the flesh, is a garment put on or congealed by the fallen will and a medium in which the eternal wisdom of God is mirrored. Spirit, as a conscious life, is the ascending, sublimated aspect of the root torment of the will. Even the basest sexual desire is a longing for something higher, a longing for the eternal light and a flight from death and darkness. From the human vantage, the angels represent the fulfillment of all betterment, be it of the soul in need of redemption or of the world in need of improvement.

All of Boehme's work was done to explain the contradiction inherent in reality, "to grasp the possibility, indeed the necessity of evil in the highest Good." He found that "in the being of all being, there is strife and opposition;" any revelation is possible only in division. The will of the Nothing looks out in search of Something as light (love) and, having achieved self-revelation in the Son, draws it back to itself in desire as fire. Yet, the two exist in union. They are a coincidence of opposites. God rests, as Boehme puts it, in love-play. All of life is endowed by an imprint. The KABBALAH calls it Tav, the mark of the SHEKINAH, or divine presence in the world. Boehme calls it *Signatura rerum,* the seal or signature of the eternal within things. The rediscovered harmonies of nature are a model for restoring harmony to the strife-torn world, a theme that would be taken up by the Romantic philosophers and poets a few generations later.

FURTHER READING
Stoudt, John Joseph. *Jacob Boehme: His Life and Thought.* New York: Seabury Press, 1968.
Weeks, Andrew. *Boehme: An Intellectual Biography.* Albany: State University of New York Press, 1991.

Botis (Otis)

One of the FALLEN ANGELS and 72 spirits of SOLOMON. As a great president and earl of HELL, Botis commands 60 legions. He appears in the shape of an ugly viper, but he will take on human form with large teeth and horns when commanded to do so. He carries a sharp sword. He sees past, present, and future, and he reconciles friends and enemies.

Bounteous Immortals See AMARAHSPANDS.

Briah See KABBALAH.

Briathos

In the Testament of SOLOMON, angel who thwarts the dog demon Scepter. Briathos is not mentioned elsewhere in APOCRYPHA AND PSEUDEPIGRAPHA TEXTS.

Buer

One of the FALLEN ANGELS and 72 spirits of SOLOMON. Buer is a president of HELL who appears when the sun is in Sagittarius. He teaches philosophy, ethics, logic, and the virtues of herbs. He heals all diseases and gives good FAMILIARS. In the Pseudo-Monarchia he is the seventh spirit.

Bune

One of the FALLEN ANGELS and 72 spirits of SOLOMON. A duke in HELL, Bune appears as a dragon with three heads, one of them being that of a man. Despite his frightening appearance, he speaks with a divine voice. He can bring a man riches and make him eloquent and wise. He changes the places of the dead, causing DEMONS to crowd around the sepulchres. Bune answers to all demands. He commands 30 legions of demons.

Byron, Lord George See LITERATURE AND ANGELS.

Caddy, Eileen and Peter See FINDHORN.

Cahethel (Cahetel)
One of the SERAPHIM and the 72 SCHEMHAMPHORAE. Cahetel rules over agriculture and is invoked for the increase of crops.

Caim (Caym, Camio)
One of the FALLEN ANGELS and 72 spirits of SOLOMON. Prior to his fall, Caim was in the order of ANGELS. In HELL he is a great president with 30 legions. He appears first as a thrush and then as a man carrying a sharp sword. The LEMEGETON says that he answers questions in burning ashes. He is good at settling disputes. He gives men the understanding of the songs of bird, the lowing of cattle, the barking of dogs, and the voice of waters. He gives true answers about the future. Martin Luther is alleged to have had an encounter with Caim.

Camael (Camiel, Camiul, Chamuel, Kemuel, Khamael, Camniel, Cancel)
Angel who is chief of the POWERS, one of the sephirot of the TREE OF LIFE, and ruler of Mars. Camael means "he who sees God."

FRANCIS BARRETT lists Camael as one of the seven angels who stand before God. As Chamuel, he wrestles with JACOB and appears to Jesus in the Garden of Gethsemane. As Kemuel, he guards the gate of HEAVEN and gives way to MOSES when the patriarch comes to receive the Torah from God.

In occultism, Camael is assigned to the FALLEN ANGELS, whom he rules as a Count Palatine. He can appear in the guises of a leopard crouched upon a rock. He is a god of war. His name is invoked for divine justice.

caretaking angels
Angels who care for infants of "untimely birth" and the children of adultery.

See CHILDBIRTH ANGELS; TEMELUCH.

Cassiel (Casiel, Casziel, Kafziel)
Angel of Saturn, a ruling prince of the seventh HEAVEN, and a PRINCE of the order of POWERS. Cassiel also rules Saturday along with Machatan and Uriel. He sometimes appears as the angel of temperature or the ANGEL OF TIME.

Cayce, Edgar (1877–1945)
American psychic, called "the sleeping prophet," renowned for his trance readings in which he diagnosed illness, prescribed remedies, and discussed past

Edgar Cayce (Photograph copyrighted 1978, Edgar Cayce Foundation Archives. Used by permission)

lives and spiritual wisdom. Edgar Cayce had only a grammar school education, but from a trance state he could accurately prescribe drugs and treatments. His calling was initiated by an ANGELOPHANY. On occasion angels came through in his trance sessions, including one who created disruption and divisiveness among Cayce's supporters.

Cayce was born on March 18, 1877, in Hopkinsville, Kentucky. He had psychic powers from an early age, including the ability to see nonphysical beings, who were his childhood companions, and the auras of others.

As a child, Cayce received religious instruction along with his family, who attended the Liberty Christian Church in Hopkinsville. He was given a Bible at age 10 and quickly read it in its entirety over and over again. His biblical background formed the foundation of his spiritual work in his adult years, and it is evident in his trance readings.

One of Cayce's favorite activities was to go off alone in the woods to read. One afternoon when he was 13,

he did just that with the Bible. He suddenly became aware of a woman standing before him. At first he thought it was his mother; then he noticed that something on her back made shadows shaped like wings. "Your prayers have been heard," the woman said to him in a voice that sounded like music. "Tell me what you would like most of all, so that I may give it to you." Frightened, Cayce could barely respond, "Most of all I would like to be helpful to others, and especially to children when they are sick." The woman vanished, and Cayce ran home. He shared the story with his mother, who accepted it.

The next day, Cayce—who was a poor student—heard the woman's voice as he struggled with his spelling lessons. She told him, "If you can sleep a little, we can help you." Cayce put his spelling book beneath his head and fell asleep. When he awoke, he discovered that he mysteriously knew his lessons. He began sleeping with all his school books beneath his head. He would always awaken with the contents learned.

Cayce's powers to give diagnoses and remedies manifested in 1898 when he was 21 and working as a salesman. He suffered a persistent hoarse throat and intermittent laryngitis that resisted medical treatment and forced him to give up his job. As a last resort, he tried hypnosis. Under trance, he was asked for the cause of his affliction and a cure. He gave the answers, and at the end of the session he had his voice back. He began giving trance readings for others on March 31, 1901.

On June 17, 1903, he married Gertrude Evans, with whom he had two sons, Edgar Evans and Hugh Lynn.

Cayce's success was so great that thousands began seeking him out for help. He could read for anyone anywhere in the world—he needed only a name and address.

In 1911, he made his first reference in a reading to karma as a cause of physical ailment, and from then on, many of his readings concerned past-life karma. He sometimes spoke about the fabled civilizations of Lemuria and Atlantis, and how the latter's inhabitants had misused their high-tech power. He came to believe in reincarnation, and his readings revealed that some of his own past lives were as one of the first celestial beings to descend to earth prior to Adam and Eve; as an Atlantean; as Ra-Ta, a high priest in Egypt 10,600 years ago; as a Persian ruler; as a Trojan warrior; as Lucius of Cyrene, mentioned in the New Testament as a minor disciple of Jesus; and various other lives. He believed his scientific knowledge in readings came from a former life as a chemist in Grecian Troy.

Cayce and his family moved to Virginia Beach, Virginia, where in 1928 he established the beginnings of the Association for Research and Enlightenment (A.R.E.).

On July 15, 1928, at a trance session with his study group, the archangel Michael made an appearance, speaking through Cayce: "I am Michael, Lord of the Way! Bend thy head, O ye children of men! Give heed unto the way as is set before you in that sermon on the mount, in that on yon hill this enlightenment may come among me . . . for in Zion thy names are written, and in service will come truth!"

The hill referred to the site of what was to become the headquarters for the A.R.E., which was officially founded in 1931.

Michael made other appearances during Cayce readings. His voice was so loud and booming that dishes rattled in the kitchen. Son Hugh Lynn asked his father who was Michael, and received the answer: "Michael is an archangel that stands before the throne of the Father . . . Michael is the lord or guard of the change that comes in every soul that seeks the [spiritual] way, even as in those period when His manifestations came in the earth."

The gist of Michael's messages was that the people present at the sessions had been chosen for service in a time when spiritual renewal was needed. He admonished people to hold to high spiritual values, and said he would protect those who sought to know the face of God. He was not tolerant of using readings for material gain. In 1940, Cayce gave a series of business readings for the purpose of locating oil wells in Texas in order to raise funds for the work of Cayce and others. Michael manifested and warned that this amounted to a deviation in the search for God.

Michael was sometimes harsh. In one of Cayce's last readings of his life, when his health was rapidly failing and his staff was quarreling, Michael lashed out, "Bow thine heads, ye children of men! For I, Michael, Lord of the Way, would speak with thee! Ye generation of vipers, ye adulterous generation, be warned! There is today before thee good and evil! Choose thou whom ye will serve! Walk in the way of the Lord! Or else there will come that sudden reckoning, as ye have seen! Bow thine heads, ye who are ungracious, unrepentant! For the glory of the Lord is at hand! The opportunity is before thee! Accept or reject! But don't be pigs!"

In the mid-1930s, Cayce's study group began collecting material from the readings that eventually was published in the two-volume work, A Search for God. A new angel, who identified itself as Halaliel, manifested through Cayce with a commanding tone that made some of the group uneasy. Halaliel indicated to the study group that he had been appointed to teach and guide them, and their acceptance of him would mark a change in the course of the group. Bitter arguments ensued, but ultimately the group voted to reject him.

Cayce also gave 24 readings dealing with the book of REVELATION. He interpreted the symbols described by John of Patmos as representative of forces that war within the human psyche. The fallen angels represent fallen ideals, which are necessary in order to attain the "new Jerusalem" of a higher state of spiritual consciousness.

Cayce prophesied the Second Coming of Christ in 1998, accompanied by cataclysmic earth changes.

Cayce drove himself to try to keep up with the demand for readings. In August 1944, he collapsed from exhaustion. He went to the mountains near Roanoke, Virginia, to recuperate, returning home in November 1944. On January 1, 1945, he told friends he would be "healed" on January 5, and they took it to mean his death. He died peacefully on January 3, 1945, at the age of 67. Gertrude died the following April 1. The A.R.E. now is under the direction of his grandson by Hugh Lynn, Charles Thomas Cayce.

Three organizations are dedicated to Cayce's work. Atlantic University, chartered in 1930 in Virginia Beach, offers graduate level transpersonal studies. The Edgar Cayce Foundation, chartered in 1948 in Virginia Beach, provides permanent custodial ownership for the Cayce readings and their supporting documentation. The Harold J. Reilly School of Massotherapy opened in 1986 under the auspices of Atlantic University, offering a diploma program certified by the Commonwealth of Virginia in massage, hydrotherapy, diet, and preventive health care practices based on the Cayce readings.

FURTHER READING
Grant, Robert J. Are We Listening to the Angels? Virginia Beach: A.R.E. Press, 1994.

Sugrue, Thomas. There Is a River. New York: Holt, Rinehart and Winston, 1942.

Candomblé See ORISHAS.

celestial hierarchies

Systems organizing angels into ranks (choirs) with designated duties, powers, and rulers. There is no general agreement on a single system, either in Judaism or Christianity. The Bible gives the names of nine groups—ANGELS, ARCHANGELS, PRINCIPALITIES, POWERS, DOMINIONS, VIRTUES, THRONES, CHERUBIM, and SERAPHIM—but does not specify their respective rankings or their celestial duties. Those details have been filled in by theologians, philosophers, and artists.

Jewish literature from the Second Temple period begins to differentiate classes of angels, perhaps due to influences from the angelologies of Persia and Babylonia. In the KABBALAH, angels are organized into 10

Angel, from Eastern Orthodox Church, Romania (Author's collection)

classes; some of the names overlap with Christian designations. The TREE OF LIFE has 10 stations, or sephirot, each of which has an archangel and angelic order assigned to it, as well as an archdemon and a demonic order. The Hebrew names of the ranks have equivalents in the Christian hierarchies. The great Jewish philosopher MAIMONIDES, who identified angels with the INTELLIGENCES who govern the celestial spheres, named the 10 orders from highest to lowest as HAYYOTH, OPHANIM, ERELIM, HASMALIM, ELOHIM, BENE ELOHIM, cherubim, and ISHIM.

In Christianity, the best-known hierarchy was elaborated by PSEUDO-DIONYSIUS (Dionysius the Areopagite), said to be a man converted to Christianity by St. PAUL in Athens, but more likely an anonymous Christian Platonist and Gnostic writer of the fifth or sixth century. Pseudo-Dionysius was heavily influenced by Platonic thought and also by some of the opinions expressed in previous centuries by early church fathers. Pseudo-Dionysius said that the hierarchy implies a holy order that aims to achieve the greatest possible assimilation to

and union with God. Only God could know the true number of angels, their ranks and duties. Pseudo-Dionysius's celestial hierarchy survived at the forefront of angelic lore thanks in large part to its adoption several centuries later by St. THOMAS AQUINAS, one of the most influential theologians of the church.

Other early Christian theologians addressed the organization of angels as well. St. Ignatius Martyr made direct reference to ranks and hierarchies of angels. Saints Jerome, Ambrose, and Gregory the Great wrote about the rankings of angels, but they did not concur. St. Ambrose organized the nine groups in ascending order from angels to seraphim. St. Jerome specified only seven choirs, leaving out principalities and virtues, and wondered about the real differences between ranks. The *Apostolic Constitutions,* which also predate Pseudo-Dionysius, list 10 choirs, adding AEONS and hosts but omitting dominions, and at another time give 11 choirs, adding dominions back in. St. AUGUSTINE said he did not know the difference between the ranks of thrones, dominions, principalities, and powers.

The church fathers argued over whether or not scripture had included all of the choirs, pointing to a vague statement by St. Paul. In Ephesians 1:21, Paul refers to Christ sitting at God's right hand "far above all principality and power and virtue and dominion, and above every name that is named, not only in this age but also in that which is to come." Some argued that the statement implies an infinite number of angelic choirs while others argued that Paul didn't know all of the choirs and mentioned only those that he did know. Still others suggested that Paul deliberately concealed the true numbers of choirs.

In the Pseudo-Dionysian scheme, the hierarchy of nine choirs is split into three tiers. The higher tiers possess all of the wisdom, abilities, and illumination of the lower tiers, which in turn depend upon the immediate higher choirs for dispensation of the light and love of God. In the highest tier, the seraphim, cherubim, and thrones receive illumination directly from God and send it down through the layers. The second tier of virtues, dominions, and powers are concerned with heavenly order, the ruling of other angels, and miracles. The third and lowest tier of principalities, archangels, and angels are concerned with the affairs of humanity.

FURTHER READING

Scholem, Gershom. *Kabbalah*. New York: Dorset Press, 1987. First published 1974.

Trachtenberg, Joshua. *Jewish Magic and Superstition: A Study in Folk Religion*. New York: Berhman's Jewish Book House, 1939.

Cellini, Benvenuto (1500–1571)

Celebrated goldsmith, sculptor, and author during the Renaissance, who credited his GUARDIAN ANGEL with saving his life.

Benvenuto Cellini tells in his flamboyant autobiography, *The Life of Benvenuto Cellini* (published posthumously in 1728), how an angel rescued him while he served time in prison. Cellini, a hotheaded man, was constantly engaging in scrapes and fights with other people. On several occasions he was imprisoned, and once was condemned to death. He was absolved once for murder, by Pope Paul III.

In 1535, he was jailed in Rome on charges of stealing the jewels of Pope Clement. Cellini was incarcerated high in the towers of the Castel Sant' Angelo. He made a daring attempt to escape by scaling down the castle walls on a rope made of bedsheets tied together. He suffered a broken leg, was captured, and thrown into a wretched dungeon. The dungeon lay below a garden that was filled with water, and Cellini's cell was damp and populated by "big spiders and many venomous worms." His mattress quickly became watersoaked. A tiny shaft of sunlight trickled through a narrow opening for about an hour and a half every day, enabling him to read his Bible.

In these horrible conditions, Cellini sank into despair and resolved to kill himself. As he wrote:

> Once, notwithstanding, I took and propped a wooden pole I found there, in position like a trap. I meant to make it topple over on my head, and it would certainly have dashed my brains out; but when I had arranged the whole machine, and was approaching to put it in motion, just at the moment of my setting my hand to it, I was seized by an invisible power and flung four cubits from the spot, in such terror that I lay half dead. Like that I remained from dawn until the nineteenth hour, when they brought my food.

Upon reflection, Cellini said, "I came to the conclusion that it must have been some power divine and my good guardian angel."

Seraph, from Eastern Orthodox Church, Romania (Author's collection)

This angel manifested several times to Cellini while he was in prison:

> During the following night there appeared to me in dreams a marvellous being in the form of a most lovely youth, who cried, as though he wanted to reprove me: "Knowest thou who lent thee that body, which thou wouldst have spoiled before its time?" I seemed to answer that I recognized all things pertaining to me as gifts from the God of nature. "So then," he said, "thou hast contempt for His handiwork, through this thy will to spoil it? Commit thyself unto His guidance, and lose not hope in His great goodness!" Much more he added in words of marvellous efficacy, the thousandth part of which I cannot now remember.

Cellini took the angel's advice to heart. He began to ignore his suffering and to sing the praises of God throughout the day and night instead. His good spirits continued, despite the fact that his teeth were rotting and falling out, his gums perforating and bleeding, and his nails growing so long that he wounded himself every time he touched himself.

Cellini's good humor confounded his jailors. Once a party came to visit him:

> They found me on my knees; I did not turn at their approach, but went on praying my orisons before God the Father, surrounded with angels, and a Christ arising victorious from the grave, which I had sketched upon the wall with a little piece of charcoal I had found covered up with earth. This was after I had lain four months upon my back in bed with my leg broken, and had so often dreamed that angels came and ministered to me, that at the end of those four months the limb became as sound as though it had never been fractured.

Cellini said he prayed daily, and every night he was visited by his guardian angel in his dreams. He told the angel that he had but one request, to see the sun again, and then he would be content to die. On October 3, 1539, he awoke to be taken away by his invisible angel, who was like a whirlwind. A vision then unfolded: Cellini was taken by the angel first to a large room and then into the sunlight. An image of Christ upon the cross formed itself out of the light, followed by a Madonna and child. Cellini basked in the vision for about fifteen minutes, he said, before it faded.

According to Cellini, these celestial visitations and visions sustained him through the darkest period of his imprisonment. Not long after the sun-vision, he was released from the dungeon by the pope on the personal request of a cardinal. He went on to become one of the most celebrated artists of the Renaissance.

The tone of Cellini's autobiography is florid, and some scholars opine that he exaggerated or fabricated some of the events he related. Whether or not the angel episodes were experience or exaggeration remains unknown.

FURTHER READING
Cellini, Benvenuto. *Autobiography.* New York: P. F. Collier, c. 1910.

Cerviel (Cervihel, Zeruel)
According to PHILO, the angel who was sent to David to help him slay Goliath. Cerviel also rules the order of PRINCIPALITIES; other rulers of this order are Haniel and Nisroc.

chalkydri (kalkydras)
In 2 ENOCH, 12-winged angels or brass serpents of the flying sun, mentioned with PHOENIXES as the ones who pull the chariot of the sun through the sky. The chalkydri are associated with CHERUBIM and SERAPHIM and live in the fourth HEAVEN. When the sun rises, they burst into song at the Lord's command:

> The light-giver is coming,
> to give radiance to the whole world;
> and the morning watch appears.
> which is the sun's rays.
> And the sun comes out over the face of the earth,
> and retrieves his radiance,
> to give light to all the face of the earth.

The song of the chalkydri and phoenixes is the reason why birds sing in the morning. In GNOSTICISM, the chalkydri are demonic serpents with crocodile heads.

Chamuel (Haniel, Camuel, Simiel)
One of the seven ARCHANGELS and ruler of the order of DOMINATIONS and the order of POWERS. Chamuel means "He who seeks God." Like Gabriel, Chamuel is named as the angel who appears to JESUS in the Garden of Gethsemane to give him strength.

Chax See SHAX.

chayot, chayoth, chayyoth See HAYYOTH.

Chayyliel (Chayyliel H', Hayyiel, Hayyal, Haileal)
In 3 ENOCH, Chayyliel is the ruling PRINCE of the HAYYOTH. The name Chayyliel means "army." A powerful angel, Chayyliel has the capability to swallow the entire earth in one mouthful. The other angels in HEAVEN tremble before him, and if the MINISTERING

ANGELS do not chant the trisagion (see QEDUSSAH) at the right time he flogs them with whips of fire.

cherubim (kerubim)

In the Pseudo-Dionysian hierarchy of angels, the second highest angels to God. The etymology of the name "cherub" (cherubim in plural) is uncertain. The Hebrew term "kerub," which means either "fullness of knowledge" or "one who intercedes," is thought to be derived from the Akkadian term KARABU, a winged guardian being of Assyria. Karabu had the bodies of sphinxes or bulls and the heads of humans, and they guarded entrances to buildings. The cherubim of the Israelites corresponds to the sphinxes of the ancient Near East, serving as both guardian and throne.

Cherubim are mentioned 91 times in the Hebrew Bible. They also are described in REVELATION in the New Testament. The cherubim are not specifically called angels. They make their first appearance in the Bible in Genesis 3:22. God places them at the east entrance to the Garden of Eden, guarding it with flaming sword.

In Exodus 25:10–22, God gives MOSES instructions for building the ARK OF THE COVENANT, a gilded wooden chest that shall bear the mercy seat of God with cherubim made of hammered gold on its two ends:

> The cherubim shall spread out their wings above, overshadowing the mercy seat with their wings, their faces one to another; toward the mercy seat shall the faces of the cherubim be. (25:20)

The mercy seat, from which God speaks to Israel, is to be placed on the top of the ark.

1 Kings 6:23–35 describes the cherubim King SOLOMON placed in his temple. Two gilded olivewood cherubim 10 cubits high are placed in the inner sanctuary. Each wing spans five cubits, and they are spaced so that their wing tips touch the walls on each side and each other in the middle. The inner wings form the throne seat for the invisible deity. Carved and gilded figures of cherubim are placed in the inner and outer rooms. The doorposts to the entrance of the nave are carved with cherubim, palm trees, and open flowers, all of which are gilded. The Ark of the Covenant is placed beneath the wings of the two large cherubim.

According to 2 Chronicles 3:13–14, the Solomonic cherubim stand on their feet facing the nave, giving the impression that they are sphinxlike in form and are on their two back legs instead of on all fours; there is no throne formed by them.

In EZEKIEL 1:4–28, the cherubim as carriers of the throne God appear as living creatures having four faces and four wings. Ezekiel is by the river Chebar when he has a vision of a great cloud flashing fire, and a fire gleaming like bronze in the middle. The four living creatures each have the faces of a man, an ox, a lion, and an eagle. They have four wings, two of which touch the other creatures and two of which cover the body. They stand on straight legs that end in calf's feet. They are like burnished bronze. They have beside them four wheels with spokes that seem like wheels within wheels and gleam like chrysolite. The creatures and wheels move in any direction simultaneously without turning, and with flashes of lightning and sounds of thunder. Over their heads is a firmament shinning like crystal. Above that is a throne like sapphire bearing the likeness of a human form like gleaming bronze and enclosed by fire: This is the glory of the Lord, who speaks to Ezekiel. In Ezekiel 10:1–22, Ezekiel sees the cherubim again on a journey to heaven, and he gives the same description of them. They seem to have human hands under their wings.

A cherub (Toome, in Heyward's *Hierarchie of the Blessed Angells*, 17th c.)

Cherub with thrones depicted as wheels with eyes (Copyright 1995 by Robert Michael Place, from *The Angels Tarot* by Rosemary Ellen Guiley and Robert Michael Place. Reprinted courtesy of HarperSan Francisco)

In 3 ENOCH the cherubim are under the rule of Kerubiel, who beautifies them and sings their praises. The cherubim stand beside the hayyoth with their wings raised up to the tops of their heads. The SHEK-INAH rests upon their backs and illuminates their faces. Their hands are under their wings and their feet are covered by their wings; they have horns of glory upon their heads. They are surrounded by pillars of fire and sapphire stones. They enfold each other in their wings and sing constantly songs of praise and glory to God.

In other lore, the cherubim are the voice of divine wisdom, possessing a deep insight into God' secrets. They enlighten the lower levels of angels. They emanate holiness through the universe in order to ensure the success of universal truths. They personify the winds. The Testament of ADAM includes them in the hierarchy of angels, making them second in rank. They stand before God and reverence his throne, keep the seals, and sing the hourly "holy, holy, holy." (See QEDUSSAH.)

Chiefs of the cherubim are Ophaniel, Rikbiel, Cherubiel, Raphael, Gabriel, Zophiel, and Satan before his fall.

AGRIPPA says that the cherubim are associated with the earth element. They assist humans in the contemplation of the divine, by enabling "light of mind, power of wisdom, very high fantasies and figures."

According to the Koran, the tears Michael cries over the sins of the faithful form the cherubim.

See ST. TERESA OF AVILA.

FURTHER READING

van der Toorn, Karel, Bob Becking, and Pieter W. van der Horst, eds. *Dictionary of Deities and Demons in the Bible.* 2d ed. Grand Rapids, Mich.: William B. Eerdmans, 1999.

Kaplan, Aryeh. *Sepher Yetzirah: The Book of Creation.* Rev. ed. York Beach, Maine: Samuel Weiser, 1997.

Chesed   See TREE OF LIFE.

childbirth angels

In Jewish lore, angels invoked in MAGIC and inscribed on AMULETS to protect mothers and their newborn infants. Childbirth angels ward off illness and misfortune, usually attributed to demons. They are also invoked to aid the process of childbirth and prevent miscarriages and stillbirth.

The magical names of the angels are written on some object and placed on the body of the woman. For example, one formula for easing labor pains calls for the inscription of an angel name upon virgin clay, which is then fastened to the navel of the woman. The amulet is to be removed as soon as the child is deliv-

The cherubim appear before he is lifted up to the east gate of HEAVEN.

Revelation 4:6–8 describes the four living creatures seen by Ezekiel, but with six wings instead of four. They are "full of eyes all around and within," and they ceaselessly sing, "Holy, holy, holy is the Lord God Almighty, who was and is to come!" They are not named as cherubim, however, but only as "four living creatures."

In Hebrew lore, the cherubim are sometimes equated with the HAYYOTH. In the KABBALAH, the cherubim govern Yesod (Foundation), the ninth sephirah of the TREE OF LIFE, where they are under the rule of Gabriel.

ered. A formula for easy delivery calls for inscribing an angel name on the woman's wedding ring. She places it under the tongue and repeats 10 times "go out, you and all the company of your followers and then I will go out." The child will then be delivered without interference from negative spirits such as Lilith.

In MERKABAH lore, there are 70 childbirth angels, The SEFER RAZIEL gives the following 70 names, several of which repeat:

Michael	Gabriel	Raphael
Nuriel	Kidumiel	Malkiel
Tzadkiel	Padiel	Zumiel
Chafriel	Zuriel	Ramuel
Yofiel	Sturiel	Gazriel
Udriel	Lahariel	Chaskiel
Rachmiah	Katzhiel	Schachniel
Krkiel	Ahiel	Chaniel
Lahal	Malchiel	Shebniel
Rachsiel	Rumiel	Kadmiel
Kadal	Chachmiel	Ramal
Katchiel	Aniel	Azriel
Chachmal	Machnia	Kaniel
Griel	Tzartak	Ofiel
Rachmiel	Sensenya	Udrgazyia
Rsassiel	Ramiel	Sniel
Tahariel	Yezriel	Neriah
Samchia	Ygal	Tsirya
Rigal	Tsuria	Psisya
Oriel	Samchia	Machnia
Kenunit	Yeruel	Tatrusia
Chaniel	Zechriel	Variel
Diniel	Gdiel	Briel
Ahaniel		

See LAYLAH.

FURTHER READING

Savedow, Steve. *Sepher Rezial Hemelach: The Book of the Angel Rezial.* York Beach, Maine: Samuel Weiser, 2000.

Trachtenberg, Joshua. *Jewish Magic and Superstition: A Study in Folk Religion.* New York: Berhman's Jewish Book House, 1939.

Chockmah See TREE OF LIFE.

choirs See CELESTIAL HIERARCHIES.

Chonae See MICHAEL.

Christianity, angels in See ANGELOLOGY.

Cimeries

One of the FALLEN ANGELS and 72 spirits of SOLOMON. Cimeries rules 20 legions as a marquis in HELL. He also rules spirits in Africa. He rides a black horse and teaches grammar, logic, and rhetoric. He finds lost objects and buried treasures. He can make a man appear as one of his own soldiers.

Cochabiel (Coahabiath)

According to AGRIPPA, one of seven PRINCES who stand before God and to whom are given the spirit names of the planet. Cochabiel probably was originally a deity in Babylonian lore; in Kabbalistic lore he is angel of the planet Mercury.

Coleridge, Samuel Taylor See LITERATURE AND ANGELS.

confessors

One of 12 orders of angels named in Thomas Heywood's *The Hierarchy of the Blessed Angels.* The confessors are ruled by the angel Barakiel.

Crosell See PROCEL.

curetes See POWERS.

Curson See PURSON.

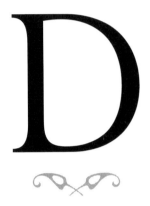

Dabriel

Angel who rules over Monday and resides in the first HEAVEN. Dabriel is sometimes equated with Vretiel (Pravuil), the wise archangel who keeps God's records and dictates heavenly wisdom to ENOCH.

Dagiel (Daghiel, Daiel)

Angel who rules over fish. In magical rites, Dagiel is invoked on Friday. He is supplicated in the name of Venus.

daimones

In Greek mythology and religion, one of many supernatural agents or INTELLIGENCES, lower in rank than a god, and holding a middle place between gods and humans. The name "daimones" originally meant "divine beings." Early texts do not always distinguish between "daimon" and "theos," or "god." It was not until the Hellenistic period that the two terms became distinctly different. "Daimon" can have either a masculine or a feminine gender; a related and neuter term, "daimonion," refers also to "divine beings." Daimones, along with other gods and demigods, were assigned into the ranks of DEMONS in Christianity.

Daimones include such entities as the corybantes, curetes, dactyls, satyrs, sileni, GENII, or spirits of place, and spirits of forests, rivers, glades, mountains, and cities, where they presided over public and family life. They also are ministering spirits similar to MINISTERING ANGELS, godlike beings; and souls of the dead.

Daimones are protective and/or attending spirits much like GUARDIAN ANGELS or Plotinus's notion of tutelary spirits. However, they can be either good or evil, but even good ones are capable of evil acts if they are angered by humans. Matthew 8:31 is the only New Testament reference to cast the term "daimones" in an evil light: "And the demons begged him [Jesus], 'If you cast us out, send us away into the herd of swine.'"

Belief in daimones dates to ancient Mesopotamia. The Babylonians had an elaborate daemonology, in which daimones were organized into armies and hierarchies, and, like angels, had specific duties.

The Greeks also had a large daemonology. Daimones were said to haunt locales. For example, in Laws II. 914b, Plato warns pious Greeks not to disturb abandoned property, as it is guarded by the spirit of the wayside. Daimones could take over human bodies in the form of possession (especially for oracular prophecies), and they could also possess humans to cause physical and mental illness. Some were vampiric in nature.

Daimones also were associated with the dead and the ghosts of the dead. The Greeks believed that the remains of dead people retained for a time a spark of life force, which could be conjured in magical practices. Such daemonic entities could be asked for advice or dispatched on errands through necromantic rituals.

Other daimones were akin to angels and were associated with stars and planets and plants and minerals of the earth. The term "angelos," or "messenger"—and the root of the word angel—could refer to either a human or a supernatural agent sent out to deliver messages. If supernatural, an "angelos" might be a higher being or a daimon, depending on who might be dispatching it and for what purpose.

In the Hellenistic period, there was a popular belief in a good daimon, called an *agathodaimon*, who functioned as a kind of guardian angel. An evil daimon was referred to as a *kakodaimon*.

Plato

In *Epinomis* 984–985, Plato distinguishes daimones as a middle rank of being. First comes the stars as visible gods:

> after them and below them, come in order the daimones and the creatures of the air, who hold the third and midmost rank, doing the office of interpreters, and should be peculiarly honored in our prayers that they may transmit comfortable messages. Both sorts of creature, those of aether and those of air, who hold the rank next to them, we shall say, are wholly transparent; however close they are to use, they go undiscerned. Being, however, of a kind that is quick to learn and of retentive memory, they read all our thoughts and regard the good and noble with signal favor, but the very evil with deep aversion. For *they* are not exempt from feeling pain, whereas a god who enjoys the fullness of deity is clearly above both pain and pleasure, though possessed of all-embracing wisdom and knowledge. The universe being thus full throughout of living creatures, they all, so we shall say, act as interpreters, and interpreters of all things, to one another and to the highest gods, seeing that the middle ranks of creatures can flit so lightly over the earth and the whole universe. As for the fifth and last of our substances, water, the safest guess would be that what is formed from it is a demigod.

Plato concludes:

> these five sorts of creatures must surely exist, when it comes to beliefs of individuals or whole societies originating in the intercourse of some of them with us— appearance in dreams of the night, oracular and prophetic voices heard by the whole or the sick, or communications in the last hours of life—and those have been, as they will be hereafter, the resources of many a widespread cult.

He adds that rulers need to be sensitive to these worship needs, "inherited usages."

Mnemonic figure with good and bad angels at head, similar to daimones (Author's collection)

In *Statesman* 274 Plato retells a creation and fall myth that suggests humankind's failings are explained by its presence in a cycle "bereft of the guardian care of the daemon who had governed and reared us up, . . . [and regressed to] become weak and helpless."

In *Timaeus* 41 he gives another creation myth, saying in the voice of the creator of the universe speaking to the first gods that their job is to create three tribes of mortal beings, but:

> the part of them worthy of the name immortal, which is called divine and is the guiding principle of those who are willing to follow justice and you—of that divine part I will myself sow the seed, and having made a beginning, I will hand the work over to you. And do ye then interweave the mortal with the immortal and make and beget living creature.

Socrates

Socrates described his daimonion as an inner voice that warned him whenever he was about to do something wrong.

In *Cratylus* 397–398 Socrates begins a definition of daimones as "the golden [good] race of men who came first" by quoting Hesiod's *Words and Days* 121:

> But now that Fate has closed over this race,/ They are holy daimones upon the earth,/ Beneficent, averters of ills, guardians, of mortal men. I have the most entire conviction that he [Hesiod] called them daimones, because they were [Greek daemon, meaning knowing or wise] . . . and other poets say truly that when a good men dies he has honor and a mighty portion among the dead, and becomes a daemon . . . signifying wisdom. And I say too, that every wise man who happens to be a good man is more than human both in life and death, and is rightly called a daimon.

In *Apology* 26–27, Socrates defends himself against a charge that he does not believe in daimones, or demigods, by explaining that daimones are to gods as flute-playing is to flute-players, or horsemanship is to horses, therefore belief in supernatural and divine activities implies belief in supernatural and divine beings, and vice versa.

In *Phaedo* 107–108, Socrates discusses the immortality of the soul and explains that when anyone dies, the GUARDIAN SPIRIT, which was given charge of him in life, tries to bring the deceased to a place of assembly for judgment, and then sets out to Hades in the company of a guide whose job is escorting souls from this world to the other. The soul, which is deeply attached to the body, will not leave readily, and only after much resistance and suffering is it at last led forcibly away by its appointed guardian spirit.

Iamblichus
In *On the Mysteries of Egypt,* Iamblichus distinguishes daimones from visible gods (intelligible gods) and invisible gods (who transcend rational knowledge and perception tied to matter), and from heroes, a semi-divine mortal. Though invisible, daimones are inferior to both visible and invisible gods. Daimones are produced according to the generative and creative power of the gods, while heroes are produced according to the vital principles in divine beings. Daimones fashion cosmic organisms and complete the authority of every single creature, whereas heroes are more concerned with the disposition souls.

Other Views
Daimones appear in the works of other early philosophers, such as Homer, Porphyry, Pausanias, Seneca, Apuleius, Philostratus, Plotinus, Eusebius, and others, and also in the works of Christian theologians.

Plutarch developed a complex daemonology that assigns daimones functions traditionally assigned to gods. Daimones are spiritual beings that lived for centuries, he says, and their thoughts are so intense that vibrations are created that can be picked up by other spiritual beings and highly sensitive humans as well.

St. AUGUSTINE devotes several chapters of Books 8 and 9 of *The City of God* to Greek and Neoplatonist beliefs and practices on daimones. His purpose is to discredit them and imply the superiority of Christian cosmology and theology.

The church's blanket condemnation of all pagan daimones was complete by medieval times, though Christians continued to believe in their existence. Demons, as they became known, were usually considered messengers and assistants of a single devil, in the same relationship to the devil as the angels to God.

St. THOMAS AQUINAS declared as a dogma of faith that all bad weather and natural catastrophes are brought about by demons. Pope Eugene IV issued a bull against human "agents of Satan" who control weather-demons, and Pope John XXII complained of wizards trying to kill him through the agency of demons sent into inanimate objects.

FURTHER READING
Levinson, Ronald B., ed. *A Plato Reader.* Translated by B. Jowett. Boston: Houghton Mifflin, 1967.
Luck, Goerg. *Arcana Mundi: Magic and the Occult in the Greek and Roman Worlds.* Baltimore: Johns Hopkins University Press, 1985.

Dalkiel
Angel of HELL and ruler of SHEOL, who serves under Duma, the angel of the stillness of death. In hell, Dalkiel punishes nations. He is equated with Rugziel.

Dalquiel
In Kabbalistic lore, one of three PRINCES of the third HEAVEN along with Jabniel and Rabacyal. The princes rule over fire and serve under Anahel. Dalquiel is aided by the angel Oul.

Damabiath
Angel in the order of ANGELS who rules over naval construction. Damabiath also is one of the 72 angels of the SCHEMHAMPHORAE.

Daniel
Apocalyptic book in the Old Testament, featuring six stories and four dream visions narrated by Daniel, a pious Jew. The book of Daniel is the first great apoca-

lyptic work, followed by REVELATION, 1 ENOCH, and the Syrian manuscript of BARUCH. It is the first book in the Bible to give individual identities and names to angels (PRINCES).

One of the last books to be included in the Old Testament canon, Daniel was written in Aramaic about 165 B.C.E. It depicts some of the sufferings of the Jews under Hellenic domination, especially pressure to conform to idolatry. Daniel is purported to be present at the court of Nebuchadnezzar (604–562 B.C.E.), but much of the allegorical prophecy actually describes events that were well past by the second century B.C.E.

In the first chapters, Daniel, Hananiah, Mishael, and Azariah are young Hebrews who have been educated and found favor in the Babylonian court and have been given the Babylonian names, respectively, of Belteshazzar, Shadrach, Meshach, and Abednego. Daniel successfully interprets Nebuchadnezzar's dreams, where the king's Chaldean priests fail to do so. The king makes a golden idol and orders people to worship it or be thrown into a furnace. They are pressured to worship idols or ordered not to worship any god besides the king. Shadrach, Meshach, and Abednego refuse to worship the idol, and the furious king has them cast into the fiery furnace. The flames are so hot that the king's men are burned up, but the three youths remain unharmed and walk about the flames singing praises to God. Nebuchadnezzar sees four men in the furnace; the fourth is "like a son of the gods."

The Aramaic word used in this phrase (chapter 3:25) is *ir,* usually translated as "WATCHER," a term for angels that appears in the apocrypha, where it refers to FALLEN ANGELS. In the canonical Bible it is used only in Daniel. This word was associated in the ancient [Aramaic] Ugaritic language with irim, local protecting gods. The Israelite monotheists transformed these watchers into angels, and their old name, its meaning lost, came to be understood as "wakeful." It was interpreted by some to mean archangels, and sometimes as fallen archangels in the apocrypha. In later tradition the "watchers" became GUARDIAN ANGELS. Nebuchadnezzar himself declares that God has sent his angel to protect the three youths. (Later in Daniel, in 7:15, it is "one of those who stand by"—a watcher—who interprets a complex dream for Daniel.)

The Hebrews remain safe and practically rule Babylonia while Nebuchadnezzar lives, but Daniel is thrown into a lion pit by the next ruler, Darius, for praying to his own God instead of to the king. Daniel is protected: "My God sent his angel who sealed the lions' jaws, they did me no harm, since in his sight I am blameless, and I have never done you any harm either, O king" (6:17–24). The villains who plotted to trap Daniel are thrown to the lions and eaten immediately.

THE DREAM VISIONS

Daniel's initial visionary experience is described in 7:1 as "a dream and visions of his head as he lay in bed." He has a complex apocalyptic vision with four beasts and the ANCIENT OF DAYS. In 7:13–14 there appears a much-discussed manlike figure:

> I gazed into the visions of the night, and I saw, coming on the clouds of heaven, one like a son of man. He came to the one of great age and was led into his presence. On him was conferred sovereignty, glory and kingship, and men of all people, nations and languages because his servants. His sovereignty is an eternal sovereignty which shall never pass away, nor will his empire ever be destroyed.

In all the Old Testament, Jewish, and Talmudic literature, heavenly beings do not emerge from the transcendent sphere on clouds except to show themselves to man. Interpretations of this figure include the faithful of Israel, the Messiah, and an angel.

In 7:15–18, a figure who is "one of those standing" (a watcher) interprets the vision for Daniel: The four great beasts are the four kings who shall possess the earth, but the saints of the Most High will receive the kingdom and possess it forever. Some interpretations identify the interpreter as the archangel Michael, and the meaning of this passage to imply that the world will be ruled by HEAVEN and not by the evil host.

Angel sent to protect Daniel from the lions, from a 19th-century Bible (Author's collection)

Chapter 8 presents a second vision, which he has when he is on the banks of the river Ulai. He sees a ram and a he-goat fight. The he-goat wins, but it is replaced by four horns toward the four winds of heaven. A small horn appears and rises up to the heavenly host, where it throws down stars and tramples them.

Puzzled, Daniel then hears a man's voice command, "Gabriel, make this man understand the meaning of the vision" (8:16). Daniel falls on his face as Gabriel explains that the vision is for "the time of the end." Daniel falls into a deep sleep, but the angel picks him up and sets him on his feet while he explains the symbolisms. The experience ends with Daniel falling into unconsciousness and being ill for several weeks. When he recovers, he is "appalled" by the vision.

MAIMONIDES observes that Daniel's falling into a deep sleep is consistent with visionary prophecy. When God or an angel speaks to man, the senses are depressed.

In chapter 9, Daniel is in deep prayer, confessing his sins and the sins of the Israelites, when Gabriel suddenly appears in swift flight at the time of the evening sacrifice. The angel says he has come to give Daniel wisdom and understanding: "therefore consider the word and understand the vision" (9:23). Gabriel goes on to discuss the restoration of Jerusalem and the "coming of an anointed one, a prince" (9:25).

Daniel's fourth vision occurs during the third year of Cyrus the king of Persia. After three weeks of deep mourning, Daniel is on the banks of the Tigris River when he sees above the waters

> a man clothed in linen, whose loins were girded with gold of Uphaz. His body was like beryl, his face like the appearance of lightning, his eyes like flaming torches, his arms and legs like the gleam of burnished bronze, and the sound of his words like the noise of the multitude. (10:5–6)

Daniel knows he is the only one who can see this vision. The men with him know something strange is happening, however, for they start to tremble and then they flee. When this apparition speaks, Daniel falls to the ground unconscious, but then he feels a hand touching him, setting his knees and hands trembling. The man/angel tells Daniel that he is again specially chosen to receive the prophetic news about the times to come.

He tells Daniel he is fighting against the prince of Persia (possibly one of the PRINCIPALITIES who govern nations) and after that he will face the prince of Greece. He is aided only by Michael, "your prince" who has charge of Daniel's people. This championing of opposed sides by different angels signifies that the fate of nations is a secret awaiting God's revelation and hidden from the angels themselves.

The man/angel tells about the battles and kings to come. Finally, Michael shall arise and the Israelites will be delivered, "every one whose name shall be found written in the book" (12:1). The dead shall awake, the righteous ones to everlasting life and the sinners to shame and everlasting contempt. The wise will shine like the brightness of the firmament, and those who turn many to righteousness will become like the stars. Finishing the prophecy, the man/angel instructs Daniel to shut up the words and seal the book.

Daniel asks when the end will come, but he does not understand the answer: "a time, two times, and a half time; and that when the shattering of the power of the holy people comes to an end all these things would be accomplished" (12:7). Daniel is told to go, and he shall have his "allotted place at the end of the days."

Apocalypse of Daniel

The Apocalypse of Daniel is a late Byzantine apocalypse written in the ninth century C.E., based upon the Byzanto-Arba wars of the eighth century, culminating in the coronation of Charlemagne in Rome in 800. It is primarily historical and political in nature, offering little in the way of theology or ANGELOLOGY. Its odd description of the origins and appearance of the Antichrist are noteworthy, however.

The apocalypse describes how the Antichrist will rise up and lead a final assault upon Christians. Chapter 9 describes how the Antichrist comes out of the chasms of Hades and enters into a type of small fish called a garidion (also gabridion). The fish is caught by 12 fishermen, who then fall into fighting among themselves. The one named Judas prevails, and he takes the fish as his inheritance. He sells it for 30 pieces of silver to a virgin named Injustice, and whose last name is Perdition. She touches the head of the fish and becomes pregnant, giving birth to the Antichrist in three months. He suckles for four months, and then goes to Jerusalem and becomes a false teacher, appearing quiet, gentle, and guileless.

In appearance, the Antichrist is 15 feet tall with hair down to his big feet. One eye is like the morning star (Venus) and one eye is like a lion's. His lower teeth are iron and his lower jaw diamond. His right arm is iron and his left arm copper, and his right hand is four-and-a-half feet long. He is long-faced, long-nosed, and disorderly, and his forehead is stamped with three letters, A, K, and T. A signifies "I deny"; K signifies "And I completely reject"; and T signifies "the foul dragon."

The Jews make him king and worship him. He reigns for three years, and demons come out of the abyss to tempt and kill Christians, especially babies. Then three men condemn him as a liar and expose him as the Antichrist. The great day of judgment arrives and the devil falls. The light and glory of Christ is established forever.

See DREAMS AND VISIONS.

FURTHER READING

Beasley-Murray, G. R. "The Interpretation of Daniel 7." *The Catholic Biblical Quarterly* 45, no. 1 (January 1985).

Charlesworth, James H., ed. *The Old Testament Pseudepigrapha*. Vols. 1 and 2. New York: Doubleday, 1983, 1985.

Introduction and Notes. *Jerusalem Bible*. Garden City, New York: Doubleday, 1966.

Dantanian

One of the FALLEN ANGELS and 72 spirits of SOLOMON. According to the LEMEGETON, Dantanian is a mighty duke who appears in the form of a man with many faces, of men and women, carrying a book in hand. He knows human thoughts and can change them at will. He makes people fall in love, and can show visions of people to others. He teaches all arts and sciences.

Dante Alighieri (1265–1321)

Italian poet and writer, considered one of the greatest of the late Middle Ages. T. S. Eliot remarked once that Shakespeare and Dante divide the modern world between them, allowing no third. Dante's epic *The Divine Comedy* (*La Divina Commedia*) established his Tuscan dialect as the literary tongue of Italy and gave readers a detailed exposition of medieval man's conception of God and his perfect, changeless universe. Dante's travels into hell, purgatory, and heaven not only glorify God but also illuminate the follies and sins of past and present political and church figures, clarify the Catholic Church's position on supposed heresies of the day, and extol and sanctify the memory of Beatrice Portinari, Dante's greatest love.

Life

Born in Florence in 1265 to a noble but impoverished family, Dante studied at the university in Bologna. He took an active interest in the byzantine world of Florentine politics about 1295, siding with the Guelphs, or the bourgeoisie, in their struggles against the aristocratic Ghibellines. When the Black Guelphs defeated the White faction in 1302, Dante went into exile in Ravenna, where he wrote *The Divine Comedy*.

He first met Beatrice in 1274, encountering her again in 1281, and again in 1283. Even though Dante

Beatrice and Dante before the Empyrean (Gustave Doré)

married Gemma Donati in 1284, his unrequited but pure passion continued. Beatrice died in June 1290.

Grief-stricken, Dante immersed himself in the study of philosophy and Provençal poetry. He became active in politics in Florence, which led to his banishment from the city in 1302. He became a citizen of all Italy. He died in 1321 in Ravenna.

Works

Dante's most important work is *The Divine Comedy,* a vernacular poem in 100 cantos, more than 14,000 lines. It is an excellent representation of the medieval outlook of a changeless universe ordered by God.

Virgil, the ancient Roman poet, accompanies Dante in his journeys through the *Inferno* and *Purgatorio,* but the angelic Beatrice guides his voyage into heaven's holy spheres in the *Paradiso.* Along the way, she introduces him to various biblical and contemporary spirits who have earned the right to approach God at the center of the universe. These spirits populate several lower spheres; the highest sphere is the EMPYREAN.

When Dante and Beatrice arrive at the Ninth Sphere, or the Primum Mobile, Dante sees a brilliant point of light surrounded by nine spinning, dazzling spheres. Conversely to what he would expect, the closer spheres are more radiant than those farther away, leading Beatrice to explain that they are more brilliant because of their absorption of God's essence.

These nine spheres are the Angel Hierarchy, organized into the nine ranks traditional in medieval thought: SERAPHIM, CHERUBIM, THRONES, DOMINIONS or dominations, VIRTUES, POWERS, PRINCIPALITIES, ARCHANGELS, AND ANGELS. They are too numerous to count, always concentrating on God and singing and praising his name. Beatrice explains that love created the angels as "pure act" without potential for further greatness.

Since all Creation occurred simultaneously, according to Beatrice, Lucifer's fall from grace happened before a person could count to 20. Dante calls him a principality, or PRINCE of HEAVEN, instead of an archangel. He fell because of pride, she explains to Dante, and those angels that remain do so because:

These you see here were humble, undemanding,
and prompt in their acknowledgment of the Good
that made them capable of such understanding;

whereby their vision was exalted higher
by illuminating grace and their own merit,
in which their wills are changeless and entire.

(*Paradiso*, Canto XXIX: 59–63)

Totally focused on God's light and secure in their own eternity, these angels have no understanding, memory, or will, as man comprehends these attributes.

. . . these beings, since their first bliss in the sight
of God's face, in which all things are revealed,
have never turned their eyes from their delight.

No angel's eye, it follows, can be caught
by a new object; hence, they have no need
of memory, as does divided thought.

(*Paradiso*, Canto XXIX: 76–81)

Proceeding upward into the lower levels of the Empyrean, Dante learns that the angels he first saw are what Beatrice describes as the "sacred soldiery": those mortal souls who, through their sanctity, encircle God the Father within their nine spheres. Beatrice sits as a Throne in the third sphere.

Within the Empyrean are the Angelic Host: those angels created by God who never left Paradise. Instead of encircling the Father they fly rapidly back and forth between God and his Son, represented by a mystic rose, much as bees swarm between the hive and the flowers. Dante's translator and critic, John Ciardi, describes this swarming as taking the sweetness of God's hive to the flowers and returning to God the bliss of heaven's souls.

In Dante's vision, as opposed to Milton's in *Paradise Lost,* there are two angelic congregations: one created by God and one dedicated to God. Both, however, appear as beautiful, shining, gold-winged, and dazzling creatures. And all receive their happiness and grace through the redeeming ardor of love:

Like living flame their faces seemed to glow.
Their wings were gold. And all their bodies shone
more dazzling white than any earthly snow.

On entering the great flower they spread about them,
from tier to tier, the ardor and the peace
they had acquired in flying close to Him.

(*Paradiso*, Canto XXXI: 13–18)

Dante was also an accomplished painter and sculptor. He writes in *La Vita Nuova* (ca. 1294), a work celebrating Beatrice and love that preceded *The Divine Comedy,* that as he was reflecting on Beatrice's ascension into heaven, "among the angels in the realm of peace," he was painting angels on boards—perhaps part of a larger work commissioned for a church.

See LITERATURE AND ANGELS.

FURTHER READING
Arthos, John. *Dante, Michaelangelo and Milton.* London: Routledge and Kegan Paul, 1963.
Dante Alighieri. *La Vita Nuova.* Translated by Barbara Reynolds. Harmondsworth, Middlesex, England: Penguin Books, 1969.
———. *The Divine Comedy.* Translated by John Ciardi. New York: W. W. Norton, 1961.
Elledge, Scott, ed. *John Milton: Paradise Lost, An Authoritative Text.* New York: W. W. Norton, 1975.
Levey, Judith S., and Agnes Greenhall, eds. *The Concise Columbia Encyclopedia.* New York: Columbia University Press, 1983.

Dardariel

In the LEGEMETON, the ruling angel of the 11th hour of the night, called Alacho. Dardariel governs hundreds of dukes and lesser dukes.

Dark Angel

The angel or angel-man who wrestles with JACOB at Peniel. Different angels have been identified as the Dark Angel, including Michael, Gabriel, Uriel, Metatron, Samael, or even God himself. St. Clement of Alexandria identified the Dark Angel as the Holy Ghost.

Daveithe

In GNOSTICISM, one of four great LUMINARIES who surround the self-begotten, the savior, or God. The other three are Oroiael, Harmozy, and Eleleth.

Dead Sea Scrolls See QUMRAN TEXTS.

deathbed visions

Apparitions of angels, gods, religious figures, and the dead experienced by the dying. Deathbed visions have

Angel taking away the soul of a child (Reprinted courtesy of U.S. Library of Congress)

been recorded since antiquity and share common characteristics regardless of racial, cultural, religious, educational, age, and socioeconomic factors.

The first scientific study of deathbed visions was done in the early 20th century by William Barrett, an English professor of physics and psychical researcher. Barrett became interested in deathbed visions in 1924 when his wife, a physician specializing in obstetrical surgery, told him about a woman patient who spoke of seeing visions of a place of great beauty, and of her dead father and sister, shortly before she died. The visions were real to the patient, and transformed her into a state of great radiance and peace. Barrett was struck by the fact that the woman had not known that her sister had died about three weeks earlier.

Several decades later, Barrett's research interested Karlis Osis, then director of research for Eileen Garrett's Parapsychology Foundation. Under the auspices of the Foundation in 1959–60, and later the American Society for Psychical Research in 1961–64 and 1972–73, Osis collected information from doctors and nurses on tens of thousands of deathbed and near-death experiences in the United States and India. The Indian survey (1972–73) was conducted with Erlendur Haraldsson. Of those cases, more than a thousand were examined in detail. The findings of these studies confirmed Barrett's findings, as well as research of the NEAR-DEATH EXPERIENCE (NDE) and research with the terminally ill.

Deathbed visions may occur to individuals who die gradually, as from terminal illness or injuries, rather than those who die suddenly, as from heart attacks. The majority of visions are of apparitions of the dead, who usually are close family members and appear to be glowing and dressed in white. Other apparitions are of angels and other religious figures, such as JESUS, the Virgin MARY, and gods and semi-divine beings pertinent to a person's background.

The primary purpose of these apparitions is to beckon or command the dying to come with them; thus, they are frequently called "take-away apparitions." The dying person usually is happy and willing to go, especially if the individual believes in an afterlife. (However, deathbed visions do occur to people who do not believe in an afterlife.) If the person has been in great pain or depression, a complete turnaround of mood is observed, and pain vanishes. The dying one literally seems to "light up" with radiance. Osis and Haraldsson, in their book *At the Hour of Death,* relate this story:

> The condition of one man, suffering from a heart attack, had been serious for the last few days. Suddenly he gained consciousness. He looked better and cheerful. He

Angel guarding a tomb (Author's collection)

talked nicely to his relatives and requested them to go home. He said, "I shall go to my home. Angels have come to take me." He looked relieved and cheerful.

Other persons present usually cannot see the apparitions. Sometimes people see a cloud or mist form over the patient at the moment of death, and they usually interpret it as the soul leaving the body.

Approximately one-third of deathbed visions involve total visions, in which the patient sees another world—heaven or a heavenly place, such as beautiful gardens or alpine meadows. Some people also see gates, bridges, rivers, and boats, which are symbolic of transition, as well as castles and beautiful cities. Sometimes these places are filled with angels or glowing souls of the dead.

Such visions are resplendent with intense and vivid colors and bright light. They either unfold before the patient, or the patient feels transported out-of-body to them. As with apparitional figures, visions of ethereal places fill the person with radiant joy and anticipation.

Few total visions conform to religious expectations about the nature of the afterlife. Researcher Osis found only one case of a vision described as hell, from a Catholic woman who seemed to be carrying a great burden of guilt about her "sins."

A small number of persons in the Osis-Haraldsson research reported hearing heavenly or angelic music. The incidence of music is higher in cases collected around the turn of the century by earlier psychical researchers, and may reflect the different tastes in music then.

Most deathbed visions are short: Approximately 50 percent last five minutes or less; 17 percent last from six to fifteen minutes; and 17 percent last more than one hour. The visions usually appear just minutes before death: Approximately 76 percent of the patients studied died within ten minutes of their vision, and nearly all of the rest died within one or several hours. The appearance of the vision seems to have little connection with the physical condition of the patient. Some who seemed to be recovering, then had visions, quickly fell into comas and died. Consider the following anecdote from *At the Hour of Death,* involving a girl of 10 dying from pneumonia:

> The mother saw that her child seemed to be sinking and called us [nurses]. She said that the child had just told her she had seen an angel who had taken her by the hand—and she was gone, died immediately. That just astounded us because there was no sign of imminent death. She was so calm, serene—and so close to death! We were all concerned.

Natural explanations of deathbed visions include drugs, fever, disease-induced hallucinations, oxygen deprivation to the brain, wish-fulfillment, and depersonalization. These factors can cause hallucinations, but rarely do the hallucinations concern the afterlife. The Osis-Haraldsson research found that deathbed visions are most likely to occur in patients who are fully conscious.

Deathbed visions are significant to thanatology, the scientific study of death and dying, and also provide evidence in support of survival after death.

The literature on Christian saints includes numerous accounts of saints who saw and heard angels prior to their deaths; sometimes the angels were heard or witnessed by others. St. Vincent Ferrar, a Dominican, was able to see and converse with the Guardian Angel of Barcelona, which caused a devotional cult for that angel to spring up there. Upon St. Vincent's death, a multitude of angels gathered at his deathbed in the form of beautiful white birds. The birds vanished at the moment the saint expired.

Hagiographies of early martyrs credit angels with providing comfort during their unspeakable torture, and with standing by as they faced death. St. Lawrence was being beaten and stretched on a rack when a voice suddenly boomed out of nowhere that he was reserved for still greater trials. The voice, attributed to an angel, surprised bystanders and convinced at least one soldier, Romanus, to convert to Christianity. St. Lawrence was then roasted slowly on a gridiron, and died. St. Eulalia, who was only 12 when she was threatened with horrible tortures if she did not renounce her faith, was consoled by three angels who told her to suffer with courage. She was burned alive, and angels reportedly took her soul to HEAVEN.

See ANGEL OF DEATH.

FURTHER READING

Barrett, William. *Death-Bed Visions: The Psychical Experiences of the Dying.* Wellingborough, Northamptonshire, England: The Aquarian Press, 1986. First published 1926.

Osis, Karlis. *Deathbed Observations by Physicians and Nurses.* Monograph No. 3. New York: Parapsychology Foundation, 1961.

Osis, Karlis, and Erlendur Haraldsson. *At the Hour of Death.* Rev. ed. New York: Hastings House, 1986.

O'Sullivan, Fr. Paul. *All about the Angels.* Rockford, Ill.: Tan Books and Publishers, 1990. First published 1945.

decans of the zodiac

Thirty-six degrees dividing the 12 signs of the zodiac. The decans have ruling angels.

In the Testament of Solomon, the deities of the decans are reduced to secondary DEMONS. King SOLOMON summons them to appear before him for interrogation to learn what they do and the names of the angels who thwart them. They appear with heads of formless dogs and also as humans, bulls, dragons with bird faces, beasts, and sphinxes. The demons are, by order of decan:

1st Ruax (also Rhyx), or "the Lord": He causes headaches and is dispatched by the words "Michael, imprison Ruax."

2nd Barsafael: He causes those who live in his time period to have pains in the sides of their heads. He is repelled by the words "Gabriel, imprison Barsafael."

3rd Artosael: He damages eyes and is sent away by the words "Uriel, imprison Artosael."

4th Oropel: He causes sore throats and mucus, and is thwarted by the words "Raphael, imprison Oropel."

5th Kairoxanondalon: He causes ear problems and is dispatched by the words "Ourouel (Uriel), imprison Kairoxanondalon."

6th Sphendonael: He causes tumors of the parotid gland and tetanic recurvation, and is quelled by the words "Sabael, imprison Sphendonael."

7th Sphandor: He paralyzes limbs, deadens the nerves in hands, and weakens shoulders. He is subdued by the words "Arael, imprison Sphandor."

8th Belbel: He perverts the hearts and minds of men and is dispatched by the words "Karael, imprison Belbel."

9th Kourtael: He causes bowel colic and pain and retreats when he hears the words "Iaoth, imprison Kourtael."

10th Methathiax: He causes kidney pains and is sent away by the words, "Adonael, imprison Methatiax."

11th Katanikotael: He causes domestic fights and unhappiness. To dispel him, write on seven laurel leaves the names of the angels who thwart him: Angel, Eae, Ieo, Sabaoth.

12th Saphthorael: He causes mental confusion. To get rid of him, write down the words "Iae, Ieo, sons of Sabaoth," and wear the AMULET around the neck.

13th Phobothel: He causes loosening of the tendons and retreats when he hears the word "Adonai."

14th Leroel: He causes fever, chills, shivering, and sore throats, and he retreats when he hears the words "Iax, do not stand fast, do not be fervent, because Solomon is fairer than eleven fathers."

15th Soubelti: He causes shivering and numbness, and is dispatched by the words "Rizoel, imprison Soubelt."

16th Katrax: He causes fatal fevers. He can be averted by rubbing pulverized coriander on the lips and saying, "I adjure you by Zeus, retreat from the image of God."

17th Ieropa: He causes men to collapse and creates stomach problems that cause convulsions in the bath. He retreats if the words "Iouda Zizabou" are repeated three times in the right ear of the afflicted person.

18th Modebel: He causes married couples to separate, but will retreat if the names of the eight fathers are written down and posted in doorways.

19th Mardeo: He causes incurable fevers and is sent away by writing his name down in the house.

20th Rhyx Nathotho: He causes knee problems and is repelled if the word "Phounebiel" is written on a piece of papyrus.

21st Rhyx Alath: He causes croup in infants and is dispelled if the word "Rarideris" is written down and carried on a person.

22nd Rhyx Audameoth: He causes heart pain and is dispatched by the written word "Raiouoth."

23rd Rhyx Manthado: He causes kidney disease and is thwarted by the written words "Ioath, Uriel."

24th Rhyx Atonkme: He causes rib pain. If a person writes "Marmaraoth of mist" on a piece of wood from a ship that has run aground, the demon retreats.

25th Rhyx Anatreth: He causes bowel distress and is quelled by the words "Arara, Arare."

26th Rhyx, the Enautha: He alters hearts and "makes off" with minds. He is thwarted by the written word "Kalazael."

27th Rhyx Axesbuth: He causes diarrhea and hemorrhoids. If he is adjured in pure wine given to the sufferer, he retreats.

28th Rhyx Hapax: He causes insomnia, and is subdued by the written words "Kok; Phedisomos."

29th Rhyx Anoster: He causes hysteria and bladder pain, and is thwarted when someone mashes

laurel seeds into oil and massages it into the body, and calls upon Mamaroth.

30th Rhyx Physikoreth: He causes long-term illnesses, but retreats when the sick person massages his body with salted olive oil while saying, "CHERUBIM, SERAPHIM, help me."

31st Rhyx Aleureth: He causes choking on fish bones. If one puts a fish bone into the breasts of the afflicted one, the demon retreats.

32nd Rhyx Ichthuron: He detaches tendons and retreats when he hears the words "Adaonai, malthe."

33rd Rhyx Achoneoth: He causes sore throats and tonsillitis. He is sent away by writing "Leikourgos" on ivy leaves and heaping them into a pile.

34th Rhyx Autoth: He causes jealousy and fights between people who love each other. He is subdued by writing the letters Alpha and Beta.

35th Rhyx Phtheneoth: He cast the evil eye on everyone, and is thwarted by the "much suffering eye" amulet.

36th Rhyx Mianeth: He holds grudges against the body, causes flesh to rot, and demolishes houses. He flees when the words "Melto Ardad Anaath" are written on the front of the house.

King Solomon orders the demons of the decans to bear water and prayed that they would go to the Temple of God (Jerusalem).

FURTHER READING
Charlesworth, James H., ed. *The Old Testament Pseudepigrapha*. Vols. 1 and 2. New York: Doubleday, 1983, 1985.

Decarabia (Carabia)

One of the FALLEN ANGELS and 72 spirits of SOLOMON. Decarabia is a marquis in HELL with 30 legions reporting to him. He appears as a star in a pentacle, but changes into a man when ordered to do so. He makes magical birds fly before a magician and leaves them as FAMILIARS, singing and eating like ordinary birds. Decarabia knows the virtues of herbs and precious stones.

Dee, John (1527–1608)

English alchemist, mathematician, astronomer, and astrologer, who devoted most of his life to trying to communicate with the angelic realm. He was a credulous man, and his desire to speak with angels, coupled by his failure to do so on his own, made him a gullible target for fraudulent mediums.

John Dee exhibited scholastic brilliance at an early age; he was made one of the original fellows at Trinity College at Cambridge. He was a respected lecturer at home and abroad. He was fascinated by the occult and MAGIC, and he was well versed in Neoplatonic, Hermetic, and kabbalistic philosophy. He was sometimes called "the last royal magician" because of his astrological services to Queen Elizabeth I. His occult interests, however, landed him in trouble. In 1555 he was imprisoned on accusations that he had cast death spells on Queen Mary I. In 1583, a mob whipped up by witch-frenzy ransacked his home in Montlake, burning many of his valuable books. Queen Elizabeth reimbursed him for some of the £2,000 in damages. He was able to salvage some 3,000 books, most of which are currently in British museums.

Dee suffered from continuous financial problems, and he turned to alchemy for a solution. He desired to contact angels who would help him find the philosopher's stone (a mysterious substance that allegedly could turn base metals into silver and gold) or else discover buried treasure. He was influenced by Cornelius Agrippa's *Three Books of Occult Philosophy,* which describe the cosmic ladder of angels (see JACOB) and how one might ascend to the level of angels through magic. Dee also paid great attention to his DREAMS and to scrying with a mirror of black obsidian.

Dee could not cultivate his own mediumistic ability, and so he advertised for mediums. His first partnership was with a young man named Barnabas Saul, who got into trouble with the law after a few months. His second partner was Edward Talbot (who became known as Edward Kelly), a hot-tempered Irishman who'd lost his ears as punishment for forgery. Kelly came to Dee's house and demonstrated his ability by scrying into a stone. After about fifteen minutes he said he could see an angel, who identified himself as Uriel. Dee felt uneasy about Kelly, and dismissed him. But Kelly persisted, and Dee then relented. For seven years, the two had an uneasy partnership which Kelly dominated and for which Dee paid Kelly a salary.

Kelly would gaze into a crystal stone and summon spirits with incantations, or "calls" in a complex and secret magical language, Enochian, of unknown origin. It is a real language with its own grammar and syntax, and similar in sound to Sanskrit, Arabic, or Greek. Many believe Kelly and Dee invented it. Dee would ask the spirits questions and Kelly, as the medium, would relay their answers, which Dee took down in dictation. They conjured the angels with the Nineteen Calls or Keys of Enochian. The first two keys conjured the element Spirit, and the next 16 keys conjured the four Elements of nature, each of which was also subdivided into four classes. The 19th key invoked any of 30 "aethyrs" or "aires" which they never defined, but which probably represent levels of consciousness, or are comparable to the AEONS of GNOSTICISM.

When the angels appeared in Kelly's crystal, he communicated with them in Enochian by using charts of squares either filled with letters or left blank. The angels would spell out messages by having Kelly point with a rod to various squares.

To further add to the air of mystery that he liked to engender, Kelly claimed the messages were always dictated backward, because to communicate them directly would unleash dangerous and powerful forces beyond control. When the messages were finished, he and Dee rewrote them in reverse order.

In one of Dee's own, few psychic experiences, he saw Uriel floating outside his window, holding a pale pink crystal about the size of an orange. The archangel Michael appeared and told Dee to use it for scrying. This crystal, and Dee's obsidian "magic mirror" and other instruments, are in the British Museum.

Dee's *Spiritual Diaries* form an intriguing, firsthand account of alleged communication with angels. Many encounters are suspect; the angels wax on at great length, and some of the entries appear to have been rewritten in a neat, not scribbled, hand. Curiously, Dee, who professed to be on a search for spiritual truth, peppered the angels with the most mundane and trivial questions, of the kind one might pose to a fortune-teller. The occasional mystical philosophies and revelations of the angels seem to be regurgitations of material that could have been found in magical and kabbalistic texts available at the time.

Kelly exhibited an unbalanced personality and was prone to fits of rage and darkness, which were reflected in his sessions with the spirits. He offered up dark prophecies—many of which never came to pass—and descriptions of horrible, demonic beings. Sometimes he said he felt possessed by demonic beings and wanted to be exorcised of them. Dee, a devout Christian, was often wary of Kelly's visions. Concerned that he might be tricked by evil spirits, he put various tests to screen them out. However, if Dee thought that Kelly was accessing good angels, he tended to accept whatever was transmitted without question.

Dee and Kelly sold their services to a variety of noblemen, including Count Albert Laski of Poland, who brought them to Poland. From 1585 to 1589 Dee, Kelly, and their families toured the Continent, performing for royalty and nobility, but with only modest success. Whenever Dee and Kelly quarreled, Kelly would stop scrying for a time. The pope accused Dee of necromancy (conjuring the dead), and they were thrown out of Prague. Kelly and Dee parted company shortly after Kelly announced that Madimi, one of their chief spirits, had ordered them to share wives, and that if anyone objected, God would strike them dead. Both wives were hysterical at the idea, and Dee himself was not pleased. Nonetheless he acquiesced, and convinced his wife to do the same. But before the swap could be consummated, Dee and Kelly split up. The Dees returned to England and Kelly remained in Europe. He was killed in 1595 while trying to escape from prison in Prague.

Back in England, Dee found a new medium partner, Batholomew Hickman. Queen Elizabeth made Dee warden of Christ's College in Manchester in 1595, but Dee did not like the job. In 1604, he unwisely challenged James I, successor to Elizabeth, to try him for sorcery, but nothing happened. He was, however, dismissed from his college post a years later in 1605. He died in poverty and obscurity in 1608. His story has been resurrected in more recent times by historians of the Western magical and mystery tradition.

The language Enochian sank into oblivion until the 19th century, when it was revived by the Hermetic Order of the Golden Dawn, a magical order in England. Enochian also was studied at length by Aleister Crowley, who said the Keys were genuine, and worked. Crowley said that only properly initiated adepts could invoke all of the aethyrs in the Nineteenth Key (he claimed to be able to do this himself), which would produce visions of spirits and astral beings.

Enochian magic as a path of inner work continues to be practiced by magical adepts who use the Keys for astral travel to different levels of consciousness. (See MAGIC.)

FURTHER READING

Cavendish, Richard. *The Black Arts*. New York: Perigee Books, 1967.

Guiley, Rosemary Ellen. *The Encyclopedia of Witches and Witchcraft*. New York: Facts On File, 1989.

Harkness, Deborah E. *John Dee's Conversations With Angels*. Cambridge: Cambridge University Press, 1999.

demiurge   See GNOSTICISM.

demons

Lesser spirits usually regarded as malevolent, and also associated with FALLEN ANGELS.

Pagan demons, called DAIMONES or daemones, are both good and evil according to their inherent nature, and they include a broad range of beings, from spirits to spirits of the dead to gods. But the Christian view, condemning all pagan spirits as evil, regards demons as agents of the devil whose purpose is to ruin souls so that they are condemned to HELL.

Jewish demonologies have long and complex histories; popular beliefs were influenced by exposure to the

Demon harassing a woman, from Chartres Cathedral, France (Author's collection)

lore of the Babylonians, Persians, and Egyptians. In Talmudic times, demons were ever-present enemies posing constant dangers to humanity—but not working under the aegis of any archfiend. Like angels, demons were held to be numberless, and could be invoked in MAGIC; however, demon-magic was met with strong disapproval.

According to Talmudic tradition, demons were created by God on the first Sabbath eve at twilight. Dusk fell before he finished them, and thus they have no bodies. They have wings and exist between humans and angels—roughly between the earth and the moon—and are less powerful than angels. They frequent uninhabited and unclean places, and once they attach themselves to a person or family, bad luck follows.

By the Middle Ages, rabbinic writings had elaborated upon demons. Some demons, who were produced by ADAM and Lilith or other female demons, had

Demons (Gustave Doré)

bodies. There were different classes and types of demons, some of which were absorbed from French and German lore, including their names. Demons have their own duties, such as governing the night hours, causing diseases and malfortune, and sexually harassing people. The Zohar states that every pollution of semen spawns demons.

According to KABBALAH, evil powers emanate from the left pillar of the TREE OF LIFE, especially from Geburah, the sephirah of the wrath of God. By the 13th century, the idea had developed of 10 evil sephirot to counter the 10 holy sephirot of the Tree.

But medieval demon magic fell to a minor role in the larger scope of Jewish magic, surpassed by the magic of the NAMES of God and angels. They retained importance in divination.

Apocryphal texts such as ENOCH and JUBILEES associate demons with fallen angels (see WATCHERS) and malicious beings who populate the lower air.

In Christianity, demons are unrelentingly evil and are the minions of Satan, the devil. They live in hell but can prowl the world actively looking for souls to subvert. By the end of the New Testament period, demons were synonymous with fallen angels, the one-third of the heavenly host cast out of heaven along with Lucifer (later identified as Satan), who all descended into hell. As Christianity spread, the ranks of demons swelled to include the gods and demons of the ancient Middle Eastern and Jewish traditions, and all pagan deities and NATURE SPIRITS.

The fall of Satan and his angels is related in the book of REVELATION: "And the great dragon was thrown down, that ancient serpent, who is called the Devil and Satan, the deceiver of the whole world—he was thrown down to the earth, and his angels were thrown down with him" (Revelation 12:9).

St. AUGUSTINE attributed this fall to pride and will: "good and bad angels have arisen, not from a difference in their nature and origin . . . but from a difference in their wills and desires. . . . While some steadfastly continued in that which was the common good of all, namely, in God himself, and in His eternity, truth, and love; others . . . became proud, deceived, envious."

The church fathers and theologians who followed them wrote extensively on the evil nature and dangers of demons, whose attacks were certain to be caused by moral failings.

Both demons and angels play roles in the Western magical tradition that evolved from the practical Kabbalah, alchemy, GNOSTICISM, Neoplatonism, and other influences. The magical GRIMOIRES give NAMES, duties, SEALS, and incantations for demons as well as angels. In this respect, demons are negative entities but have useful functions when commanded, such as the procurement of treasures and lost objects.

During the Inquisition, demons especially became associated with witches, who also were regarded as agents of the devil. Much was written about the specific ways demons tormented humans, especially by sexual assault. Male demons (incubi) and female demons (succubi) were believed to visit people in their beds at night to copulate with them. Monstrous births were explained away as the products of human-demon intercourse.

The preeminent guide of the day, *The Malleus Maleficarum* ("The Witch Hammer"), goes into great detail about the offenses of demons and witches. Written by two Dominican inquisitors, James Sprenger and Heinrich Kramer, *The Malleus Maleficarum* was first published in Germany in 1486, and it quickly spread throughout Europe in dozens of editions.

The book is divided into three parts. Part I concerns how the devil and his demons and witches, with God's permission, perpetrate a variety of evils upon men and animals, including sexual assaults, instilling hatred, obstructing or destroying fertility, and changing humans into beasts. According to the authors, God permits these acts, otherwise the devil would have unlimited power and destroy the world. Part II concerns details of how witches cast spells and bewitchments—such as conjuring and controlling demons—and how these actions may be prevented or remedied. Part III sets forth the legal procedures for trying witches, including the taking of testimony, admission of evidence, procedures for interrogation and torture, and guidelines for sentencing.

Sex with Demons

The Inquisition devoted attention to sex between humans and demons. Prior to the 12th century, the church denied the possibility of intercourse with demons. By the 14th century, as the Inquisition gained force and witchcraft was decreed a punishable heresy, intercourse with demons became accepted. Enemies of the church were said to not only have sex with demons but also copulate wildly and frequently with them and to worship them. In many cases, the distinction between the devil himself and demons was blurry, and witches said to copulate with "the devil" probably were accused of having sex with an incubus or succubus type of demon. Such tales served the church's purpose of consolidating its power over the populace by branding all pagan deities and rites, and all acts of magic and sorcery, as instruments of the devil.

Sex with demons invariably was portrayed as unpleasant and painful. Sometimes demons deceived people by appearing in the forms of spouses or lovers. After copulation, they would reveal their true identities and blackmail the victims into continuing the sexual liaison.

Incubi were especially attracted to women with beautiful hair, young virgins, chaste widows, and all "devout" females. Nuns were among the most vulnerable, and could be molested in the confessional as well as in bed. While the majority of women were said to be forced into sex by the incubi, it was believed that some of them submitted willingly and even enjoyed the act. Incubi had huge phalluses, sometimes made of horn or covered with scales, and which ejaculated icy semen. When they appeared as demons and not as human imposters, they were described as ugly, hairy, and foul-smelling.

Incubi were believed to have the ability to impregnate women. They did not possess their own semen, but collected it from men in nocturnal emissions, masturbation, or in coitus while masquerading as succubi. The demons preserved semen and used it later on one of their victims.

Succubi were less prevalent. Because of the inherent evil of women, in the view of Christianity, women were morally weak and therefore more licentious than men. If a man was assaulted by a succubus, it was most likely not his fault. The sex act itself with a succubus was often described as penetrating a cavern of ice. There are accounts of men being forced to perform cunnilingus on succubi, whose vaginas dripped urine, dung, and other vile juices and smells.

The wild copulation between witches (usually female) and demons was lamented in *The Malleus Maleficarum,* which noted that "in times long past the Incubus devils used to infest women against their wills [but] modern witches . . . willingly embrace this most foul and miserable servitude." Some incubi served as familiars to witches, who sent them to torment specific individuals.

The church prescribed five ways to get rid of sexual demons: sacramental confession, making the sign of the cross, reciting the Ave Maria, moving away, and exorcism. Reciting the Lord's Prayer and sprinkling holy water also were effective.

Sexual molestation by demons continues to be reported in modern times, often in connection with hauntings and poltergeist activities.

FURTHER READING

Flint, Valerie I. J. *The Rise of Magic in Early Medieval Europe.* Princeton, N.J.: Princeton University Press, 1991.

Guiley, Rosemary Ellen. *The Encyclopedia of Witches and Witchcraft.* Rev. ed. New York: Facts On File, 1989.

Russell, Jeffrey Burton. *A History of Witchcraft.* London: Thames and Hudson, 1980.

Thomas, Keith. *Religion and the Decline of Magic.* New York: Charles Scribner's Sons, 1971.

Trachtenberg, Joshua. *Jewish Magic and Superstition: A Study in Folk Religion.* New York: Berhman's Jewish Book House, 1939.

deputy angels See MEMUNIM; MINISTERING ANGELS.

destroying angel See ANGELS OF DESTRUCTION.

devas

Advanced spirits or god-beings who govern the ELEMENTALS and the well-being of all things in nature. In Sanskrit, *deva* means "shining one."

In HINDUISM, the term *deva* has various meanings. It is a brahman in the form of a personal God. A brahman is an abstract concept expressing absolute being or absolute consciousness, a state of pure transcendence that defies precise description. A deva also is a mortal who has attained a state of divinity, but remains mortal. A deva also is an enlightened person who has realized God.

In Buddhism, a deva is a god who lives in one of the good celestial realms (there are 28 altogether). Such devas enjoy a long and happy life in these realms as a reward for having lived good lives while mortals. How-

ever, they are subject to the wheel of reincarnation. Their very happiness in their realm is an obstacle to their enlightenment, for they cannot come to terms with the truth of suffering, one of the four noble truths that form the basis of Buddhist philosophy. The truth of suffering holds that everything is suffering: birth, illness, death, dislikes, desires, and attachments of the personality.

Devas in Theosophy

Devas are discussed at length in the writings of Helena P. Blavatsky, cofounder of the Theosophical Society. According to Blavatsky, devas are types of angels or gods who can neither be propitiated nor worshiped by men. She quotes an Ascended Master, one of her mentors, as describing the devas, also called "Dhyan-Chohans," as progressed entities from a previous

Deva (Copyright 2003 by Robert M. Place. Used by permission)

planetary period. In the evolution of new solar systems, the devas arrive before either elementals or man, and they remain dormant until a certain stage of human evolution is reached. At that time the devas become an active force, and they integrate with the elementals—(spirits of nature) to further the development of man. In classical Greece, Blavatsky says, a class of devas became symbolized by Prometheus, symbol of the purely spiritual man.

Theosophists believe that all religions stem from the same roots of ancient wisdom, and they find a belief in angels common to many religions. In fact the gods of ancient Greece and Rome, Assyria and Mexico, and those worshiped today by Indians, Native Americans, and practitioners of Vodun, Santería, and Candomblé may actually be angels. Such beings are rays or emanations of the Divine Absolute, an impersonal, eternal ONE much different from the intensely personal God of Judeo-Christian tradition.

However, the idea of Divine Breath, of a sending forth of the Word of God, does not differ from the Logos doctrine of Christianity:

> In the beginning was the Word, and the Word was with God, and the Word was God. He was in the beginning with God; all things were made through him, and without him was not anything made that was made. In him was life, and the life was the light of men. . . . And the Word became flesh and dwelt among us, full of grace and truth.
>
> John 1:1–4, 14

According to Blavatsky in her book *The Secret Doctrine,* creation is the utterance of the Word, the Great Breath of the Absolute, into nothingness. The Divine Idea subdivides into three aspects—masculine, feminine, and androgyne—eventually forming great patterns, called Archetypes, which are the basis of all life. These Archetypes first become the Archangels, who transmit the Divine Will and Intelligence and serve as Lords of the planetary systems.

As energy is sent outward, and an organized hierarchy of devas, nature spirits, humans, animals, plants, and minerals eventually forms under the ministry of the Archangels. This vast army of solar and planetary angels is called the Army of the Light, or the Hosts of the Logos. Each plant, each solar system, each type of being has an archangelic regent, supported by legions of lesser devas. Eternal emanations of the Word are continually transmitted, organized, and refined by the Archangels and angels. GEOFFREY HODSON, a Theosophist and clairvoyant, described this process of creation as a performance by the celestial symphony, conducted by the ONE as Divine Musician.

Devas appeared before the creation of man and are not the spirits of former humans. They are the ministers and messengers of the Absolute and have no personality separate from the Divine Will. Although they were patterned after the same archetypes as humans, devas have no clearly defined bodies or gender, differing solely by the order to which they belong.

There are orders of devas or gods responsible for every minute thing in the universe. Mountain Gods preside over the peaks, while Landscape Angels rule over the divisions and areas of the earth's surface. Builder Angels use the Archetypes to create the lesser spirits, humans, animals, plants, and rocks. Guardian Angels watch over humans, their homes, children, and endeavors, while Healing Angels tend the sick, heal the wounded, and console the bereaved. Ruler Angels guide and direct nations in the fulfillment of their destiny. Devas of Nature provide the spark of life to the Builders' creations and nurture each being's existence. Within this category are the nature spirits who tend the earth, air, fire, and water, as well as the gods of storms, fire, and weather. Devas of Art and Beauty lift up the beautiful in all things, while the Angels of Music bear the Voice of God, in all its complicated melodies, to mankind.

Borrowing from the KABBALAH, Theosophy also organized the devas into seven sephirot, usually designated the first emanations from the Divine ONE. These Seven Sephirot are called the Archangels of the Face, the Mighty Spirits Before the Throne, the Seven Viceroys, the Cosmocratores. Along with the Three Supernal Aspects or the Trinity—the Masculine, Feminine, and Androgyne; the Father, Mother, and Holy Spirit—the Seven become the Ten.

The first three sephirot are the primary ones, as follows:

1. *The Sons of Will.* Imbued with omnipotence, the First Sephirah includes the agents of Manifested Will. They are robed in white radiance and are also called the Morning Stars. By directing creation's rays they bring those forces together and atoms into being.
2. *The Sons of Wisdom.* The Second Sephirah forces embody and manifest cohesion, balance, and harmony. They also direct the vitalizing current of solar energy by which substances and forms are given coordination and life. They preserve the balance of Nature and are forever wise.
3. *The Sons of Intelligence.* The Third Sephirah forces order the patterns of formation and fashion the forms according to transcendental dreams. They are the artists and craftsmen of the universe, producing innumerable progeny of lesser devas and

the nature spirits. They mold Nature according to the Archetypes and control thought and law.

Skipping to the secondary sephirot:

5. *Fifth Sephirah.* This order conceives of evolving forms. Through this emanation, Divine Ideation goes from the Archetype to the concrete. Whereas the Ideation, or Thought, was eternal in the First Sephirah, everlasting in the Second, and durational in the Third, it is controlled in the Fifth by Time. The Fifth Sephirah is the soul of the Third, containing many gods and devas in perpetual creative activity and represented by fire.

6. *Sixth Sephirah.* This order, like the rhythmic waves of the ocean, constantly expresses the One Life at the lower levels, including the physical world, saturating it with divine, vitalizing fluid. The Sixth Sephirah corresponds to the Second as the sustaining life-blood of Nature and is represented by air and water.

7. *Seventh Sephirah.* This order is the Lord of all Nature and the physical universe. The angels of this group are responsible for matter and the construction and maintenance of physical forms, representing the Logos in physical substance, and are symbolized by earth. The Seventh Sephirah expresses the Immanence of God, the Indwelling Presence, while the other six show God's Transcendence.

The Fourth Sephirah links the primary and secondary orders, acting as a powerful intermediary to maintain the Archetypes. All the powers, offices, and attributes of the other six sephirot must be mastered by the fourth. It is the Center.

As noted above, the gods or devas, in one way or the other, are associated with all major religions and the practice of many lesser faiths. To the ancient Mayans of Pre-Columbian Mexico, Ekxhuah was the god of travelers, a name quite similar to the Exus of Brazilian Candomblé and the Eshus of Santería. In Hindu India, the *devarajas* are worshiped as gods or goddesses, but they may also be considered angels. All these religions share a belief in an all-powerful, distant Absolute, but they invoke the intervention of lesser gods or angels to deal with the more mundane affairs of humans. Angels will respond to any human, religious or not, who calls them through prayer, study, and meditation, and the practice of ceremony and ritual.

Modern Concepts of Devas

Through Theosophy, devas came to be regarded as high-level nature spirits. Modern views vary as to whether devas are part of, or work under, the angel kingdom. Channeling messages from devas increased during the latter 20th century, as part of the New Age movement. Such messages have tended to focus on the devas' displeasure with humanity's pollution of the earth and disrespect for nature.

Devas as nature spirits received attention in the activities at FINDHORN, a community in northern Scotland that became renowned in the 1970s for spectacular produce grown with the advice of devas. Findhorn became the model for other similar gardens and communities, such as PERELANDRA, near Washington, D.C., and GREEN HOPE FARM in New Hampshire.

Descriptions and impressions about devas are, like angels, subjective and dependent upon the experiencer. Some individuals perceive detailed hierarchies of beings, while others say that devas, angels, and nature beings are facets of a whole—like a diamond—and resist categorization. Devas themselves may remain invisible to the percipient, or manifest as humanlike bodies of light, balls or points of light, or diffuse fields or grids of energy. They communicate via mental impressions, intuitions, the inner voice, or sometimes a clairaudient external voice, much like the DAIMONES who whispered in Socrates' ear.

See ELEMENTALS; MINISTERING ANGELS; NATURE SPIRITS.

FURTHER READING

Blavatsky, H. P. *The Secret Doctrine.* Pasadena, Calif.: Theosophical University Press, 1977. First published 1888.

Findhorn Community. *The Findhorn Garden.* New York: Harper and Row Perennial Library, 1975.

Hawken, Paul. *The Magic of Findhorn.* New York: Bantam Books, 1976.

Hodson, Geoffrey. *The Brotherhood of Angels and Men.* Wheaton, Ill.: The Theosophical Publishing House, 1982.

———. *The Kingdom of the Gods.* Adyar, Madras, India: The Theosophical Publishing House, 1972.

Maclean, Dorothy. *To Hear the Angels Sing.* Hudson, N.Y.: Lindisfarne Press, 1990. First published by Lorian Press, 1980. 2d ed. by Morningtown Press, 1988.

Wright, Machaelle Small. *Behaving As If the God in All Life Mattered.* Jeffersonton, Va.: Perelandra, 1987.

devotional cults

Special devotion and veneration of the angels have been permitted, even sometimes encouraged, in Christianity since its beginnings. Catholic tradition regards angels as conscious beings of high intelligence, not bound by the limitations of physical laws, who can be of help to humanity—but who must not be worshiped or adored, or placed above Christ or God. Devotion to angels centers on imitating them, for they in turn imitate God. Veneration of saints is closely associated with angelic devotion, for saints are considered to be the real friends of angels and models of piety to men and women.

The early Christian Church looked to St. PAUL as setting the standard for veneration of angels. On various occasions, Paul referred to angels within a context of respect and veneration. In 1 Corinthians 11:1–16, Paul discusses proper ways to worship. Women should worship with their heads covered, he says in 11:10, "because of the angels." In this way, they would show respect for the divine order, which is administered by angels (also, women are assigned a lower status than men, whose heads signify Christ; men should not worship with their heads covered).

Early church fathers were sometimes cautious about encouraging veneration of angels out of fear that it would lead to idolatry. The celestial intermediaries proved convenient substitutes for pagan gods and spir-

Angel guarding a cathedral (Author's collection)

its, but the fathers did not wish to see worship of pagan gods transferred to angels. Consequently, angel cults were occasionally suppressed. St. Justin Martyr defended veneration of angels, and the philosopher Celsus declared that angels were different from gods, else they would be called DEMONS.

ORIGEN distinguished between worship of God and devotion to angels. In his *Contra Celsum* (IV, 5), he states:

> We indeed acknowledge that Angels are ministering spirits, and we say they are sent forth to minister for them who shall be heirs of salvation, and that they ascend, bearing the supplications of men, to the purest of the heavenly places in the universe, or even to the supercelestial regions purer still, and they come down from these, conveying to each one, according to his deserts, something enjoined by God to be conferred by them upon those who are to be the recipients of His benefits. . . . For every prayer and supplication and intercession is to be sent up to the Supreme God through the High Priest, who is above all the Angels, the living Word and God. . . . It is enough to secure that the holy Angels be propitious to us, and that they do all things on our behalf, that our disposition of mind toward God should imitate, as far as possible for human nature, the example of these holy Angels, who themselves imitate the example of their God.

St. AUGUSTINE was among those who feared that veneration of angels would be confused with worship of pagan gods. "We honor them out of charity not out of servitude," he said in *De Vera Religione*.

Once the CELESTIAL HIERARCHY of PSEUDO-DIONYSIUS became established and accepted, veneration of angels achieved a level of comfort in Christianity. From about the sixth century on, devotion to the angels grew steadily. St. Benedict and Pope St. Gregory fostered this practice. By the eighth century, however, angels were so popular that prayer to them was discouraged, again out of fears of idolatry. Devotion to the angels still climbed, and reached a height during the Middle Ages; St. Bernard of Clairvaux was especially ardent about the GUARDIAN ANGEL. Citing Psalm 90:11, which states, "God has given his angels charge over thee, to keep thee in all thy ways," Bernard advocated lavishing great respect, gratitude, and love upon angels.

Devotion to angels also has been expressed in the dedication of churches; many of these dedications sprang from apparitional experiences (see MICHAEL; DREAMS AND VISIONS). In Constantinople, a shrine to the archangel Michael was erected outside the city, and 15 churches within city limits were dedicated in his honor. In Rome, Michael had seven churches dedicated to him by the ninth century.

Catholics observe a number of feast days in honor of angels. Only three individual angels are thus honored: the archangels Michael, Gabriel, and Raphael. There are feast days for guardian angels in general and all angels in general, but no feast days for any of the orders in the celestial hierarchy, such as SERAPHIM, CHERUBIM, and so forth.

The feast of the GUARDIAN ANGELS (October 2) once was not separate from the feast of Michael (September 29 in the West and May 8 in the East). The custom began in Spain and spread. In 1518, Pope Leo X issued a bull creating a special office in honor of the guardian angels. The office was raised in rank by Pope Clement IX in 1667, Pope Clement X in 1670, and Pope Leo XIII in 1883.

In places where veneration of the angels is particularly high, feasts also are held in honor of the guardian angel of the place.

NAMES of angels have always been held in high regard for the power they invoke, but the Catholic Church has not encouraged litanies, in which the names of all the choirs of angels are invoked. Litanies were even forbidden in earlier centuries (such as by Pope Clement VIII and Pope Benedict XIV in the 17th and 18th centuries, respectively). However, certain litanies of the angels are allowed for private use if approved by a local bishop.

Veneration of the angels also led to the establishment of confraternities, legal and approved associations whose purpose is works of piety or charity and advancement of public worship. The first Archconfraternity of Saint Michael was established in 1878 in Italy (an archconfraternity has the right to affiliate other confraternities). Confraternities were particularly popular during the 19th century; they have had renewed interest in the latter 20th century.

In 1950, Philangeli was established in England with Episcopal approval, and it has spread worldwide. Members seek to become real friends with angels.

The Opus Sanctorum Angelorum ("The Work of the Holy Angels") is one of the newer Catholic movements intended to renew and bolster belief in guardian angels and to foster a collaboration between angels and humans for the glory of God, the salvation of humanity, and the regeneration of all creation.

The Opus Sanctorum Angelorum was sanctioned by Pope Paul VI in 1968, who probably was influenced by POPE PIUS XII, who advocated a renewal of devotion to angels. Other sources of inspiration are the experiences of Padre Pio, and the appearance of the angel in Fatima, Portugal (see MARIAN APPARITIONS).

The goal of the Opus is a divine conjugation—a *hieros gamos*—between humanity and the angelic kingdom. The Opus teaches that the guardian angel will "ward off danger to body and soul; prevent Satan's suggestion of evil thoughts; remove occasion of sin; enlighten and instruct; offer our prayers for us; correct us if we sin; help us in the agony of death; conduct us to God or purgatory at death."

Initiates are guided by priests who are part of the Opus.

There are three phases.

In the first phase, "the Promise," initiates make a promise to God and their angels that they will love their guardian angels and will respond to their instructions when heard through the voice of conscience. The Promise is done in the presence of a priest. This initial phase lasts for one year, during which time the initiates strive to learn to hear the voice of their guardian angels.

The second phase involves a consecration to the guardian angel. The initiates participate in a candlelight ceremony in the presence of the Blessed Sacrament, in which they consecrate themselves to their "holy guardians." They pledge to become like angels, and to venerate angels, who have been given to humanity by God "in a very special way in these days of spiritual combat for the Kingdom of God." The initiates ask their angels to obtain for them "a love so strong that I may be inflamed by it."

In the third phase, the initiates participate in a ceremony of consecration to all the angel kingdom, which will enable the initiates to live in sacred communion with all things.

What the Opus accomplishes is the bringing to life of powerful psychic forces within the individual—the unmanifest creative potential.

FURTHER READING

Grosso, Michael. "The Cult of the Guardian Angel." In *Angels and Mortals: Their Co-Creative Power*, compiled by Maria Parisen. Wheaton, Ill.: Quest Books Theosophical Publishing House, 1990.

Parente, Fr. Pascal P. *The Angels: The Catholic Teaching on the Angels*. Rockford, Ill.: Tan Books and Publishers, 1973. First published 1961.

directions, angels of See NATURE SPIRITS.

Diniel

In Syriac magical rites, angel invoked to protect newborn infants, and also to bind tongues.

See CHILDBIRTH ANGELS.

Divine Wisdom See WISDOM.

djinn (genii, ginn, jann, jinn, shayatin)
In Arabic lore, a type of spirit demonized in Christianity. Like the DAIMONES, djinn are self-propagating and can be either good or evil. They possess supernatural powers and can be conjured in magical rites to perform various tasks and services. A djinnee (singular) appears as a wish-granting "genie" in many Arabic folktales such as the *Arabian Nights*.

In pre-Islamic lore, the djinn are malicious, are born of liquid fire, and are not immortal. They live with other supernatural beings in the Kaf, a mythical range of emerald mountains that encircles the earth. They like to roam the deserts and wilderness. They are usually invisible, but they have the power to shapeshift to any form, be it insect, animal, or human.

Islamic theology absorbed and modified the djinn; some became beautiful and good-natured. According to lore, they were created 2,000 years before ADAM AND EVE, and they are equal to angels in stature. Their ruler, Iblis, refused to worship Adam, and so was cast out of HEAVEN, along with his followers. Iblis became the equivalent of the devil and the followers all became DEMONS.

The djinn can be converted, as Surah 72 of the Koran indicates: "It has been revealed to me that a company of the Djinn gave ear, then they said 'we have indeed heard a Koran wonderful, guiding to rectitude.'"

King SOLOMON used a magic ring to control djinn and protect him from them. The ring was set with a gem, probably a diamond, that had a living force of its own. With the ring, Solomon branded the necks of the djinn as his slaves.

One story tells that a jealous djinee (sometimes identified as Asmodeus) stole his ring while he bathed in the Jordan River. The djinnee seated himself on Solomon's throne at his palace and reigned over his kingdom, forcing Solomon to become a wanderer. God compelled the djinnee to throw the ring into the sea. Solomon retrieved it and punished the djinnee by imprisoning him in a bottle.

According to another story, Solomon brought djinn to his crystal-paved palace, where they sat at tables made of iron. The Koran tells how the king made them work at building palaces and making carpets, ponds, statues, and gardens. Whenever he wanted to travel to faraway places, the djinn carried him there on their backs.

FURTHER READING
de Givry, Emile Grillot. *Witchcraft, Magic and Alchemy.* New York: Dover Publications, 1971. First published 1931.

Domiel (Abir Gahidrion, Dumiel)
In Jewish lore, angel who guards the sixth hall of the seventh HEAVEN. In GNOSTICISM, Domiel is an ARCHON who rules the four elements and is a PRINCE of majesty, fear, and trembling.

dominions (dominations, lords, lordships)
In the Pseudo-Dionysian hierarchy, the fourth highest order of angels, who regulate the duties of other angels and make known the commands of God. Dominions also are channels of mercy. The term *dominion* refers to "lordship," "rule," or "special meaning." Use of the term *dominions* as a class of angels occurs in apocryphal writings influenced by the New Testament passages that suggest designations of heavenly powers. For example, Ephesians 1:21 states that God has raised Christ far above "all rule and authority and power and dominion and every name that is named" and Colossians 1:16 states that in Jesus Christ all things visible and invisible in heaven and earth are created, "whether thrones or dominions or rulers or powers."

Dominion or domination (From *The Hierarchie of the Blessed Angells* by Thomas Heywood [1635])

The Testament of ADAM describes dominions as rulers over earthly kingdoms who decide the outcome of wars; in battles they are angels riding on red horses. 2 ENOCH states that when Enoch is taken to the seventh HEAVEN, he sees "an exceptionally great light, and all the fiery armies of the great archangels, and the incorporeal forces and the dominions and the ORIGINS and the AUTHORITIES, the CHERUBIM and the SERAPHIM and the many-eyed THRONES." (20:1). The Ethiopic translation of 1 Enoch refers to "angels of dominions." The Apocalypse of ZEPHANIAH sees "angels who are called lords" when he is taken to the fifth heaven.

In RUDOLPH STEINER's three-tiered structure of the angelic realm, the kyriotates may equate with dominions.

St. AUGUSTINE agreed with St. PAUL that there exist seats (THRONES), dominions, PRINCIPALITIES, and POWERS in the heavens, but he did not know specifically what they are or the differences between them.

According to AGRIPPA, dominions are associated with the air element. They help humans overcome their enemies.

In Kabbalistic lore, dominions—along with Powers and VIRTUES—form one of four triplicities of intelligible hierarchies. They are one of the ruling angelic orders of Hesed (Mercy), the fourth sephirah of the TREE OF LIFE.

Dominions are sometimes equated with HASMALIM.

FURTHER READING

van der Toorn, Karel, Bob Becking, and Pieter W. van der Horst, eds. *Dictionary of Deities and Demons in the Bible.* 2d ed. Grand Rapids, Mich.: William B. Eerdmans, 1999.

The Vision of St. Joseph (Philippe de Champaigne; reprinted courtesy of the National Gallery, London)

dreams and visions

Traditional means by which apocalyptic trips to HEAVEN and HELL take place, as well as revelations, prophecies, and messages/instructions from God. Angels serve as guides, interpreters, and messengers.

Dreams were especially important for divination and prophecy in the ancient cultures of Egypt, Babylonia, Greece, Rome, and the Middle East. The divine will was held to be constantly revealed in dreams, and incubation procedures were followed to obtain dream answers to questions. Because of the connection between dreams and idol priests (who incubated and interpreted dreams, and who also practiced MAGIC), the Israelites were warned against them. Nonetheless, God often revealed himself through dreams, sometimes using angels as the messengers.

Dreams in Judaism

The early Jews placed a high value on dreams as real experiences of the direct voice of God. The Old Testament has many examples of dreams and visions, affirming these as primary ways that a concerned God speaks to human beings to provide direction and guidance. It is often difficult to distinguish between dreams and visions, however. Some are referred to as "dreams," "night visions," and simply "visions." The recipient may "awaken" from sleep to have the vision, which may describe a lucid dream-within-a-dream. Some are clearly trance states, perhaps induced by consciousness-altering techniques such as found in MERKABAH. Descriptions such as a "vision of the night" (1 Samuel 3:5; Job 20:8; Isaiah 29:7; and Daniel 2:19 and 7:2), or "in the night I saw" (Zechariah 1:8), or "in the visions of my head as I lay in bed" (Daniel 4:13) probably refer to dreams.

These biblical dreams/visions are characterized by the voice of God (direct audition); the appearance of angels as messengers; bright lights, fire; and other-

The Angel of Dreams (Copyright 1995 by Robert M. Place; from *The Angels Tarot* by Rosemary Ellen Guiley and Robert M. Place)

worldly images of heaven and hell. These images still appear in transpersonal dreams today.

The first biblical reference to a dream is found in Genesis 15:12–16. While the prophet Abram (later renamed Abraham) is in a deep sleep, God gives him the prophecy that Abram's descendants will be enslaved in a foreign land (Egypt) for 400 years, but that they will be liberated with great possessions and return to their own land.

Abraham's grandson, JACOB, had significant dreams. Hunted by his twin brother, Esau, Jacob escapes to his uncle. En route, he has a dream of angels ascending and descending a ladder to heaven. God promises him and his descendants the land upon which he sleeps: "I will not leave you until I have done all that I promised you" (Genesis 28:15). Jacob is so awestruck by the dream that he declares the spot as "the house of

God . . . the gate of heaven." An angel again addresses Jacob in a dream in Genesis 31:11–13, instructing him to return to the land of his birth.

Jacob's son Joseph, sold into slavery in Egypt by his brothers, excels in dream interpretation, and thus gains the pharaoh's favor.

The tradition for God to address prophets through dreams is established in Numbers 12:6, when God tells MOSES, Miriam, and Aaron, "Hear my words: If there is a prophet among you, I the Lord make myself known to him in a vision, I speak with him in a dream." God goes on to say that Moses is different from other prophets, for God speaks directly ("mouth to mouth") to him. (See ARK OF THE COVENANT.)

Many other biblical prophets, patriarchs, and rulers were inspired and directed by dreams or visions, among them Samuel, Saul, SOLOMON, ELIJAH, Jeremiah, Job, ISAIAH, EZEKIEL, and DANIEL. Their experiences include the voice of God, the appearances of angels, and visions of heaven. These dreams were not experienced for personal enrichment, but were the instruments by which God speaks to the people; the prophets had a responsibility to report their dreams.

In apocalyptic literature, the dream vision is reported in a formula: the initial dream-vision is experienced; questions are raised by the percipient; and answers and interpretations are given, usually by an angelic guide. Sometimes questions are answered by additional dream-visionary experiences.

Losing contact with God through dreams was a crisis—a serious loss of power. Saul, the first king of Israel, suddenly finds that God no longer speaks to him in dreams. In desperation for guidance, he breaks his own law and hires a medium to perform necromancy, the summoning of the dead for divination. Saul seeks out the spirit of the prophet and judge Samuel.

In apocryphal Jewish-Christian texts, the action takes place within dreams and visions. The prophets/visionaries see the heavens and hells first-hand, learn the secrets of the workings of the universe, and the secret names and duties of angels, and are taken into God's presence. (See APOCRYPHA AND PSEUDEPIGRAPHA TEXTS.)

MAIMONIDES, writing in the 12th century C.E., interpreted angelic appearances in general as prophetic visions or dreams. According to Maimonides's cosmology, angels are intermediaries between God and man, but operate through the visionary imaginative plane in the human mind to convey God's wishes to the patriarchs and prophets. Maimonides explains in *Guide of the Perplexed:*

> It is all the same whether the particular passage says first
> that he saw an angel, or the phrasing implies that he

thought at first it was a human being and then in the end he realized it was an angel. Whenever it turns out in the end that what he saw, and was addressed by, was an angel, you must accept it as true that this was from the outset a prophetic vision or prophetic dream. In such a prophetic vision or prophetic dream the prophet sometimes sees God speaking to him . . . or he may see an angel who speaks to him, or hear someone speak to him without seeing anyone speaking, or he may see a human being speaking to him and afterwards he realizes that the one who spoke to him was an angel. (XLII)

Despite the importance of dreams, scholars and theologians debated their reliability: How could it be proved that a dream was true and genuinely from God, or false and the work of demons? Many authorities, including the prophet Jeremiah were skeptical of dreams. However, after centuries of debate, dreams have continued to be held in high estimation. For example, the Zohar reaffirmed dreams as a valid source of divine inspiration: "Nothing takes place in the world but what has previously been made know, either by means of a dream, or by means of a proclamation, for it has been affirmed that before any event comes to pass in the world, it is first announced in heaven, whence it is proclaimed to the world." (See KABBALAH.)

Dreams in Christianity

Initially, Christianity continued its inherited tradition of dreams and visions as a primary way in which God communicates with humans. Dreams and visions shaped the birthing and early development of Christianity. As in the Old Testament, distinctions are not always made between dreams and other kinds of visionary experiences.

Christianity begins with a visionary experience in which Zechariah is visited by the angel Gabriel and told that his elderly wife will have a son, to be named John, who will become John the Baptist (Luke 1:1–11). Later, Gabriel is sent by God to inform the virgin that she will conceive a child through the Holy Spirit (Luke 1:26–38). Her betrothed, Joseph, decides to leave her when he discovers she is pregnant. But an angel appears to him specifically in a dream and tells him to marry her, that she has conceived with the Holy Spirit, and will bear a son to be named JESUS who will "save his people from his sins" (Matthew 1:18–25). Joseph, in keeping with time-honored tradition to follow divine directives given in dreams, acts accordingly when he awakens. After Jesus is born, Joseph is again contacted by an angel through his dreams. The angel tells him to take Mary and Jesus and flee to Egypt until instructed otherwise, for King Herod will search for the child to destroy him (Matthew 2:13). Joseph fol-

lows directions; they remain in Egypt until Herod is dead. An angel appears in a dream to Joseph, telling him Herod is dead, and he should take his family and return to Israel (Matthew 2:19–20). Other passages in Matthew (2:12 and 2:22) refer to Joseph receiving warnings in dreams, but do not state the messages are delivered by angels. In light of his other dreams, it is likely they were.

Angels proclaim the birth of Jesus and direct people to where he can be found (Luke 2:9; 13). Joseph is given another dream warning him to take his family and flee to Egypt in order to save the baby Jesus from death at the hand of the jealous Herod (Matthew 2:13–14), and he is told in yet another dream to return to Israel when Herod has died and it is safe (Matthew 2:19–23).

Jesus has numerous visionary experiences during his life, some of which involved the audition of the voice of God, and which were shared by others. He encounters angels and Satan, hears the direct voice of God speaking from the heavens, and becomes filled with radiant light in a transfiguration involving the presences of Elijah and Moses. After the arrest of Jesus, Pontius Pilate's wife is warned in a dream that her husband should have nothing to do with him (Matthew 2 and 19).

Acts is full of dream/visionary experiences—in fact, all major events are marked by them. When the apostles are filled with the Holy Spirit at Pentecost (2:3–11), it is seen as a fulfillment of a prophecy in the Old Testament book of Joel: "And it shall come to pass afterward, that I will pour out my spirit on all flesh; your sons and your daughters shall prophesy, your old men shall dream dreams, and your young men shall see visions" (Joel 2:28). Saul's conversion into the evangelist PAUL is a visionary experience. Throughout his ministry, Paul is guided by nighttime visions that may have been dreams. Paul's epistles, and the book of REVELATION (attributed to John), are instructions and prophecy based upon direct visionary experience.

Though early Christians accepted dreams and visions, they also had doubts about how to discern true and false dreams. Many church fathers wrote positively about dreams and visions, among them Justin Martyr, Irenaeus, Clement of Alexandria, Origen, Tertullian, Athanasius, AUGUSTINE, John Chrysostom, Anthony, Basil the Great, Gregory of Nazianzus, Gregory of Nyssa, Ambrose, Gregory the Great, and John Cassian.

Views on dreams shifted significantly in the fourth century C.E. with St. Jerome, who translated the Bible from Greek and Hebrew into the Latin Vulgate. Jerome called himself a Christian but was an avid scholar of pagan classics. During a severe illness, he had a dream vision that changed the course of his life:

Suddenly I was caught up in the spirit and dragged before the judgment seat of the Judge; and here the light was so bright, and those who stood around were so radiant, that I cast myself upon the ground and did not dare to look up. Asked who and what I was I replied: "I am a Christian." But he who presided said: "Thou liest, thou art a follower of Cicero and not of Christ. For 'where thy treasure is, there will thy heart be also.'" Instantly I became dumb, and amid the strokes of the lash—for He had ordered me to be scourged—I was tortured more severely still by the fire of conscience, considering with myself that verse, "In the grave who shall give thee thanks?" Yet for all that I began to cry and to bewail myself, saying: "Have mercy upon me, O Lord: have mercy upon me." Amid the sound of the scourges this cry still made itself heard. At last the bystanders, falling down before the knees of Him who presided, prayed that He would have pity on my youth, and that He would give me space to repent of my error. He might still, they urged, inflict torture on me, should I ever again read the works of the Gentiles. . . .

Accordingly I made an oath and called upon His name, saying "Lord, if ever again I possess worldly books, or if ever again I read such, I have denied Thee." Dismissed, then, on taking this oath, I returned to the upper world, and, to the surprise of all, I opened upon them eyes so drenched with tears that my distress served to convince even the credulous. And that this was no sleep nor idle dream, such as those by which we are often mocked, I call to witness the tribunal before which I lay, and the terrible judgment which I feared. . . . I profess that my shoulders were black and blue, that I felt the bruises long after I awoke from my sleep, and that thenceforth I read the books of God with a zeal greater than I had previously given to the books of men.

After the realistic experience of rebuke by God and severe beating by angels, Jerome retired to the desert as a hermit for several years. He then resumed his career as scholar and biblical consultant, and headed a monastic community in Bethlehem. Despite his own dream experience, Jerome sided with skeptics and said that dreams can be a vehicle of revelation to a soul, but the impure and unrighteous can twist dreams for their own self-serving ends. He declared that the word of God could not be sought through pagan practices of dream incubation. In his translation of the Bible, Jerome placed dreams with forbidden activities such as witchcraft.

As Christianity spread, the church took an increasingly strong opposition to pagan and Jewish traditions that could hinder the authority of the new religion, especially MAGIC (including divination) and dreams and visions. The latter, dreams and visions, would still retain an accepted place, such as in the lives of saints and martyrs, in inspired instructions (see MICHAEL),

and especially in the practice of sleeping at churches and shrines in order to be healed—a form of dream incubation. But for the average person, divine experience through dreams and visions was discouraged. The church preached against dreams as dangerous instruments of deception caused by Satan and his demons. (However, in the Middle Ages, dreams of the dead were useful for promoting the doctrine of purgatory and the necessity of praying for the suffering souls there.)

Dreams and visions remain outside religious importance in mainstream Christianity, though they still are pivotal experiences. For example, Ellen G. White, the founder of the Seventh Day Adventists, had significant visionary experiences, as did JOSEPH SMITH JR., the founder of MORMONISM.

See HERMAS.

Dreams and Visions in Islam

One of the finest examples of divine inspiration from an angel in dreams occurred to MUHAMMAD (c. 570 or 571–632), the founder of Islam, who received the revelations that became the Koran in a series of angelic visions. In 610, Muhammad was 40 years old and living a life of asceticism when, one night in his dreams, the archangel Gabriel appeared and gave him the first revelation of the Koran, the holy book that contains the doctrine of Islam.

In Islamic tradition, the soul goes to Allah every night. Angels are recognized as the messengers of Allah, who enter dreams when appropriate. There are three types of dreams:

1. *Good dreams containing good tidings from Allah.* Only those who are on the true and righteous path are favored with these dreams; one need not to be a prophet or imam (teacher), however, to achieve the right closeness with Allah. In "true" dreams, Allah transmits wisdom, knowledge of the future, and tidings of reward. In "pleasing" dreams, a step lower than true dreams, a person is satisfied and happy. According to Muhammad, when the Resurrection is near, the dreams of believers will not be false.
2. *Suggestions from one's own mind.* These are mainly evil in nature and spring from desires, fantasies, and material attachments.
3. *Evil dreams caused by Satan.* These contain nightmarish or unpleasant themes or imagery—essentially any dream not liked by the dreamer. They can occur because Allah is angry with the dreamer, and devils and Satan take advantage of the situation. The traditional folk remedy is to spit three times without saliva over the left shoulder, seek refuge in Allah in prayer, and refrain from revealing the dream to anyone.

Tradition holds that while some dreams are simple and true, most dreams are of a superior code not understood by the average person; only a person specially empowered by Allah can interpret dreams.

Divine Healing in Dreams

Modern researchers of ANGELOLOGY, prayer, and healing have found anecdotal cases of dream angels being instrumental in a healing process. People who pray to be healed of an illness or problem sometimes have dreams in which angels tell them they are healed, or give them encouragement or information to help them heal.

The appearance of angels in dreams can be interpreted from different perspectives. Many societies have, since ancient times, considered dreams not to be imaginary, but to be real events in a separate reality. The early Greeks and Romans believed that the soul traveled while the body was asleep. The soul would go to otherworldly realms wherein dwelled the lesser spirits who mediated between humans and the gods. Plato called this realm "the between." Here the human soul had experiences and encounters that had the same validity as experiences had during waking life. In dreams, it was possible to meet the gods, to see the distant past or future, and to be healed of illness and disease.

In psychology angels in dreams might be explained as a manifestation of the higher self, imparting wisdom already within and known to the dreamer, but buried. The angel is an archetypal construct that makes it possible for the dreamer to access this buried wisdom.

See ARCHETYPES; DUMA; NICHOLAS FLAMEL.

FURTHER READING

Azam, Umar. *Dreams in Islam.* Pittsburgh: Dorrance Publishing, 1992.

Fox, Robin Lane. *Pagans and Christians.* San Francisco: Harper and Row, 1986.

Guiley, Rosemary Ellen. *Dreamwork for the Soul.* New York: Berkley Books, 1998.

Kelsey, Morton. *God, Dreams and Revelation: A Christian Interpretation of Dreams.* Minneapolis: Augsburg Publishing House, 1968, 1974, 1991.

Maimonides. *Guide of the Perplexed.* Abridged. Introduction by Julius Guttmann. London: East and West Library, 1952.

Dubbiel (Dubiel, Dobiel)

GUARDIAN ANGEL of Persia and accuser of Israel. Dubbiel means "bear-god." According to lore, Dubbiel became corrupted and fell along with other angels of nations, with the exception of Michael.

Duma

Angel who is the PRINCE of dreams. Duma is invoked for dream incubation, the solicitation of advice, and answers to questions in dreams. The ritual must be done only on Sunday nights and only for important and urgent matters. The invocation is: "I conjure you, Duma, prince of dreams, in the name of the Almighty God, that you come to me this night and answer my question. And when you wish to indicate good or evil, show me for evil: priests and churches, wells, cisterns, caves, and graves; but for a favorable sign show me: schools, synagogues, open books, and scholars studying them; and let me not forget the apparition."

See DREAMS AND VISIONS.

Dumah (Douma)

Angel of silence, the stillness of death, and vindication; the tutelary spirit of Egypt. In Aramaic, Dumah's name means "silence." He is a prince of HELL; in Babylonian legend he guards the 14th gate. The Zohar describes him as a chief of Gehenna (hell) with tens of thousands of ANGELS OF DESTRUCTION under his command, and 12,000 myriads of attendants whose job it is to punish sinners. A small reference in the Talmud holds that even sinners get a day of rest on the Sabbath and are released to roam the earth. At evening, Dumah herds them back into hell. In a midrash, Dumah releases all souls of the dead, not just sinners, to the earth each evening for the first year after their deaths.

dynameis

Greek term for "powers" used as an appellation for supernatural powers and deities, and also to describe the powers of spirits, gods, stars, the elemental forces and forces of nature, and the Holy Spirit. References to dynameis are sometimes translated as the POWERS class of angels. The term also is applied to DEMONS: the DYNAMEIS of HELL and Satan. Plato uses the term to describe "supernatural powers." Aristotle equates DAIMONES (spirits or INTELLIGENCES) with dynameis, or "powers." In the New Testament, God's power (dynamis) is transmitted through Christ, who stands above all other powers, celestial and earthly.

The term "dynamis" also refers to the power to effect miracles or MAGIC, and the results of miracle power and magical power.

See PRINCIPALITIES.

FURTHER READING

Luck, Goerg. *Arcana Mundi: Magic and the Occult in the Greek and Roman Worlds.* Baltimore: Johns Hopkins University Press, 1985.

van der Toorn, Karel, Bob Becking and Pieter W. van der Horst, eds. *Dictionary of Deities and Demons in the Bible.* 2d ed. Grand Rapids, Mich.: William B. Eerdmans, 1999

Eae

In the testament of SOLOMON, one of the angels who thwarts Katanikotael, one of the DEMONS of the DECANS OF THE ZODIAC.

eating and angels See ANGELS.

eblis See IBLIS.

Eiael

Angel who rules the occult sciences. Eiael is one of the 72 angels of the SCHEMHAMPHORAE.

Eisheth Zenumim (Iseth Zenumim) See ANGELS OF PROSTITUTION; SAMUEL.

El

One of the Hebrew NAMES of God; also the name of an angel. El is one of the most powerful names of God and is used frequently in invocations, AMULETS, TALISMANS, and MAGIC. According to the Talmud, reciting sentences beginning and ending in "El" protects one from being harmed by any enchantment or sorcery. "El" is affixed to the end of many angel names; "-iel" means "of God."

El is one of the divine names of Chesed, the fourth sephirah of the TREE OF LIFE.

El is an angel who impregnated a mortal a woman, who bore two children, Shahar and Shalim.

The plural of El is ELOHIM.

See ANGEL OF THE LORD; ELYON.

El Roi See ANGEL OF THE LORD.

Eleazar of Worms See SEFER RAZIEL.

Eleleth (Heleleth)

In GNOSTICISM, one of four great LUMINARIES who surround the self-begotten, the savior, or God. The other three are Oroiael, Daveithe, and Harmozy.

elementals

A lower order of spirit beings that is the life-force in the natural world and whose task it is to maintain harmony. In occult lore, elementals are said to govern minerals, plants, and animals; the four elements of earth, air, fire, and water; the planets, stars, signs of the zodiac; and hours of the day and night. They are ruled by angels. Most are viewed as benevolent, though some are malicious or tricksterlike in behavior.

The Neoplatonic Greeks grouped elementals according to the four elements of life. Earth elementals are gnomes, ruled by the angel Ariel; air elementals are sylphs, ruled by Cherub; water elementals are undines, ruled by Tharsis; and fire elementals are salamanders, ruled by Nathaniel or Seraph. In the fifth century, Proclus added a fifth group which lives beneath the ground, and in the eleventh century, Psellus added a sixth group, the *lucifugum,* which means "fly-the-light."

The term "elemental" is applied to a broad range of spirit beings, also including elves, who live in the woods and along the seashore, and household spirits such as brownies, goblins, bogles and kobolds, and FAIRIES.

Elementals appear in a variety of forms. Some are humanlike, such as the dwarfish gnomes. Sylphs appear as butterflies and undines as waves. Some are more like angels and are amorphous shapes of white light surrounded by flowing, colorful auras of energy. British Spiritualist Grace Cooke said that elementals enjoy human company, can understand human speech, and respond to music. They have their own karmic evolutions, progressing toward higher forms of life.

British medium Geraldine Cummins channeled information about elementals, purportedly from the deceased Frederic W. H. Myers, one of the founders of the Society for Psychical Research in London. In automatic writing, "Myers" described elementals as the essence which emanates from forms of life such as trees and plants, and which coalesces into a form perceived by the human mind as a sprite.

See DEVAS; FINDHORN; NATURE SPIRITS.

FURTHER READING

Hall, Manly P. *Paracelsus: His Mystical and Medical Philosophy.* Los Angeles: The Philosophical Research Society, 1964.

Steiner, Rudolph. *The Influence of Spiritual Beings upon Man.* Spring Valley, N.Y.: Anthroposophic Press, 1961.

Eligor (Abigor)

One of the FALLEN ANGELS and 72 spirits of SOLOMON. Eligor is a duke who appears as a goodly knight carrying a lance, pennon, and scepter. He discovers hidden objects, kindles love and lust, and procures the favor of lords and knights. He marshal armies and causes war. He has 60 legions under his command.

Elijah

Prophet who is translated directly to heaven in a fiery chariot. The name Elijah means "my God is Jehovah." Elijah is the forerunner of the Messiah, preparing the

way by spreading repentance, peace, and justice among Israelites.

The biblical story of Elijah is told in 1 Kings and 2 Kings. Elijah is a prophet in Israel during the reign of King Ahab. Ahab and his foreign wife, Jezebel, sin by worshiping Baal and killing God's prophets. God sends Elijah to warn of punishment by drought.

Elijah departs the land, but returns in three years to find the drought still going on. Ahab accuses him of causing it. Elijah challenges the king's prophets to prove that their god, Baal, is real. Both they and Elijah will prepare sacrifices on Mt. Carmel. Whichever God sets the sacrifices afire will be declared the real god.

The prophets of Baal dance, pray, and ritually cut themselves all day, but nothing happens to their sacrifice. When Elijah prays, God sends fire and burns his sacrifice. The people turn on the priests of Baal, and they and Elijah slay them.

The killings infuriate Jezebel, and Elijah flees for his life. After a day of wandering, he sits down and

Angel bringing food to Elijah (Gustav Doré)

asks God to let him die. He sleeps, during which an ANGEL OF THE LORD appears and tells him to arise and eat. Elijah awakes to find a jar of water and a cake baked on hot stones. The angel urges him to eat and drink more in preparation for his journey. The food and water last him for 40 days and nights as he journeys to Mount Horeb. God tells Elijah that he has much work to do: He must anoint a new king, and train the prophet Elisha to carry on his work.

Ahab is later killed in battle, and his son Ahaziah succeeds him to the throne.

In 2 Kings 2:9–11, Elijah passes his role to Elisha in a dramatic scene. He strikes the waters of the Jordan River with his rolled-up mantle, causing them to part. The two cross. A chariot of fire and horses descends from the sky, separating the two. It takes Elijah to heaven in a whirlwind.

In Malachi 4:5–6, the prophet Malachi foretells the return of Elijah. In the New Testament, it is inferred that JESUS is "Elijah, who is to come" (Matthew 11:13). In Luke 9:28–33, Jesus, on the Mount of Transfiguration, appears to his disciples in a vision along with MOSES and Elijah.

In rabbinic lore, Elijah is credited with being an angel from his beginnings; he becomes Sandalphon, the angel of prayer, in heaven. He also serves as a guide for the souls of the dead: he stands at the crossways of Paradise and helps the righteous find heaven. In midrashim, Elijah often is synonymous with the prophet ENOCH, who also translated directly to HEAVEN, and became the angel Metatron.

Elijah translating to heaven in a fiery chariot driven by an angel, from a 19th-century Bible (Author's collection)

In Kabbalistic lore, the ANGEL OF DEATH is not happy with Elijah's translation, insisting that humans must die under his jurisdiction. God tells the angel that Elijah is not like other men, and can even replace the angel of death if challenged to do so. Elijah and the Angel of Death confront each other, but God holds Elijah back to prevent him from destroying the Angel of Death. God instructs Elijah to be the guardian of his children and to make himself known as God's messenger throughout the world. Elijah then receives the name Sandalphon.

In Talmudic lore, Elijah is a champion of the poor, losers, and victims.

As the forerunner of the Messiah, Elijah will give three proclamations in Israel three days prior to the Messiah's appearance, according to Jewish lore. The archangel Michael will blow a trumpet, and Elijah will appear and introduce the Messiah. During the reign of peace, Elijah will be one of eight princes in the Messiah's cabinet.

Apocalypse of Elijah

The Apocalypse of Elijah is a composite work written between the first and fourth centuries C.E. It is not typical of the apocalyptic style in that it is not a revelation transmitted by an angel to a prophet; rather, it is the "word of the Lord" delivered to the supposed author, who is identified simply as a "son of man." It draws upon the book of REVELATION. The text mentions two angels by name, Gabriel and Uriel, and also refers to the prophets Elijah and Enoch. The text discusses the final judgment, the punishment of sinners, and the rewards of the righteous who follow Christ. It describes the Antichrist and also contains a homily on the benefits of fasting and prayer.

The apocalypse opens with the call to the author/prophet, in which the Lord directs him to ask the people why they sin against the Lord God. God says he will have mercy upon the people, for he sent his son to the world to save them from the captivity of the age. God did not even inform an angel, an archangel, or any principality about his plans to send his son to the world; he changed himself to be like a man. The faithful will be rewarded and will have the Lord's name written upon their foreheads and sealed on their right hands. The Lord exhorts people to fast and says that those whose fasts are not pure anger both him and the angels. A pure fast releases sin, heals diseases, and casts out DEMONS. As for prayer, those who are not single-minded in devotion to the Lord are mistrusted by the angels.

The Lord discusses all of the evils that will befall the world under the Antichrist. The evil one will be recognized by his appearance: "a skinny-legged young lad, having a tuft of gray hair at the front of his bald head. His eyebrows will reach to his ears. There is a leprous bare spot on the front of his hands" (3:15–16). The Antichrist will have the ability to transform himself in appearance and age, but the signs of his head will not be able to change and therefore he will always be recognized. The Antichrist will deceive people by imitating all of the miracles of Christ except for one: he will not be able to raise the dead.

The true Christ will come surrounded and crowned by doves. He will walk in the clouds with the sign of the cross leading him, shining like the sun from one horizon to the other. His multitudes of angels will surround him.

Elijah and Enoch will oppose the Antichrist. After seven days of fighting, the prophets will lie dead in the public marketplace for three-and-on-half days. On the fourth day they will rise up and denounce the Antichrist, who will not be able to prevail over them. He will then vent his fury on the saints.

Sixty righteous ones will be martyred by being burned on altars. Christ will send to them 64,000 angels, each of whom has six wings. They will take the martyrs to heaven upon their wings. Gabriel and Uriel will become a pillar of light leading them into the holy land. (This is reminiscent of the ANGEL OF THE LORD who manifests as a pillar of fire and a pillar of cloud to help MOSES lead the Jews to the promised land in the exodus from Egypt.) The righteous ones will be clothed in white and will eat from the Tree of Life in Paradise.

The salvation of the righteous martyrs will be followed by great destruction upon the earth. The sun will darken, birds will fall dead, and the seas will dry up. Knowing his time is at end, the Antichrist will make one final campaign against the saints, pursuing them upon his fiery wings. Angels will come down from heaven and fight him with swords. The wrathful Lord will send fire out upon the earth to consume all the sinners and devils. The last judgment will be rendered.

Elijah and Enoch will receive their spiritual bodies and will kill the Antichrist, who will dissolve in their presence like ice in a fire. He and all of his followers will be cast into the bottom of an abyss, which will close over them.

Christ and his saints will burn the earth. Christ will spend 1,000 years upon it and create a new heaven and a new earth devoid of devils. Christ will rule with his saints, who ascend and descend (reminiscent of the ladder of angels dreamed by JACOB) in the company of angels.

FURTHER READING
Charlesworth, James H., ed. *The Old Testament Pseudepigrapha.* Vols. 1 and 2. New York: Doubleday, 1983, 1985.

Margolies, Morris B. *A Gathering of Angels.* New York: Ballantine, 1994.

Elim (alim,'elim)

The proper name of an angel, and the name of a high order of angel whose name means "mighty ones" or "gods." The term *elim* in the Bible has been translated in different ways: in Exodus 15:11 and Daniel 11:36 it is "gods;" in Psalms 29:1 it is "heavenly beings;" and in Psalms 89:7 it is "holy ones." In 3 Enoch 14:1–3, the PRINCES of the elim (alim) order, along with the princes of the ERELIM and TAPSARIM, pay homage to Metatron.

Elim is the proper name of the guardian angel of Libbeus the Apostle. Elim also is a divine name answering to the numbers of the moon.

Elohim

A Hebrew name for Yahweh and the name of an angelic order. As a proper name, Elohim denotes God's anodrogynous nature. It is a divine name of Binah (Intelligence/Understanding), the third sephirah of the TREE OF LIFE, and also Tipareth (Beauty), the sixth sephirah. Elohim implies a plurality of forces and is used in Genesis in conjunction with the act of creation. Elohim Chaim (Chayim) is the "Living God."

The angelic order of the elohim ranks seventh in importance, and it is the order by which God produces vegetables. They rule Netzach (Victory), the seventh sephirah of the Tree of Life, ruled by the archangel Haniel. The elohim are sometimes equated with PRINCIPALITIES.

See EL.

Elyon (Elion)

A Hebrew name of God and also the name of an angel. Elyon means "Supreme or Most High."

Elyon is one of the MINISTERING ANGELS, and he was invoked by MOSES to cause hail to rain down on Egypt during the plagues. He also is MELCHIZEDEK, whom ABRAHAM identified with Yahweh. Elyon is frequently invoked in magical rituals.

See ANGEL OF THE LORD.

Emmanuel

In the Testament of SOLOMON, the angel who thwarts the Lion-Shaped Demon and the legions of demons under his command. Emmanuel's name means "God with us." Emmanuel also is the angel of Malkuth, the tenth sephirah of the TREE OF LIFE. The name refers as well to Christ, the Son of God.

Though not named in the Bible, Emmanuel is considered to be the ANGEL OF THE LORD who appears in the furnace of King Nebuchadnezzar. DANIEL 3:13–30 tells how the king summons three men, Shadrach, Meshach, and Abednego, and sentences them to be burned alive in his furnace for their refusal to worship his pagan gods and idols. The furnace is heated seven times hotter than normal, and the three men, bound in their clothing, are cast into it. The fire is so hot that the king's men near the furnace are killed. But Shadrach, Mesach, and Abednego are then seen walking loose in the flames, unharmed, accompanied by a fourth and unknown man who has the appearance "like a son of the gods." The three men are pulled out, and they and their God are honored by the king.

In other angel lore, Emmanuel is said to be the son of an angel and a human woman. In MAGIC he is conjured under the third Seal. In GEMATRIA, his name adds up to 644.

Empyrean

In Christian ANGELOLOGY, the residence of God and the angels.

See DANTE ALIGHIERI; FIRMAMENT; MILTON, JOHN.

encounter phenomenon See EXTRATERRESTRIALS.

Enepsigos

DEMON in the shape of a woman with two heads. Enepsigos has countless other names and can shapeshift into a goddess and other forms. Most often she takes three forms because she hovers near the moon (which has three forms: waxing, full, and new). Enepsigos is conjured up as Kronos, Greek god of time, and is thwarted by the angel Rathanael.

In the Testament of Solomon, Enepsigos is bound by King SOLOMON with a triple-link chain and is made to prophesy. She predicts that Solomon's kingdom will be divided and the Temple of Jerusalem will be destroyed by the kings of the Persians, Medes, and Chaldeans. The tools in the temple will be used to serve other gods. The vessels used to trap all the demons will be broken by men, and the freed demons will go throughout the world, leading men astray until the Son of God is crucified. This Son of God shall be born of a virgin and shall be the only one to hold power over demons. His name is Emmanuel.

Solomon does not believe Enepsigos and has her bound in unbreakable chains. But later he witnesses the truth of part of her prophecy, when he is led astray by women to worship pagan gods, and his kingdom is divided by God.

See INCANTATION BOWLS.

Enoch

Patriarch taken to HEAVEN on the orders of God, and transformed into the great angel Metatron. Enoch's detailed descriptions of the heavens and HELLS he encountered, and the angels therein, are given in three versions of the apocalyptic book of Enoch, also called the "Chronicles of Enoch," part of the MERKABAH literature. The book of Enoch offers a rich ANGELOLOGY. It also was a significant influence on the development of doctrines in the New Testament.

Historical Background

According to Genesis (5:18–24), Enoch was of the seventh generation from Adam in the long-lived lineage of patriarchs. His father, Jared, was 162 years old when he was born, and he lived for another 800 years. Enoch fathered Methuselah at age 65, and lived another 300 years before translating directly to heaven. Genesis 5:24 says that "Enoch walked with God; and he was not, for God took him."

The book of JUBILEES, a Jewish text from the second century B.C.E., says that Enoch was "conducted into the Garden of Eden in majesty and honor, and behold there he writes down the condemnation and judgment of the world."

The Enochian manuscripts were written by anonymous authors between the second century B.C.E. and sixth century C.E. (or much later according to some scholars) in Hebrew and possibly Aramaic; translations were made into Greek, Ethiopic, and Slavonic. The writings carried great authority. Tertullian, a Roman Christian theologian of the late first and early second centuries C.E., said the book was divinely inspired, and it had either been preserved by NOAH on the ark during the Flood or had been reproduced by Noah through the inspiration of the Holy Spirit. ORIGEN, a second-century Christian philosopher, gave the same weight to the Enochian writings as he did to Psalms. Clement of Alexandria, a Greek theologian who converted to Christianity, and who died ca. 215, referred to the chronicles as a sacred text.

The chronicles were declared apocryphal in the fourth century by St. Jerome, a father and doctor of the church. One of the chief objections to them was that they portray a multilayered heaven that contains hells populated by fallen angels—concept contradictory to the heaven-above, hell-below model set forth in Christianity.

St. AUGUSTINE, a doctor of the church and a contemporary of St. Jerome, said in his opus *The City of God* that certain Scriptures, such as the book of Enoch, were declared apocryphal because their origins were obscure and their errors many. He also considered

Enoch to be too old to be of any value to Christianity. Augustine states:

> We cannot deny that Enoch, the seventh from Adam, left some divine writings, for this is asserted by the Apostle Jude in his canonical epistle. But it is not without reason that these writings have no place in that canon of Scripture which was preserved in the temple of the Hebrew people by the diligence of successive priests; for their antiquity brought them under suspicion, and it was impossible to ascertain whether these were his genuine writings, and they were not brought forward as genuine by the persons who were found to have carefully preserved the canonical books by a successive transmission. (XV:23)

Thus kept out of the canon, along with the book of Jude, which quotes once from it (Jude 1:9), the book of Enoch subsequently fell into obscurity for hundreds of years. Today the different manuscripts of the book are of continuing scholarly and theological interest around the world. New translations and numerous commentaries have been written.

General Story
Enoch, the son of Jared and seventh descendant of ADAM AND EVE, is taken to heaven by angels, for God has chosen him to be a scribe and a witness to the consequences of sin and the rewards of righteousness. He makes one or more journeys—accounts vary—and has many visions. He is taken to the different levels of heaven and hell, learns the mysteries of the cosmos and the celestial realms, and sees the future, including the Flood, the end of the world, and the Last Judgment. He is given a heavenly body of light and shown the books of knowledge.

After these revelations, Enoch is sent back to earth in order to pass on the teachings to his sons and others. God then takes Enoch back into heaven. In some accounts God transforms him into Metatron, giving him 365,000 eyes and 36 pairs of wings. One of his functions as Metatron is to be the scribe of heaven.

1 Enoch
1 Enoch, also called the Ethiopic Book of Enoch, is the oldest of the three Enochian writings, and was authored between the second century B.C.E. and the first century C.E. Scholars disagree as to whether it was originally written in Hebrew or Aramaic; it may have been composed in both. It is a composite work created in Judea, predating the Dead Sea Scrolls (see QUMRAN TEXTS). It was known to Jews, early Christians, and Essenes. 1 Enoch was important in the early church, and it was cited by numerous church fathers and

philosophers as well as the authors of other apocalyptic works, such as the Assumption of MOSES, Testaments of the Twelve Patriarchs, 4 EZRA and 2 BARUCH, as well as JUBILEES. The oldest copies of 1 Enoch date only to the 15th century; earlier copies were lost or destroyed.

1 Enoch influenced the language and thought of the New Testament, such as the doctrines of the nature of the Messiah and Son of Man, eschatology, demonology, and the messianic kingdom. In Ethiopian Christian theology, it shaped the ideas that Satan and his minions are equally responsible for the Fall, and that good angels are active in our defense.

1 Enoch has 107 chapters that are divided into five books:

THE BOOK OF THE WATCHERS (CHAP. 1–36)
The first book opens with the prophecy of the fall of the WATCHERS, their judgment, and the destruction of all wicked ones. It describes how the Watchers, led by Semyaza, take human wives, beget giants (see NEPHILIM), and corrupt humans. Azazel teaches them the arts of metals, weaponry, dying, textiles, chemistry, sciences, herbology, magic, astrology, deception, and so on. Michael, Gabriel, and Surafel notice the resulting corruption, adultery, and bloodshed on earth and hear the people's prayers for help. They appeal to God.

God issues instructions to the angels. He sends Asuryal (Asuriel) to the son of Lamech NOAH) to warn him of the coming destruction of the earth and the Flood. He sends Raphael to bind Azazel and cast him into darkness. He sends Gabriel to destroy the children of adultery an expel the children of the Watchers. He sends Michael to tell Semyaza that the Watchers will be punished; they and all who are corrupt and unjust will be destroyed.

In a dream vision (see DREAMS AND VISIONS) Enoch attempts to intercede on behalf of the fallen angels. He warns Azazel of God's wrath, and the angels are frightened. But God tells Enoch that the prayers of the angels will not be heard. Their punishment is that they will not ascend into heaven for all eternity but shall remain imprisoned inside the earth.

In another vision Enoch is take into heaven, where he beholds fiery CHERUBIM and is taken before God, who is a brilliant shining being on a throne. God tells Enoch not to be frightened and explains to him why the Watchers and their children must be punished.

Enoch is taken on a heavenly tour by angels. He is shown the foundations of the earth and the FIRMAMENT of heaven. He is told the names of the holy archangels: Suruel (Uriel), Raphael, Raguel, Michael, Saraqael, and Gabriel.

Enoch takes a second journey to heaven. He is shown a terrible place where the fallen angels will be imprisoned forever. He is shown another place where the souls are gathered until the judgment day. Michael takes Enoch to the Tree of Life involved in the fall of ADAM AND EVE. The fragrance of this tree and its fruit will be given to the righteous. Enoch travels to the four directions.

BOOK OF THE SIMILITUDES (CHAP. 37–71)

Enoch is carried by whirlwinds into the ultimate ends of the heavens. He is told about the coming judgment of the wicked and is shown the heavenly home of the righteous. He beholds multitudes of angels—a hundred thousand times a hundred thousand, 10 million times 10 million—standing before the glory of the Lord of the Spirits. He sees all the cosmic secrets in heaven: the mysteries of lightning and thunder, the elements, the sun, and the stars and planets. Those who deny the name of the Lord will not ascend into heaven.

Enoch meets the Son of man, who has existed before time and before the creation of the world. He is like the angels and full of grace. The angels tell Enoch that the Son of man shall be sent to depose kings from their thrones, and that the righteous will be saved in his name. The unrepentant shall perish. The righteous dead shall be resurrected.

Enoch sees angels preparing iron chains of great weight for the imprisonment of the fallen angels. The ANGEL OF PEACE says that Michael, Raphael, Gabriel, and Phanuel will seize the fallen ones, bind them, and cast them into a furnace of fire. Flood waters shall be opened upon the earth to destroy the wicked.

Enoch prophesies God's promise to Noah that his seed will be strengthened forever upon the face of the earth. Angels are involved in the construction of an ark of wood and they protect it against the floodwaters.

Enoch is shown a valley full of turbulent sulfurous water where fallen angels will be punished. The water will be like poison to the bodies of the angels. Michael discusses the judgment with Raphael. The names and sins of the fallen angels are enumerated.

In another vision Enoch is carried off in spirit to the heaven of heavens. There he sees a structure of crystal between crystal tongues of living fire. It is encircled by rivers of living fire. The SERAPHIM, cherubim, OPHANIM, and countless myriads of angels are present to guard the throne of God's glory. Enoch beholds the Antecedent of Time: his head is white and pure like wool and his garment is indescribable. Enoch falls on his face to worship him. An angel tells him he is born in righteousness and the Antecedent of Time will not forsake him. He shall have peace forever and ever.

THE BOOK OF THE ASTRONOMICAL WRITINGS (CHAP. 72–82)

In this book, Enoch describes in detail the workings of the cosmos that are revealed to him: the sun, the moon, the winds and elements, the stars and constellations, the four directions, and all astronomical laws.

Enoch is instructed by the angels to reveal his experiences to his son Methuselah. Enoch shall be allowed to stay with his son for one year in order to write down his revelations and deliver warnings of God's judgment. In the second year he shall be taken away from the people.

THE BOOK OF THE DREAM VISIONS (CHAP. 83–90)

Enoch relates to Methuselah all the visions he has ever experienced, including those before the time of his marriage. Couched in symbols of animals, the visions relate history including the Flood, the exodus of the Jews from Egypt, their arrival in Canaan, the building of the temple of Jerusalem, the two kingdoms of Israel and Judah, the destruction of Jerusalem, the return of the Jews from exile, the Maccabean revolt, and the establishment of the messianic kingdom.

THE BOOK OF THE EPISTLE OF ENOCH (CHAP. 91–107)

Enoch warns his children about the consequences of sin. He foretells the coming oppression and trials, and how a great plague will be visited upon the earth by the wrathful Lord. Sinners will be judged and thrown into eternal fire and the righteous shall be rewarded with eternal glory. The eternal judgment will be executed by the angels. The first heaven shall pass away, and a new heaven shall appear. Enoch admonishes his children to follow the ways of the righteous, and he describes the many woes that will befall the sinners. He says, "I swear unto you that in heaven the angels will remember you for good before the glory of the Great One; and your names shall be written before the glory of the Great One. Be hopeful, because formerly you have pined away through evil and toil. But now you shall shine like the lights of heaven and you shall be seen, and the windows of heaven shall be opened for you. Your cry shall be heard."

Methuselah's son Lamech fathers a son, Noah. Lamech is distressed because the infant looks like an angel. Enoch assures him that Noah has been born righteous and is the one who shall survive the coming Deluge.

The book ends with the reassurance that the righteous will be seated on a throne of honor in heaven.

2 Enoch

2 Enoch, also called The Slavonic Apocalypse of Enoch, is a text of mysterious origins. It probably dates to the late first century C.E., although some scholars think it was written in the Middle Ages because it exists only in

Slavonic. Most Slavonic manuscripts of this nature were translated from Greek, and no Greek text for 2 Enoch has been found. The Slavonic text exists in 20 manuscripts of varying lengths and completeness. The oldest of these manuscripts dates to the 14th century.

2 Enoch covers the events in the life of Enoch to the beginning of the Flood, and it includes the story of the birth and ascension of MELCHIZEDEK. It describes Enoch's journey to the seven heavens, which takes place when Enoch is 365 years old.

Enoch relates that one day when he is asleep on his couch, a "great distress" comes into his heart, which he cannot understand. Two huge beings appear before him:

> And there appeared to me two men, exceedingly big, so that I never saw such on earth; their faces were shining like the sun, their eyes too were like a burning light [lamps], and from their lips was fire coming forth with clothing and singing of various kinds in appearance purple, their wings were brighter than gold, their hands whiter than snow.

Enoch is frightened, but the angels call him by name and assure him to fear not, for they have been sent by God to take him into heaven. They bear him up on their wings to the clouds. Enoch is shown seven heavens with seven corresponding earths, all united to each other by hooks. Beyond the seventh heaven are three more heavens. The 10 heavens are:

FIRST HEAVEN
Ruled by Gabriel, this heaven is the one closest to earth, and it contains the winds and the clouds. The angels who live here are astronomers and rule the stars and heavenly bodies. There also are angels who are guardians of ice, snow, flowers, and dew.

SECOND HEAVEN
The second heaven is ruled by Raphael and is a dark penal area where FALLEN ANGELS await judgment. They are 200 myriads of attendants to the Watchers, who are imprisoned in the fifth heaven. Enoch says his guiding angels

> showed me darkness, and there I saw prisoners hanging, watched, awaiting the great and boundless judgment, and these angels were dark-looking, more than earthly darkness, and incessantly making weeping through all hours.

Enoch is told that these prisoners are "God's apostates," fallen angels who have turned away from God with their prince, who is fastened in the fifth heaven. The fallen angels ask Enoch to pray for them, but he wonders how he, a mere mortal man, can do for angels what angels are supposed to do for humankind.

THIRD HEAVEN
The third heaven is ruled by Anahel and is a land of contrasts. One part of this heaven, the northern section, is actually hell, ice cold and sulfurous, filled with torturing angels who punish the evil souls who reside there. The condemned include those who dishonor God, sin against nature, and practice enchantments and witchcraft. However, the rest of this heaven is an Eden-like garden where manna (see ANGEL BREAD) is made and the souls of the holy—those who are righteous and compassionate—reside. Angels of light watch over this heaven.

FOURTH HEAVEN
The fourth heaven, under the jurisdiction of Archangel Michael, contains Holy Jerusalem and its Temple, all made of gold, surrounded by rivers made of milk, honey, wine, and oil. The Tree of Life is to be found in this heaven, as well as the sun and the moon. Here Enoch hears the singing of angels:

> In the midst of the heavens I saw armed soldiers, serving the Lord, with tympana and organs, with incessant voice, with sweet voice, with sweet and incessant voice and various singing, which is impossible to describe, and which astonishes every mind, so wonderful and marvelous is the singing of those angels, and I was delighted listening to it.

Enoch also sees the workings of the sun, moon, and celestial bodies. The chariot of the sun carries dew and heat for the earth and is accompanied by 8,000 stars and 150,000 angels during the day and by 1,000 angels at night. In front of the chariot are 100 six-winged angels of flaming fire. There are also numerous PHOENIXES and CHALKYDRI, who pull the chariot.

FIFTH HEAVEN
The fifth heaven is another prison, a fiery ravine where 200 myriads of huge Watchers are imprisoned with their leader Satanail (Satan). They are dejected, miserable, and silent, and they perform no liturgy. Enoch urges them to perform the liturgy so that they will not enrage God to his limit. The Watchers respond and burst into song in unison. The scene, says Enoch, is piteous and touching.

SIXTH HEAVEN
The sixth heaven has seven brilliant, scholarly angels who study astronomy, nature, and the human race. They are the archangels who govern the angels of the cycles and functions of nature: the seasons, the calendar, the rivers and seas, the fruits of the earth, the grass, and so forth. The archangels also govern celestial

speech, and they harmonize all existence in the heavens and on earth.

There also are angels who record all the lives and deeds of every human soul, to set forth before God.

SEVENTH HEAVEN

The seventh heaven is a place of exceptionally great light. Enoch sees the higher orders of angels, such as the THRONES, CHERUBIM, SERAPHIM, ORIGINS, AUTHORITIES, OPHANIM, and DOMINIONS, as well a "fiery troops of great ARCHANGELS." The angelic hosts bow down before the Lord, singing his praises. Enoch is frightened, but his guides tell him to be brave. He is shown a glimpse of God in the tenth heaven.

Enoch's two guides leave him at the end of the seventh heaven, however, and he falls down terrified. Gabriel appears before him, catches him up as though a leaf in the wind, and transports him higher.

EIGHTH HEAVEN

In the eighth heaven, called Muzaloth, Enoch sees the "changer of the seasons, of drought, and of wet, and of the twelve signs of the zodiac."

NINTH HEAVEN

The ninth heaven, called Kuchavim, holds the heavenly homes of the twelve signs of the zodiac.

TENTH HEAVEN

Michael escorts Enoch to the tenth heaven, where he beholds the face of God. It is

> like iron made to glow in fire, and brought out, emitting sparks, and it burns.
>
> Thus I saw the Lord's face, but the Lord's face is ineffable, marvelous and very awful, and very, very terrible.
>
> And I cannot tell the quantity of his many instructions, and various voices, the Lord's throne very great and not made with hands, nor the quantity of those standing round him, troops of cherubim and seraphim, nor their incessant singing, nor his immutable beauty, and who shall tell of the ineffable greatness of his glory?

God instructs Michael to "take Enoch from out of his earthly garments, and anoint him with my sweet ointment, and put him into the garments of my Glory." The oil is like sweet dew, smells like myrrh, and is like the glittering rays of the sun. Enoch takes on a shining appearance like the angels around him.

God summons the angel Vrevoil (Vretiel or Pravuil), "whose knowledge was quicker in wisdom than the other archangels, who wrote all the deeds of the Lord," to bring out the books of knowledge for Enoch to read and a pen for "speed-writing."

Vrevoil teaches Enoch all the cosmic secrets, talking for 30 days and 30 nights without stopping. Enoch writes 366 books in 30 days and 30 nights with his speed-writing pen. He tells the creation story, the Fall, and that the world will end on the eighth day of creation (or after 8,000 years), when time will cease and the righteous and the wicked will be judged. He tells all the rules of morality and righteousness for humans to live by.

When Enoch is done instructing his sons and all the people, a gloom comes upon the earth, and angels come and carry Enoch into heaven for eternity. The light returns, and people find a scroll entitled, "The Invisible God."

2 Enoch relates the passing of Methuselah, his appointment of the priest Nir as the people's leader, and the miraculous birth of Nir's son, Melchizedek. It ends with a brief description of Noah surviving the Flood.

3 Enoch

3 Enoch is also called the Hebrew Apocalypse of Enoch, the Sefer Hekalot (the Book of the Palaces), and the Chapters of Rabbi Ishmael. It is written in Hebrew and it most probably dates to the fifth or sixth century C.E., although some scholars place it much later in the ninth century and even as late as the 15th century. It is the most complex and significant of the three versions of the Book of Enoch, and it is an important work in the body of MERKABAH literature.

3 Enoch is attributed to Rabbi Ishmael and constitutes an account of his journey into the highest heaven to the throne of God and revelations made to him by the great angel Metatron. Rabbi Ishmael was an historical figure, a famous Palestinian scholar who died in 132 C.E. His name was used by the unknown author(s) of 3 Enoch to lend it authority.

The text has four main sections: The first section concerns Ishmael's ascension through the layers of heaven to the throne where he participates in the reciting of the QEDUSSAH (Sanctus). The second section reveals that Ishmael is Enoch and describes his translation. The third gives an elaborate description of the angelic hierarchies, the activities of the heavenly court of law, and the performance of the Qedussah. The fourth provides a tour of heaven.

3 Enoch begins with Rabbi Ishmael's arrival at the seventh palace in the seventh heaven; there is no explanation as to how he makes his ascent. He prays to God the Holy One that Prince Qaspiel, an ANGEL OF DESTRUCTION, and the angels with him will not cast him from heaven. God summons Metatron, Prince of

the Divine Presence, to come to his aid. Metatron takes him to the camp of the SHEKINAH and presents him to the throne of glory so that he can behold the chariot. But the princes of the chariot—the SERAPHIM, CHERUBIM, and OPHANIM,—fix their fiery and disapproving gaze on him and Ishmael shrinks back in terror, stunned by the brilliance of their faces and the radiance of their eyes. God rebukes the angels and tells them to hide their eyes, calling Ishmael his beloved friend. God opens the gates of Shekinah.

Still disapproving, the angels challenge Metatron and ask him why a human has been allowed to come before the chariot. Metatron answers that Ishmael is blessed and has been chosen to minister in God's presence.

Metatron tells Ishmael that he has 70 names and once was the prophet Enoch. The angels protested Enoch's translation but God appointed him as a prince and ruler among the MINISTERING ANGELS. Metatron relates that after the Fall and before the Flood he was taken up to the highest heaven and set by God to serve the throne of glory. God bestowed many blessings and great wisdom upon him and gave him a luminous body of splendor. Metatron describes in detail how he was physically transformed from Enoch into Metatron. Metatron was made to understand the mysteries of all things and was shown the letters (of the Hebrew alphabet) by which all things are created. (See gematria; names.) Metatron's elevation in stature was opposed by scholars on earth. God reduced him by sending the angel Anapiel to strike Metatron with 60 lashes of fire.

Metatron reveals to Ishmael the names of the angelic PRINCES who guide the world. He names the seven princes of the seven heavens and the angels who serve under them, the various orders of angels and their chiefs, and how the angels must bow down when they see a higher-ranking angel. He describes the WATCHERS and their roles and many names; these Watchers, however, are not the fallen ones of 1 Enoch, but rather four great princes who are God's primary advisers in the heavenly court of law.

Metatron explains that in the seventh heaven of Arabot, God covers his face, otherwise his brilliance would cause the heaven to burst open in the middle. Standing opposite his throne are 660 thousands of myriads of angels made of flaming fire. A bridge is laid across the heaven and the ministering angels—a thousand thousand and myriads of myriads of them—cross over it to sing the Qedussah. There are 12,000 myriads of bridges, six above and six below; 12,000 myriads of rivers of fire, six above and six below; 12,000 treasuries of snow, six above and six below; and 24,000 myriads of wheels of fire, 12 above and 12 below, which sur-

round everything. At each entrance there are six MINISTERING ANGELS for every single person, and they face the paths of heaven.

Ishmael is shown how angels bathe in the RIVER OF FIRE that flows beneath the throne of Glory, and how the angels perform their devotional song, the Qeddusah. He learns how the heavenly law court functions, and how souls are judged and punished by angels of destruction.

When the heavenly law court convenes only the great angelic princes who are called YHVH by the name of the Holy One are permitted to speak. There are 72 of these princes who rule kingdoms in the world, not counting the PRINCE OF THE WORLD, who is an advocate for the world. God sits on the throne of judgment with Justice on his right, Mercy on his left, and Truth directly facing him. The angels of destruction also face him and a scribe stands below him and a scribe stands above him. Seraphim surround the throne with walls of lightning and ophanim surround them like torches; clouds of fire and flame surround them all. Beneath them are the holy creatures who bear up the throne of glory, each with three fingers, the height of each one of which is 8,766 PARASANGS. The rivers of fire flow out beneath them.

When a man comes for judgment the splendor of Mercy takes a position in front of him. The man falls prostrate and all the angels of destruction shrink from him. When God opens the book of judgment—half of which is fire and half of which is flame—the angels of destruction go out immediately to execute judgment against the wicked. Their unsheathed swords have the brilliance of lightning and pass through the world from end to end, striking fear in all the inhabitants of the world.

Metatron says that God has 496,000 myriads of camps of angels in the seventh heaven and each camp has 496,000 angels. Every angel is as tall as the Great Sea (probably the Mediterranean) and has a face like lightning, eyes like torches of fire, arms and feet like burnished bronze, and a roaring voice. They stand before the throne of glory in four rows and when time comes to say "Holy," a storm wind goes out from God.

Metatron reveals to Ishmael the cosmic letters by which all of creation comes into being, including the angels, and the cosmic power of divine names. Ishmael sees the souls of the patriarchs and the righteous, who have been raised from their graves and have ascended into heaven. They are praying to God for mercy upon the world.

3 Enoch ends with Ishmael reading all of earth's history to the end of time, including the coming of the messianic kingdom, that is inscribed on the pargod, the curtain that veils God.

FURTHER READING

Augustine, St. *The City of God*. New York: The Modern Library, 1950.

Blavatsky, H. P. *The Secret Doctrine*. Pasadena, Calif.: Theosophical University Press, 1977. First published 1888.

Charlesworth, James H., ed. *The Old Testament Pseudepigrapha*. Vols. 1 and 2. New York: Doubleday, 1983, 1985.

ephemerae

Angels who live for a day or less. The ephemerae chant the Te Deum and expire as soon as they are finished.

See MUSIC AND ANGELS.

Ephippas

Arabian wind DEMON captured by King SOLOMON. In the Testament of Solomon, the cornerstone for the Temple of Jerusalem is so heavy that all the artisans and demon laborers cannot move it. Solomon sends a servant out into the Arabian desert to capture a wind demon in a flask. Solomon is astonished when the flask has the ability to move about on its own. The demon gives his name as Ephippas, and says he is thwarted by "the one who is going to be born from a virgin and crucified by the Jews" (JESUS).

Ephippas tells Solomon that he has the ability to move mountains, carry houses from place to place, and overthrow kings. Solomon bids him to move the cornerstone. The demon says not only will he do that but he will also raise up the pillar of air from the Red Sea and place it wherever the king wants. Ephippas inserts the cornerstone at the entrance of the temple. Solomon takes this as a profound sign according to Scripture; Psalm 118:22 says: "The stone which the builders rejected has become the head of the corner."

Ephippas goes out with the demon of the Red Sea, Abezethibou, to raise up the pillar. They have been outwitted by Solomon, who binds the two of them to the pillar so that they remain suspended in air holding it up until the end of time. The pillar of air may be the same as the "pillar of cloud" referenced in the Old Testament, and it may mean the Milky Way.

Erathaol (Erathaoth)

According to ORIGEN, one of the seven great ARCHONS of GNOSTICISM along with Michael, Raphael, Gabriel, Suriel, Onoel, and Thauthabaoth. Erathaol appears in the form of a dog.

erelim (aralim, arelim, erellim)

Angels made of white fire who are 70,000 myriads strong and are equated with BENE ELOHIM, ISSIM, and THRONES. Erelim means "valiant ones" (though some sources say it is uncertain) and comes from Isaiah 33:7: "Behold, the valiant ones cry without; the envoys of peace weep bitterly."

The erelim are said to live in either the third, fourth, or fifth HEAVEN, from whence they govern grass, trees, fruit, and grain. They were involved in the capture of the sacred ark. Their chiefs are said to be either Michael or Raziel. The Maseket Aziluth names them 10th (last) in rank in the CELESTIAL HIERARCHY.

In 3 ENOCH 14:1–3, the PRINCES of the erelim, along with the princes of the ELIM and TAPSARIM, pay homage to Metatron.

The erelim are the angelic order of Binah (Intelligence), the third sephirah of the Kabbalistic TREE OF LIFE. They are under the rule of the archangel Tzaphkiel.

Eremiel (Jeremiel, Jerimiel, Remiel, Hierimiel)

In the Apocalypse of ZEPHANIAH, the great angel who presides over the abyss and Hades and cares for all of the souls who are trapped there from the end of the Flood to the present. Eremiel has a brilliant face like the sun and feet like melted bronze, and he wears a golden girdle. He serves the same function as Jeremiel in 4 EZRA to oversee the souls in Hades and forecast the coming of the new age. Similarly, Eremiel serves the same function as Ramiel in 2 BARUCH.

In the Apocalypse of Elias, Eremiel is equated with Uriel. In REVELATION, he has a strong resemblance to the Son of Man.

Eros

The Greek god of love, called Cupid by the Romans. The name Eros means "erotic love." Eros is often mistaken for an angel because of his occasional portrayal in art as an infant with wings, reminiscent of the Italian PUTTI. In mythology, Eros is the son of Aphrodite and Ares, and he is married to Psyche (soul). His brother Anteros is the god of mutual love.

Eros often is portrayed as being about to shoot an arrow of love into a mortal. Once shot, the victim falls in love with the first thing he or she sees.

In MAGIC lore, the angel of love is Theliel. The invocation of Theliel's name will secure the love of someone desired.

erotes

Winged, boyish figures prominent in Roman funerary art, and an inspiration for the IMAGES OF ANGELS.

Erotes are ministers of the dead, and they help to transport the souls to the land of the dead or the Chris-

Winged Eros served as a model for angel art (Reprinted courtesy of U.S. Library of Congress)

tian HEAVEN. They are based on the myth of Psyche (soul), who marries Eros (erotic love). They function as "eros psychophoros," or escorts of the soul. Sometimes they are called GENII comparable to the DAI-MONES, though the association is not entirely accurate).

Erotes were common on sarcophagi and funerary altars into the early centuries post-Christ. They were portrayed in pairs, either standing or hovering, and carrying one of three items: a gorgoneion, or Minerva's shield with the severed head of the Gorgon, which was believed to be a powerful AMULET against evil; an inscribed tablet; or an image of the deceased. Typically they were shown nude, with mantles reaching down to the feet.

Erotes often were depicted along with VICTORY, another early inspiration for the winged angel. They also were associated with the winged Roman goddess Aeternitas (Eternity), who functioned as a psychopomp to the dead.

See EROS; PSYCHOPOMPOI.

FURTHER READING
Berefelt, Gunnar. *A Study on the Winged Angel: The Origin of a Motif.* Stockholm: Almquist and Wiksell, 1968.

excellencies

In the Life of ADAM AND EVE, angels equated with VIRTUES who appear to Eve when she gives birth to Cain. The name "excellencies" may be a translation of the Hebrew term for "partakers of the divine glory." The text says that 12 angels and two excellencies attend Eve.

exousiai

Greek term for celestial beings of authority, often equated with AUTHORITIES, DOMINIONS, POWERS, and VIRTUES. RUDOLF STEINER said exousiai are part of the CELESTIAL HIERARCHY, and he called them "Spirits of Form."

extraterrestrials (ETs)

Alien "angels." Since the advent of ufology around the time of World War II, hypotheses have been advanced that biblical descriptions of angels, and other ancient writings relating to shining beings and gods who come from the sky, were referring to extraterrestrial visitors from space. It is argued that advanced beings from other planets would have seemed godlike to earlier peoples, and their high-tech spacecraft would have been described in such nontechnical terms as "flying disks" and "wheels."

As a social phenomenon, ET encounters, which are reported worldwide, are as significant as encounters with the devil or with angels, and reported sightings of the Virgin Mary throughout history.

The age of modern interest in ETs began in 1947. On June 26, a Boise, Idaho, businessman and pilot, Kenneth Arnold, sighted a chain of nine bright objects while flying over the Cascade Mountains in Washington State. He estimated their speed to be at 1,600 miles per hour. Arnold said the objects' motion resembled saucers that had been skipped over water, which gave rise to the popular term "flying saucer" to describe unidentified flying objects (UFOs).

Since then more than 70,000 sightings and encounters have been reported—probably a small fraction of the actual number. Approximately 95 percent of the cases have been explained as natural phenomena, aircraft, weather balloons, or hoaxes. The U.S. Air Force set up a project in the late 1940s to analyze UFO reports; the project ended in 1969. It was advised by J. Allen Hynek, chairman of the Astronomy Department at Northwestern University. Even though most cases appeared to have natural explanations, the minority that did not eventually led Hynek to conclude that UFOs were a reality.

Parallels have been drawn between ancient descriptions of angels and aerial gods and modern-day descriptions of encounters with extraterrestrials; many modern encounters contain religious, especially Christian, elements. Passages in the Bible involving angels have been reinterpreted in modern ufological terms.

Among the parallels cited by some ufologists are the following: Visitations by both angels and ETs are preceded by brilliant light. The visiting beings also are radiant or are clothed in radiant garments. They have large, burning eyes. They are superior to humans and travel about in the sky. Paranormal phenomena occur (telepathy, levitation, psychokinesis, out-of-body experience, etc.). Unusual physical effects occur (blindness, paralysis, heat, light, suspended animation, spontaneous healing, etc.). The beings present themselves as custodians who are always watching over the earth, know what people are doing, and can be anywhere instantaneously. The beings often seem to have a mission of imparting important information—moral codes, apocalyptic warnings—that must be disseminated to others. Sometimes people are taken away with the beings, instructed, and then returned. The visiting beings may or may not be kindly. The encounters often have a dreamlike quality.

The characteristics of ET encounters have changed over the decades. Early encounters were more likely to include benevolent, beautiful beings with angelic characteristics. Contactees who were unfamiliar with ufology interpreted visiting beings as angels. One of the most notable cases in ufology is that of Betty Andreasson Luca, who reported that her first encounter occurred in 1944 at the age of seven, involving voices and a ball of light. According to Luca, numerous subsequent encounters took place over ensuing decades, all with a broad purpose of anointing Betty as a messenger to the world. The key event took place in 1967, when several small beings came through the wall of her house. Betty, a devout Christian, assumed them to be angels. They took her aboard their saucerlike craft, where she underwent some highly symbolic and religious experiences. She entered rooms and tunnels full of crystals, and she was shown a reenactment of the phoenix myth.

Eight years elapsed before Betty reported her experience to UFO researchers. Through hypnosis, details of that and other encounters were uncovered. Betty later referred to her visitors as "ETs." However, in their communication with her they exhibit knowledge of Christianity, and they seem to approve of her Christian background. Their "message," like that of other ETs

and otherworldly beings, is to wake up humanity to its multidimensional and spiritual nature, and to warn of dire apocalyptic events that will occur if people do not respond.

Since the late 1970s another type of encounter—decidedly unpleasant—has dominated ufology. Small beings with gray, rubbery skin and large, insectlike slanted eyes (called "the Grays") reportedly abduct humans and subject them to terrifying and painful medical procedures and forced sex with other humans. They also extract semen and ova, allegedly for the purpose of creating a hybrid race of half-human, half-alien beings.

Some ufologists equate these encounters with medieval stories of encounters with demons. The sexual cross-fertilization also is reminiscent of the fallen SONS OF GOD. Some Christians hold that these ETs are diabolical and are part of Satan's FALLEN ANGELS, sent to earth to corrupt humanity and steal souls. Their warnings and their messages of "salvation" are tricks to lure people into spiritual enslavement.

One way of looking at the angel-ET connection is through the "encounter phenomenon" hypothesis, which holds that encounters with otherworldly beings —regardless of type of being or culture—share fundamental common characteristics that pertain to the psychospiritual evolution of humanity. The encounters occur in a mythic, alternate reality springing from the human unconscious. The particulars—types of beings, what happens, and so forth—take on a framework that can be accepted by the society of the moment. It is argued that ETs, with their high technology, fit our present-day mind-set.

According to the encounter phenomenon hypothesis, such encounters are need-driven, on both an individual and a collective level. Individuals may unconsciously seek an otherworldly event in order to enhance their sense of purpose and self-esteem and give direction to their lives. On a collective level, these encounters may spring from the collective unconscious in answer to very deep longings for a sense of connection to the ineffable, and for spiritual development. It is interesting that ETs deliver apocalyptic messages to people just as angels did to prophets. These harbingers of the "end times" may represent an evolutionary or paradigm shift in human consciousness. (See similarities in NEAR-DEATH EXPERIENCE.)

CARL G. JUNG considered the possibility that UFOs are truly extraterrestrial, but he emphasized their psychological implications, observing that they are "a modern myth of things seen in the sky," a direct psychological consequence of man's intense interest in space. ET encounters cut across all social, educational, and cultural lines, but so far as is known, occur only to individuals who already are aware of the possibility of ET existence and contact. Jung also said that UFOs are harbingers of collective psychic transformation. (See ARCHETYPES.)

The numerous descriptions of ETs who resemble sick and starving children—such as the Grays, who are small beings with enlarged heads, big eyes and spindly limbs—can also be placed within the context of the encounter phenomenon hypothesis. Philosopher Michael Grosso suggests that ETs are mythical projections of the Child archetype, who in myth is the bearer of extraordinary powers, the harbinger of the future and always under threat. ETs may be symptoms of a racial self-healing (human beings putting themselves on the operating table) and the emergence of a new mythology.

FURTHER READING

Bramley, William. *The Gods of Eden*. San Jose, Calif.: Dahlin Family Press, 1989.

Downing, Barry H. *The Bible & Flying Saucers*. New York: Lippincott, 1968.

Evans, Hilary. *Gods, Spirits, Cosmic Guardians: A Comparative Study of the Encounter Experience*. Wellingborough, Northamptonshire, England: The Aquarian Press, 1987.

Fowler, Raymond. *The Watchers*. New York: Bantam Books, 1990.

Godwin, Malcolm. *Angels: An Endangered Species*. New York: Simon and Schuster, 1990.

Grosso, Michael. "UFOs and the Myth of the New Age." *ReVision*, 11, no. 3 (Winter 1989): 5–13.

Guiley, Rosemary Ellen. *Harper's Encyclopedia of Mystical and Paranormal Experience*. San Francisco: HarperSanFrancisco, 1991.

Little, Gregory L. *People of the Web*. Memphis: White Buffalo Books, 1990.

Ezekiel

Jewish prophet taken to HEAVEN by CHERUBIM and THRONES. His account is one of the richest in angel lore of books included in the Bible.

Ezekiel lived in Jerusalem, and he was taken captive by the Babylonians when Nebuchadnezzar invaded in 597 B.C.E. After about four years in Babylon, he received the call to be a prophet. In numerous visions and trances, he received apocalyptic messages with themes that were common among the Jews of the day. Ezekiel preached repentance; his main prophecy was that Jerusalem would fall because of the wickedness of its inhabitants (the city did fall in 586 B.C.E.). "Thus says the Lord God" became his signature line.

The book of Ezekiel gives a dramatic description of Ezekiel's ascent to heaven:

As I looked, behold, a stormy wind came out of the north, and a great cloud, with brightness round about it, and fire flashing forth continually, and in the midst of the fire, as it were gleaming bronze. And from the midst of it came the likeness of four living creatures. And this was their appearance: they had the form of men, but each had four faces, and each of them had four wings. Their legs were straight, and the soles of their feet were like the sole of a calf's foot; and they sparkled like burnished bronze. Under their wings on their fours sides they had human hands. . . . [T]heir wings touched one another; they went every one straight forward, without turning as they went.

[E]ach had the face of a man in the front . . . the face of a lion on the right side . . . the face of an ox on the left side . . . the face of an eagle at the back . . . And their wings were spread out above; each creature had two wings, each of which touched the wing of another, while two covered their bodies. And each went straight forward; wherever the spirit would go, they went, without

Ezekiel's vision (17th c. Bear Bible)

turning as they went. In the midst of the living creatures there was something that looked like burning coals of fire, like torches moving to and from among the living creatures; and the fire was bright, and out of the fire went forth lightning. And the living creatures darted to and fro, like a flash of lightning. (1:4–14)

Ezekiel then sees four WHEELS beside each of the living creatures. They gleam like chrysolite and have rims full of eyes. They go in any direction without turning. When the living creatures rise, the wheels rise with them. When the living creatures stand still, so do the wheels. The flapping of the wings sounds like many waters, like the thunder of the Almighty.

There is a FIRMAMENT over the heads of the living creatures, and there appears a throne like sapphire, and a human likeness seated upon it, glowing like fire and surrounded by a RAINBOW. This is the glory of the Lord. Ezekiel receives a scroll, which he eats and which tastes like honey, and he also receives instructions to act as prophet. When the message is over, there is a sound of earthquakes, the cherubim rise up, and Ezekiel is deposited back among the exiles in Babylon. "And I sat there overwhelmed among them seven days," he states (3:15).

Ezekiel has other visions in which he is in the presence of God and is shown the evil ways of the Israelites. Once again he sees the winged cherubim and the whirling wheels, as well as a "man clothed in linen" who carries out the instructions of God to punish wrongdoers on earth.

The four living creatures are also referenced in REVELATION 4:7. The wheels are the THRONES, third in the highest hierarchy of angels, who carry God. Four wheels also symbolize omnidirectional ability, and the four faces of the cherubim symbolize the ability to see in all directions at once. The man in linen is described also in Daniel 10:5 and is probably a reference to an angel, perhaps the ANGEL OF THE LORD.

Ezekiel's vision forms an important part of the MERKABAH mysticism.

Apocryphon of Ezekiel

The Apocryphon of Ezekiel is a text of Jewish origin probably written in the first century C.E. and circulated to a Christian audience in the early centuries of Christianity. It survives only in five fragments written in Hebrew and Greek, the longest of which concerns resurrection and judgment. According to some scholars, the Apocryphon of Ezekiel may have originally been a midrash on the canonical Ezekiel.

The story in the longest fragment appears also in rabbinic literature and was quoted by St. Clement of Alexandria. The story goes that a king invites everyone in his kingdom except for two cripples, a lame man and a blind man, to attend a great feast. The cripples are offended and vow revenge. The lame man climbs onto the shoulders of the blind man; thus the two are able to enter into the garden of the king and eat his best fruit, or, by some accounts tear down his fruit trees. The two men are brought before the king. Each points to his handicap as proof that he could not have committed the crime. The king figures out how they did it, and he punishes them by flogging. As they are flogged the men accuse each other of being responsible for the deed. The moral of the story is that the crippled men are like body and soul: they must cooperate together in all deeds. Thus, when judgment comes, body and soul must be reunited in resurrection in order to receive their due.

FURTHER READING

May, Herbert G., and Bruce M. Metzger, eds. *The New Oxford Annotated Bible with Apocrypha*. New York: Oxford University Press, 1977.

Scholem, Gershom. *Kabbalah*. New York: Dorset Press, 1974.

eye writing See ANGEL ALPHABETS.

Ezra

Jewish priest and teacher of the Law during the exile in Babylon. King Artaxerxes gave Ezra permission to take a group of Jews back to Jerusalem. There Ezra was dismayed to find many people, including priests, had married outside the Jewish faith, and he ended many of these unions. Several apocalyptic pseudepigrapha are attributed to Ezra, in which angels assist in his visions and take him on tours of HEAVEN and HELL.

4 Ezra

4 Ezra—also known as 2 Esdras, 4 Esdras, and 5 Esdras—was written at the end of the first century C.E. by a Jewish author, probably in Hebrew or Aramaic; additional Christian chapters were added in Greek in the second and third centuries. 1 Esdras and 2 Esdras are considered part of the apocrypha. (See APOCRYPHA AND PSEUDEPIGRAPHA TEXTS.)

Ezra is called by God to admonish the Jews who sin despite God's mercies shown them. The Jews reject him and he turns to the gentiles. An angel—probably Uriel, who is later identified as his guide—shows him a vision in which the righteous receive their crowns in heaven from the Son of God. The angel commands Ezra to go and tell the people about the wonders and greatness of the Lord.

The text then describes seven apocalyptic visions shown to Salathiel, also called Ezra. The visions concern Ezra's questions about the origins of sin, the ultimate fate of sinners, those who will be the saved, and the coming of the new age. He intercedes for sinners and asks for God's mercy on them. Throughout, he is guided by Uriel. On one occasion, the angel Jeremiel comes forward when Ezra asks if he will be alive when the new age comes. Jeremiel replies, "Concerning the signs about which you ask me, I can tell you in part; but I was not sent to tell you concerning your life, for I do not know" (4:52).

In the seventh vision, Ezra is sitting beneath an oak tree when he is addressed by the voice of the Lord emanating from a bush opposite him. The voice tells him about MOSES and directs Ezra to be like Moses and reveal what he has been shown. He is to take five men as scribes and write in seclusion for 40 days. Some of the material is to be made public and some to be delivered in secret only to the wise.

Ezra does as directed. Divine inspiration pours into him like fire, and he dictates 94 books to the scribes, who write in a new script unknown to them. When he is finished, God tells him to give the first 24 books to the public and reserve the last 70 books for the wise.

Greek Apocalypse of Ezra

The Greek Apocalypse of Ezra is a Christian composition based on Jewish and Christian sources, written between the second and ninth centuries C.E. Angels figure prominently in it as guides and participants in Ezra's journeys to heaven and Tartarus (hell).

The text opens with Ezra's petition to God for a vision to see God's mysteries. That night—presumably in a dream vision—the angel Michael appears and tells Ezra to fast for 70 weeks. Ezra does as directed. The angel Raphael appears and gives him a staff, after which he fasts "twice sixty weeks." Ezra is then granted his request and sees the mysteries of God and his angels. He says he wishes to plead with God on behalf of the Christian people.

Ezra is taken up into the first heaven where a great command of angels lead him to the judgments. He sees the fates of sinners and asks God for mercy for them, but God refuses, saying they are punished as they deserve.

Michael, Gabriel, and all the apostles appear and greet Ezra. Ezra tells God that they all shall plead the case for mercy. The sins of ADAM and the punishment of SODOM AND GOMORRAH are discussed. Ezra again pleads for mercy for the sinners but God says, "How can I have mercy upon them? They gave me vinegar and gall to drink and [not then] they repented" (2:25).

Ezra asks God to reveal his CHERUBIM and show him the character of the day of judgment. He says he will never cease to argue his case on behalf of sinners. God

relates how he created men and beasts, and how men fell into corruption. The opponent of men—the Antichrist—will rise up from Tartarus and deceive men. Ezra says he wants to see Tartarus. Michael, Gabriel, and 34 other angels take him down 85 steps and then another 500 steps.

At that level Ezra sees King Herod being punished for his sin of killing infants. Herod is an old man seated on a fiery throne. The angels take Ezra lower still, too many steps to count, where he sees old men with fiery axles revolving on their ears. They are being punished for being eavesdroppers. Ezra is taken down another 500 steps and sees there "the unsleeping worm and fire consuming the sinners" (4:21). The angels take Ezra down to the Foundation of Destruction where he is shown the "twelvefold blow of the abyss" (probably a reference to the 12 last plagues of hell). A man hangs from his eyelids and is beaten by angels. Michael explains the man is being punished for incest.

Ezra is taken to another spot and shown a man restrained by iron bars. He is the Antichrist who deceives people as the Christ. Ezra is told to tell others what he looks like. He has the face of a wild man with a right eye like a star rising at dawn and the left eye fixed. His mouth is one cubit, his teeth are a span long, his fingers are like scythes, the soles of his feet are two span, and his forehead is inscribed with the word "Antichrist." He has the ability to take on many guises, even those of a child or an old man.

Ezra is shown more punishments, including that of a woman suspended in air with four wild beasts sucking upon her breasts. Her sins were not giving her milk and throwing infants into rivers. Ezra sees many other judgments that cause him to weep bitterly. God tells him he will not pardon sinners.

Ezra then asks to see Paradise and is led away by angels to the east where he sees the Tree of Life. He also sees apostles, prophets, and patriarchs—including ENOCH, ELIJAH, MOSES, Peter, PAUL, Luke, and Matthew, as well as the righteous. He is told the names of the "angels who are over the consummation": Michael, Gabriel, Uriel, Raphael, Gabuthelon, Aker, Arphugitonos, Beburos, and Zebuleon.

A voice tells Ezra he must die. He resists, demanding to know how his soul can be taken. He argues with the angels. They tell him they can draw his soul forth through his mouth, nostrils, eyes, feet, and toenails, but he give reasons why they cannot do so, saying he has experienced God with all of those parts of the body. The angels leave and tell God they cannot take his soul. God then tells Christ to go with a host of angels to take the soul of Ezra. Still Ezra protests, asking God who then will plead on behalf of sinners. Ezra argues with God and makes a final prayer that all those who pay attention to this book will be forgiven their sins on the day of judgment, but those who do not believe will be burned like Sodom and Gomorrah. God agrees and so Ezra gives up his soul. He is buried with incense and psalms.

The apocalypse ends with a doxology: "Glory, might, honor and worship to him for whom it is fitting, for the Father and the Son and the Holy Spirit now and always and forever and ever Amen."

Vision of Ezra

The Vision of Ezra is a Christian text written between the fourth and seventh centuries C.E. The original language was Greek; the surviving manuscripts are in Latin, dating from the 11th to 13th, centuries. Like the Greek Apocalypse of Ezra, the Vision of Ezra describes his visits to heaven and Tartarus, and his pleading on behalf of sinners. The vision dwells upon hell and is exceptionally dark and filled with terrible images; scant attention is paid to heaven. As every terrifying scene unfolds in hell, Ezra prays for mercy for those in torment.

The text opens with Ezra praying to God for courage so that he does not fear when he sees the judgments of sinners. Seven angels of hell carry him beyond the 70th grade of Tartarus. There he sees fiery gates guarded by fire-breathing lions. He sees powerful men passing through the fires unharmed and is told by the angels that these men are the just whose repute has ascended to heaven. But those who have denied the Lord and sinned with women on the Lord's Day are consumed by the fire and ripped apart by dogs.

The angels take Ezra lower, beyond the 50th grade (which implies that the worst of Tartarus is lower at ground zero), where he sees men standing in torments. Angels throw fire in their faces and whip them with fiery scourges. The sinners are men who committed adultery with married women; the women are those who adorned themselves to please others besides their husbands.

Ezra also sees women hanging and being whipped by angels with fiery clubs. Further down is a cauldron boiling with sulfur and bitumen; sinners are burned in it but the righteous can pass freely over it. The sinners punished here committed lust, refused hospitality to strangers, did not give alms to the poor, and were generally selfish. Sinners who performed no confession or penitence stand in front of a giant, immortal worm which continually inhales and exhales them like flies.

Ezra sees King Herod sitting on a fiery throne attended by his counselors who are immersed in fire. Elsewhere are bound men having their eyes pricked with thorns by the angels of hell. Women who had premarital sex are encased in 500-pound neck irons. Old men are lying prostrate with molten iron and lead poured continually over them. Great furnaces contain kings, princes, and other sinners who are burning with pitch and sulphur. Some of them are adulterers and some have killed their children.

After this tour of the horrors of hell, Michael and Gabriel come and invite Ezra to see heaven. He refuses, vowing that he will not come until he sees every judgment of sinners. The angels oblige, leading him downward beyond the 14th level, where he sees lions and little dogs lying around fiery flames. The righteous come through them and cross over into Paradise.

Ezra is then lifted up into heaven where a multitude of angels instruct him to pray to God for the sinners. They take him to the Lord and he beseeches God for mercy. God says that those who break his commandments against sin are justly punished in torments. The text ends with the admonition to readers that eternal punishment can be avoided by following the ways of the Lord.

Questions of Ezra

Questions of Ezra concerns the fate of souls after death and at the end of time, presented in a dialogue between Ezra and the ANGEL OF THE LORD. The date of its composition and its original language are not known; surviving texts are in Armenian.

Ezra sees the angel of God and begins asking him questions about the fates of the righteous and the sinners. The angel, who is not identified by name, says that the righteous shall enjoy great joy and eternal light and the sinners shall be punished with great darkness and eternal fire. Noting that all people are sinners at some point, Ezra asks for mercy for those who have been seized by Satan. The angel says not to wait to do good deeds for the end can come unexpectedly. When it comes a good angel comes to take the good soul and an evil angel comes to take away the evil soul. The angel stresses that the angels who come for evil souls are not evil in and of themselves—for everything that God has created is good—but their role relates to the evil deeds of men.

After death the souls pass through trials of elements, storms, hosts of Satan, high mountains, and fiery rivers. There are seven camps and seven steps to the divinity. The first are lodgings bad and wondrous; the second holds fearsome obstacles; the third is a hell of icy cold; and the fourth holds quarrels and wars. In the fifth camp the soul is inspected. If the soul is just it shines and if it is a sinner it is darkened. In the sixth camp the righteous souls sparkle like the sun and in the seventh camp they can approach the great throne of the Divinity from the garden opposite the glory of God.

Ezra wonders why the souls who pass successfully through all the harrowing cannot meet God instead of just approach the throne. The angel replies:

> You are one of the foolish and you think according to human nature. I am an angel and I perpetually serve God and I have not seen the face of God. How do you say that sinful man should be cause to meet Divinity. For the Divinity and wondrous and who dares to look toward the uncreated Divinity. If a man should look he will melt like wax before the face of God: for the Divinity is fiery and wondrous. For such guardians stand around the throne of the Divinity. (23–26)

The guardians include incorporeal SERAPHIM and six-winged (not the four wings cited in other texts) cherubim. Of the cherubim, two wings cover their face, two wings cover their feet, and with two they fly. The guardians constantly sing, "Holy, Holy, Holy Lord of Hosts, the heaven and earth are full of your glory." (See QEDUSSAH.)

Ezra asks what will become of all sinners. The angel says that they can receive rest and mercy if their families or any other Christians offer prayers for them with fasts for 40 days. The angel likens prayer to the sowing of a crop that produces great fruit. The cares of the world and its deceits are like weeds that choke it.

See DREAMS AND VISIONS.

FURTHER READING

Charlesworth, James H., ed. *The Old Testament Pseudepigrapha*. Vols. 1 and 2. New York: Doubleday, 1983, 1985.

fairies

Supernatural beings both helpful and harmful who are attached to the earth, and who sometimes are associated with angels. Fairy beliefs are universal and strikingly similar; they attempt to explain the reasons for illnesses, deformities, and untimely deaths among children; epidemics among livestock; and various disasters of weather. The term "fairy" comes from the Latin *fata*, or fate, which refers to the Fates of mythology, three women who spin, twist, and cut the threads of life.

Contemporary popular Western beliefs about angels link fairies to angels as a subordinate class of beings, in accordance with the idea of MINISTERING ANGELS—everything in nature has its guiding angel. In folklore tradition, fairies are not a type of heavenly angel, but a separate class of being; conceivably an angel might be invoked to protect against the tricks and malice of fairies.

Folklore traditions give various origins of fairies. They are:

- souls of the pagan dead, caught between heaven and earth because they were not baptized;
- guardians of the dead;
- ghosts of venerated ancestors;
- FALLEN ANGELS, cast out of heaven with Lucifer but condemned by God to remain in the elements of the earth;
- NATURE SPIRITS who are attached to particular places or elements;
- Small-statured human beings.

Fairies are especially known for their roles in enchantments and bewitchments; in witch lore they are sometimes said to be the FAMILIARS of witches.

Fairies have many names and descriptions; most are diminutive or even tiny. They may be beautiful or ugly, may resemble humans, or have wings and carry wands and pipes. Wings are small and not feathered as in depictions of angels, but more resemble butterfly or gossamer dragonfly wings. They usually are invisible save to those with clairvoyant sight; they can make themselves visible to humans if they so desire. Some are morally ambivalent, whereas others are always benevolent, and still others are always malevolent.

Some live as a fairy race or nation; the Land of Fairy, also called Elfland, has characteristics of the land of the dead: it exists underground and is accessed through barrows and mounds; time ceases there. The fairies come out at night to dance, sing, travel about, make merry, and make mischief. They steal human women for wives, and also steal unprotected human children, leaving their own children (changelings) in exchange. In order to stay in the good graces of "the little people," "the good people" and "the good neighbors," as they are called, humans are to keep clean houses and leave out food and drink. In return, fairies bestow gifts and money and help humans with their chores. Fairies also are propitiated with offerings and rites at sacred wells, fountains, lakes, and tree groves so that humans may ward off illness and misfortune.

FURTHER READING

Briggs, Katherine Briggs. *The Vanishing People.* New York: Pantheon Books, 1978.

———. *An Encyclopedia of Fairies: Hobgoblins, Brownies, Bogies, and Other Supernatural Creatures.* New York: Pantheon Books, 1976.

Evans-Wentz, W. Y. *The Fairy Faith in Celtic Countries.* New York: Carroll Publishing Group, 1990. First published 1911.

fallen angels

Angels who fall from God's grace and are punished by banishment from HEAVEN.

The three versions of the book of ENOCH associate fallen angels with the WATCHERS, 200 angels who come down from heaven to cohabitate with women and corrupt humanity. They are severely punished by God.

2 Enoch speaks of four grades of fallen angels:

1. Satanail, the prince of the fallen one. Satanail was once a high angel who thought he could be greater than God and thus was cast out of heaven on the second day of creation. He is imprisoned in the fifth heaven.
2. The Watchers, who also are imprisoned in the fifth heaven, dejected and silent.
3. The apostate angels, the followers of Satanail who plotted with him and turned away from God's commandments. They are imprisoned in the second heaven, a place of "darkness greater than earthly darkness." There they hang under guard, waiting for the "measureless judgment." The fallen angels are dark in appearance, and they weep unceasingly. They ask Enoch to pray for them.
4. Angels—possibly some of the Watchers—who are sentenced to be imprisoned "under the earth."

In Christian lore, Lucifer is the arrogant, prideful angel cast out of heaven; he becomes identified with Satan. (See REVELATION.) The fallen angels become DEMONS who seek to ruin men's souls, a view reinforced by the influential theologian St. THOMAS AQUINAS. One-third of the heavenly host—133,306,668 angels—are fallen; according to lore, they fall for nine days. Various theologians have posited that a portion of each of the nine orders of angels fall; some said the fallen ones comprise a 10th order.

The Letter of Jude references the fallen angels of Genesis, the Watchers, as examples of the fate that befalls immoral ones:

> And the angels that did not keep their own position but left their proper dwelling have been kept by him in eternal chains in the nether gloom until the judgment of the great day; just as Sodom and Gomorrah and the surrounding cities, which likewise acted immorally and indulged in unnatural lust, served as an example by undergoing a punishment of eternal fire. (6–7)

Jude, attributed to Jude brother of the apostle James, was written by an unknown author to warn against false teachers in early Christianity.

falling stars

In The Testament of Solomon, DEMONS who have no way station in which to rest. The demon Ornias explains to SOLOMON that demons have the capability of flying up to heaven in order to eavesdrop upon God and learn his plans. But because they have no place to rest, they become exhausted and fall to earth like flashes of lightning, burning fields and cities. People think they are falling stars.

Folklore traditions through history hold that falling stars are the souls of those who have just died, or who are coming to earth to be reborn.

See LUCIFER.

familiars

Low-ranking servant DEMONS who assume an animal or insect form. In magical lore, familiars are summoned into the regular service of a magician, sorcerer, or witch to perform various tasks, such as carrying out spells and bewitchments. The ability to "give good familiars" is an asset in descriptions of FALLEN ANGELS and other spirits in magical texts known as GRIMOIRES.

During the Inquisition, familiars were associated with evil. Accused witches were thought to have familiars, also called imps, usually in the forms of cats, toads, owl, mice, and dogs. In witchcraft trials, even a fly buzzing in the room was said to be a familiar, given by the devil or bought or inherited from other witches. The inquisitors took the Bible to heart: those who had familiars were "an abomination unto the Lord" (Deuteronomy 23:10–12), and should be "put to death: they shall stone them with stones: their blood shall be upon them" (Leviticus 20:27).

feather crown See ANGEL WREATH.

film, television, and drama

Like their literary counterparts, angels play roles in film and television and onstage. They serve as ways for God to act in the world, Fate to play out, and humans to become inspired.

Several thematic patterns have dominated angel films: the HEAVEN-to-earth trip of a dead person's soul to revisit and rectify errors with angelic help and perspective; direct angelic intervention by angels to inspire people, usually on spiritual matters; comic or ironic twists of situations from angelic lore, such as Gabriel blowing the horn for the last judgment; battles with Satan for a troubled soul.

A highly original Great Depression–era plot, *Gabriel over the White House* (1933), tells the story of a comatose president who revives and becomes a benevolent dictator via Gabriel. He gets jobs for the unemployed, conquers crime, collects foreign debts, and dies after signing an international peace treaty.

The toll taken by World War II was felt deeply, and Hollywood produced many films that dealt with death and bereavement in a variety of themes. An early classic in the angel-come-to-earth genre is *Here Comes Mr. Jordan* (1941). Boxer Robert Montgomery crashes his plane and a heavenly messenger escorts him to heaven, where an error is discovered—it is not his time to die. Mr. Jordan, the "man in charge" (Claude Rains), accompanies him back to earth to search for a suitable replacement body and uncover and rectify wrongdoings in his former lifetime. The true nature of Mr. Jordan is ambiguous. He is invisible to all but those who need to see him; the viewer is left to assume he is an angel. Montgomery takes over the body of another boxer, loses his previous identity, and resumes the activities the old Montgomery was meant to do. In 1947 a musical sequel, *Down to Earth*, reprises several roles from *Here Comes Mr. Jordan*, featuring Rita Hayworth as the muse Terpsichore who comes to earth because she is dissatisfied with a Broadway producer's jazz treatment of the nine muses. *Heaven Can Wait* (1978), starring Warren Beatty, is a remake of *Here Comes Mr. Jordan*. The title comes from the Henry Seegal play from which the 1941 movie is adapted. In the 1978 version, Mr. Jordan (James Mason) is clearly identified as an archangel.

Stephen Vincent Benét's novel *The Devil and Daniel Webster*, first adapted into a folk opera by Douglas Stuart Moore, became a 1941 film featuring Eddie Arnold as mid-19th-century American statesman Daniel Webster undergoing Faustian despair and temptations by Mr. Scratch, played by Walter Huston.

I Married an Angel (1942), a Jeanette MacDonald–Nelson Eddy musical based on a Hungarian play by Vaszary Janos, was adapted into a Rodgers and Hart musical for Broadway. A playboy dreams he is married to an angel and wakes up to discover the love of a plain girl he has been ignoring.

Heaven Can Wait (1943) features Don Ameche as a bon vivant reviewing his supposedly unworthy human existence on the doorstep of hell. In *Happy Land* (1943), Ameche plays a father who has lost his son in the war and who is helped through his grief by his long-dead grandfather Harry Carey, a Civil War veteran who has received permission from "the authorities" to intervene.

A Guy Named Joe (1943) adds patriotism to the angelic agenda of assisting humans through bereavement. Joe, a pilot—played by Spencer Tracy—dies and becomes the GUARDIAN ANGEL of new pilots during World War II, including a rival pilot played by Van Johnson, with whom he fixes up his grieving girlfriend, played by Irene Dunne. In 1989 director Steven Spielberg made *Always*, a remake of *A Guy Named Joe*. It stars Audrey Hepburn as a guardian angel who assists a dead pilot played by Richard Dreyfuss to fix up his girlfriend (played by Holly Hunter) with the right man.

Cabin in the Sky, originally a Broadway musical in the early 1940s, was released as a movie in 1943 with an all-black cast in 1943: Ethel Waters, Lena Horne, Duke Ellington, and Eddie "Rochester" Anderson. Lucifer and the Lord's General battle for a soul. *Liliom* went from a European play in 1921 to a Rogers and Hammerstein stage musical, *Carousel,* in 1945, to a film—also titled *Carousel*—in 1956. Dead carousel barker Billy Bigelow gets permission from the Starkeeper in heaven to go help his family on earth.

The Horn Blows at Midnight (1945) features Jack Benny as Athanael, angel junior third grade, a nightclub trumpet player who fights with two FALLEN ANGELS to prevent the earth from being blown up by a trumpet blast.

The most famous film with an angel is Frank Capra's *It's a Wonderful Life* (1946). James Stewart depicts George, a man of moral worth rediscovering his own life at Christmas after his suicide attempt is foiled by his guardian angel Clarence Oddbody, played by Henry Travers, an apprentice trying to get his wings. When financially pressed George declares, "I wish I had never been born," Clarence shows George what life in his hometown of Bedford Falls would be like without him. *It Happened One Christmas* (1977) is a made-for-television movie remake of *It's a Wonderful Life* with a gender switch: Marlo Thomas plays the beleaguered lead, Mary Bailey Hatch. *Clarence* (1990), a made-for-cable television film, develops the character of Clarence Oddbody. This script added a new twist: Guardian angels get younger as they gain rank with every good deed, and they reach the ultimate state of grace as cherubs.

The Bishop's Wife (1947) features Cary Grant as Dudley, an angel who intervenes when an Episcopal bishop, Henry Brougham (played by David Niven) loses his faith at Christmas season, making his wife Julia (played by Loretta Young) feel neglected. A remake is *The Preacher's Wife* in 1996, starring Denzel Washington and Whitney Houston.

In *For Heaven's Sake* (1950) Clifton Webb and Edmund Gwenn play disguised angels doing good on earth. In *The Angel Levine* (1970), Harry Belafonte plays a Jewish angel on probation. *Brother John* (1971) features Sidney Poitier as an angel or an even higher ranking being who undoes wrongs in a southern town full of bigotry and strife. In *Angels in the Outfield* (1951, remake 1994) angels intervene to assist a losing baseball team to victory. *Two of a Kind* (1983) combines the biblical Flood and SODOM AND GOMORRAH: Four angels beg God to spare earth if they find two souls who will perform a great deed of sacrifice for one another. John Travolta and Olivia Newton-John play the two humans chosen at random to prove to God (played by Gene Hackman) that he should not destroy earth with a second flood.

In *One Magic Christmas* (1985) angel Gideon (Harry Dean Stanton dressed as a cowboy who plays the harmonica up in a tree), stops time, saves lives, takes a little girl to the North Pole to see Santa Claus, and reverses history to rekindle the spirit of Christmas in an embittered midwestern housewife, played by Mary Steenburgen.

A spate of 1980s films about angels interacting with adolescents sought to appeal to the teenage market: *The Kid with the Broken Halo* (1982), *Somewhere Tomorrow* (1983), *School Spirit* (1985), *Date with an Angel* (1987), and *The Heavenly Kid* (1985). *Earth Angel,* a 1991 made-for-television movie, tells of a prom queen killed in a car crash, who returns 28 years later to perform good deeds.

The German author/director Wim Wenders released *Wings of Desire* in 1987 and *Far Away, So Close!* in 1993. Both films revisit literary and biblical apocryphal themes of angels desiring to come down to earth. In these films, angels want to become more familiar with the world and people of West Berlin. One falls in love with a trapeze artist and forgoes his immortality to be with her. Along similar lines is *City of Angels* (1998), in which a restless angel, Seth, played by Nicolas Cage, falls for a mortal woman who is a doctor, played by Meg Ryan.

The height of popular angel interest was matched by the nadir of angel movies in 1996 with the release of *Michael,* scripted by Nora Ephron. John Travolta plays the archangel Michael, who is an unappealing slob. He comes to earth to intervene in the lives of three writers for a tabloid. His chief mission is to play matchmaker for two lonely hearts, played by William Hurt and Andie McDowell. The scratching, belching Michael does a disservice to the dignity of angels.

People acting like angels is a popular theme in movies. In *Angels with Dirty Faces* (1938), James Cagney is Rocky Sullivan, a criminal who goes back to his old neighborhood and is challenged by friends to become a better person; he passes the tests of character and becomes a role model for young boys. In *Dear God* (1996), Greg Kinnear plays Tom Turner, a con man forced by a judge to get a job. He goes to work in the dead letter office of the postal service. "Dear God" letters lead him into the role of an angel-like miracle-worker.

In television, the angel-helper theme has been used as the basis of several series, the most popular of which is *Touched by an Angel,* which aired from 1994–2003. A team of angels, including a gentle and friendly ANGEL OF DEATH, help people through their spiritual and moral crises.

Onstage, Tony Kushner's *Angels in America* received Tony awards in 1993 and 1994. The first part of the musical, "Millennium Approaches," had a sensational season in London in 1991. The full work, adding part two, "Perestroika," comprising a seven-hour epic in total, had its world premiere in Los Angeles in November 1992, and ran a successful two years more on Broadway. The play ranges from earth to heaven, politics, sex, and religion, switches between realism and fantasy, treating the tragedy of AIDS and the death of, or at least the absence of, God. The subtitle, "A Gay Fantasia on National Themes," summarizes its intellectual content: a critique of America's soul from a political perspective. One character says: "There are no angels in America, no spiritual past, no racial past, there's only the political."

At the heart of the drama of the lives of several mainly gay characters is Lucifer-figure Roy Cohn, the McCarthy-era lawyer and ruthless power broker, a vicious bigot who was secretly gay but persecuted homosexuals in public. At the end of part one, the character with AIDS is visited by an angel who emerges from an unzipped earth and flies down to hail him as a new prophet; Cohn gasps "*very* Steven Spielberg." In "Perestroika," the fantasia continues with the angel revealing herself as the Angel of Death, and the task of the AIDS patient to make sense of death and "face loss with grace." Part of this grace is humor, moving toward resolutions that are darkly comic. Cohn is relentlessly conniving even in death, bursting into the afterlife to offer his legal services to the runaway God.

FURTHER READING

Parish, James Robert. *Ghosts and Angels in Hollywood Films.* Jefferson, N.C.: McFarland, 1994.

Teague, Raymond. *Reel Spirit: A Guide to Movies That Inspire, Explore and Empower.* Lee's Summit, Mo.: Unity House, 2000.

Findhorn

Experimental spiritual community in northern Scotland near the Arctic Circle, made famous in the 1960s and 1970s by the gardening guidance given by the overlighting DEVAS and NATURE SPIRITS that yielded spectacular produce in inhospitable terrain. Findhorn has grown beyond community to a foundation and college, attracting about 70,000 visitors annually from around the world.

The Findhorn founders were Peter and Eileen Caddy, husband and wife, and their friend DOROTHY MACLEAN. The three never intended to establish a spiritual colony. Rather, Findhorn came into being after they were all laid off from their jobs running a resort hotel in Scotland. Out of work and with nowhere to go, they banded together in the Findhorn Bay Caravan Travel Park, where the Caddys had their trailer. The trailer park was a desolate place, situated next to a rubbish dump and a rundown building. However, the Caddys had moved there because of spiritual guidance received by Eileen in meditation, namely, that a purpose would unfold there.

The Caddys and Maclean had known each other for years and had studied under the same spiritual teacher, a Quaker woman named Sheena Govan, who was Peter's wife for five years; she terminated the marriage, but they retained a close relationship. In addition, Peter Caddy, a Royal Air Force officer, had studied Rosicrucianism. Maclean was steeped in Sufism. Both Eileen Caddy and Maclean had developed mediumistic gifts; of the two, Maclean's dominated at Findhorn.

Unable to find work, Caddy turned to gardening in 1962 to pass the time, even though Findhorn was ill-suited for it. The area is located on a narrow sandy peninsula jutting into the North Sea, and it is exposed to near-constant winds from all sides. The soil is mostly sand and gravel.

In May 1963, Maclean, while meditating, received a message from an angelic being—whom she later referred to as both "angel" and "deva"—instructing her to tune into the nature spirits, and a cooperation could begin. Maclean did so, and she began to receive regular advice from an assortment of angelic spirits on how to cultivate the garden. Peter Caddy would pose questions for the devas, and Maclean would obtain the answers. The chief coordinating entity was a being Maclean called the "Landscape Angel."

Within a year, Findhorn was transformed. Cabbages, which normally reach four pounds at maturity, weighed over 40 pounds. Broccoli grew so large they were too heavy to lift from the ground. Flowers were nearly twice their normal size. Word of the Findhorn successes spread, but agronomists were at a loss to explain them.

In 1966, a friend of Peter Caddy's, scholar R. Ogilvie Crombie, paid a visit to Findhorn, an experience that opened him psychically. Shortly afterward, Crombie was sitting in the Royal Botanic Gardens near his home in Edinburgh, Scotland, when he saw a nature spirit dancing in front of him. The three-foot high, half-man, half-animal gave his name as Kurmos, and said he lived in the gardens and helped trees to grow. This meeting paved the way for a subsequent meeting with Pan, chief of the nature spirits. Pan told Crombie that he had been chosen to help renew the lost contact between mankind and the nature spirits. Crombie passed on to Caddy and the others at Findhorn what he learned from Pan about the spirits who lived and worked in the garden.

For several years, the Caddys and Maclean were reluctant to talk about their invisible helpers, though word of their spectacular gardening successes spread. Agronomists could not explain their results, based just on the composition of the soil, and the methods they used. When they finally began to talk of the devas, they attracted disciples who wanted to live and work with them.

Over time, Maclean sensed the creation of a new entity, the "Angel of Findhorn," which started as a nebulous impression and grew slowly over the years. The Landscape Angel told Maclean that the Angel of Findhorn was being fed by the growth in the gardens, as well as the love generated by the human beings present. Maclean clairvoyantly perceived this being developing almost like a fetus, until it had acquired sufficient power to open to all devic knowledge. The angel took on a masculine presence, and, when it communicated with Maclean, described itself as "the Spirit of a place."

Findhorn became a model community for proponents of the New Age movement. By the early 1970s, it had more than 300 residents. Among them was the American philosopher and visionary David Spangler, who arrived in 1970 with his spiritual partner, Myrtle Glines. Residents viewed themselves as the vanguard of a new society based on the principles of cooperation between man and the kingdom of nature.

After Spangler's arrival, an angelic presence called Limitless Love and Truth manifested. The being provided revelations that had first appeared, independently, to another man in Britain. Spangler published some of the transmissions in his book, *Revelation: The Birth of a New Age* (1976).

By 1980, the Findhorn community had declined, due in part to the departures of some of the principals, including Maclean, Peter Caddy (he and Eileen divorced), and Spangler. Eileen remained, but she took a background position so that Findhorn could be cared for by a new generation of residents. Without someone like Maclean as a focal point, interest and involvement in the nature kingdoms faded. But a decade later, around 1990, interest and growth renewed as part of a broader upswing in interest in human cooperation with angelic and nature realms.

Presently, Findhorn is an ecovillage residential community, a foundation that operates educational programs, and a college that offers a combination of mainstream academic and alternative experiential education courses. It has served as a model for other similar enterprises and communities, such as PERELANDRA, near Washington, D.C., and GREEN HOPE FARM in Meriden, New Hampshire.

FURTHER READING

"The Findhorn Foundation: Who Are We?" URL: http://www.findhorn.org. Downloaded December 18, 2002.

Findhorn Community. *The Findhorn Garden*. New York: Harper and Row, 1975.

Hawken, Paul. *The Magic of Findhorn*. New York: Bantam Books, 1976.

Maclean, Dorothy. *To Hear the Angels Sing*. Hudson, N.Y.: Lindisfarne Press, 1990. First published by Lorian Press, 1980. 2d ed. by Morningtown Press, 1988.

Spangler, David. *Revelation: The Birth of a New Age*. Elgin, Ill.: The Lorian Press, 1976.

firmament

The vault of sky or space that separates HEAVEN and earth; or heaven itself.

In Genesis 1:6–8 God creates the firmament and calls it heaven. In the Martyrdom and Ascension of Isaiah, the firmament refers to the space that separates the seven heavens from earth, and it is where dark angels struggle for control. As an angel escorts ISAIAH heavenward in his vision, the prophet sees Samael (Satan) and his hosts in the firmament, envying each other and struggling with each other. Isaiah is told by his escort angel that the struggle mirrors the struggles and darkness on earth ("as above, so also on earth"). The angel tells Isaiah that the struggle will last until the coming of "the one," or Christ.

Flamel, Nicolas (1330–1416)

French scribe, alchemist, and adept, whose successful career as an alchemist was launched by an angel, according to legend.

Nicolas Flamel was born in 1330 in Pontoise, 18 miles north of Paris, to a modest family. As a young man he set up business in Paris as a public scribe, copying and illuminating manuscripts and performing other publishing services. He enjoyed a good reputation. Through his work he met Madame Pernelle Lethas, an older woman who was twice widowed and left with comfortable means. He fell in love with her. They married, and led a quiet and thrifty life.

Alchemy, the transmutation of base metals to gold and silver, was popular at the time, and Flamel undoubtedly copied various alchemical manuscripts. He showed little interest in the subject, however, until he experienced a dream one night. An angel appeared to him and held out a beautiful book of obvious antiquity. The angel said, "Flamel, look at this book. You will not in the least understand it, neither will anyone else; but a day will come when you will see in it something that no one else will see." In the dream Flamel reached out to take the book, but both it and the angel vanished in a golden cloud.

Flamel paid scant attention to the dream until sometime later, in 1357, when an event occurred. For two florins, he acquired from a vendor a mysterious gilded book that was large, very old, and made not of paper or parchment but from the thin bark of tender shrubs. Its cover was made of copper, and it was engraved with strange symbols. Its contents included equally strange drawings, and a claim that it was authored by Abraham Eleazar, or "Abraham the Jew," a prince, astrologer and philosopher. It also delivered curses against anyone who should set his eyes on the book, lest he be a sacrificer or scribe.

Feeling exempted from the curses, Flamel examined the book and determined that it was an alchemical text that told how to transmute metals into gold, so that Jews could pay levies due to the Roman Empire. The secret remained hidden in the drawings, some of which were not accompanied by explanatory text. On every seventh leaf there was an illustration of one of three icons: a caduceus (staff) with intertwined serpents; a serpent crucified on a cross; or a snake-infested desert with beautiful mountains. Among other drawings was one of a winged Mercury with Saturn holding an hourglass and scythe, and a mountain with a rose (with a blue stalk and red and white flowers) blowing in the north wind.

The book remained inscrutable to Flamel and his wife for years. In 1378, Flamel made a pilgrimage to Spain, hoping to meet a learned Jew who was versed in the Kabbalah who could help him to decipher the alchemical book. After a year of wandering he met a converted Jew, Maitre Canches, who identified copies of some of the drawings from the book as coming from an old Kabbalistic text, the *Asch Mezareph,* written by a Rabbi Abraham and believed to be lost. Maitre Canches decided to return to France with Flamel, but became ill on the journey and died when they reached Orleans. According to Flamel, Canches revealed enough secrets before he died so that Flamel could then decipher his book on his own.

It took Flamel, assisted by Pernelle, three years of hard labor to make a successful projection of the philosopher's stone. In 1382, Flamel claimed, they turned lead (according to some accounts it was mercury) first into silver and then, on a second occasion, into gold. Legend has it that they made three projections, which gave them a handsome amount of gold, so much that they founded and endowed 14 hospitals, built three chapels, made generous gifts to seven churches, and paid for the repair of numerous church buildings. They made similar grants in Bologne, where Pernelle had been born.

Flamel wrote about his experiences in a book, but he gave away no secrets. In addition, he painted some of the drawings from the book as frescoes in an archway he had built in the Cemetery of the Holy Innocents in Paris. The painting symbolizes the Great Secret, and was the object of many pilgrimages by alchemists into the 17th and 18th centuries.

Pernelle died in 1397. Flamel died on November 22, 1416 (he is also said to have died in 1417 or 1418). His house was futilely ransacked by fortune hunters seeking the secrets of transmutation. It was widely believed by other alchemists that Flamel did achieve the philosopher's stone—the substance that transmutes metals into gold—but apparently his secrets died with him, and his success was not achieved by others.

Legend has it that Flamel did give some of his philosopher's stone to a nephew of his wife named Perrier, who passed it on to a Dr. Perrier. When he died, his grandson, named Dubois, found it among his effects. He took it to Louis XVII, and he successfully transmuted some base metal into gold in the king's presence. The king asked him to make some more of the philosopher's stone, which Dubois promised but failed to do. He was hanged, according to the story.

Flamel and Pernelle entered legend, and they reputedly attained immortality—the spiritual side of the philosopher's stone. Stories about them circulated for centuries. They were reported to be alive in India in the 17th century, and to have been seen attending an opera in Paris in 1761.

See DREAMS AND VISIONS.

FURTHER READING

Burckhardt, Titus. *Alchemy: Science of the Cosmos, Science of the Soul.* London: Stuart and Watkins, 1967.

Grillot de Givry. *Witchcraft, Magic & Alchemy.* New York: Dover Publications, 1971. First published 1931.

Holmyard, E. J. *Alchemy.* Mineola, N.Y.: Dover Publications, 1990. First published 1957.

Seligmann, Kurt. *The Mirror of Magic.* New York: Pantheon Books, 1948.

Thompson, C.J.S. *The Lure and Romance of Alchemy.* New York: Bell Publishing, 1990. First published 1932.

Flauros (Hauras, Haurus, Havres)

One of the FALLEN ANGELS and 72 spirits of SOLOMON. Flauros reigns as a duke with 20 (or 36) legions. He appears first as a terrible leopard, but, if commanded, will change shape into a man with fiery eyes and a terrible countenance. If invoked into the magician's triangle, he will give true answers to questions about the past, present, and future; outside the triangle, he will lie. Flauros will talk openly of divinity, the creation of the world, and the fall of the angels, including his own fall. He will destroy and burn one's enemies, but he will protect those who invoke him from temptation, spirits, and other dangers.

Focalor (Forcalor, Furcalor)

One of the FALLEN ANGELS and 72 spirits of SOLOMON. In hell Focalor reigns as a duke with three legions (according to Davidson, 30 legions). He appears as a man with griffin wings. He has the power of the wind and the sea, drowns men, and sinks warships. If commanded, he will not harm anyone. Prior to his fall, he was in the order of THRONES. After 1,000 years, he hopes to return to the seventh HEAVEN.

Forcas (Foras, Furcas, Fourcas)

One of the FALLEN ANGELS and 72 spirits of SOLOMON. The LEMEGETON describes Forcas as a president who commands 29 legions and appears as a strong man. He teaches logic, ethics, and the virtues of herbs and precious stones. He makes people invisible, discovers hidden treasures and lost objects, and imparts wit, wisdom, eloquence, and longevity.

forces See SERAPHIM.

Forneus

One of the FALLEN ANGELS and 72 spirits of SOLOMON. Forneus is a marquis of HELL who appears as a sea monster. He teaches rhetoric, art, and languages and gives a good reputation. He causes people to be loved by their enemies. Prior to his fall Forneus was in the order of THRONES and also partly in the order of ANGELS.

Frances of Rome, St. (1384–1440)

Christian saint who was guided daily by angels. She reportedly was given two GUARDIAN ANGELS at birth, but neither one of these presented themselves in a dramatic way. Rather, she was guided first by an ARCHANGEL and then by a POWER.

Frances's frequent angelic visits began with the death of her first son, Evangelista, at age nine. Just before dying, he exclaimed that angels had arrived to take him to heaven (see DEATHBED VISIONS). On the one-year anniversary of his death, Frances had an extraordinary hour-long vision. Her oratory was filled with a brilliant light at dawn, and she beheld her son accompanied by a beautiful boy. Evangelista said that he now resided in the second choir of the first hierarchy of angels, and introduced his companion as an archangel who had a place above his. He told his mother that God was sending her this archangel, who would not leave her day or night, and that she would be blessed by seeing the archangel with her "bodily eyes." Evangelista then said he had to return to HEAVEN, but the sight of the angel would always remind his mother of him.

Evangelista disappeared, never to manifest to Frances again. The angel remained, standing with arms folded across his chest. Frances fell to her knees, and begged for his help in guiding her spiritual growth and in defending against the devil. When she left the oratory the angel followed her, enveloping her in a halo of light. The angel, and this halo around Frances, could not be perceived by other people. (See ANGELOPHANIES.)

Frances could not look upon the angel's brightness without its hurting her eyes, so, she looked upon the glow around him. Over time she was able to more directly see his features while she was at prayer; it seemed that the angel purposefully dimmed his own light to help her. He looked like a boy of nine, with sparkling eyes, an ever-present sweet expression upon his face, and his eyes turned constantly toward heaven. He wore a white robe covered by a tunic that reached to his feet. He was clear as light, and an ethereal color like sky-blue and flaming red. His hair, like spun gold, fell across his shoulders. The light coming from his hair was so bright that Frances frequently did not need a candle, even at night.

She wrote that the angel was never soiled by dirt or mud when he walked beside her. If she committed even the slightest fault, however, he disappeared from her sight, and would reappear only after she had confessed her transgressions. If she was plagued by doubts, he gave her a kind look that immediately made her feel better. When he talked, she could see his lips move; his voice was incredibly sweet.

Much of the angel's guidance centered around Frances's worries as head of a family. The angel assured her that she was not lost in God's sight. He also enabled her to supernaturally discern the thoughts of others. Thus she reportedly was able to short-circuit evil intent, reconcile enemies, and help wandering souls return to the fold.

Frances also was engaged in a constant struggle against evil spirits. Whenever the devil would particularly plague her, she would appeal to the archangel for help. Like Samson, the angel's power also lay in his hair, for when Frances asked him for protection, the angel shook his hair and frightened the evil spirits away.

The archangel—who never offered a name—stayed with Frances for 24 years. In 1436 she joined her own community and was granted a vision in which she saw God seated on a high throne and surrounded by myriads of angels. God appointed one of the high-ranking powers to replace the archangel. In his human form, the power was even more beautiful than the archangel, and he exhibited greater power and courage. He did not have to shake his hair to scare away evil spirits; his mere presence accomplished that. He carried in his left hand three golden palm branches, which symbolized three virtues that he helped Frances to cultivate: charity, firmness, and prudence.

The power stayed with Frances for four years until she died. Her angelic experiences are characteristic of hagiographies.

FURTHER READING

Guiley, Rosemary Ellen. *The Encyclopedia of Saints.* New York: Facts On File, 2001.
Parente, Fr. Pascal P. *The Angels: The Catholic Teaching on the Angels.* Rockford, Ill.: Tan Books and Publishers, 1973. First published 1961.
O'Sullivan, Fr. Paul. *All about the Angels.* Rockford, Ill.: Tan Books and Publishers, 1990. First published 1945.

Francis of Assisi, St. (1181?–1226)

Often called the most Christ-like of all the saints, Francis of Assisi is known for his love of animals and for his stigmata, given to him by an angel.

Francis of Assisi was born in either 1181 or 1182 in the town of Assisi in Umbria, Italy, to Pietro Bernardone and his wife Pica. Although baptized Giovanni,

The Stigmatization of St. Francis (Stefano di Giovanni, called Sassetta, reprinted courtesy of the National Gallery, London)

signs that he should change his ways. Upon recovery he outfitted himself to join the forces of Walter de Brienne, who was fighting in southern Italy, but instead ended up trading his fine clothes and armor for the rags of a poor former knight he met on his journey.

By 1204 he had stolen one of his father's horses and a large amount of cloth, which he sold to rebuild the ruined church of San Damiano de Assisi. His father tried everything to dissuade Francis from his "mad" ideas, including beatings and shackles, but Francis was immovable. By 1206 he had completely renounced his patrimony and had taken a vow of absolute poverty. He and his growing band of followers wore long, rough tunics of undyed wool, shaved the tops of their heads, and preached as itinerants among the poor and sick, depending solely on the generosity of strangers.

St. Francis's commitment to Christ caught the imagination of his day. Familiar with court poetry and the songs of the troubadours, St. Francis introduced into medieval worship a love of nature and creation, of song and praise, and of higher chivalric love. His poem the "Canticle of the Sun" is still sung in Christian churches all over the world. He introduced a crèche at a Nativity Mass in Greccio in 1223, as a memorial to Jesus' humble birth. St. Francis's simple appeal and total devotion, as well as the stories of his prophecies and miraculous healings, continue to attract followers to this day.

Perhaps his most unusual achievement was the acquisition of stigmata after an ecstatic vision in 1224. During the summer of that year, close to the Feast of the Assumption (August 15), St. Francis returned in seclusion to a tiny hut on Monte La Verna, part of the property of Orlando, count of Chiusi. He intended to suffer a long fast in honor of the archangel Michael, requesting that he be left alone until the angel's feast day on September 29. St. Francis was then 42 years old, racked with disease and fevers, and quite thin from self-mortification.

On September 14, the Feast of the Exaltation of the Holy Cross, St. Francis continued his fasting and prayer by concentrating on Christ's sufferings on the cross. As described in the *Little Flowers of St. Francis of Assisi*, he was contemplating the Passion so fervently that he believed himself transformed into JESUS. While in such an ecstatic state, his vision continued with the appearance of a seraph. The angel's six fiery wings descended from heaven, and as they drew closer to St. Francis they revealed the crucified Jesus within their folds. St. Francis was filled with fear, joy, and sorrow. When the vision ended, the saint found to his amazement that his hands and feet were

or John, the boy was called Francesco, "the Frenchman," because his father was often in that country conducting his successful cloth trade.

Francis spent his early years in song, drink, and extravagance, going through his father's money but showing no interest in his father's business. In 1201 war broke out between Assisi and neighboring Perugia, and Francis was captured. He languished for a year in prison, then suffered a long illness after his release. During his convalescence he kept receiving marked with black excrescences in the form of nail heads and bent nails, and that a wound on his side oozed blood frequently.

St. Francis was embarrassed and frightened by these stigmata, and for the remaining two years of his life kept his hands within his habit and wore shoes and stockings. He told none of his followers about the miracle, but they finally deduced the situation after finding blood on his clothing and after noting St. Francis's inability to walk without hobbling.

Modern research suggests that the marks were scar tissue from earlier, unknown wounds. In the days of the early church, any disfigurement was known as "stigmata." Today, stigmata are believed to result from the auto-suggestion of worshippers who brood intensely on Christ's sufferings. Yet several surviving accounts from various of St. Francis's followers refer to his bleeding wounds, the saint's inability to walk, and the blackness of the marks.

St. Francis died on October 3, 1226, and he was canonized two years later by Pope Gregory IX. St. Francis's biographer, Thomas of Celano, reported that black marks resembling nails even appeared on St. Francis's flesh after death. Two paintings of St. Francis, painted within 10 years of his death, both show the stigmata.

FURTHER READING

Guiley, Rosemary Ellen. *The Encyclopedia of Saints.* New York: Facts On File, 2001.

Walsh, Michael, ed. *Butler's Lives of the Saints,* Concise Edition. San Francisco: Harper and Row, 1985, pp. 314–320.

Wilson, Ian. *Stigmata: An Investigation into the Mysterious Appearance of Christ's Wounds in Hundreds of People from Medieval Italy to Modern America.* San Francisco: Harper and Row, 1989.

fravashis (farohars, favashis, ferchers, ferouers, pravashi) In ZOROASTRIANISM and Persian lore, preexistent souls and the spiritual primeval images of humans independent of the body. Fravashis, who reside in homes and communities, have both human and angel characteristics. They serve as GUARDIAN ANGELS to the faithful and to the seed of the prophet Zarathrustra, and his future saviors Hushedar, Hushedar-man, and Soshyant. They protect procreation and childbirth (see CHILDBIRTH ANGELS), do battle, and are invoked against miscarriage and danger. In the Zend Avesta (a commentary on passages from the Avesta, the sacred book of Zoroastrianism), the fravashis are described as female GENII who dwell in all things and are protectors of mankind.

Furcas

One of the FALLEN ANGELS. According to JOHANN WEYER, Forcas is a knight who commands 20 legions and who appears as a cruel man with a long beard and hoary head. He rides on a pale horse and carries a sharp weapon. Weyer says Forcas teaches rhetoric, philosophy, logic, astronomy, chiromancy (divination of the hands), and pyromancy (divination with fire).

Furfur

One of the FALLEN ANGELS and the 72 spirits of SOLOMON. Furfur is an earl with 26 legions under his command. He appears as a hart with a fiery tail. When summoned, he must be placed within the magician's triangle, or what he says—if he speaks at all—will be false. Once in the triangle, he changes form to that of a beautiful angel who speaks with a hoarse voice. Furfur causes love between a husband and a wife. He will give true answers about secret and divine things. He can raise thunder, lightning, and great winds.

Gaap (Goap, Taap, Tap)

One of the FALLEN ANGELS and 72 spirits of SOLOMON. Once a member of the order of POWERS, Gaap is a president and mighty PRINCE in HELL, ruling 66 legions. He appears when the sun is in the southern signs as a human with huge bat's wings and preceded by four powerful kings. Gaap teaches liberal sciences and philosophy, excites love and hatred, makes men insensible, gives true answers about the past, present, and future, and takes FAMILIARS away from other magicians. Upon command he will move people quickly from place to place. Gaap gives instruction in the consecration of things that belong to the divination of his master, Amaymon.

Gabriel

One of the three principal angels of Christianity—along with Michael and Raphael—and the most important angel in Islamic ANGELOLOGY. Gabriel also appears in Jewish angelology. The name Gabriel means "hero of God" or "the mighty one." Gabriel is the angel of revelation, wisdom, mercy, redemption, glad tidings, and promise. He sits at the left hand of God. He is mentioned four times in the Bible in connection with important news.

Gabriel is among the angels identified as the ANGEL OF DEATH; ANGEL OF GREAT COUNSEL; ANGEL OF PEACE; ANGEL OF PRAYER; ANGEL OF TRUTH; and as one of the ANGELS OF THE EARTH; ANGELS OF THE LORD OF THE SPIRITS; ANGELS OVER THE CONSUMMATION; ANGELS OF MERCY; and one of the ANGELS OF DESTRUCTION sent to destroy SODOM AND GOMORRAH. He is an angel of January, the moon, Mars, winter, and Aquarius.

Gabriel in Jewish Lore

In the Old Testament, Gabriel is named as Daniel's frequent visitor, bringing prophetic visions of apocalyptic proportion (Daniel 8:16, 9:21). Angelic attribution of the visions, which were treasonous at the time of the writing of the book of DANIEL, might explain Gabriel's prominent presence.

Gabriel's messenger mission probably inspired his presence in apocryphal and MERKABAH literature, where Gabriel figures in the stories of Adam's creation, the punishment of the FALLEN ANGELS (see ENOCH; WATCHERS), the burials of ADAM, Abel, and ABRAHAM, and other events. The four archangels (Michael, Gabriel, Uriel, and Raphael) bury Abraham; Michael and Gabriel witness the contract between Esau and JACOB. Gabriel also is among the candidates to be the dark angel who fights with Jacob.

Gabriel figures in various Hebrew folktales as well. There is a chain of midrashim concerning Gabriel and a magical stone that begins with Abram (later Abraham). Abram is left in a cave by his mother because of the

The Annunciation (Eustache Le Sueur, c. 1650; reprinted courtesy Toledo Museum of Art, Toledo, Ohio; gift of Edward Drummo Libbey)

slaughter of newborn males by the king Nimrod. God sends Gabriel to tend the infant, feeding him with his thumb through which milk and honey flow. This enables the boy to grow at a spectacular rate of a year a day. The archangel also talks with him, so when his mother Amitlai returns, she is amazed at her son's speech.

On his third day in the cave, Abram finds a glowing stone, which Gabriel places around his neck. This is the Zohar ("light" or "window"), the light of the Garden of Eden preserved by God after the fall of ADAM AND EVE. The angel Raziel gives the Zohar to Adam, who gives it to his son Seth, who uses it to become a great prophet. Eventually the stone is given to Enoch, who uses its light to read the Celestial Torah on his trip to the HEAVENS. Enoch gives it to his son Methuselah, who gives it to his son Lamech, who gives it to his son NOAH, who places it in his ark. After Noah lands on Mount Ararat, he celebrates with wine, gets drunk, and lets the Zohar slip into the sea. It eventually finds its way into the cave in which Abram is being hidden.

Abraham wears the stone for his entire life, and all who look upon it are healed. He uses it as an astrolabe with which to study the heavens. He passes the stone to ISAAC, who passes it to Jacob, who wears it during his famous dream of the angels going up and down the ladder to heaven. Jacob gives it to his son Joseph, but does not tell him of its power. When Joseph's brothers take his coat of many colors and throw him into a dark pit, the stone begins to glow. Suddenly Joseph finds himself transported to an incandescent palace. Gabriel, a glowing being, announces himself and says this is his palace, and Joseph will remain there as long as he is held prisoner in the pit. Gabriel creates a cloth woven from the stone's light and so Joseph is clothed. Gabriel points to a window, and there Joseph sees revelations of future generations.

For three days and nights, Joseph remains in the palace, studying the Torah and the future of Israel. At the end of the third day, Joseph is rescued from the pit and sold into slavery. He keeps the Zohar inside a silver cup, and he prophesies the future and interprets DREAMS by gazing upon it. When Joseph dies, the stone is buried with it, but MOSES recovers it and hangs it in the Tabernacle.

Gabriel's palace figures in another Jewish mystical tale from the oral tradition in Germany. According to the story, Rabbi Meir of Rothenburg is imprisoned and declines to be ransomed. Instead, he asks only to be given scribe's tools so that he can write down his thoughts on the Torah. One night, his soul ascends to Gabriel's brilliant palace. Gabriel, also brilliant in light, introduces himself and says Rabbi Meir has been brought here to receive a Torah. In fact, he is getting one of the 13 Torahs that Moses wrote before his death, the one that was intended for the celestial academy.

When Rabbi Meir awakens, he finds a Torah in his cell. He follows Gabriel's instructions, and reads from it loudly enough for the heavenly host to hear him. When he does so, his cell fills with a holy light. He discovers numerous truths that can be obtained only from that celestial Torah.

Rabbi Meir copies the Torah; as soon as he is done, Gabriel comes in the night and takes the original back to heaven. Rabbi Meir seals his copy in a waterproof wooden ark and sets it afloat down the Rhine River. It comes to Worms. Gentiles cannot catch it, and, after Jews capture it, Gentiles cannot lift it or open it. The Jews open it. The Torah remains in the city for many generations.

In other midrashim, Gabriel is the angel who destroys Sodom, although he is not specifically named in the Genesis account.

In the courtship of Rebekah by Abraham's agent Eliezer, Gabriel is credited with exchanging a plate of poison food planned by Laban.

Like the angel Sandalphon who weaves garlands of prayers, Gabriel weaves shoes from the feet of Jews who dance to commemorate the Giving of the Torah. In the fervor of dancing, the shoes fly off to the Garden of Eden, where they are swept up by angels and delivered to Gabriel.

Gabriel in Christian Lore and Art

In the New Testament, Gabriel gives his name when he appears to Zechariah to announce the coming birth of John the Baptist: "I am Gabriel who stand in God's presence" (Luke 1:19). He is identified as the ANGEL OF THE LORD who makes the annunciation to MARY of the coming birth of JESUS (Luke 1:26–38). Gabriel appears to her, tells her she has found favor with God, and she will become pregnant with a son who is to be named Jesus. When Mary wonders how this can happen, since she is a virgin, Gabriel tells her the Holy Spirit will come upon her, and the child will be holy. When she consents ("Behold, I am the handmaid of the Lord; let it be done to me according to your word.") the angel departs. Though the angel who announces the birth of Jesus to the shepherds (Luke 2:8–14) is called only an "angel of the Lord," Catholic tradition credits that to Gabriel.

Gabriel also is credited with other major acts of unnamed angels concerning Jesus: as the angel who appears in a dream to Joseph, warning him to take his family and flee to Egypt to avoid Herod's hunt for the baby Jesus (Matthew 2:13); as the angel who appears in the Garden of Gethsemane to provide strength and support to Jesus in his agony (Luke 22:43); and as the "angel of the Lord" who has a countenance as lightning and a raiment as snow, who rolls back the stone from the tomb of Jesus and sits upon it (Matthew 28:2). In addition, Gabriel is said to be the unnamed archangel in 1 Thessalonians 4:15 who sounds the trumpet of judgment and the Resurrection.

In Catholic devotion to angels, Gabriel is a saint and has a prominent place because of his role in the Annunciation. Gabriel's salutation, "Hail, O favored one, the Lord is with you!" became the basis of the Hail Mary ("Hail Mary, full of grace, the Lord is with thee, blessed art thou among women."). Gabriel's feast day is March 24. He is patron saint to telecommunications workers, radio broadcasters, messengers, postal workers, clerics, diplomats, and stamp collectors.

Because of his role in the Annunciation, other lore about Gabriel holds that he guides the soul from Paradise to the womb and there instruct it for the nine months prior to birth.

It is in his role as annunciator of the coming of the birth of Christ to Mary that Gabriel is best known and best depicted in art. In art, he is shown holding a lily, the symbol of purity.

Gabriel in Islamic Lore

In Islamic angelology, Gabriel—who has 140 pairs of wings—is equated with the Holy Spirit and dictates the Koran to MUHAMMAD. Gabriel is the Angel of Knowledge and Revelation, to whom the philosophers trace back their active INTELLIGENCE. He is the personal Holy Spirit, the companion and celestial guide.

See RUDOLF STEINER.

FURTHER READING

Giudici, Maria Pia. *The Angels: Spiritual and Exegetical Notes*. New York: Alba House, 1993.

Graves, Robert, and Raphael Patai. *Hebrew Myths*. New York: Doubleday Anchor Books, 1964.

O'Sullivan, Fr. Paul. *All about the Angels*. Rockford, Ill.: Tan Books and Publishers, 1990. First published 1945.

Schwartz, Howard. *Gabriel's Palace: Jewish Mystical Tales*. New York: Oxford University Press, 1993.

Galgani, Gemma, St. See ANGELOPHANY.

genii

In Roman mythology, GUARDIAN SPIRITS comparable to GUARDIAN ANGELS, but attached to people, places, or things. The genius (singular) presides over the birth of a person, place, or thing and shapes its character and destiny. If attached to a person, the genius stays with him or her through life, and becomes the person's living soul after death. The genius of a place is perceived as the living spirit that animates a locale and gives it its unique powers and atmosphere. The Romans used a figure of a human being to symbolize the genius of a person, and a serpent to symbolize the genius of a place.

See DAIMONES.

George, St. See MONS, ANGELS OF.

Gideon

The book of Judges tells the story of Gideon and his encounter with the ANGEL OF THE LORD.

In Judges 6, Gideon is commissioned by God to deliver Israel from the Midianites, their greatest enemy at the time. He is threshing his wheat at Ophrah when the angel of the Lord appears and apprises him of his mission. Gideon protests that his clan is weak, and asks for a sign that it is the Lord who is speaking.

Gideon retires to his house, where he prepares food: a kid, unleavened cakes of bread, and broth. He returns to the angel and presents them. The angel tells him to place the meat and cakes on a rock and pour the broth over them. Judges 6:21: "Then the angel of the Lord reached out the tip of the staff that was in his hand, and touched the meat and the unleavened cakes; and there sprang up fire from the rock and consumed the flesh and the unleavened cakes, and the angel of the Lord vanished from his sight." This is proof to Gideon, and he builds an altar on the site.

To fulfill God's mission, he assembles an army of 300 men. Armed with trumpets, empty pitchers and torches, they storm the enemy at night, shouting, "A sword for the Lord and for Gideon!" (Judges 7:20) The Midianites fall into panic and flee. Under Gideon's rule, peace reigns for forty years until his death.

As in other biblical encounters involving angels, there is ambiguity over whether the divine entity is an angel or the Lord himself. "Angel of the Lord" often is interpreted as being another description of God.

FURTHER READING

Harper's Bible Commentary. James L. Mays, gen. ed. San Francisco: HarperSanFrancisco, 1988.

The New Oxford Annotated Bible with the Apocrypha. Herbert G. May and Bruce M. Metzger, eds. New York: Oxford University Press, 1977.

ginn See DJINN.

Gadreel (Gadriel)

In 1 ENOCH, a FALLEN ANGEL. Gadreel means "God is my helper." Gadreel leads Eve astray and teaches men how to make weapons of war.

Gadriel

Angel who rules the fifth HEAVEN, where he crowns prayers and takes them to the sixth heaven. Gadriel also governs the wars among nations on earth.

Galgaliel (Galgalliel)

Angel who is PRINCE of the sun—a duty also ascribed to Raphael—and chief of the order of GALGALIM. According to 3 ENOCH 17:4, Galgaliel serves directly under the seven princes of the seven HEAVENS (Michael, Gabriel, Satqiel, Sahaqiel, Baradiel, Baraqiel, and Sidrel). He governs 96 angels who make the orb of the sun run 365,000 PARASANGS through the heavens each day.

galgalim (galgallim)

In Jewish lore, a high-ranking order of angels equal to the SERAPHIM. Galgalim, which means "spheres," is a later name for the OPHANIM, the "Many-Eyed Ones" who are the wheels of the Merkabah (THRONES). Their principal duty is to sing the QEDUSSAH. The order ruled by Galgaliel or Rikbiel.

In 3 ENOCH, Rikbiel rules the eight wheels (galgalim) of the chariot of the throne of Glory. There are two wheels for each direction, and they are enclosed by the four winds: Storm, Tempest, Hurricane, and Gale. Four rivers flow out beneath them and four clouds encircle them: the Clouds of Fire, Clouds of Firebrand, Clouds of Glowing Coal, and Clouds of Brimstone. The movement of the wheels creates earthquake roars and thunder rumbling. When the time comes to recite the Qedussah, the wheels tremble and angels writhe in agony. Voices issue forth from beside the wheels.

Galizur (Akrasiel, Gallitzur, Gallisur YHVH, Gallizur, Raguil, Raziel)

In Talmudic lore, a great angel who rules the second HEAVEN and elaborates on the Torah. MOSES meets Galizur in heaven. In 3 ENOCH, he is Gallisur YHVH, a great angelic PRINCE of the seventh heaven who reveals all the secrets of the Torah, and who bows down to Zakzakiel.

Galizur is sometimes equated with Raziel, the angel who gives ADAM the SEFER RAZIEL, the book of great secrets. Galizur spreads his wings over the HAYYOTH in order to prevent their fiery breath from burning up the MINISTERING ANGELS.

Gamaliel ("recompense of God")

In the Nag Hammadi and other Gnostic literature, a great AEON whose NAME is mentioned frequently for graciousness and protection. With Abraxas and Sablo, Gamaliel takes the elect into HEAVEN. The occultist Eliphas Levi described Gamaliel as an evil adversary of the CHERUBIM who serves under Lilith.

Gamygyn (Gamigin)

One of the FALLEN ANGELS and 72 spirits of SOLOMON. In HELL Gamygyn is a duke with 30 legions of demons. He appears in the form of a small horse or ass, and he then changes into a human. His voice is hoarse. Gamygyn teaches liberal sciences, and he delivers news about people who have died in sin. According to JOHANN WEYER, he can summon the souls of drowned men and those who are in purgatory. These souls appear as aerial bodies before the magician and give answers to questions.

Gazardiel (Casardia, Gazardiya)

According to the Zohar, angel who supervises the east and kisses the prayers of the faithful and takes them to heaven. In Talmudic lore, Gazardiel oversees the rising and setting of the sun.

Geburah See TREE OF LIFE.

Geburatiel YHVH (Geburathiel)

In 3 ENOCH, one of the PRINCES who guards the seventh HEAVEN. Geburatiel represents divine power and strength. He bows down to Arapiel.

Gehenna See HELL.

gematria

A Kabbalistic system for discovering the secret and mystical truths of words and the NAMES of God and angels, and for interpreting biblical words and passages according to their numerical values. Each letter of the Hebrew alphabet has a numerical value and a certain spiritual, creative power; God creates everything in the universe by uttering certain words. The values of words and names are totaled, then equated with other words and names that have the same numerical values. These are analyzed within the context of Scripture and other factors.

Gematria was developed into a sophisticated system by German Kabbalists during the 13th century, but it was known and used much earlier by other cultures. King Sargon II, who ruled Babylonia in the eighth century B.C.E., used the numerical value of his name to determine that the wall of Khorsabad should be built to the same equivalent, or 16,283 cubits. The ancient Greeks, Persians, Gnostics, and early Christians used gematria for a variety of purposes. The Greeks applied it to dream interpretation and the Gnostics to the names of deities. Early Christians arrived at the dove for the symbol of Christ because the Greek letters of alpha and omega (the Beginning and the End) and the Greek term for dove (*peristera*) add up to the same number, 801.

The Kabbalistic system of gematria derived from Near Eastern Gnostic and Hellenistic cultures. It is more complex than merely tallying up numerical values of letters; it involves various methods of analysis by which the mystical purposes of the Scriptures, buildings, and objects may be determined. Not only are the numerical values considered but also the size and strokes of the letters. The Kabbalists of the 13th century, most notably Eleazar of Worms, applied gematria to the Scriptures, which were held to have been inspired by God and written in code. Thus, "And lo, three men" from Genesis 18:2 is interpreted as referring to the archangels Michael, Gabriel, and Raphael, for "And lo, three men" and "Elo Michael Gabriel Ve-Raphael" each have the same numerical value of 701.

Gematria was used to ascertain the secret, ineffable, and indescribably powerful names of God. These names were incorporated into the incantations of MAGIC, used for conjuring and controlling DEMONS. Some names of angels also are secret names of God, such as Azbogah.

Different systems of gematria were developed; Moses Cordovero said there were nine. Gematria spread into alchemical and esoteric Christian works. Hebrew words—with or without gematria—took on greater importance for their mystical power or hidden meanings and connections.

Lesser known than gematria are notarikon and temurah, other systems of decoding and analyzing mystical truths. Various methods exist in both systems. In notarikon, the first letter of words may be extracted and combined to form new words; or, the first, last, and sometime middle letters of words are combined to create new words or phrases. Names of God and angels

Final Letters.	Figure.		Names.	Corresponding Letters.	Numerical Power.
Mother	א	1	Aleph	- - -	1
	בּ	} 2	Baith	B	2
	בֿ		Vaith	V	- -
Double	ג	3	Gimmel	G	3
	ד	4	Daleth	D	4
	ה	5	Hay	H	5
	ו	6	Wav	W	6
	ז	7	Zayin	Z	7
Single	ח	8	Cheth	Ch	8
	ט	9	Teth	T	9
	י	10	Yood	Y	10
Double	כ	} 11	Caph	C	20
	כֿ		Chaph	Ch	- -
Single	ל	12	Lamed	L	30
Mother	מ	13	Mem	M	40
Single	נ	14	Noon	N	50
	ס	15	Samech	S	60
	ע	16	Ayin	- - -	70
Double	פ	} 17	Pay	P	80
	פֿ		Phay	Ph	- -
Single	צ	18	Tzadè	Tz	90
	ק	19	Koof	K	100
Double	ר	20	Raish	R	200
Mother	שׁ	} 21	Sheen	Sh	300
	שׂ		Seen	S	- -
Double	ת	} 22	Tav	T	400
	תֿ		Thav	Th	- -

Table of numerical values of Hebrew letters (Author's collection)

are revealed in this fashion (see AGLA). In temurah, letters are organized in tables or mathematical arrangements, which are then substituted for the letters in words; or, letters are rearranged into anagrams. For example, such tables can be used to discover the names of the good and evil angels of the planets and signs of the zodiac.

FURTHER READING

Patai, Raphael. *The Jewish Alchemists*. Princeton, N.J.: Princeton University Press, 1994.

Scholem, Gershom. *Kabbalah*. New York: New American Library, 1974.

Three Books of Occult Philosophy Written by Henry Cornelius Agrippa of Nettesheim. Translated by James Freake. Edited and annotated by Donald Tyson. St. Paul, Minn.: Llewellyn Publications, 1995.

Gemma Galgani, St. (1878–1903)

Italian saint known as the Passion Flower of Lucca, who had a strong relationship with her GUARDIAN ANGEL.

Gemma Galgani was born on March 12, 1878, in Camigliano, a small town near Lucca in Tuscany, Italy, to a poor family. She was chronically ill, and, from an early age, she exhibited supernatural gifts: visitations, visits by Christ, assaults by the devil, and stigmata. Her ill health caused her to be turned away by the Passionists.

At age 19, Gemma fell seriously ill with meningitis. She was miraculously cured, and she credited the intercession of the Venerable Passionist Francis Possenti (later canonized as St. Gabriel of Our Lady of Sorrows), to whom she had prayed for help.

The stigmata appeared on her wrists, feet, and side from 1899 to 1901. The first visionary episode occurred on June 8, 1899. Gemma felt an intense sorrow for her sins and a willingness to suffer. She had a vision of her guardian angel and the Blessed Virgin Mary. MARY opened her mantle and covered her, and told Gemma she was much loved by Jesus, who was giving her a special grace. Then JESUS appeared with his wounds open; flames, not blood, issued forth. The flames touched Gemma's hands, feet, and heart, and she felt as though she were dying. Mary supported her for several hours. The vision ended, and Gemma found herself on her knees, a sharp pain in her hands, feet, and heart. Her guardian angel helped her into bed, and blood began to flow from her wounds.

Thereafter, every Thursday evening to Friday afternoon, Gemma would fall into a rapture and the five wounds would open and issue a bright red blood. She would utter the words of Jesus and Mary. The wounds would abruptly stop bleeding, close, and leave only white marks. Sometimes the obliteration took until Saturday or Sunday to complete. When the ecstasies ended, Gemma would serenely go about her normal business. However, she suffered great inner torments and trials from the devil. Throughout these difficult experiences, she maintained a great serenity and peace.

A Passionist, Father Germano, took an interest in Gemma and became her spiritual director and confessor. An expert on fraudulent mystical phenomena, he had Gemma thoroughly tested and was convinced her experiences were genuine. He recorded her utterances and later became her biographer. With Germano's help, Gemma went to live with a family as a mother's helper, where she was shielded from unfriendly attention and had the freedom to experience her ecstasies.

In 1901, Germano forbade her to accept the stigmata. She prayed and the phenomenon ceased, though the white marks remained. In 1903, she was diagnosed with tuberculosis of the spine. She died on April 11, 1903.

Gemma's rich visionary life was recorded in detail in her diaries and letters, as well as in Germano's writings. She was especially known for her angelic visions. She saw her guardian angel and heard his voice. Her conversations with her angel were observed and recorded by others who could only hear her side of the conversation. Germano commented that whenever she saw or listened to her angel, she entered into an ecstatic state of consciousness, lost in another world; as soon as she turned her eyes away, she resumed her usual personality.

Gemma's angel was her constant companion, so familiar that she often treated him like a brother. She was once admonished by Germano—who overheard one of her one-way conversations—that she should treat him with more respect. She agreed, and vowed to remain 100 steps behind the angel whenever she saw him coming.

Whenever Gemma was plagued by evil spirits, she called upon her angel. In 1900 she recorded an episode in which she was harassed for hours by the devil in the form of a horrible "little fellow." She was assaulted by blows upon her shoulders while she prayed. Her angel appeared but attempted to beg off her request to stay with her all night. He told her he had to sleep. When she replied that the "angels of Jesus do not need to sleep," he said he still needed to rest. Nonetheless, he remained and spread his wings over her while she slept.

Sometimes the angel was severe with her, in word or expression, as a way of trying to keep her on the straight and narrow spiritual path. He would find fault with her and tell her he was ashamed of her. If she strayed from the path, he would depart from her presence for awhile (this departure of divine grace, either in the form of the presence of an angel or the presence of God, appears often in the literature of saints).

Perhaps the most remarkable trademark of Gemma's angel was his couriership. She would send him off on errands to deliver verbal messages to people in distant places, and he would return with their replies. Gemma considered this angelic postal service to be a natural thing. Others reportedly received the messages. Sometimes replies were delivered back to her by the guardian angel of Father Germano. When some suggested this was the work of the devil, Germano subjected Gemma to various spiritual tests, asking for irrefutable signs, and got them.

For one test, Germano told Gemma to give a letter addressed to him to her aunt Cecilia, who was to lock it in a place unknown to her. The aunt gave the letter to a priest who locked it in a chest in his room and pocketed the key. The next day Gemma sensed that the angel passed with her letter. She notified the surprised priest, who found the letter missing from the chest. The letter was received by Germano—apparently by angelic post. This test was successfully repeated a second time using different circumstances.

Gemma was visited by other angels, and often by Germano's guardian angel, who, she said, had a brilliant star over his head. No thought or deed of hers ever escaped angelic attention. If she was distracted in prayer, her angel would punish her. If she did not feel well, or if she would not eat enough, the angel exhibited a tender side, inquiring after her welfare and urging her to eat.

Though she never officially was a Passionist, Gemma's remains are interred at the Passionist monastery at Lucca. She had accurately predicted it would be built two years after her death.

Gemma was beatified in 1933 and canonized on May 2, 1940. Her feast day is April 11. She is the patron saint of pharmacists and tuberculosis sufferers.

FURTHER READING

Cruz, Joan Carroll. *Mysteries, Marvels, Miracles in the Lives of the Saints.* Rockford, Ill.: TAN Books, 1997.

Guiley, Rosemary Ellen. *The Encyclopedia of Saints.* New York: Facts On File, 2001.

Glasyalabolas (Caacrinolaas, Caassimola)

One of the FALLEN ANGELS and 72 spirits of SOLOMON. Glasyalabolas is a president in HELL. He appears as a winged dog. He can make men invisible and discern the past and the future. He is the leader of all homicides and incites people to bloodshed. He teaches all arts and science instantly. Glasyalabolas commands 36 legions of DEMONS.

Gnosticism

A popular cult of beliefs and practices contemporary with early Christianity, with older roots in the mythologies and philosophies of Egypt, Babylonia, Persia, and Greece. The term *Gnosis* means "knowledge," and Gnosticism refers to the restoration of the truth of humanity's situation of being cut off from its real nature and God.

Angels play prominent roles in Gnostic cosmology. When the Gnostics viewed the night sky, they saw the stars as angels who had erred and the heavens as a vault barring them from their soul's home. Exalted higher beings caused mankind's fall, created the world, and facilitated the means for redemption.

Background

Gnosticism arose in the Hellenic Middle East, particularly Alexandria, an intellectual crossroads of cultures, and it was propelled by philosophical debates on the presence and power of ignorance, evil, and suffering on earth. The Gnostics were thoroughly familiar with the Scriptures of Christianity and Judaism, Neoplatonism, Hermeticism, and probably the religions of the East. The Gnostics wrote gospels and epistles. They combined lore and practices from many sources, expanding limits as they wished. The most notable proponents were Simon Magus (who met Peter in Acts 8); Basilides, who taught in Alexandria ca. 120–140; and Valentinus, who was born Christian and who taught in Rome ca. 140–160.

Gnosticism developed both within Christianity and outside of it; evidence exists of Jewish Gnostic sects as well. Gnosticism eventually was pushed out of Christianity as a heresy, but it continued to exist alongside of it in the second and third centuries. Some remnants survived to the Middle Ages, and its followers were often considered sorcerers. Church fathers wrote extensively on it, mostly to denounce it.

NAG HAMMADI LITERATURE

Contemporary interest in Gnosticism was rekindled in 1945 when a cache of Gnostic documents was discovered in Nag Hammadi in Upper Egypt. Two brothers out fertilizing their fields found a jar. Hoping it contained gold but fearing it really contained a djinnee (see DJINN), they opened it, only to find papyrus fragments and dust. The jar resided in homes for a time; pieces of papyrus were even burned in an oven by a superstitious housewife. The texts were written in

Coptic—Egyptian mixed with Greek—and contained Christian references. The Coptic Museum in Cairo acquired some of the texts. Others, considered worthless, were sold for low prices. More jars were found at Nag Hammadi. Eventually the Jung Institute in Zurich acquired in 1952 what became known as the "Jung Codex." The texts eventually were returned to the Coptic Museum. While the QUMRAN TEXTS found near the Dead Sea are in scrolls, the Nag Hammadi texts are codices, or bound pages. It took more than 20 years for scholars to access, translate, and begin to analyze them. CARL G. JUNG was among many scholars who compared Gnosticism to modern psychology.

CENTRAL CONCEPTS

There is no organized, definitive statement of Gnostic beliefs. Its several strains share a primary vision of the origin of humankind as inherently flawed by earthly elements, yet keeping a spark of divinity, a "touch of light" from its exalted origin, and thus a breath of hope. Christian Gnosticism seeks transcendence to an ideal world from a physical world that has become dark and evil. Gnosticism is similar to Hinduism and Buddhism and differs from most Western religions in this negative view of the material world and its yearning toward an unknowable mystery. The feminine principle is honored and important; the women around JESUS, including his mother MARY, are figures of authority.

Like Eastern practices, Gnosticism had many degrees of commitment and initiation. Basilides once required his advanced students to spend five years in complete silence. For some, learning the magic NAMES of angels and partaking in rituals were sufficient.

Gnostic Angelology

Like the Platonists, the Gnostics viewed the cosmos as a series of concentric spheres. The spheres are called AEONS, each with its own ruler also called an aeon, who is comparable to a high angel. The 365th aeon is the highest and is ruled by Abraxas, the chief of the heavens. At the summit, or the center, is the good God, otherwise called the Father, unknowable to humans.

Aeons can combine and subdivide and multiply themselves in a process called syzygy. Descending in tiers down to the terrestrial world are 30 circles, which, according to Valentinus, constitute the Pleroma.

Sophia is the aeon of the 30th circle. According to her story, she desires to contemplate on her own the splendor of the Pleroma. This is an ill-fated wish, for when she crosses the last circle, she is dazzled by light and falls down to our world. Sophia is made pregnant by the Pleroma and gives birth to a creature, the Demiurge, who, after modifications by the aeons of the Pleroma, creates humankind. Gnostics associated their

many versions of this "accursed god" with the God of the Old Testament.

Another version says that Sophia (the active principle) desires to create a work without her consort (the passive Unknown good God). When she does so her thought became a work, an image of HEAVEN. But a shadow is cast; the shadow is envious of heaven, being superior to itself. Thus the beginning (arche) of envy enters all the regions in chaos and becomes matter. This Demiurge has no spirit. It creates the visible world and withholds knowledge from humanity, beginning with the warning to ADAM AND EVE not to eat of the tree of knowledge of good and evil (Tree of Gnosis). When Sophia sees the resulting horror, she has compassion and breathes life into the world of matter.

The Nag Hammadi text the Apocryphon Johannis, said to be a vision given to the apostle John, gives another variation on this story. Sophia is the third aeon of the fourth light, and, without the consent of the spirit or approval of her partner, she has a son, Ialdabaoth ("child, pass through to here") of whom Sophia is ashamed because he is a being unlike her. She hides him in a cloud so other aeons will not see him. Ialdabaoth creates his own world with 12 angels after the pattern of the immortal aeons and subordinate angels for each of them. He also appoints seven kings of the heaven and five to rule over the chaos of the underworld, all the hierarchies of heaven (ARCHONS). Their NAMES are taken variously from the Old Testament and magical texts: Iao, Sabaoth, Eloaeus (ELOHIM), Adonaeus (ADONAI), Astapheus, Horaeus.

But Ialdabaoth gives his creatures no part of the power that he has inherited from his mother, and so he is able to rule over them. Ignorant of any higher being, he declares, "I am a jealous God; beside me there is no other." By the time Sophia reencounters Ialdabaoth, he is full of power in himself and has created the lower heavens and earth. He states he needs no help: "I have need of no one. I am God, and there is no other apart from me." Sophia cries out against him, "You are Wrong, Samael."

"Samael" means "the blind god." This passage is crucial to comprehending the Gnostics, who regarded blindness or ignorance, not sin, as the seat of evil. Ignorance leads to pride, vanity, greed, ambition, and so forth. From a psychological perspective, the Gnostics projected the evil in the human heart onto the archons, the bad angel rulers under Samael's control.

The archons abuse Sophia and she becomes blind. At length she understands all this has happened because she separated herself from her consort. She repents, asking the "Father" to hear her prayer. The highest God hears her and sends to Sophia redemption in the form of the Logos, who takes the form of Jesus. Jesus restores Sophia's sight with a touch and she begins the process that will bring redemption to all mankind. This reunification of Logos (masculine) and Eros (feminine) is another great Gnostic theme, which recurs when the creation story moves to the Garden of Eden.

The Gnostics considered the first man Adam to be an earlier and superior being to the Demiurge. He comes from the Unknowable God through the spheres, gaining more materiality at each stage. He is associated with the three son-ship scheme, wherein Jesus is superior to the Demiurge, but he has no real life in him until he is imbued by the pneumatic life substance by Holy Eve, the emanation of Sophia.

The Apochryphon Johannis says that the Father reveals to Ialdaboath's seven archons his own image revealed in water, and they are so impressed that they resolve, "Let us make a man after the image and likeness of God." Each of them contributes of his power, so that man has the powers of the seven. However, he is lifeless and neither the archons nor their 60 angels can quicken him to life. The Mother, however, intervenes with the Father, who sends Christ with his four great lights to Ialdabaoth in the form of Ialdabaoth's angels. They advise him to breathe into the face of the new creature the power that he inherited from his mother. Ialdabaoth does so, and he transfers to Adam this power, so that Adam becomes superior both to his creators—the seven archons—and to Ialdabaoth himself.

Ialdabaoth and his powers bring Adam down into the material world and fashion him a body made of the four elements. God in his mercy sends him a helper (the soul or spirit within), the Epinoia of light, whom he calls Zoe. This is hidden in Adam so the archons will not become aware of it. Ialdabaoth sets Adam in Paradise to deceive him, for its bliss is illusory. The Tree of Life is intended to lead Adam astray and keep him from reaching perfection; the tree of knowledge of good and evil (Tree of Gnosis) is Epinoia of light—hence the command from Ialdabaoth not to eat of it. It is Christ, not the serpent, who encourages man to eat of it.

To prevent Adam from perceiving the truth, Ialdabaoth brings forgetfulness upon him and then creates another human being in the form of a woman. Epinoia influences them to eat of the Tree of Gnosis, and they become aware of their true being. Realizing his failure, Ialdabaoth curses man and expells him. Ialdabaoth desires Adam's wife and begets two sons, the righteous Eloim and the unrighteous Jave, whom men call Cain and Abel. He sets them over the four elements from which the material body of man has been made. Ialdabaoth also implants sexual passion in Adam, whose son is Seth. There are now two spirits in man, one divine and the other material. The former inspires him

from his sleep and forgetfulness to Gnosis; the latter is the sexual instinct that serves the ends of Ialdabaoth.

Other versions emphasize Sophia's role, blending her with the soul (Epinoia) and the Holy Eve. She hides herself in the Tree of Gnosis when threatened by the archons, seeking to escape domination by Adam. They seek to defile her so that they will have control over her children, but they instead defile an image of herself that she creates. The archons tell Adam and Eve not to eat of the Tree of Gnosis, but the serpent intervenes and convinces Eve to eat. She gives Gnosis to her husband and their understanding is opened. In dismay, the archons cast them out of Paradise. Sophia drives the archons out of heaven and casts them down into the sinful cosmos, so they become the wicked DEMONS of the earth.

In one of Basilides's several versions of creation, the unknowable God desires to create a world in seed form via its spoken word, inherent in which is the threefold son-ship that manifests in archons of greater and lesser purity. They bring matter into being, with angels emanating from them, and create spheres and rule over their realms, which eventually number 365. The Great Archon rules the Ogdoad (the eighth aeon) and is the father of Jesus, who is superior to all other sons. The Holy Spirit emanates from the Ogdoad into the Gospel. From the least sons come the Demiurge, who rules the Hebdomad (seventh aeon) and orders the earth. The Great Archon discovered from his son that he is inferior to him.

In another version attributed to Basilides, the unknowable God (the Father) sends his first-born son Nous (Jesus) to confront the God of the Jews. He performs wonders but does not suffer, for Simon of Cyrene is transformed to take the place of Jesus at the Crucifixion.

Hierarchical switches and revelations with different names in different spheres pervade Gnosticism and vary from sect to sect. Thus, there is no one definitive myth of Gnosticism.

Many Gnostics believed that prophecy was inspired by both creator angels (aeons) and Satan. They regarded Satan with ambivalence because he had so opposed the Old Testament God. The Gnostics' reputed sorcery arose from their ability to name and invoke various aeons and archons (see MAGIC). Spells and passwords enabled the Gnostic to ascend through the aeons to the highest realms. These were secrets of initiation.

The Gnostics practiced rituals to celebrate the union of Logos and Eros. Simon Magus and his companion Helen represented themselves, and were regarded by some as the apotheosis of the Father and Mother of the Universe, Logos and Sophia. Like many

Gnostics, Simon was an advocate of unbridled sexuality. Whereas the Christian fathers accused the Gnostics of "free love," all impure acts and abominations, later Gnostics were to adopt a practice of total asceticism, or the refusal to procreate. These poles indicate the Gnostics' ambivalence toward human behavior, and their belief that redemption comes through grace and not through good works. Therefore, either asceticism or debauchery might be the right path for an individual at a particular time, depending on their Gnosis, or their current holistic apprehension of existence.

The fact that the Gnostics were persecuted by the Romans along with the Christians led them to become more and more secretive. Their long-hidden documents have come to light in an age that can appreciate and apprehend more clearly the forces behind the stories they used to explain life.

Islamic Gnosticism

Similar to the worldview of Christian Gnosticism, one sect of Shia Gnostics, the Ismaili community, explains human esoteric history as a recovery from a catastrophic prehistoric mistake made by an angel, the Third Intelligence, *Adam ruhani,* the celestial spiritual Adam and angel-archetype of humanity. *Adam ruhani* refuses to respond to the summons of the First Intelligence and remains motionless in a state of bedazzlement. He finally recovers only to realize he has been overtaken and has fallen behind himself, and was now the Tenth Intelligence. This interval of time in stupor he must redeem, corresponding to seven other INTELLIGENCES, who are called the Seven CHERUBIM, the Seven Divine Worlds, and who assist the Angel-Adam to come to himself.

This delay introduces into a being of light an alien dimension that expresses itself in the form of an opaqueness. Each archangelic intelligence in the Pleroma contains a pleroma of innumerable forms of light. All the forms who comprise the Pleroma of the celestial Adam are immobilized with him in the same delay. He communicates to them the eternal summons. They angrily reject him, and their denial darkens the essential ground of their incandescent being. The Angel-Adam realizes that if they are to remain in the pure spiritual world, they will never free themselves of their darkness. He makes himself the Demiurge of the physical cosmos, the instrument through which the Forms who had once been of Light will find their salvation.

Through several cycles of rulership of the three dimensions of cosmic space, the first human being arises like a plant growing out of the earth, to be distinguished from both his celestial archetype (the spiritual Adam, the Third Intelligence who became the

Tenth), and from the partial Adam who inaugurates our present cycle. He is described as the integral primordial Adam (*Adam al-awwal al-kulli*), who is surrounded by 27 companions, who in physical forms are the faithful humanity of the Tenth Angel, and whose fidelity is manifested by their physical and spiritual superiority over all other humans of other climes. The first earthly Adam is simultaneously the epiphanic (manifest) form and the veil of the celestial Adam. He is the founder of the permanent esoteric hierarchy, uninterrupted from cycle to cycle, up to and since Islam.

After having invested his successor, the first Adam is transferred to the Pleroma, where he succeeds the Tenth Angel, the celestial Adam, who rises with the entire hierarchy of intelligences to a level higher. This ascending movement will not cease until the Third Angel Intelligence has regained the sphere of Second Intelligence. The cycle of epiphany is followed by one of occultation (necessitating the arcane sciences and philosophy, for most of humanity is unworthy of the revelations), which is followed by a new cycle of epiphany and so on in rotary succession. This will continue until the ultimate Resurrection of Resurrections, which will be the consummation of our Aion and will restore humanity and its Angel to their initial state.

FURTHER READING

Hurtak, J. J. *Pistis Sophia: A Coptic Gnostic Text with Commentary.* Los Gatos, Calif.: The Academy for Future Science, 1999.

Jonas, Hans. *The Gnostic Religion.* 2d. ed. Boston: Beacon Press, 1963.

Laccarriere, Jacques. *The Gnostics.* Translated by Nina Rootes. New York: City Lights, 1989.

Pagels, Elaine. *The Gnostic Gospels.* New York: Random House, 1979.

Robinson, James M., ed. *The Nag Hammadi Library in English.* San Francisco: Harper and Row, 1977.

Singer, June. *Seeing through the Visible World: Jung, Gnosis, and Chaos.* San Francisco: Harper and Row, 1990.

Goethe, Johann Wolfgang von (1749–1832)

German writer and poet with strong mystical interests. Johann Wolfgang von Goethe's *Faust* ranks with JOHN MILTON's *Paradise Lost* and DANTE's *Divina Commedia* as the spiritual manifesto of a great poet of an epoch.

Life

Goethe was born at Frankfurt-on-the-Main on August 28, 1749. His father was a lawyer. At an early age, he demonstrated an ability to draw and an interest in drama. By his early teens, he was writing and also learning several languages: Italian, Greek, Latin, English, and Hebrew.

Goethe entered the university at Leipzig with the intent of becoming a lawyer. Although he successfully became an advocate, he preferred studying the classics and writing prose and verse. In 1771 he returned to Frankfurt; he wrote poems and also critiques for the newspapers. The publication of his love poems for Lilli Schonemann, the daughter of a local banker, made him instantly famous, and Duke Carl August invited him to court at Weimar. He performed numerous administrative duties and founded a court theater. He maintained a rigorous schedule of writing, producing some of his best works.

In 1795 Goethe met Frederich von Schiller, noted poet and playwright, and entered into a collaboration with him to produce a literary magazine intended to educate the masses. He wrote plays. His work impressed Napoleon Bonaparte, who decorated him with the cross of the Legion of Honor.

In 1806, Goethe—famous also for his love affairs—married. He enjoyed a celebrated life and met other famous people, such as Beethoven and William Makepeace Thackeray. In his later years his health declined, and he died on March 22, 1832.

Works
Goethe produced numerous plays, poems, prose works, and translations of other works. In relation to angels, his most significant work is the one most familiar, *Faust,* about a man's pact with the devil and his redemption. It shows Goethe's knowledge of religion and alchemy—he actually had an alchemical laboratory where he conducted long experiments—and his mystical speculations.

Goethe began *Faust* in 1774 and worked on it for 60 years, leaving parts of it to be opened posthumously. Its poetic heights, virtuosity, breadth and complexity, gripping drama, and philosophical vigor are unparalleled in the German language, and it ranks among the world's greatest literary achievements. The story is of a genius made sport of by the devil, who sells his soul, then sins, repents, dies, and is redeemed. Faust the man projects a noble aspiration of the human spirit, despite his sinister side.

In a poem called "Dedication" at the head of his collected poems of 1794, Goethe described being dazzled by an apparition whom he recognizes as the Goddess of Truth, comparable to Sophia. She says to him, "you see how necessary it was to reveal only a small part of my essence to you. . . . Scarcely having overcome the crudest error, scarcely having mastered thy first childish willfulness, thou deemest thyself straight-

way a superman who can afford to ignore the ordinary duties. Art thou really so different from the others? Get to know thyself. Live in peace with the world." *Faust* acts out a next step toward development of national self-consciousness and the self-consciousness of mankind.

The Prologue in Heaven (probably written in 1799 after Goethe read *Paradise Lost* by John Milton) presents God with Michael, Raphael, and Gabriel. Mephistopheles, the devil, enters as a court jester and asks the Lord about mankind's wretchedness. God mentions Faust, "my serf," and agrees to let Mephistopheles try to sway him. Faust is "doctor" of all knowledge of all the realms, but he has no solace.

Goethe's faith in the future of mankind was unshakable, but he was not sentimental. He sees the struggle between good and evil as a necessary part of evolution. Mephistopheles says he himself is "a part of that force which always wills evil and always produces good."

The seeds of good can lie hidden in evil, but at the same time, there can be something satanic in the most lofty feeling, or the satanic can even grow out of it. This balancing on the razor's edge is what constitutes the inner drama of *Faust.*

In Part I, Faust is in despair with weariness and emptiness; his immense knowledge and magical power have been rebuffed by the Earth Spirit, the lesser deity that dwells in the earth. He is miffed that he, "godhead's likeness," "more than cherub," has been "withered" by the Earth Spirit's rejection. Faust is about to commit suicide when Easter bells and a chorus of angels interrupt him. Mephistopheles—a symbol of the libido's greed for gold and lust—arrives on the scene with attendant spirits he calls "my airy cherubim." The seduction of Faust through his limitations begins and Faust sells him his soul. His youthful vigor restored by a witch, he descends into sensuality, which destroys Gretchen, an innocent woman who loves him. Faust attends a witches' sabbat. He watches Gretchen die and pray to the heavenly hosts for protection. A heavenly voice proclaims she is redeemed while Mephistopheles insists she is damned.

As Part II opens, it seems lifetimes later. Faust wakes in a charming landscape with fairies and Ariel (the same spirit of the air from Shakespeare's play). Mephistopheles next takes Faust to Greece for an inside view of an Emperor, lovemaking with Helen of Troy, frolic among the gods, satyrs, fauns, and nymphs. His steady movement to damnation contrasts with the glories of knowledge and sensuality. After Faust dies he is buried by angels and DEMONS.

In Act V, the heavenly angels confront Mephistopheles and his devils to seize Faust's soul and carry it off. In the epilogue male and female saints and blessed children sing of God's plan as the ranks of angels comment on the ascent of Faust's immortal essence. Gretchen is heard among the chorus of penitent women, and Faust's soul is received by the Sophia-like "Woman Eternal."

Both Goethe and his contemporary, the philosopher Georg Hegel, held the Enlightenment conviction that the human race is capable of indefinite perfection once it has freed itself from the fetters of the Middle Ages. Goethe wrote in *Conversations with Eckermann*, "Man must be ruined again. Every exceptional man has a certain mission . . . once he has done so, he is no longer needed on earth in this figure." Hegel wrote in *The Phenomenology of Mind*, "From the struggle, from the destruction of the particular, the universal results." For Goethe and Hegel both, the unceasing progress of the human species results from a chain of individual tragedies. "Man ever errs the while he strives," says the Lord to Mephistopheles.

Faust is a tool of divine progress. Goethe wrote in *Conversations with Eckermann* that "all supreme productivity, every important observation, every invention, every great idea that bears fruit and has lasting effect, stands not in anyone's power and is above earthly force. Man must regard these things as gifts from on high, as pure children of God, and he must receive and venerate them with joyful gratitude. It is related to the daemonic which can overpower him and do with him as it pleases and to which he gives himself up unconsciously, while believing himself to be active under his own power. In such cases man can often be regarded as the tool of a higher world government, as a vessel that has been found worthy to receive a divine influence."

Goethe's view of life is expressed in "Parade of Masks": "I gave him to understand that life is properly given to us to live. . . . While we have life, let us be alive!"

FURTHER READING

Goethe, Johann Wolfgang von. *Faust.* Edited by Cyrus Hamlin. Translated by Walter Arendt. New York: Norton, 1976.

———. *The Autobiography of Johann Wolfgang von Goethe.* Vols. 1 and 2. Chicago: University of Chicago Press, 1976.

Lukacs, Georg. *Goethe and His Age.* New York: Grosset and Dunlap, 1969.

Gomory

One of the FALLEN ANGELS and the 72 spirits of SOLOMON. Gomory is a powerful duke in HELL with 26 legions. He appears as a beautiful woman with a duchess crown, who rides a camel. He discovers hidden treasures and gives true answers about the past, present, and future. He procures the love of women, especially girls.

Graham, Rev. Billy (1918–)

Prominent American Protestant evangelist. Reverend Billy Graham's classic book *Angels: God's Secret Agents,* written in 1975 and revised in 1986 (the second edition was republished in 1994 under the title *Angels*), outlines his belief that angels are with people at all times and all places. In it, Graham comments on the rise of evil, Satanism, UFOs, and other supernatural phenomena, but bemoans the lack of interest—at least in the mid-1970s—in the existence and power of angels. Angels, he says, act on God's behalf to perform supernatural feats of healing and salvation, to provide comfort and guidance at death, to fight the devil's evil intentions, to serve as God's messengers, and to dispense justice as God's avengers.

Graham has been an evangelist nearly all his life. Born William Franklin Graham on November 7, 1918, he was ordained a Southern Baptist minister in 1939 and received his first church in Western Springs, Illinois, in 1943. Since that time Graham has founded various religious and evangelical organizations, written several books and columns, and produced the "Hour of Decision" radio broadcast. He has spoken to hundreds of thousands at Billy Graham Crusades over the years and reached millions more by television. He embodies Christian living for many, having never been implicated in the scandals that have soiled the reputations of other televangelists.

Graham uses Scripture to describe the angels' characteristics and how they differ from humans. He notes the ironic situation that while humans were created lower than the angels, the angels were created to serve humankind, who are the only real heirs to salvation. Graham asks how can angels—holy beings that know no sin—be redeemed at the Final Judgment by people who were first sinners? He comments that although the angels serve God and his son JESUS, they do not fully comprehend Jesus' power as Savior. Nevertheless, until that day, angels remain superior to humans.

Graham says that God is not "Father" to the angels because they cannot look to Him for redemption from sin: They are not sinners. And while there is eventual redemption for sinful man, the sinful angels were not enticed as ADAM AND EVE were into sin, so they cannot be forgiven their choice to defy God. As God's ministering spirits, angels will remain exalted at the Final Judgment, but only man, who has tasted death, can receive everlasting life. And while Graham reports that the angels rejoice each time someone accepts Jesus as his or her savior, they cannot personally attest to the saving grace of God, as they have never experienced the need for such salvation. Neither do they receive the Holy Spirit, for the same reason.

Based on Jesus' observation in Matthew 22:30 that at the resurrection men neither marry nor are given in marriage but become as the angels in HEAVEN, Graham deduces that angels neither marry nor procreate. Since the obedient angels do not die, their numbers are fixed. Although medieval scholars tried to count them, Graham simply says that the host is innumerable. They do not need food, but when occasionally in human form they eat and drink.

Graham ascribes great knowledge and power to angels, but they are neither omniscient nor omnipotent. They cannot be in more than one place at one time. They do not know when the Lord will return to make his Final Judgment. But at that time, one angel, probably Michael, will take a chain and bind Satan, throwing him into the bottomless pit. And while the heavenly choirs may refer only to the various ranks of angels, Graham believes that the angels' capacity for praise does make them singers.

The angels' work is personal, ministering to a particular group or even one individual. He cites the biblical struggles of JACOB with angels; the angel who closed the lion's mouth and saved DANIEL; the angels who appeared to ABRAHAM and MOSES; and the angels who ministered to the disciples after Jesus' resurrection.

Graham tells of a woman and her daughter who called on the angels for protection in the Nazi concentration camp at Ravensbruck. The angels shielded her and her daughter and allowed them to keep their woolen underwear and a small Bible. While everyone else in line was searched, the guards appeared not even to see the woman and her daughter and their hidden "treasure."

Angels protect everyone, whether they are Christians or not, according to Graham. They also stand in judgment, warning of God's power, and carry out his dreadful commands against the wicked. Graham cites the near destruction of Jerusalem after David counted the Israelites; the angel who killed all the Egyptian firstborn before the Exodus; and the angels who will separate the good from the evil at the Final Day.

Principally, however, angels are messengers. They brought the message of Jesus' conception and birth, and the birth of John the Baptist. They spoke to the apostles and directed them to people who were eager to accept the gospel of Jesus. Angels announced Jesus' Resurrection to the women at the tomb, and they explained the Ascension to the bewildered disciples.

Graham says that angels also will prophesy and bring the message of upcoming salvation to a weary world.

Perhaps the angels' greatest ministry, according to Graham, is to help the dying cross over into their new life. Often described today as NEAR-DEATH EXPERIENCES, several stories of the dying seeing Jesus and a light ahead are recounted by Graham. Jesus is surrounded by angels. Angels also bring balm to the bereaved, helping them to deal with loss and giving them hope of the life to come.

Finally, Graham issues this warning: Remember that evidence of the devil is everywhere, but do not let the sometimes overwhelming presence of evil lead man to forget the holy angels. They are a mighty force for good, and a bright promise that God's goodness and mercy will overcome.

FURTHER READING

Graham, Rev. Billy. *Angels: God's Secret Agents.* Garden City, N.Y.: Doubleday & Co., Inc., 1975.

Great Angel   See ANGEL OF YAHWEH.

Green Hope Farm

"Cocreative" garden in Meriden, New Hampshire, similar in concept to FINDHORN and PERELANDRA in that its activities are guided by INTELLIGENCES of nature. The garden is privately owned and is not open to the public. It produces plants for flower essences.

Green Hope Farm was founded by Molly and Jim Sheehan. Molly Sheehan, a longtime gardening enthusiast who grew up on a farm in Connecticut, experienced a psychic opening in 1984, and she began a spiritual quest that led to communion with the devic and angelic kingdoms. One day something shifted in her consciousness, and she began getting "little messages" from the plants. She was then able to identify the voices as those of angels, DEVAS, and ELEMENTALS, who began to give her gardening guidance. They told her what, how, and when to plant, how to cultivate, and also how to design gardens.

Sheehan prefers not to precisely define the beings—such terms as "angels" and "devas" are human labels, she says—but defines them only as "a spectrum of energy" whose nuances can be detected by shifts in vibrations. She senses that devas possess a "bigger" energy than do angels, and they are more evolved. But there are contradictions, for the energy of the archangel Michael is bigger yet.

Initially, Sheehan spent hours in meditation in order to communicate with the intelligences. Over time, she perfected her ability so that communication became easier, especially through automatic writing. In

Deva departing the gardens, top of photo (Reprinted courtesy of Molly Sheehan)

1990 the intelligences began guiding her in the design of certain geometric patterns for gardens that would enhance the energetic properties of the flower essences.

In 1993 the gardens were opened formally to the public, but were closed the following year; the angels and nature spirits felt it was in the best interests of maintaining the energetic levels of the plants.

The purpose of Green Hope Farm is to demonstrate how the angelic, elemental, and human kingdoms can work harmoniously together and with God. The angelic kingdom holds the vision and divine plan for the place and inspires the human kingdom with love and inspiration. The elementals bring the divine plan into physical form, using humans as their "hands and feet."

FURTHER READING
Guiley, Rosemary Ellen. "Behold the Kingdom of the Nature Gods, Parts I and II." *FATE* (May 1994): 46–55; (June 1994): 37–41.

Sheehan, Molly. "The History of Green Hope Farm." URL: http://www.greenhopeessences.com. Downloaded October 7, 2002.

Grigori See WATCHERS.

grimoires
Handbooks of MAGIC that include the lore and NAMES of angels, DEMONS, and spirits, and instructions for invoking them for various purposes. Grimoires, some of which reputely date to ancient sources, came into common circulation in the Middle Ages and were particularly popular from the 17th to early 19th centuries. The "black books" as they were often called, were used by magicians, sorcerers, alchemists, physicians, noblemen, and students of the occult and mystical. Grimoires still are sometimes consulted by students of ceremonial magic in modern times, though newer books have replaced them.

The purpose of most grimoires is to conjure and control spirits and cosmic forces for protection, wealth, luck, power, curses on enemies, and so forth. Grimoires give precise and sometimes laborious instructions for various rituals, instructing the magician what to wear, what tools to use, and what prayers and incantations to recite at precise astrological times and various hours of the day and night, according to the ruling angels and intelligences. They give recipes for incenses to burn, descriptions of the creation of magic circles, AMULETS, TALISMANS, SEALS and sigils, instructions on the slaughtering and sacrifices of animals, and ways to deal with unruly demons. They admonish the magician to prepare with periods of fasting, sexual abstinence, cleanliness, and prayer, and to use only virgin materials in rituals. They describe the duties and powers of angels, demons, and spirits.

The material in grimoires is drawn largely from Hellenistic Greek and Egyptian magical texts, and from Hebrew and Latin sources. The ancient Jews had a rich magical lore involving the invocation of the names of God and the angelic forces of good against the interferences of demons.

Some grimoires are devoted to theurgy, or white magic, while others concern goety, or black magic. Some include both. The greatest grimoire is The Greater Key of Solomon, which has provided material for many other grimoires. The book is attributed to the legendary King SOLOMON, who asked God for wisdom and commanded an army of demons to do his bidding and build great works. A book of incantations for summoning and thwarting demons attributed to the authorship of Solomon was in existence in the first century C.E. It is mentioned in literature throughout the centuries, growing in size and content. So many versions of this grimoire were written that it is difficult to ascertain the contents of the original text. A Greek version which dates to 1100–1200 C.E. is part of the collection in the British Museum. Around 1350, Pope Innocent VI ordered a grimoire called The Book of Solomon to be burned; later, in 1559, Solomon's grimoire was condemned by the church again as dangerous. The Greater Key of Solomon was widely distributed in the 17th century.

Another grimoire attributed to Solomon is the LEMEGETON, or Lesser Key of Solomon.

A major Jewish magical text is the SEFER RAZIEL, supposedly based on the cosmic secrets passed to ADAM and said to be the book passed to Solomon. With the rise of the KABBALAH in the Middle Ages, a system of magic called "practical Kabbalah" emerged, though it had little to do with the theoretical Kabbalah.

AGRIPPA's *Occult Philosophy* is one of the greatest Western works on occult and magical lore, published in 1531. FRANCIS BARRETT drew heavily upon *Occult Philosophy* for his book *The Magus*, published in 1801.

Other major grimoires are:

Grimorium Verum. Drawn on The Greater Key of Solomon and written in French, this book probably was written in the mid-18th century, though claims were made that it was translated from Hebrew by a Dominican priest and was published by "Alibeck the Egyptian" in 1517.

Grimoire of Honorius. First published in Rome between 1629 and 1670, it gained wide circulation during the 17th century. The authorship is attributed to Pope Honorius, a reputed sorcerer, though this is doubtful. It claims to be based on the practical Kabbalah, but its connection is tenuous. As a magical text, it is viewed as having little foundation.

The Book of Sacred Magic of Abra-Melin the Mage. Authorship is attributed to Abramelin (Abra-Melin), a Jewish mage of Würzburg who supposedly wrote the grimoire for his son in 1458; most likely, it was written in the 18th century. The book was a major influence in the 19th-century occult revival carried out by the Hermetic Order of the Golden Dawn in England.

The Book of Black Magic and of Pacts. This text was written in 1898 by Arthur Edward Waite, a leader of the Hermetic Order of the Golden Dawn. In the first part of the book, Waite discusses other grimoires; the second part comprises a "Complete Grimoire of Black Magic."

True Black Magic, also called *The Secrets of Secrets.* An 18th-century grimoire that draws heavily upon The Greater Key of Solomon.

Grand Grimoire. A French grimoire probably authored in the 17th century. A book of black magic, this grimoire includes instructions for necromancy that "only a dangerous maniac or an irreclaimable criminal" would attempt, according to Waite.

Red Dragon. Published in 1822 but reported to date back to 1522, this is nearly identical to the *Grand Grimoire*.

The Black Pullet. Probably authored in the late 18th century in Rome, The Black Pullet does not claim to be a manuscript of antiquity. It places particular emphasis on magic talismans and rings. It has appeared in altered versions as *Treasure of the Old Man of the Pyramids* and *Black Screech Owl*.

FURTHER READING

Grillot de Givry, Emile. *Witchcraft, Magic and Alchemy.* New York: Dover Publications, 1971. First published 1931.

James, Geoffrey. *Angel Magic: The Ancient Art of Summoning and Communicating with Angelic Beings.* St. Paul, Minn.: Llewellyn Publications, 1999.

Trachtenberg, Joshua. *Jewish Magic and Superstition: A Study in Folk Religion.* New York: Berhman's Jewish Book House, 1939.

guardian angels

Angels who are attached to a person from birth to death, providing constant guidance, protection, and companionship. The concept of GUARDIAN SPIRITS is ancient and universal; guardian angels are developed most in Christianity and are particularly prominent in Catholicism.

The Judeo-Christian guardian angel evolved from guardian beings of other cultures, such as the FRAVISHIS of ZOROASTRIANISM, the KARABU of the Assyrians, the DAIMONES of the Greeks, and the GENII of the Romans. Guardian spirits and SPIRIT GUIDES also are comparable to the guardian angel.

Guardian Angels of Individuals

Guardian angels are not expressly named so in the Bible, but the concept of personal angels is established in various passages. Genesis 32:1 tells that "JACOB went on his way and the angels of God met him," implying that he had personal angels protecting him on his journey. In Psalm 91:11–13, God "will give his angels charge of you to guard you in all your ways. On their hands they will bear you up, lest you dash your foot against a stone. You will tread on the lion and the adder, the young lion and the serpent you will trample under foot."

In the New Testament, JESUS also refers to the personal angels of children: "See that you do not despise one of these little ones; for I tell you that in heaven their angels always behold the face of my Father who is in heaven" (Matthew 18:10–11). In Acts 13:6–17, St. Peter, imprisoned by Herod, is freed by an angel who wakes Peter up, causes the chains to fall off of him, and takes him outside. Peter thinks he is having a vision. Once in the street, the angel vanishes, and Peter realizes the experience is real. He refers to the angel as one of God's: "Now I am sure that the Lord has sent his angel and rescued me from the hand of Herod and all that the Jewish people were expecting" (13:11). But when Peter shows up at the house of MARY, mother of John, people mistake him for his own personal angel. Rhoda the maid announces he is at the gate, but the people present in the house say, "You are mad. . . . It is

Victorian postcard of guardian angel and children

his angel!" (13:15) Peter convinces them it is himself in the flesh.

Apocryphal texts such as The Shepherd of HERMAS speak of companion angels similar to the daimones, in that one is good and one is bad. Hermas says, "The good angel is sensitive, modest, sweet, calm . . . the wicked angel, by contrast, is prone to anger, is bitter and rash. When anger or bitterness takes possession of you, know that the evil angel is within you!" (Precept VI, 2, 4).

Islam's RECORDING ANGELS, who watch all of a person's activities, are a type of guardian angel.

OPINIONS OF CHURCH FATHERS

The church fathers agreed about the existence of personal, or guardian, angels. They disagreed, however, over whether pagans and the unbaptized were entitled to guardian angels, and also when exactly a guardian angel assumed his duties over one's life. St. Basil the Great, citing Matthew 18:10–11, said that "each one of the faithful has an Angel who directs his life." St. John Chrysostom concurred. ORIGEN states in *De Principia* that all the faithful receive guardian angels: "Every one of the faithful we are told, however insignificant he may be in the Church, is assisted by an angel, and Christ is our witness that these angels behold the Father's face continually" (II, 10, 7). St. Hilary of Poitiers associated guardian angels with the ANGEL OF THE LORD: "All the faithful are helped in a very considerable way by these divine messengers in accordance with what has been written, namely, that the angel of the Lord stays near those who fear the Lord" (*Treatise on Psalm 124*).

Saints Basil and Cyril of Alexandria likewise believed that only the faithful qualified. St. Jerome made no distinction between souls of the righteous and souls of sinners as deserving of guardian angels, but he agreed with St. Basil that mortal sin would put guardian angels "into flight." St. Ambrose said that God sometimes withdraws a guardian angel in order to give someone the "opportunity" to struggle alone, and thus gain more glory. St. THOMAS AQUINAS qualified that view by stating that he did not believe that a guardian angel would completely abandon a person, but an angel might leave temporarily. Some church fathers believed that the guardian angel was installed at baptism, whereas others, such as Aquinas, Jerome, and Anselm, believed that the guardian angel appears at birth. Aquinas also said that out of envy, a demon also appears at the time of birth. After baptism the good angel is strengthened.

DUTIES OF GUARDIAN ANGELS

The primary purpose of the guardian angel is the salvation of the soul. It serves as messenger, bringing God's inspiration and guidance, and as protector against harm and evil. The guardian angel has also been called the ANGEL OF PRAYER, ANGEL OF PEACE, and ANGEL OF REPENTANCE.

CATHOLIC TEACHINGS

The Catholic Church has taught from the Middle Ages on that every person has a guardian angel. There are no exceptions for any reason, not race, age, religion, sex, or virtue. Even the most wicked people on the earth have guardian angels. While guardian angels protect and guide, their ultimate purpose is to enlighten and help the soul achieve salvation (thus it could be argued that the wicked need guardian angels more than the righteous). Hebrews 1:14 states, "Are they [angels] not all ministering spirits sent forth to serve, for the sake of those who are to obtain salvation?" and 1 Timothy 2:4 notes that God "desires all men to be saved and to come to knowledge of the truth."

The Catholic Church teaches that guardian angels watch over humanity as a shepherd watches his flocks. Jacob's ladder (Genesis 28:12) provides testimony to this; his dream shows angels descending from heaven

The Angel of Hope (Reprinted courtesy of U.S. Library of Congress)

to protect and ascending back up to sing praise to God (see JACOB). Angels are joyful and happy to promote the welfare of human souls, for it is the will of God, and angels serve God. The church further teaches that "the dignity of the angels given to us depends on the dignity of the persons to whom they are assigned. Ordinary Christians have one of the lower order of angels; priests, bishops, kings, and so forth have nobler spirits to guard them. Feasts of the guardian angels are observed on October 2 and in some places on the first Sunday of September.

There are several primary ways that guardian angels help people, according to the catechism:

1. *They put good thoughts into minds, and move will to what is good.* Although angels manifest when necessary, such as their appearance to the shepherds at Bethlehem to announce the birth of Jesus, and their appearances at his tomb and after his Ascension, guardian angels influence us without being seen or heard. They accomplish this through "secret impulse," or what otherwise would be described as intuition. They incite pious and salutary thoughts and desires, and, when necessary, fear of God's judgment. Guardian angels correct people when they stray.
2. *They pray with people and for people, and offer their prayers and good works to God.* It is not that God doesn't hear people when they pray, but the angels mingle human prayers with theirs and thus make them "more acceptable to God." Aquinas, who wrote extensively on angels, observed that angels help people obtain all of God's benefits.
3. *They protect in danger.* Guardian angels rescue people from the dangers in the physical world, but their chief task in this regard is to protect from the "snares of the devil." People must commit themselves to the care of their guardian angels at all times, especially when undertaking a journey or starting any new enterprise.
4. *They reveal the will of God.* Among the biblical examples of this are ABRAHAM's attempt to sacrifice ISAAC, in which an angel stays his hand at the moment of slaughter (Genesis 22:11–12); the angel who interprets the word of God for the prophet Zechariah in the Book of Zechariah; and Gabriel's annunciation to MARY of the birth of Jesus (Luke 1:28–38). The appearance of angels in such circumstances often causes fear initially, but that soon gives way to joy and consolation. With evil angels, the effect is the reverse: they engender feelings of consolation at first, which then disintegrate into fear and confusion. The way to obtain the protection of guardian angels is to imitate them by living

a holy life, to honor them, and to always invoke their aid. They are attracted to innocence; evil drives them away like smoke drives away bees. The Church advocates that people congratulate their guardian angels on their faithfulness to God, and thank them for all their benefits.

5. *They receive and protect the soul at the moment of death.* The guardian angel guides it to the afterworld, protecting it from the onslaught of demons who attempt to steal it away to HELL. The biblical basis for this belief can be found in Luke 16:22 concerning the death of the beggarman Lazarus: "The poor man died and was carried by the angels to Abraham's bosom." (The rich man who refused to feed Lazarus, meanwhile, died and went to hell, and was refused mercy by Abraham.)

According to Catholic belief, if the soul goes to purgatory, the guardian angel visits it frequently to bring relief and comfort. When the soul becomes purified of all debt of sin, the guardian angel will, at the request of Mary, Queen of Angels, fly it to heaven, accompanied by jubilant martyrs and choirs of angels.

Numerous liturgical prayers to guardian angels ask for their presence at the hour of death.

(This role of PSYCHOPOMPOI overlaps with the official ANGEL OF DEATH, one of the many titles held by Michael.)

6. *Guardian angels praise God.* Angels continuously sing the glory of God, and they encourage humans to do the same.

Various popes have publicly acknowledged their close relationships with their guardian angels, and they have advocated that others cultivate the same (see Popes PIUS XI, PIUS XII, and JOHN XXIII).

EXPERIENCES OF SAINTS
The hagiographies of the Christian saints feature guardian angels (see St. GEMMA GALGANI). Descriptions speak of guardian angels who were not always cheerful, but capable of remonstration. In accordance with the opinion of St. Ambrose, they even withdrew their presence whenever the saints in question acted in a displeasing or ungodly manner (see St. FRANCES OF ROME).

St. Francis de Sales, prior to preaching, would silently address the guardian angels of everyone present and ask that the listeners be well disposed to what they were about to say.

St. Padre Pio, following the advice of Pius XII, had a constant and close relationship with his guardian angel. Lore has it that God used the angel to make it possible for Pio to understand foreign languages he had not learned, and to have clairvoyant knowledge of

secrets within the heart (especially useful to him during confessions). Pio would tell people that whenever they were in need of his prayer, to address his guardian angel through their guardian angels. One story goes that a busload of pilgrims, enroute to San Giovanni Rotondo where Pio lived, got caught at night in a violent lightning storm in the Apennine Mountains. They followed his advice, and weathered the storm unscathed. When they arrived the next day, and before they could tell their story, Pio announced that he had been awakened by his guardian angel during the night and had prayed for them.

Similarly, St. Theresa Neumann used her guardian angel to discover whatever she needed to know about the secrets and hidden lives of her visitors. She could see her own angel as well as the guardian angels of others.

Aquinas acknowledged that the mere presence of our angels influences us for the better; however, if we are not aware that we are being enlightened, then we are not enlightened. St. Ignatius of Loyola observed that the more we advance ourselves spiritually, the more we are able to discern the subtle influences of our angels, and thus the more receptive we are to their help. St. John of the Cross opined that when we attain higher spiritual levels, we no longer need the mediation of angels, but obtain our enlightenment directly from God. Not only are angels no longer necessary, but words, forms, and images fall away as well.

GUARDIAN ANGELS IN EASTERN ORTHODOXY
Guardian angels have a presence in the Eastern Orthodox Church. A liturgical prayer in the Litany before the Communion of the Faithful asks, "For an angel of peace, a faithful guide, a guardian of our souls and bodies, let us entreat the Lord."

OTHER VIEWS
The visionary EMMANUEL SWEDENBORG states in *Arcana Coelestia* everyone has two angels, one to affect what is our will and one to affect what is our understanding.

In *Angeloglia*, Karl Rahner, a contemporary Christian theologian, speaks approvingly of the human–guardian angel relationship "providing that we do not try to visualize this relationship in too anthropomorphic or infantile a manner."

Modern popular thought casts guardian angels as ever-present and ever-loving beings.

Guardian Angels of Stars and Nations
People are not the only recipients of guardian angels; the early church fathers assigned a particular angel to the stars and everything in the heavens; to everything in the natural world; and to the elements. Aquinas

thought such a belief to be rather exaggerated, but he opined that there were guardian angels for every species of living things, and for nations, cities, churches, and communities. The heads of state and church thus had two guardian angels, one for themselves and one for their offices. Earlier, Clement of Alexandria supported the idea of guardian angels for countries and cities, but he said they "perchance" might be assigned to some individuals as well.

The existence of guardian angels of nations is established in Deuteronomy 32:8: "When the Most High gave to the nations their inheritance, when he separated the sons of men, he fixed the bounds of the peoples according to the number of the SONS OF GOD" (a reference to angels). Other biblical references to guardian angels of nations refer to them as PRINCES. DANIEL 10:13 refers to the "prince of Persia" and to the archangel Michael as "one of the chief princes" who is guardian of Israel.

St. Paul's vision of the "man of Macedonia" in Acts 16:9 is widely interpreted to refer to the guardian angel of Macedonia: "And a vision appeared to Paul in the night: a man of Macedonia was standing beseeching him and saying, 'Come over to Macedonia and help us.'"

See DEVOTIONAL CULTS.

FURTHER READING

Giudici, Maria Pia. *The Angels: Spiritual and Exegetical Notes.* New York: Alba House, 1993.

Huber, Georges. *My Angel Will Go Before You.* Westminster, Md.: Christian Classics, 1983.

Lang, Judith. *The Angels of God: Understanding the Bible.* Hyde Park, N.Y.: New City Press, 1997.

Parente, Fr. Pascal P. *The Angels: The Catholic Teaching on the Angels.* Rockford, Ill.: Tan Books and Publishers, 1973. First published 1961.

The Catechism Explained. Rockford, Ill.: Tan Books and Publishers, 1921.

guardian spirits

Spirits that protect individuals, tribes, and clans, or provides magical or shamanic power. In terms of their abilities, guardian spirits are the approximate equivalent of angels; however, they usually have animal forms, which stems from a deep belief that humans and animals are related to one another.

The purpose of guardian spirits is to help in the spiritual development of a person and to provide sources of spiritual and psychic power. Other names for them are totems, power animals, spirit helpers, tutelary spirits (in Siberian shamanism), assistant totems (among Australian Aborigines), "spirits of the head" (used by the Vasyugan of Siberia), and *nagual* (used among Mexican and Guatemalan shamans, from the Aztec term *nahualli*).

Guardian spirits are considered to dwell within the body, rather than exist externally. Unlike GUARDIAN ANGELS, who come at birth and remain until death, guardian spirits change during the course of a person's life, depending on spiritual development and needs.

Like angels, guardian spirits represent the human conscious and the unconscious, what is obvious and what is hidden. They are sources of knowledge, wisdom, and inspiration, and they help human beings to connect to otherworldly realms. As intermediaries between the physical world and the Creator, or "Great Mystery," they are sources of power that can be tapped by the individual.

Guardian spirits can shapeshift to other forms, including human, when necessary. The innate animal form of a guardian spirit represents the collective power of an entire species or genus, which has magical powers that enables the guardian spirit to perform extraordinary feats. Guardian spirits can converse with humans, regardless of their form.

Beliefs about guardian spirits vary. In many tribes it is more important for males than females to have guardian spirits. Such spirits are acquired during rites of passage into adulthood (which are more elaborate for males than for females) and during vision quests. Males who do not acquire guardian spirits will suffer weakness and failure in life.

Some tribal societies have totem guardian spirits that protect entire tribes or clans on both a collective and individual basis.

Shamans must acquire guardian spirits, who empower them with magical powers, in order to function in their roles. The guardian spirits share much in common with angels in terms of their powers and roles. The guardian spirit serves as the shaman's "power animal," or his alter ego. When the shaman enters an altered state of consciousness he merges with his power animal and uses it for guidance. It accompanies him on his journey to the Underworld, where he searches for sick or lost souls, or on his mystical ascents to the sky, where he goes to obtain revelation and prophecy.

Communication with guardian spirits is made through ecstatic dancing, in which the dancer enters a trance state and assumes the form of the animal, and also through drumming and chanting, and in meditation.

"Spirit helpers" are minor powers with specialized functions, as the healing of specific illnesses or diseases. The spirit helpers are used collectively by a shaman, who in turn works with his guardian spirit, or power animal.

FURTHER READING

Eliade, Mircea. *Shamanism*. Princeton, N.J.: Princeton University Press, 1964.

Harner, Michael. *The Way of the Shaman*. New York: Bantam, 1986.

Hultkrantz, Ake. *The Religions of the American Indians*. Berkeley, Calif.: University of California Press, 1979. First published 1967.

guardians of the doors (guardians of the palaces)

Angels who guard the gates of the seven palaces of God in the seventh HEAVEN. The guardians of the doors appear in MERKABAH literature. According to the Hekalot Rabbati, there are eight guardians at each of the seven gates and each group has its own leader. 3 ENOCH mentions the guardians but names only one leader, Prince Qaspiel, of the seventh palace. (See PRINCES.)

In general, angels are guardians of the doors of consciousness; the door is a symbol of a passageway or portal to another place. In Christian art of the Annunciation, Gabriel and MARY are in the foreground and open doorways and arches often are in the background. The openings reveal perhaps a river, treed landscape, or castle in the distance, which evoke the kingdom to come, a return to Eden—but only if one passes through the thresholds of higher spiritual consciousness.

FURTHER READING

Lang, Judith. *The Angels of God: Understanding the Bible*. Hyde Park, N.Y.: New City Press, 1997.

Guriel

Angel of the zodiac sign of Leo. Guriel means "whelp of God."

Gusion (Gusayn)

One of the FALLEN ANGELS and 72 spirits of SOLOMON. In HELL Gusion is a duke who appears as a cynocephalus (*Xenophilus*). He discerns the past, present, and future, answers all questions, gives honor and dignity, and reconciles enemies. He commands 40 legions of DEMONS.

Gzrel

Angel who can countermand any evil decree that has been issued against a person in HEAVEN. Grzel is taken from part of the 42-letter name of God.

See NAMES.

Hadraniel (Hadariel, Hadarniel, Hadriel)
Angel who stands at the second gate in HEAVEN. Hadraniel means "majesty of God." Hadraniel is a large angel, bigger than Kemuel but smaller than Sandalphon, the twin of Metatron. He is sometimes identified with Metatron, and his name is one of Metraton's many names. Hadraniel is mentioned in the Zohar in connection with the SEFER RAZIEL; he is sent by God to ADAM to tell him to keep the book secret, even from the angels.

Tradition holds that Hadraniel proclaims the will of God with 12,000 flashes of lightning emanating from his mouth; his voice penetrates 200,000 firmaments.

MOSES sees Hadraniel in heaven and is awestruck, but he makes the angel tremble when he speaks the Supreme Name. (See NAMES.)

Hadriel (Hadraniel)
In GNOSTICISM, angel who is among the guardians of the gates of the East Wind.

Hagar
The Egyptian handmaid of Sarai (Sarah), wife of Abram (ABRAHAM). Hagar was aided by an ANGEL OF THE LORD in her times of distress. The story is told in the Old Testament book of Genesis 14 and 21.

Sarai is old and childless when she suggests to Abram, who is 86, that he conceive children through Hagar. Abram agrees. When Hagar becomes pregnant, she considers herself better than her mistress. Enraged, Sarai curses Abram. He tells his wife to do as she pleases with Hagar. Sarai punishes the maid, who flees into the wilderness.

As Hagar rests by a spring, an Angel of the Lord appears to her and inquires where she has come from, and where she is going. When Hagar replies, the angel instructs her to return to Sarai and submit to her punishment. As reward, the angel says he will "so greatly multiply your descendants that they cannot be numbered for multitude" (Genesis 16:10). He also tells her she will bear a son, and should name him Ishmael. "He shall be a wild ass of a man, his hand against every man and every man's hand against him; and he shall dwell over all his kinsmen" (Genesis 16:12).

Hagar calls the angel "a God of seeing," and wonders, "Have I really seen God and remained alive after seeing him?" (Genesis 16:13). The spring becomes known as Beerlaharoi, which means "the well of one who sees and lives."

Hagar follows the angel's instructions. Her troubles, however, are not over; the story resumes in Genesis 21.

Fourteen years later, Sarai bears a son, ISAAC, following a visit by three angels. By the time Isaac is weaned, Sarah (as she was renamed by God) frets that his inheritance will be threatened by Ishmael. She orders Abraham (as he is renamed) to cast out Hagar and Ishmael. Abraham does not wish to do so, but he is reassured by God that Ishmael shall have his own nation. Abraham packs bread and water and sends the two off into the wilderness of Beersheba.

When the water runs out, Hagar sets Ishmael under a bush. Certain they will die, she cries out loud that she cannot bear to look upon the death of her child. Ishmael begins to cry. God hears the weeping. An angel calls from heaven to Hagar, "What troubles you, Hagar? Fear not; for God has heard the voice of the lad where he is. Arise, lift up the lad, and hold him fast with your hand; for I will make him a great nation" (Genesis 21:17–18).

To Hagar's astonishment, she sees a water well. They have plenty of water and survive. Ishmael grows up and becomes an expert archer. Hagar secures for him an Egyptian wife, and Ishmael lives in the wilderness of Paran.

The moral of this tale is to call upon one's inner strength to survive adversity. The role of the angel here is not to rescue, but rather to call attention to self-reliance.

FURTHER READING
Ginzburg, Louis. *Legends of the Bible*. Philadelphia: The Jewish Publication Society, 1992.
Margolies, Morris B. *A Gathering of Angels*. New York: Ballantine Books, 1994.

Hagenti

One of the FALLEN ANGELS and 72 spirits of SOLOMON. Hagenti is a president who commands 33 legions. He appears in the shape of a bull with griffin wings but can change into human form. He turns wine into water, transmutes all metals, and imparts wisdom.

Hagith

One of the seven ruling angels of the 196 Olympic provinces of HEAVEN, according to the Arbatel of Magic. As the fifth angel, Hagith rules all matters pertaining to Venus, 21 provinces and 4,000 legions of spirits, each legion having 490 beings. Hagith has the ability to transmute gold into copper and copper into gold.

Halahel

In the LEMEGETON, a spirit who is part good and part evil, and under the rule of Bael. In the Zohar Halahel is equated with the archangel Raphael, but in the demonology of JOHANN WEYER, he is a king of HELL.

Halaliel

In the EDGAR CAYCE readings, an archangel who as the Lord of Karma governs the law of karma. The name "Halaliel" has no known etymology and is not mentioned elsewhere in angel literature.

Halaliel appeared suddenly in the mid-1930s during a session of Cayce's study group, which was collecting material for a spiritual study guide. Cayce, in trance, would give answers to questions. Halaliel made his debut in a commanding tone:

Come, my children! Ye no doubt have gained from the comment this day that a new initiate has spoken in or through this channel [Cayce]; Halaliel, that was with those in the beginning who warred with those that separated themselves and became naught.

In a subsequent session, the angel further identified himself as coming from the higher spiritual realms, and being on the side of Michael's righteous angels who fought against the FALLEN ANGELS:

One in and with whose courts Ariel fought when there was the rebellion in heaven. Where is Ariel, and who was he? A companion of Lucifer or Satan.

In a reading Cayce refined Halaliel's role, saying he "has made the ways that have been made heavy—but as the means for understand," a reference to his governance of the law of karma.

Halaliel also indicated that he was as important on other worlds as Christ is on this one.

Members of the study group, including Cayce himself and his immediate family—especially his son, Hugh Lynn Cayce—were alienated by the commanding and dark tone of Halaliel. They were uncertain whether the angel intended to intervene in the group or interfere with it. The angel said he had been appointed to serve as their teacher and guide who could give clearer and better organized material. Disagreement broke out over whether to accept or reject him; accepting him would mean a marked change in the direction of the group. Those who wanted to accept Halaliel pointed out that Cayce had been giving messages from Michael, and so perhaps Halaliel, as Lord of Karma, would help them in their struggle with hard lessons about karma.

Meanwhile, the Cayce readings took on a darker character with predictions of dire disasters and catastrophes in the world.

Hugh Lynn Cayce consulted noted medium Eileen J. Garrett to ask if it would be wise to follow Halaliel. Garrett's spirit control, Uvani, had corroborated that the angel would be able to give clearer material than the group had been receiving in the past. But the answer given to Hugh Lynn's question was a question:

"Does Uvani claim to know better than the Master who made him?" Hugh Lynn interpreted it to mean that the group should send Halaliel away.

The study group remained divided and undecided. Halaliel became irritated at the group's indecision and then forced the question. All but two members of the group voted to reject Halaliel and stay focused on "the Christ Consciousness" as the source of their material received through Cayce. The dissenters left the group, and Halaliel withdrew his presence.

Cayce scholars have cast Halaliel in a positive light as an important teacher whose duty is to make people face their spiritual lessons and shortcomings.

FURTHER READING
Grant, Robert J. *Are We Listening to the Angels?* Virginia Beach, Va.: A.R.E. Press, 1994.

haloes See IMAGES OF ANGELS.

Halpas

One of the FALLEN ANGELS and 72 spirits of SOLOMON. In HELL Halpas is an earl who appears in the form of a stork and speaks with a hoarse voice. He burns towns; it is also said that he builds towns and fills them with armed men. Halpas takes a sword to the wicked, and he sends men to either the fields of war or other places. He rules 26 legions.

Hamaliel

Angel who rules the order of VIRTUES, the month of August, and the sign of Virgo.

Hamon

In 3 ENOCH, a "great, terrible, honored, beautiful and dreaded PRINCE" who makes all other angels in HEAVEN quake when it comes time to recite the QEDUSSAH. Hamon bows down to Tatrasiel. St. Jerome said Hamon is another name for Gabriel.

Haniel (Aniel, Hanael, Hamiel, Onoel, Simiel)

One of the seven ARCHANGELS and the 10 sephirot of the TREE OF LIFE. Haniel means "glory or of God" or "he who sees God." Haniel rules the orders of PRINCIPALITIES and VIRTUES and also all innocence. He is sometimes said to be the angel who carries the prophet ENOCH to HEAVEN, a role usually ascribed to Anafiel. He governs the planet Venus, the month of December, and the signs of Libra and Taurus.

In magical lore Haniel is an angel of benevolence, grace, and mercy who is invoked for the winning of favor. Haniel also rules love and beauty and is invoked in spells for the increase of love and affection, peace and harmony.

Harahel

In the KABBALAH, the angel who oversees libraries, archives, and rare cabinets. Harahel also is one of the 72 angels of the SCHEMHAMPHORAE who bear the name of God.

Harmozy (Harmozel, Armogen)

In GNOSTICISM, one of four great LUMINARIES who surround the self-begotten, the savior, or God. The other three are Oroiael, Daveithe, and Eleleth.

Hasdiel

Angel of benevolence who also is a ruler of the planet Venus. Hasdiel is named as angel of benevolence in MEZUZOT of Germany; another angel of benevolence is Zadkiel. In the Zohar, Hasdiel also acts as one of two angelic chiefs who accompanies Uriel into battle as he carries his standard.

Hasmal (Hashmal)

Ruling angel of the HASMALIM. Hasmal is a fire-speaking angel who surrounds the throne of God. "Hasmal" denotes primeval wisdom and wonderful light. According to the Zohar, Hasmal is associated with a hidden, inner sphere in which the mysteries of the celestial letters of the Holy Name are suspended.

hasmalim (chasmalim; hasmallim)

In Jewish lore, a high-ranking order of angels, along with the CHERUBIM and SERAPHIM. The hasmalim are sometimes equated with DOMINIONS. Their name means "brilliant ones" and the "HAYYOTH" or "living creatures," also a reference to a high class of MERKABAH angels (see SERAPHIM).

The fiery hasmalim support the throne of God. In his heavenly journey, the prophet EZEKIEL sees a sapphirelike throne occupied by a humanlike form, in a reference to the "glory of the Lord" or also one of the hasmalim:

> And upward from what had the appearance of his loins I saw as it were gleaming bronze, like the appearance of fire enclosed round about; and downward from what had the appearance of his loins I saw as it was a brightness round about him. (Ezekiel 1:27)

Hasmalim have been given different rankings. The Zohar places them sixth highest; the Maseket Azilut seventh; and the Berith Menucha fourth, by which EL (God) framed the effigies of bodies.

Angels named as rulers of the hasmalim are Hasmal, Zadkiel, and Zacharael. In the KABBALAH, the hasmalim belong to Yetzirah, the World of Formation, ruled by Metatron. Their sweat from carrying the throne of God forms a fiery river, Dinur.

Hasmed

Angel of annihilation and one of the ANGELS OF PUNISHMENT.

Hasmoday See ASMODAY.

Haurus See FLAUROS.

Haurvatat

In ZOROASTRIANISM, one of the AMARAHSPANDS, who is a spirit of the waters and personifies salvation. Haurvatat is a female angel who may be the precursor of the fallen angel Harut in Islamic lore.

Hayliel YHVH (Chayyiel, Hashmal, Hayyel, Hayyliel, Johiel, Yayael)

Great angelic PRINCE in the seventh HEAVEN and chief angel of the HAYYOTH. Hayliel rules wild beasts whom he whips with lashes of fire. He extols the beasts when they offer praise and glory. He is able to swallow the entire world in one gulp.

hayyoth (chaioth ha-qadesh; chayoh; chayot; chayyoth; chiva; haioth hacadosch)

High-ranking MERKABAH angels who live in the seventh HEAVEN, and who are sometimes equated with CHERUBIM, HASMALIM, and SERAPHIM. Hayyoth means "holy living creatures" or "creature of holiness." EZEKIEL refers to the "four living creatures" in his heavenly visions who are "running and returning, like the appearance of lightning" (Ezekiel 1:14).

The hayyoth are angels of fire and support the throne of Glory; they move the wheels and support the universe. According to the Zohar, there are 36 hayyoth. 3 ENOCH cites only four, who comprise the "camp of the SHEKINAH." The four "holy creatures" face the four winds. Each one has four faces and every face looks like the sunrise. Each one has four wings and every single wing would cover the world. Each one has faces within faces and wings within wings. The size of each face is 248 faces and the size of each wing is 365 wings. Each creature wears 2,000 crowns, each of which is like the rainbow and as bright as the sun.

On the TREE OF LIFE, the hayyoth are rulers of the sephirah Kether (Crown), and are governed by Metatron.

According to the Sefer Yetzirah, the hayyoth exist in the universe of Yetzirah (Formation). They rank below the seraphim and above the OPHANIM.

Haziel

Angel who is both good and bad. The name "Haziel" is Hebrew for "vision of God," and probably was taken from the man named Haziel in 1 Chronicles 23:9. As a good angel, Haziel is one of the CHERUBIM who governs the pity of God, and is one of the 72 SCHEMHAMPHORAE who bear the name of God. Haziel is an angel of darkness when he is equated with Bernael.

Head of the Dragons

Name of a DEMON in the form of a three-headed dragon with awful skin. In the Testament of SOLOMON, the Head of the Dragons describes himself as a three-pronged spirit who is responsible for birth defects and epilepsy. He can enter the wombs of women and blind the unborn as well as turn their ears around backwards and make them deaf and dumb. He makes men fall down, grind their teeth, and foam at the mouth. The Head of the Dragons is thwarted by an "angel of the Counselor" (Christ) at Golgotha. The demon tells King SOLOMON that a great deal of gold lies beneath the foundation of the Temple of Jerusalem, which Solomon has under construction. Solomon finds the gold and seals the demon with his magical ring. He sentences the demon to make bricks for the temple.

heaven

Abode of souls in the afterlife. In Christianity there is one heaven, a place of eternal rest and reward for the righteous in the presence of God and JESUS and in the company of angels. The opposite of heaven is HELL, a separate and lower realm of terrible, eternal punishment ruled by Satan and DEMONS. In GNOSTICISM and Jewish mysticism, there are multiple heavens, each of which is different and may be pleasant or unpleasant. Some levels are more hellish places where different kinds of sinners and FALLEN ANGELS are punished.

In Jewish mysticism, an early belief held that all souls are initially woven into the curtain (*pargod*) that veils God's throne of Glory. (In 3 ENOCH, all of history is written upon the curtain.) The past history and future destiny of each soul is recorded. Wicked souls, however, will not have a home in the curtain. The "curtain of souls" appears in KABBALAH works.

Angel showing the New Jerusalem heavenly city to St. John
(Gustave Doré)

In later Kabbalistic doctrine, the soul first crosses a purgatorial RIVER OF FIRE, then ascends to a terrestrial paradise—"the world of souls"—where it retains its individuality, and then to an eternal celestial paradise—"the world to come"—sometime interpreted as one of the sephirot of the TREE OF LIFE, in which the soul partakes of life in the Godhead.

Jewish apocryphal and MERKABAH texts describe ascents into the heavens with detailed descriptions of the characteristics and angels therein. There usually are seven heavens, each of which has seven halls or palaces; God resides in the seventh hall of the seventh heaven. The heavens have names and ruling angels; texts are inconsistent.

3 Enoch gives the names of the PRINCES and their heavens as follows:

Sidriel, prince of the first heaven, Wilon
Baraqiel, prince of the second heaven, Raqia
Baradiel, prince of the third heaven, Sehaqim

Sahaqiel, prince of the fourth heaven, Zebul
Satqiel, prince of the fifth heaven, Maon
Gabriel, prince of the sixth heaven, Makon
Michael, prince of the seventh heaven, Arabot

Each of the seven princes of the heavens is attended by 496,000 myriads of MINISTERING ANGELS.

The Midrash Konen says that the heavens are all fixed and vaulted over earth, one above the other. Wilon, the lowest, shades the uppermost earth from the heat, but at sundown it is rolled back to enable the moon and stars to shine from Raqia, the second heaven.

According to the Hagiga, Sehaqim, the third heaven, holds a pair of millstones that grind manna for the righteous. Zebul, the fourth heaven, is home to the heavenly Jerusalem, the temple and altar, and the angels Sandalphon, Michael, Zazagel, Shamsiel, and Sapiel. In Maon, the fifth heaven, hosts of ministering angels sing hymns to God's mercy all night long, but fall silent at dawn, thus allowing him to hear his praises sung by Israel below. Makhon, the sixth heaven, contains storehouses of snow and hailstones, lofts of dews and rains, chambers of storms, and caves of fog. In the seventh heaven, Arabot, abide Justice, Law, and Charity, the treasures of Life, Peace and Blessing, the souls of the righteous, the souls of the yet unborn, the dew with which God will revive the dead, the chariot seen by EZEKIEL in a vision, the ministering angels, and the Divine Throne.

Mystical literature describes seven palaces in the garden of Eden; souls go there both in prayer and after death.

Seven heavens also are referenced in the Koran (sura 23) and in ancient Persian and Babylonian lore.

In 2 Enoch there are 10 heavens. The garden of Eden and the paradise Tree of Life are in the third heaven. The eighth heaven is Muzaloth, although this is sometimes interpreted as really the seventh heaven. The ninth heaven, called Kukhavim, contains the 12 signs of the zodiac. The tenth heaven, called Aravoth, is where Enoch sees "the vision of the face of the Lord." The name Aravoth refers to the 12 signs of the zodiac thus causing confusion with the ninth heaven.

Fewer or more heavens are described in some texts; for example, in the Testament of the Twelve Patriarchs the prophet LEVI references only three heavens. The Zohar speaks of 390 heavens and 70,000 worlds. In Gnostic cosmology, there are 365 heavenly spheres or AEONS.

Characteristics of Heaven

In Scripture and apocryphal texts, heaven can be a place of lush, earthlike abundance in the fashion of the garden of Eden enjoyed by ADAM AND EVE before their fall; or can be a realm of brilliant light and gold in which souls enter the presence of God. It is the new city or the new Jerusalem from which evil is permanently banished. Heaven is filled with myriads of brilliant angels who constantly sing praises to God. (See MUSIC AND ANGELS; QEDUSSAH.) Souls in heaven are rewarded with eternal rest, peace, love, and happiness.

Other views of heaven present it as more like an idealized earth. EMANUEL SWEDENBORG saw heaven as multilayered and a happier continuation of life on earth, but in the form of angels. (See also INSTRUMENTAL TRANSCOMMUNICATION.)

See BARUCH; DREAMS AND VISIONS; ISAIAH; EZRA; REVELATION; SHEOL.

FURTHER READING

Charlesworth, James H., ed. *The Old Testament Pseudepigrapha*. Vols. 1 and 2. New York: Doubleday, 1983, 1985.

Scholem, Gershom. *Kabbalah*. New York: Dorset Press, 1987. First published 1974.

heavenly bodies

In the Testament of Solomon, DEMONS of the world of darkness, which cause misery and strife in the world.

Chapter 8 describes seven heavenly bodies who are demonic powers of the world. Interrogated by King SOLOMON, the demons say they live together in Lydia or on Mount Olympus, and their stars in heaven look small. Six of them are thwarted (nullified) by certain angels.

The seven are:

1. Deception, who deceives and causes heresies. He is thwarted by the angel Lamechiel.
2. Strife, who provides weapons for fighting and warfare. He is thwarted by the angel Baruchiel.
3. Fate, who causes men to fight instead of make peace with those who are winning. He is thwarted by the Angel Marmaroth.
4. Distress, who divides and separates men into opposing factions and creates jealousy, and who is followed by Strife. He is thwarted by the angel Balthioul.
5. Error, who leads men astray by causing them to kill each other, dig up graves, and do other wicked things. He is thwarted by the archangel Uriel.
6. Power, who feeds the greed for power, establishes tyrants, and deposes kings. He is thwarted by the Angel Asteraoth.
7. The Worst, who tells Solomon he will harm the king by causing him to be bound with the bonds of

Artemis. The Worst does not name a thwarting angel.

Solomon sentences the seven demons to dig the foundation of the Temple of Jerusalem.

Chapter 18 describes 36 heavenly bodies, demons who correspond to the DECANS OF THE ZODIAC and call themselves the world rulers of darkness. Solomon forces them to bear water for the Temple of Jerusalem.

FURTHER READING

Charlesworth, James H., ed. *The Old Testament Pseudepigrapha*. Vols. 1 and 2. New York: Doubleday, 1983, 1985.

heavenly court of law See ENOCH.

The archangel Michael weighs souls of the dead (By Johann Weissenburger, *Ars Moriendi*, 1514)

Heleleth See ELELETH.

hell

The underworld, which in Christianity is the home of Satan and the FALLEN ANGELS, as well as of the souls of all the sinners throughout eternity. The geographic location of hell is unknown; it is "down" somewhere, perhaps inside the earth according to some descriptions. The name "hell" comes from the Scandinavian death goddess Hel, whose name refers to her home.

The concept of hell, or someplace where souls go after death, probably predates written history. The first extant accounts of a Land of the Dead appear on Sumerian clay tablets found in the valley of the Tigris and Euphrates Rivers in what is modern-day Iraq. The peoples from that area—Sumerians, Akkadians, Babylonians, and Assyrians, collectively called Mesopotamians—had underworlds that shared many characteristics that reappeared in later civilizations and religions: mountain barriers, rivers, boats and boatmen, bridges, gates and guardians, and an important tree. Hell or the Land of the Dead is somewhere in the Great Below.

For the Greeks, Hades, the underworld, was not a place of punishment but simply the land of the dead; souls, or shades, were believed to be generally unhappy there, longing continually for physical life. The blessed dead, including the souls of the valiant killed in battle, went to a happier place, the Elysian Fields.

Stories of descents into hell symbolize a conquering of death. The most famous Babylonian epic is *Gilgamesh,* in which Inanna, the Queen of Heaven and Earth (Queen Ishtar in Akkadia and Astarte in Assyria, both goddesses of fertility), goes to visit her sister Ereshkigal, the ruler of the dead. Inanna seems destined to stay below until her faithful vizier petitions Ereshkigal for his mistress's rescue. Reluctantly, Ereshkigal lets her go, provided she can provide ransom. Inanna sends her lover, Dumuzi, who stays below for six months and returns to the Great Above for six months. This descent story closely resembles the Greek myths of Demeter and Persephone, Orpheus and Eurydice; the Egyptian stories of Isis and Osiris; and the Roman myth of Ceres and Proserpina. Such accounts explained the perpetual changes of seasons and the resurrection of the soul.

Christ made the same journey in his harrowing of the souls of hell after his crucifixion.

Judgments and Battles

The idea of judgment after death may have originated with the Egyptians. In order to reach paradise, or

Sekhet Hetepet, the body and soul travel by the boat of Ra, the sun, along the river of the Milky Way, much like later Greek souls navigated the river Styx. Upon disembarking, the dead must pass through seven gates, each with a gatekeeper, watcher, and herald, then enter the Hall of Justice. Thoth, god of wisdom, prosecutes the case of the soul before Osiris the Judge, and the soul may defend itself. Eventually Anubis places the petitioner's heart on the scales of justice, and if the heart sinks lower than a feather from the headdress of Maat, goddess of truth, the soul is eaten by the horrid monster Ammit. Christian parallels are St. Peter as gatekeeper of heaven, and the archangel Michael as psychopomp and weigher of souls. (See PSYCHOPOMPOI.)

The cult founded by the prophet Zoroaster (Zarathustra) in Babylon, called ZOROASTRIANISM, influenced the later concept of Christian hell. Zoroastrianism introduced dualism, in which the forces of good continually battle the forces of evil. The divine Good, Ahura Mazda ("wise lord"), lives in the Great Above with his seven AMARAHSPANDS, or angels. On the other side is Angra Mainyu or Ahriman ("evil spirit"), the Lord of Lies who dwells under the earth and sends out his daevas or devils to torment the world. Law, love, and light oppose darkness, chaos, filth, and death in an epic struggle for man's soul.

In another powerful parallel to Christianity, Zoroaster taught there will be a final cosmic battle between good and evil, and that evil will be conquered. A savior named Soshyans, born of a virgin impregnated by Zoroaster, will harrow hell, forgive sinners, and facilitate a universal resurrection of the body and reunion with the soul. Hell will be destroyed and the kingdom of God will reign forever.

Similarly, Isaiah 7:14 and 9:6 tell, "Behold, a young woman shall conceive and bear a son, and shall call his name Immanuel . . . and his name will be called "Wonderful Counselor, Mighty God, Everlasting Father, Prince of Peace." REVELATION 20:7–10 says, "And when the thousand years are ended, Satan will be loosed from his prison and will come to deceive the nations which are at the four corners of the earth . . . to gather them for battle; their number is like the sand of the sea. . . . And the devil who had deceived them was thrown into the lake of fire and brimstone where the beast and the false prophet were, and they will be tormented day and night for ever and ever."

Afterlife Punishments in Jewish Mysticism

SHEOL is the initial destination of most souls. Some move on to paradises. Sinning souls go to Gehenna, where subtle spiritual fires burn off their sins. Moses de Leon, a 13th-century Spanish Jew who authored the

Zohar (see KABBALAH), argued against the idea of eternal punishment, contending that the soul is consubstantial with God and God would not inflict such suffering on himself. The Zohar states that the highest part of the soul, the *neshamah,* is not capable of sinning; it leaves the sinner the moment a sin is committed; after death it returns to its home in the Garden of Eden.

The atonement of sins also is accomplished through transmigration (*gilgul*), a reincarnational recycling into new lives in which the sins are punished through misfortunes and suffering. The Kabbalah does not make clear which sins are expiated by Gehenna and which are expiated by transmigration. (Some medieval Kabbalists held that *gilgul* affected all life from angels to inorganic matter.)

In Jewish apocryphal texts, certain levels of heaven are places of punishment. For example, 2 ENOCH tells that the second heaven is where the WATCHERS are being punished, and the third heaven is half paradise and half hell. More Watchers, miserable and dejected, are in the fifth heaven.

The Horrors of Christian Hell

Central to the Christian concept of damnation is the Fall, both the descent into hell by Lucifer and his angelic followers and the Fall from Paradise by ADAM AND EVE. The torments of hell were quick to be emphasized in early Christianity. Most of the Gospel references to hell occur in Matthew, wherein JESUS warns his listeners over and over again about the certainty of damnation to those who do not believe. Matthew 13:41–42 states, "The Son of man will send his angels and they will gather out of his kingdom all causes of sin and all evildoers, and throw them into the furnace of fire; there men will weep and gnash their teeth."

Some of the starkest and darkest early descriptions of the tortures in hell (Tartarus) are in the Greek Apocalypse of EZRA, a Christian work written between the second and ninth centuries C.E. Sinners are hung by their eyelashes, repeatedly eaten by a fire-breathing worm, beaten and continually attacked by wild beasts and punishing angels. (See ANGELS OF DESTRUCTION.)

Eventually, the concepts of death, hell, Satan, and sin became merged, so that no one would be spared unless he had truly believed and lived a godly life. The church's position that all people are born in original sin became so strong that, by the Middle Ages, few people expected to go to heaven, and lived in fear of spending eternity in the unspeakable horror of hell. Dying became a terrifying prospect, with a good angel and bad angel or demon wrestling for control of the soul in one's final moments.

Priests lavishly detailed hell's fires and punishments, and religious art and drama portrayed heinous aspects of Satan's minions. The most colorful aspect of such religious theater was the "hellmouth," or the entryway into the pit of hell. The hellmouth was an elaborate creation, usually a papier-mâché beast's head with wide jaws that opened and closed with winches. Smoke, flames, foul smells, and noise emitted from it, and actors playing demons would dance out on stage from the opening. Very low humor accompanied the antics of the devils. The hellmouth's finest moment came when Christ descended through its fetid doorway to release the Old Testament prophets.

Perhaps the greatest literary visit to hell was DANTE Alighieri's *Inferno* (ca. 1300), wherein Dante is led by the Roman poet Virgil through the nine levels of hell, narrowing to the final center at Satan himself. The architecture of Dante's Inferno together with the author's extensive knowledge of classical mythology and his involvement in Renaissance Italy's turbulent

Last judgment scene with devil and hell in foreground, from Eastern Orthodox Church, Romania (Author's collection)

politics make his the most exhaustive and fascinating portrait of hell. But although the church embraced his vision, Dante's presentation of hell as an allegory, not revelation, paved the way for later intellectuals to reject hell's threat.

The PROTESTANT REFORMATION focused even greater attention on hell. Authors both Catholic and Protestant wrote extensively on hell, describing in gruesome detail the terrors there and identifying contemporary sinners, usually politicians, tax collectors, and corrupt church officials, as some of hell's more colorful and deserving inhabitants.

By the late 16th and early 17th centuries, the Jesuits had reformed hell into a less dramatic place devoid of cavorting demons. Instead they made it a fiery landscape overrun with diseased, repugnant, foul-smelling peasants, merchants, aristocrats, and all types of sinners, crowded together like grapes in a wine press. Many were heretics, Protestants and scientists.

The English poet JOHN MILTON redefined hell in his mammoth work *Paradise Lost*. Unlike the vision literature of the past, which concentrated on the tortures of damnation, Milton fleshed out the story of Lucifer's battle with God and the Fall of Adam and Even. Lucifer is a proud man, jealous of the power God gives his Son, and he chooses to fight God rather than obey. When he loses, Lucifer turns his wiles upon innocent man. Milton's hell is dark and dreary, inhospitable, both frozen and fiery, a parched desert. It is a cavernous underworld, more notable for its separation from God than for its diabolic creatures.

Although fire-and-brimstone preachers exhorted their congregations to seek salvation, many intellectuals of the 1700s viewed hell as more Miltonian than Dantean. The mystic EMANUEL SWEDENBORG described hell as a place peopled with monsters and monstrous activities, but it was a place created by the humans who had chosen lives of evil and self-love rather than as a place into which sinners were cast. Evil itself was Satan and hell, so there was no need for a separate devilish leader. Sinners made their own misery.

By the 19th century, the Industrial Revolution led many to speculate that life was hell on earth. There was no much filth, poverty, degradation, and economic disparity that no one need fear another place after death. And if there were no longer a social contract, no accountability, then anything was possible, even the cruel fantasies of the Marquis de Sade, the horror of Bram Stoker's vampiric count, or even the ghoulish experiments of Mary Shelley's Dr. Frankenstein. In contrast to their ugly surroundings, the Romantic poets retrieved the shining gods and heroes of classic mythology, but they still equated hell with the ravages of government and poverty they saw around them.

Some groups optimistically reject any notions of hell, saying that a just and loving Christ will save all people, not just the godly elect, and that there is no hell for a loving God. Some have taken a Swedenborgian bent, believing that hell is what a person chooses who denies love and charity. Others believe that at death souls do not go to either heaven or hell but simply into the abyss of nothingness.

See DREAMS AND VISIONS; HEAVEN; LITERATURE AND ANGELS.

FURTHER READING

May, Herbert G., and Bruce M. Metzger, eds. *The Oxford Annotated Bible with the Apocrypha*. Revised Standard Version. New York: Oxford University Press, 1965.

Scholem, Gershom. *Kabbalah*. New York: Dorset Press, 1987. First published 1974.

Swedenborg, Emanuel. *Heaven and Hell*. Translated by George F. Dole. New York: Swedenborg Foundation Inc., 1976.

Turner, Alice K. *The History of Hell*. New York: Harcourt Brace and Co., 1993.

Hemah

Angel of wrath, fury, and destruction who governs the death of domestic animals. In Jewish lore, Hemah lives in the seventh HEAVEN; he is 500 PARASANGS tall and is made of chains of black and red fire.

In the Zohar, Hemah is one of three angels in Gehenna (HELL)—along with Af and Mashit—who punish those who sin by idolatry, incest, and murder. Hemah swallows MOSES with the help of his brother angel Af. God intervenes and forces him to spit Moses back out. Moses then kills Hemah.

See ANGELS OF PUNISHMENT.

Heman

In 3 ENOCH, the leader of a heavenly choir who sings hosannas every morning. Heman means "trust."

Hermas

Converted slave and author of an important Christian visionary work known as The Shepherd of Hermas, in which angelic guides interpret visions that convey church teachings. The text, which appeared in the late first century C.E., probably was composed as an aid to the early church in convincing people to convert and to renounce sinful behavior. The Shepherd of Hermas describes the importance of the church and central teachings for all Christians. It was widely circulated among Christians; however, it was omitted from the canon. Written in Greek, no full text has survived.

Hermas, most probably a Jew, was sold as a slave to a Roman woman named Rhoda in the late first century C.E. He describes how he became aware of his sins and desired to purify himself of them. After being sold to Rhoda, he "recognizes" her, that is, he realizes she is a Christian. He then "loves her as a sister," which probably refers to his own conversion.

One day he sees Rhoda bathing in the Tiber and helps her from the water. He has sinful thoughts, complicated by the fact that he is married himself. Later he walks toward Cumae, praising God's creations. He enters into a sort of slumber or trance and is seized by the Spirit and lifted up out of the countryside to a level plain. This marks the beginning of his visionary life. (See DREAMS AND VISIONS.)

Hermas prays and sees a vision of Rhoda, who tells him she has been taken up, probably in death, to denounce his sins against her. He does not know what she means until she reminds him of the "wicked desire in his heart." The heavens shut and Rhoda disappears. Hermas is terrified that he will not be able to overcome his sin in the eyes of God.

While he worries about this, another vision appears: a white chair covered with white wool fleece, occupied by an old woman in white who is reading a book. She asks him why he is upset. She tells him that even though his sin is grave, God is even more displeased with his wife and children, who are not believers. The woman prophesies terrible things to come upon the earth, which will end in the imminent rule of God. While she speaks, four young men—probably the four great angels of the inner host of HEAVEN—appear and lift her by the elbows, taking her away to the East, which is the center of Paradise. The vision ends.

Hermas spends a year reflecting on this experience, not writing anything about it. One day while walking to Cumae, he has another trance and is transported again to the same realm, where he sees the same old woman. She asks him if he can still preach her message, but he tells her he cannot remember it and must be given her book to copy. She does so.

Hermas still cannot understand the message and prays and fasts for its meaning to be revealed. After 15 days it becomes clear. He is told to discipline his family and his wife and to "live with her as with a sister," that is, to remain chaste. He is also told that every Christian who genuinely repents will be forgiven for all sins up to the day upon which Hermas reveals his book; but after that, they will have no such opportunity for unconditional mercy. Hermas himself will be saved despite his "bad dealings and neglect of his family," thanks to his chastity and simplicity of heart.

Until now, Hermas has believed the old woman to be the Sibyl, a prophetess of pagan and Jewish tradition whose center was near Cumae. That night Hermas has a dream in which a beautiful young man—probably an angel—corrects this misconception, and tells him that the woman is actually the church; she looks old because she has existed since creation. The old woman appears and tells Hermas to send out two copies of his book: one to Clement, probably the bishop of Rome, and one to a man named Grapte, who will teach it to widows and orphans. Hermas also must give a public reading of the book in the presence of the elders of an unspecified city.

The old woman promises Hermas another vision. After a period of fasting, Hermas has a dream vision in which the woman agrees to meet him at his chosen place, "a remote and beautiful field." There Hermas finds an ivory bench with linen rugs and cushions. He becomes frightened and confesses his sins over and over again. The woman arrives accompanied by six angels. She sits on the bench and invites Hermas to sit on her left, the place normally reserved for elders—an indication of Hermas's privileged status. She raises a shining staff and a vision unfolds before him.

Hermas sees a body of water upon which a tower is being constructed from stones of different qualities. The woman explains that the tower is the church and the stones represent different classes of Christian sinners and penitents. Some of the sins are so great that the stones are unusable, and soon the building will stop. By publishing his visions, Hermas will help wavering Christians. He must do so after three days have passed. The woman denounces the leaders of the churches, whom she describes as sorcerers with poison in their hearts. Christians, she says, should not eat excessively while others go hungry—a reference to spiritual food, not literal food. The woman disappears and then returns by night to tell Hermas he must undergo strict fasting in order to receive answers to any additional questions.

That night, a young man—again probably an angel—appears to Hermas in a dream vision and explains more about the woman, for each time Hermas sees her she becomes younger and fairer. These changes are due to spiritual improvements in Hermas himself. Another vision follows in which Hermas is pursued by a terrible monster and the woman appears as a fair virgin. The monster symbolizes the fate of Christian sinners at the end of the world; the virgin is their hope and salvation. Hermas escapes the monster, which symbolizes his salvation by his faith; he returns home. This is not the last vision, however, for after praying he sees a glorious figure dressed as a shepherd.

The man identifies himself as the ANGEL OF REPENTANCE, who has been sent to be with Hermas for the rest of his life.

Thus begins a new phase of revelations. The Angel of Repentance teaches Hermas 12 new commandments, which are not laws or rules but rather admonitions to virtues. Hermas asks the angel questions. For example, if a man has a Christian wife who commits adultery, is it a sin to continue to live with her? This question concerned a despised Roman law that mandated divorce under such circumstances. Hermas learns that the angels agree with this law; a man must divorce his adulterous wife.

Hermas also learns that Christians have two conflicting angels with them throughout life, a good angel and a bad angel (similar to DAIMONES). He learns that fasting alone is not a sufficient spiritual practice but must be combined with giving to the poor the food that would have been eaten.

In one vision Hermas travels on a plain where he sees angel shepherds guarding sheep. One mean-looking angel has a knotted staff and a huge whip. Whenever a sheep seems happy and well fed, he forces it down a ravine full of briars. This is the Angel of Punishment (see ANGELS OF PUNISHMENT), who will also remain with Hermas throughout his life to chasten him for the sins of his family.

Another important lesson learned by Hermas, one central to the teachings of the church, is that the rich should give to the poor and the poor should pray for the souls of the rich.

After much instruction, the shepherd Angel of Repentance tells Hermas that he has become virtuous enough to see his visions directly from the Holy Spirit. He is taken away immediately in spirit to Arcadia, where there are 12 mountains. Hermas sees a giant white rock on which six men are handing stones to a group of virgins, who are building the tower that Hermas had seen in his earlier vision. A giant inspector comes along and orders the shepherd angel to sort the stones. Hermas spends the night with the virgins, the holy powers, and the virtues of God. Though kissed and embraced by the virgins, he remains chaste and in the process becomes a younger man. Hermas is told that he will continue to prosper if he lives blamelessly in the company of the shepherd (the Angel of Repentance) and the virgins.

After the completion of his visions, Hermas sent his account of them to the churches. His message of a final repentance was circulated by other contemporary visionaries, who also couched their messages within the context of visions and interpreting angels. Though the Shepherd of Hermas was an important work in the early history of the Church, it has received little attention from contemporary scholars.

FURTHER READING
Fox, Robin Lane. *Pagans and Christians*. San Francisco: Harper & Row, 1986.
Koester, Helmut, ed. *Shepherd of Hermas: A Commentary*. Minneapolis: Augsburg Fortress Publications, 1999.

Hermesiel

Angel who leads one of the heavenly choirs along with Hemah, Metatron, Radueriel, Tagas, and other angels. The name Hermesiel is derived from Hermes, the Greek god who invented the lyre.

Hinduism

Hindu cosmology has no exact counterpart to the angel, but acknowledges major and minor deities (DEVAS or shining ones) and numerous other INTELLIGENCES: demigods, spirits, attendants, and a host of infernal and celestial beings, all of whom have the corresponding characteristics and functions found in the angelic realm.

Hinduism is nondual and does not share the Christian concept of absolute evil. According to one's choices, certain powers will be obstacles or helpers. Suras (gods) and devas generally are helpful and embody godly qualities. Among the various entities in this pantheon are krda (play), vijigisa (supremacy), vyapara (relation), dyuti (light), stuti (praise), moda (joy), mada (ecstasy), svapna (dream), kanti (radiance), gati (movement). Asuras (antigods) are associated with powerful instincts and attachments that keep humans within the power of Nature. The main kinds of asuras are daityas (GENII), danavas (giants), kalakanjas (stellar spirits), kalejas (demons of Time), khalins (threshers), nagas (serpents), nivata-kavacas (wearers of impenetrable armor), and raksasas (night wanderers). Serpent kings and queens are half-snake, half-human. They are beautiful, richly adorned, and dangerous, and they defend their sumptuous underground cities fiercely against both gods and men. They are the guardians of the scriptures and esoteric knowledge, and often they live under water.

Later Vedic mythology explains the asuras similarly to the fall of the angels in the Judaic-Christian story. As they multiplied, they became jealous of the devas and proud; a series of struggles with the gods followed, and they gradually became incorporated with the demons, spirits, and ghosts worshiped by the aboriginal tribes, as well as non-Vedic gods of the other Indian populations. However, the functions of devas and asuras are more mixed than in the Judaic-Christian belief system. The asuras can win boons from the gods by penance, and, if they repent, they may end up as great devotees, or benefactors of mankind.

Hindu metaphysics takes up questions of "reality" in ancient Sanskrit scripture, the Vedas and Upanishads. The Vedic seers stated what Buddhists, Plato, the Neoplatonists, Sufis, and Christian mystics were to observe centuries later: deities are both projections of our minds and objectively outside us. These divine and/or infernal beings are experienced as outside one's individual ego, but as the consciousness expands, one realizes the gods' true nature to be that unbounded Consciousness in which everything exists; the gods are within us, as everything else in the universe. The infinitely complex web of relationships that is the universe operates through a network of correspondences that connect each part of the whole and link the subtle to the gross levels. The system operates as a vast hologram. Thus each deity, itself an aspect of the universal Consciousness, is at the same time intimately associated with particulars through its connections with elements, senses, names, sounds, colors, diagrams, symbols, and so forth. Traditionally, a devout believer will worship three kinds of deity: the local deity, the family deity, and the personal deity.

The outer world of "reality" and the inner world of "imagination" are equally real, continuously influencing and shaping each other, polarities in a unified field that is itself the dream of the Divine. The epic poems the Puranas the Ramayana, and the Mahabharata contain all aspects of Hindu lore—religious, ritual, spiritual, mystical, scientific, philosophical, legal, and historical—in their thousands of legends and stories.

Beyond the solar sphere are immense spheres that no longer belong to the world of man, representing the transcendent aspects of the Cosmic Being, the boundless powers from which universes are born, the Unknowable. The higher principles, the higher gods, dwell in these supersolar worlds known as the spheres of the stars, as to the spirits of the Ancestors. Mountains, trees, rivers, animals have in them a common yet multiple life and are guided by conscious beings who are attendants of the earth goddess.

The Adityas (sovereign principles) are the sons of the Primordial-Vastness (Aditi) which is the primal power, the unbroken totality, the boundless HEAVEN. The 12 sovereign principles are generally given as Mitra (solidarity), Varuna (fate), Aryaman (chivalry), Daksa (ritual skill), Bhagra (the inherited share), Amsa (the gods' given share), Tvastr (craftsmanship), Savitr (the magic power of words), Pusan (prosperity), Sakra (courage), Vivasvat (social laws), and Visnu (cosmic law). The regents of the directions are: east/Indra (power, courage), south/Yama, (justice, lord of dead), west/Varuna (knowledge), north/Kubera (wealth), northeast/Siva (purity), southeast/Agni (ritual sacri-

fice), southwest/Surya (the sun) and/or Nirrti (misery), and northwest/Vayu (life, health).

All of these gods and demigods have beings under them who intervene in human affairs under their various dominions of influence. For instance, Kubera, god of wealth, has dominion over the yaksas (the speedy ones, spirits of the earth), guardians of the earth's treasures. Legend has it that Kubera and they were originally asuras (antigods), but they withdrew from the raksasas (night wanderers).

The Maruts and the Rudras are the divinities of the subtle world, the middle sphere, or sphere of space, situated between earth and sky. The Rudras appear as faithful companions of Rudra-Shiva (an aspect of the third person of the Hindu Trinity, Shiva). They are his friends, his messengers, whom everyone fears. The Rudras are not celestial aristocrats but the working class of heaven. The Maruts (immortals) are a restless, warlike horde of flashy young men, the embodiment of heroism and youthful exuberance.

The Vedic polytheistic universe became organized under the Trinity of Brahma the Immense Being, Vishnu the Redeemer, and Shiva the Destroyer/Transformer. Hindu metaphysics associated them with cohesion (Vishnu), disintegration (Shiva), and balance (Brahma). In addition, the tension between the opposites, the creative aspect of divinity, Shakti, the all-pervading divine Energy, had been personified in the great goddess since the early Rig Veda. The Trinity was thus one of divine couples: Brahma and Sarasvati (the Flowing One, goddess of speech, poetry, music, representing the union of power and intelligence); Vishnu and Lakshmi (Fortune, the power of multiplicity); Shiva and Shakti (all pervading active energy), Parvati (Daughter of the Mountain, peaceful, permanent energy, ether personified), and Kali (Power-of-Time); subaspects of the gods and goddesses were personified in further versions of the couples.

One manifold name of the goddess as Star, Golden Embryo—the cosmic location from which the world develops—and the power of hunger (not just for food, but for transcendence) is Tara, who is also worshiped by Jains and Buddhists. Minor forms of the goddess were Yoginis (ogresses or sorceresses, powers of realization), dakinis (female imps, eaters of raw flesh), grahis (seizers, witches who cause new babies to die), bhairavis (fearful ones, servants of Durga and Siva), and sakinis (able ones, female attendants of Durga). Dakinis have important functions in Tantric Buddhism, far more elevated than in Hindu lore.

A panoply of demigods (devatas), spirits, and fabulous creatures also have been featured since earliest Hindu times. The ghandarvas (Fragrances, or celestial harmonies) and apsaras (Essences, or unmanifest potentialities) are the celestial beings born of the centripetal sattva tendency, the tendency toward light. They are minor forms of Vishnu. The apsaras are essences of the waters, forms that take shape within the causal ocean. In later myth they are represented as water nymphs, eternally young women who are the courtesans and dancers of heaven. They are also called the women of the gods (surangana) and the daughters of pleasure (sumad-atmaja). They are depicted as uncommonly beautiful, with lotus eyes, slender waists, and large hips. By their languid postures and sweet seductiveness they rob those who see them of their wisdom and intellect. Apsaras have been known on several occasions to have been sent by the gods to lure from their austerities ascetics who might endanger their supremacy, the most famous being Menaka, who succeeded in bringing down the great sage Vishwamitra.

The number of apsaras is large; one source records 35 million. They choose lovers among the dead fallen on the battlefield. They have the power of changing their form, are fond of playing dice, and give luck to those whom they favor. They produce madness, and the Atharva Veda gives charms against them.

The ghandarvas are said to possess limitless sexual power and to be attracted by women. They play the part of lovers, give or refuse fecundity. Varuna is said to have regained his virility by an aphrodisiac provided by a ghandarva. Ghandarvas' vibrations soothe and nourish the earth plane. Amorous intelligences, the ghandarvas like scented oils and incense. They gave the gift of music to mankind. Their preferred instrument is the vina, whose sweet tones refine emotions of love and devotion.

The charanas ("wanderers") are the bardic historians of the heavens. Their speciality is to recount ancient tales, sing the praises of heroes, and teach the arts of dance, at which they excel.

The attendants of Siva are the ganas, which include all the minor deities that are counted in groups: the Adityas, the Rudras, and the Vasus, which are, respectively, the divinities of the sky, the atmosphere, and the earth. In addition there are the Visvadevas, the 10 Universal Principles, the Satisfied (Tusitas), the 64 Shining Ones (Abhasvaras), the 49 divinities of the winds (Anilas), the Princely Ones (Maharajikas), and the Means-of-Realization (Sadhyas).

Realized human beings who have attained liberation are known as Siddhas. They are perfect and blessed spirits, also defined as divinities, but there remains a difference between beings who have become deities after having been through the bondage of life and gods eternally unbound. The human being may dissolve into Basic Nature, while a divinity is forever free.

Ribhus were men who attained immortality by performing with skill a large number of propitiatory rites; they are guardians of the ritual sacrifice, clever craftsmen who dwell in the solar sphere. Vidyadharas resemble men but have magic powers and change form at their fancy. They are generally benevolent aerial spirits. They can marry with humans, who then themselves become Vidyadharas.

Village-Angels (grama-devata) and Village-Goddesses (grama-kali) are local tutelary deities. The latter are also divinities of forests. Many temple guardians are fabulous hybrids, *yalis,* often the heraldic emblem of the temple builder. They combine various powerful creatures—dragons, elephants, lions, horses—and are usually shown destroying enemies, with the pop-eyes of a god expecting blood sacrifices. Tree spirits (yakshis) abound in both Hindu and Buddhist art, as fertility icons and protagonists in myths and legends.

FURTHER READING
MacKenzie, Donald A. *Indian Myth and Legend.* Boston: Longwood Press, 1978.
Shearer, Alistair. *The Hindu Vision.* London: Thames and Hudson, 1993.
Zimmer, Heinrich. *Myths and Symbols in Indian Art and Civilization.* Princeton, N.J.: University Press, 1946.

Hod See TREE OF LIFE.

Hodson, Geoffrey (1886–1983)

English clairvoyant and Theosophist who wrote more than 40 books on the occult and, most especially, angels and nature spirits. Geoffrey Hodson believed he was contacted by the angels in the mid-1920s, and he spent much of the rest of his life trying to see angels and understand their universal wisdom.

Hodson was born on March 12, 1886, in Wainfleet, Lincolnshire, England, to a family of yeomen farmers. He was the oldest of five children. When he was 15, his family suffered hard times, and he was forced to quit school and go into business to earn a living.

During his childhood years, he had several psychic experiences that showed natural clairvoyant abilities. Perhaps these experiences led to his early interest in metaphysics. He sampled Spiritualism, but it did not appeal to him. Around 1912, he heard Theosophist Annie Besant lecture on "The Great White Brotherhood," and decided to join the Theosophical Society lodge in Manchester. He later became an important figure in the society.

From 1914 to 1918, Hodson served as an infantry trooper for the British in World War I. In 1919, he resumed a civilian life, marrying Jane Carter, whom he had met during his military training. The couple lived in Preston.

The Hodsons would take frequent trips to the countryside, researching local fairy and nature spirit lore. These experiences opened Hodson's awareness of the angelic realms.

In 1924, Hodson began a series of clairvoyant experiments at the behest of the London Research Group of the Theosophical Society. He and his wife moved to London. For the next five years, he worked in the clairvoyant diagnosis and occult treatment of disease. He invoked divine and angelic aid for patients. Also, he used his clairvoyance in researching angelology, embryology, anthropology, geology, psychology, physics, and astronomy.

In 1929, Jane fell ill with multiple sclerosis. Her illness, however, did not prevent the couple from touring America for three years, during which time Hodson lectured and pursued studies of occultism and Native American history and archaeology.

Hodson's fame as a clairvoyant spread, and international lecture invitations arrived. The couple traveled around the world. Hodson distinguished himself in the 1960s when he used his clairvoyance on fossils found in South Africa.

The Hodsons settled permanently in New Zealand. Jane's health deteriorated, and she died on October 27, 1962, in Auckland. Hodson later married Sandra Chase, a friend of the couple who took care of Jane during her long illness.

Hodson's later years were full of international travel, lecturing, research, and writing. He wrote 47 books, plus scores of articles and pamphlets. He became active in animal welfare rights. From 1953 to 1955 and in 1961, he served as director of studies of the Theosophists' School of the Wisdom in Adyar, India. He was awarded the Theosophical Society's Subba Row gold medal for his contributions to theosophical literature.

Hodson began his angel research in 1921. In 1924 or 1926 (Hodson gives both dates in two different books), he was sitting quietly on a hillside in Sheepscombe, Gloucestershire, gazing at the countryside. Through meditation Hodson hoped to enter nature's hidden life and see fairies, gnomes, and other spirits at work. Suddenly the skies were filled with light, and his consciousness was completely subsumed by that brilliant radiance. Gradually he became aware of a shape, a "Heavenly Being," within that light, who blended its mind with Hodson's to impart the wisdom of the universe. Hodson claimed he was completely awake and able to write. The Being, who called itself Bethelda, was godlike, beautiful, and majestic, yet at the same time quite passive and impersonal.

Bethelda explained to Hodson the organization of the Heavenly Host, their purposes and activities, and the close relationship angels have to man—even though most of mankind is completely blind to the angels' ministrations. The angels stand ready at all times to foster cooperation between themselves and mankind to uplift the human race. But, Bethelda told Hodson, man must quietly listen and watch. If man's consciousness melds with that of Nature, concentrating on purity, simplicity, directness, and impersonality, he will perceive the angels, for they are always there. Angels have no personality separate from the Divine Will and are ministers and messengers of the Divine Ideation. They were present before mankind and are not the spirits of deceased humans.

Geoffrey Hodson (Reprinted courtesy of Theosophical Publishing House)

In Hodson's book *The Brotherhood of Angels and Men,* published in 1927, he organized the angels into categories, groupings he believed were the easiest to contact by man and the most beneficial.

The Angels of Power are those able to teach men and women how to release the deeper levels of spiritual energy within them and to inspire them to infuse their entire lives with the angels' fiery and motivating energy. These angels are attracted to ceremonial and religious functions and use such gatherings as channels for their power. If the mental attitudes of all participants in a ceremony are in harmony, the angels' ability to transmit this energy is increased.

The Angels of Healing are those that work tirelessly to heal the sick and injured, stand ready to provide a healing touch, suffer with those who are dying, and offer consolation to the bereaved. Healing angels serve under Raphael, whom Hodson identified as an archangel. Unfortunately, too few healing angels actually get the chance to help mankind, for overcoming the barriers erected by mankind's closed minds and hearts dissipates the energy necessary for healing.

The Guardian Angels of the Home are those that delight in man's labors, the laughter of children, the warmth and security of shelter and sustenance. They guard against danger and disease, against strife and discord, and hear each simple prayer. Harmony and love are their watchwords.

The Builder Angels are those that supervise the creation of all forms and worlds, from the greatest planetary system to the smallest grain of sand. They take on the universal ARCHETYPES, the patterns for all life forms, and aid in the incarnation of each being. Angelic organization is hierarchical, and builder angels especially have their assigned levels of work and responsibility.

At the point of human conception, the angels take the divine emanations from the Word and attach the cells of the person's physical and his etheric, or spiritual, bodies together. At childbirth, Builder Angels working under their Queen help mothers to deliver children in joy, not pain. Hodson does not identify the Queen as the Virgin MARY per se, but describes her as a Holy One who has won freedom from the burdens of the flesh and ascended to the Angel Hosts. In the name of Him (most probably Christ) whom she bore long ago, she uplifts all womanhood and stands ready, through her angelic assistants, at every human birth.

The Angels of Nature breathe life into the Builders' creations. This order's hierarchy includes the lower nature spirits, such as brownies, sylphs, undines, gnomes, and salamanders, who control agriculture, the growth of fruit and flowers, the formation of earth and minerals, water and fire. Hodson said that if man would only understand these spirits' presence and influence, he could learn to control the weather and other natural disasters.

The Angels of Music embody the creative Word of God and the expression of his divine Voice. They sing God's Word, sounding like a million harps or the rolling of the sea. Their songs emanate from the center of the Universe in great, glorious waves, giving harmony to the world and providing the radiance of light and sound which is the Voice of God. Their mission is to pour forth this heavenly music; it is up to mankind to hear.

The Angels of Beauty and Art express the perfect beauty of the Absolute Divinity that is in everything. They help the Builders to hone and perfect each form so that even more loveliness is revealed. Beauty is eternal, and one of God's most treasured offerings. Each time mankind attempts to create anything, no matter how insignificant, that object or act should be judged beautiful. And when that search for the beautiful becomes man's permanent aspiration, he comes closer to the angels at the Hand of God.

Bethelda told Hodson that in order to foster this brotherhood between angels and men, humans must take the initiative. For their part, the angels always are ready and eager to work with mankind. But in order to build a bridge of communication, first there must be more humans willing to try. They must be quiet and listen to Nature, approaching it from within as well as from without. They must practice such angelic communication daily, always choosing the path to the highest sensibility.

Ceremony and ritual are very important. Supplicants would be wise to set up a shrine exclusively for the invocation of the angels, decorated with religious symbols, pictures of the holy ones in each religion, flowers, and candles—flowers and a single beautiful object at the very least. Prayers of invocation should be offered in the morning, and those of thanksgiving at night. Communicants must be completely clean and pure, much as any priest should be. In *The Brotherhood* Hodson provides simple prayers for contacting each order of angels and suggests that supplicants wear certain colors associated with the orders, much as the priests and priestesses of Santería and Candomblé do when they call upon their ORISHAS, or gods: rose and soft green for the Guardian Angels, deep sapphire blue for the Healers, sky blue for the Builder Angels associated with childbirth, white for both ceremony and Angels of Music, apple green for the Nature Angels, and yellow (the color of wisdom) for the Angels of Beauty and Art.

Much as Virgil guided DANTE through hell and purgatory, Bethelda revealed different types of angels to Hodson, who continued to see angels and nature spirits long after Bethelda departed. Hodson claimed that Mountain Gods in the Sierra Nevada range of California were colossal, rising 30 to 60 feet in height. They were surrounded on every side by brilliantly colored auric forces, resembling wings emanating from a golden center, which changed color as the energy ebbed and flowed. Each had a visible face with a broad brow, wide-set eyes, and a square jaw. Fire Lords, masters of the salamanders (nature spirits of fire are called "salamanders" after mythical beings, especially lizards or reptiles, which were thought to be able to live in fire), stood like enormous human blast-furnaces. Bethelda guided Hodson through their searing flames unscathed. Storm Angels, who resembled bats and had terrifying expressions, controlled the elemental forces. Gods of gold appeared as feminine in shape, with radiating auras that resembled flaxen hair.

Bethelda taught Hodson about the angels' mental communications and their use of auric color to convey emotion. Rose is the color of love. Illustrations by Ethelwynne M. Quail of all the angels and nature spirits Hodson has described appeared in his book *The Kingdom of the Gods*.

The angels, said Hodson, ask only to receive love from mankind, and to have humans always seek the highest, the best, the most beautiful, the most loving and giving in all their endeavors. Angels are eager to impart the Divine Fire of healing, power and beauty. Through humanity's search for the angels, Hodson concluded they will develop patience, peace, wisdom, joy, vision, thoroughness, unity and complete knowledge of the Self and its oneness with the Divine.

FURTHER READING

Hodson, Geoffrey. *The Brotherhood of Angels and Men.* Wheaton, Ill.: The Theosophical Publishing House, 1982.

———. *The Kingdom of the Gods.* Adyar, Madras, India: The Theosophical Publishing House, 1972.

"Geoffrey Hodson—Man of Words 1886–1983," *Theosophy in New Zealand*, Vol. 44, No. 2, April–June, 1983, pp. 38–40.

Hofniel

Angel who rules the order of the BENE ELOHIM, according to the Zohar. Hofniel means "fighter for God."

Holy Living Ones   See CHERUBIM; HASMALIM; HAYYOTH.

Holy Ones   See ARCHANGELS.

Holy Spirit   See ANGEL OF THE LORD.

huarna

In Persian lore, a protective force or power. In ZOROASTRIANISM, the huarna is symbolized by the luminous, winged emblem of OHRMAZD. In Persian art, angels often hold rings which symbolize the huarna.

See IMAGES OF ANGELS.

Hurdat   See AMARAHSPANDS.

Hutriel

One of the ANGELS OF PUNISHMENT who lives in the fifth camp of HELL and helps to punish the 10 nations. Hutriel means "rod of god." Hutriel is sometimes equated with Oniel.

Ialdabaoth See GNOSTICISM.

Iameth
Angel who has the power to thwart the sea-horse demon Kunopegos.

Iaoel
In the Apocalypse of Abraham, the ANGEL OF THE LORD sent to take ABRAHAM to HEAVEN in a visionary experience. Iaoel appears in the likeness of a man whose "body was like sapphire, and the aspect of his face was like chrysolite, and the hair of his head like snow. And a kidaris [headdress] (was) on his head, its look like that of a RAINBOW, and the clothing of his garments (was) purple; and a golden staff (was) in his right hand" (11:1–4).
Iaoel describes himself:

> I am Iaoel and I was called so by him who causes those with me on the seventh expanse, on the firmament, to shake, a power through the medium of his ineffable name in me. I am the one who has been charged according to his commandment, to restrain the threats of the living creatures of the cherubim against one another, and I teach those who carry the song through the medium of man's night of the seventh hour. I am appointed to hold the Leviathans, because through me is subjugated the attack and menace of every reptile. I am ordered to loosen Hades

and to destroy those who wondered at the dead. I am the one who ordered your father's house to be burned with him, for he honored the dead. I am sent to you now to bless you and the land which he whom you have called the Eternal One has prepared for you. (10:7–16)

Iaoel is visible to Abraham as he accompanies him on a 40-day fast and purification, but after Abraham makes a required sacrifice to God, the angel becomes invisible forever.

Iaoth
In the Testament of SOLOMON, one of seven ARCHANGELS, and the angel who has the power to thwart Kourtael, DEMON of the ninth DECAN OF THE ZODIAC.

Iblis
In Persian and Arabic lore, angel who is the equivalent of Satan or the devil. Variations of his name are Eblis and Haris.
In Islamic lore, Iblis/Eblis was known as Azazel, and once was one of the most exalted of angels, serving as treasurer of Paradise. But when God created Adam and commanded the angels to worship him, he refused and was cast out of heaven along with a band of his followers. They all became DJINN.

ibn Sina (980–1037)

Great Islamic philosopher and physician. For centuries ibn Sina was known by his Latinized name, Avicenna; his Arabic name has returned to usage. His full name is Abu Ali al-Husain ibn 'Abdallah ibn Sina.

Life

Ibn Sina was born in Kharmaithen near Bukhara (Bokhara), now part of Uzbekistan. His father, a Persian, governed a village in one of the estates of the Samanid ruler, Nuh ibn Mansur, the sultan of Bukhara. Ibn Sina was quick student—later in life he claimed to have been largely self-taught—and by age 10 he had completely memorized the Koran and various poems. He gravitated to Aristotlean and Neoplatonic philosophies, metaphysics, and logic. By age 13, he was studying medicine, and at 16 he performed charitable medical work with the sick. He often would spend nights in a mosque praying for answers to his questions about metaphysics, aided by wine.

In 997 the sultan fell seriously ill with colic and his own physicians were unable to cure him. Ibn Sina succeeded, and he was granted his desired reward, to have access to the royal library of the Samanids.

But two years later Bukhara fell to invading Turkish Qarakhanids, and within five years the Samanids had suffered complete defeat. Ibn Sina's father died, and both that and the fall of his royal patrons caused him to wander about, working as a physician and writing. He also indulged his passions for wine and women in a sensuous lifestyle.

In Hamadan (now in Iran) he was made court physician. He was appointed twice as vizier by Shams ad-Dawlah, the ruling Buyid prince. Ibn Sina did not do well in politics; he spent time hiding from his opponents and even was jailed as a political prisoner. He escaped prison disguised as a Sufi.

In 1022 the prince died and ibn Sina left Hamadan and went to Isfahan, where he joined the court of Prince Abu Ya'far 'Ala Addaula. He completed his major works and wrote additional ones. As court physician, he had to accompany the prince on military campaigns. On a military march to Hamadan, he was stricken with colic and died, despite his attempts to minister to himself. According to some sources, he may have been poisoned by a servant. On his deathbed he repented his licentious ways, freed his slaves, and gave all his belongings to the poor.

Works

Ibn Sina is credited with authoring more than 450 works, of which about 240 have survived. Of those, 150 are on philosophy and 40 are on medicine, the two topics on which he wrote most frequently. His greatest works are *Qanun fi al-Tibb (Canon of Medicine)*, an encyclopedic text that influenced medicine for centuries, and *Kitab al-Shifa*, an encyclopedic work on philosophy, science, metaphysics, and Muslim theology. He also composed works on alchemy, philosophy, theology, philology, astronomy, music, physics, and mathematics.

Ibn Sina's *Recital of Hayy ibn Yaqzan* is a visionary recital (in which an angel speaks to a human) that concerns the journey into the Orient, the soul's return to its "home" under the conduct of its Guide, its celestial Self.

This metaphoric journey aligns the emanation of origin, spheres of existence, and the subtle dynamics of the soul with ANGELOLOGY. It features the archangels or pure INTELLIGENCES, the CHERUBIM, and the angels who emanate from them and who are the moving the souls of the celestial spheres. The human souls are "terrestrial angels" who move and govern earthly human bodies. Human souls are in the same relation to the angel from whom they emanate as is each soul to the intelligence from whose thought its being is an emanation. Human souls also harbor the domain of the demonic agencies. The human soul has the ability to realize its angelic nature, or to develop demonic qualities.

Celestial souls and human souls share the function of ruling and governing physical bodies. To do this they must imagine, and the imagination can be either angel or demon. The whole immense world of the imaginable, the universe of symbol (*'alam al-mithal*), would not exist without the soul. The celestial souls are superior, for their bodies are made of celestial matter. Unlike human imaginations, they are not dependent on sensible knowledge; their imaginations are true.

The love between the angelic intelligence and the soul is compared not only to the affection between parent and child, between master and disciple, but also to the reciprocal love of lovers. The celestial souls offer themselves as models to be imitated; the human soul is to hear and obey. These two complementary aspects define the journey into the Orient, in the terms of the *Recital of Hayy ibn Yaqzan*, as "traveling in company with the Angel."

Below the greater Orient of the pure cherubinic intelligences, there is an intermediate Orient, the world of symbols, which is the "clime" of the celestial angels or souls. These inspire humans and make visible to the imagination the symbolic visions of prophets and sages in a "seal of prophecy."

The human soul can raise itself step by step toward the world of pure intelligence after death by becoming enveloped in the subtle celestial body that will have been organized for it by the images, the symbols, and the DREAMS dispensed by the celestial souls. The world of symbols and of archetypal images is also the world of remembrance, and it is the celestial souls who preserve the traces of all particular things. (See ARCHETYPES.) The relation of the soul to the active intelligence is like child to parent.

See AL-SUHRAWARDI; ANGELOLOGY.

FURTHER READING

Corbin, Henry. *Avicenna and the Visionary Recital.* Translated by William R. Trask. Bollingen Series 66. Princeton, N.J.: Princeton University Press, 1968, 1988.

Goodman, Lenn Evan. *Avicenna.* London: Routledge, 1992.

Morewedge, Parvis. *The Mystical Philosophy of Avicenna.* Binghamton: Global Publications at State University of New York Binghamton, 2001.

leo

In the Testament of SOLOMON, one of the angels who thwarts Katanikotael, one of the DEMON DECANS OF THE ZODIAC.

Illuminator

In Gnostic literature, the *Photor*, the bringer of knowledge and redeemer of souls. More than one Illuminator is mentioned: Jesseus, Mazareus, and Jessedekeus, the latter of whom is the "living water." The Illuminator comes from various origins, and descends to the water, or the material world.

The Apocalypse of ADAM gives the origin of the Illuminator according to the 13 kingdoms of man:

First kingdom: The lines pertaining to origin are missing, but the text says the Illuminator was nourished in heaven and received his power and glory of "that one." He came to the bosom of his mother, and then into the world.

Second kingdom: The Illuminator came from a prophet. A bird carried him to a high mountain and nourished him. He received his strength and glory from an angel.

Third kingdom: He came from a virgin womb, was cast out of his city, and went to a desert place with his mother. There he was nourished and received his power and glory.

Fourth kingdom: He came from a virgin womb and was nourished in the desert. The demon armies of SOLOMON were sent to look for the virgin. The DEMONS did not find her but found another virgin, whom Solomon impregnated. She nourished the child on the edge of the desert, and he received his power and glory.

Fifth kingdom: He came from a drop from HEAVEN, was cast into the sea, and then taken to heaven, where he was nourished and received his power and glory.

Sixth kingdom: The text concerning the origin is missing; the Illuminator was nourished by the angels of the flower garden, where he received his power and glory.

Seventh kingdom: He came from a drop from heaven, brought down to caves by dragons (similar to the story of Zeus being hidden and nourished in a cave). A spirit took him back to the place in heaven from whence he came, and he received his power and glory.

Eighth kingdom: He came from a cloud that came upon the earth and enveloped a rock. Angels nourished him and he received his power and glory.

Ninth kingdom: A Muse went away to a mountain by herself in order to become androgynous. She conceived from her own desire and brought forth the Illuminator. He was nourished by angels and received his power and glory.

Tenth kingdom: The god of the Illuminator loved a cloud and begot him in his hand. The god cast some of the drop on the cloud near him, and the Illuminator was brought forth. He received his power and glory.

Eleventh kingdom: The text says "the father desired his own daughter. She also conceived from her father." The daughter put the child in a tomb in the desert, where he was nourished by angels and received his power and glory.

Twelfth kingdom. He came from two LUMINARIES, the sun and the moon. He was nourished there and received his power and glory.

Thirteenth kingdom: The text says that "every birth of their ruler is a word, and this word received a mandate there." He received his power and glory.

The text says that the race without a king says that God chose the Illuminator from all the AEONS to carry the undefiled knowledge of truth, for the benefit of the race of men.

Those people who accept the Illuminator's knowledge of truth will live for "aeons and aeons," or forever and ever.

FURTHER READING

Charlesworth, James H., ed. *The Old Testament Pseudepigrapha.* Vols. 1 and 2. New York: Doubleday, 1983, 1985.

images of angels

The representation of angels in art has undergone many changes since the inception of Christianity.

Angel images of contemporary times differ significantly from the angels of 2,000 years ago. That angels can be depicted at all was the subject of a heated controversy in early Christianity.

In Judaism, figurative representations of religious concepts, including angels, are prohibited. Angels are described in various mystical texts, but images of them are not in religious devotion.

The fathers of the early Christian church inherited a flourishing angel cult based on Jewish and pagan beliefs. Though Jews eschewed images, the pagans—the great masses to be converted—expected them. The faithful were attracted to numerous angel shrines, especially those devoted to Michael, where images abounded.

The church fathers were divided on the desirability of any images of the sacred. Many, such as Theodotus of the second century and Methodius (d. 311) pointed to the scriptural evidence that angels have no form. For example, Psalm 104:4 establishes angels as incorporeal: "who makest the winds thy messengers, flame and fire thy ministers," as does Hebrews 1:7, "And of the angels he saith, Who maketh his angels spirits, and his ministers a flame of fire."

Thus, as beings of pure spirit, fire, or even intellectual fire, angels cannot be represented correctly by an image, for artists can never perceive their true form. Christ, being part human, at least had "bones and sinew," and saints were entirely mortal; both could be accurately portrayed in images. But angels were never incarnate and have only assumed humanlike form as a symbolic representation and a matter of necessity—a concession to the limitations of human perception. The human mind cannot possibly fully understand divine things, and the only way to approach the unknowable is through inner contemplation, not through incomplete or inaccurate images that could lead people astray.

Many church fathers also were concerned about the dangers of idolatry posed by images. Angels essentially

Angel at Père Lachaise Cemetery, Paris (Author's collection)

Cathedral angel with censer (Author's collection)

Gabriel, from Eastern Orthodox Church, Romania (Author's collection)

had absorbed the characteristics and functions of pagan gods, and images of angels might easily encourage angel worship. The worship done at the shrines to Michael pointed to those dangers.

In 325 the Council of Nicaea decreed belief in angels a part of dogma, which stimulated more theological debate for several centuries. Particularly influential were the anti-image views of Epiphanus of Salamis (ca. 315–403), an esteemed orthodox theologian. Epiphanus stated point-blank that anyone who "endeavors to perceive the divine character of the holy Logos in the flesh," should be anathematized. Divinity, he said, can only be worshiped "in spirit and truth," as stated in John 4:24: "God is spirit, and those who worship him must worship in spirit and truth."

The disagreements over images—which extended beyond angels—reached a peak in the eighth and ninth centuries in the Iconoclasm dispute, one of the major factors leading to the eventual split between the Western (Latin) church based in Rome and the Eastern (Byzantine) church based in Constantinople. The issue of images was especially volatile in the East, where opponents held that images (icons) were idols that fostered superstition and hindered the conversion of the Jews and Muslims. Emperor Leo III (the Isaurian) instigated persecutions against icon worship.

In 731 Pope Gregory III defended images by holding a synod in Rome that declared that anyone who broke or defiled holy images would be excommunicated. The response of Leo III was to send a fleet to Rome to punish the pope, but it was wrecked by storms. When Leo III died in 741, his persecutions were carried on by his son Constantine V. In 754 a synod in Constantinople declared that the only lawful image of Christ was the Eucharist; all others were heretical, since they confounded or divorced his two natures. Furthermore, names alone—such as Christ, and by inference angels—constitute an "image" acceptable for worship.

Iconophiles countered that there was an unwritten tradition in the church from its beginnings condoning images. The earlier writings of PSEUDO-DIONYSIUS provided support for their position. In discussing the angelic orders, Pseudo-Dionysius said that symbols offer the primary access to God; thus, angel images give people access to God in a way they can understand. Nicephorus (ca. 750–828) argued that images of angels had existed throughout the church's history (see discussion of "Wings" below) and contributed to Christians' correct discrimination. St. John Damascus was among iconophiles who argued that image raises consciousness to a higher level. Damascus—like other iconophiles—also cited God's instructions for the building of the ARK OF THE COVENANT with its two golden CHERUBIM as evidence supporting the use of material images. Because of his views, Damascus was anathematized by the iconoclastic council of Hiereia in 754.

Nonetheless, the destruction of images and relics continued in the East. When Constantine V died in 775, his son Leo V maintained the persecutions, though less vigorously than his father.

Leo V died in 780 and the throne went to his nine-year-old son, Constantine VI. The boy's mother, Empress Irene, served as regent. She began a campaign to reverse Iconoclasm and reopen and restore the monasteries. Pope Adrian I demanded restitution of the property confiscated by Leo III.

The lawfulness of venerating holy images was reestablished at a synod at Nicaea in 787. But peace did not last, for the Iconoclast party still existed, especially in the army. Twenty-seven years later, a second Iconoclastic persecution erupted. There were countering synods that rejected and upheld icons, and much fighting. The Iconoclasts regained the upper hand. The persecutions became so great that many monks fled to the West.

The situation did not change until 842, when another empress regent, Theodora, gained control and restored icon worship. The Iconoclasts were excommunicated. The Feast of Orthodoxy was established to commemorate the defeat of Iconoclasm, and became symbolic of the defeat of all heresies. The Iconoclast party gradually died out.

Images of the divine, including angels, are now incorporated into both Eastern and Western churches. Angel images bring them nearer to humans; however, their fundamental bodiless state makes them absent from their images.

Artistic styles differ between East and West. Eastern icons have a distinctive style that attempts to portray the tension between reality and abstraction, physicality and incorporeality. The Western angel has become a model of human perfection with wings. Both styles represent different aspects of the angel. The Eastern angel is transcendent and mysterious; the Western angel is the idealized human.

Wings

The image of angels as humanlike beings with wings—more or less taken for granted in contemporary times—did not become established in art until the fourth century C.E. The evolution of the angel wing has a long history.

Wings denote spirituality and divine purpose, speed, and the ability to mediate between physical and nonphysical realms. The endowment of wings on spiritual beings is an ancient idea, but one that developed in the West more so than in the East. Eastern deities, saints, and spiritual beings move about without the benefit of wings, which are not necessary to navigate in

Fifteenth-century stone carving of angel guarding a house in Dinan, France (Author's collection)

the world of illusion. In art, they are shown descending from the sky or hovering in the air, held up by the weightlessness of their own divinity.

Wings also indicate mystic or shamanic travel. India's Garuda, the golden-winged sun bird, was a mysterious figure similar to the Persian simurgh. Garuda was variously pictured as a man, a bird, a man riding a bird, or a curious combination of human and avian characteristics. Though probably older than the religion of Vishnu, Garuda is now regarded as the vehicle of Vishnu, bearing the god either within or upon his back. In Egypt, the BA was one of each person's seven souls. Its usual form was that of a human-headed bird, and linked to the ancient worldwide concept of ancestors and ancestral divinities in bird shapes. The hawk was the totemic form of the god Horus, shown as a man's body with a falcon or hawk head. Thoth, the Egyptian god comparable to Hermes, god of magic, spells, writing, and recordkeeping, was depicted with the head of an ibis.

In the ninth century B.C.E., the Assyrians began placing wings on the shoulders of their protective geniuses, despite the fact that their bodies seemed too heavy and muscle-bound for celestial flight. These divine beings were depicted in art as human figures with wings. The KARABU, a half-human, half-animal figure that guarded buildingserpahs, also had wings.

In about the eighth century B.C.E., the figure of a lordly helmeted four-winged man carrying corn and oil, called a "genius of blessing" by historians, (see GENII), was carved and painted in the Assyrian palace of Sargon and now rests in the Louvre. In the same museum stands a bronze statue of a demon with a similar wing arrangement from the same area and period. In Persepolis is a stone relief of Ohrmazd, the upper half of a man on a winged sun-disc. Winged lions, griffins, sphinxes, centaurs, bulls, enthroned or standing guard, abound in the ancient Middle East, along with bird-headed demons with wings. Wings can often be found on East Asian gods and demons.

In Judaism, the angels of the MERKABAH are described as having fiery, brilliant, human-like forms with multiple, even thousands of wings. (See ENOCH.) Some of them have "angel faces" but bodies of eagles. (The NEPHILIM, the offspring of angels and mortal women, fly like eagles in the QUMRAN TEXTS, suggesting mystical or shamanistic ascent.) The Old Testament gives scant information on the appearance of angels. There are the four-faced, winged creatures seen by ISAIAH, six-winged and sometimes serpent-like SERAPHIM, and four-winged CHERUBIM; otherwise angels appear like men.

See ABRAHAM; DANIEL; JACOB; SODOM AND GOMORRAH.

In Greek and Roman mythologies, wings commonly denoted divine or semi-divine status and ability to access the realms of the gods. A winged siren-handled cauldron dates from the eighth century B.C.E., a winged sphinx from 560 B.C.E. NIKE, the victory aspect of Athena, goddess of war, was always pictured or sculpted as winged. Nike was adopted as Victory by the Romans, who saw her as the symbol of the invincibility of the Roman Empire. In art, the winged Victory was shown with one breast exposed and was sometimes depicted naked with a mantle or drapery flowing around her. Her image was adopted into sacred art in Egypt and Syria.

EROS, son of Aphrodite, is a winged messenger, both ANCIENT OF DAYS and naked graceful boy. In other contexts, like winged shamanic figures from diverse cultures, Eros acts as guide of the soul, the guardian or spiritual double of man, representing both spiritual master and beloved, and also trickster and magician.

Some of these qualities and many more were ascribed to Hermes (a universal Indo-European god much older than Greece, the original Hermaphrodite) whose iconography called for a helmet with wings and wings on the feet of his naked body. Dark-winged figures include the Furies, also called the Eumenides, and the Erinyes, the personification of the vengeful aspect of Demeter.

In *Phaedo* Plato associates the wing with qualities that apply to spiritual ascent:

> The wing is the corporeal element which is most akin to the divine, and which by nature tends to soar aloft and carry that which gravitates downwards into the upper

A haloed angel shows Mary Magdalene, Salome, and Mary the empty tomb of Jesus.

region, which is the habitation of the gods. The divine is beauty, wisdom, and the like; and by these the wing of the soul is nourished, and grows apace. (246)

Plato adds the aspect that became important to the concept of angelic INTELLIGENCES:

the mind of the philosopher alone has wings; and this is just, for he is always, according to the measure of his abilities, clinging in recollection to those things in which God abides, and in beholding which He is what He is. And he who employs aright these memories is ever being initiated into perfect mysteries and alone becomes truly perfect. But as he forgets earthly interests and is rapt in the divine, the vulgar deem him mad, and rebuke him; they do not see that he is inspired. (249)

In Rome, Mercurius (Hermes), the genii of the seasons and the four directions, Fate and Victory continued to be winged. Winged figures were painted on the walls of Pompeii.

The New Testament sheds little light on the appearances of angels. Gabriel, in announcing the pending birth of JESUS to MARY, merely "comes in" and "departs." The angel who announces the birth of Jesus to the shepherds just appears "suddenly" and "came upon them" in the night. Early angel art portrays angels as ennobled, ethereal male humans without wings. The earliest such extant image dates to the early third century C.E. in the Catacomb of Priscilla in Rome. It portrays the Annunciation, with Gabriel looking like a tunic-clad man standing on the earth.

Though angels played an important role in Christian piety from a very early stage, they acquired greater importance in 325 with the Council of Nicaea's approval of them. Art mirrored the theological debate. The manlike angel evolved into the winged, hovering angel during the fourth century. By the end of the fourth century, Christian artists had turned to the pagan religions for inspiration. They borrowed heavily from the Greek idea that divinity has shape, and it is human-like, and from the Roman image of Victory. However, they refrained from frank nakedness and sexuality. Their angels were adult males but without pronounced sexual characteristics—almost androgynous in appearance—and were fully clothed, with a standard tunic and mantle. Their wings often were not pronounced in size or detail. By the end of the fifth century, the winged, hovering angel had become standard, even in Persian art that was absorbed into Islam (Persian angels tend to have smaller, thinner wings than Christian angels).

The androgynous, hovering winged angel dominated angel art through the sixth century. This formula reappeared again in Carolingian art (eighth century) and the Romanesque art of Italy and southern France (mid-11th to mid-12th centuries).

Angels sometimes appeared alongside images of Victory and the EROTES in funerary art, especially in early art. They were readily distinguished from those figures by their maturity, clothing, and lack of sexual features. They were often shown in pairs, holding wreaths with the medallion of Christ, or the wreaths with the cross of Christ, or other ceremonial symbols. Generally, however, angels were reserved for depiction of the central themes in Christianity and not the mundane affairs of humans.

The purposes of these winged angels included demonstration of their role as:

- divine messengers of God sent to execute the will of God
- guardians of, and attendants to, Christ
- guides of the soul to eternity, or HEAVEN
- important participants in ceremonies
- heralds of the Last Judgment

By the 14th century, theological interest in angels had peaked and began to decline. The Inquisition focused attention on FALLEN ANGELS—the DEMONS who tempted people into sin and witchcraft. These beings were given ugly, batlike wings by artists. The Reformation of the 16th century further diminished the importance of the heavenly angel.

This decline was mirrored in changes in angel art. Renaissance artists began portraying angels as male youths and especially women, signifying that angels no longer held a central stage in theology. Ironically, this shift produced some of the greatest and most beautiful angel art: glorious beings with enormous, elegant wings and exquisite, flowing garments. Artists turned to birds such as the eagle and swan for models of wings. They gave them RAINBOW hues. The rainbow is a symbol of the bridge to heaven, and it underscores the angel's role as intermediary between heaven and earth.

The Renaissance started the stylization of angels that remains in Western art: the idealized human form, winged, rendered somehow more genuinely mystical. Botticelli, Raphael, Fra Angelico (who was given his name for his beautiful angels), Titian, Tintoretto, Veronese, Perugino, Murillo, Rembrandt, Rubens, El Greco, and other artists created images that continue to serve as models. Angels in art are just as likely to be feminine as they are masculine; children often are used as models as well. (See PUTTI.)

One contemporary trend in media and popular art has been to make angels as humanlike as possible. These depictions show cute figures in country dress with pigtails, and as winged human children and adults performing ordinary tasks of daily life. This type of art removes angels from the incorporeal realms of celestial fire and places them in the domain of earth. It remains to be seen whether this descent from heaven ultimately will enhance the angel (in terms of human ability to relate to it) or will lead to its demise (as a figure that is reduced in stature and thus in respect).

Haloes

The halo signifies divine radiance and nearness to God. One prototype of the halo is the HUARNA, an angel-like protective power symbolized by the luminous, winged emblem of Ohrmazd in ZOROASTRIANISM.

The ancient Egyptians, Greeks, and Romans used halos to depict supernatural force, mystical states, and superior intellect. In Egypt and Greece, the halo was associated with the sun and resurrection. In the Eleusinian mysteries, the sacrificed and reborn god, usually Dionysus, was portrayed with a halo.

In Christian art, the became a common feature of the angel and all heavenly beings around the fourth century C.E.

Symbols of Angels

Persian angels often are shown with rings, which, like haloes, symbolize the huarna power. Various symbols or details have become identified with certain angels or types of angels, such as in the following descriptions:

Seraphim
The seraphim have six wings of fiery red and bear a flaming sword; their feet are bare.

Cherubim
Cherubim have two blue wings and shod feet, and they may hold open books representing their fullness of knowledge. They may stand on wheels.

Thrones
Thrones are two fiery wheels with four eye-filled wings each; they may carry thrones or scales representing divine justice.

Dominions
Dominions are two-winged, wear long albs, golden girdles, and green stoles, hold the seal of Jesus Christ in their right hands and a golden staff topped by a cross in their left hands. They also have crowns and they carry scepters, orbs, swords, or books.

Virtues
Like dominions, virtues are two-winged, wear long albs, golden girdles, and green stoles, hold the seal of JESUS Christ in their right hands and a golden staff topped by a cross in their left hands. Virtues are vested in the garments of high ecclesiastics and

carry other liturgical items, including lilies or red roses symbolic of Christ's passion.

Powers
Like dominions and virtues, powers are two-winged, wear long albs, golden girdles, and green stoles, hold the seal of Jesus Christ in their right hands and a golden staff topped by a cross in their left hands. Powers sometimes hold rods or swords, wear knightly armor, and lead demons in chains.

Principalities
Principalities appear as soldiers with two wings, golden belts, and lance-headed javelins. They wear princely robes over armor, with crowns and sword or scepter.

Archangels
Archangels appear as soldiers in armor with two wings, golden belts, and lance-headed javelins, and also as deacons in albs.

Angels
Angels are two-winged and may appear as soldiers, or they may wear ecclesiastical garments. They frequently wear a diadem with a cross in the front. A late medieval variation was to show them in clothing made of feathers. They carry many objects: candles, musical instruments, scrolls, and inscribed shields.

Michael
Michael, whose office of PRINCE of the Hebrew nation became, after Christian revelation, the

Seraph (Copyright 1995 by Robert M. Place; from *The Angels Tarot* by Rosemary Ellen Guiley and Robert M. Place)

guardian of the Church Militant in Christendom, is depicted as young, beautiful, and powerful. He is usually clothed in a coat of mail with sword, spear, and shield, wings rising from his shoulders and sometimes wearing a jeweled crown. Frequently he is battling with Satan, represented as a dragon, serpent, or DEMON. Medieval and Renaissance paintings also depicted his intercession in the Old Testament in scenes from ABRAHAM, JACOB, MOSES, and the battles led by Joshua. He plays an important role in the legends of the Virgin, as it is Michael who is sent to announce to MARY her approaching death and then carry her body to heaven.

Gabriel

Gabriel is the guardian of the celestial treasury, the Angel of Redemption, and the Chief Messenger. He is most often portrayed in his role as the angel of the Annunciation to Mary. In fact, the Annunciation is the most frequently depicted scene in all of Western art. Gabriel is a majestic figure who wears a crown and is richly robed. He evokes purity with a lily—a detail not mentioned in the Gospels.

Raphael

Raphael, the guardian angel of all humanity, is represented as a benign friend and fellow traveler, protector of the young and innocent, rendered in episodes from the book of TOBIT. He is dressed as a pilgrim, wears sandals, and carries a staff and some supplies on his belt or slung over his shoulder. He is often shown with a fish, a significant element in the story of Tobias.

When he is portrayed as a guardian spirit, he is richly dressed, has a casket of provisions, holds a sword in one hand, and makes a gesture of warning with the other. Christian tradition holds that it is Raphael who announces to the shepherds the arrival of the Savior on Christmas night: "Fear not; for behold, I bring you tidings of great joy" (Luke 2:10), although the text identifies the angel anonymously as the ANGEL OF THE LORD.

Uriel

Uriel, an important angel in Jewish mystical literature but not part of the official Catholic canon, appears less frequently in art than the aforementioned three archangels. Early legend holds that it is Uriel who, as ambassador of Christ, appears to the disciples at Emmaus (Luke 24:13–16). In art, Uriel is usually represented carrying a scroll and a book indicating his role as interpreter of judgments and prophecies.

Islamic Images of Angels

Islam does not prohibit images. In Sufi iconography Israfil, the Angel of the Day of Judgment, has hairs and tongues over which are stretched veils. He glorifies Allah with each tongue in a thousand languages, and Allah creates from his breath a million angels who glorify him.

Israfil looks each day and each night toward HELL, approaches without being seen and weeps. His trumpet or horn has the form of a beast's horn and contains cells like a bee's honeycomb, in which the souls of the dead repose.

Mika'il (Michael) has hairs of saffron from his head to his feet, and his wings are of green topaz. On each hair he has a million faces and on each face a million eyes, from which fall 70,000 tears each, and a million tongues, which speak a million languages. The tears become the kerubim, who lean down and rain over the flowers, trees, and fruit.

Jibra'il (Gabriel) has 1,600 wings and hair of saffron. The sun is between his eyes. Each day he enters the Ocean of Light 360 times. When he comes forth, a million drops fall from each wing to become angels who glorify Allah. When he appeared to the Prophet to reveal the Koran, his wings stretched from the East to the West. His feet were yellow, his wings, green, and he wore a necklace of rubies or coral. Between his two eyes were written the words: "There is no God but Allah, and MUHAMMAD is the Prophet of God." In icons and late medieval paintings, he takes his more usual shape, that of a delicate and beautiful youth. One Sufi vision of Jibra'il showed him "like a maiden, or like the moon amongst the stars. His hair was like a woman's falling in long tresses. . . . He is the most beautiful of angels. . . . His face is like a red rose."

Azrael, the ANGEL OF DEATH, is veiled before the creatures of God with a million veils. His immensity is vaster than the heavens, and the East and West are between his hands like a dish on which all things have been set, and he eats what he wishes. He has four faces, one before him, one on his head, one behind him, and one beneath his feet. He has four wings, and his body is covered with innumerable eyes. When one of these eyes closes, a creature dies.

Angel Images in Visionary Encounters

If angels have no physical form and no consistent symbolic shape, how can they be recognized in a visionary encounter? (See ANGELOPHANY.) Ancient descriptions associate angels with fire, pillars of light, and sensational displays of the elements, such as thunder and lightning. From these phenomena, one might infer the presence of an angel in certain circumstances. In many ancient encounters, however, angels are not recognized unless they identify themselves, such as the three "men" who visit Abraham and the "man" who accompanies Tobias on his journey. (See TOBIT.) In the legendary apparition of Michael at the Monte Gargano sanctuary in southern Italy (see MICHAEL), the archangel appears as a fearsome man riding a white horse, and he is not recognized as an angel unless he identifies himself to the man who is having the vision.

Contemporary appearances of angels in visionary experiences have been heavily influenced by Western art and the media, though they can range from pillars of light to MYSTERIOUS STRANGERS who look like ordinary people to human figures with wings.

FURTHER READING
Berefelt, Gunnar. *A Study on the Winged Angel: The Origin of a Motif.* Stockholm: Almquist and Wiksell, 1968.
Cicciari, Massimo. *The Necessary Angel.* Albany: State University of New York Press, 1994.
Guiley, Rosemary Ellen. *Angels of Mercy.* New York: Pocket Books, 1994.
Halewood, William H. *Six Subjects of Reformation Art.* Toronto: University of Toronto Press, 1982.
Highet, Gilbert. "An Iconography of Heavenly Beings," *Horizon* 3, no. 2 (November 1960): 26–49.
Peers, Glenn. *Subtle Bodies: Representing Angels in Byzantium.* Berkeley, Calif.: University of California Press, 2001.
Wilson, Peter Lamborn. *Angels.* New York: Pantheon, 1980.

Imamiah

In the KABBALAH, a FALLEN ANGEL who was once in the order of PRINCIPALITIES and also formerly one of the 72 angels of the SCHEMHAMPHORAE. As a fallen angel, Imamiah governs voyages and destroys and humiliates enemies.

incantation bowls

In early Jewish and Babylonian MAGIC, bowls inscribed with charms for capturing DEMONS or invoking angelic powers for protection. The bowls, about the size of soup tureens, were placed upside down at the four corners of houses and in cemeteries. Presumably the bowls caught or overturned demons who caused a variety of ills and problems. The bowls are inscribed in ink in a spiral from the inside out; some centers contain drawings of chained demons. The charms specify protection of homes, families, and possessions against witchcraft, diseases, and demons. They call upon powerful angels or SOLOMON and the power of the seal of his magical ring. Dating of incantation bowls is uncertain; they were in use in the fourth and fifth centuries C.E. and as late as the seventh century.

Metatron's name appears often on incantation bowls in invocations for angelic help. Various titles given him are the Great Prince of the Whole World, PRINCE OF THE WORLD, and Great Prince of God's Throne.

Some bowls inscribed in Jewish Aramaic seem to refer to the ANGEL OF THE LORD with this or similar inscriptions: "YYY the Great, the angel who has eleven names."

FURTHER READING
Barker, Margaret. *The Great Angel: A Study of Israel's Second God.* Louisville, Ky.: Westminster/John Knox Press, 1992.
Charlesworth, James H., ed. *The Old Testament Pseudepigrapha.* Vols. 1 and 2. New York: Doubleday, 1983, 1985.

Inias

One of the seven REPROBATE ANGELS in a church council trial in 745 in Rome.

instrumental transcommunication

Electronic communication with nonphysical beings, the dead and angels. Instrumental transcommunication (ITC) involves a three-way partnership: living people, people who have died and now exist on the astral plane, and spiritual beings who act as guides, advisors and facilitators. Communication, often two way, is made via telephone, radio, television, fax, and computer.

Historical Background

Human beings have always sought to communicate with otherworldly realms, including the abodes of angels and the dead. In ancient times, visions, dreams, raptures, divination, and oracles were the primary means of communication. When photography was invented, people used it to try to capture spirit images on film. Mediumship and channelling, which turn human beings into mouthpiece for the delivery of messages, enjoy contemporary popularity.

ITC evolved from the electronic voice phenomenon (EVP), which is the receiving of voices on audio tape for which there is no known physical source. The voices are captured by a tape recorder left on for periods of time. They often are very faint and are heard only on playback. Words, phrases, and short sentences are captured.

The first recorded experiments in EVP date to the 1930s and involved record players rather than tape recorders. In the 1950s, EVP was popularized by Friedrich Jurgenson, a Swedish opera singer, painter, and film producer. In 1959, Jurgenson tape recorded bird songs in the countryside near his villa. On playback, he heard a male voice discussing "nocturnal bird songs" in Norwegian. Jurgenson conducted more experiments and captured more voices.

In 1965, he met Konstantin Raudive, a Latvian psychologist and philosopher, and influenced him to devote himself to EVP. Over a period of years, Raudive recorded more than 100,000 voices. His and Jurgenson's successes influenced others all over the globe to research EVP.

Spiricom and Beyond

One of the persons fascinated by EVP was George W. Meek, an American engineer whose interest in survival after death led him to meet medium William O'Neill in 1977. At a séance, a deceased guide told Meek he would provide instructions for building a device that could communicate with the dead. The result was "Spiricom," a device built in a partnership between Meek and O'Neill. Meek founded the MetaScience Foundation to pursue more research.

Meek also explored metaphysics. He saw creation as hundreds of universes that share space with our universe. Each has its own frequency. The spirit worlds have much higher frequencies than we have on earth. They remain imperceptible to us, even to our technology. Special technology and assistance from the other side can make a communications bridge possible. Such communication would be pure rather than filtered through a human medium. Mediumship had failed to provide solid proof of survival after death, but direct communication via technology promised to provide evidence that could not be refuted.

Spiricom enabled two-way conversations to take place between the living and the dead, which Meek recorded on tape. He gave others the instructions for building the device, but no one who did reported any success. The Spiricom work began in 1979 and ended in 1982.

Meek then sought to establish communication with higher realms populated by angels and beings of light. "Project Lifeline" involved the development of sophisticated equipment that could send and receive the higher frequencies possible. Meek hired psychics and mediums to get technical advice from the other side. But despite all efforts, no technical contacts were made.

Timestream

What became known as ITC began in 1985 in Luxembourg. Interested in EVP, Maggy Harsch-Fischbach began experimenting with audio tape. She was immediately successful, and soon a single, recognizable voice appeared repeatedly. The voice began talking authoritatively on a broad range of topics, surprising Maggy with its wisdom. The voice eventually identified itself as TECHNICIAN, a member of THE SEVEN, a council of angel-like, higher beings who were seeking to estab-

lish a reliable communications link with the living on earth. The Seven referred to their spiritual brethren as RAINBOW PEOPLE, so named because when they lowered their vibration to manifest on the astral plane, they shimmered in rainbow colors.

According to Technician, the Rainbow People were attracted to her sincerity and interest, and they had chosen her to assist in their efforts to build a communications bridge to earth. She would be aided by Timestream, a team of deceased scientists, relatives, technical experts, celebrities, and others who live on the astral plane. The ultimate goal would be to set up receiving stations around the world. Maggy's home would be the first fully functioning receiving station.

Maggy was joined by her husband, Jules Fischbach, in setting up a system of televisions, radios, telephones, and computers for the experiments. Within a few years, they were receiving photos from the spirit world on their TV set, phone calls, and long and clear messages through their radio. Most of the phone calls came from Raudive.

The Seven told them that humanity was at crucial stage in its development. This was the seventh era; the preceding six, extending back beyond recorded time, had all ended badly. ITC would be the most important way to wake up human consciousness in order to survive the "End Time." The only way for ITC to be successful would be to establish a harmonious, unified partnership of researchers in many countries.

Efforts to Organize

Maggy and Jules began quietly publicizing their work, attracting the attention of Meek and other prominent researchers in the field, many of whom were getting high-tech communications of their own. At first, an international cooperative effort looked promising. Breakthroughs with computer technology expanded communications.

The researchers had difficulty uniting, however. Despite many good intentions and meetings, ITC never took firm hold as a unified international effort. The researchers disagreed over agendas, research protocols, what to make public, and how to handle the media. Some were skeptical of the results obtained by others.

Meanwhile, the higher beings and Timestream kept stressing that without a unified consciousness of sincerity, ethics, morals, and harmony among the researchers, the work ultimately would not succeed. ITC transmissions continued, however, while researchers tried to organize and collaborate.

In 1991, Mark H. Macy, who would head American ITC interests, met Meek, who was living in North Carolina. Macy's interest in spiritual matters had been expanded after overcoming cancer of the colon in

1988. Through Meek, Macy—who was already successful in EVP taping—met the European ITC researchers a year later. Maggy and Jules authorized Macy to disseminate and promote their work in North America, which he did from his base in Colorado.

By 1995, serious rifts had developed among the researchers. In September that year, a group of them—including Maggy, Jules, and Macy—met at a symposium and made another attempt to organize. They established the International Network for Instrumental Transcommunication (INIT), with headquarters in Luxembourg. Macy was named head of the North American effort.

Membership doubled in INIT's first two years. But friction and problems continued, and the organization lasted only four years. Most of the researchers went their separate ways or formed small collaborations.

In 1999, Macy met Jack Stucki, who had developed a machine called the "Luminator" for facilitating spirit photography with Polaroid cameras. The advantage of the Polaroid is that film cannot be double-exposed. The two began a collaboration. In 2000 a special Luminator was developed for Macy's research—the GT-21 (Galileo's Telescope of the Twenty-first Century). Images obtained with the Luminator show a spiritual world superimposed upon the physical world.

After INIT ended, Maggy Harsch-Fischbach and Jules Fischbach continued to receive communications from Timestream and The Seven. ITC research organizations in various countries have continued their own independent work, as have many independent researchers.

The Afterlife

According to Timestream, after death humans go to the astral plane, which is much like earth but with different physics and more of a paradise. This conforms with nearly all the major spiritual traditions, which hold that earth is a reflection of the spiritual world.

On the astral plane, people continue to do many of the same things they did on earth; they live in houses, work at jobs, have relationships and families, and share common interests with others. But they are not limited by time and space. They can shed their astral body to merge with the environment—though they retain their individuality—and move freely through time and space.

Images of this astral existence transmitted to televisions and computers proved to be a significant topic of dispute among ITC researchers involved in Timestream. It was hard for some researchers to believe that "heaven" or afterlife would so closely duplicate life on earth. The Seven explained that material things exist in many dimensions simultaneously. If pictures were sent directly from the higher realms, nothing would be recognizable to people on earth.

After death people may spend a long time on the astral level, but at some point they feel a need to move on. Some may reincarnate on earth. Others seek to raise their vibration and ascend to more subtle realms. In these higher reaches, forms become more ethereal and then give way to pure consciousness. In order to attain these levels, souls must purge themselves of negativity.

Some souls who go higher become what would be called angels. They acquire white ethereal bodies and live in love, peace, and beauty, immersed in Light. These souls shimmer in gold and white or in rainbow colors when they move down to the lower astral planes.

Earth's History

The Seven provided information about the history of the earth that corroborated some of the writings of Zecharia Zitchin, Erich von Daniken, and others. A planet named Marduk had once existed between Mars and Jupiter, with a highly sophisticated and advanced human civilization. Their world was a paradise free of disease, aging, and even the need to eat or procreate. Their consciousness enabled them to have knowledge of the spiritual realms and the afterlife. They could travel through a time-space doorway into subtler dimensions.

The people of Marduk visited Mars (also inhabited) and earth, which was populated by various primates, including primitive humans. They colonized earth. But back on the home planet, science and technology took a dangerous turn and destroyed Marduk in a gigantic explosion. The explosion also destroyed the life on Mars. The marooned earth colonies survived and interbred with the humans. The colonists developed the civilization of Atlantis. But the Marduk technology also destroyed Atlantis—the true fall of humankind.

FURTHER READING

Macy, Mark H. *Miracles in the Storm: Talking to the Other Side with the New Technology of Spiritual Contact.* New York: New American Library, 2001.

Macy, Mark. "Welcome to World ITC!" World ITC website. Available online. URL: http://www.worlditc.org. Downloaded on October 10, 1999.

Macy, Mark. "How ITC Works," *Contact!* 97, no. 2 (1997): 8–10.

"Miracles in Europe." World ITC website. Available online. URL: http://www.worlditc.org/miracles.htm. Downloaded on October 10, 1999.

"Our Seven Colleagues from the Ethereal Realms," *Contact!* 96, no. 3 (1996): 8–9.

intelligences

A type of astral power or intercessor of God. "Intelligences" can refer to cosmic powers that rule the celestial bodies and forces of nature, to the ARCHONS of GNOSTICISM, and to intercessory beings such as angels. Intelligences, or "active intelligences," also refers to forces acting within human consciousness in terms of opening to divine and imaginal realms. (See ARCHETYPES.) Intelligences figure prominently in Neoplatonic philosophy.

Plato understood that certain governing aspects of human consciousness exist beyond the physical. In *Phaedo,* he states that:

> in the heaven which is above the heavens . . . there abides the very being with which true knowledge is concerned; the colorless, formless, intangible essence, visible only to mind, the pilot of the soul. The divine intelligence, being nurtured upon mind and pure knowledge, and the intelligence of every soul which is capable of receiving the food proper to it, rejoices at beholding reality once more. (247)

Plato's most famous student, Aristotle, considered intelligences as "secondary movers" of the heavenly bodies (the prime move is God). In *Metaphysics,* Aristotle says:

> there are other spatial movements—those of the planets—which are eternal . . . each of these movements also must be caused by a substance both unmovable in itself and eternal. . . . Evidently, then, there must be substances which are of the same number as the movements of the stars, and in their nature eternal, and in themselves unmovable. (XII, 7, 1073a)

Intelligences are developed in the work of Plotinus, an Egyptian who taught philosophy in Rome in the third century C.E. and the first and most influential of Neoplatonists. Plotinus used the term Divine Thought (in Greek *ho Nous,* variously translated Mind, Divine Mind, Intellect, or Intelligence) is a sort of mediation to human beings of the Unknowable One, and connotes the highest reality knowable. Universal Intelligence contains all particular intelligences, and the totality of the Divine Thoughts known in the language of Plato as Ideas or Ideals. "Intelligence" or "Intelligible" applies to various expressions of the Divine Thought (*Nous*).

Plotinus rejected the idea of astral intelligences influencing people, but he believed people to be guided by increasingly powerful higher forces—indwelling tutorial spirits—as they ascended to Divine Mind. These forces or intelligences kept the soul focused on God. In his treatise *On Our Tutelary Spirit,* Plotinus said:

> Our tutelary spirit is not entirely outside of ourselves, is not bound up with our nature, is not the agent in our action; it belongs to us as belonging to our soul, as "the power which consummates the chosen life"; for while its presidency saves us from falling deeper into evil, the direct agent within us is something neither above nor equal to it, but under it; man cannot cease to be characteristically man.

PSEUDO-DIONYSIUS (fifth–sixth centuries C.E.), referred in *The Celestial Hierarchy* to angels as "heavenly and godlike intelligences" and said the sacred truth about them was hidden to the masses. His three-tiered hierarchy of nine orders of angels influenced Christian philosophy, including the works of St. THOMAS AQUINAS.

The Islamic philosopher IBN SINA was influenced by Neoplatonic ideas on intelligences. He associated the "Active Intelligence" with the Holy Spirit, and with Gabriel, the Angel of Humanity and Angel of Knowledge and Revelation. The Islamic theosophists following him looked upon the Angel as intimately related to the spiritual existence of humanity.

The Active Intelligence is the 10th in the hierarchy of the CHERUBIM or pure separate Intelligences, and this hierarchy is paralleled by the secondary hierarchy of the Angels who are the Souls which move the celestial Spheres; at every degree of these hierarchies couples or *syzygai* are formed between them. These celestial Souls have no sense perception but possess Imagination; they are Imagination in its pure state. They are the Angels of the intermediate world, where prophetic inspiration and theophanic visions have their place.

The Holy Spirit is the source from which human souls emanate, the source at once of their existence and their light. All knowledge and all reminiscence are a light projected by the Intelligence upon the soul. Through the Intelligence the human individual is attached directly to the celestial pleroma without the mediation of any teacher or ecclesiastical reality.

This radical spiritual autonomy of the individual alarmed orthodoxy and created an adverse reaction to the ibn Sina line, led by Averroës in the 12th century. Averroës accepted the existence of a human intelligence independent of the organic world, but he said this intelligence is not the individual, who is perishable. The eternal in the individual pertains exclusively to the separate Active Intelligence. He also excluded from his cosmology the entire second angelic hierarchy, that of the celestial Angel-Souls, who govern the world of the active Imagination: visionary events and archetypal beings. He was inspired by the idea that all minds have not the same degree of discernment; to

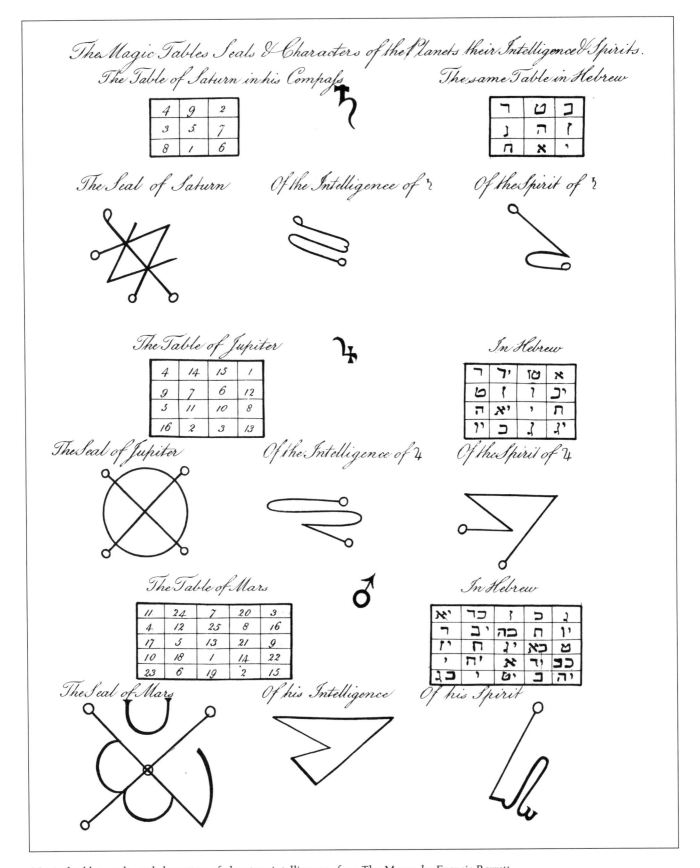

Magical tables, seals, and characters of planetary intelligences, from The Magus *by Francis Barrett*

some men the literal aspect, the *zahir*, is addressed, while others are capable of understanding the hidden meaning, the *batin*. Psychoses and social disasters result from the revelation of the hidden to those who cannot understand it.

One who gained the best insight into the matter of the Active Intelligence was Abu'l-Barakat, a 12th-century Jewish philosopher who converted to Islam toward the end of his life. He envisioned neither the separate Active Intelligence nor an active Intelligence immanent in each individual, but a plurality of separate and transcendent active Intelligences, corresponding to the differences among the multitude of souls. He wrote that:

> some souls . . . have learned everything from invisible guides, known only to themselves. . . . The ancient Sages . . . taught that for each individual soul, or perhaps for a number of souls with the same nature and affinity, there is a being of the spiritual world who, throughout their existence, adopts a special solicitude and tenderness toward that soul or group of souls; it is he who initiates them into knowledge, protects, guides, defends, comforts them, brings them to final victory, and it is this being whom the Sages called the *Perfect Nature*. And it is this friend, this defender and protector, who in religious language is called the *Angel*.

MAIMONIDES, the great Jewish rabbi and legal scholar educated in Islamic Spain in the 12th century, was well acquainted with the works of Plato, Aristotle, the Neoplatonists, ibn Sina, and Averroës. He held that Intelligences were pure form, existing in their own plane, that of the angels, which is arranged in a causal hierarchy. Angelic Intelligences are the medium through which humans experience prophecy and vision, sometimes in DREAMS. (See ANGELOLOGY.)

Maimonides points out that dreams and prophecy both involve the seeing of aspects and the reception of experiences that, unlike most imagination, are not under the control of the people involved. This process is almost entirely a natural phenomenon, but it involves a complex system like that of ibn Sina, of interconnecting spheres.

AGRIPPA, one of the leading European occultists (15th–16th centuries) described intelligences in his great work *Occult Philosophy* as forces governing all things. They are "an intelligible substance, free from all gross and putrifying mass of a body, immortal, insensible, assisting all, having influence over all; and the nature of all intelligences, spirits and angels in the same."

FURTHER READING

Corbin, Henry. *Avicenna and the Visionary Recital.* Translated by Willard R. Trask. Bollingen Series 66. Princeton, N.J.: Princeton University Press, 1960.
Corbin, Henry. *Creative Imagination in the Sufism of Ibn Arabi.* Translated by Ralph Manheim. Bollingen Series 91. Princeton, N.J.: Princeton University Press, 1969.
Leaman, Oliver. *Moses Maimonides.* New York: Routledge, 1990.
Levinsion, Ronald B., ed. *A Plato Reader.* Translated by B. Jowett. Boston: Houghton Mifflin, 1967.
Turnbull, Grace H., ed. *The Essence of Plotinus.* Translated by Stephen MacKenna. New York: Oxford University Press, 1948.

Iofiel

One of the seven ARCHANGELS, a companion to Metatron, a prince of the law, ruler of Saturn and INTELLIGENCE of Jupiter. Iofiel means "beauty of God."

Ipos

One of the FALLEN ANGELS and 72 spirits of SOLOMON. Ipos is an earl and PRINCE who rules 36 legions. The LEMEGETON gives his appearance as an angel with a lion's head, goose feet and a hare's tail; JOHANN WEYER said he appears either as an angel or an evil and crafty lion. Ipos knows the past and future and imparts wisdom and courage.

irin (irin qaddisin)

Twin angels who live in either the sixth or seventh HEAVEN and who act as the supreme judgement of the heavenly court. Irin means "watchers"; they are the WATCHERS mentioned in Daniel 4:17. The irin have a higher rank than Metatron. In the Revelation of Moses, Metatron shows MOSES the irin in the sixth heaven.

Isaac

In the Old Testament, the son of ABRAHAM and Sarah, whose life is saved by an intervening ANGEL OF THE LORD.

In Genesis 22, God tests Abraham's obedience by ordering him to take Isaac to the land of Moriah and sacrifice him to the Lord. Abraham does as ordered, binding Isaac and placing wood on him for a sacrificial fire. He raises his knife to slit the boy's throat, but at the last moment, the Angel of the Lord intervenes and stops the sacrifice: "Then Abraham put forth his hand, and took the knife to slay his son. But the angel of the Lord called to him from HEAVEN, and said, Abraham, Abraham!' And he said, 'Here am I.' He [the angel] said, 'Do not lay your hand on the lad or do anything to him; for now I know that you fear God, seeing you have not withheld your son, your only son from me'" (22:10–12).

Abraham then spies a ram caught in the thicket, and he sacrifices it to the Lord instead.

God reiterates his earlier covenant with Abraham: "And the angel of the Lord called to Abraham a second time from heaven and said, 'By myself I have sworn, says the Lord, because you have done this, and have not withheld your son, your only son, I will indeed bless you, and I will multiply your descendants as the stars of heaven and as the sand which is on the seashore. And your descendants shall possess the gate of their enemies, and by your descendants shall all the nations of the earth bless themselves, because you have obeyed my voice'" (22:15–18).

In rabbinic literature, a midrash from the eighth century tells the story of what happens to Isaac at the moment he is about to be slain. Abraham's knife touches the boy's throat, and at that moment, his soul flies out of his body and rises into heaven. There angels take him to the celestial academy of Shem and Eber. He remains there for three years studying the Torah as a reward for his suffering. All of the treasuries of heaven are opened to him: the treasuries of prayer, souls, ice, and snow; as well as the palaces of heaven, the celestial Temple that has existed since creation, and the "Chambers of the Chariot" (perhaps a description of the throne of God). Isaac is shown his past lineage on earth as well as the future generations that would come from Abraham. The End of Days also is revealed.

Meanwhile, Abraham stands frozen, his hand upraised. Though three years pass for Isaac, only a single breath transpires for Abraham. The instant the angel speaks and tells him not to lay a hand on the lad, Isaac's soul returns to his body. When he is back in his body, Isaac realizes the dead will have future life and exclaims, "Blessed is He who quickens the dead!" Abraham unbinds the boy and he arises as if reborn.

Christian influence is apparent in this story, which underscores the theme of death and resurrection as well as passage of time marked by three: three years for Isaac, three days between Jesus's crucifixion and his resurrection.

The story also resembles modern-day accounts of the NEAR-DEATH EXPERIENCE. There is the ascent to heaven and the meeting with the angels; the revelation of mystical secrets; the life review; the revelation of the future and the end of times. The distortion of time also is characteristic of an NDE. Near-death experiencers often feel that time is expanded or stretched, and that what takes place during their encounters is over a much longer period of time than what actually passes on earth.

Testament of Isaac

The Testament of Isaac is a pseudepigraphon written in the second century and tells the end of his life. It is sometimes in the voice of Isaac and sometimes in the voice of a narrator.

When it is time for Isaac to die, God sends Michael to take his soul, as he did with Isaac's father, Abraham (see ANGEL OF DEATH). Michael casts sleep over the household and comes to Isaac in his bed. He says that in heaven Isaac will be with the saints and will have a throne beside his father, and a throne shall be prepared for Isaac's son Jacob. Isaac will be entrusted with the name of the Patriarchs, the name of all future generations and the fathers to all the world.

Isaac mistakes Michael for Abraham, but the angel corrects him and tells him to make his house ready. Isaac asks what he should do about Jacob (in terms of taking away his brother Esau's birthright), and the angel says the blessing upon him cannot be undone, and he will create 12 tribes.

After Michael leaves, Jacob awakens and Isaac breaks the news of his departure. Isaac weeps and wants to come along, but Isaac dissuades him, telling him of his destiny.

Isaac dispenses advice about righteous living to throngs that gather around him. When he stops to rest, an angel of God appears and takes him to the heavens, where he beholds things in fear: strange, wild beasts who are pursuing people. Several times Isaac is eaten and swallowed by a beast, but each time he returns to his original state. This punishment, endured by the people here, is visited upon those who hated their neighbors without reconciliation before death. They are punished one year for every hour of their enmity.

Isaac then beholds a great river of fire that rolls with the sound of thunder. It is filled with crying and groaning souls of sinners. At the bottom are the weeping and screaming souls of those who committed the sin of Sodom. They are, says the angel, "due a drastic punishment."

The "overseer of punishment" is a being of fire who urges his minions on to greater torments of the damned. The angel commands Isaac to look at all the punishments but he cannot do so. The angel says the punishments will go on until God has mercy on the souls.

The angel takes Isaac to heaven, where he sees Abraham and the saints, who take him to the curtained throne of God. They prostrate themselves and worship. God blesses the lineage of Abraham.

Abraham delivers a discourse on how to gain entry into heaven. When he is done, God asks Michael to call in all the angels and saints. God mounts the chariot of the seraphim and goes to

Isaac, with the cherubim preceding, and Isaac is filled with radiant joy. He gives Isaac some final instructions about his covenant.

God takes Isaac's soul, white as snow, and ascends to the heavens in his chariot, while the cherubim and other angels sing praises. The kingdom of heaven and the fulfillment of the covenant are bestowed upon Isaac.

FURTHER READING

Charlesworth, James H., ed. *The Old Testament Pseudepigrapha.* Vols. 1 and 2. New York: Doubleday, 1983, 1985.

Schwartz, Howard. *Gabriel's Palace: Jewish Mystical Tales.* New York: Oxford University Press, 1993.

Isaiah

One of the great prophets of the Old Testament, whose call to duty involved a grand vision of the heavenly court attended by SERAPHIM, the highest of angels. Isaiah received his call in 740 B.C.E., the year the Uzziah, king of Judah, died. He prophesied for 40 years, and he had the ear of kings.

In Isaiah 6:1–8, the prophet describes his initial heavenly vision:

I saw the Lord sitting upon a throne, high and lifted up; and his train filled the temple. Above him stood the seraphim; each had six wings: with two he covered his face, and with two he covered his feet, and with two he flew. And one called to another and said: "Holy, holy, holy is the Lord of Hosts; the whole earth is full of his glory."

And the foundations of the thresholds shook at the voice of him who called, and the house was filled with smoke. And I said: "Woe is me! For I am lost; for I am a man of unclean lips, and I dwell in the midst of a people of unclean lips; for my eyes have seen the King, the Lord of hosts!"

Then flew one of the seraphim to me, having in his hand a burning coal which he had taken with tongs from the altar. And he touched my mouth, and said: "Behold, this has touched your lips; your guilt is taken away, and your sin is forgiven." And I heard the voice of the Lord saying, "Whom shall I send, and who will go for us?" Then I said, "Here I am! Send me."

God then endorses Isaiah as a messenger and instructs him to make people listen to the word and warnings of God.

The main thrust of Isaiah's many prophecies is that the nation must depend on God alone, and God will judge all who turn away from him. However, he also says that God loves to forgive. Isaiah prophesies the coming of the Messiah (9:6) and the creation of a new heaven and new earth (65:17–25) in which "the wolf and the lamb shall feed together."

A fuller account of Isaiah's journey through the seven HEAVENS is given in the Martyrdom and Ascension of Isaiah, a composite apocryphal work written between the second and fourth centuries. Part one of the text tells how Isaiah suffers at that hands of Manasseh, son of the king Hezekiah of Jerusalem. Isaiah prophesies that Manasseh is under the influence of Beliar and Samael. Inspired by Beliar, he will cause the death of Isaiah.

Isaiah has a vision in which he is shown the seven heavens and sees the Lord and the Holy Spirit. He hears God commission the Lord (Christ) to descend to the world, and then he witnesses the miraculous birth of JESUS, and his life, death, resurrection, and ascension.

It is Isaiah's claim that he saw God in his vision and lived that serves as one reason for Manasseh's hatred of him. According to MOSES, no one can see the face of God and survive. But Isaiah claims to see more than did Moses. Beliar also is angry at Isaiah because his vision revealed the coming of the Lord to the world. Beliar would attempt to reign as a false king, but he would be cast into Gehenna (HELL).

For these and other prophecies, Beliar inflames the heart of Manasseh against Isaiah. When a Samaritan accuses Isaiah of treason and blasphemy, Manasseh has him arrested and executed by being sawed in half.

Part two of the text describes the prophet's heavenly vision, which takes place six years before his execution. Isaiah visits Hezekiah. Before a large assembly of the king and his counselors and prophets, Isaiah enters a trance and begins speaking in the voice of the Holy Spirit. He then falls silent as his vision begins with the appearance of an angel from the seventh heaven.

The angel tells Isaiah he is going to take him up into the heavens. Isaiah asks his name, but the angel does not give it, saying only that when the journey is completed the prophet will understand who is the angel and what is the purpose of the vision; but he cannot divulge his name because Isaiah must return to his body.

Isaiah first sees the firmament, where Samael and his evil hosts struggle with one another in envy. The angel says that this struggle will last "until the one come whom you are to see, and he will destroy him" (7:12). The prophet then sees the seven heavens (7–9):

First Heaven

A throne sits in the middle of the heaven with angels on both sides. The angels sing the praises of

God in the seventh heaven. The angels on the right are more glorious than the angels on the left.

Second Heaven

The second heaven is as tall as the distance from the first heaven to earth. There is another throne, more glorious than the first, and angels on the right and left who have a greater glory than the angels of the first heaven, and give more glorious praise to the throne. Isaiah falls on his knees to worship God, but the angel tells him to wait until he is in the seventh heaven, where his robes and crown of martyrdom await him.

Third Heaven

The third heaven is like the lower two, only more glorious yet.

Fourth Heaven

The height from the third to the fourth heaven is greater than the distance between earth and the firmament. The fourth heaven is like the lower ones, only still more glorious.

Fifth Heaven

In the still more glorious fifth heaven, Isaiah praises God who cannot be named.

Sixth Heaven

In the sixth heaven, there is no longer a throne and angels on the right and left. The more glorious angels here are directed upward to the seventh heaven, wherein dwell God and Christ. The escort angel tells Isaiah that no man can see the sixth heaven and return to the body, but the angel has been empowered to make an exception for Isaiah, who will become equal to the angels in the seventh heaven. Entry to the sixth heaven is made via going first into the heaven's air. The heaven itself is so brilliant that the lower heavens are dark by comparison. Isaiah is so overwhelmed that he wishes to remain, but the angel tells him that it is not yet time for him to come there. The thought of returning to his body makes him sad.

Seventh Heaven

As Isaiah enters the air of the seventh heaven, the angel in charge of praise in the sixth heaven challenges his right to ascend higher. The Lord answers that he has permission, for his robes are in the seventh heaven. In this highest heaven, Isaiah sees angels without number and all the righteous from the time of ADAM onward, including ENOCH. They are clothed in brilliant robes like the angels, but they have no thrones or crowns. Isaiah is told about the descent of Christ into the world, and his persecution, crucifixion, resurrection, and ascension. At that time, the righteous will rise with him and receive their crowns and robes. Isaiah is shown record books that contain all the deeds of the children of Israel. He also sees arrayed the crowns and thrones that await the righteous when Christ will ascend into the seventh heaven.

Isaiah then beholds the Lord, who becomes like an angel, and he joins in the worship and praise of him. He sees a second brilliant figure who is also worshiped and praised; this is the angel of the Holy Spirit.

Isaiah hears the worship and praises sent up by the lower six heavens. He then is given a vision of the descent of Christ, his life and return to the seventh heaven (10–11).

Reminded that he has seen things witnessed by no other man, Isaiah is returned to his body. The text ends with the assertion that because of his vision and what he witnessed, Samael, by corrupting Manasseh, caused him to be executed.

See DREAMS AND VISIONS; MERKABAH; QEDUSSAH.

FURTHER READING

Charlesworth, James H., ed. *The Old Testament Pseudepigrapha.* Vol. 2. New York: Doubleday, 1985.

May, Herbert G., and Bruce M. Metzger, eds. *The New Oxford Annotated Bible with the Apocrypha.* New York: Oxford University Press, 1977.

Islam, angels in See ANGELOLOGY.

issim (aishim; ashim; ischim; izachim)

Angels who live in the fifth HEAVEN and who are made of snow and ice. Their primary duty is to extol the glory of God. Issim means "valorous men" or "men of God," and is applied to both saintly men and angels. In the KABBALAH they are the beautiful souls of just men (saints). The Zohar equates them with the BENE ELOHIM (THRONES) and says they are ruled by Azazel and also Zephaniah as their chief. The issim are ranked the 10th order of angels in importance in the Zohar; sixth in the Maset Azilut; and second in the Berith Menucha. They also are sometimes equated with the ERELIM.

The issim are known as the "Flaming Ones" and "the Souls of Fire," and are referenced in Psalms 104:4: "who makest the winds thy messengers, fire and flame thy ministers."

The issim are mentioned in the Book of Judges. Manoah and his wife, who are childless, are visited by an "ANGEL OF THE LORD" or "man of God" who tells them they will have a son. The wife tells Manoah:

A man of God came to me, and his countenance of the angel of God, very terrible; I did not ask him whence he came, and he did not tell me his name, but he said to me, "Behold, you shall conceive and bear a son." (Judges 13:6–7)

MOSES sees the issim where he visits the fifth heaven.

The issim also is a name of the ANIMISTICS (*dii animalie*) or "Blessed Souls," who are half human and half angel or god and who rule the 10th sephirah, Malkuth (Kingdom), governed by Metatron.

Israfil

Angel prominent in Islamic lore, though not named in the Koran. Israfil means "the burning one." Israfil serves as the angel of resurrection who blows the trumpet on Judgment Day—to bring of his own demise, for he and other angels supposedly will be destroyed in the universal conflagration that will be unleashed.

According to lore, Israfil served as a companion to the prophet MUHAMMAD for three years before being succeeded by Gabriel.

A well-known Islamic story says that Allah dispatched Michael, Gabriel, Israfil and Azrael to the four corners of the earth, to get seven handfuls of dust for the creation of ADAM. However only Azrael, the ANGEL OF DEATH, was able to accomplish this.

izads (izeds)

In ZOROASTRIANISM, 27 or 28 angels who comprise the second level of emanations below the AMARAHSPANDS. Sometimes equated with the CHERUBIM, the izads are charged with governing the innocence, happiness, and preservation of the world, and with protecting GENII and guardians. The chief of this order is Mithras.

Izra'il

The Islamic ANGEL OF DEATH. Izra'il's name is mentioned in the Koran, and his characteristics and duties are elaborated upon by commentators. He is one of the four principal ARCHANGELS of Islamic angelology. In Hebrew lore, he is known as Azrael, whose name means "whom God helps."

While the angel Israfil breathes life into souls, Izra'il takes breath away. He is associated with writing, in the idea that writers "take away" ideas from the realm of thought and cause them to fall into the world of matter.

On the macrocosmic level, Izra'il represents the human soul. He removes the soul from the world and delivers it to God's forgiveness, and thus the soul is displayed in a nobler form. In this respect, Izra'il is considered the bringer of good news, because he helps the soul on its path to spiritual perfection.

Izra'il is supposed to be the biggest of the angels, with his shape pleasing to the believer, in order to facilitate the release from life. Sufi teacher Abdul Karim Jili says that Izra'il appears to the soul in a form provided by its most powerful metaphors. He may even manifest invisibly, "so that a man may die of a rose in aromatic pain"—or of a rotting stench. When the soul sees Izra'il it "falls in love," and its gaze is thus withdrawn from the body as if by seduction. Great prophets and saints may be invited politely by Izra'il in corporeal form, as he did to MOSES and MUHAMMAD.

When the Sufi poet Rumi lay on his deathbed, Izra'il appeared as a beautiful youth: "I am come by divine command to inquire what commission the Master may have to entrust to me." Rumi's human companions almost fainted with fear, but the Sufi master replied: "Come in, come in, thou messenger of my King. Do that which thou art bidden, and God willing thou shalt find me one of the patient."

Islamic angelology holds that Izra'il is another form of RAPHAEL, and possesses 70,000 feet and 40,000 wings. He has as many eyes and tongues as there are people. Arabic mythology tells that Izra'il constantly writes and erases in a large book. The writing brings birth and the erasing brings death.

Still another story, regarding the creation of Adam, has Izra'il fulfilling a crucial task. The angels Michael, Gabriel and Israfil do not produce seven handfuls of earth necessary to make Adam; Izra'il does. Thus, he is endowed with the power to separate the soul from the body.

See DEATHBED APPARITIONS.

FURTHER READING

Klein, F. A. *The Religion of Islam*. London: 1906, reprint 1971.

Nasr, Seyyed Hossein, ed. *Islamic Spirituality*. New York: Crossroad, 1987.

Jacob

Son of the patriarch ISAAC, grandson of ABRAHAM, and father of Joseph. Jacob's dream of angels on a ladder to heaven (Genesis 28:10–17) and his wrestling with an angel (Genesis 32:22–31) are two of the most striking angel stories in the Bible.

Jacob's Dream Ladder

After stealing his twin brother Esau's birthright with the aid of his mother Rebekah, Jacob leaves to escape his father Isaac's shame and Esau's wrath. Rebekah suggests her brother as a destination. On his way to his uncle Laban's country, Jacob stops for the night, taking a stone as his pillow. He dreams: "a ladder was there, standing on the ground with its top reaching to HEAVEN; and there were angels of God going up it and coming down" (Genesis 10:12). Next in the dream Jacob hears the voice of Yahweh explaining his high spiritual destiny: this land will be the dwelling of his innumerable descendants and Yahweh will never desert him. When he wakes up Jacob calls the place Bethel, the gate of heaven, anoints the stone pillow with oil, and sets it up as a monument, with which he promises faithfulness and to give a 10th of his wealth to Yahweh in return for his preservation and safe return to his father.

There are many rabbinic and midrash comments on this dream and its context. Some note the union of the land and the people destined for it, signified by Jacob placing his head on the stone. Some rabbis interpret the ladder as a symbol of the angels' constant interventions and frustration with the previous patriarchs from the beginning of creation up until this point, when Jacob at last is found worthy. Jacob's acceptability is signified by the choice of him as the model for the man-faced angel on the chariot of EZEKIEL. Some see the ladder as a political allegory, a prophecy of the ascent and descent of Israel that was to come.

In John 1:51, JESUS tells his disciples: "I tell you most solemnly, you will see heaven laid open and, above the Son of Man, the angels of God ascending and descending." MAIMONIDES interprets the ladder to represent the hierarchy of the INTELLIGENCES. A glimpse of angelic activities, particularly the image of a ladder, denoted the interdependence of the angelic hierarchies, and it was an obvious interpretation in ANGELOLOGY. Analogies were applied to stages of spiritual ascent for human seekers, for example by St. Bonaventure. Various scholars since have taken the ladder to represent every kind of correspondence, system, and parallelism between worlds and planes of being, ranging from the esoteric motto "as above, so below" to the rough model of 18th-century science, "the Great Chain of Being."

Jacob Wrestling With the Angel

After working 14 years to win Rachel, the bride of his choice (having had first to marry Leah by Laban's deception), fathering 12 sons, and working many more years with the help of the ANGEL OF THE LORD to gain great flocks of his own (Genesis 31:11), Jacob departs from Laban with all his wives, children, and flocks of livestock to return to his father and the unknown factor, his brother Esau. Along the way "angels of God met him, and on seeing them he said 'this is God's camp,' and he named the place Mahanaim" (Genesis 32:2–3). Jacob had sent a party out to meet Esau and has found out that Esau is coming to meet him with 400 men. After sending gifts ahead to Esau, and praying, Jacob leaves everyone on one side of the Jacob River and goes alone to the other side.

> And there was one [literally, "a man"] that wrestled with him until daybreak who, seeing that he could not master him, struck him in the socket of his hip, and Jacob's hip was dislocated as he wrestled with him. He said, "Let me go, for day is breaking." But Jacob answered "I will not let you go unless you bless me." He then asked, "what is your name?" "Jacob," he replied. He said, "your name shall no longer be Jacob but Israel, because you have been strong against God, you shall prevail against men." Jacob then made this request, "I beg you, tell me your name," but he replied, "Why do you ask my name?" And he blessed him there. (Genesis 24–29)

Jacob names the place Peniel because he had seen God face to face and had survived. The sun rises as he leaves Peniel, limping because of his hip. "That is the reason why to this day the Israelites do not eat the sciatic nerve which is in the socket of the hip; because he had struck Jacob in the socket of the hip in the sciatic nerve" (Genesis 32:30–32).

This dramatic scene has spurred much commentary from Judaic, Catholic, and Protestant theologians, biblical scholars, and literary critics. Does Jacob wrestle with God or with an angel? If it is an angel, is it one of the heavenly host such as Michael, Gabriel, or Uriel, or is it a fallen angel such as Samael? There is no definitive answer, but the story has been rationalized, romanticized, treated as myth, and treated symbolically.

Angels on Jacob's ladder

Jacob wrestling with the angel (Gustave Doré)

A midrash presents Esau as Jacob's unknown adversary at Peniel, continuing their competitive relationship from birth, a struggle that Jacob ultimately wins.

Another midrash (Rabbah) identifies the assailant as Esau's guardian angel. The implication is that Jacob knew with whom he was wrestling and was reassured by his success that he would have nothing to fear from his imminent reunion. The reason why the angel is required to depart before dawn is that he is required to be present among the heavenly host to praise God. "Let your brothers praise him," objects Jacob, to which the angel replies that if he does not praise God today, the angels will not let him do so tomorrow. According to this midrash the injury to Jacob is only temporary.

Early Christian commentaries identified the angel who wrestled with Jacob as a figure of Christ. Jacob's victory, which is with the angel's consent, indicates that the Jews would appear to overcome Christ at his passion. St. AUGUSTINE understands the name "Israel" to mean "seeing God," and this will be the reward of the saints. The paradox that Jacob emerges from the encounter both blessed and lame points forward to the fact that some Jews will believe in Christ and others will reject him.

MAIMONIDES treats Jacob's wrestling match as he treats other angelic visitations, namely, as a prophetic vision. The wrestling match is foreshadowed when the angels meet Jacob in Genesis 32:2.

In his lectures on Genesis of 1542–44, Martin Luther rejects the Jewish interpretations as well as the allegories of his Christian predecessors. He assumes the assailant is Christ, even though Jacob thinks it is a man, and that the assailant had tried to convince Jacob that the promises to him had been revoked. Anguish from this causes Jacob to fight beyond his normal physical strength and enables him to overcome his opponent. The request for a blessing is a demand that the assailant should revoke the earlier suggestion that Jacob has been forsaken by God and is without hope. Only when Jacob's name is changed does Jacob realize who his opponent was, and that during his struggle he has been close to heaven as well as hell. In his joy at dawn he exclaims that he has seen God. For Luther, this means that there is a dark side to the nature of God, and it is a mystery that the aspiring soul must encounter and struggle with while clinging to faith.

John Calvin regards the incident as a vision and states that Jacob is wounded so that the content of the vision would leave a permanent visible mark on him. God knows what the outcome will be, so Jacob really does not overcome God. Calvin holds that if God fights with us, he provides us with the means of resistance. Thus, God fights both against us and for us.

Another idea put forward is that the angel is Gabriel, who symbolizes the coming of Christ consciousness.

Thus the wrestling match represents the soul's struggle to free itself from the prison of darkness. Yet another twist is that the struggle is not Jacob's, but God's struggle with Jacob. God graciously gives Jacob a new name and courage to face the future.

Jacob in Apocryphal Texts

TESTAMENT OF JACOB

The Testament of Jacob is a pseudepigraphon probably written in the second or third centuries C.E. Like the Apocalypse of Abraham and Testament of Isaac, the text concerns the death of Jacob, preceded by a tour of heaven.

Jacob is in Egypt when his life nears an end. God sends Michael, as he did for Abraham and Isaac, to announce to Jacob his impending death and that he must close his affairs. By now Jacob is accustomed to speaking with angels, and he says he is ready to die, especially since he has been able to visit his son Joseph in Egypt. But when another angel resembling Isaac appears, Jacob is frightened. The angel introduces himself as Jacob's GUARDIAN ANGEL who has been with him throughout his life and has saved him from many crises.

Jacob prepares Joseph for his death and requests to be buried in the ancestral tomb in Canaan. He delivers a blessing to his 12 sons.

Jacob is taken on a heavenly tour, first to see the torments of HELL and then to preview the rewards of heaven. The text does not offer the detail found in the Apocalypse of Abraham and Testament of Isaac, though more description is devoted to the suffering sinners than to the heavenly realms. In heaven Jacob sees Abraham and Isaac and is shown "all the joys of the redeemed."

He returns to earth and dies at age 147. God sends Michael and Gabriel to take his soul to heaven. His body is embalmed according to Egyptian technique and is taken to Canaan for burial.

THE LADDER OF JACOB

This is a short text that elaborates on Jacob's dream at Bethel. The date of its composition is unknown but is thought to be around the first century C.E. Portions of the text have been corrupted and are considered by some scholars to be unreliable. Its final portion, chapter 7, most probably is a separate work that was appended to it.

According to the text, Jacob's dream includes four-faced CHERUBIM, many-eyed SERAPHIM, and God's throne of glory. There are 12 steps on the ladder and on each step there are two human faces on the right and on the left, so there are 24 faces altogether. Angels ascend and descend the ladder.

Jacob prays to God for an interpretation of the dream. God sends the angel Sariel, who is in charge of dreams, to explain the meaning. Jacob says, "And Sariel the ARCHANGEL came to me and I saw (him), and his appearance was very beautiful and awesome. But I was not astonished by his appearance, for the vision I had seen in my dream was more terrible than he and I did not fear the vision of the angel" (3:3–5).

Sariel tells Jacob that his name shall now be Israel. He says the ladder represents this age and its 12 steps are the periods of the age. The 24 faces are the kings of the ungodly nations of the age. The sins of Jacob's grandsons will make the place desolate. A palace will be built, a temple in the name of God, but it will become deserted. God will raise up kings from the grandsons of Jacob's brother Esau and they will receive the nobles of the tribes of the earth who will mistreat Jacob's descendants. Jacob's descendants will be exiled into slavery, but the Lord will judge the people who enslave them. The descendants will be released. Angels and archangels will hurl bolts of lightning before them for the sake of the salvation of Jacob's tribe. God will grant his mercy upon them and fight on their behalf. He will punish the enslavers with famine, swarms of reptiles and deadly things, and earthquakes and destruction. Jacob's children will walk in justice.

The final chapter that is probably a separate text concerns a prophecy that speaks in symbolic terms of Christ's descent to earth.

PRAYER OF JACOB

The Prayer of Jacob, written sometime between the first to fourth centuries C.E., consists of four invocations, three petitions, and one injunction and is similar to charm prayers found in Greco-Egyptian and Jewish magical texts. The prayer uses secret NAMES OF GOD and asks for the petitioner to be filled with wisdom and power "as an earthly angel," as having become immortal.

See DREAMS AND VISIONS.

FURTHER READING

Charlesworth, James H., ed. *The Old Testament Pseud-epigrapha.* Vol. 2. New York: Doubleday, 1985.

Corbin, Henry. *Creative Imagination in the Sufism of Ibn'Arabi.* Translated by Ralph Manheim. Princeton, N.J.: Princeton University Press, 1969.

Graves, Robert, and Raphael Patai. *Hebrew Myths.* New York: Doubleday Anchor Books, 1964.

Luther, Martin. *Luther's Works.* St. Louis: Concordia, 1971.

Maimonides. *Guide of the Perplexed.* Abridged. Introduction by Julius Guttmann. London: East and West Library, 1952.

Rogerson, John. "Wrestling With the Angel: A Study in Historical and Literary Interpretation," *Hermeneutics, the Bible, and Literary Criticism.* Edited by Ann Loades and Michael McLain. New York: St. Martin's Press, 1992.

Jael (Joel)

Cherub who, with his twin Zarall, guards the ARK OF THE COVENANT. Jael also is the angel of the zodiac constellation Libra. The Apocalypse of MOSES gives Jael as a name of God.

Jahoel (Jehoel, Shemuel, Kemuel, Yaoel, and Metatron)

A member of the ANGELS OF THE PRESENCE, who mediates the ineffable name of God. The name Jahoel may have been an early form of Metatron.

Jahoel is said to be chief of the SERAPHIM (a job also held by Seraphiel), and governs heavenly singing. He is responsible for holding in check Leviathan, the monster of evil who will swallow the souls of sinners on Judgment Day.

Jaoel (Joel, Yahoel, Yahoel Yah)

Great angel, GUARDIAN ANGEL, and ARCHANGEL who lives in the seventh HEAVEN; also a proper name of God. Jaoel the angel is associated with Michael and Metatron.

In the Apocalypse of Abraham, Jaoel is the angel sent by God to guide ABRAHAM on his heavenly journey of revelation. He has the likeness of a man and is robed in purple with a turban of RAINBOW around his head. His hair is white and his body is like sapphire. He carries a golden scepter. Jaoel reveals to Abraham the history of his people, and he brings the blessings of Michael as well as of himself.

In the Slavonic Life of ADAM AND EVE, the angels Joel and Michael pray for the couple. The Apocalypse of MOSES also names an archangel Joel.

In 3 ENOCH, the angel is called Yahoel and Yahoel Yah, also names for Metatron.

The Apocalypse of Abraham gives EL, El, Jahoel as one of the names of God.

FURTHER READING

Barker, Margaret. *The Great Angel: A Study of Israel's Second God.* Louisville, Ky.: Westminster/John Knox Press, 1992.

Jeduthun

In Kabbalistic lore, angel known as the "Master of Howling" who leads myriads of angels in the chanting of hymns of praise of God every evening. Originally, Jeduthun was a man who served as a director of music in the temple and was transformed into an angel with similar duties.

Jefischa

In the LEGEMETON, the ruling angel of the fourth hour of the night, called Ramersy. Jefischa rules 101,550 dukes and other servants who are divided into 12 orders.

Jehudiel

Angel who is sometimes included in the seven ARCHANGELS and who rules the movements of the celestial spheres.

Jeremiel

Archangel whose name means "mercy of God" or "whom God sets up." Jeremiel is included in the earliest lists of the seven ARCHANGELS who stand before God.

In 4 Ezra (4:36ff) Jeremiel is equated with Eremiel, the angel who watches over the souls in the underworld. When EZRA asks how long he must wait until the new age, Jeremiel answers that the righteous are in the underworld and the chambers of the souls, which, like wombs, will bear their fruit when the time is ready. Jeremiel shows Ezra a parable, but says he cannot say if Ezra will be alive when the new age comes, for he does not know.

1 ENOCH and 2 Edras equate Jeremiel with Remiel and Uriel.

Jerome, St. See DREAMS AND VISIONS.

Jesus

Son of God in Christianity. Both divine and human, Jesus is higher than all angels. He supplants many of the functions of angels, especially their intercessory and intermediary roles between God and humanity. The New Testament portrays angels mostly in secondary roles in the life of Jesus, with the exception of the devil, Satan, who tempts Jesus.

Angels are messengers and supporters. The ANGEL OF THE LORD announces the coming birth of Jesus' forerunner, John the Baptist, to John's father Zechariah, instructing him on the name and upbringing (Luke 1:11–22). The angel says, "I am Gabriel who stand in God's presence," and strikes Zechariah dumb because he has doubted the message. Gabriel is sent to MARY in the sixth month of Elizabeth's pregnancy with John (Luke 1:26–38) to tell her not only of her own impending conception of Jesus, "Son of the Most High," but also that her cousin Elizabeth is with child. When John is circumcised, Zechariah regains his speech after he follows the angel's instructions, writing on a tablet that the child is named John.

The Angel of the Lord next appears to the shepherds the night Jesus is born (Luke 2:9–14) and announces his birth; a "great throng of the heavenly host" then appears to sing praises to God.

The Angel of the Lord appears three times to Joseph in dreams: before the birth of Jesus to explain that Mary has conceived by the Holy Spirit (Matthew 1:20–21); to warn him to take Mary and Jesus away to Egypt to avoid the wrath of Herod, which would unleash the slaughter of Innocents (Matthew 2:13); and to tell Joseph when it is safe to return to Israel (Matthew 2:19). Joseph has a fourth dream warning (Matthew 2:23) that causes him to go to Galilee for safety. Though an angel is not mentioned as the messenger, it can be assumed so based on the pattern of the other three dreams. (See DREAMS AND VISIONS.)

In Matthew 4:1–11 and Luke 4:1–12, Satan tempts Jesus three times in the wilderness in a key confrontation between good and evil. The devil appears after Jesus has fasted for 40 days and 40 nights. First the devil challenges Jesus to turn stones into bread, but Jesus declines, saying, "It is written, 'Man shall not live

Angel with swanlike wings announcing birth of Jesus

by bread alone, but by every word that proceeds from the mouth of God'" (Matthew 4:4).

The devil then challenges Jesus to prove he is the Son of God by throwing himself off a parapet. The devil quotes Psalm 91: "He will put you in his angels' charge." Jesus deflects, "You shall not tempt the Lord your God" (Matthew 4:7).

Finally, the devil takes Jesus to a high mountain where they can see "all the kingdoms of the world and the glory of them," and promises them to Jesus if he will fall down and worship him. Jesus declares, "Begone, Satan! for it is written, 'You shall worship the Lord your God and him only shall you serve'" (Matthew 4:8–10).

Satan departs, and at that point angels make their appearance, ministering to Jesus.

Angels do not participate in the activities of Jesus' ministry, though Jesus does acknowledge them. In Matthew 18:10 he tells his disciples "never despise any of these little ones [children], for I tell you that their angels in heaven are continually in the presence of my Father in heaven." This passage is one of the key scriptural proofs for the belief in GUARDIAN ANGELS.

John 5:1–9 relates that Jesus goes to a pool in Jerusalem (Bethzatha, or Bethesda) where he heals a paralyzed man. The text implies that healing occurs at the pool when the water is "troubled," that is, when there is some sort of divine intervention. Some ancient authorities inserted into the text at 5:4, "for an angel of the Lord went down at certain seasons into the pool and troubled the water: whoever was the first person after the troubling of the water was healed of whatever disease he had." The episode involving Jesus has no angelic presence, however. The paralyzed man tells Jesus that there is no one to help him be first in the water. Jesus says, "Rise, take up your pallet and walk," whereupon the man is instantly healed.

In the Garden of Gethsemane, Jesus prays about his ensuing passion and death and surrenders to God's will. Some ancient authorities inserted into the text at Luke 22:43, "And there appeared to him an angel from heaven, strengthening him."

Jesus does not call on angels for help when he is betrayed by the kiss of Judas Iscariot, who has been taken over by Satan. Jesus is arrested by priests and a mob. One of Jesus's disciples—Simon Peter according to John 18:10—attempts to defend him by cutting off the ear of a slave of the high priest. Jesus says, "Put your sword back. . . . Do you think that I cannot appeal to my Father and he will at once send more than twelve legions of angels? But how then should the scriptures be fulfilled, that it must be so?" (Matthew 26:52–54). (According to Luke 22:51, Jesus heals the man's severed ear.)

After Jesus is crucified and buried, Mary Magdalene and "the other Mary" go to the tomb on the third day. According to Matthew 28:2–7:

> And behold, there was a great earthquake; for an angel of the Lord descended from heaven and came and rolled back the stone, and sat upon it. His appearance was like lightning, and his raiment white as snow. And for fear of him the guards trembled and became like dead men. But the angel said to the women, "Do not be afraid; for I know that you seek Jesus who was crucified. He is not here; for he has risen, as he said. Come, see the place where he lay. Then go quickly and tell his disciples that he has risen from the dead, and behold, he is going before you to Galilee; there you will see him. Lo, I have told you."

Mark 16:5–6 says that "a young man in a white robe" greets the women. Luke 24:4–5 says that "two men in brilliant clothes suddenly appeared at their

The Agony in the Garden (Albrecht Dürer, 1508)

Angels holding image of Christ, from Eastern Orthodox Church, Romania (Author's collection)

side." John 20:11–14 says that Mary Magdalene finds "two angels in white sitting where the body of Jesus had been, one at the head, the other at the feet." They speak with her just before Jesus appears to her.

A controversy arose in Christian theology about the identity of the Angel of the Lord. Some authorities said it was the pre-incarnated Christ, although this would make him the announcer of his own birth and would make him a presence throughout the Old Testament.

In portraying scenes in the life of Jesus, artists throughout the centuries have taken license to insert angels. They guard him as an infant, are in the background as witnesses to his experiences, weep bitterly at his crucifixion, and rejoice at his ascension.

See ANGELOLOGY; IMAGES OF ANGELS.

Joan of Arc (1412–1431)

French peasant girl, known as "the Maid of Orleans," whose communion with saints and an angel led her to become a military hero of France. Joan of Arc's success was short-lived, for her enemies succeeded in executing her as a heretic. Her story is especially interesting to scholars because of the extensive documentation of her trial, in which she was interrogated in depth about her visions and voices.

Joan was born to a farming family in Domremy, a village between the Champagne and Lorraine regions. At the time, France was torn by civil war and had an unstable throne. Henry V of England had invaded and was claiming the crown of the insane King Charles VI. Charles VII, or the dauphin, put up no resistance. Joan's mission, guided by her supernatural aides, appears to have been ensuring the coronation of the dauphin and the defeat of the English.

At the age of 13 she began to experience visions and voices. At first it was a single voice accompanied by a brilliant light. Other voices manifested. They instructed her to "be a good girl, and go often to church." The voices then began to intervene often in her life, and to be accompanied by forms that Joan identified as the archangel St. Michael and saints Catherine and Margaret. The voices usually came to her during a waking state, but sometimes they roused her from sleep. Sometimes they were unintelligible. They manifested almost daily.

Over time the voices gave Joan more instructions and predictions of the future, and they revealed her mission. She was to take up arms like a man, raise the English siege of Orleans, and see that the dauphin was crowned king of France. The voices told her that she would be wounded in battle, and that a great victory would be won over the English within seven years.

When Joan protested to the voices that she could not possibly accomplish these things, the voices replied, "It is God who commands it." The voices became so insistent that she finally sought an audience with Robert Baudricourt, who commanded the king's forces in the town of Valcouleurs. Baudricourt dismissed her with laughter.

But when one of her prophecies later came true—a serious defeat for the French in battle—Baudricourt

Joan of Arc (Jules Bastien-Lepage, c. 1879; reprinted courtesy of Metropolitan Museum of Art, New York, gift of Erwin Davis, 1889)

agreed to send her to the dauphin. For protection she traveled in male clothing, something that later would contribute to her demise.

She had an audience with the dauphin on March 8, 1429. He purposely disguised himself, but she recognized him instantly. She impressed him because she knew his daily personal prayer to God, which she had received from the voices. She persuaded him about her mission, and asked for troops to lead to Orleans.

Court advisers considered her a lunatic, so Charles sent her to a council of theologians for interrogation. They found no quarrel with her and sent her back to Charles. According to Joan, Charles accepted her not because of the clergy, but because she had presented him with a divine sign. She said Michael had accompanied her to her meeting with Charles, and had bowed to him and presented him with a marvelous crown. The angel had told him that with Joan's help, the English would be banished from France.

Charles gave her troops, which she led into battle against the English at Orleans, flying a special standard that bore the words "Jesus: Maria" and a representation of the Eternal Father being presented a fleur-de-lis by two angels.

Joan raised the siege of Orleans in May 1429, and won another important campaign against the English on the Loire River. Charles was crowned Charles VII on July 17 of that year. In gratitude, he ennobled Joan and her family. Among the people, she was hailed as the savior of France.

Despite the victories, the English retained a firm hold on Paris and parts of Normandy and Burgundy. Joan attempted to wrest control of Paris, but she was ordered to retreat before the battle was decided. She then attempted to raise the English siege of Compiégne on May 23, 1430, but she was wounded, unhorsed, and captured. The duke of Burgundy, an ally of the English, imprisoned her in the tower of Beaurevoir castle. Joan attempted to escape twice by jumping out of the tower—against the instructions of her saints—and was apprehended. For several months, she languished in the tower; Charles VII never made a single effort on her behalf. The English, still stung by their defeat at her hands, persuaded the duke of Burgundy to sell her to them for 10,000 francs. She was delivered to the bishop of Beauvais, an English ally.

Joan was imprisoned in Castle Rouen. At first she was placed in an iron cage, and then she was chained to a bed and watched around the clock by guards. On February 21, 1431, she appeared before an ecclesiastical tribunal, who interrogated her about her visions, voices, wearing of male clothing, and faith in the church. Joan honestly described her communication

with the saints and said that she could see, hear, kiss, and embrace them. When it came to answering questions, Joan demurred until she was permitted to do so by her voices. She admitted to hearing them daily. The tribunal declared her revelations diabolical; she also was vehemently denounced by the University of Paris.

Joan's interrogators were especially interested in why she thought her spirits were saints rather than demonic deceptions. Had she been given a sure sign? A consultant to the investigations, the bishop of Lisieux, had stated that prophets should be believed only if there were accompanying signs, miracles, and references to Scriptures. A sign would be something imprinted on the physical world, which could be perceived by at least one of the five senses and could be verified independently.

Joan could offer no such evidence. She said she knew her spirits were good because they always helped her. She could identify Michael, she said, by his angelic speech and language. However, she also admitted that initially she was uncertain that it was indeed Michael; she was afraid; she saw him many times before she knew it was Saint Michael.

The interrogators were not impressed by the alleged sign given to Charles, for no testimony was forthcoming from the court as to the verity of what she claimed. Joan's world may have been full of visions, voices, apparitions, and a crown, but no one else could—or would—verify the truthfulness of it all.

From the outset the interrogators were inclined to believe that Joan's experiences were of evil spirits, and they relentlessly attempted to link them with FAIRIES (because fairies were pagan, they were evil in the view of the church). Joan testified over and over again that the spirits filled her with joy and guided her. When Michael appeared, she said, she felt carefree and not in a state of mortal sin; she was always unhappy to see him depart. The spirits even kissed and embraced her, she said. The alleged physical contact repulsed the interrogators, who associated that too with evil. Furthermore they were put off by the spirits' instruction to her to wear men's clothing and to ignore many of their questions. Ultimately what sealed her fate was her spirits' counsel to fight the English.

Joan was charged with 70 counts of sorcery, witchcraft, divining, pseudo-prophecy, invoking of evil spirits, conjuring, being "given to the arts of magic," and heresy. The charges of sorcery and witchcraft could not be substantiated, and they were dropped. The remaining charges were reduced to 12, chief among them being heresy, the wearing of men's clothing, and the ability to see apparitions. She remained unrepentant and refused to recant, even when threatened with torture. On May 24, 1431, she did make a partial recantation before a large, jeering crowd at the cemetery of St. Ouen. She was sentenced to life in prison. But upon returning to her cell, she resumed male dress. She declared again that the voices were from God, and that God had sent her on her mission.

She was accused again of dressing as a man on the instructions of her saints. (Some modern historians speculate that guards stole her own clothing and left her nothing but men's clothing to wear.) On May 28, 1431, Joan was condemned as a relapsed heretic. On May 30 she recanted her confession and was excommunicated from the church. She was burned at the stake the same day in Rouen.

According to legend her heart refused to burn, and the executioner discovered it whole in the ashes. The ashes were cast into the Seine.

Nearly 20 years after her execution, at the behest of Joan's mother and two brothers, Charles VII initiated an investigation into her rehabilitation. The report, written in 1449, takes a much more sympathetic view of her experiences. It emphasizes as a virtue, not a sin, her willingness to accept the counsel of her saints, her distaste for violence, and the accuracy of her prophecies. It also emphasizes that she possessed five saintly virtues that were deemed signs at the time: humility, willingness to accept counsel, patience, accuracy, and charity. It notes her lack of fear whenever she dealt with her spirits, which various experts throughout the centuries had stated was characteristic of a good rather than an evil person.

Pope Calixtus III annulled her sentence in 1450. She was canonized in 1920 by Pope Benedict XV. A national festival in her honor is held in France on the second Sunday in May. Her feast day is May 30.

Frederic W. H. Myers, a founder of the Society for Psychical Research in 1882 in London, hypothesized that Joan's visions and voices were externalizations of her own inner voice coming from her subconscious, which Myers called "the sublimal self." He compared her saint-guides to the DAIMON of Socrates, an inner voice Socrates credited to a guiding spirit that had been with him from childhood. Joan's case, Myers said, exhibited characteristics of motor automatism, in which voices are accompanied by an "overwhelming impulse to act in obedience to them."

FURTHER READING

Butler, Alban. *One Hundred Saints*. Boston: Little, Brown & Co., 1994.

Christian, William A., Jr. *Apparitions in Late Medieval and Renaissance Spain*. Princeton, N.J.: Princeton University Press, 1981.

Myers, Frederic W. H. Myers. *Human Personality and Its Survival of Bodily Death*. Vols. I and II. New ed. New York: Longmans, Green, 1954. First published 1903.

Pernoud, Regine. *Joan of Arc: By Herself and Her Witnesses*. New York: Dorset, 1964. First published 1962.

John XXIII (1881–1963)

Pope John XXIII (1958–63) maintained a deep and abiding faith in GUARDIAN ANGELS, thanks to the influence of Pope PIUS XI. John XXIII often used his radio addresses to exhort followers never to neglect devotion to their guardian angels, who, he said, stand ready at all times to help. He particularly urged parents to educate their children that they were not alone but always in the company of their guardian angels.

Like Pius XI, John XXIII brought his guardian angel into all his dealings with other persons, especially those with whom he was having trouble. He followed the advice given to him by Pius XI and asked the guardian angels of both him and the other person to work out an accord between them on the angelic level, which then would manifest on the physical level. Even if no difficulties were present, John XXIII always at least acknowledged and paid respect to all guardian angels present at any meeting or gathering. He often acknowledged to his secretary how his guardian angel had inspired him to do various things. He confided to a Canadian bishop that his angel had given him the idea to call the Second Vatican Council in 1962, which became the high point of his pontificate.

John XXIII was warm and outgoing, and one of the best-loved popes of modern times. He worked for world peace, dialogue with other faiths, and social welfare causes around the world.

FURTHER READING

Huber, Georges. *My Angel Will Go before You*. Westminster, Md.: Christian Classics, 1983.

Jubilees

Apocryphal text that sets forth an account of the revelations of chronology and law made to MOSES during his 40 days on Mount Sinai. Forty-nine of the 50 chapters are a long revelation made directly to Moses by one of the ANGELS OF THE PRESENCE, who instructs Moses to record what he says in a book. Though the angel is not named, he is thought by some to be Michael.

The book of Jubilees is so named because it divides history into periods of jubilees, or about 50 years. Called "The Little Genesis," the book probably was written by a priest between 160–140 B.C.E. The earliest mention of it appears in the QUMRAN TEXTS, which include five fragments of the book written in Hebrew. The book draws upon the Old Testament and also the first book of ENOCH.

Jubilees gives stories about the creation of the world and ADAM AND EVE; NOAH and the flood; ABRAHAM; JACOB and his family; Enoch; the trials of Joseph; and Moses. It also tells about the creation of angels and demons, their characteristics, duties, and activities. According to Jubilees, evil originates in the angelic kingdom and not with the fall of Adam and Eve.

Angels are described only by their ranks; the only angel to be named is Mastema, or Satan, whose origin is not disclosed. "Beliar" is mentioned, but this is a reference to "worthless men" and not Satan or a demonic power (1:20).

The angels are created on the first day, along with the HEAVENS, the earth, and the waters. There are two high ranks of angels, the angels of the presence and ANGELS OF SANCTIFICATION. These angels are born circumcised, which enables them to participate with Israel in all its religious observances. Lesser ranks of angels govern the forces of nature: the angels of the spirits of fire; the spirit of the winds; the spirit of the clouds and darkness and snow and hail and frost; resoundings and thunder and lightning; cold and heat and winter and springtime and harvest and summer; and all the spirits of his creatures that are in heaven and on earth. Seeing the wonders of creation, the angels praise and bless God (2:1–3).

After creation, God tells the angels of the presence and the angels of sanctification that they are to keep the sabbath with him in heaven and on earth. He announces his intention to separate a nation of people to keep the sabbath; this is Israel (2:19).

Jubilees describes the many duties of the good angels. Besides governing the forces of nature and providing knowledge and skill instruction to humans, they convey God's will to people, test them, report their sins to God, reveal the future, disclose secret cosmic knowledge, bind evil spirits, guard men, and assist those who are attacked by the forces of evil. Angels are assigned to rule over nations, but no angel is assigned to rule over Israel, because God has a direct connection to that nation. Angels who are assigned to the nations of gentiles lead those peoples astray (15:32).

A particular class of angels called the WATCHERS are sent to give instruction to humanity, but they fall in love with women and corrupt themselves, spawning giants called the NEPHILIM and a host of evil DEMONS Revolted by the corruption that has spread across the earth, God decides to open the seven floodgates of heaven and send floodwaters to wipe out every living thing save NOAH and his ark. Enoch, taken up into the heavens by angels to see all of creation, bears witness against the Watchers and condemns them for their evil. Enoch is taken to Eden, and, because of his presence there, the waters of the flood spare Eden (5–6). The corruption of the Watchers marks the beginning of evil upon earth.

Two generations later, the polluted demons begin leading the children of Noah's sons astray. Noah prays to God to shut the demons up so that they do not have power over the "children of the righteous." God tells the angels to bind the demons. But Mastema appeals to God to let him to keep one-tenth of the demons to be subject to him on earth. This request is granted. The angels bind nine-tenths of the demons into the place of judgment and let Mastema have the rest. The angels then teach herbal healing lore to Noah, so that the remaining evil spirits could be restrained (10:1–14).

Jubilees treats dreams as important events; they serve as a medium of communication with God and provide information about the future. Abraham is told by God in a dream that his reward will be great (14:1–5); Rebecca learns in a dream that Esau intends to kill Jacob, and she warns him to go away (27:1–12); Jacob is sent away, and he has his famous dream of the angels ascending and descending a ladder (27:19–27); later he dreams that he has been appointed and ordained priest of the Most High God, he and his sons forever (32:1–2); Rebecca dreams the time of her own death (35:6); Joseph impresses the Egyptian pharaoh with his dream interpretation (39:16ff).

See DREAMS AND VISIONS; HAGAR.

FURTHER READING

Charlesworth, James H., ed. *The Old Testament Pseudepigrapha*. Vol. 2. New York: Doubleday, 1985.

Judaism, angels in See ANGELOLOGY.

Jung, Carl Gustav (1875–1961)

Swiss psychiatrist, founder of depth psychology, and one of the most influential minds of the 20th century. Carl Jung was unique among his peers, possessing immense knowledge of ancient and modern world mythology, Eastern and Western mysticism, alchemy, GNOSTICISM, poetry, music, art and architecture, anthropology, and cross-cultural spiritual experience and practice. From an early age he had numerous extraordinary experiences of his own. He believed that science and religion could be compatible.

Life

Jung was born on July 26, 1875, in Kesswil, Switzerland, and he grew up in Klein-Huningen near Basel. In early childhood, he began to experience mystical realms in dreams. He felt he had two personalities. One was a wise old man who stayed with him and had increasing influence on his thought throughout his entire life.

Jung experienced precognition, clairvoyance, psychokinesis, and hauntings. His psychic sensitivity may have been hereditary, for both his mother and maternal grandmother were known as "ghost seers."

Jung began to take serious interest in occult phenomena in 1898. In 1890, he decided to become a psychiatrist, and he did his medical training at Basel. Throughout his career, the paranormal played a significant role in his vision of humanity's psychic realm.

He married in 1903. In 1906, he published one of his most significant early works, *The Psychology of Dementia Praecox.*

Jung became interested in mythology around 1909, the year he resigned a post at Burgholzki Mental Clinic, where he had been practicing for nine years. Also in 1909, he traveled to the United States with his mentor, Sigmund Freud, and received an honorary degree from Clark University in Worcester, Massachusetts. (Jung also received an honorary doctorate from Harvard in 1936, Oxford in 1938, and the University of Geneva in 1945.)

In 1910 he was appointed permanent president of the International Congress of Psycho-Analysis. Jung resigned this position in 1914, one year after he also resigned a professorship at the University of Zurich.

From 1907 to 1913, Jung was greatly influenced by Freud, but then they parted company over diverging viewpoints, especially concerning the spiritual aspects of the psyche. The break with Freud had a profoundly disturbing effect on Jung, and he suffered a six-year-long breakdown during which he had psychotic fantasies. He was labeled a "mystic" and was shunned by his peers. During this psychotic phase of Jung's life, he experienced numerous paranormal phenomena.

Following his emergence from this period, Jung pursued work on his own theories, guided in part by his visionary dreams. He also was intensely interested in GNOSTICISM, particularly its Sophia or WISDOM. This interest, joined with an interest in alchemy, paved the way for a modern revival of interest in the spiritual dimensions of both subjects. Jung also became intensely interested in mandala symbolism.

In 1944, Jung suffered a heart attack. He recovered, and he later recounted a NEAR-DEATH EXPERIENCE (NDE) in which he attained a mystical understanding of the meaning of his life. In the aftermath, he experienced a remarkable transformation in which he felt he was in the happy state felt by the unborn. He had a vision in which he was Adam and a Jew, and his nurse was his Magna Mater, who proceeded to teach him the mystery of the *hieros gamos,* or sacred marriage with the divine.

After the death of his wife, Jung built a castle of stone on newly acquired property in Bollingen, Switzerland. He carved numerous alchemical and mystical symbols into the stone. The ongoing building and altering of his tower signified for him an extension of consciousness achieved in old age. The tower and its symbolic role in his life is a leitmotif in Jung's writings. During his retirement at Bollingen, Jung reworked many earlier papers and developed further his ideas on many topics.

Jung believed in reincarnation and was influenced by *The Tibetan Book of the Dead.* He believed his own incarnation was not due to karma, however, but a passionate drive for understanding in order to piece together mythic conceptions. He feared greatly for the future of mankind, and said the only salvation lay in becoming more conscious. He said he believed his work proved that the pattern of God exists in every person.

Three days before he died, Jung had the last of his visionary dreams, and a portent of his own impending death. In the dream, he had become whole. A significant symbol was tree roots interlaced with gold, the alchemical symbol of completion. When he died in his room in Zurich on June 6, 1961, a great storm arose on Lake Geneva and lightning struck a favorite tree of his.

Works

Jungian principles have been found to be applicable to nearly all academic disciplines from mythology to religion to quantum physics, and to nearly all aspects of modern life. His prolific writings have been collected into 20 volumes plus a supplement.

One of his most important contributions was his general theory of psychological types, first published in 1921. He distinguished two basic psychological types, extroverts and introverts, who could be grouped according to four basic functions: thinking, feeling, sensation, and intuition. Other significant theories include the anima (feminine principle) and animus (masculine principle), psychic images that exist in everyone as feminine and masculine aspects; the collective unconscious; and ARCHETYPES. Of symbols, Jung termed them "an intuitive idea that cannot yet be formulated in any other or better way." Of dreams, he maintained that they are the private property of the dreamer and seek a private language that only the dreamer can interpret; some dreams, however, come from the collective unconscious and belong to all mankind.

In *Aion* (1951), Jung summarizes the roles of the "archetypes of the unconscious;" his observations on the Christ image as symbolized in the fish had a major influence on Christian scholarship. Religious themes are developed by Jung in another major work of the period, "Answer to Job" (1952) as well as in *Mysterium Coniunctionis* (1955–56), which concerns alchemy. In the latter, his last masterpiece, he states that he was satisfied that his psychology was at last "given its place in reality and established upon its historical foundations."

Jung's personal experiences are recorded in his autobiography, *Memories, Dreams, Reflections* (1961).

Visionary Experiences

During his lifetime Jung concealed the origins of his discoveries. He said everything he wrote was based on empirical evidence, indicating that no matter how esoteric or mystical much of his work appeared, it always rested on experience from the psychiatric and psychological field. His heirs have not released the corpus containing Jung's original experiences of the unconscious. But after his death and the publication of his autobiographical fragments entitled *Memories, Dreams, Reflections,* progressively more daring revelations began to appear from his disciples and his posthumous letters and notes disclosing that between 1912 and 1917 Jung underwent a period of psychic intensity that involved a tremendous flooding of his consciousness from within by forces that he called archetypal, but which previous ages would have declared to be divine and demonic.

He called this cycle of experiences his *Nekyia,* using the term with which Homer described the descent of Odysseus into the underworld. His handwriting changed to a style used in the 14th century, and he painted with pigments he himself made. According to eye-witnesses, Jung had bound his most beautiful scriptures and paintings in red leather, which became known as the *Red Book,* and they fell into two distinct categories. Some were bright and angelic, whereas others are dark and demonic in form. One document that has surfaced from this period, entitled *Seven Sermons to the Dead,* purports to be dictated by the second-century Gnostic Basilides in Alexandria (see ABRAXAS). The influence of visionary revelations on Jung's work can be compared to EMANUEL SWEDENBORG, JAKOB BOEHME, WILLIAM BLAKE, RUDOLF STEINER, Islamic theosophists such as IBN SINA and AL-SUHRAWARDI, as well as all the mystics from around the world whose works he knew so well.

In the context of the Judeo-Christian myth, Jung found the role of angels remarkable in their pointing to a disturbance on "the other side," that is, in the unconscious. In his autobiography, he calls the fall of the angels "a premature invasion of the human world by unconscious contents. The angels are a strange genus: they are precisely what they are and cannot be anything else. They are in themselves soulless beings who represent nothing but the thoughts and intuitions of their Lord. Angels who fall, then, are exclusively 'bad' angels. These release the well-known effect of 'inflation,' which we can also observe nowadays in the megalomania of dictators; the angels beget with men *a race of giants* which ends by threatening to devour mankind, as is told in the book of ENOCH."

The self-realization of God in human form to rectify the situation picks up the ancient idea of the divine marriage and its consequences; the possibility of "Christ within us" means "the unconscious wholeness penetrated into the psychic realm of inner experience, and man was made aware of all that entered into his true configuration. This was a decisive step, not only for man, but also for the Creator, who, in the eyes of those who had been delivered from darkness, cast off His dark qualities and became the *summum bonum.*"

Jung saw the task of middle and later age as achievement of insight, wholeness, and spiritual depth, the rounding out of the psyche, which he called the individuation process, and which can only be accomplished through self-knowledge, the road to knowledge of God.

Jung's concept of the unconscious was much more elaborate than Freud's. There is a personal unconscious of dimmed memories and repressed materials, a transpersonal or collective unconscious at a deeper level, evidenced by emotions and visions erupting from its depth, and a fathomless part beyond. By collective unconscious Jung meant "the inherited possibility of psychical functioning . . . namely . . . the brain structure." This shared human heritage is not the dark chaos of impulse that Freud had assumed. Jung's unconscious has a primordial structure and coherence, like a burial chamber of priceless antiques whose luster is revealed by the light of consciousness probing the darkness of the womb.

One cannot directly observe the unconscious mind, but there are persistent hints of its archetypal structure. Jung defines archetypes as primordial psychic processes that have their own independent lives, and are made known to us when transformed into images that consciousness can grasp, but only in symbol and metaphor. Angels and ARCHONS are example of archetypal images.

In *Psychology and Alchemy* (*Collected Works* volume 12), Jung describes meditation in an alchemical sense as "an inner dialogue with someone unseen. It may be God, when He is invoked, or with himself, or with his good angel. . . . [T]he psychologist is familiar with this 'inner dialogue'; it is an essential part of the technique for coming to terms with the unconscious." In another alchemical context in *Alchemical Studies* (*Collected Works* volume 13) Jung says that "the angel, as a winged or spiritual being, represents, like Mercurius, the volatile substance, the pneuma, the disembodied. Spirit in alchemy almost invariably has a relation to water or to the radical moisture, a fact that may be explained simply by the empirical nature of the oldest form of 'chemistry,' namely the art of cooking. The steam arising . . . conveys the first vivid impression of 'metasomatosis,' the transformation of the corporeal into the incorporeal, into spirit or pneuma." Thus, the angel or spiritual being is an archetype who mediates and activates the spiritual inner power to the conscious being.

A striking example of an archetype that Jung calls a symbol of the immortal self is the Koranic figure Khidr, the "long-lived one" who is analogous to ELIJAH, Osiris, a Second Adam, a counselor, a Paraclete whom MOSES accepts as a higher consciousness and looks up to for instruction. Jung tells of the headman of a safari he met in East Africa, a Somali raised in the Sufi faith, who regarded the Khidr as a living person whom one could meet at any time in various guises. The man dreams of Khidr and respectfully salutes him, and a few days later his wish for employment was fulfilled. Jung compares this figure to an angel, a messenger. He says this shows how even in our own day, the archetype lives on in the religion of the people.

See INTELLIGENCES.

FURTHER READING

Hoeller, Stephan A. *The Gnostic Jung and the Seven Sermons of the Dead.* Wheaton, Ill.: Quest Books, 1982.

Jung, Carl G. *Collected Works.* Edited by Sir Herbert Read. Translated by R.F. C. Hull. Bollingen Series 20 Vols. 1–20. Princeton, N.J.: Princeton University Press, 1958– .

Jung, Carl G. *Memories, Dreams and Reflections.* Edited by Aniela Jaffe. Translated by Richard and Clara Winston. New York: Pantheon, 1961.

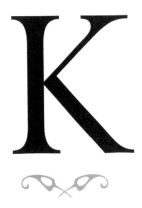

Kabbalah (Cabala, Kabala, Qabalah)

The mysticism of classical Judaism. "Kabbalah" is derived from the Hebrew word *QBL,* meaning "to receive" or "that which is received." It refers especially to a secret oral tradition handed down from teacher to pupil. The term "Kabbalah" was first applied to secret, mystical teachings in the 11th century by Ibn Gabirol, a Spanish philosopher, and it has since become applied to all Jewish mystical practice. Though the Kabbalah is founded on the Torah, it is not an intellectual discipline; nor does it instruct the mystic to withdraw from humanity to pursue enlightenment. The Kabbalist seeks union with God while maintaining a full social, family, and community life.

According to lore, God taught the Kabbalah to angels, who, after the Fall, taught it to ADAM in order to provide man with a way back to God. It was passed to NOAH, then to ABRAHAM and MOSES, who in turn initiated 70 Elders. Kings David and SOLOMON were initiates.

History

The theosophical and mystical lore which grew into the Kabbalah was influenced by GNOSTICISM and Neoplatonism.

The earliest form of mystical literature is found in the tradition of the MERKABAH mystics (ca. 100 B.C.E.–1000 C.E.). Merkabah means "God's Throne–Chariot" and refers to the chariot of Ezekiel's vision. The goal of the Merkabah mystic was to enter the throne world, which was reached after passing through seven HEAVENS as seven hekalot, or heavenly mansions. Merkabah mysticism was shamanistic in nature and required fasting and repetitious recitation of hymns and prayers to achieve a trance state. The Merkabah-rider then sent his soul upwards (later mystics said downwards) to pierce the veil around the Merkabah throne. The soul was assailed along the way by evil DEMONS and spirits, and, to protect it, the mystic prepared in advance magical TALISMANS and SEALS and recited incantations.

The historical origin of the true Kabbalah centers on a short book titled Sefer Yetzirah ("Book of Creation"). Its exact date is unknown; it was in use in the 10th century, but it may have been authored as early as the 3rd century. It is attributed to Rabbi Akiba, whom the Romans martyred. Sefer Yetzirah presents a discussion on cosmology and cosmogony and sets forth the central structure of the Kabbalah. It also is reputed to contain the formula for creation of a golem, an artificial human. A golem can be created only with divine permission; the ritual is performed only by the purest of practitioners.

In 917, a form of practical Kabbalism was introduced by Aaron ben Samuel in Italy; it later spread through Germany and became known as German Kabbalism or Early Hasidim. It drew upon the Merkabah practices in that it was ecstatic, had MAGIC rituals, and had as primary techniques prayer, contemplation, and meditation. The magical power of words assumed great importance, and it gave rise to the techniques of GEMATRIA, notarikon, and temura.

The German Kabbalists held that God was too exalted for man to comprehend. However, mystics could perceive God's presence in the form of a divine fire or light, which is the first creation, SHEKINAH, the Mother, God's female aspect. The mystic sought to unite with this glory. The German Kabbalists also conceived of four worlds: God's glory, angels, the animal soul, and the intellectual soul.

Classical Kabbalah was born in the 13th century in Provence, France, and it moved into Spain, where it was developed most extensively by medieval Spanish Jews. The primary work from which classical Kabbalah developed is Sefer Zohar ("Book of Splendor"), attributed to a second-century sage, Rabbi Simeon bar Yohai, but actually written between 1280 and 1286 by the Spanish Kabbalist, Moses de Leon. According to the story, Rabbi Simeon and his son, Eleazar, persecuted by the Roman emperor Trajan, hid in a cave for 13 years

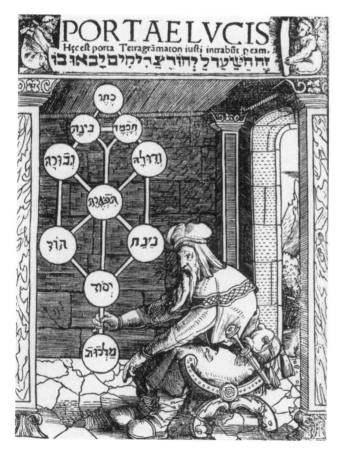

Kabbalist and the Tree of Life (From *Portae Lucius* by Paulus Ricius [1516])

where the Ben-Gurion Airport now stands in Lod, Israel. After Trajan's death, the two emerged, but Rabbi Simeon was so distraught at the lack of spirituality among Jews that he returned to the cave to meditate. After a year, a voice told him to let the ordinary people go their own way, but to teach those who were ready. The Zohar is said to comprise those teachings, which were recorded by disciples.

The Spanish Kabbalah—the teachings of the Zohar—spread into Europe in the 14th and 15th centuries. After the expulsion of Jews from Spain in 1492, Kabbalah study became more public. The most important post-expulsion figure to influence what was to become modern Kabbalah was Isaac Luria Ashkenazi (1534–72), called the Ari. Luria, a student of the great Kabbalist, Moses Cordovero (1522–70), conceived of bold new theories which gave the Kabbalah a new terminology and complex new symbolism. He emphasized letter combinations as a medium for meditation and mystical prayer.

The Hasidic movement emerged from the Lurianic Kabbalah, and it made Kabbalah accessible to the masses. The Hasidim are the only major branch of modern Judaism to follow mystical practices. The principle figure in this emergence was Israel ben Eleazar (1698–1760), called the Baal Shem Tov ("the Master of the Holy Name"), whose teaching centered on *devekuth*, or cleaving to God, but in a more personal and emotional way than before. *Devekuth* centers in the here and now; thus, concentrated awareness and prayer were reinterpreted in order to be made part of everyday life. For the Hasidim, constant prayer is the vehicle to mystical awareness.

Interest in the Kabbalah among Jews began to decline after the 18th century. The Reconstructionist movement, founded in 1922 by Rabbi Mordecai M. Kaplan, borrows from Hasidic traditions and espouses a more mystical Judaism. Interest in Kabbalah enjoyed a cross-cultural renewal beginning in the late 20th century as part of a broad interest in esoteric subjects.

Practical Kabbalah

A form of Kabbalah called "practical Kabbalah" is the core of the Western magical tradition. Magical applications grew first out of German Kabbalism and then Lurianic Kabbalism. Christian occultists were attracted to the magical AMULETS, incantations, demonology, seals, and letter permutations, and they used practical Kabbalah as the basis for ritual magical texts. The Tetragrammaton was held in great awe for its power over all things in the universe, including demons.

Beginning in the late 15th century, the Kabbalah was harmonized with Christian doctrines to form a Christian Kabbalah, which supposedly proved the divinity of Christ. AGRIPPA included Kabbalah in his monumental work, *Occult Philosophy* (1531). Also in the 16th century, alchemical symbols were integrated into the Christian Kabbalah.

Interest in the Kabbalah received renewed attention in the 19th century from non-Jewish occultists such as FRANCIS BARRETT, Eliphas Levi, and Papus. Kabbalah influenced the Hermetic Order of the Golden Dawn; occultist Dion Fortune called it the "Yoga of the West."

Central Concepts

God is Ain Soph ("without end" or "unending"), who is unknowable, unnameable, and beyond representation. God created the world out of himself but is not diminished in any way through the act of creation; everything remains within him. The aim of man is to realize union with the Divine. All things are reflected in a higher world, and nothing can exist independently of all else. Thus, man, by elevating his soul to unite with God, also elevates all other entities in the cosmos.

One of the mysteries of Kabbalah is why God chose to create imperfect, lower worlds, though it is held that he did so because he wished to show the measure of his goodness. He created the world by means of 32 secret paths of wisdom, which are formed of letters and numbers: the 22 letters of the Hebrew alphabet and 10 sephirot, which are vessels bearing the emanations of God, or are expressions of God. They form a language that substitutes for God. The sephirot are the source from which all numbers emanate and by which all reality is structured.

The sephirot form the central image of Kabbalistic meditation, the TREE OF LIFE, a map that depicts the descent of the Divine into the material world, and the path by which man can ascend to the Divine while still in the flesh. Kabbalists meditate on arrays of numbers and letters—every letter has its own numerical value—to achieve the different states of consciousness of the 32 paths. Fingers and toes, each of which correspond to a sephirah, also can be used in meditation. Meditational arrays are precise and must be meditated upon in exact order at the right time, and to completion. Some arrays make take hours or even days to complete.

The sephirot comprise the sacred, unknowable, and unspeakable personal name of God: YHVH (Yahweh), the Tetragrammaton. So sacred is the Tetragrammaton that other names, such as ELOHIM, ADONAI, and Jehovah, are substituted in its place in scripture. The letters YHVH correspond to the Four Worlds that constitute the cosmos:

- Atziluth is the world of archetypes and emanation, from which are derived all forms of manifestation. The sephirot themselves exist here.

- Briah (also Beriyah) is the world of creation, in which archetypal ideas become patterns. The Throne of God is here, and God sits upon it and lowers his essence to the rest of his creation.
- Yetzirah is the world of formation, in which the patterns are expressed. It is the world of speech.
- Assiah is the world of the material.

Each sephirah has its own title and divine names, and each is divided into four sections in which operate the Four Worlds.

Angels in Kabbalistic Teachings

Angels belong to the world of Yetzirah, the highest realm that can be visualized. In Yetzirah, one can glimpse only a reflection of the higher worlds. The prophet EZEKIEL attained this state of consciousness in his mystical experience, in which he saw the "likeness of the Throne" (Ezekiel 1:26), which is Briah, the realm of the Throne. Ezekiel also saw a "likeness of the appearance of a man," which is the anthropomorphic array of the sephirot.

According to the Talmud, every word of God creates an angel. God's word is his interaction with lower creation, and the spiritual force he creates in this interaction is the angel. The Sefer Yetzirah says that angels are made of breaths, and they carry out the function of direct and reflected breaths.

Angels exist purely on a spiritual plane and are the ARCHETYPE of the nonphysical being. However, they are inferior to man in that they are assigned a station and can go no higher, and they know nothing outside of their own domain. Descriptions are given in various texts of angels having to consult other angels in order to answer questions, or of not knowing answers to questions. Man has the capability of expanding his knowledge. He is capable of ascent, and, by applying himself spiritually, he can achieve greater closeness to God.

There are two types of angels, temporary and permanent. Temporary angels were created for the first time on the second day. Temporary angels are created every morning for a day. They have no proper names and each has a single mission, which differentiates it from the other angels. No two angels can share the same mission. MINISTERING ANGELS are visualized as flames and fire.

Permanent angels were created on the fifth day. These angels have proper names and can perform multiple tasks. They are associated with the stars (including planetary bodies) and work through these celestial entities. They act like souls for the stars, and the stars act as their bodies, helping to keep their tasks integrated and unified. According to the Zohar, every star has its own name; the midrashim teach that these names correspond to the names of the permanent angels. The Sefer Yetzirah says that the names are formed by permutations of the letters of the Hebrew alphabet; there are approximately 1 sextillion possible permutations.

The angels and stars form the lowest level of interaction between God and creation. The stars channel spiritual energy down to the physical world. They govern everything; nothing is too small. The stars and their angels are assigned relationships to the elements, seasons, hours, days, months, body parts, and everything imaginable. According to midrashim, every blade of grass has a constellation over it, telling it how to grow.

The NAMES of angels, along with names of God, are used in meditation arrays and magical incantations. Western magical texts called GRIMOIRES describe formulae for rituals and spells.

FURTHER READING

Bloom, Harold. *Kabbalah and Criticism.* New York: Continuum, 1984.

Epstein, Perle. *Kabbalah: The Way of the Jewish Mystic.* Boston: Shambhala, 1988.

Kaplan, Aryeh. *Sefer Yetzirah: The Book of Creation.* Rev. ed. York Beach, Maine: Samuel Weiser, 1997.

Scholem, Gershom. *Kabbalah.* New York: New American Library, 1974.

Three Books of Occult Philosophy Written by Henry Cornelius Agrippa of Nettesheim. Translated by James Freake. Edited and annotated by Donald Tyson. St. Paul, Minn.: Llewellyn Publications, 1995.

Zohar: The Book of Enlightenment. Translated by Daniel Chanan Matt. Ramsey, N.J.: Paulist Press, 1983.

Kabshiel

Angel invoked for grace and favor. Kabshiel's name is inscribed on old Jewish AMULETS. One magical formula instructs that the petitioner write the following charm on a piece of deer skin:

> By Thy universal name of grace and favor YHVH, set Thy grace YHVH upon (name), son of (name), as it rested upon Joseph, the righteous one, as it is said, "And the Lord was with Joseph, and showed kindness unto him and gave him favor" in the sight of all those who beheld him. In the name of Michael, Gabriel, Raphael, Uriel, Kabshiel, Yah (repeated eight times), Ehyeh, Ahah (repeated four times), Yehu (nine times.)

kadishim (kadashim) See QADDASIN.

Kafziel (Cassiel, Qaphsiel)

One of the seven ARCHANGELS and a ruler of the planet Saturn. As Qaphsiel, he governs the moon. Kafziel rules over the death of kings. In the Zohar, he and Hizikiel are the chief aides to Gabriel during times when Gabriel takes his standard into battle.

Kakabel (Kabaiel, Kochab, Kochbiel, Kokbiel)

Angel who is both good and bad. In the SEFER RAZIEL, Kakabel is a high angel and PRINCE who rules over stars and constellations. In 1 ENOCH he is a FALLEN ANGEL who commands 365,000 spirits. Kakabel also teaches astrology.

Kalaziel

In the Testament of SOLOMON, the angel who has the power to thwart Rhyx, the Enautha, a disease-causing DEMON who is among the DECANS OF THE ZODIAC.

karabu

Winged Assyrian deity of protection. The term *karabu* is Assyrian and means "bless, consecrate." The term CHERUBIM is derived from it.

The male kari-bu is a "blessed/consecrated one" and the female kuribi is a protector goddess. The kari-bu have the bodies of sphinxes or bulls and the heads

Kari-bu guarding a temple, from a 19th-century Bible (Author's collection)

of humans, and they guarded entrances to temples, homes, and buildings.

Karael

In the Testament of SOLOMON, angel who has the power to thwart Belbel, the DEMON of the eighth DECAN OF THE ZODIAC.

Kedushah See QEDUSSAH.

Kelly, Edward See JOHN DEE.

Kemuel (Camael, Shemuel, Seraphiel)

ARCHON, chief of the SERAPHIM and one of the 10 sephirot of the Kabbalistic TREE OF LIFE. In rabbinic lore of the ninth century, Kemuel guards the gate to HEAVEN. When MOSES reaches the top of Mount Sinai to receive the law from God, he sees a cloud floating there and steps inside it. He is at once in the presence of a great light similar to that of the burning bush. The cloud bears him up to heaven, and he loses track of time. The cloud stops at the gate of the FIRMAMENT and he gets out. The angel Kemuel, who guards the gate, admonishes him for trying to enter heaven. Moses tells the angel he has come to receive the Torah, and the gate opens instantly. Seeing that it is God's will, Kemuel allows Moses to come through. The angels, who were not happy to see the creation of humanity, likewise are not happy to see the Torah passed into human hands.

As an archon, Kemuel stands at the windows of heaven. He mediates the prayers of Israel with the princes of the seventh heaven.

In the Revelation of Moses, Kemuel is the leader of 12,000 ANGELS OF DESTRUCTION.

See ARCHONS.

Kerubiel YHVH (Cherubiel)

PRINCE of the CHERUBIM. 3 ENOCH describes Kerubiel as a being as high and as wide as the seven HEAVENS. His body is full of burning coals; when he opens his mouth it blazes like a fiery torch and his tongue is of fire. His entire face looks like a blazing fire, his eyes are brilliant sparks and his eyelashes are like lightning. The sacred name of Yahweh is engraved upon his crown of lightning. The splendor of the SHEKINAH is on his face and he wears the bow of the Shekinah upon his shoulders. Flames and lightnings shoot from his face and his body. Wherever Kerubiel goes he is accompanied by thunderclaps and earthquakes. When he is angry the earth shakes.

Kerubiel is attended by two princes of the chariot; one of them is Sarbiel. Kerubiel is in charge of the cherubim whom he increases in beauty and glory. He sings their praises, shines their crowns, and praises them and thus prepares the throne of glory that rests upon the tops of the heads of the cherubim.

Kether See TREE OF LIFE.

Kezef

In Jewish lore, the angel of wrath, an ANGEL OF DEATH, and one of five ANGELS OF DESTRUCTION or ANGELS OF PUNISHMENT, with Af, Hemah, Mashit, and Haron-Peor. Kezef fights against MOSES and, as the ANGEL OF DEATH, is imprisoned in the Holy Tabernacle by Aaron.

Kokabiel (Kabiel, Kakabiel, Kochab, Kochbiel, Kokbiel)

Angel who is PRINCE of the stars (kochab); also a FALLEN ANGEL. The name "Kokabiel" means "star of God." In 1 ENOCH Kokabiel is a fallen angel who commands 365,000 demons. In 3 Enoch he is prince of the stars, ranking below Rahatiel, the prince of the constellations. 3 Enoch 17:7 says Kokabiel commands 365,000 myriads of MINISTERING ANGELS who make the stars run from city to city and from state to state in the Raqia' level of the HEAVENS. In SEFER RAZIEL, Kokabiel is a high-ranking angel.

Kunopegos (Kunopaston)

DEMON in the shape of a sea horse. Kunopegos raises himself up a great waves in the open seas, causes seasickness among sailors, and sinks boats in order to claim the bodies of men and their treasures. He consults with the Prince of Demons, Beelzebub. He can come up to shore as waves and shapeshift into the form of a man. He is thwarted by the angel Iameth.

In the Testament of Solomon, King SOLOMON confines Kunopegos by casting him into a broad flat bowl filled with 10 receptacles of seawater. The top is fortified with marble and the bowl's mouth is covered with asphalt, pitch, and hemp rope. The vessel is stored in the Temple of Jerusalem.

Kutiel

Angel of divining rods. Kutiel is invoked in Yiddish-Deutsch rituals for the making of divining rods.

kyriotates See DOMINIONS; STEINER, RUDOLF.

Labbiel

The original name of the archangel Raphael. According to Jewish lore, Labbiel was renamed Raphael by God when he obeyed God's command concerning the creation of man.

Lahabiel

Angel who protects against evil spirits and who assists Raphael in the rulership of the first day. As a protector, Lahabiel is often invoked with Phaniel, Rahabiel, and Ariel.

Lahash

Angel who, with the help of Zakun, attempts to interfere with divine will by leading 184 myriads of angels to steal the prayer of MOSES before it could reach God. Lahash and Zakun were punished with 60 lashes of fire. According to another version of the story the angel Sammael binds Lahash with chains of fire, flogs him with 70 stripes of fire, and expels him from the divine presence.

Lamechiel (Lamechalal)

In the Testament of SOLOMON, angel who thwarts Deception, of the seven demonic HEAVENLY BODIES. In 3 ENOCH, Lamechiel is one of the PLANETARY RULERS.

Lassuarim

In the LEGEMETON, the ruling angel of the 10th hour of the night, called Malcho. Lassuarim rules 100 chief dukes and 100 lesser dukes who are attended by thousands of servants.

Laylah (Lailah, Lailahel, Leliel)

Angel who oversees and protects childbirth. The name Laylah derives from the Hebrew word *layil*, meaning "night." In Jewish lore, Laylah is portrayed as being both good and bad. In the Zohar and Talmud, he guards birth and the newborn, and he proclaims if the individual will be strong or weak, wise or foolish, and rich or poor. Elsewhere he is said to fight for ABRAHAM in his battle against kings. In other Jewish lore, Laylah is similar to Lilith as a DEMON of the night who attacks those who sleep alone and as a "prince of conception."

See CHILDBIRTH ANGELS.

Lemegeton

A handbook of magic, or GRIMOIRE, attributed to SOLOMON. Also known as the Lesser Key of Solomon.

Lerajie (Leraie, Oray)

One of the FALLEN ANGELS and 72 spirits of SOLOMON. Lerajie is a marquis who appears as an archer, dressed in green, and carrying a bow and quiver. He causes battles and causes arrow wounds to putrefy. He commands 30 legions.

Lesser Yahweh See ANGEL OF THE LORD; METATRON.

Levi

Third son of JACOB and Leah, and progenitor of the priestly line of Israel. Levi received his calling to the priesthood in a dream vision in which an angel took him into the HEAVENS. He was initiated in another dream vision by seven angels.

The dream visions are described in the Testament of the Twelve Patriarchs, a pseudepigraphon that comprises the last statements of the 12 sons of Jacob and Leah.

Levi's vision of the ascent to heaven originally told of three heavens, but later versions of the text expanded it to include seven heavens, though not all heavens are described.

Levi is out tending sheep in Abel-Maoul (also Abel-Meholah), when a spirit of understanding from the Lord comes to him, and he sees how all human beings are living in sin, deceit, and injustice. Lamenting this, he prays to the Lord for deliverance. He falls asleep and has his visionary experience.

Levi beholds that he is on a high mountain. The heavens open and an ANGEL OF THE LORD invites him to enter. He sees the first heaven, where much water is suspended, and the second heaven, which is measureless and much brighter and more lustrous. The angel tells him that he shall see yet another heaven, even more lustrous and beyond compare, where he shall stand near the Lord. The angel says:

> You shall be his priest and you shall tell forth his mysteries to me. You shall announce the one who is about to redeem Israel. Through you and Judah [Levi's brother] the Lord will be seen by men. . . . Your life shall be from the Lord's provision; he shall be to you as field and vineyard and produce, as silver and gold. (2:10–12)

The angel goes on to describe the heavens that have been shown to Levi. The first heaven is dark because it sees all the injustices of humankind, and it contains fire, snow, and ice, ready for the day of judgment. The first heaven also contains all the spirits who are instruments of God's judgment, who are dispatched for the punishment of mankind.

The second heaven contains the armies arrayed for judgment day to "work vengeance on the spirits of error and of Beliar."

In the third heaven are the angels, or Holy Ones.

In the sixth heaven are the messengers who carry responses to the ANGELS OF THE PRESENCE and the THRONES and AUTHORITIES who offer eternal praise to God.

The seventh heaven contains the Great Glory, or God, in the Holy of Holies superior to all holiness. The ARCHANGELS attend God and offer propitiatory sacrifices on behalf of all the sins of ignorance of the righteous ones.

The angel who is with Levi tells him that when the Lord looks upon the angels, they all tremble. Even the earth and abysses tremble, but the sons of men remain insensitive and continue their sinful ways. Consequently, God's judgment will be delivered upon them. Levi, however, is delivered from wrongdoing so that he can bring light into Israel.

The angel opens the gates of heaven, and Levi beholds the Holy Most High sitting on his throne. God says, "Levi, to you I have given the blessing of the priesthood until I shall come and dwell in the midst of Israel" (5:2–3).

The angel takes Levi back to earth and gives him a sword and shield, with instructions to take vengeance on the city of Shechem for the sake of his sister Dinah, who has been defiled by the men there. Levi obeys, putting an end to the sons of Hamor. He asks the angel for his NAME so that he can call upon him again for help. The angel replies, "I am the angel who makes intercession for the nation Israel, that they might not be beaten" (5:6–7). Levi awakens, and he blesses God for the vision.

Levi takes action on his dream vision. He destroys Shechem, and his brother Simeon and others destroy Hamor. Jacob is not happy, but Levi maintains that God's sentence upon the cities was "guilty."

Levi goes to Bethel, and, after 70 days, he has another dream vision in which he sees seven "men in white clothing" who are God's agents (and are probably angels). They initiate him into the priesthood. The men tell him to put on the vestments of the priest, the crown of righteousness, the oracle of understanding, the robe of truth, the breastplate of faith, the miter for the head, and the apron for prophetic power.

The first man anoints him with holy oil and gives him a staff. The second man washes him with pure water, feeds him by hand with bread and holy wine, and puts on him a glorious vestment. The third man gives him a linen garment. The fourth places on him a purple girdle. The fifth gives him a branch of olive wood. The sixth places a wreath on his head. The seventh places the priestly diadem on him and fills his hands with incense.

The men tell Levi that from his posterity will come priests, judges, and scribes, and that they will be blessed and have everything desired in Israel.

When Levi awakens, he understands that this dream vision is like the first one. He resolves to tell no one about it, and he does not do so until he delivers his last words in his testament. As the dream visions foretell, he does establish the great priestly lineage in Israel.

See DREAMS AND VISIONS.

FURTHER READING

Charlesworth, James H., ed. *The Old Testament Pseudepigrapha.* Vols. 1 and 2. New York: Doubleday, 1983, 1985.

Leviathan

One of the demonic angels who is associated with the primordial deep of the seas. The name Leviathan means in Hebrew "that which gathers itself together in folds." In rabbinic lore, he is associated with the Rahab, angel of the sea. Leviathan is personified as an enormous whale who is impervious to all weapons.

In Job, Leviathan is a sea DEMON. In Jonah, Leviathan is a whale who swallows Jonah and keeps him in its belly for three days, until God orders Jonah to be vomited up. In Isaiah, Leviathan is the "fleeing serpent" and "twisting serpent," "the dragon that is in sea," whom God will slay at the end of time. (27:1)

Both Leviathan and Behemoth were created on the fifth day.

Lilith

Winged female DEMON of the night who flies about searching for newborn children to kidnap or strangle, and sleeping men to seduce in order to produce demon sons.

Lilith evolved from Babylonian and perhaps Sumerian demonologies, which included male and female evil spirits that molested children. Lilith figures prominently in Jewish demonology.

Lilith has a female face, wings, and long hair. She flies about at night with a horde of demons, using tens of thousands of names to disguise herself. She visits women in childbirth and sleeping men, from whose nocturnal emissions she creates her demon sons.

There are different versions of the story of how Lilith came into being. According to one, she encountered Adam after his split with Eve and had sexual relations with him that produced the demon sons who fill the world. According to another version she was the first woman to have sexual relations with Adam, and thus was his wife. Lilith demanded equality with Adam, and, and failing to get it, she left him in anger. She said the Ineffable Name of God and flew off into the air. Adam complained to God that his wife had deserted him. God then sent three angels, Sanvi, Sansanvi, and Semangelaf (Snwy, Snswy, and Smnglf), to bring Lilith back to Eden. The angels found her in the Red Sea, and threatened her with the loss of 100 of her demon children every day unless she returned to Adam. She refused and was punished accordingly. Lilith took revenge by launching a reign of terror against women in childbirth, newborn infants—particularly males—and men who slept alone. She was forced, however, to swear to the three angels that whenever she saw their NAMES or images on an AMULET, she would leave infants and mothers alone.

This story has Christian versions, in which the name of Lilith varies and the angels are replaced by the saints Sines, Sisinnios, and Synodoros.

A Kabbalistic story tells that Lilith became the bride of Samael (Satan). She will exist until the Messianic day, when God will cleanse evil from the face of the earth.

Various charms and AMULETS protected the vulnerable against her predations. Women in childbirth were protected by amulets bearing not only the names of the three angels but also their form, wings, hands, and legs, which were affixed to all four walls of the birthing room. The incantation "To her that flies in rooms of darkness—pass quickly quickly Lil[ith]" was said to protect homes. New marriages were protected from Lilith by the tossing of four coins on the marriage bed and saying "Adam and Eve" and "Avaunt thee, Lilith!"

As late as the 18th century, it was a common practice in many countries to protect new mothers and infants with amulets against Lilith. Male infants were vulnerable for the first week of life; girls for the first three weeks. Sometimes a MAGIC circle was drawn around the lying-in bed, with a charm inscribed with the names of the three angels, ADAM AND EVE, and the words "barring Lilith" or "protect this newborn child from all harm." Sometimes amulets with such inscriptions were placed in all corners of and throughout the bedchamber. If a child laughed in its sleep, it was a sign that Lilith was present. Tapping the child on the nose made the demon go away. (See CHILDBIRTH ANGELS.)

Men who had nocturnal emissions believed they had been seduced by Lilith during the night, and had to say incantations to prevent the offspring from becoming demons. Lilith was believed to be assisted by succubi in her bloodthirsty nocturnal quests, and these gathered with her near the "mountains of darkness" to frolic with Samael. The Zohar describes Lilith's powers as being at their height when the moon is on the wane.

Lilith also could be repelled by the saying of any of her numberless names. The basis for this comes from the story (probably Christian Byzantine in origin) about how the prophet ELIJAH confronted her as she was en route to attack a woman's newborn son, and "to give her the sleep of death, to take her son and drink his blood, to suck the marrow of his bones and to eat his flesh." Elijah forced her to reveal some of her names. Then he excommunicated her.

Lilith probably is related to the Judeo-Hellenistic demon Obizoth, who is repelled by an amulet bearing one of the mystical names of the archangel Raphael.

According to Islamic mythology, her sexual relations with her infernal husband, IBLIS, created the demonic DJINN.

Lilith-like demons appear in mythologies around the world. She also is associated with other characters in legend and myth, including the Queen of Sheba and Helen of Troy. In medieval Europe she often was portrayed as the wife, concubine, or grandmother of Satan. In the late 17th century she was described as a screech owl (probably originating from a reference in Isaiah), blind by day, who sucked the breasts or navels of young children or the dugs of goats.

Some of Lilith's best-known names are: Abeko, Abito, Abro, Abyzu, Ailo, Alu, Amiz, Amizo, Amizu, Ardad Lili, Avitu, Batna, Bituah, Eilo, Gallu, Gelou, Gilou, 'Ik, 'Ils, Ita, Izorpo, Kalee, Kali, Kakash, Kea, Kema, Kokos, Lamassu, Odom, Partasah, Partashah, Patrota, Petrota, Podo, Pods, Raphi, Satrina(h), Talto, Thiltho, Zahriel, Zefonith.

FURTHER READING

Mercatante, Anthony S. *An Encyclopedia of World Mythology and Legend*. Frenchs Forest, Australia: Child & Associates Publishing, 1988.

Scholem, Gershom. *Kabbalah*. 1974. Reprint, New York: Dorset Press, 1987.

Lincoln Imp

Famous carved stone DEMON on a column in the Angel Choir at Lincoln Cathedral in Lincoln, England. According to lore, a rampaging demon was turned to stone there by an angel. The cathedral, once the tallest structure in the world, dates to the 11th century. The Angel Choir was consecrated in 1280.

There are different versions of the legend. On version tells in rhyme that one day the devil was in good spirits and let his young demons out to play. One rode on the wind to Lindum (Lincoln) and ordered the wind to take him into the church, intending to wreak havoc there. The wind demurred and dropped him off outside. The imp entered the church and set about tearing and breaking things, especially in the Angel Choir. Spying angels, the imp boasted, "Pretty things,/A sackful of feathers I'll

pluck from your wings/To make me a couch when I'm tired of this joke." At that, the "tiniest angel" with amethyst eyes and hair of spun gold rose up before the altar and declared, "O impious Imp, be ye turned into stone!" The imp immediately was turned to stone and frozen on a column high above the choir.

The legend goes on to make points about several morals of the story: Don't meddle in the affairs of the church; don't play tricks on the clergy; don't chum with low people, and don't be clever but seek to be good. About angels, the legend says,

> To angels—when met—be extremely polite,
> Attentions too forward they'll keenly requite;
> Don't ruffle their feathers: just let them alone,
> Else, if you're converted, 'twill be into stone.

Another version says that in the 14th century the devil sent two imps out to make mischief. First they went to Chesterfield and twisted the spire of the church there. Then they went to Lincoln Cathedral. They tripped the bishop and smashed tables and chairs. They set about destroying the Angel Choir. An angel immediately appeared and told them to stop. One of the imps defiantly flew up to a stone pillar and began to throw heavy objects at the angel. The angel turned him into stone, leaving him there forever. The second imp hid in the wreckage and made his escape by latching onto the broomstick of a passing witch. The witch turned him into a black cat for companionship. This part of the legend explains why all witches are portrayed with black cats on their broomsticks.

The grinning imp is carved in a seated position with one leg crossed over the other. He is associated with both good luck and bad luck. The imp has been used in jewelry and even worn by royalty. In 1928 the Prince of Wales (the future King Edward VII) was given an Imp tie pin. It was noted that the next year two of his horses won major races, the Grand National and the Epsom Derby.

FURTHER READING

Kesson, H. J. *The Legend of the Lincoln Imp*. Lincoln: J. W. Ruddock and Sons, 1904.

"The Real Story of the Lincoln Imp." Available online. URL: http://www.theimp.lincolnfans.co.uk/lincoln.shtml. Downloaded August 5, 2002.

Lindbergh, Charles (1902–1974)

The man who was first to fly solo nonstop across the Atlantic Ocean may have done so with the help of angels. On his flight from New York to Paris in 1927,

Charles Lindbergh had profound mystical experiences, which he kept secret for 26 years. Lindbergh then revealed that vaporous beings had appeared to aid him; while he did not call them "angels," they can be interpreted as such.

Lindbergh did not mention his supernatural experiences in his first book about the flight, *We, Pilot and Plane,* published later in 1927. He did in *The Spirit of St. Louis,* published in 1953, and he discussed it again in *Autobiography of Values,* published posthumously in 1977. His reluctance reflects in part the prevailing lack of social acceptance of such experiences.

The historic flight took 33 1/2 hours. As he related it, Lindbergh had to remain alert at all times; there was no such thing as automatic pilot, and to doze off at the controls meant certain death by plummeting into the ocean. At one point over the Atlantic, fatigue and tension altered Lindbergh's perception of reality. By the ninth hour, he felt both very detached from and very near to the world below, and it made him think of "the nearness of death" and "the longness of life."

Lindbergh slipped into an altered state of consciousness that to him seemed both wakefulness and sleep. He was conscious of being three elements: body, which was fatigued; mind, which made decisions; and spirit, a driving force that told him sleep was not needed, and that his body would be sustained through relaxation.

While he was in this twilight state, he became aware that the fuselage behind him was filled with ghostly presences that were humanlike but vaguely outlined, transparent and seemingly weightless. They did not appear suddenly. One moment, they were not present, another moment they were, as if they had always been there. Lindbergh, who felt caught in some "unearthly age of time," was not surprised or afraid. In *The Spirit of St. Louis* he states:

> Without turning my head, I see them as clearly as though in my normal field of vision. There's no limit to my sight—my skull is one great eye, seeing everywhere at once.

> These phantoms speak with human voices—friendly, vaporlike shapes, without substance, able to vanish or appear at will, to pass in and out through the walls of the fuselage as though no walls were there. Now, many are crowded behind me. Now, only a few remain. First one and then another presses forward to my shoulder to speak above the engine's noise, and then draws back among the group behind. At times, voices come out of the air itself, clear yet far away, traveling through distances that can't be measured by the scale of human miles; familiar voices, conversing and advising on my flight, discussing problems of my navigation, reassuring

me, giving me messages of importance unattainable in ordinary life.

The ability of the spirits to appear and disappear; their friendly demeanor and helpful advice; and their imparting of mystical wisdom "unattainable in ordinary life" are all characteristic of angelophanies, as well as encounters with other types of spirit beings. Lindbergh seemed to associate them, however, with the dead, for he often wondered whether he had crossed the boundary between life and death and was in the land of the dead.

As his altered state continued, Lindbergh felt weightless himself, independent of physical laws: "I'm almost one with these vaporlike forms behind me, less tangible than air, universal as aether. I'm still attached to life; they, not at all; but at any moment some thin band may snap and there'll be no difference between us."

Lindbergh also offers a description of the beings that makes them sound archetypal: "The spirits have no rigid bodies, yet they remain human in outline form—emanations from the experience of ages, inhabitants of a universe closed to mortal men. I'm on the borderline of life and a greater realm beyond, as though caught in the field of gravitation between two planets, acted on by forces I can't control, forces too weak to be measured by any means at my command, yet representing powers incomparably stronger than I've ever known."

Lindbergh acknowledged that at another time, these visions would have startle him, but he felt so separated from earthly life that they seemed normal:

> [T]he emissaries from a spirit world are neither intruders nor strangers. It's more like a gathering of family and friends after years of separation, as though I've known all of them before in some past incarnation. . . . They belong with the towering thunderheads and moonlit corridors of sky. . . . What strange connection exists between us? If they're so concerned with my welfare, why didn't they introduce themselves before?

Here is another characteristic of an ANGELOPHANY: the appearance of angels only at a moment of great need, and when the percipient is in an altered or receptive state of consciousness.

Says Lindbergh: "I live in the past, the present, and the future, here and in different places, all at once. Around me are old associations, bygone friendships, voices from ancestrally distant times."

If Lindbergh had lived in another era, he might have immediately interpreted the helping beings as angels. Instead, he struggled to place them in a context he could understand.

The experience changed his views about life after death. He said that death no longer seemed final, but rather the entrance to a "new and free existence which includes all space, all time."

FURTHER READING

Lindbergh, Charles. *The Spirit of St. Louis*. New York: Charles Scribner's Sons, 1953.

Murphy, Michael, and Rhea A. White. *The Psychic Side of Sports*. Reading, Mass.: Addison-Wesley, 1978.

Lion-Shaped Demon

FALLEN ANGEL in the shape of a roaring lion, who commands legions of DEMONS and makes it impossible for sick men to recover from their diseases. In the Testament of Solomon, the Lion-Shaped Demon appears before King SOLOMON and says he cannot be bound. But the king, invoking the name of "the great God Most High," forces the demon to reveal that he is thwarted by the angel Emmanuel. Solomon sentences the demon's legions to carrying wood from a grove of trees, and he sentences the Lion-shaped Demon to use his claws to saw it into kindling and throw it under a perpetually burning kiln.

literature and angels

Supernatural and divine beings have always played roles in stories about human destiny, nature, dramas, and struggle with evil. The specific roles of angels have changed in accordance with changing beliefs about them. In earlier times they were more neutral to individual problems and concerned with a larger, more cosmic perspective. In popular literature of the late 20th century, angels are more like personal friends.

All the gods and demigods of classical literature can be interpreted as angels of varying rank. Greek mythology begins with a war in HEAVEN. The Hindu *Ramayana* pits the avatar Rama against DEMON Ravana. The most famous section of the *Mahabharata* is the *Bhagavad-Gita,* the "song of God," actually a conversation between Khrisna, the charioteer, and Arjuna, the peerless Pandava archer, on the battlefield at Kurakshetra. Two intermarried families whose members are guided by certain gods or swayed by demonic beings have assembled to fight it out after many generations of strife and treachery, and Krishna briefs Arjuna on the cosmic situation before the conch shell blows to signify the battle's start.

Whereas Hindu and Greek myth allowed the gods to have intercourse and offspring with humans, the Judaic story line eliminates these "abominations" with Noah's flood. (See SEX AND ANGELS; WATCHERS.) Hindu and Buddhist deities are still very much alive in rituals today, including parts of the epic *Gita* and the Sanskrit *sutras,* the oldest literature in the world. The members of the Greek pantheon are referred to, invoked, adored in hymns, and are featured prominently in the works of Aeschylus, Sophocles, and Euripides, the dialogues of Plato, the Homeric hymns, and of course the *Illiad* and the *Odyssey.*

The intervention of Apollo, Aphrodite, Ares, Athena in the Trojan wars, the arrival of Hermes or Iris with messages, appear similar to the comings and goings of the ANGEL OF THE LORD and Gabriel in the Old and New Testaments. The plots of both the *Illiad* and the *Odyssey* are driven by rivalries among the gods; throughout the epics intercessory actions of the gods abound. Where Athene is the special goddess who guides and protects Odysseus, Venus is the mother-guardian angel of Aeneas in Virgil's epic, with several appearances of the "messenger with wings," Mercury.

The *Aeneid*'s underworld provided DANTE ALIGHIERI a working model for the Christian inferno he molded in his *Divina Commedia* in the early 14th century. Both *El Cid* and the *Chanson de Roland* invoke the Christian angels during their battles. The German *Nibelungenlied* (to be taken up in the 19th century operas of Richard Wagner) with its FAIRIES, nymphs, and demons, and the Anglo-Saxon *Beowulf* both convey folk cosmology before Christianity. *Beowulf* shows the dawning of a Christian revisioning of the local demonic GENII as the Christlike heros Beowulf and Wiglaf destroy Grendel and his mother. The epic romances of the Italian Renaissance by Vegio, Sannazaro, Vida, and Tasso include interventions by the Christian archangels. Ariosto's early 16th-century *Orlando Furioso* includes an irreverent treatment of Michael's assistance to the Christians against the Moors.

Among significant English writers, Shakespeare has fairies and genii (Ariel and Caliban in *The Tempest*). Edmund Spenser develops an elaborate allegorical universe in his *Faerie Queene* (1590). In that work, good and evil forces are cloaked in angelic and demonic symbolism derived from Celtic, Arthurian, Anglo-Saxon, and French-Norman folklore, Catholic and Protestant politicotheology, and there are literary allusions from the classics, Dante, and the Italian epic romance writers, especially Ariosto's *Orlando Furioso.*

Spenser's *Fowre Hymns* ("Of Heavenly Love" and "Of Heavenly Beautie") are spectacular cosmic visions invoking Platonic Ideas and INTELLIGENCES and the nine choirs of angels (Hymn 4). "Love, lift me up upon thy golden wings,/ From this base world unto thy heaven's height,/ Where I may see those admirable things/ Which there thou workest by thy sovereign might (Hymn 3)." The "Mutabilitie Cantos" of the

Faerie Queene (Book VII, Cantos 6 and 7) present parallels between physical nature, human nature, and heaven.

JOHN MILTON paints a romantic picture of good and fallen angels in his epic treatment of the fall of ADAM AND EVE in *Paradise Lost* and the redemption in *Paradise Regained*. Milton was steeped in the works of Spenser, calling him "my original," and "a better teacher than Scotus or Aquinas." Milton was inspired by Spenser's mission as a poet to embody moral lessons in beautiful imaginative forms. There is a striking analogy between Milton's interpretation of the struggle of forces involved in Adam's fall and the representation of virtue under trial in the person of Sir Guyon (*Faerie Queene*, Book II). Both advocate temperance as the supremacy of the rational over the passionate principle in the soul.

Several lesser-known English religious epic poets known as Spenserians also influenced Milton, namely, Giles and Phineas Fletcher. Phineas Fletcher's *Apollyonists* and its Latin counterpart *Locustae* include a representation of Satan as a majestic and defiant being. The theme of Giles Fletcher's *Christ's Victory in Heaven* is the same as that of Book III of *Paradise Lost,* except that Milton casts the heavenly debate over man's fate into the mouths of the Father and the Son.

Lyric Poetry

Although angels receive recognition along with MARY and the other saints in medieval and Renaissance court and folk lyrics, some 17th and 18th-century English poets literally achieved celestial heights in image and melody (see MUSIC AND ANGELS). Milton's youthful lyric "On the Morning of Christ's Nativity" (1645) and mature "At a Solemn Music" (1673) both aspire to recreate the music and magic of the angelic presence.

Milton's Catholic contemporary Richard Crashaw (1612–49) wrote two famous lyrics celebrating angels. "Musicks Duell" parallels a lute player's song with the angelic music of the spheres. "In the Holy Nativity" the shepherds sing of their vision of the angels. Crashaw also wrote two poems about St. Teresa of Avila's visionary experiences. "The Flaming Heart" attempts to recapture the saint's visitation by a seraph: "O sweet incendiary! . . . By all thy dower of Lights and Fires;/ By all the eagle in thee, all the dove . . ./ By all thy brim-fill'd bowls of fierce desire/ By thy last Morning's draught of liquid fire."

George Herbert's "Easter Wings" is actually shaped like wings. John Donne's "The Dream" brings celestial qualities to the bed of lovers and "The Relique" refers to the asexuality of the lovers' guardian angels. Donne's "Anniversary Poems" on the death of a young girl survey the upper and lower realms and find her soul so pure that she has "Tutelar Angels" assigned to each of her limbs (Second Anniversary, 43–45). In "Holy Sonnet 5" Donne says "I am a little world made cunningly/ Of Elements and an Angelike spright" and in "Holy Sonnet 7" he cries "At the round earth's imagin'd corners, blow/ Your trumpets, Angels." Thomas Traherne's "Wonder" recounts heaven from the point of view of a soul: "How like an Angel came I down!" Henry Vaughan's "The Retreate," "Peace," and especially "The World" convey the elevated consciousness of a mystical partnership with angels.

John Dryden's "Ode in Honour of St. Cecilia's Day" is a comprehensive gathering of classical and Christian images surrounding music into an orchestra elevating the patron saint of music. He repeats "He [the old pagan musical god] rais'd a Mortal to the Skies;/ She [St. Cecilia] drew an Angel down."

With the Romantic poets of Germany, France, Italy, and England, another wave of mythological symbolism, supernatural, magical, and mystical experiences entered into literature. Angels of every rank—and nymphs, demons, vampires, and the like—symbolized not only themselves but also emotions, psychic forces, and even physical forces for the scientifically informed Percy Bysshe Shelley. Classical mythology continued to influence many poets, such as Friedrich Holderlin's *Hyperion* and John Keats's *Hyperion* and *Endymion*, Shelley's *Prometheus Unbound* and legions of others. After all, an education still covered the Greek and Latin classics.

Shelley was haunted "by the awful shadow of some unseen Power," and he was passionately convinced of the living presence of "that Light whose smile kindles the universe." He asserts an intimate relation between this "interfused and over-ruling Spirit" and the souls of individual human beings. Man does not have to stand alone. "I vowed that I would dedicate my powers/ to thee and thine—. . . ." The "phantoms of a thousand hours" are called upon to bear witness "that never joy illumed my brow/ Unlinked with hope that thou wouldst free/ This world from its dark slavery" ("Hymn to Intellectual Beauty").

Lord Byron's verse drama *Cain* was one of many Romantic works reapproaching good and evil, in this case via the characters the ANGEL OF THE LORD and Lucifer. Another work of Byron's, "Heaven and Earth," is a "mystery" based on Genesis 6:2 with Samuel Taylor Coleridge's line from "Kubla Khan" as an epigraph: "And woman wailing for her demon lover," a theme Coleridge might have treated fully had he developed the fragmentary "Christabel" and Keats did develop in "La Belle Dame Sans Merci." Commenting on this theme in Byron, CARL G. JUNG said: "as a power which transcends consciousness the libido is by nature daemonic; it is both God and devil." (See ABRAXAS.)

Angel offering inspiration (reprinted courtesy of U.S. Library of Congress)

Coleridge intended to write a critical essay on the supernatural as a preface to *The Rime of the Ancient Mariner*, but he did not leave one. William Wordsworth and Coleridge planned for the *Lyrical Ballads* (1798) to treat natural and supernatural experiences, with Coleridge covering the latter. In *Biographia Literaria*, Coleridge treats this project and states his objective was "to transfer from our inward nature a human interest and a semblance of truth sufficient to procure for these shadows of imagination that willing suspension of disbelief for the moment, which constitutes poetic faith." The *Rime* certainly achieved that purpose, with demonic figures of Life in Death, tutelary spirits of the oceans, and much more. When the bodies of the mariners come to life again, it happens "not by the souls of the men, not by daemons of earth or middle air, but by a blessed troop of angelic spirits, sent down by the invocation of their guardian saints."

Coleridge's translation of Burnet's *Archaeologiae Philosophicae* sums up the situation of the Western intellectual with an open imagination: "I easily believe that there are more invisible Natures than visible ones in the universe. But who will explain to us the rank, relations, characteristics and powers of each? What do they do? Where do they live? The human mind has always circled around the knowledge of these things, but never achieved it."

Visionary Literature

Poets, saints, and mystics of various philosophies and faiths have recorded their visionary experiences with supernatural beings. The Koran was dictated to MUHAMMAD by Gabriel. The visionary recitals of the patriarchs, the writers of apocryphal works, IBN SINA, Ibn Arabi, AL-SUHRAWARDI, and others purport to be recited to them by angels. The Native American shaman Black Elk's vision at age nine involved two angelic figures who show him the shaman's world. The works of Rumi, Kabir, Sri Aurobindo, Rabindranath Tagore, WILLIAM BLAKE, William Butler Yeats, and his friend A. E. (George William Russell) reveal familiarity with multiple worlds and beings.

In the West, Gnostic and Hermetic lore is believed by some to have been preserved in the Grail cycle, a series of medieval and Renaissance documents set in a magic time and place, the spiritual Britain. In the introduction to his Grail romance, Robert de Boron claims that it was given to him by the Angel of the Lord. The book then vanished and he searched to find it again by journeying through the Angelic World, and by following the Questing Beast through a visionary landscape.

To a certain extent, all good poets have some visionary intuitive capacity, and all great ones possess an integration of language, inner vision, and energy, which they may or may not attribute to angels or higher beings. Probably Yeats and Blake are the best exemplars of this capacity in the English language and GOETHE and Rainer Maria Rilke in German. Rilke's *Duino Elegies*, even in translation, are extraordinary poems about the human longing for transcendence, using angels as its unifying symbol. When a friend tried to persuade Rilke to undergo psychotherapy, he wrote back: "I am afraid it would exorcise my angels along with my demons."

FURTHER READING

Chessman, Harriett Scott, ed. *Literary Angels*. New York: Fawcett Columbine, 1994.

Hillman, James. *Archetypal Psychology*. Dallas, Tex.: Spring Publications, 1983.

Greene, Thomas. *The Descent from Heaven: A Study of Epic Continuity*. New Haven, Conn.: Yale University Press, 1963.

Sugg, Richard P., ed. *Jungian Literary Criticism*. Evanston, Ill.: Northwestern University Press, 1992.

Wilson, Peter Lamborn. *Angels*. New York: Pantheon Books, 1980.

Lix Tetrax

A FALLEN ANGEL and DEMON of the wind. In the Testament of Solomon, Lix Tetrax is summoned to the presence of King SOLOMON by Beelzebub, at the king's orders. The demon appears with his face high in the air and his body crawling like a small snail. He raises up clouds of dust and wind and hurls them at Solomon until he is forced to stop by the king, who seals the demon with his magical ring.

Lix Tetrax claims he is "the direct offspring of the Great One," perhaps a reference to Beelzebub, the Prince of Demons. He lives at the tip of the horn of the moon when it is in the south. He says he divides men, creates whirlwinds, starts fires, sets fields on fire, and renders households nonfunctional. He is especially busy during the summertime. He has the power to heal the "day-and-a-half fever" if invoked to do so. He is thwarted by the angel Azael.

Solomon sentences Lix Tetrax to throw stones up to the workmen at the heights of the Temple of Jerusalem, under construction.

FURTHER READING

Charlesworth, James H., ed. *The Old Testament Pseudepigrapha*. Vols. 1 and 2. New York: Doubleday, 1983, 1985.

loa See ORISHAS.

Lot See SODOM AND GOMORRAH.

Lucifer

Angel equated with Satan. The name Lucifer means "bearer of light" or "bearer of fire," "Son of the Morning" or "Morning Star." In Hebrew, Lucifer is Helel ben Sahar: "Bright Son of the Morning." Rabbinical literature of the fourth and fifth centuries C.E. describes him as Samael, the highest of those angels around the throne of God and created above the SERAPHIM. He was distinguished from all his other angelic brethren by possessing 12 wings.

There is only one reference to Lucifer in the Bible, in Isaiah 14:12–15: "How you are fallen from HEAVEN, O Day Star, son of Dawn! How you are cut down to the ground, you who laid the nations low! You said in your heart, 'I will ascend to heaven; above the stars of God I will set my throne on high; I will sit on the mount of assembly in the far north; I will ascend above the heights of the clouds, I will make myself like the Most High.' But you are brought down to SHEOL [the underworld], to the depths of the Pit."

St. Jerome, one of the church fathers (ca. 347–420) identified the Isaiah passage with Satan, the leader of the fallen angels. From that time on "Lucifer" became one of the names of the devil. The identification was further reinforced by JOHN MILTON who made Lucifer the protagonist of *Paradise Lost*.

The 18th-century mystic EMANUEL SWEDENBORG denied the existence of any Satan or demon. He attributed all power to the Divine True and Good, or the Lord, and claimed that there was no controlling devil responsible for hell. He said that while a literal reading of Scripture seemed to tell the story of Lucifer's fall, in reality "devil" and "Satan" simply mean hell, the place of evil and falsehood chose by those who go down the path of self-love and lack of charity. For Swedenborg, "Lucifer" meant "people from Babylon."

FURTHER READING

Every, George. *Christian Mythology*. London: The Hamlyn Publish Group Ltd., 1970.

Swedenborg, Emanuel. *Heaven and Hell*. Trans. George F. Dole. New York: Swedenborg Foundation, 1976.

Turner, Alice K. *The History of Hell*. New York: Harcourt Brace, 1993.

luminaries

In Gnostic literature, the celestial lights, especially the sun and the moon. The luminaries are personified and have powers. The Apocalypse of Adam relates that, according to the 12th kingdom, the ILLUMINATOR, or JESUS, came from two luminaries (the sun and the moon), where he was nourished and received his glory and power.

Luther, Martin See PROTESTANT REFORMATION.

Machidiel (Malchedael, Malchidiel, Malahidael, Melkeial, Melkejal)

Angel who governs the month of March and the sign of Aries. Machidel means "fullness of God." In Kabbalistic lore he is one of the four angels of the sephirah Malkuth in the TREE OF LIFE, along with the angels Sandalphon, Messiah, and Emmanuel. In MAGIC Machidiel is invoked in love spells to require a desired maiden to appear at a certain time and place.

Maclean, Dorothy (1920–)

A founder of FINDHORN, whose mediumistic abilities enabled her to communicate with angels and DEVAS. Maclean relayed the beings' instructions for growing unusual produce in a harsh Scottish climate, and she also spread their teachings about humankind's co-creative relationship with the spirit world.

Dorothy Maclean was born on January 8, 1920, in Guelph, a small town in Ontario, Canada. She had no particular psychic gifts as a child; these were to develop in adulthood through years of spiritual study and practice.

Maclean studied business at the University of Western Ontario, and after graduation in 1940 became a secretary for the British Intelligence Service. Her work took her from Toronto to New York City, and she was chaperoned by the woman who was to become her spiritual mentor, Sheena Govan, a Quaker whose parents had founded an evangelical movement, the Faith Mission. Maclean's job eventually took her to Panama, South America and England. In Panama she met an Englishman, John Wood, also working for the intelligence service. Though he was distant and somewhat secretive about himself, Maclean felt compelled to accept his proposal of marriage. After they were married, she discovered that John followed Sufi teachings. She became immersed in the study and practice of these herself, as well as other philosophies practiced by other spiritual groups, particularly after the couple moved to England.

Through these studies, Maclean learned to develop her spiritual attunement to the still center within, and to practice telepathic communication with people around the world. Govan taught her about unconditional love, and Sufi teachings taught her about "love in action," or seeking to do everything in life with purity of heart for the greater glory of God.

The marriage was emotionally unsustaining, and Maclean began to see that her best course of action would be to express an unconditional love for Wood and set him free. She focused a great deal of energy on achieving that state. One day she suddenly had her first awareness of the God within. It changed her life and set the stage for her subsequent experiences at Findhorn.

Dorothy Maclean (Reprinted courtesy of Dorothy Maclean)

Maclean also was influenced by Govan, who had a substantial following in the United Kingdom. Govan introduced Maclean to many people, including Peter and Eileen Caddy, with whom Maclean would later establish Findhorn. Peter Caddy, a Royal Air Force officer, was steeped in Rosicrucianism and its teachings on the power of positive thought. He had been married to Govan for five years; Govan had terminated the marriage, but they retained a close relationship.

After her divorce from Wood, Maclean worked as a secretary on Fleet Street in London. She began to get inner promptings to write down her inspirations. She showed these to Govan, who recognized her budding mediumistic gifts and encouraged her to develop them by channeling spiritual messages for others. Following Govan's guidance, Maclean quit her secretarial work to live "according to God's will." She worked as a kitchen maid and then as a mother's helper—a most humbling

change, but one that taught her to trust that she would be led to do what God intended her to do.

When Govan's group disbanded, Maclean joined up with the Caddys in Glasgow. They spent six years working at the Cluny Hill Hotel, a Victorian resort open only during the summer. Maclean served as secretary and receptionist. The hotel flourished, and the Caddys and Maclean spent their spare time working on spiritual attunement and telepathically communicating around the world in the "Network of Light," a loose collection of people who shared similar spiritual ideals and who had telepathic abilities. They also communicated with "space beings," who said they were alien beings from elsewhere in the universe, and with the "Masters of the Seven Rays," who were highly developed humans who had undertaken to aid humanity in its spiritual quest.

Maclean and the Caddys moved to another hotel in Scotland but could not repeat their success—they were fired in 1962. Their only recourse was to band together four miles away at Findhorn, a small fishing village located on an inhospitable strip of the north Scottish coast, where the Caddys lived in a caravan with their three children. The Caddys and Maclean scraped out a living. Peter began to cultivate a garden, with mixed success.

In May 1963, Maclean, in her daily meditation, received an unusual message about the "forces of Nature." She learned that one of her jobs was to attune and harmonize with those forces, who would be friendly in their greeting to her. Peter interpreted this as meaning that she could receive guidance from Nature on what to do in the garden. This was immediately affirmed in her next meditation, with the following message, told in Maclean's autobiography *To Hear the Angels Sing:*

> Yes, you can cooperate in the garden. Begin by thinking about the nature spirits, the higher overlighting nature spirits, and tune into them. That will be so unusual as to draw their interest here. They will be overjoyed to find some members of the human race eager for their help.

> By the higher nature spirits I mean the spirits of differing physical forms such as clouds, rain, vegetables. The smaller individual nature spirits are under their jurisdiction. In the new world to come these realms will be open to humans—or should I say, humans will be open to them. Just be open and seek into the glorious realms of Nature with sympathy and understanding, knowing that these beings are of the Light, willing to help but suspicious of humans and on the lookout for the false. Keep with me and they will not find it, and you will all build towards the new.

Maclean did as instructed, and so began a long and fruitful relationship with the angelic and devic kingdoms. The first nature spirit to come into her awareness was what she called the "Pea Deva," which she described as holding the archetypal pattern in place for all the peas in the world. Her primary contact was the "Landscape Angel," who acted as control and had a broad, holistic outlook. The Landscape Angel often facilitated communication with other beings. All communications were on the inner planes.

Initially Maclean did not know what to call the beings with whom she came in contact. She thought them to be angels, but to her the term "angel" conjured up hackneyed religious and pop-culture images. These beings seemed too glorious. She settled on the term "deva," though in talking about them she used the terms "angel," "deva," and "nature spirit" interchangeably. Later in life she felt that "angel" better expressed the beings she experienced.

With the advice of the devas (Maclean's favored term during her Findhorn years), Peter's garden grew lush and robust. They produced bumper crops of produce, some of fantastical size, which they sold in the local community. Agricultural experts, who examined the produce and the soil, could not explain their success. When they began to publicly acknowledge their spiritual help others were attracted to Findhorn, and they established a spiritual colony. After a couple of years Peter no longer needed angelic messages, but had learned enough from them to work the garden. Maclean worked in the office and continued to receive varied messages from the devas, expanding her own consciousness. She was able to contact the devas of animals, stones, and inanimate objects ("machine devas").

Maclean left Findhorn in 1973 and commenced work as a writer and lecturer. She settled for a time in the High Sierras of California to work on her autobiography. She joined about 15 other Findhorn veterans, including mystic David Spangler, to form the Lorian Association in the San Francisco Bay area. The group offered public performances of talks, songs, and dance drawn from their Findhorn experiences.

In 1976, Maclean returned to Canada and lived in Toronto for eight years. She then moved to Issaquah, Washington, near Seattle, where Spangler and other members of the Lorian Association had moved. She occasionally revisits Findhorn to deliver workshops and lectures.

After returning to North America, Maclean began to attune to angels of cities and countries (see PSEUDO-DIONYSIUS). These experiences gave her insights into the characters and group destinies of collections of humans.

Her autobiography, *To Hear the Angels Sing,* was published in 1980. In it, Maclean acknowledges the uncertainties and doubts that accompanied her experiences with the angelic realm. At Findhorn she often feared that she would pose the wrong questions on behalf of Peter, or not get the information straight. Sometimes she was skeptical of her own abilities and results, and she worried that others would think her strange.

Nonetheless, Maclean's own spiritual understanding deepened tremendously due to her Findhorn experiences, and she passed this wisdom on to others. She provided a unique look into the workings of the angelic and devic kingdoms. Though she was by no means the first to have extensive contact with these realms, she was able to gain a large public platform thanks to the success and popularity of Findhorn.

Maclean realized that to attune to angels and devas is to attune to one's own higher self, the God-essence that dwells within each soul. Finding the God within is the important achievement, she said; angels are a subsidiary part of that attunement. She acknowledged that all perceptions received are colored by the recipient, in terms of beliefs, biases, vocabulary, the subconscious and other factors.

Maclean described devas as "the builders of our world. Embodiments of creative intelligence, they wield or transmute what we might call energy (vibrating waves or particles in patterns) into increasingly more 'physical' structures (including emotional and mental structures) and finally into what we call matter (which is pattern in space). They build vehicles for the expression of life on all levels: mineral, vegetable, animal, human and suprahuman." The beings she encountered were not small in relative stature, as one might think of FAIRIES and elves; some, she said, were awesome beings whose scope stretched into the infinite universe. Her primary contacts were the overlighting angels/devas of a species, rather than the spirits that tend to individual life-forms.

The devas told Maclean to think of plant life in terms of light and of vital patterns of energy. She learned that everything can be viewed in the same way—including humans. The devas hold these patterns in place so that form can manifest. According to Maclean, the devas do their work with joy and love, despite the counterproductive acts of humankind that destroy their work. They are wary of humans, but most seem willing to help if a sincere plea is put to them. Humans, they said, must be the ones to initiate contact with their realms, and then they will respond. They said that frequently humans enter the devic realms without knowing it, for fleeting moments. Such occasions are walks in nature, for example, where one is suddenly uplifted with euphoric feelings.

The devas also told Maclean that human beings ultimately have greater powers than they, but also more limitations, the latter being imposed by our destructive thoughts and ways. Humans cannot access their true powers of creativity because they have cut themselves off from the divine source of power, God. The devas emphasized the need to approach everything from the standpoint of love, which opens one to knowledge of the unity of all things.

Maclean said that through her contact with the angelic/devic realms she was able to unify her higher and lower selves into a wholeness. She connected with the God-source within, and she learned that humans can truly create their own reality in a joyous partnership not only with each other but with the higher realms as well.

FURTHER READING
Hawken, Paul. *The Magic of Findhorn.* New York: Bantam Books, 1976.
Maclean, Dorothy. *To Hear the Angels Sing.* Hudson, N.Y.: Lindisfarne Press, 1990. First published by Lorian Press, 1980. 2d ed. by Morningtown Press, 1988.

magic

The harnessing of supernatural powers and beings—deities, angels, DEMONS, and the forces of nature—to effect change in the physical world. The petitioning of both good and FALLEN ANGELS plays a prominent role in the Western tradition of magic. Important are the secret NAMES of angels and God, written and spoke at precise times in precise ways, such as with symbols and ritual tools.

General Background
The term *magic* comes either from the Greek *megus,* which means "great" (as in "great" science), or from the Greek term *magein,* referring to ZOROASTRIANISM. Many systems of magic exist, each with its own procedures, rules, and proscriptions. Magic is neither "white" nor "black" but reflects the intent of the magician.

Anthropologist Bronislaw Malinowski defined magic as having three functions and three elements. The three functions are to produce, protect, and destroy. The three elements are spells or incantations; rites or procedures; and the altered state of the magician. Altered states are accomplished through fasting, meditating, chanting, visualizing symbols, sleep deprivation, breath control, dancing, staring into flames, inhaling fumes, and so forth.

The primary intents of folk magic are to ensure good luck; protect against misfortune, illness, and death; and ask for blessings. Folk magic also is used to harm others.

In religious and mystical practices, magic is used to communicate with and invoke the presence and help of higher and supernatural powers. A thin line separates magic and religion. The Bible inveighs against magic and sorcery, but the miracles in the Bible—the intervention and action of God in the world—have the same characteristics as the "magic" of other cultures and religions. A prime example of this is the confrontation between MOSES and his son Aaron and the Egyptian priests in Exodus. Instructed by God, Moses and Aaron produce magic (though it is not named magic) that outperforms the magic of the Egyptians, thus securing the liberation of the Jews. In the New Testament, JESUS performs feats that are considered sacred and miraculous acts, but in different cultural clothing would be what Western theologians condemn as magic.

The very reverence for the Bible itself can be considered a type of magical practice. Copies of the Bible have amuletic and healing properties, as do specific verses and prayers. (See AMULETS; MEZUZOT.) The Lord's Prayer taught by Jesus protects the believer against harm, and it was especially believed in the Middle Ages to protect against attack by demons and witches.

Pagans Roots of Western Magic
Ancient man saw himself as at the mercy of cosmic and natural forces; magic and religion grew out of efforts to bend and defend against these forces and communicate

Magical seal of Agrippa with sacred names (Author's collection)

with the gods or INTELLIGENCES controlling them. Western magic emerged from Egyptian, Babylonian, Persian, and Greek cosmologies rich with deities and spirits. The Romans, however, disapproved of magic and vigorously prosecuted laws against it. They tolerated magic done for benefit, but condemned magic that was used for manipulation or harm. Pliny the Elder, writing in the first century C.E., was a major authority against magic.

Magic in Jewish Lore

Magical practices among the early Jews developed from the superstitions of the Canaanites and the traditions of the Babylonians, Egyptians, and later the Hellenistic-Gnostic lore. There was no initial organized system of magic, but a collection of beliefs and practices related to protecting against evil forces (demons) and procuring beneficent blessings. (See INCANTATION BOWLS). Magical lore attributed to the wisdom of King SOLOMON was in circulation as early as the first century C.E.

The Tanakh—the Old Testament—condemns sorcery, the use of spirits; some references seem designed to protect the Jews against the magic of their enemies while others offer instructions for obtaining God's help and blessings. Notable antimagic references are Exodus 7:10–12, against all forms of enchantments and shapeshifting; Numbers 22:7 and 22:23, against divination; Leviticus 19:31, 20:6, and 27, against mediums and wizards; and Deuteronomy 18:10, against necromancy. Apocryphal literature also casts magic in a negative light. The book of ENOCH, for example, tells how the magical arts were taught to humans by FALLEN ANGELS.

Talmudic law interpreted biblical sorcery into different categories. Magic that manipulated and enchanted and required the help of demons was forbidden and deserved the biblical penalty of death. Magic that did not require demons was still forbidden, but it did not deserve such severe punishment. The distinction between these two magics often was not clear. Magic involving the "Laws of Creation" was tacitly permitted; later, the use of mystical names of God and angels fell into this category as more acceptable to religious practices. Verses of scripture were recited along with the addition of mystical names.

Organized magic emerged in the Geonic period, which succeeded the Talmudic period around 500 C.E. At that time, Jewish mysticism, influenced by GNOSTICISM, was taking more shape. MERKABAH practices of mystical ascent to the throne of God centered on the proper use and recitation of sacred names, combined with other spiritual practices such as postures and breath control. The letters of the Hebrew alphabet were recognized as having unique properties by which all things were created.

See GEMATRIA.

By the Middle Ages, Jewish magic depended almost entirely on the use of names and interventions of spirits. The KABBALAH does not expressly forbid magic, but various kabbalistic writings warn of the dangers of it, and they state that only the most virtuous persons should perform magic and do so only in times of public emergency and need, never for private gain. How strictly these admonitions were followed is questionable, as extensive literature exists on what is called the "practical Kabbalah," an important source to Western magic in general. Some Kabbalists argued that the invocation of demons was acceptable, for there is little difference between an angel and a demon. Thus, many rituals found in the Western magic tradition involve the aid of "dukes of HELL" and other fallen angels.

The practical Kabbalah evolved from about the 14th century on, reaching a peak in the Renaissance. A master of practical Kabbalah is called a *ba'al shem* ("master of the name") who is adept at making amulets, invoking angels or demons and exorcizing evil spirits.

Practical Kabbalah is complex; its relationship to angels includes the use of many ANGEL ALPHABETS, secret codes of communication whose mythical origin is in texts such as the SEFER RAZIEL, a magical book written in the Middle Ages but said to be handed down from heaven at the time of ADAM AND EVE.

Numerous magical texts, or GRIMOIRES, flourished in the Middle Ages and later, all of which owe their basis to elements found in "Jewish" magic.

So-called black magic is called "apocryphal science" in the Kabbalah. It is strictly forbidden and only theoretical knowledge is permitted. According to the Zohar, those who choose to practice it become sorcerers who journey to the "mountains of darkness" where live the fallen angels Aza and Azael, to study under a sorcerer-witch. In the Bible, the archetypal sorcerer is Balaam.

By the Middle Ages, Jews were renowned among Christians for being adepts at magic, including the ability to heal by magic. There were no Jewish professional magicians or "sorcerers" or "witches," though Christians believed in such. Rather, those adept in this lore were rabbis, doctors, philosophers, teachers, and students of oral transmission of mystical and esoteric knowledge. These Jewish "magicians" were sought out; if their magic worked, they were feared, and if it failed, they were punished.

Magic in Christian Lore

Christianity also condemned magic, but, like Judaism, developed paradoxical attitudes. Manipulative "low" magic was absolutely forbidden, but helpful magic, such as for healing, was practiced within certain limits. Especially noxious to the church fathers was divination, which took one's destiny out of the hands of Christ-oriented faith.

Christian magic placed more emphasis on nature, such as herbal lore, and did not emphasize mystical names. The body of Christ, as represented by the Eucharist, held the biggest magic, as did the name of JESUS and relics (body parts and possessions) of saints.

Medieval Europe was rife with magic of all sorts: folk practitioners, wizards, cunning men and women, alchemists, and others. The "practical Kabbalah," along with Gnostic and Neoplatonic lore, served as important foundations of ceremonial magic. (See AGRIPPA.) In this, names of angels and demons, SEALS, TALISMANS, symbols, incantations, and so forth retained importance. Magical texts written in Arabic influenced the development of Kabbalah and alchemy.

But popular reliance on magic—spellcasting, divination, charms, and so forth—was attended by great fear and distrust. Any and every misfortune, problem, and setback was blamed on malefic magic or witchcraft. During the Inquisition, this fear became a useful tool: the charge of witchcraft was made a heresy, and it was virtually impossible to refute. Witches were portrayed as the servants of Satan with armies of demons at their command to wreak havoc.

Magic was further discredited by the scientific revolution of the 18th century, but interest in ceremonial magic was revived in the 19th century by occultists such as FRANCIS BARRETT and Eliphas Levi, whose respective works, *The Magus* (1801) and *Dogma and Ritual of High Magic* (1856) were influential. In the late 19th century, magical fraternities and lodges rose in prominence, the best known of which was the Hermetic Order of the Golden Dawn in England.

In contemporary times, many schools of magic are studied and practiced. Most draw upon the Judeo-Christian traditions, but many new systems are developed, such as within the different streams of Paganism. Angels and FAIRIES constitute part of many of these schools.

See JOHN DEE.

FURTHER READING

Flint, Valerie I. J. *The Rise of Magic in Early Medieval Europe.* Princeton, N.J.: Princeton University Press, 1991.

Guiley, Rosemary Ellen. *The Encyclopedia of Witches and Witchcraft.* Rev. ed. New York: Facts On File, 1999.

James, Geoffrey. *Angel Magic: The Ancient Art of Summoning and Communicating with Angelic Beings.* St. Paul, Minn.: Llewellyn Publications, 1999.

McLean, Adam, ed. *A Treatise on Angel Magic.* Grand Rapids, Mich.: Phanes Press, 1990.

Scholem, Gershom. *Kabbalah.* New York: Dorset Press, 1987. First published 1974.

Thomas, Keith. *Religion and the Decline of Magic.* New York: Charles Scribner's Sons, 1971.

Trachtenberg, Joshua. *Jewish Magic and Superstition: A Study in Folk Religion.* New York: Berhman's Jewish Book House, 1939.

Maimonides, Rabbi Moses (1135–1204)

Great Jewish scholar, philosopher, and rabbi of the Middle Ages, who wrote extensively on angels.

Life

Moses ben Maimon (also called Rambam) was born on April 6, 1135, in Cordova, Spain, during a time of Arab rule. He learned Hebrew and Jewish scholarship from his father, a well-to-do gem merchant, and also Arab teachers. In 1148 Cordova fell to a fanatical sect of Islam, and the climate of learning ceased to flourish in the face of increasing persecutions. By 1160 the family had endured enough, and they moved to Fez.

In Fez Maimonides launched his literary career, but his views against Jewish assimilation were not popular. In 1165 he moved to Cairo, where he enjoyed great success in court and as a rabbi. However, the family fortune was destroyed when a consignment of gems was lost in a shipwreck. Maimonides went to work as a physician. His success in this endeavor also was great, and he was able to decline an offer to become court physician to Richard I in England.

In 1185 he married; the couple had a son, Abraham, in 1186. In his later years, Maimonides became a prolific writer, but he sought to avoid controversy. He is said to have been interested in KABBALAH. He died on December 13, 1204.

Works

Maimonides authored numerous books and treatises writing in Arabic with Hebrew characters. His most important works are *Mishneh Torah* (*Code of Law*)—the first systematic organization of Jewish oral law—and *Guide for the Perplexed* (also given as *Guide of the Perplexed*). He sought to align Judaism and philosophy, demonstrating how Islamic Aristotlean philosophy, widely accepted at the time, was reflected in the Bible and the rabbinic tradition.

Guide of the Perplexed, published in 1190, was quickly translated into Hebrew. It had a profound influence on Jewish, Arabic, and Christian philosophers for centuries. In the 13th century, it impressed Albertus Magnus and his famous pupil, St. THOMAS AQUINAS. Aquinas refers often to Maimonides ("the rabbi") in his own monumental works.

Like Aquinas, Maimonides viewed the Bible as the authority on all metaphysical questions and on divine revelation; philosophy is the key to revealing and understanding these truths. And, like Aquinas, he was aware of the limits of human understanding. He identifies knowledge and love of God as one and the same, thus establishing sound philosophical knowledge as a commandment of God and as an act of piety for any religious Jew. He accepts the existence of angels because the Torah says they exist.

Maimonides organizes the universe into three parts: the sublunar world, the supernal realm, and the realm of the INTELLIGENCES, who oversee the movement of the spheres. Maimonides identifies angels with the intelligences; they are the intermediaries between God and creation, and they exist in pure form only. They are organized in their own hierarchy of 10 orders, the names of which refer both to the orders and to the angels governing them. The orders are, from highest to lowest:

HAYYOTH (hayyot ha-Qodesh)
OPHANIM
ERELIM
HASMALIM
ELOHIM
BENE ELOHIM
CHERUBIM
ISSIM (ishim)

Because angels exist in pure form only, they cannot have tangible bodies; thus, the descriptions of their appearances in the Bible and rabbinical writings are only metaphors. The lowest level of angels, the issim, speak to humans in prophecy and are part of prophetic visions. Visions, says Maimonides, are a function of the imagination and not the senses. He is emphatic that angels cannot be seen or heard except in visions or dreams. In cases where angels are described without direct reference to a vision or dream, one must assume that a vision or dream is responsible. (See DREAMS AND VISIONS.)

In describing the process of prophecy, Maimonides calls the imagination an angel, the intellect a cherub, and the soul common sense. Soul receives impressions through the senses, which are passed to the imagination, and then are transformed by the intellect into intellectual concepts. The prophetic message is "real, but the angelic appearance is just an impression which helps the recipient understand the message."

A critic of Maimonides, Isaac Abrabanel, held that prophecy is not a natural event, but a miracle divinely brought about by God, and that dreams and prophecy are different things. Maimonides's predecessor, IBN SINA, refers to angels as existing in both their own right and relative to us, but he makes the same distinction between actuality and prophecy as does Maimonides.

Maimonides denies the reality of many miracles. He accepts miracles as the means by which God demonstrates his intervention in the world, but he questions many of miracles in the Bible, viewing them as natural events or folklore metaphors. He rejects the type of miracle in which God and angels talk to men as equals, and in which angels appear in bodily form. These are not natural or supernatural events, but prophetic visions, and thus are imaginary.

See CELESTIAL HIERARCHIES.

FURTHER READING
Arbel, Ilil. *Maimonides: A Spiritual Legacy.* New York: Crossroad/Herder and Herder, 2001.
Leaman, Oliver. *Moses Maimonides.* London: Routledge, 1990.
Maimonides. *Guide of the Perplexed.* Vols. I and II. Translated by Shlomo Pines. Chicago: University of Chicago Press, 1974.

Makatiel

One of the ANGELS OF PUNISHMENT. Makatiel means "the plague of God."

malachim (malakim)

In Jewish lore, an order of angels, through whom God Eloha makes metals. Malachim means "kings" (gods) and possibly derives from *malak*, the Hebrew term for "messenger" or angel. The book of Malachi, written circa 500–450 B.C.E. by an anonymous Jewish priest, is a proper name converted from the Hebrew term for "my messenger."

Malachim are given different ranks: sixth highest (MAIMONIDES); first (the Zohar); eighth (the Maseket Azilut); and fourth (the Berith Menucha).

The malachim are one of the angelic orders ruling Tiphareth (Beauty), the sixth sephirah of the TREE OF LIFE in the KABBALAH. Malachim are sometimes equated with VIRTUES. Their ruling princes are Peliel, Raphael, Uriel, and Uzziel.

Malachim is a name of an ANGEL ALPHABET used in magical texts.

Malephar See VALEFOR.

Malkira

In the Martyrdom and Ascension of ISAIAH, Malkira is another name for Samael. It means "king of evil."

Malkuth See TREE OF LIFE.

Malpas (Malphas)
One of the FALLEN ANGELS and 72 spirits of SOLOMON. Malpas is a powerful president in HELL who appears first as a crow and then, when commanded, as a human who speaks in a hoarse voice. He skillfully builds houses and high towers, and he brings down the temples and towers of enemies. He will bring artificers together quickly. Malpas gives good FAMILIARS. He will receive a sacrifice kindly, but then deceive the one who offers it. Malpas commands 40 legions.

Mammon
FALLEN ANGEL who rules in HELL as an archdemon and prince of tempters. The name Mammon means in Aramaic "riches." Mammon is equated with Lucifer, Satan, and Beelzebub and rules over avarice. He serves as hell's ambassador to England.

manna See ANGEL BREAD.

mansions of the moon
In MAGIC, the 28 mansions, or spheres of influence of the moon, based upon its 28-day cycle of phases. Each mansion is governed by an angel, has positive or negative influences over certain activities, and is ascribed talismans for working specific kinds of magical spells. In magical ritual, the magician calls upon the appropriate ruling angel of the mansion involved to help effect the spell.

The mansions of the moon are fixed in the eighth sphere of heaven. As the moon wanders the sky, it obtains the powers and virtues of the signs of the zodiac and the stars contained in them. Each mansion measures 12 degrees, 51 minutes and nearly 26 seconds, according to the Kabbalists.

The mansions, their names, their ruling angels, their zodiac signs, and their influences are as follows:

First Mansion
Name: Alnath (horns of Aries)
Angel: Geniel
Zodiac sign: Aries
Influences: Causes prosperous journeys; creates discords; helps in the giving of medicines, especially laxatives

Second Mansion
Name: Allothaim or Albochan (belly of Aries)
Angel: Enediel
Zodiac sign: Aries
Influences: Helps in the finding of treasures and the holding of captives; aids voyages, sowing, and planting; hinders purging and vomiting

Third Mansion
Name: Alchaomazon or Athoray (showering or Pleiades)
Angel: Anixiel
Zodiac sign: Aries
Influences: Profitable to sailors, hunters, and alchemists

Fourth Mansion
Name: Aldebaram or Aldelamen (eye or head of Taurus)
Angel: Azariel
Zodiac sign: Taurus
Influences: Causes the destruction and hindrances of buildings, fountains, wells, gold mines, and the flight of creeping things (insects), and begets discord

Fifth Mansion
Name: Alchatay or Albachay
Angel: Gabriel
Zodiac sign: Taurus
Influences: Helps the return from a journey and the instruction of scholars; confirms edifices; gives health and goodwill to persons of quality

Sixth Mansion
Name: Athanna or Alchaya (little star of great light)
Angel: Dirachiel
Zodiac sign: Gemini
Influences: Helps hunting, the besieging of towns and the revenge of princes; destroys harvests and fruits, hinders the operations of physicians

Seventh Mansion
Name: Aldimiach or Alazarch (arm of Gemini)
Angel: Schliel
Zodiac sign: Gemini
Influences: Confirms gain and friendship, is profitable to lovers, destroys magistracies

Eighth Mansion
Name: Alnaza or Anatrachya (misty or cloudy)
Angel: Amnediel
Zodiac sign: Cancer
Influences: Causes love, friendship, and the society of fellow travelers; drives away mice, afflicts captives, and confirms their imprisonment

Ninth Mansion
Name: Archaam or Arcaph (eye of the Lion)
Angel: Barbiel
Zodiac sign: Cancer-Leo
Influences: Hinders harvest and travelers, puts discord between humans

Tenth Mansion
Name: Algelioche or Albegh (neck or forehead of the Lion)
Angel: Ardifiel

Zodiac sign: Leo
Influences: Strengthens buildings, promotes love and benevolence, helps against enemies

Eleventh Mansion
Name: Azobra or Ardaf (hair of the Lion's head)
Angel: Neciel
Zodiac sign: Leo
Influences: Good for voyages, gain by merchandise, and redemption of captives

Twelfth Mansion
Name: Alzarpha or Azarpha (tail of the Lion)
Angel: Abdizuel
Zodiac sign: Leo
Influences: Gives prosperity to harvests and plantations, is good for the bettering of servants, captives, and companions; hinders seamen

Thirteenth Mansion
Name: Alhaire (Dog stars, or wings of Virgo)
Angel: Jazeriel
Zodiac sign: Virgo
Influences: Aids benevolence, gain, voyages, harvests, and freedom of captives

Fourteenth Mansion
Name: Alchureth or Arimet, Azimeth, Althumech or Alcheymech (spike of Virgo)
Angel: Ergediel
Zodiac sign: Virgo
Influences: Causes the love of married folk; cures the sick; is profitable to sailors; hinders journeys by land

Fifteenth Mansion
Name: Agrapha or Algrapha (covered or covered flying)
Angel: Atliel
Zodiac sign: Libra
Influences: Helps in the extracting of treasures and the digging of pits; assists in divorce, discord, and the destruction of houses and enemies; hinders travelers

Sixteenth Mansion
Name: Azubene or Ahubene (horns of Scorpio)
Angel: Azeruel
Zodiac sign: Scorpio
Influences: Hinders journeys, wedlock, harvest, and merchandise; prevails for redemption of captives

Seventeenth Mansion
Name: Alchil (crown of Scorpio)
Angel: Adriel
Zodiac sign: Scorpio
Influences: Betters a bad fortune; makes love durable; strengthens buildings; helps seamen

Eighteenth Mansion
Name: Alchas or Altob (heart of Scorpio)

Angel: Egibiel
Zodiac sign: Scorpio
Influences: Causes discord, sedition, conspiracy against princes and mighty ones, and revenge from enemies; frees captives; helps edifices

Nineteenth Mansion
Name: Allatha or Achala (tail of Scorpio)
Angel: Amutiel
Zodiac sign: Scorpio
Influences: Helps in the besieging of cities, the taking of towns, the driving of humans from their places, the destruction of seamen, and the perdition of captives

Twentieth Mansion
Name: Abnahaya (a beam)
Angel: Kyriel
Zodiac sign: Sagittarius
Influences: Helps in the taming of wild beasts and the strengthening of prisons; destroys the wealth of societies; compels a person to come to a certain place

Twenty-first Mansion
Name: Abeda or Albedach (a desert)
Angel: Bethnael
Zodiac sign: Capricorn
Influences: Good for harvest, gain, buildings, and travelers; causes divorce

Twenty-second Mansion
Name: Sadahacha, Zodeboluch or Zandeldena (a pastor)
Angel: Geliel
Zodiac sign: Capricorn
Influences: Promotes the flight of servants and captives in their escape; helps the curing of diseases

Twenty-third Mansion
Name: Zabadola or Zobrach (swallowing)
Angel: Requiel
Zodiac sign: Capricorn
Influences: Helps divorce, the liberty of captives; promotes health to the sick

Twenty-fourth Mansion
Name: Sadabath or Chadezoad (star of fortune)
Angel: Abrinael
Zodiac sign: Aquarius
Influences: Aids the benevolence of married people and the victory of soldiers; hurts the execution of government and prevents its being exercised

Twenty-fifth Mansion
Name: Sadalabra or Sadalachia (butterfly or spreading forth)
Angel: Aziel
Zodiac sign: Aquarius
Influences: Favors besieging and revenge; destroys enemies; causes divorce; confirms prisons and buildings;

hastens messengers; conduces to spells against copulation; binds a human being so that he or she cannot perform a duty

Twenty-sixth Mansion
Name: Alpharg or Phragal Mocaden (first drawing)
Angel: Tagriel
Zodiac sign: Aquarius-Pisces
Influences: Causes union and the health of captives; destroys buildings and prisons

Twenty-seventh Mansion
Name: Alchara or Alyhalgalmoad (second drawing)
Angel: Atheniel
Zodiac sign: Pisces
Influences: Increases harvest, revenues, and gain; heals infirmities; hinders buildings; prolongs prison sentences; causes danger to seamen; helps to cause mischief to anyone

Twenty-eighth Mansion
Name: Albotham or Alchalcy (Pisces)
Angel: Amnixiel
Zodiac sign: Pisces
Influences: Increases harvest and merchandise; secures travelers through dangerous places; makes for the joy of married people; strengthens prisons; causes the loss of treasures.

FURTHER READING
Barrett, Francis. *The Magus.* Secaucus, N.J.: The Citadel Press, 1967. First published 1801.
McLean, Adam, ed. *A Treatise on Angel Magic.* Grand Rapids, Mich.: Phanes Press, 1990.

Marbas (Barbas)
One of the FALLEN ANGELS and 72 spirits of SOLOMON. Marbas is a president who rules 36 legions. He appears as a lion but will change into a man. He knows about hidden and secret things and both causes and cures diseases. He imparts wisdom and knowledge of the mechanical arts. He can change men into different shapes.

Marchosias
One of the FALLEN ANGELS and 72 spirits of SOLOMON. Marchosias is a marquis ruling 30 legions. He appears as a cruel she-wolf with griffin wings and a serpent's tail, with fire spewing from his mouth. He will take a human form if commanded to do so. He faithfully serves the magician and gives true answers to all questions. Once a member of the order of DOMINIONS, Marchosias holds the futile hope that he will return to the Seventh Throne after 1,200 years.

Marian apparitions
Visions or supernatural manifestations of the Blessed Virgin MARY. The experiences are accompanied by other paranormal phenomena, such as visions of angels, heavenly music and singing, miraculous healing, luminosities, and on the part of the percipients, extrasensory perception, prophesying, and mediumship. The apparitions tend to be apocalyptic in nature, with Mary exhorting people to prayer and righteous living, and to the building of churches in her honor. She warns of dire consequences if people continue in their sinful ways. She bestows secret prophecies on a select few who perceive her (frequently children). In this respect Mary has taken over the primary functions of the prophets of old, who were transported to HEAVEN to receive the same admonitions and prophecies from God. But Mary, out of her love for humanity and her loyalty to those devoted to her, is able to intercede with an angry God on humanity's behalf.

Our Lady of Guadalupe (Reprinted courtesy of U.S. Library of Congress)

Marian apparitions have been reported worldwide over the centuries, but only eight have been deemed authentic by the Catholic Church. In the latter 20th century, reports of Marian apparitions escalated dramatically. Two major reasons behind this increase are the Catholic Church's acceptance of Mary's assumption into heaven as an article of faith in 1950, thereby raising her spiritual stature; and the general trend toward apocalyptic thinking with the approach of a new millennium. The latter involves a need to turn to a spiritual savior figure.

The Catholic Church holds that religious apparitions are mystical phenomena permitted by God. Both corporeal and incorporeal apparitions are recognized, and they are mentioned in both Old and New Testaments of the Bible. Marian apparitions are not accepted as articles of faith, but those that are deemed authentic are celebrated. The church is painstaking in its investigation of Marian apparitions.

Authentic sightings approved by the church are: Guadalupe, Mexico, 1531; Paris, 1830; La Salette, France, 1846; Lourdes, France, 1858; Knock, Ireland, 1879; Fatima, Portugal, 1917; Beauraing, Belgium, 1932–33; and Banneaux, Belgium, 1933. Appearances of angels are especially associated with four of those (Paris, Guadalupe, Knock, and Fatima), and with numerous unauthenticated sightings as well.

At Guadalupe, Mary's appearances were accompanied by heavenly singing, and one of her miraculous signs involved an angel. She appeared five times to Juan Diego, a middle-aged Aztec convert to Catholicism. The first episode occurred in the predawn one morning, as Juan was on his way to attend Mass. He suddenly heard a heavenly choir, and then a lady's voice calling out to him by name. Diego then saw a woman standing in a luminous cloud of mist iridescent with rainbow hues. She identified herself immediately as Mary.

On another occasion Mary appeared and told Diego to pick flowers, despite the fact that it was too cold a time of the year. Miraculously, he found a garden of roses at a site where no flowers had grown before. He followed her instructions to wrap the flowers in his cape and take them to the bishop. Unwrapped, the cape was imprinted with a beautiful image of the Immaculate Conception: a woman with the sun and stars, standing on a new moon, with an angel at her feet. The cape remains preserved at the shrine built at Guadalupe.

In Paris, the percipient was Catherine Labouré, a nun with the Sisters of Charity in the rue du Bac. She entered the convent in 1830, shortly before the sighting. Within a few days of her arrival she had a vision of the heart of St. Vincent, glowing above a case containing some of his relics. She prayed to St. Vincent and to her GUARDIAN ANGEL to be granted a vision of Mary, her greatest ambition.

On July 18, Labouré was awakened at 11:30 P.M. by the sound of her name being called. She saw a child of about four or five years of age with golden hair, whom she took to be her guardian angel. The angel told her to go to the convent chapel; upon arrival, she found it brilliantly lit. Mary appeared at midnight and delivered her customary messages of exhortation to prayer, the appointment of Labouré to a mission that would require her suffering, and various prophecies.

Mary appeared to Labouré again on November 27 in a glorious vision while Labouré was praying in the chapel at about 5:30 P.M. She told Labouré to have a medal struck of her vision, and that all who wore it would receive graces. Labouré was not able to do this until six months before her death in 1876. The medal, called "the Miraculous Medal," is now worn by millions worldwide.

Marian apparition at Reus, Spain

At Fatima in 1917—the most dramatic of the authenticated sightings—three children were paid three visits by an angel who identified itself as the Angel of Portugal, who acted as an annunciating figure. Mary then appeared to the children: Lucia dos Santos, 10, and her two cousins, Jacinta and Francisco Marto, seven and nine, respectively. The two girls saw a "young lady" and heard her speak; the boy saw her but did not hear her speak. The children said the lady was dressed in white and stood above a small tree. She asked them to return to the same place at the same hour of the same day for six consecutive months. Tens of thousands of spectators showed up at the appointed time and place to witness the six apparitions.

At the final sighting on October 13, a crowd of 50,000 or more gathered in the rain. Mary appeared to the children and told them to build a chapel in her honor. She said she was the "Lady of the Rosary," and that people must say the rosary daily. Then the rain stopped, and a phenomenon now known as the "miracle of the sun" occurred. The sun appeared suddenly through a rift in the clouds and seemed to spin, throwing off multicolored light. It appeared to plunge to the earth, giving off heat, and then returned to normal in the sky.

A devotional cult to the Angel of Portugal, the guardian angel of the state, was sanctioned by the Catholic Church (see DEVOTIONAL CULTS).

Lucia wrote four memoirs between 1935 and 1941. In her *Second Memoir* she made the new claim that she and her cousins had been visited by an angel in 1916. This "Angel of Peace," as he identified himself, taught the children a special prayer and said that the hearts of Jesus and Mary were attentive to them. Lucia described him as looking to be about 14 or 15 years of age, whiter than snow, transparent as crystal, and quite beautiful when the sun shone through him. She warned the other two that the visit must be kept secret (secret visits, messages, and prophecies are an integral part of Marian apparitions, and conform with apocalyptic experiences).

On a second visit the angel urged them to pray constantly to God and said that the hearts of Jesus and Mary had "designs of mercy" on them. He instructed them to turn everything they could into a sacrifice offered to God, which would be reparation for the sins that offend God and supplication for the conversion of sinners. The angel said that if they did this, their country would have peace. He then identified himself as the Angel of Portugal. He ended his visit by telling them to bear the suffering that God would send them.

On a third visit, the angel gave them communion. Lucia received the consecrated host, and Jacinta and Francisco were allowed to share the chalice.

At Knock, Ireland, Mary, other figures, and perhaps angels were seen on August 21, 1879, by 15 people by the village chapel at dusk. Besides Mary there were figures of St. Joseph, and a bishop or St. John the Evangelist (accounts differ). There also was an altar, above which was a lamb with a halo of gold stars; behind the lamb was a cross. Mary had her hands raised in prayer. Although it was raining, no rain fell where the apparition appeared. One witness, Patrick Hill, was 11 years old. Interviewed again in 1897, he embellished his account with visions of winged angels who fluttered in the air for some 90 minutes.

In 1961, apparitions appeared at San Sebastian de Garabandal in northern Spain; they are unauthenticated. The sightings involve the archangel Michael, who, like the Angel of Portugal at Fatima, gave the witnesses communion. The case began on June 18 when four girls reported that they had seen an angel. Over the next two weeks, the angel made nine appearances. In the two years following, there were more than 2,000 reports of Marian apparitions by the girls.

One of the chief documents is the *Diary* of one of the witnesses, Conchita Gonzalez, who was 12 at the time. She began to write the account in September of 1962 and finished it in 1963.

According to Gonzalez, she and the other seers were stealing apples on June 18—and arguing over whether it was right to do so—when a beautiful figure appeared, brilliant in light. The girls told others about this angel, and they were ridiculed by some. The girls returned to the spot the next day to pray, but the angel did not reappear. Gonzalez was consoled by a voice that night that assured her that she would see the angel again. The angel did appear on the following day, causing some disbelievers to recant.

Others joined them in prayer at the site, and over the next eleven days the girls had various ecstasies and eight more sightings of the angel, in front of numerous witnesses who could not see the phenomena themselves. On six of the eight appearances, the angel only smiled at the girls. On June 24, he appeared with a sign beneath him; they could only remember that the first line began with "Hay" and the second line contained roman numerals.

On July 1 the angel appeared with the sign again and spoke for the first time, telling the girls that he had come to announce the arrival of Mary on the following day. Mary appeared on July 2, accompanied by two angels who looked like twins. One was Michael—the angel who had been appearing to them; the other was not recognized (Gonzalez never said how she was able to identify the angel as Michael). On Mary's right side was a large eye of God.

During these and other visions the girls were subjected to crude experiments by researchers, to test their ecstatic states by measuring their sensitivity to pain. During the June 25 appearance of the angel, Gonzalez was dropped on her knees, pricked and scratched with needles and subjected to strong electric light, none of which broke her trance or made her feel any pain.

On May 18, 1962, the girls began to announce that they had been receiving communion from Michael. Mari Loli was the first to make the claim. She said Michael had told her he would give her communion while the local priest was absent. The four girls said that from then on they received frequent communions from the angel.

Gonzalez said that Michael used unconsecrated hosts in order to teach them how the host should be received. One day the angel told them to fast, and to bring another child along as a witness. He then gave them consecrated hosts. These reports generated much controversy. Priests said that angels did not have the ability to consecrate a host. Gonzalez took this objection to Michael, who then told her he had taken consecrated hosts from tabernacles on earth. Nonetheless, some people doubted the story.

Prior to their public admission of communion from Michael, the girls were witnessed going through gestures of putting their hands together, sticking out their tongues and swallowing, all of which now made sense. After the admission, numerous photos were taken of them receiving invisible communion.

On June 22, 1962, the angel told Gonzalez—who had been asking for a miracle as a sign of proof—that during the next communion God would perform a miracle through the angel's intercession by making a host visible on her tongue. (Until then, Gonzalez had never realized that no one else could see the hosts given them by the angel.) She told the angel that this would be a tiny miracle, and he laughed. On July 18, a host appeared on her tongue and was seen by witnesses.

Though the girls later retracted some of their statements about their experiences, believers were not dissuaded. Even the retractions seemed to be part of the overall experience, with Gonzalez's diary claiming that Mary had predicted that retractions would be made. Supporters of the apparitions at Garabandal have worked to try to convince the Catholic Church to authenticate the sightings.

Other famous apparition sites not authenticated are Zeitoun, Egypt, and Medjugorje, Bosnia-Herzegovina. The Zeitoun sightings in 1968–69 included more than 70 Marian apparitions and other unusual phenomena in the vicinity of the St. Mary's Coptic Church in Zeitoun, a suburb of Cairo. The first eyewitnesses were three Muslim mechanics, who reported seeing a woman dressed in dazzling white, standing on top of the central dome of the church in the late night hours. The light was so brilliant that they could not make out facial features. Other witnesses recognized the apparition as Mary. The crowd shouted and the figure acknowledged by bowing. After a few minutes, it ascended rapidly into the night sky and disappeared.

The first sighting was followed by hundreds of alleged spontaneous cures of all manner of diseases and illnesses. Other notable phenomena were reddish clouds of sweet incense which appeared and disappeared with great rapidity; unusual lights shooting across the sky; and luminous doves or dovelike objects of silver and other brilliant colors, some of which appeared in the shape of a Christian cross. The total number of eyewitnesses was estimated at 250,000 to 500,000. The General Information and Complaints Department of the Egyptian government investigated and declared it "an undeniable fact" that Mary had appeared to both Christians and Muslims.

The Medjugorje apparitions began in 1981, when Mary first appeared on a hill to six adolescents on June 24. Four were girls and two were boys; they ranged in age from 10 to 17. For the next 18 months, there were daily apparitions to one or more of the adolescents, who came to be called the "seers" or "visionaries." Thousands of apparitions have been witnessed by pilgrims. Many have occurred in the "chapel of apparitions," the rectory behind the St. James Roman Catholic Church in Medjugorje. Other phenomena include miraculous healings; the appearance of the Croatian word for peace, *Mir*, in the sky at night; a spinning sun; and a spontaneous ignition of a bush, the fire of which left no charring.

As in other apparitional cases, the messages from Mary at Medjugorje are apocalyptic: repent, pray, and return to the ways of God (peace and love) before it is too late and the people of the world will suffer the consequences of their evil.

See ANGELOPHANIES.

FURTHER READING

Arintero, Juan. *Mystical Evolution in the Development and Vitality of the Church.* Vol. I. St. Louis: B. Herder, 1949.

Attwater, Donald. *A Dictionary of Mary.* New York: P.J. Kennedy, 1960.

McClure, Kevin. *The Evidence for Visions of the Virgin Mary.* Wellingborough, England: Aquarian Press, 1983.

Zimdars-Swartz, Sandra L. *Encountering Mary.* Princeton, N.J.: Princeton University Press, 1991.

Marmaroth (Marmarath, Marmaraoth)
In the Testament of SOLOMON, the angel who has the power to thwart Fate, one of the seven demonic HEAVENLY BODIES, who incites warfare, and also the disease-causing DEMON Rhyx Anoster, one of the DECANS OF THE ZODIAC. Marmaroth is one of the PLANETARY RULERS.

Mary

The mother of JESUS. Mary has numerous titles, among them "Queen of Angels," "Our Lady of the Angels," and "Queen of Martyrs." She also is called "Blessed Virgin," "Virgin Mary," or simply "Our Lady." Early church councils, including those at Ephesus in 431 and at Chalcedon in 451, gave her the title *Theotokos* ("God-bearer"); the title "Mother of God" is widely used, especially among Catholics. Devotion to Mary is a vital part of the Catholic liturgical life, especially in the Eastern Orthodox churches.

According to Catholic doctrine, Mary's Immaculate Conception makes her the one exception to the state of Original Sin (the state in which all humankind is born, due to the fall of ADAM AND EVE). Because Mary was destined to be the mother of Christ, God infused her soul with grace at the moment of her conception in the womb of her mother, St. Anne, which freed her from lust, slavery to the devil, depraved nature, darkness of intellect, and other consequences of Original Sin. Her Immaculate Conception is announced by the archangel Gabriel (Luke 1:26–38). Gabriel tells her that the Holy Spirit will come upon her in order that she may conceive her Son.

The Immaculate Conception was rejected by St. THOMAS AQUINAS in the 13th century. Many modern theologians, challenging doctrines, consider the Immaculate Conception to be symbolic and not literal.

Similarly, the church sanitized her sexuality. Besides conceiving Jesus without human intercourse, she became "the Virgin" who never defiled her body with sexual intercourse—despite the fact that the Bible refers to Jesus' brothers and sisters.

Furthermore, Mary did not die as a mere mortal but was raised from the dead by Jesus and assumed into heaven as a live woman (the Assumption became an article of faith in 1950). In other lore, her death is announced by the archangel Michael.

Mary and her proper place in Christian theology have been a subject of much controversy over the centuries. She absorbed the characteristics of previous pagan goddesses, thus fulfilling that universal need for worship of a Mother-figure, which otherwise is curiously absent from Christianity. Early church fathers attempted to discourage worship of her by saying that

Mary and Jesus (Albrecht Dürer)

God would never be born of a woman. For the first five centuries after Christ, Mary was depicted as lower in status even than the Magi, who were graced by haloes in sacred art. The Marianite sect, which considered her divine, was persecuted for heresy. In the early fourth century, Constantine I ordered all goddess temples destroyed and forbade the worship of Mary, so that she would not overshadow her Son. The people, however, refused to accept Christianity without the worship of Mary. She was prayed to as a mother who intercedes for her children. By the sixth century she had been given a halo in art, and by the ninth century she had been designated the Queen of Heaven. By the 11th century she had eclipsed Jesus in popularity as the savior of mankind, and the great Gothic cathedrals were built to her greater glory.

In Catholic tradition Mary reigns in the splendor of heaven, where angels behold her glory and are ravished at the sight of her. She is second only to Jesus in suffering, and so commands the obedience of the angelic host. It may be Michael who leads the good angels in the celestial war against evil (see REVELATION), but he is under the command of Mary. The Queen of Paradise may even be considered to be the Mother of Angels, since she loves them and treats them as her own children. The Precious Blood shed by Jesus is the song of angels, the light of Mary, and the jubilee of her woes.

Countless visions of Mary have been reported worldwide; the numbers rose dramatically in the latter part of the 20th century. The Catholic Church has authenticated only a handful of them (see MARIAN APPARITIONS). Numerous saints have seen visions of Mary, often accompanied by angels. Frequently she exhorts people to pray, to counter the evil loosed in the world.

In Catholic tradition an unnamed Bernadine sister had a vision in which she saw the desolation wrought by evil. She heard Mary tell her that the time had come to pray to her as the Queen of the Angels, to ask her for the assistance of the angels in fighting the foes of God and men. The sister asked why Mary, who is so kind, could not send the angels without being asked. Mary responded that she could not because prayer is one of the conditions God requires for the obtaining of favors. Mary then communicated the following prayer, which is part of the many devotions to Mary:

> August Queen of Heaven! Sovereign Mistress of the angels! Thou who from the beginning hast received from God the power and mission to crush the head of Satan, we humbly beseech thee to send thy holy Legions, that, under thy command and by thy power, they may pursue the evil spirits, encounter them on every side, resist their bold attacks and drive them hence into the abyss of eternal woe. Amen.

Several feast days are observed in Mary's honor: the Immaculate Conception, her Nativity, Purification, Annunciation, and Assumption. The most popular devotion to Mary is the rosary, which is the saying of 50 "Hail Marys," five "Our Fathers," and five doxologies ("Glory be to the Father . . .") while meditating on specific traditional mysteries. This association with the rosary stems from apparitions of Mary seen at Fatima, Portugal, in 1917, in which she identified herself as the Lady of the Rosary and asked that believers say the rosary every day.

Ex-canonical works such as the Book of John the Evangelist refer to Mary as being an angel herself. The Apocryphal New Testament says that she is the angel sent by God to receive the Lord, who enters her through the ear.

FURTHER READING

Arintero, Juan. *Mystical Evolution in the Development and Vitality of the Church*, Vol. I. St. Louis: B. Herder, 1949.

Attwater, Donald. *A Dictionary of Mary.* New York: P. J. Kennedy, 1960.

St. Michael and the Angels. Rockford, Ill.: Tan Books and Publishers, 1983. First published 1977.

Warner, Marina. *Alone of All Her Sex: The Myth and the Cult of the Virgin Mary.* New York: Vintage, 1983.

Mashit

ANGEL OF DESTRUCTION and one of the ANGELS OF PUNISHMENT. Mashit means "destroyer." Mashit governs the death of children. According to the Zohar, he is one of three angels in Gehenna (HELL)—along with Af and Hemah—who punish those who sin by idolatry, incest, and murder.

maskim

In Akkadian lore, seven great princes of HELL or princes of the abyss. Azza, Azael, and Mephistopheles are among the maskim.

Mastema (Mastemah, Mansemat)

Angel of evil, hostility, adversity, and destruction; the accuser; a PRINCE of DEMONS and injustice. The proper name of Mastema comes from the same Hebrew noun, which means "hostility," its use in two references in the Old Testament (Hosea 9:7–8).

According to lore, Mastema once was the ANGEL OF THE LORD who delivered the punishments of the Lord and became demonized.

In ten references in the QUMRAN TEXTS, Mastema is equated with Belial, whose purpose is to destroy. He also is described as existing between the Prince of Light and the Angel of Darkness and ruling the children of falsehood. He leads the children of righteousness astray.

In JUBILEES, Mastema is the only angel who is named; he is equated with the ANGEL OF HOSTILITY. His origins are not explained, though he is equated with Satan and is the prince of evil beings who menace and harass humankind. As a satan, Mastema urges God to test ABRAHAM with the sacrifice of his son ISAAC. Mastema also aids the Egyptians in opposition to MOSES, and he tries to kill him. He helps the pharaoh's magicians compete with Moses and Aaron. His demons lead the sons of NOAH astray to commit sin, idolatry, and pollution.

One legend holds that Mastema asked God to give him some demons so that he might have power over humankind; God gave him one-tenth of the fallen ones to be under his command.

FURTHER READING

van der Toon, Karel, Bob Becking, and Pieter W. van der Horst, eds. *Dictionary of Deities and Demons in the Bible.* 2d ed. Grand Rapids, Mich.: William B. Eerdmans, 1999.

Matanbukus (Mekembukus)

In the Martyrdom and Ascension of Isaiah, Matanbukus is given as another name for Beliar. It possibly means "gift of desolation."

See ISAIAH.

Mefathiel

Angel whose name means "opener of doors" in Hebrew. Mefathiel was a favorite of thieves, who invoked him to aid their entries.

Melchizedek (Melkisedek, Melchisedec, Melch-Zadok)

A king and priest in the Old Testament, who in angel lore is associated with angels. Melchizedek means "the god Zedek is my king," and he is described in the New Testament as the "king of righteousness" and the "king of peace."

There are only two references to Melchizedek in the Old Testament. In Genesis 14:18–20, Melchizedek is identified as the king of Salem (Jerusalem)—the priest of EL ELYON—who blesses Abram (see ABRAHAM) after a battle. Abram then tithes to the king. Psalm 110:4 declares, "You are a priest forever after the order of Melchizedek." These words are echoed in the New Testament book of Hebrews (5:6–10), in which Jesus is declared the high priest successor, "Thou art a priest forever, after the order of Melchizedek" for offering the sacrifice of his life. Hebrews 7:1 says that Melchizedek has not father or mother or genealogy, "and has neither beginning of days nor end of life, but resembling the Son of God he continues a priest forever."

According to 2 ENOCH, Melchizedek is the supernatural son of the priest Nir, brother of NOAH. When Methuselah, the grandfather of Nir and Noah, is near death he appoints Nir as the leader of his people. For 202 years there is peace and order, and then the people turn away from the ways of the Lord. Nir is distressed for this turbulence has been prophesied.

Nir's elderly wife Sopanim becomes pregnant, despite being sterile and having had no sexual relations with Nir for many years. Ashamed, she hides herself away, even from Nir. Toward the end of her pregnancy,

Nir summons her to him, and when he sees that she is pregnant he is ashamed and angry. Sopanim tries to explain that she does not understand how she became pregnant, but he does not believe her. He sends her away.

Sopanim dies. Nir and Noah decide to bury her secretly to hide the scandal of her pregnancy. They wrap her body in black garments and go out to dig a grave in secret. When they return they find that a child has issued from her corpse. He has been born fully formed and about the size of a three-year-old child. He is sitting on the bed beside his dead mother. He speaks and blesses the Lord.

Nir and Noah are terrified. Then they see that he wears a glorious badge of priesthood on his chest. They believe that God is renewing the priesthood from their bloodline. They name him Melchizedek. They wash the boy, dress him in the garments of a priest, and give him holy bread to eat.

Nir and Noah take the black clothing off the body of Sopanim, wash her, reclothe her in a bright garment, and build a shrine for her. They bury her publicly. Noah tells Nir to look after Melchizedek in secret because the people who have turned away from God will put him to death.

Nir prays to the Lord to ask what is the destiny of his son. God appears to him in a DREAM and tells him that he will send the angel Michael to take the boy away to Eden where he will be safe from the destruction and punishment planned for the sinners. Melchizedek will be the priest to all holy priests and he will be the head of the priests of the future. Melchizedek will be the head of the 13 priests who existed before. In the last generation there will be another Melchizedek, the first of 12 priests. The last will be the head of all, a great archpriest, the Word and Power of God, who will perform great and glorious miracles.

After 40 days, Michael appears to Nir in a dream and announces he will take Melchizedek. When Nir arises in the morning he finds the boy gone. He grieves for Melchizedek is his only son. Nir passes away and after him there is no priest among the people. A great confusion exists on the earth, to be followed by the Flood.

Midrashim identify Melchizedek as a son of Noah, and the feeder of the beasts aboard the Ark. Phoenician mythology identifies him as the father of the seven ANGELS OF THE PRESENCE. Early Greek writers called him a VIRTUE and PRINCE OF PEACE.

In a QUMRAN TEXT, 11QMelch, Melchizedek is not a mortal but an angel. He is an exalted being over all other angels who presides over the heavenly court and meets out punishment from Belial and his DEMONS on the Day of Judgment. In this respect, Melchizedek is like Metatron, who also had an earthly life prior to his translation into HEAVEN as the highest of all angels.

Melchizedek was regarded as an angel by some groups in early Christianity, although St. Jerome rejected this idea. ORIGEN considered Melchizedek an angel.

Melchizedek also is associated with the ANGEL OF THE LORD.

FURTHER READING
Barker, Margaret. *The Great Angel: A Study of Israel's Second God.* Louisville, Ky.: Westminster/John Knox Press, 1992.
Charlesworth, James H., ed. *The Old Testament Pseudepigrapha.* Vols. 1 and 2. New York: Doubleday, 1983, 1985.

memunim

In Jewish lore, deputy angels or MINISTERING ANGELS who are the agents through whom the universe operates. Memunim in Hebrew means "appointed ones." Every single thing in creation is assigned its all-powerful memuneh (singular). Most important of all is the memuneh of the star assigned to a person, which governs his existence; this memuneh is the equivalent of a GUARDIAN ANGEL.

Besides influencing all affairs and activities, the memunim represent and defend their charges in the heavenly court of law (see ENOCH). If an animal or human has been wronged, for example, their memunim take up their case with God to see that justice is done. Memunim who watch over places are held responsible if a man injures himself there. Prayers cannot be answered unless the memunim offer them directly before the Throne of Glory. Memunim help to bring about good fortune by influencing people to take favorable actions; in this function they are similar to the DAIMONES. The memunim like familiarity and habit, for one must be careful when renovating a building or home, so that familiar doors and windows are not disturbed and the memunim become upset. And, when a person dies, his memuneh of his guiding star will ask for a reprieve so as not to be held accountable for his death.

The first appearances of memunim in rabbinic sources date to the 10th century in southern Italy. The concept of memunim was developed and expanded by German Jews in the 13th century as part of an elaborate structure of angel MAGIC. In magic, a practitioner commanded the elements by commanding memunim and DEMONS. In casting a spell on a person, the magician commanded his memuneh to deliver it to the memuneh of the victim. Memunim could also be employed to dispatch dreams to others, reveal the will of God in dreams, and serve in other magical intermediary duties (see DREAMS AND VISIONS). If a magician desires information, he commands his memuneh to bring it to him. The memuneh does not appear but impresses the information mentally by mingling his thoughts with those of the magician.

FURTHER READING
Trachtenberg, Joshua. *Jewish Magic and Superstition: A Study in Folk Religion.* New York: Berhman's Jewish Book House, 1939.

Mendrion

In the LEMEGETON, the ruling angel of the seventh hour of the night, called Venaydor. Mendrion rules 101,550 dukes and other servants who are divided into 12 orders.

Mephistopheles

One of the seven great princes of HELL, and a representative of Satan in legend and literature. Mephistopheles means in Hebrew "he who loves not the light."

Mephistopheles is best known for the part he plays in the legend of Dr. Johann Faust, which has been turned into plays, poems, operas, and symphonies. The story concerns the way in which vanity can lead to easy seduction by the devil. Perhaps the best-known of these artistic creations is GOETHE's *Faust.*

According to the story, Faust lives in 15th-century Weimar, Germany, where he is an astrologer, alchemist, and magician. In his youth he exhausted all the knowledge of his time, and so he turned to sorcery. Now in old age, he is bitter and disillusioned. Using his skill in sorcery, he conjures up Mephistopheles in the name of beelzebub. The DEMON is friendly and consoling. Faust conjures him a second time, and Mephistopheles promises him all the worldly pleasures and sensations he desires—in exchange for his soul at the end of 24 years' time. Faust agrees.

For the next 24 years, Faust lives a splendid life. He has youth, wealth, magical powers, and the satiation of all his physical desires. He can magically transport himself anywhere in the world, conjure up any woman, have anything. Then the demon comes to collect his due.

Goethe allows redemption for Faust. He has the doctor seduce a young woman named Margaret. She bears a child, but is so overcome with shame that she kills it. She is arrested and imprisoned, and in prison she becomes insane.

Faust, meanwhile, continues to live the high life. He conjures up Helen of Troy. Mephistopheles takes

Faust on an adventure and shows him the creation of the universe, and the secrets of the homunculus (an artificial man created by magic).

Faust tries to save Margaret, but to no avail. She goes to her death and her sacrifice redeems them both.

FURTHER READING

Hyatt, Victoria, and Joseph W. Charles. *The Book of Demons.* New York: Fireside, 1974.

Merkabah (Merkavah)

A form of Jewish mysticism. Merkabah focuses on the ascent to God's throne of glory through knowledge of the secret NAMES of angels and God, breath control and the rhythmic repetition of hymns, prayers, and invocations. The term *Merkabah* refers to the chariot that bears the throne of God. Merkabah originated in Palestine and was active prior to time of the destruction of the Temple of Jerusalem in 70 C.E. Influenced by GNOSTICISM, it spread into the Jewish communities in Babylonia and flourished through the eighth century or the ninth century C.E. It was a significant influence upon the development of the KABBALAH in medieval Spain. Merkabah terminology is found in Dead Sea Scrolls. (See QUMRAN TEXTS.)

In Merkabah cosmology, God's throne of glory resides in the center of seven concentric halls or palaces (hekalot) in the seventh or highest HEAVEN. (Some references imply the existence of higher heavens.) Descriptions of the throne are more impressionistic than specific, and are intended to convey the majesty of the throne. A curtain, the *pargod*, separates the throne from the rest of heaven. It's purpose is to shield the angels around God from the intensity of his glory. It also symbolizes mysteries known only to God. His palaces contain many treasures, among them the phenomena of the natural world, the archives of the heavenly court of law, (see ENOCH) and spiritual gifts such as wisdom. A RIVER OF FIRE flows out from beneath the throne; it is a symbol of the wrath of God in matters of divine judgment. Angels bath in the river when they perform the QEDUSSAH (Sanctus), a devotion that is their most important duty.

Below God is a complex organization of hierarchies of angels. Although angels are central to Merkabah mysticism, the various texts have no uniform ANGELOLOGY. There is general agreement that angels are made of a fiery substance and the higher ones can appear in a human-like form. The numbers of angels are infinite, and different angels are identified as filling certain offices. The function of angels is to worship and serve God; they attempt to obstruct the direct access of humans to the throne. Only the highest angels have access to God near or inside the curtain. In 3 Enoch, Metatron holds the privilege of access inside the curtain. In the Maseket Hekalot, the seven angels who were created first sit in front of the curtain.

In order to reach the throne the mystic must alter consciousness by going into trance. This is accomplished by preparatory fasting, assuming certain postures such as placing his head between his knees, breath control, and reciting certain prayers or hymns. He passes through the gates of each heaven, which are guarded by powerful, hostile angels. To get past the angels, the mystic must know the right SEALS and secret magical names, hymns, and prayers to recite; some are the songs of the HAYYOTH, and almost all conclude with the QEDUSSAH. There is great emphasis on angels' names, many of which are composed from number and letter magic. (See GEMATRIA.) Failure to pass through a gate poses a danger to the mystic.

With its emphasis on direct access to God, Merkabah mysticism was not entirely embraced by orthodoxy. According to tradition, Merkabah techniques could be undertaken only by those who were steeped in spiritual learning and who had properly purified themselves by days of fasting, eating special food, and bathing. With its strict procedures and shamanistic trances, Merkabah likely was confined to a small number of practitioners.

Merkabah literature emphasizes the mysteries of heaven and the ascent to God's throne. It is less concerned with eschatological and apocalyptic themes such as the last judgment, the resurrection of the dead, the messianic kingdom, and the world to come, though those themes are dealt with in some texts. Among the most significant Merkabah texts are the Hekalot Zutrati ("Lesser Hekalot"), the Hekalot Rabbati ("the Greater Hekalot"), the Merkavah Rabbah, the SEFER RAZIEL, and 3 Enoch, the latter of which is also known as the Sefer Hekalot (the Book of the Palaces) and the Chapters of Rabbi Ishmael. Merkabah mysticism also is found in apocryphal texts.

Merkabah's parallels to Gnosticism can be found in the heavenly ascent and the layers of heaven. In Gnosticism the ascent to heaven is not made during life, however, but after death. The soul passes through the realms of seven ARCHONS to reach the eighth sphere of the Ogdoad, a nameless being known as the "first power."

Other parallels can be found between Merkabah, mysticism and the Hermetica, Roman Mithraism and Neoplatonism.

Merkabah mysticism also made significant contributions to synagogue liturgy and to the theology of medieval Jewish mystics in Germany known as the Haside 'Askenaz.

FURTHER READING

Charlesworth, James H., ed. *The Old Testament Pseud-epigrapha.* Vols. 1 and 2. New York: Doubleday, 1983, 1985.

Scholem, Gershom. *Kabbalah.* New York: Dorset Press, 1987. First published 1974.

Merkabah Angels

In 3 ENOCH, six classes of angels who guard the throne of Glory, among them the CHERUBIM, GALGALIM, HAYYOTH, OPHANIM, and SERAPHIM.

Metatron

In Jewish lore, one of the four great ARCHANGELS and the greatest of angels, second only to God and a "Lesser Yahweh" in stature and power. In various accounts about Metatron, scarcely an angelic duty or function is not related to him. Primarily, he sustains the physical world and carries Jewish prayers through 900 HEAVENS to God. He is an important angelic figure in the MERKABAH and KABBALAH literature and the Talmud.

Metatron apparently absorbed characteristics originally ascribed to the angel Jahoel. He is huge in size, a pillar of fire with 36 pairs of wings and myriad eyes. His face is more dazzling than the sun. As PRINCE OF THE DIVINE PRESENCE, he is the only angel who has the high privilege of serving in God's immediate presence inside the curtain (*pargod*) that surrounds God on his throne of Glory.

Metatron stands at the top of the TREE OF LIFE as the ANGEL OF YAHWEH. He also is identified with the "tree of knowledge of good and bad," which means he embodies both human and angelic perfection. This enables him to be an excellent interface between the two realms, but his success depends on the righteousness of humans. The good deeds of people generate a spiritual energy that literally vitalizes Metatron, and, without it, he grows weak and less effective.

Metatron is the representative of God who led the tribes of Israel through the wilderness, and he is one of the angels identified as the dark angel who wrestles with JACOB. He is sometimes identified as the angel who stays the hand of ABRAHAM as he is about to sacrifice his son, ISAAC, and he is credited with ordering the angelic announcement of the coming of the Flood. (See URIEL.) Metatron also is said to have given the wisdom of the Kabbalah to humanity.

Metatron is sometimes called THE PRINCE OF THE COUNTENANCE, meaning he is the chief angel of those angels who are privileged to look upon the face of God. He serves as God's ANGEL OF DEATH, instructing Gabriel and Samael which human souls to take at any

Metatron (Copyright 1995 by Robert Michael Place, from *The Angels Tarot* by Rosemary Ellen Guiley and Robert Michael Place, 1995. Used with permission.)

given moment. The flames that issue from him create legions of angels. He is minister to the Throne of Glory, on which God sits; High Priest of the heavenly Temple (a role also ascribed to the archangel Michael); minister of wisdom, who holds the secrets to all divine affairs; and minister of the GUARDIAN ANGELS of the "70 peoples of the world." In addition, he teaches prematurely dead children who arrive in Paradise.

The etymology of the name Metatron is unclear. The name appears in two forms, Mttrwn and Myttrwn. Possibly, the name itself was intended to be a secret, and may have been produced through a glossolalia type of altered state of consciousness. Glossolalia is speaking in tongues, and it is perhaps best known for its part in charismatic religions. According to the Zohar, the name of Metatron is the equivalent of Shaddai, one of the NAMES of God. This association is derived from the mystical numerology called GEMATRIA, which assigns a numerical value to each letter in the Hebrew alphabet. Names and words that have the same numerical value have a mystical connection. Both Shaddai and Metatron equal 314. As another aspect of God, Metatron is sometimes called the "shining light of the SHEKINAH" and he "whose name is like that of his Master." Eleazar of Worms speculated that "Metatron" comes from the Latin term *metator,* which means a guide, measurer, or one who prepares the way, an apt description of this important angel. Other possible etymologies are the Greek term *metaturannos,* which means "the one next to the ruler," and the Greek term (*ho*) *meta thronon,* which means "(the throne) next to the (divine) throne" or "the second throne."

The earliest references to Metatron in literature use the term as a simple noun and not as a proper name. "Metatron" is a guide or function. In the Sifre Deuteronomy, an early-third-century work from Palestine, God's finger is a "metatron to MOSES and showed him the whole land of Israel" (32:49). The Genesis Rabbah says "the voice of God was made a metatron over the waters" (5:4).

According to the book of Enoch, Metatron originally was the human prophet ENOCH, who is so righteous that God transforms him directly into an angel. Enoch had been a scribe, and as Metatron he continues as a heavenly scribe, residing in the seventh heaven where he logs all celestial and earthly events. The Zohar says that Enoch was able to be transformed into Metatron because the divine spark lost by Adam in the Fall entered Enoch. Since mortals cannot contain the divine spark of perfection, it was then necessary for God to take Enoch into heaven and turn him into an angel.

3 Enoch gives a detailed description of the transformation of Enoch into Metatron. God sends the angel Anapiel to bring Enoch to heaven on the wings of the Shekinah. But as soon as he reaches the heavenly heights the holy angels who attend the throne of God—the OPHANIM, SERAPHIM, CHERUBIM, THRONES, and the ministers of consuming fire—smell his human odor 365,000 myriads of PARASANGS away. They ask God why a human being has been brought up to heaven. God says that due to the corruption of mankind he has removed his Shekinah from their midst but Enoch is righteous and worth all the rest of the people.

In heaven Enoch is transformed into fire. Metatron describes the transformation:

at once my flesh turned to flame, my sinews to blazing fire, my bones to juniper coals, my eyelashes to lightning flashes, my eyeballs to fiery torches, the hairs of my head to hot flames, all my limbs to wings of burning fire, and the substance of my body to blazing fire. On my right—those who cleave flames of fire—on my left—burning brands—round about me swept wind, tempest, and storm; and the roar of earthquake upon earthquake was before and behind me. (15:1–2)

God places his hand on Enoch and gives him 1,365,000 blessings. Enoch becomes enlarged and increases in size until he reaches the world in length and breadth. He grows 72 wings, 36 on each side, and each single wing covers the entire world. Metatron is given 365,000 eyes, and each eye is like the Great Light. He is given a brilliant robe and a crown of 49 stones each like the orb of the sun and that shine into the four quarters of heaven.

There is no splendor, brilliance, brightness or beauty that God does not bestow upon Metatron: wisdom, power, all the virtues, and 300,000 gates each of understanding, prudence, life, grace and favor, love, Torah, humility, sustenance, mercy, and reverence. He is given to know all the mysteries, including the thoughts of people before they have them.

God names Metatron "the Lesser Yahweh" before the entire heavenly court and proclaims, "My name is in him." Metatron is set above all angels to serve the throne of glory; he has the privilege of accessing God behind the curtain of mystery that surrounds him. But when scholars on earth object to his status as a second power in heaven, God reduces his stature by having him lashed with a whip of fire by the angel Anapiel.

In 3 Enoch Metatron serves as the heavenly guide to Rabbi Ishmael.

In the Visions of Ezekiel, a composite work probably dating from the fourth century C.E., Metatron is identified with Michael and also with the DYNAMEIS, an order of angels.

Metatron has numerous alternative names; from 70 to more than 100 are mentioned in various texts. The following are 93 names given in 3 Enoch:

Yahoel Yah	Yoppiel	Apapel
Margayel	Geyorel	Tanduel
Tatnadiel	Tatriel	Tabtabiel
Ozahyah	Zahzahyah	Ebed
Zebuliel	Sapsapiel	Sopriel
Paspasiel	Senigron	Sarpupirin
Mitatron	Sigron	Adrigon
Astas	Saqpas	Saqpus

Mikon	Miton	Ruah Pisqonit
Atatyah	Asasyah	Zazzazyah
Paspasyah	Mesamyah	Masmasyah
Absannis	Mebargas	Bardas
Mekarkar	Maspad	Tasgas
Tasbas	Metarpits	Paspisahu
Besihi	Itmon	Pisqon
Sapsapyah	Zerah Zerahyah	Ababyah
Habhabyah	Pepatpalyah	Rakrakyah
Hashasyah	Taptapyah	Tamtamyah
Sahsahyah	Araryah	Alalyah
Zazruyah	Aramyah	Sebar Suhasyah
Razrazyah	Tahsanyah	Sasrasyah
Sabsebibyah	Qeliqalyah	Hahhahyah
Warwahyah	Zakzakyah	Titrisyah
Sewiryah	Zehapnuryah	Zazayah
Galrazyah	Melakmelapyah	Attaryah
Perisyah	Amqaqyah	Salsalyah
Sabsabyah	Geit Zeityah	Geityay
Perisperisyah	Sepat Sepatyah	Hasamyah
Sar Saryah	Gebir Geburyah	Gurtaryah
Ziwa Rabba	Naar Neeman	Lesser Yhvh
Rabrakiel	Neamiel	Seganzagel, Prince of Wisdom

FURTHER READING

Barker, Margaret. *The Great Angel: A Study of Israel's Second God.* Louisville, Ky.: Westminster/John Knox Press, 1992.

Charlesworth, James H., ed. *The Old Testament Pseudepigrapha.* Vols. 1 and 2. New York: Doubleday, 1983, 1985.

Margolies, Morris B. *A Gathering of Angels.* New York: Ballantine Books, 1994.

Scholem, Gershom. *Kabbalah.* New York: Dorset Press, 1987. First published 1974.

mezuzot

Biblical inscriptions attached to doorposts, which in the Middle Ages acquired great power as a Jewish AMULET protecting against DEMONS.

According to historian Joshua Trachtenberg, the mezuzah (singular) descended from a primitive charm, which rabbinic leaders imparted with religious significance, based on Deuteronomy 6:9: "And you shall write them on the doorposts of your house and on your gates." The mezuzah was inscribed with the verses Deuteronomy 6:4–19 and 11:13–20—the delivery of the commandments from the one and only God, and his instructions to obey them—to remind Jews of the principle of monotheism. By the Middle Ages the people clearly preferred it as an amulet. So powerful was the mezuzah in its ability to keep demons away that gentiles and Jews alike used it. It was believed also to prevent premature death. Many homes had mezuzot in every room. People also carried small mezuzot as personal protective charms.

Strict procedures were set forth for the making of a mezuzah. It was to be written on deer parchment according to an amulet table in the SEFER RAZIEL and under certain astrological and angelic influences. One set of 10th century instructions were: "It is to be written only on Monday, in the fifth hour, over which the sun and the angel Raphael preside, or on Thursday, in the fourth hour, presided over by Venus and the angel Anael."

Mezuzot were encapsulated in cases. While it was forbidden to alter the face of the mezuzah, it was permissible to write on the back of the parchment. One popular medieval addition was the name Shaddai, held to be especially powerful in repelling demons. Small windows were cut in the backs of the mezuzot cases so that the name Shaddai would show. Other additions were names of God, other Bible verses, NAMES of angels, and magical symbols. Frequently named angels were Michael, Gabriel, Azriel, Zadkiel, Sarfiel, Raphael, Anael, Uriel, Yofiel, and Hasdiel.

Mezuzot are still in use as both a religious object and an amulet.

FURTHER READING

Trachtenberg, Joshua. *Jewish Magic and Superstition: A Study in Folk Religion.* New York: Berhman's Jewish Book House, 1939.

Michael

The most prominent and greatest angel in Christian, Jewish, and Islamic lore. Michael means in Hebrew "who is like God" or "who is as God." Michael is Chaldean in origin. In ANGELOLOGIES, his chief roles are many: he is warrior, priest, protector, healer, guardian. He holds numerous offices in heaven: he is chief of the VIRTUES and ARCHANGELS, one of the ANGELS OF THE PRESENCE, a PRINCE OF LIGHT, ANGEL OF TRUTH, and angel of repentance, righteousness, mercy, and salvation. Some of his roles overlap with those of other great archangels, Uriel, Gabriel, and Raphael; of the four, he is the primary aspect of the ANGEL OF THE LORD. Michael also shares similarities with Metatron and Melchizedek. He also has duties as the ANGEL OF DEATH.

Biblical References to Michael

Michael is mentioned by name in the Old Testament books of DANIEL and the New Testament books of Jude and REVELATION. In Daniel, he is the GUARDIAN ANGEL or PRINCE of the people of God [Israel]. In Daniel 10:13, Michael is named and described as "one of the chief princes, and in 10:21, "one having the appearance of a man" tells Daniel "there is none who contends by my side except Michael, your prince." In Daniel 12:1, the prophecy of "the time of the end" states that:

> At that time shall arise Michael, the great prince who has charge of your people. And there shall be a time of trouble, such as never has been since there was a nation till that time; but at that time your people shall be delivered, every one whose name shall be found written in the book.

This refers to the Israelites' departure from Egypt, led by MOSES and guided by a pillar of cloud during the day and a pillar of fire at night, as told in the book of Exodus. In Exodus 23:20, God promises to send his angel before them. Though Michael is not named here, it is widely interpreted that he is that angel.

Jude 1:8 makes a reference to the archangel Michael contending with Satan over the body of MOSES. According to Jewish lore, Michael became angry at Satan's contention that Moses was a murderer and therefore was not worthy of burial. Michael says to Satan, "The Lord rebuke you."

In REVELATION 12:7–12, Michael and his legions battle Satan and his forces, and defeat them; they are thrown down.

Numerous other biblical references to "the Angel of Yahweh" and "the Angel of the Lord" are interpreted as meaning Michael. In ZECHARIAH 3:1–2, an Angel of the Lord who is interpreted as Michael confronts Satan before God and the high priest Joshua, and he serves as guide to Zechariah in his vision.

Michael in Other Texts and Lore

Numerous references in apocryphal writings to the Angel of the Lord and to unnamed but important angels are widely interpreted to be Michael. In the Slavonic Life of ADAM AND EVE, he prays for the couple after their fall. In 2 ENOCH he is a chief and captain of angels; in 3 Enoch, he is called the Great Prince who is in charge of the seventh HEAVEN. In 1 Enoch he joins Gabriel and Surufel (Suriel/Uriel) in petitioning God to take action against the WATCHERS.

The QUMRAN TEXT 4Q529 is a visionary recital by Michael on his journey to the highest heaven; Gabriel serves as mystic guide and interpreter of the vision. Michael then descends to lower angels to report what he has seen. He tells them that in the highest heaven he beheld troops of fire and nine mountains. Gabriel appeared and told him that a city (interpreted to be the heavenly Jerusalem) will be built for the Name of the Great One (the Lord), in whose presence no evil shall be committed.

In the Midrash Konen, Michael offers sacrifices on an altar in the heavenly Temple of Jerusalem in Zebhul, the fourth heaven.

In Jewish legend the two primeval monsters, Leviathan and Behemoth, will murder each other, but variations of the story predict that God will send Michael and Gabriel against both creatures, and that when they fail to dispatch either, God will shoulder the task Himself.

Some midrashim state that God commands the archangel Michael to "bring me dust from my sanctuary" to make Adam. Others say God disdains to fetch Adam's dust himself and sends an angel instead, either Michael to Mount Moriah or Gabriel to the world's

Michael subduing Satan

Michael, from Eastern Orthodox Church, Romania (Author's collection)

four corners. Nevertheless earth opposed the angels, knowing she will be cursed on Adam's account, and God stretches forth his own hand to gather it.

When Cain kills Abel, some midrashim say that when he tries to bury the corpse earth spews it up again and cries, "I will receive no other body until the clay that was fashioned into Adam has been restored to me!" At this Cain flees, and Michael, Gabriel, Uriel, and Raphael place the corpse upon a rock, where it remains many years without corrupting. When Adam dies, these same archangels bury both bodies at Hebron side by side, in the very field from which God had taken Adam's dust.

The midrashim say that the FALLEN ANGELS Azael and Semyaza (see WATCHERS) cause such wickedness on earth among the Canaanites that the four archangels tell God, and God sends Raphael to bind

Azael hand and foot, heaping jagged rocks over him in the dark Cave of Dudael, where he now abides until the Last Days. Gabriel destroys the Fallen Ones by inciting them to civil war. Michael chains Semyaza and his fellows in other dark caves for 70 generations. Uriel becomes the messenger of salvation who visit NOAH.

One midrash said that when JACOB and Esau are in Rebekah's womb and fight, that Michael intervenes on Jacob's behalf and saves him from death. Samael intervenes on behalf of Esau. Rabbinic lore says that Gabriel and Michael were witnesses to the contract in which Esau sold Jacob his birthright.

The Testament of ABRAHAM relates that when Michael comes to fetch Abraham's soul, the patriarch boldly insists on seeing the whole world. God commands Michael to let Abraham ride across the heavens in a chariot drawn by CHERUBIM, and so his wish is fulfilled, yet Abraham is still reluctant to die. God then sends the Angel of Death disguised as a fair youth, and when his true aspect is revealed Abraham faints in horror. Death draws out Abraham's soul through his fingers. Michael wraps it in a divinely woven kerchief and conveys it to heaven.

The Yalqut Genesis and the Pirqe Rabbi Eliezer say that it is Michael who fights with Jacob at Peniel. When God asks Michael, "What have you done to my firstborn son? Michael answers, "I shrank a sinew in your honor." God says, "It is good. Henceforth, until the end of time, you shall have charge of Israel and his posterity! For the prince of angels should guard the prince of men; fire should guard fire, and head should guard head!"

Hebrew midrashim and folklore sources tell that when Jacob's daughter Dinah is raped by the Canaanite Sechem, she gives birth to a daughter. Her brothers wishes to kill the child but Jacob restrains them and puts a silver disk about her neck, laying her underneath a thornbush (hence her name "Asenath" for the bush). Michael, in the shape of an eagle, takes off with Asenath to Egypt and leaves her beside God's altar, where a priest finds her and brings her up. Many years later when Joseph saves Egypt from famine, he makes a trip throughout Egypt and the women throw him tokens of gratitude. Asenath throws him her silver disk and he recognizes it. Knowing she must be his own niece, he marries her.

Michael in Christian Lore

Christianity recognizes Michael as the Guardian Angel of the Hebrew nation, and the angel who wages ceaseless war against the forces of Satan. He is the special defender of Christians (and particularly Catholics) and the Catholic Church. Satan trembles at the mere mention of his name, and all the angels of heaven bow down before him in obedience. Michael inspires fidelity to God. St. Francis de Sales wrote that veneration of Michael is the greatest remedy against despising the rights of God, insubordination, skepticism, and infidelity.

In Catholic devotion, there is no greater angel than Michael, who is canonized as a saint. The Catholic Church refers to him as "Prince of the heavenly hosts." Churches were built and dedicated to him from the fifth century on. So intense was adoration of Michael that many devotional cults sprang up all over Europe, peaking in popularity in the late Middle Ages. Devotion to Michael (as well as to Gabriel and Raphael) is still carried out by Catholic DEVOTIONAL CULTS and in prayer and Mass.

At Mass, Michael presides over the worship of adoration to the Most High, and he sends to God the prayers of the faithful, symbolized by the smoke from incense. The prayer to St. Michael asking him to defend Christians in battle is a condensed form of the general exorcism against Satan and evil spirits composed by Pope Leo XIII.

One of Michael's important duties is guiding the souls of the newly departed to the afterlife. In this capacity, he resembles the Greek/Roman god Hermes/Mercury and the Egyptian god Thoth. (See PSYCHOPOMPOI.) Michael weighs the souls for righteousness. He is associated with benevolent aspects of the Angel of Death and has the ability to shapeshift when he comes to take a soul away (as in the case of Abraham). In lore, Michael is the angel designated to appear to MARY to announce her death. Michael also guards the gates of purgatory and has pity on the souls therein. Legends tells of prayers made to Michael for souls in purgatory; he appears and takes them into heaven.

Michael shares with Raphael special healing duties, a function naturally associated with him as protector of the general welfare. (See descriptions of some of his apparitions below.) Michael was considered the great heavenly physician at Constantinople, and he is credited with banishing a pestilence in Rome during the days of St. Gregory the Great.

Michael has two feast days: May 8, which commemorates the dedication of a basilica in honor of him on the Salarian Way about six miles outside of Rome; and September 29, known as Michaelmas. He is the patron saint of grocers, mariners, paratroopers, police, and sickness.

In Christian art, Michael is usually portrayed in warrior garb, holding a sword and scales and trampling Satan.

Apparitions of Michael
Numerous apparitions of Michael have been reported over the centuries, especially in the first millennium of

Christianity as he supplanted pagan gods of protection, battle, and healing. These apparitions usually occurred on or near mountaintops or rocky outcrops, which became the sites of healing springs and miracles. Shrines, churches, and even great abbeys were built at these places and were dedicated to Michael. They have attracted countless pilgrims.

Some of the most famous Michael sites and their legends are:

MICHAELION, CONSTANTINOPLE
The Michaelion church near Constantinople was built in the fifth century C.E. by the Emperor Constantine because of an apparition of Michael. At the command of Mary, Queen of the Angels, Michael came to the aid of Constantine in his battle against the pagan emperor Maxentius. Constantine built the church for Michael in

Michael slaying the dragon (Author's collection)

gratitude. After its completion, Michael appeared there to the emperor and said, "I am Michael, the chief of the angelic legions of the Lord of hosts, the protector of the Christian religion, who while you were battling against godless tyrants, placed the weapons in your hands."

Miracles attributed to Michael have been reported at the Michaelion over the centuries.

EUSEBIOS, CONSTANTINOPLE

The church of Michael at Eusebios, Constantinople, acquired its importance from an apparition of Michael that occurred during the reign of Emperor Michael III (842–867) under the regency of his mother, Theodora. Since the use of icons had recently been restored in Byzantine worship (see IMAGES OF ANGELS), the story may have served to help reestablish the importance of sacred images.

The story concerns a candlemaker named Marcianus, who was a pious servant of the shrine of Michael. Marcianus was never ill. If he felt the slightest discomfort he would go into the church and immediately recover. On one occasion when he felt poorly he went into the church but took with him a medicinal poultice because doctors had convinced him it was necessary to do so. As he slept that night in the shrine—a customary practice at healing centers—he had a terrible dream vision (see DREAMS AND VISIONS). The doors of the church suddenly flew open and in rushed "a fearful man as out of the heaven, descending on a white and terrible steed." The man dismounted and entered the church, escorted by men dressed in the garb of court officials. The church became filled with a strange unworldly odor.

The mysterious man walked to where Marcianus lay on his cot. He examined him and asked Marcianus about the poultice. He demanded to know who had dared to bring such medicine into his house thus identifying himself as the namesake of the shrine, Michael. Marcianus told him about the doctor who had insisted on the poultice and Michael ordered his assistants to find him. Michael then led Marcianus to an icon of himself, which had a lit candle and small dish of oil beside it. Michael dipped his finger in the oil and made the sign of the cross on Marcianus's forehead. He then got back on his horse and rode off into the sky, the church doors closing by themselves behind him. The next morning, Marcianus had a cross on his forehead, which proved to the deacon the truth of his vision. The deacon learned that the offending doctor had become mysteriously and seriously ill during the night. Marcianus visited the doctor and then brought him on his bed into the church and told him to beg Michael for forgiveness and mercy. He then imitated his own heal-

ing by dipping his finger in the icon oil and drawing a cross on the forehead of the doctor. The doctor was miraculously healed, thus establishing the model for successful healing.

CHONAE, PHRYGIA, ASIA MINOR

The most important center of Michael devotion in the Byzantine world developed in Phrygia in a syncretic mix of pagan, Jewish, and Christian angel cults popular in the early centuries after Christ. The apostles Philip and John came to the town of Colossae (Chairetopa) and prophesied the appearance of Michael there.

Michael caused a medicinal spring to appear; anyone who bathed there and invoked the Blessed Trinity and Michael was said to be cured. The miracles, conversions, and baptisms at the spring aroused the jealousy of the pagan Hellenes. They gathered a mob and dammed two rivers to combine them. The waters were directed onto Colossae and the church at the spring. But Archippus, a God-fearing hermit who had settled at the spring when just a boy, heard the roaring waters and called upon Michael (the Archistrategos) for help.

Michael appeared immediately in a clap of thunder, in the appearance of a pillar of fire reaching from earth to heaven. He told Archippus to leave before he is covered by water. But the sight of the awesome angel caused the hermit to fall on the ground as though lifeless.

Michael then told him to stand firm and witness the power of God. He commanded the waters to stop, and they formed a wall as high as 10 persons. He struck the rock with his staff, which sounded like thunder and shook the entire land. The rock opened. Michael commanded the water, "Funnel yourself into the funnel," and the water funneled into the chasm. Thereafter, the town was called Chonae ("funnels"). Michael promised to guard the place, and the waters were sanctified forever.

MONTE GARGANO, ITALY

Apparitions of Michael appeared to the bishop of Siponto near Monte Gargano in Apulia, near Naples, Italy, during the reign of Pope Gelasius (492–496), leading to the establishment of a healing shrine. Versions of the events, which resemble the Chonae story, date to the eighth and ninth centuries.

One day a bull belonging to a wealthy man named Garganus became lost on a mountainside. After a long search, Garganus found it inside a cave. Irritated at the bull, he shot an arrow at it, but it turned in mid-air "as if breathed upon by the wind" and hit him instead. He went back to the town of Siponto and told the story. The bishop undertook a fast of three days and three nights to learn the cause of this mysterious event.

Michael came to the bishop in a dream and said, "Let it be known to you that it occurred because I willed it. For I am the Archangel Michael, he who always stands in the presence of God. The bishop fasted a second time to be worthy of Michael's aid and presence. He had a second vision.

On the third night, Michael appeared in a dream and identified himself. He said he had intervened because he wished "to dwell in this place on earth and guard all." The next day, the bishop and some towns-folk visited the mountain and found two doors cut into its face.

In another dream, Michael told the bishop that the Sipontini and their allies, the Beneventi, would win in a war against their "heathen" enemies, the Neapoli-tans. The next day, the mountain was full of thunder, lightning, and darkness, which so frightened the Neapolitans that they fled. The locals went up to the doors in the side of the mountain and entered a cave where they found traces of the presence of Michael: "a small trace, as if the footstep of a man struck there in the marble." A shrine was begun there and was called "the place of the footprints."

The shrine was completed after a visit by Michael to the bishop. The bishop was uncertain how to con-secrate the chapel and was told by Michael in another vision not to consecrate it at all. Michael told him, "I myself have put it in order and conse-crated it. You need only come and approach with your entreaties since I am attending as master in that place." Michael told him to return the next day and he would show the townspeople how the place would guide them.

The bishop did as instructed and found a chapel ready made and carved out of the living rock "as if by the hands of the archangel." He knew the angel had made it because it was too irregular, rough, and full of corners and angles to have been made by human hands. A red cloak covered the altar. A spring erupted nearby and became known for its healing properties.

The site attracted hordes of pilgrims. In the seventh century, the shrine was at a peak of popularity, due in part to a Lombard victory over the Saracens in 663 that was attributed to the help of Michael. According to lore, the Lombards, who went to the shrine to pay thanks for their victory, found the imprint of Michael's foot near the south door of the temple.

ST. MICHAEL'S MOUNT, ENGLAND

In 495 in Cornwall, England, fishermen saw Michael standing on a ledge of rock atop a small mount off the coast near Penzance. St. Michael's Mount, as it became known, was already an important trading market and port. It took on new significance with its association with Michael and became a hallowed place. In the sixth century it was visited by St. Cadoc, one of the principal saints of Wales. According to legend, the saint needed water for his traveling party, and he struck his staff into the rock, whereupon water sprang forth.

A Benedictine priory was built atop St. Michael's Mount in 1135 by Bernard Le Bec. The community was enriched by the earls of Cornwall. But on September 11, 1275, an earthquake destroyed the church. It was rebuilt in the 14th century. Between 1349 and 1362, the religious community was nearly wiped out by the Black Plague. In 1649, the property passed into private hands, the St. Aubyn family.

From the Middle Ages, St. Michael's Mount was a favorite pilgrimage. Pilgrims came to seek answers to prayer, discharge vows, do penance, and seek healing. Many were spurred by the incentive that all those who came to St. Michael's Mount with alms and oblations would receive an indulgence of one-third of their penance. The indulgence was credited to Pope Gregory VII, though probably it was a tradition started by the monks.

A goal of many pilgrims was to prove their faith by sitting on "St. Michael's chair," a craggy spot with a precipitous drop to the sea. Monks built a stone lantern chair atop the church tower, not only to serve as a lighthouse but also perhaps as a more suitable sub-stitute for the unsafe outcropping. According to lore, the first of a married couple to sit on the chair will gain mastery in married life.

Pilgrims also were attracted to the jawbone relic of Apollonia, a martyr and patron against toothaches.

Many miracles of healing were reported at St. Michael's Mount and credited to the intercession of Michael.

The former priory is now a private residence, but much of the priory is open to public tours. The church is active and is free from episcopal jurisdiction. A stone pillar marks the spot where Michael appeared. When the tide is low, St. Michael's Mount can be accessed on foot across a sand bar.

MONT ST. MICHEL, FRANCE

In France, a similar but grander Benedictine abbey was built on Mont St. Michel, a huge quasi-island rock 1 kilometer wide and 80 feet high, off the Normandy coast. Its isolation made it a natural locale for pagan cults and hermits.

The story of Michael's apparitions bears similarities to the Monte Gargano lore, and, in fact, it serves as a continuation of that story line.

In 708, Michael appeared three times in dream visions to St. Aubert, bishop of Avranches (a nearby

The abbey of Mont St. Michel, Normandy, France (Author's collection)

town), and instructed him to build a chapel there. The bishop did not believe Michael and asked him to prove his identity. The angel pushed his finger through the bishop's skull. The bishop asked for more proof. Michael told him a stolen bull would be found at the top of the rock. It was, but still Aubert was skeptical. Michael told him to send two messengers to Monte Gargano, where they would be given the red cloak that Michael wore when he appeared there and had left upon the altar, as well as a fragment of the altar on which he had set his foot. The messengers were sent and they returned with the promised items. Convinced at last, Aubert founded an oratory.

In 966 an abbey was founded there by Richard I, duke of Normandy. Construction of the church began in 1020 and was finished in 1136. By the 12th century, Mont St. Michel was called the "City of Books" and was a great center of learning. Many of the manuscripts kept by the monks were lost during the French Revolution when the monks were expelled. In the late 18th and early 19th centuries, the abbey was used as a prison.

Between 1155 and 1424, Mont St. Michel had jurisdiction over St. Michael's Mount in Cornwall.

Access to the abbey was treacherous until the late 19th century. A slim land bridge connected the rock to the mainland. But travelers could be taken unawares by swift and terrible tides, and by constantly shifting quicksands. A causeway was built in 1879.

Mont St. Michel is now one of France's greatest tourist attractions. The spiraling road up to the abbey once walked by pilgrims is now lined on both sides by shops and restaurants. Inside the entrance to the abbey is a large marble frieze depicting Michael pushing his finger through the skull of the dreaming Aubert.

SPAIN

In Spain, where the cult of Michael peaked in popularity in about the 13th century, one of the best-known apparitions is the 1455 appearance to a shepherd about halfway between Navagamella and Fresnedillas, in the foothills of the Sierra de Guadarrama. The sighting was investigated in 1520, when some of the witnesses were still alive, and also in 1617.

According to testimony, Michael appeared late one afternoon in 1455 on a holm-oak tree and a rockrose plant to shepherd Miguel Sanchez. Michael told the shepherd not to be frightened, but to tell others that a shrine should be erected on the site and a brotherhood founded, both in honor of the angelic messengers. Sanchez protested that no one would believe him, but Michael insisted that he tell his employer. "I will make them believe you so they build a shrine here to the holy angels," he said. He then made an imprint of his hand on the tree.

However, Sanchez did not tell the story. A few days passed, and one morning he awakened crippled. His legs were folded in a bizarre manner so that the backs of his calves touched his thighs and his heels touched his buttocks. His employer, Pedro Garcia de Ayuso, tried unsuccessfully to cure him with herbs and oils. At last Sanchez told of his vision. Garcia de Ayuso consulted with authorities, and they carried the shepherd to the site of the apparition. There they found the handprint on the tree trunk. It was considered proof, and plans were made immediately for construction of a chapel. A mass was said there for the shepherd's health; when it was completed, he was cured and he stood up. Sanchez was named keeper of the shrine.

Michael in Muslim Lore

The Muslims relate that the angels Gabriel, Michael, Israfil, and Azrael bring dust from the four corners of the world, and with it Allah creates the body of Adam; to form his head and heart, however, Allah chooses dust from a site at Mecca, where the Holy Ka'aba later rises. Mecca is the navel of the earth for Muslims, as Mount Moriah is for the Hebrews, and Delphi for the Greeks.

Michael's wings are emerald green and covered with saffron hairs. Each hair contains a million faces who speak a million dialects, all imploring the pardon of Allah. When Michael cries over the sins of the faithful, his tears create CHERUBIM.

See RUDOLF STEINER.

FURTHER READING

Christian, William C. Jr. *Apparitions in Late Medieval and Renaissance Spain.* Princeton, N.J.: Princeton University Press, 1981.

Eisenman, Robert, and Michael Wise. *The Dead Sea Scrolls Uncovered.* London: Element Books, 1992.

Graves, Robert, and Raphael Patai. *Hebrew Myths.* New York: Doubleday Anchor, 1964.

Peers, Glenn. *Subtle Bodies: Representing Angels in Byzantium.* Berkeley, Calif.: University of California Press, 2001.

Schroff, Lois. *The Archangel Michael.* Herndon, Va.: Newlight Books, 1990.

Mihr (Miher, Mihir, Mithra)

In ZOROASTRIANISM, angel of divine mercy, friendship, love, and governor of September. According to Persian lore, Mihr and the angel Sorush will screen souls on Judgment Day. The angels will stand on a bridge called *al Sirat*, which is no wider than a hair and is sharper than the edge of a sword. They will examine every soul seeking to cross the bridge. Mihr will weigh the souls actions. If deemed worthy he will allow the soul to pass to paradise. Unworthy souls will be thrown into HELL by Sorush, the angel of divine justice.

Milton, John (1608–1674)

English poet. John Milton is best known for his epic poem *Paradise Lost*, the story of Lucifer's rebellion and the Fall. It is considered the greatest epic poem in the

Lucifer reigning over the souls of sinners (John Baptist Medina for *Paradise Lost*, 1688)

English language. He also wrote various political and religious treatises, served in Cromwell's Commonwealth, and fought with both the established Church of England and its reformers.

Life

Milton was born in London in 1608 to a family of comfortable circumstances. His father was a scrivener—a law writer—and a composer of music. Milton attended Christ's College in Cambridge, studying Latin, Greek, and the other classics with the intent of becoming a Puritan minister. He composed poems in Latin, Italian, and English.

By the time he finished college, Milton had abandoned the idea of the ministry, and instead he spent six years at home writing poetry and continuing his studies. In 1635 the family moved to Horton, Buckinghamshire. Milton traveled to Europe, and he met the famous astronomer Galileo Galilei in Florence. Galileo inspired his later work, *Areopagitica* (1644), which speaks against censorship.

Upon his return to London in 1639, Milton established a small school. When the Civil War broke out in 1642, he ceased writing poetry and defended the Puritan cause, writing pamphlets against episcopacy and divorce and in favor of freedom of the press and regicide. After the execution of King Charles I in 1649, Milton earned a Latin secretaryship in Oliver Cromwell's government. But in 1651 he went blind and had to depend on secretaries in order to work.

In 1660 Milton was arrested as a defender of the Commonwealth, but he was released after a short stay in prison. His fortunes declined. By this time, he was married to his third wife, Elizabeth Minshull; all of his marriages were unhappy.

Despite his blindness, Milton continued to compose poetry. He died on November 8, 1674, of "gout struck in," and he was buried in Chalfont, St. Giles, Buckinghamshire, next to his father.

Works

Milton believed in the reality of angels, who figured as prominently in the literature of his time as the mythical gods. One of his earliest poems composed at college, "Ode on the Morning of Christ's Nativity," describes the angels announcing Christ's birth as harbingers of light bringing an end to the darkness of sin and evil—an ironic twist considering that Lucifer's name means "bearer of light." The angels also fill the world with song and harmony, providing the medieval philosophers' "music of the spheres."

Paradise Lost contains his fullest descriptions of angels and their circumstances. Milton wrote his epic poem after the Restoration of King Charles II to the English throne, a period in which Milton's total blindness and his political ties to the Commonwealth left him with little to do but write the verse he had long planned. His ambition was to compose an epic poem rivaling the works of great classical writers such as Homer and Virgil. The first edition of *Paradise Lost* in 1667 filled 10 volumes; a second edition in 1674 was 12 volumes long. Difficult to read because of its style and syntax, the poem nonetheless left its mark on literary history, and it influenced such Romantic poets as WILLIAM BLAKE and Percy Bysshe Shelley.

The poem presents a sympathetic picture of Lucifer. It recounts his rebellion and the rapture of ADAM AND EVE in the Garden of Eden and their eventual shame and expulsion. Cast out of heaven, Lucifer awakens on a burning lake in HELL, his followers in shock around him.

Milton explains in great detail—some of it based on Judeo-Christian literature and some from his own imagination—the characteristics and details of the angels, the accounts of the great battles between Lucifer's armies and the followers of God, the total beauty of Eden and man's fall from grace. Most of the discourse on the angels occurs as a conversation between Adam and the archangel Raphael who had been sent by God to warn Adam and Eve of the devil's temptations. Eve prepares a feast for Adam and Raphael, and they talk of the Fall, God's grace, and what angels are like.

Raphael tells Adam that angels are the link between humans and God: "pure, Intelligential substances" rather than rational beings. They are intuitive, with great knowledge that encompasses reason. In many ways, particularly physically, angels resemble man, but their bodies are made of ether, which Milton identifies as the "fifth element": nonsolid with a liquid texture. As such they are pure spirit compared to man, but "natural" to God, since God created them.

Angels have all five of man's senses, but they experience taste, smell, sight, hearing, and touch with their whole beings and not through particular organs. They eat, enjoy music, and delight in tastes, smells, and sounds, and they even have sexual intercourse—an angelic talent original to Milton.

When Adam asks Raphael whether the angels can enjoy the sexual raptures he has experienced with Eve, Raphael answers blushingly:

> To whom the Angel, with a smile that glowed
> Celestial rosy red, love's proper hue,
> Answered: "Let it suffice thee that thou know'st
> Us happy, and without love no happiness.

Whatever pure thou in the body enjoy'st
(And pure thou wert created) we enjoy
In eminence, and obstacle find none
Of membrane, joint or limb, exclusive bars;
Easier than air with air, or spirits embrace,
Total they mix, union of pure with pure
Desiring; nor restrained conveyance need
As flesh to mix with flesh, or soul with soul."

(Book VIII: 618–629)

Angels cannot be in more than one place at the same time, but they travel at unimaginable speeds. They also are able to assume any size or shape and either gender. Angels live on planets and have been called stars. They exist as agents of divine providence, ministering to man on God's behalf or as agents of perversion if they have followed Lucifer.

But most of all, angels are winged, shining, and beautiful. In Book V, verses 277–284, Milton describes Raphael as he descends into the Garden:

A Seraph winged: six wings he wore, to shade
His lineaments divine; the pair that clad
Each shoulder broad, came mantling o'er his breast
With regal ornament; the middle pair
Girt like a starry zone his waist, and round
Skirted his loins and thighs with downy gold
And colors dipped in Heaven; the third his feet
Shadowed from either heel with feathered mail
Sky-tinctured grain.

Another characteristic of angels is their invulnerability. Each side inflicts great pain upon the other during the battles of the rebellion, but they do not suffer longer than a moment. In Book VI, verses 326–334, Lucifer marvels at his brief agony:

Then Satan first knew pain,
And writhed him to and fro convolved; so sore
The griding sword with discontinuous wound
Passed through him; but the ethereal substance closed
Not long divisible, and from the gash
A stream of nectarous humor issuing flowed
Sanguine, such as celestial spirits may bleed,
And all his armor stained, erewhile so bright.

Christian writings organized the angels in hierarchies as follows:

Seraphim	Dominions	Principalities
Cherubim	Virtues	Archangels
Thrones	Powers	Angels

Milton rejects these rankings, organizing the angels into three degrees or choirs. Lucifer often refers to the above-mentioned hierarchies when speaking of his minions; the titles are more expressions of Lucifer's power and his exercise of authority than actual rankings. Milton also describes four leading angels as archangels who rule the four corners of the world:

Michael: the first in command of God's army
Gabriel: second in command; bearer of annunciation to Mary
Uriel: viceroy of the sun
Raphael: God's chief minister.

Other loyal angels in God's service are:

Abdiel: a seraph whose name means "servant of God." Abdiel alone stands up to Lucifer when he boasts of his victory
Ithuriel: a cherub, "discovery of God"
Uzziel: like Uriel, the "eye of the Lord" and "strength of God"
Zephon: "searcher of secrets"
Zophiel: "spy of God"

See LITERATURE AND ANGELS.

FURTHER READING
Arthos, John. *Dante, Michaelangelo and Milton*. London: Routledge and Kegan Paul, 1963.
Bush, Douglas, ed. *The Portable Milton*. New York: The Viking Press, 1949.
Elledge, Scott, ed. *John Milton: Paradise Lost, An Authoritative Text*. New York: W. W. Norton, 1975.

Miniel

In magical lore, angel invoked to induce love in a reluctant girl and to make and command magic carpets.

ministering angels

An order of angels whose duties and rank vary. Ministering angels usually are placed among the lowest ranks of angels, looking after the routine affairs of daily life on earth. But they also are held to be of the highest rank and are "the hosts of the Lord." Ministering angels also are compared to GUARDIAN ANGELS.

Ministering angels are made of fire, as suggested by Psalm 104:4: "who makest the winds thy messengers, flame and fire thy ministers," and Hebrews 1:7, "And of the angels he saith, Who maketh his angels spirits, and his ministers a flame of fire."

In the Talmud Hagiga, they are born anew every day from the Dinur River, and they sing a hymn of

Angels ascending and descending the ladder in Jacob's dream.
(Gustave Doré)

praise and then perish back into the river. In the Talmud Sanhedrin, ministering angels roast meat and cool wine for Adam in Paradise. The Book of ADAM AND EVE names three ministering angels serving Adam: Aebel, Anush, and Shetel. In the Testament of the Twelve Patriarchs, God sends 70 ministering angels down from his highest HEAVEN to teach languages to the 70 children of NOAH.

In the MERKABAH, ministering angels are infinite in numbers. In 3 ENOCH, they descend from heaven in companies, bands, and cohorts to execute God's will on earth. When humans become corrupted, they protest to God: "Why did you leave the heaven of heavens above, the abode of your glory, the high and exalted throne which is in the height of Arabot [the name of the seventh heaven], and come and lodge with men who worship idols? Now you are on the earth, and the idols are on the earth; what is your business among the idolatrous of earth?" (5:11–12) God immediately removes his presence—the SHEKINAH—and the ministering angels assist its return to heaven.

3 Enoch names Azza (Semyaza), Azael, and Uzza as ministering angels, a status that may have preceded their fall.

According to the Sefer Yetzirah, the primary text of the KABBALAH, ministering angels may be seen physically, whereas all other angels can only be seen prophetically.

In the New Testament, Hebrews 1:1–14 distinguishes the exalted position of Christ compared to angels and underscores the service of ministering angels to the righteous in verse 14: "Are they not all ministering spirits sent forth to serve, for the sake of those who are to obtain salvation?"

In *Occult Philosophy*, AGRIPPA ranks ministers (ministering angels) as the lowest of three celestial tiers. They are committed to the affairs of earth, and they are associated with the four elements.

ORIGEN sees ministering angels as serving the lowly needs of earth while accessing the highest realms of heaven. The idea that ministering spirits might include other supernatural being besides angels is implied in his work *Against Celsus:*

> For we acknowledge that angels are "ministering spirits," and we say that "they are sent forth to minister for them

Ministering angels saving souls (Reprinted courtesy of U.S. Library of Congress)

who shall be heirs of salvation;" and that they ascend, bearing the supplications of men, to the purest of heavenly in the universe, of even to the supercelestial regions purer still; and that they come down from these, conveying to each one, according to his deserts, something enjoined by God to be conferred by them upon those who are to be the recipients of His benefits. Having thus learned to call these beings "angels" from their employments, we find that because they are divine they are sometimes termed "god" in the sacred Scriptures, but not so that we are commanded to honor and worship in the place of God those who minister to us, and bear to us His blessings.

See CELESTIAL HIERARCHIES; MEMUNIM.

Nun experiencing an angel in prayer

Mitatron

In the Re'uyot Yehazqe'el, a Palestinian text in the MERKABAH literature, the secret NAME of the PRINCE (angel) of the third HEAVEN. Mitatron also is named in Peter de Abano's magical work The Heptameron as an angel of the third heaven and a ruler of Wednesday who is invoked from the west. The name Mitatron may be a variation of Metatron.

Mithra (Izad, Mihir, Mihr, Mitra)

Deity who appears in various cosmologies. In Vedic lore, Mithra is a devata or shining god comparable to an angel. In GNOSTICISM he is equated with Metatron. In ZOROASTRIANISM he is one of the 27 or 28 IZADS who surround the great god Ohrmazd. He has 1,000 ears and 10,000 eyes. According to Aryan lore he is a god of light who assigns the souls of the just to their places in HEAVEN.

Moakibat

In Islamic lore, RECORDING ANGELS who write down all a person's activities. Each person has two "al Moakibat" who succeed each other every day.

Mons, angels of

Incident during World War I in which Allied soldiers reportedly were aided by heavenly soldiers and England's patron saint, St. George, mounted on horseback. The visions were not limited to British and French troops. Several captured Germans allegedly asked about the horsemen or the leader on a white horse. Whole battalions apparently retreated in fear. According to some German reports, the soldiers fell back against what appeared to be thousands of troops, not the two small Allied regiments.

The incident occurred during the battle of Mons, Belgium, on August 26–27, 1914. The Allies had only two regiments posted there, while surrounded by the better-equipped Germans. Outmanned and outgunned, the Allies expected to be slaughtered, but, although they suffered numerous losses, the numbers were many fewer than expected. Many in the companies believed their retreat was saved by hundreds of mounted, armored soldiers—spirits of the English victors at the battle of Agincourt in 1415—who came between them and the German army. Others saw or heard St. George, described as a yellow-haired man riding a white charger.

Public interest in the stories was tremendous, despite the fact that they sounded suspiciously like the plot of a fictional story, "The Bowmen," written by novelist Arthur Machen and published in the London *Evening News* barely a month after the battle, on September 29, 1914. In Machen's story, a British soldier, overwhelmed at Mons, recalls a Latin motto he once read on a plate in a vegetarian restaurant. The motto read, *Adsit Anglis Sanctus Georgius,* "May St. George be a present help to the English." No sooner had the desperate soldier invoked the motto than he heard voices roaring the same plea and adding other medieval calls for courage and preservation. The soldier looked beyond his trench and saw long lines of mounted bowmen, who shot swarms of arrows at the advancing Germans. The enemy fell by the thousands, but the German staff found no wounds on their fallen comrades.

Although Machen belatedly took credit as the only source of the angelic stories, claiming they could all be traced to his fictional tale, his protestations could not stem the increasing flood of accounts that God had taken an active stand on behalf of the Allies. Indeed, in his field notes of September 5, Brigadier-General John Charteris of the British Expeditionary Force referred to stories among his men about angelic sightings at Mons—at least three weeks before the publication of Machen's story.

Reports of angelic intervention at Mons died out about October 1914 but revived later the following spring. On April 30, the Roman Catholic newspaper *The Universe* printed an anonymous account from a supposedly reputable Catholic officer about an experience of another officer at Mons. It seemed that this second officer and about 30 of his men were trapped in a trench when they decided to make a run for it rather than be slaughtered by the advancing Germans. Yelling "St. George for England!" the men were met by a large company of bowmen who led them in a charge on the enemy's trenches. Later, a captured German prisoner asked who was the officer seated on a great white horse. The officer who told this story to the first Catholic officer said he did not see St. George but did see the archers. Again, the German dead showed no wounds.

In the May 15, 1915, issue of the parish magazine of All Saints Parish, Clifton, England, a Miss Marrable, daughter of the canon, was reported to have met two officers (although she did not know their names) who claimed they had witnessed the angelic intervention. One officer said that when the angels appeared, the German cavalry horses reared in fright and ran in all directions, no matter how determinedly the riders tried to force their horses to continue the charge.

In the same month, the Spiritualist newspaper *Light* ran a piece recounting a sermon reportedly preached by the Reverend Fielding Ould, vicar of St. Stephen's in St. Alban's. Reverend Ould heard a story from three

sources whom he believed reputable, as follows: A sergeant had often visited a branch of the Young Men's Christian Association, in which hung a picture of St. George slaying the dragon. Later, during the battle of Mons, the sergeant repeated the legend of St. George to his beleaguered men, telling how St. George was the patron saint of England and the war cry of English soldiers for centuries. Facing the advancing Germans, the men shouted "Remember St. George for England!" Shortly the Germans hesitated in their charge, then turned around and fled. One of the prisoners left behind told his captors of the horsemen in armor who led the Allies' charge—and that they could not have been Belgians.

On June 9, 1915, *Bladud, The Bath Society Paper* ran several accounts, always anonymous, of other soldiers who witnessed the same phenomenon. One officer wrote that his soldiers had fled to a place where they could stand against the Germans, even though they expected death. But instead of seeing the advancing German cavalry they saw a troop of angels and the German horses stampeding in terror. A captain in charge of German prisoners said that the Germans felt there was no use in fighting the English, for the Germans had seen angels fighting above and in front of the Allied lines, both at Mons and Ypres. Another group of German prisoners attested that they had surrendered because of the hosts of soldiers in the Allied ranks, but in truth there were only two English and French regiments.

In an interview published August 12, 1915, in the London *Daily Mail,* a wounded lance corporal told that he and his battalion were in retreat from Mons on August 28, 1914. The weather was hot and clear, and the Allied forces were waiting for the Germans to charge. While the corporal was standing guard with some others, an officer ran up to them in great agitation and asked if they'd seen anything. The guards thought he meant German soldiers, but instead the officer took the men to see something in the night sky. There was a strange light in the sky that was distinctly outlined and separate from moonlight. As the men watched, the light became brighter and more clearly defined, revealing three shapes. The one on the center had outstretched wings, and all three wore long, loose golden garments. These spirits hovered above the German lines for about an hour then disappeared.

Phyllis Campbell, a nurse who served behind the lines at Mons, contributed the following to the *Occult Review* in August 1915, a year after the battle. Campbell reported that many of the wounded, particularly the French Catholics, requested pictures of saints and angels to comfort them. Following the retreat at Mons, many of the soldiers were in an exalted state, and one

British soldier, a fusilier from Lancashire, asked for a picture of St. George. The fusilier claimed he had seen St. George on a white horse leading the British troops at Vitry-le-François. Another soldier, injured in the leg, corroborated the fusilier's claims and said that St. George had led the charge at Vitry with his sword upraised. French troops maintained the figure was St. Michael or JOAN OF ARC. Campbell claimed to hear the story again later from a priest, two officers, and three Irish soldiers.

In her booklet *Back of the Front,* Miss Campbell reported that many severely wounded soldiers, who should have been screaming in pain, were strangely calm, saying that they'd seen a great man on a white horse fighting on their behalf. Miss Campbell claimed that she'd submitted her accounts of the visions at Mons to the *Occult Review* before Machen's story appeared in late September 1914, but no record exists of any submission.

In a letter written by an unnamed lieutenant colonel to Machen, which ran in the *Daily Mail* September 14,

1915 (the lieutenant colonel's name was supposedly known to editors of the *Daily Mail* but withheld), perhaps the most believable account appeared about the angelic archers. The officer wrote that after the battle of Le Cateau on August 26, 1914, he and two other officers were riding along the column of their division during the night of August 27. Although weary, the officer did not believe that he nor the others had lost their mental faculties. While talking and joking to keep awake, the lieutenant colonel became conscious of two large bodies of cavalry riding in squadrons in the fields on both sides of the road. The lieutenant colonel did not remark on the horsemen but watched them for about 20 minutes. They marched in step with his horse and were going in the same direction.

The other two officers had also stopped talking, and at last one of them asked the lieutenant colonel if he'd seen anything in the fields. All three saw the same sight and determined to take a small party out to reconnoiter. But as soon as the men approached the cavalry, the night grew darker and the horsemen disap-

Angels at the Battle of Mons

peared. The lieutenant colonel admitted to exhaustion, but he said that several witnessed the same phenomenon, a situation he believed unlikely due simply to fatigue.

On August 24, 1915, the *Daily Mail* printed what it believed was the first account of angels at Mons that could be substantiated by a named witness. Private Robert Cleaver, of the First Cheshire Regiment, supposedly signed an affidavit in the presence of a G. S. Hazlehurst stating that he had seen the angels of Mons with his own eyes. Private Cleaver described the angels as a flash of light that confused the German cavalry and caused their lines to crumble. Unfortunately, when Hazlehurst checked with the headquarters of the Regiment at Salisbury, he found that Private Cleaver had not joined the regiment until August 22, 1914, and did not post out to France until September 6. He therefore never fought at Mons.

Private Cleaver's story ran along similar lines to previously reported accounts about mysterious clouds and lights. As early as February 14, 1915, *Light* had run an account by another unnamed officer about the strange cloud that rose up between the German and English lines. In the May 5 *Light,* a General N. stated that while his rearguard was under heavy German fire, a luminous cloud or bright light appeared between the armies. Within the cloud he saw moving shapes, but he could not tell if they were figures. Again the German horses reared and fled, saving the English from certain death.

The paper reported that another young officer—still anonymous—saw the cloud as well, convincing him that the Allies were destined for eventual victory. In a fourth story, a soldier saw a golden cloud appear between the English and German lines, enabling him to save a child who was trapped by the gunfire. In this case the cloud was accompanied by a man on a big horse, similar to the reports of St. George.

Other accounts of divine intervention included the appearance of a great cloud as well, either black or luminous, which came between the Allies and the Germans. Some of these clouds appeared to have bright beings within them. Some witnesses reported seeing true angels, with wings and flowing robes, either coming between the two sides or fighting beside or above the British and French. Other reports told of the "Comrade in White," a figure who walked the battlefields in complete calm and safety to bring aid and comfort. In some accounts the comrade was identified as Jesus Christ.

In the May 15, 1915, *Light,* a Mrs. F. H. Fitzgerald Beale of Mountmellick, Ireland, wrote that a soldier of the Dublin Fusiliers, who had returned home wounded, had seen a black cloud at Mons. The cloud was so thick that it shielded the English lines completely. Mrs. Beale also reported that every soldier who had returned home had told her that a crucifix placed on a home or building was always saved even if everything around it burned.

For some, aid and comfort did not come with a host of angels but through the offices of one man. In the June 9, 1915, issue of *Bladud* referred to above, a Dr. R. F. Horton wrote that several wounded soldiers had told him of a "Comrade in White" who walked the battlefields, even during shelling, to rescue and heal the injured. Then a Miss Stoughton wrote about the experience of her sister, who was an army nurse. The nurse said many soldiers had related seeing the "Comrade in White," whom they believed to be the Lord Himself.

Perhaps the most moving story was printed in the June 1915 issue of *Life and Work* magazine. An unnamed soldier wrote that after an especially heated battle a man in white walked among the wounded completely unfazed by sniper fire and shells. He seemed to be everywhere at once. The soldier said that later that day he was shot in both legs while charging the German trenches, and lay in a shell-hole until after dark. As night fell, he heard quiet, firm footsteps and saw the gleam of the man's white clothing. The Germans opened fire, but the stranger stretched out his arms in entreaty and then bent over and lifted the injured soldier. The soldier said he must have fainted, for when he awoke he had been carried to a little cave by a stream. The man was tenderly washing his wounds.

Then the soldier slept; when he awoke, he looked to see what he could do to help his rescuer. He found him kneeling in prayer, and was surprised to see that his hands were injured and bleeding. The man said they were old wounds that had been bothering him lately. When the soldier saw that the man's feet were bleeding as well, he realized with a shock that he had been saved by Christ.

In August 1915, Machen published a compendium of his war tales entitled *The Bowmen and Other Legends of the War.* In the introduction, Machen carefully explained the development of the Angels at Mons as his own fiction. A little later, Harold Begbie published *On the Side of the Angels: The Story of the Angels at Mons—An Answer to 'The Bowmen.'* Begbie collected all the accounts he could find and tried to show that no matter whether the visions were true or false they were not simply creations of Machen.

But the strangest twist on the stories of Mons came from the German side in an article published by the London *Daily News* on February 17, 1930. According to a colonel Friedrich Herzenwirth, a former member of the Imperial German Intelligence Service, the soldiers actually witnessed visions of soldiers and angels. But instead of heavenly intervention the images were movies projected upon the foggy white cloudbanks over Belgium. Colonel Herzenwirth said the object of the mission was to create mass hysteria and terror. He admitted that if the kaiser's officers had foreseen that the visions would strengthen the Allies' resolve, rather than weaken it, they would have tried other propaganda. He believed some of the British forces realized the trick but used it to their advantage. The next day, the *Daily News* reported that a highly placed member of the German War Intelligence Department had told the paper's Berlin correspondent that he knew of no Colonel Herzenwirth and that the entire story was a hoax.

The last "firsthand" account of angels on the battlefields of World War I appeared in *Fate* magazine in May 1968. The magazine reported on a letter from Reverend Albert H. Baller of Clinton, Massachusetts, who had spoken about UFOs to a group of engineers in New Britain, Connecticut, in the mid-1950s. Reverend Baller reported that during the lecture, one of the engineers said that he'd been in the trenches near Ypres in August 1915 when the Germans launched the first gas attack. At that time none of the soldiers knew of this new, deadly weapon and were unprepared to defend themselves. The troops panicked and ran, with many overtaken by the gas. Suddenly a figure came walking out of the gaseous mist wearing a uniform of the Royal Medical Corps but without any protection from the poison. He spoke English with a French accent.

Around his waist the man had a belt with hooks holding tin cups, and he carried a bucket of what looked like water. He slid into the trench and began removing the cups, dipping them into the liquid and telling the soldiers to drink quickly. The engineer received one of the cups, and remembered that the drink was almost too salty to swallow. But anyone who did drink the liquid was saved from any lasting effects from the gas. Reverend Baller regretted that he did not remember the engineer's name.

Was Machen responsible for the Angels of Mons, or did all these people really experience an angelic visitation? Nearly anyone who could corroborate the stories of angels at Mons is now dead, and accounts from the time are anonymous and unproven. In any case, if the tales did no more than boost the morale of the wounded, they served their purpose.

FURTHER READING

Cavendish, Richard, ed. *May, Myth & Magic: The Illustrated Encyclopedia of Mythology, Religion and the Unknown,* Vol. 11. New York: Marshall Cavendish Ltd., 1985, p. 2963.

McClure, Kevin. *Visions of Bowmen and Angels: Mons 1914.* St. Austell, Cornwall, England: The Wild Places, ca. 1992.

Mont St. Michel See MICHAEL.

Monte Gargano See MICHAEL.

months See ANGELS OF THE MONTHS.

Morael (Moriel)

In Jewish lore, the angel of awe or fear who rules the month of Elul (August–September), preceding the New Year and Day of Atonement. Morael has the power to make all things invisible.

Morax (Foraii, Forfax)

One of the FALLEN ANGELS and 72 spirits of SOLOMON. Morax is an earl and president in HELL and rules 36 legions. He appears as a bull, and, if he takes on a man's head, he will impart knowledge of astronomy and all liberal sciences. He knows the virtues of herbs and precious stones. He gives good FAMILIARS.

Mormonism

Religion better known as the Church of Christ of Latter-day Saints. The Mormons grew from six original members in 1830 to 3 million in the 1990s. The Joseph Smith family had experienced dramatic economic ups and downs, migrating from Vermont to New Hampshire and finally to upper New York in the 1820s. Joseph Smith Sr. had received visions. When in 1823 his son Joseph Smith Jr. reported receiving visions and instructions from an angel called Moroni, the father and the rest of the large close family, now located in Palmyra, New York, were receptive and believed his account.

Joseph Smith Jr.'s testimony about this series of events, which led him to believe that he had been chosen by God to restore the true church of Christ and that all other Christian groups were apostate, constitutes the introduction to The Book of Mormon, allegedly written by Mormon, a prophet-historian from the ancient Middle East. "The crowning event recorded in The Book of Mormon is the personal ministry of the Lord Jesus Christ among the Nephites soon after his resurrection. It puts forth the doctrines of the gospel, outlines the plan of salvation, and tells men what they must do to gain peace in this life and eternal salvation in the life to come. After Mormon completed his writings," the introduction continues, "he delivered the account of his son Moroni, who added a few words of his own and hid up the plates in the Hill Cumorah. On September 21, 1823, the same Moroni, then a glorified, resurrected being, appeared to the Prophet Joseph Smith and instructed him."

Moroni's first visit to Joseph Smith Jr. after the rest of the family in the crowded cabin had gone to sleep, was chiefly characterized by whiteness and brilliance, his "robe of most exquisite whiteness beyond anything earthly I had ever seen . . . and his countenance truly like lightning." Moroni repeatedly told Smith about lost scriptures preserved on plates buried nearby.

With the plates were two magical stones attached to a silver breastplate, construed by some as eyeglasses, called Urim and Thummin, which enabled Smith to translate the scriptures by 1827, after which the angel took the golden tablets away.

Smith and first three men and then another eight, hereafter official witnesses, testified to the existence of the scripture, inscribed in a strange language on gold plates. It is reported that of the first three, Oliver Cowdery and David Whitmer believed they saw an angel descend on a light bearing the plates and confirming the authenticity of the translation. Martin Harris did not claim to have had the vision, but he accepted that Smith had seen the angel. Several days later eight men—four Whitmer brothers and their brother-in-law Hiram Page, with Joseph Smith Sr. and two more of his sons, Hyrum and Samuel—were shown the plates, which they "did handle with our hands." "Seen and hefted," the plates were taken up to heaven by an angel.

Supporters took the text of the translation to a publisher in Mentor, Ohio, and it appeared as The Book of Mormon in 1830. The work quotes heavily from the authorized version of the English Bible and is couched in a similar style. It purports to tell the story of the true church of Christ on the American continent after it migrated from Jerusalem. "After thousands of years [from the destruction of the Tower of Babel] all were destroyed except the Lamanites, and they were the principal ancestors of the American Indians," states the introduction to the 1981 version of The Book of Mormon.

Mormonism underwent almost continual shifts as it started to grow under the patronage of converts. Smith Jr. continued to receive new visions and revelations, and added these dimensions to Mormon proscriptions in the 1830s and 1840s; dissenters rebelled against some of these and either left the fold voluntarily or were expelled. Meanwhile, outsiders and the law of the land often challenged the sect on business, political, moral, or religious grounds. Joseph Smith Jr. was killed in an attack on the Mormons' Nauvoo, Illinois, outpost

in 1844. A brief summary of some of the most notable Mormon beliefs, particularly in relation to the angels and celestial hierarchies, will give an idea of the uniqueness of this sect.

Mormon Beliefs and Practices

The New England settlers who became the first Mormons emerged from a long-standing group of separatists or radicals who lived on the fringes of Calvinist Puritan orthodoxy. They were well prepared for the Mormon message because they asked questions, held spiritist universalist views, and were predisposed to the occult and magical.

This was coupled with a yearning for the ancient church, a stream of thought called *restorationism*, which went back to the Middle Ages. This theme had been picked up by each Protestant declaration of independence and even Catholic revolutions, such as that of the Franciscans. Mormonism spoke to the revulsion with the "ordinary" or "gentile" church, and the passion to possess dogmatic purity in Joseph Smith's discovery and translation from an ancient language of golden scriptures buried at the time of the Tower of Babel.

Among this separatist fringe in the 18th-century New England area were also "Immortalists," who believed in human divinization, and those who practiced "spiritual wifery" or "the new covenant of spiritual union." There were strange sects who met behind closed doors and were rumored to do all manner of things. One 1793 report stated that a Nat Smith of Hopkinton, Massachusetts, "proceeded to assume and declare himself to be the Most High God and wore a cap with the word GOD inscribed on its front. His Great Chair was a Holy Chair. . . . He had a number of Adorers and Worshippers, who . . . believed he was the Great God."

Treasure-divining was a central dimension of the radical perfectionism of the New Israelite movement, which emerged in Rutland County, Vermont, at the end of the 1790s and which had a direct link to Mormonism. Nathaniel Wood, one of its leaders, prophesied after his excommunication that he had literal descent from the Lost Tribes of Israel, had a special dispensation; his family and followers began work on a temple and divined for gold "to pave the streets of the New Jerusalem" and expected that a destroying angel would bring down earthquakes and plagues on the "gentiles."

Money-diggers would locate buried treasure through divination and attempt to retrieve it. Joseph Smith Sr. had taken part in some of these expeditions, four of which were officially reported in affidavits by subsequent researchers. Martin Harris, one of the 11 official witnesses to the golden plates, reported that Joseph Smith Jr. said Moroni "told him he must quit the company of the money-diggers." An 1826 trial record shows that Joseph Smith Jr. had taken part in a treasure hunt using a certain stone. Richard L. Bushman, a sympathetic biographer, said that Smith Jr. had gotten involved because he was pressured by neighbors, his own father, and by poverty.

In treating the elements from a culture of magical practice that contributed to Joseph Smith's messages and methods, John Brooke cites treasure-divining or money-digging along with witchcraft, conjuring, counterfeiting, alchemy, and Freemasonry. John L. Brooke's thesis is that Smith "began his engagement with the supernatural as a village conjurer but transformed himself into a prophet of the 'Word,' announcing the opening of a new dispensation. Then, moving beyond his role as prophet and revelator, Smith transformed himself and the Mormon priesthood into Christian-hermetic magi, a role previously manifested in the medieval alchemist, the Renaissance hermetic philosopher and the perfectionist sectarians of the Radical Reformation."

Mystical trances producing visions of angels and saints, prophecy and the like, performed in the inner sanctum, were offered to the faithful, following the tradition of alchemy and KABBALAH that the human soul can break free from the elemental sphere of the earth and ascend through lesser celestial and supercelestial heavens of the planets, the stars, and the angels to communicate directly with the divinity. In May 1829 John the Baptist appeared to Smith and Oliver Cowdery, and they received from him divine appointments as First and Second Elders of the new church. They claimed that John the Baptist had conferred on them the Levitical, or Aaronic Priesthood. Conferred on "every worthy male member," eventually starting with boys 12 years old, these offices provided the semblance of an egalitarian order for white males in the church. Welcomed as deacons, teachers, and priests, the Aaronic Priesthood held "the keys of the ministering of angels." They were to watch over the church, teach the gospel, and perform baptisms.

In February 1832 Smith revised Genesis and reproduced the three heavens of the Kabbalah and hermeticism in the three Mormon heavens, the telestial, terrestrial, and celestial. Both hermeticism and Mormonism celebrate the mutuality of spiritual and material worlds, precreated intelligences, free will, a divine ADAM, a fortunate, sinless Fall, and the symbolism and religious efficacy of marriage and sexuality. And as in hermeticism, Adam, "the father of all, PRINCE of all, that ancient of days," would occupy a central position in the Mormon cosmology. In fact, this divine Adam

was also eventually equated with Michael the archangel by Brigham Young in April 1852:

> When our Father Adam came into the garden of Eden, he came into it with a celestial body, and brought Eve, one of his wives, with him. He helped to make and organize this world. He is Michael, the Archangel, the Ancient of Days! about whom holy men have written and spoken—he is our Father and our God, and the only God with whom we have to do.

In stark contrast to Reformation Calvinists, who stand before their omnipotent God sinful and powerless inheritors of Adam's original sin at the Fall, hermeticism promised divine power to mortal man as magus, restored to the powers of Adam in Paradise before the Fall. Freemasonry too presented a mythology where the divine Adam in the Garden of Eden communed directly with God and the angels in a state of perfection. Hermeticism and Mormonism both rejected original sin and advocated free human will. Mormonism explicitly rejected Calvinism in its advocacy of universal salvation and the freedom of the will.

Smith's authority as "Seer and Revelator" was announced in April 1830 and confirmed in September. In February and March 1831, Smith issued a series of revelations that established sacramental and institutional strictures, including the collective economy called the United Order of Enoch, or the Law of Consecration. The Council of Twelve Apostles was established in February 1835. In granting priestly powers "to seal up the Saints," Joseph Smith gave the Mormon hierarchy the same authority that the hermetic alchemist assumed: human means to immortality, indeed divinity. The men of the hierarchy, initiated into these rituals in the long attic rooms of the new temple in Kirtland, Ohio, in March 1836, testified that "they were filled with the Holy Ghost, which was like fire in their bones," and they fell into visions and prophecy. Smith had visions of Adam and Abraham, and of his deceased brother Alvin in the celestial kingdom. This experience inspired a revelation that informed the practice of baptism for the dead, begun six years later.

Joseph Smith made this revelation on July 12, 1843, at Nauvoo, Illinois:

> [I]t shall be done unto them all things whatsoever my servant hath put upon them, in time and through all eternity; and shall be of full force when they are out of the world; and they shall pass the angels and the gods, which are set there, to their exaltation and glory in all things, as hath been sealed upon their heads, which glory shall be a fullness and a continuation of the seeds forever and ever.

Then shall they be as gods, because they have no end. . . . Then shall they be above all, because all things are subject to them. Then shall they be gods, because they have all power, and the angels are subject to them.

By 1845 a successor of Smith, John Haven, had welcomed the first group of children who were to stand in for deceased ancestors, who would then become immortal Mormons by being baptized after death.

Smith's theology thus promised a radical departure from traditional Protestant Christianity. The Mormon cosmos promised universal salvation for humanity and divinity to the Mormon faithful. As a Mormon proverb later put it, capturing the doctrines of both eternity and divinization: "As man is now, so once was God; as God is now, man may become." Human salvation and Mormon divinity would be structured in a radically new configuration of the invisible world, three ascending kingdoms replacing the duality of heaven and hell.

Being endowed in the temple was the first of many secrets that would allow a Mormon to ascend toward godhead. By April 1844 only 66 people had been given the induction ceremony. Celestial marriage would seal a couple for eternity, and only those who had been granted eternal marriage would be allowed to ascend to the third heaven. On May 28, 1843, Smith was sealed to his wife Emma Hale for "time and eternity." Eternal marriage—and godhead—was guaranteed only by the marriage sealing added to the temple endowment. In heaven, Mormons without sealed eternal marriages would occupy the lowest degree of glory in the celestial kingdom, where they would simply be MINISTERING ANGELS, servants to those of higher degrees, and condemned to an unexalted existence, without prospect of progression toward and in divinity.

Finally, someone had to have authority to bestow these privileges on the uninitiated and to receive the ultimate reward. This was the high priesthood to which John the Baptist had initiated Joseph Smith and Oliver Cowdery. By 1846 almost 600 Mormons had been given a second anointing to give the kingly patriarchal powers "to seal up the Saints to eternal life." The reward of the second anointing was a virtually unconditional guarantee of godhead in the highest degree of the celestial kingdom.

In announcing a new dispensation, in assuming the revelatory powers of a prophet, in blurring the lines between spirit and matter, and in promising godhead to the faithful, Smith defied not only the established and evangelical churches but even the most ardent contemporary advocates of the imminences of the millennium. The growth of the Mormon sect, its persecution, and eventual triumph under Brigham Young, who led 30,000 of the faithful to a permanent settlement in Utah, are part of American history and folklore. The modern Church of Latter-day Saints has a large following and a vigorous campaign of proselytization.

FURTHER READING

The Book of Mormon: An Account Written by the Hand of Mormon upon Plates Taken from the Plates of Nephi. Translated by Joseph Smith, Jr. First published 1830. Salt Lake City: The Church of Christ of Latter-day Saints, 1981.

Brooke, John L. *The Refiner's Fire: The Making of Mormon Cosmology, 1644–1844.* New York: Cambridge University Press, 1994.

Bushman, Richard L. *Joseph Smith and the Beginnings of Mormonism.* Urbana: University of Illinois Press, 1984.

Paul, Erich Robert. *Science, Religion, and Mormon Cosmology.* Urbana: University of Illinois Press, 1992.

Moroni

God's heavenly messenger to Joseph Smith Jr., founder of the Church of Jesus Christ of Latter-day Saints, or MORMONISM. Moroni brought Smith the story of Christ's work in the New World. These accounts were inscribed in an ancient hieroglyphic code on golden tablets and buried near Smith's home in western New York State. Smith's translations, collected into The Book of Mormon, form the other sacred texts, besides the Bible, of the church.

The younger Smith was not the first member of his family to receive messages from divine spirits, however. Around 1811 the Smiths were living in Vermont, eking out a subsistence living as farmers. Both Joseph Sr. and his wife Lucy had come from more comfortable situations, and they deeply resented their neighbors' hostility and contempt as a result of the Smiths' current poverty. Joseph and Lucy associated such attitudes with prevailing religious thought, which equated ill fortune with bad intentions, sin, and even evil—in other words, the Smiths must be getting what they deserved.

Joseph Sr. began to have revelatory dreams that vividly showed his contempt for organized churches. The elder Smith later recounted that a heavenly messenger whom he described as an "attendant spirit" came to him with a box representing "true religion." When Smith tried to open the box, wild animals—which Smith took to represent the various established sects—rushed to attack him, and he dropped the box.

Later the attendant spirit returned and took Smith through a desolate area into a beautiful valley. In his dream, Smith gathered his large family around a tree that bore delicious fruit, much like the Tree of the Knowledge of Good and Evil in Eden. But instead of leading to sin and banishment, the fruit of this tree represented God's pure love for all those who keep His commandments. Smith was enraptured.

But his joy was marred by observing a large building in the distance, filled with finely dressed men and women who laughed contemptuously at the Smith family, much as the Smiths' neighbors had done. The angel told Joseph that the building represented Babylon, the center of evil in the book of Revelation, and that the finely dressed people inside despised God's true saints and would fall from his grace. Such black-and-white depictions of salvation, especially when the saved are the poor and downtrodden, characterize a school of thought known as Christian Primitivism.

Around 1815, Joseph and Lucy moved their family to Oneida County (now Ontario County) in western New York State, to try their luck in a new area. During the 19th century Oneida County was inflamed by one religious movement after another—from Presbyterians, Methodists, and Baptists to great revival preachers like

Moroni delivering the plates of The Book of Mormon to Joseph Smith Jr. (Reprinted courtesy of U.S. Library of Congress)

Charles Grandison Finney, and from groups like the Oneida Perfectionists to Millerites and Spiritualists. So many ideas caught fire in the area that locals called it the Burned-Over District.

By 1820–21, another revival was in progress among the Presbyterians, Methodists, and Baptists, with fire-and-brimstone preachers of each sect exhorting sinners to confess and avoid the religious lies of the other two groups. Most of the Smith family chose Presbyterianism, but Joseph could not make up his mind. Described as a literal thinker, he prayed for divine guidance to select the one church that was right.

According to Joseph Smith Jr.'s own account in *The Pearl of Great Price,* a pillar of light descended from the heavens bringing two Personages, as Smith called them, ostensibly God and Father and one whom he called "my Beloved Son." These Personages told Smith to choose no existing denomination, for they were all wrong, and like his father before him he would be shown the true church.

Smith reports that he was reviled and persecuted for his visions, but they did not stop. On the night of September 21–22, 1823, his room was filled with a brilliant white light revealing an angel, called Moroni, who appeared as a messenger from God. Moroni told Smith that he had helped to write, then bury, a history written on gold plates by his father Mormon, of an ancient people descended from Israel who had lived and died in America. Most biblical scholars maintain that God created the angels as a separate population, but Moroni apparently became an angel after death.

He told Smith that around 600 B.C.E., God forewarned the Hebrew prophet Lehi of the coming captivity in Babylon. Lehi gathered his family and followers and fled Jerusalem, wandering in the wilderness for many years until they reached the sea. With divine guidance, Lehi's family built a boat and sailed to what is now America. Upon arriving, a long-simmering family argument split Lehi's sons into two factions. Those who were righteous and obeyed God followed Nephi (Nephites); those who chose evil followed Laman (Lamanites). Each side won or lost wars for supremacy until Christ appeared to them after the Resurrection. He reunited the Nephites and Lamanites, chose 12 disciples, and instituted a 200-year period of peace, prosperity, and service to God.

But by the time Lehi's descendants had been in America for a thousand years, both factions had become corrupt and oblivious to the prophet's warnings. As the Lamanites, a fierce, dark-skinned people, were exterminating the Nephites in yet another war circa 421 C.E., the prophet and general Mormon engraved an abridged history of his people on golden plates, using Egyptian-like hieroglyphics. Shortly before he was killed, Mormon entrusted the plates to his son Moroni, who added to the history and then buried the plates in the Hill Cumorah before he too died. Victorious but without the benefit of contact with the gentler, white Nephites, the Lamanites became even more fierce. They forgot their history, Moroni told Smith, and eventually became the native Americans discovered by Columbus.

Moroni ended his narrative by telling Smith that God had chosen him to retrieve these plates, translate their stories with the accompanying seer stones, and resurrect the church to prepare for the latter days (before the Second Coming). The angel appeared to Smith three times that night, repeating the story and his instructions verbatim, and again the next day. The angel revealed the plates' hiding place—the abovementioned Hill Cumorah, miraculously near Smith's Manchester, New York, home—but forbade him to dig up the plates until four years from that date. Although eager to verify his vision, Smith did as he was told, retrieving the golden plates, the seer stones called the Urim and Thummim, and the breastplate upon which they were fastened on September 22, 1827.

Smith created a sensation when he brought home these golden plates covered in Egyptian-style hieroglyphics. He had had a reputation for finding things, maybe mythic treasures, by using a seer or "peep" stone (a crystal ball), but this prize and his revelations were too much for most of his neighbors. To avoid harrassment, Smith and his new wife Emma went to Harmony, Pennsylvania, to translate the plates. Martin Harris, a sympathetic farmer who had given the Smiths $50 to move, left his wife and family to follow the Smiths and help with the plates' translation.

By the spring of 1828, Smith and Harris had transcribed 116 pages of manuscript, which Harris begged Smith to let him take home and show to his wife. Previously Harris had taken a sample of Smith's translation to New York, where Professor Charles Anthon had identified the characters on the plates as Egyptian, Chaldean, Assyrian, and Arabic. Although warned by Moroni to guard the plates, stones and translation, Smith allowed Harris to take the manuscript—the only copy—which he then reportedly lost.

By April 1829, Smith had started over. He was still translating when Oliver Cowdery appeared, an itinerant schoolteacher who had heard to Smith's work from Smith's parents in Manchester. Intrigued, Oliver became his scribe, and the work was finished by the end of the year. David Whitmer, an early convert to Mormonism, said that Smith would put the stones in his hat and pull it around his face to simulate darkness. Then a character would appear, as if on parchment, accompanied by the English translation. Smith would read the translation to Cowdery, who wrote it down, then another character would appear in the hat. *The Book of Mormon,* hence the church's familiar name, was published in March 1830.

Once the translation of the first plates was complete, Moroni supposedly reclaimed the plates and stones, with many of the later plates still sealed. The angel never again appeared to Smith or any of his followers.

FURTHER READING

Moore, R. Laurence. "The Occult Connection? Mormonism, Christian Science and Spiritualism." In *The Occult in America.* Edited by John Godwin. New York: Doubleday, 1982.

Shipps, Jan. *Mormonism: The Story of a New Religious Tradition.* Urbana, Ill.: University of Illinois Press, 1985.

Smith, Joseph Jr., trans. *The Book of Mormon.* Salt Lake City: The Church of Jesus Christ of Latter-day Saints, 1986.

Smith, Joseph Jr. *The Pearl of Great Price.* Salt Lake City: The Church of Jesus Christ of Latter-day Saints, 1972.

Winn, Kenneth H. *Exiles in a Land of Liberty: Mormons in America 1830–1846.* Chapel Hill: University of North Carolina Press, 1991.

Moses

Biblical patriarch and great leader of the Israelites who receives the Ten Commandments and other moral rules from God. Moses has various encounters with angels.

As an infant Moses is cast adrift in a basket in bulrushes in Egypt. He is found and raised as an Egyptian by the daughter of the king. The Egyptians' cruelty toward Israeli slaves angers him, and he kills an Egyptian overseer, an act which forces him to flee from Egypt. He lives as a shepherd in the desert and marries a daughter of Jethro.

One day 40 years later, Moses is grazing his flocks on Mount Horeb, and he comes upon a burning bush:

> And the ANGEL OF THE LORD appeared to him in a flame of fire out of the midst of the bush: and he looked, and lo, the bush was burning, yet it was not consumed. And Moses said, "I will turn aside and see this great sight, why the bush is not burnt." When the Lord saw that he turned aside to see, God called to him out of the bush, "Moses, Moses!" and he said, "Here am I." Then he said, "Do not come near; put off your shoes from your feet, for the place on which you are standing is holy ground." (Exodus 3:2–5)

God tells Moses he has heard the crying and suffering of the enslaved Israelites. Moses must return to Egypt and petition the pharaoh to let the Israelites go and then lead his people to the Promised Land.

Moses beholding the Messiah and the Great Mystery (Jakob Boehme, *Mysterium magnum*)

Moses and his brother, Aaron, go to Egypt but the pharaoh refuses to let the Israelite captives go, insisting on a miracle. Aaron turns his staff into a serpent, but still the pharoah refuses. Advised by the Lord, Moses and Aaron warn the pharaoh that the Egyptians will be punished with 10 plagues unless the Israelites are released. The pharaoh is unmoved, and plagues of vermin, pests, pestilence, storms, and darkness sweep the land.

The final plague is the death of the firstborn of every family and every animal in Egypt. God instructs the Israelites how to mark their homes with the blood of a sacrificed lamb, so that they will be passed over (the origin of the Passover). The deaths are carried out by the DESTROYING ANGEL.

Broken by the death of his son, the pharaoh releases the Israelites. God helps Moses to part the waters of the Red Sea to give them easy passage. The Angel of the Lord, who is a pillar of cloud, moves between the Israelites and the Egyptians; when the pharaoh's armies try to follow, the waters of the Red Sea come in and drown them. Moses, guided by an angel (the pillar of cloud by day and the pillar of fire by night), leads the people across the desert toward Canaan, the promised land of milk and honey. They survive by eating manna (see ANGEL BREAD), which is like white wafers made with honey and tasting of coriander seed.

Finally the Israelites reach Mount Sinai in the wilderness. Moses goes up the mountain, where God gives him the Law and instructions for building the temple and the ARK OF THE COVENANT. The account of this important occasion begins in Exodus 19. The Lord comes down to the top of Mount Sinai and calls Moses to the top. The mountain is shrouded in a mystical smoke and fire that makes the entire mountaintop appear to burn. There are thunders, lightnings, and loud trumpet blasts; the mountain quakes. Moses speaks and God answers in thunder.

After his receipt of the Law, Moses continues to speak on a regular basis face to face with God as he would with any man. He constructs the ark, which serves as a portable tabernacle. He pitches his meeting tent outside the camp, and the pillar of cloud descends to the entrance of it, denoting the presence of God and lighting the ark with a brilliance.

After 40 years, Moses' leadership comes to an end. He brings the Israelites to an oasis at Kadesh and sends spies into Canaan. They return with frightening stories, and the people rebel against Moses. He turns leadership over to Joshua. He addresses the people several times, recorded in Deuteronomy; his final blessing is in chapter 33.

Moses climbs Mount Nebo (in the land of Moab), from which he can see Canaan, the promised land he will not reach himself. He dies at age 120 and the Lord secretly buries him in the valley in Moab opposite Beth-peor. His death is mourned for 30 days. Joshua succeeds in leading the Israelites into Canaan.

Testament of Moses

The Testament of Moses is a pseudepigraphon consisting of Moses' farewell exhortation prior to his death, delivered to his successor, Joshua. The text is incomplete, the last portion of it having been lost. Estimated dates of authorship range from late first century to mid-second century C.E. It was originally written in Greek. The testament is believed by some scholars to be part of the Essenes corpus, though no obvious links are found among the QUMRAN TEXTS. In relation to the Bible, it has the strongest link to the book of Deuteronomy, which features Moses' final addresses; the author also was familiar with the book of DANIEL.

The Testament of Moses gives a historical survey culminating in the destruction of evil and the establishment of the kingdom of God. Its sole reference to angels concerns the end of the devil at the hands of "the messenger, who is in the highest place appointed." This reference is taken to mean Michael, the PRINCE and GUARDIAN ANGEL of Israel.

Moses in Rabbinic Literature

A rabbinic story from the ninth century relates that when Moses reaches the top of Mount Sinai, he is taken by a cloud to the gate of HEAVEN, but he is prevented from entering by the angel Kemuel who stands guard there. But when Moses states that he has come to receive the Torah, the gates open of their own accord, and Kemuel permits him to enter.

Moses travels to the Rigyon River, made of fire that consumes both angels and humans. ANGELS OF DESTRUCTION greet him and try to incinerate him with their breath of fire. Moses cries out to God ("Master of the Universe") for help, and a wave of fire rises up and obliterates the angels.

When other angels see Moses, they too cry out to God for help. God tells them he has come for the Torah, prompting the angels to protest, "You created the Torah before You created the world. How can such a precious treasure pass into the hands of a mere man?" God replies, "It was created for that very purpose."

God pulls Moses up to Paradise. Moses apprehends God on his throne and behind him an angel so big that Moses is terrified. This is the angel Sandalphon, who, God explains, weaves garlands out of the prayers of Isreal. Calmed by God, Moses relaxes. He watches as Sandalphon finishes a garland, and it immediately rises of its own accord to rest on the head of God. This sets in motion mighty forces. The heavenly hosts shake with awe, the wheels of the throne revolve, and the creatures of the Chariot roar out like lions, "Holy holy is the Lord of hosts."

God too is weaving. He tells Moses that he weaves the crowns of the letters of the Torah, so that a thousand years into the future they will be interpreted by Rabbi Akiba ben Joseph. Moses is then shown a vision of the rabbi studying the Torah, and saying he learned it from Moses at Mount Sinai. In this way, Moses is given to comprehend the legacy he will bestow upon future generations.

God opens the portals of heaven and reveals himself to the people of Israel, who fall down and die of fright. God then dispatches a dew of Resurrection, which revives the souls of the righteous as it will at the End of Days. All are revived.

God then assigns 120 myriads of angels to act as a sort of guardian angels to the people of Israel. Each person receives two angels, one to keep the heart beating and the other to raise the head so that the glory of God can be perceived.

While the portals are open and the people below can hear, God transmits the Torah to Moses for the next 40 days. This becomes written law. For 40 nights, he explains to Moses what he has transmitted. This becomes oral law, revealing the 70 meanings of every word of the Torah.

When the task is done, a cloud takes Moses back to the top of Mount Sinai, and he delivers the word to the people.

Moses in the New Testament
Luke 9:28–36 describes the dazzling Transfiguration of JESUS during prayer, in which Moses and ELIJAH appear to him "in glory" and speak to him about his impending death. The vision is witnessed by Peter, John, and James, who fall asleep while Jesus prays but awaken in time to see the patriarchs with Jesus in a brilliant aura of light.

Moses in Art
From medieval times, artistic depictions of Moses have often shown him with hornlike rays emanating from the top of his head. Such depictions usually are of Moses after he has received the Ten Commandments, though some also are of his days in Egypt. These portrayals are based on a mistranslation of the Hebrew term *qaran,* which is derived from a term meaning horns, but in this context of Moses means "to emit rays." After being in the presence of God, Moses is transformed in splendor and the skin of his face radiates light. St. Jerome, who translated the Bible into the Latin Vulgate edition, translated *qaran* as horns, thus giving rise to centuries of misunderstanding that Moses (and Jews in general) had horns.

See ANGELS OF THE PRESENCE; JUBILEES; NEAR-DEATH EXPERIENCE.

FURTHER READING
Schwartz, Howard. *Gabriel's Palace: Jewish Mystical Tales.* New York: Oxford University Press, 1993.
Steinmetz, Dov, M.D. "Moses' 'Revelation' on Mount Horeb as a Near-Death Experience." In *Journal of Near-Death Studies* 11, no. 4 (Summer 1993): 199–203.

Mount Moriah, angel of See ISAAC.

Muhammad (ca. 570 or 571–632)
The Messenger of God and the Prophet of Islam. Tradition holds that Muhammad received his call of prophecy via DREAMS in which either God or the archangel Gabriel appeared to him.

Muhammad is believed by followers to be the last of all divine revelations before the end of the world. His name means "the Praised one" or "he who is glorified." In all, there are 200 names for Muhammad, such as "Joy of Creation," "Beloved of God," and so forth. Mention of his name is customarily followed by one of several invocations, such as "God bless him and give him peace."

Muhammad was an inspired prophet and religious reformer in the Semitic (and biblical) tradition, preaching holy war and the triumph of justice. The religion he founded borrows much from Judaism and Christianity. By some accounts he was illiterate, which made a case for his having obtained wisdom directly from God in revelations, and not from copying Judaism and Christianity. However, Muhammad was a businessman prior to becoming a prophet, and it is likely that he was at least semiliterate. It is not likely that he actually read Judeo-Christian literature, but he had heard some of the stories contained therein.

Muhammad preached a God that is both personal and transcendent. He accepted JESUS as the Messiah, the immaculate conception of MARY, and the virgin birth. However, he believed that Judaism and Christianity had distorted God's revelations to MOSES and Jesus, and that the pagan Arabs lived in ignorance of God's will. He reformed Arabic religion and life, and he established Islam as the "original" word of God.

Only two dates are certain in Muhammad's life: the year of his emigration from Mecca to Medina, 622, and the year of his death, 632. The primary source of information on his life is the Koran (Qu'ran), the holy book of Islam given to him by Allah (God) in a series of revelations.

Muhammad was born in Mecca between 567 and 572, most likely in 570 or 571. His lineage was traced back to Ishmael and ABRAHAM. His father died prior to his birth, and he was made a ward of his grandfather, Abd al-Muttalib, the founder of the pagan Hashimite tribe of the Quryash of Mecca, a cult of idols. Muhammad was given to a Bedouin foster mother to raise in the desert.

According to one account, two men dressed in white appeared one day when the boy was four or five and was out shepherding lambs. They threw him down, opened his chest, and stirred their hands around. In later years, Muhammad said the men were angels who had come to wash a dark spot from his heart with snow; thus was he purified of original sin. Muhammad also had an unusual and large mark between his shoulders. Ringed by hair, it was supposed to be the "Seal of Prophecy," the sign of the last Divine Messenger to the world.

Muhammad returned to Mecca while still a young child. He eventually became a businessman dealing in skins and raisins. At age 25, he married Khadijah, who was 19 years his senior. She bore either two or three sons, who died in infancy, and four daughters.

Muhammad began to feel the call of spirit in 610, when he reached 40 years of age. He withdrew to the mountains near Mecca to pray and meditate. He began to receive a series of divine revelations. They are not given in order in the Koran, and it is difficult to ascertain which occurred first. It is likely that he had at least several revelations before those dealing with the Koran began. In Suras 53 and 81:17–19, Muhammad describes two visions that apparently had occurred to him in the past. In the first, he is approached by a mysterious male figure first "on the high horizon" and then near a lotus tree by "the garden of the dwelling"; Muhammad says he is the figure's servant. His descriptions suggest that the figure is God; it was later in Muhammad's career that he interpreted this figure as that of Gabriel. Muslim interpreters also have favored Gabriel. The second experience was clearly visionary, in which Muhammad is transported to another realm.

It was not until after Muhammad moved to Medina in 622 that he interpreted any of his revelations as coming from Gabriel. This may have been motivated by criticism directed at him, that he was not a true prophet because God had not sent down his angels to him. His critics called him "DJINN-possessed." However, during his Mecca ascetic period, Muhammad did receive many revelations that came to him in dreams and in heavy, torporous trances. These revelations continued throughout the rest of his life.

One of his visionary experiences involved an ascent to HEAVEN to receive knowledge and revelations from God; his experience is similar to the heavenly journeys described by Hebrew prophets. Muhammad is taken to the Temple Mount in Jerusalem astride the mythical beast Buraq, and then to the seventh heaven and then face to face with God; here, it was later said, he began to receive the Koran. Another tradition holds that first the angels Michael and Gabriel appear, open his breast and wash his heart (a retelling of his alleged childhood event), thus removing doubt, polytheism, error and pre-Islamic belief, and instilling within it faith and wisdom. Then Gabriel takes Muhammad to the heavens. In the first heaven he meets ADAM; in the second heaven John and Jesus; in the third heaven the Patriarch Joseph; in the fourth heaven the prophet Idris; in the fifth heaven Aaron; in the sixth heaven Moses; and in the seventh heaven ABRAHAM. From there, he is taken to Paradise where God gives him revelations, including 50 daily prayers. On his descent, Moses urges him to ask God to reduce the number of prayers. He does so, five times, until the number is reduced to five.

Another tradition describes Muhammad's introduction to the Koran as beginning in a dream. One night the angel Gabriel appears as the Messenger of Allah. He brings a coverlet of brocade upon which there is writing. He presses it upon Muhammad and says, "Recite!" Muhammad asks, "What shall I recite?" The angel says only, "Recite!" They engage in this exercise several times, and then Gabriel finally gives him what later become the opening lines of Sura 96:

> Recite in the name of thy Lord who created,
> Who created man of blood coagulated.
> Read! Thy Lord is most beneficent,
> Who taught by the pen,
> Taught that which they knew not to men.

Muhammad reads the coverlet, and Gabriel departs. When he awakens, he hears words that seem to be written on his heart: "O Muhammad, you are the Apostle of God and I am Gabriel."

Regardless of exactly how it happened, the first night of Koran revelations is referred to as the "Night of Power." According to Muslim tradition, the Koran was revealed gradually over the rest of Muhammad's life, in nearly daily trance states, with the final revelation coming just months before his death in 632. The Koran totals 6,666 verses and forms the doctrine of Islam. Muhammad himself never explicitly stated that this was how he received it. The Koran (17:106) states that it was sent from God gradually so that it could be recited to people at intervals.

Three years after the first revelation, Muhammad began calling himself a prophet. He began preaching to his own clan, the Hashimites, that if they did not worship God instead of their idols, they would be punished. The followers of the new religion were called Muslims, which is derived from a term that means "they that surrender to God."

Muhammad was successful in converting many people, which engendered hostility from the Quryash, who guarded the Ka'bah stone in Mecca. Conflict then arose. The Quryash banned commerce with the Hashimites, and they began persecutions of the Muslims, driving them out. Muhammad went to Yathrib in 622, now observed as the year in which the Islamic era began. Yathrib became the first Islamic state, and became known as Medina, "the city of the Prophet."

A holy war erupted. Muhammad, aided by legions of angels, eventually prevailed, destroying the idols at the Ka'bah. Within weeks, Mecca officially converted to Islam. There followed conversions all over Arabia.

In March 632, Muhammad led a farewell pilgrimage to Mount Ararat, where he delivered the last revelation of the Koran. The new religion was named Islam ("surrender" or "reconciliation") and the law of Islam was established. Muhammad died on June 8, 632, and was buried in his house. His death was followed by a period of confusion and civil wars.

Islam seeks to restore the pre-Fall state of the Garden of Eden, in which man in his essence was perfect and capable of perceiving God in the Unseen. Its fundamentals are the Five Pillars: the profession of faith; the canonical prayer or worship; the fast; the legal tithe; and the pilgrimage.

See ANGELOLOGY.

FURTHER READING

Dermenghem, Emile. *Muhammad and the Islamic Tradition.* Woodstock, N.Y.: The Overlook Press, 1981. First published 1955.

Lippman, Thomas W. *Understanding Islam: An Introduction to the Moslem World.* New York: New American Library, 1982.

Peters, F. E. *Muhammad and the Origins of Islam.* Albany: State University of New York Press, 1994.

Munkar (Monker, Munker)

In Islamic lore, a blue-eyed, black angel who examines souls to determine their worthiness for Paradise. With Nakir, another blue-eyed, black angel, Munkar receives condemned souls from the angel Ruman and punishes them in HELL.

Murder

Headless DEMON who sees through his breasts and speaks with the voice taken over from his victims. In the Testament of Solomon, Murder is summoned to appear before King SOLOMON. He says that he has no head because he devours heads, and he longs for a head to do what the king does. Murder grabs hold of heads, cuts them off, and attaches them to himself. A fire (heat) that continually burns within him consumes the heads through his neck. He causes quartan fever, and inflames limbs, inflicts feet, and creates festering sores. Murder also attacks infants who cry in the night and harms them, especially if they are premature. He is thwarted by fiery flashes of lightning.

See SCEPTER.

Muriel (Murriel)

Angel who rules the order of DOMINIONS, the month of June, and the sign of Cancer. In MAGIC Muriel is invoked to produce a magic carpet.

Murmur

One of the FALLEN ANGELS and 72 spirits of SOLOMON. Murmur is a duke and earl with 30 legions. He appears as a soldier wearing a duke's crown and riding on a griffin, preceded by two ministers sounding trumpets. He teaches philosophy and makes souls of the dead appear and answer questions. Murmur once was partly a member of the order of THRONES and also of ANGELS.

music and angels

"Music is well said to be the speech of angels," wrote JOHANN WOLFGANG VON GOETHE. From ancient times, sound and ceremonial song have linked the bodily senses to the mystical and brought near the presence of God and angels. In every sect music is an essential component of ritual and liturgy. Music in all cultures—ancient or modern, Eastern or Western—began as an oral tradition. The purity and power of a human voice evokes a poetic utterance about God and sets in motion powerful vibratory forces.

Mysticism

The centerpoint of angel-related music in Jewish mysticism is the QEDUSSAH ("sanctification"), the song of praise and devotion to God sung by the angels in HEAVEN around the throne of Glory. The Qedussah appears in apocryphal literature and is given in ISAIAH 6:3: "Holy, holy, holy is the Lord of Hosts; the whole earth is full of his glory." The book of ENOCH explains that performing the Qedussah is one of the most important duties of angels and must be done correctly in order to please God. Many visionary recitals in MERKABAH literature comment on angels singing this praise. The Merkabah procedures for mystical ascent to the throne of Glory include the precise recitation of hymns, prayers, and secret NAMES of God, most of which end with the Qedussah.

Elsewhere in the heavens, multitudes of singing angels under the direction of the angelic prince Tagas create sounds of unimaginable beauty and harmony.

The belief that certain sounds transform and elevate consciousness and move the cosmic powers of creation appears universally in mythologies and cosmologies. God or the gods sing or speak the world and cosmos into being; sound and music are instrumental in the maintaining of order. The mystical importance of music is embodied in liturgy, the rites of public worship.

Liturgy

The Jewish morning service contains some ancient prayers (*yoser*), which scholars have traced back to the Essenes and which resemble *The Litany of the Angels* found among the Dead Sea Scrolls (see QUMRAN TEXTS). Jewish folklore holds that as the devout chant their prayers, choirs of angels accompany them. The *Sanctus* of the Christian Mass continues this motif.

The Litany of the Angels consists of two brief fragments. The first is based on the vision of EZEKIEL and depicts the angels rising in their several ranks to praise God aloft on his chariot/throne. The second sets forth a series of blessings evidently conceived as the angelic counterpart to the priestly benediction in Numbers

6:24–26 recited in the temple of old and now a staple element of all Jewish public worship: "The Lord bless you and keep you; The Lord make his face to shine upon you, and be gracious to you: The Lord lift up his countenance upon you, and give you peace."

Though fragmentary, *The Litany of the Angels* conveys the celestial hierarchy's presence in sound as well as vision:

> While they are soaring aloft, there sounds a murmur of angel voices . . . and the lifting of their wings is accompanied by a clamor of joyous song. It is the murmur of angels blessing the Chariot-like Throne above the firmament of the CHERUBIM, while they themselves, from below the place where the Glory dwells, go acclaiming in joyous song the splendor of that radiant expanse. . . . Like fiery apparitions are they, spirits most holy, looking like streams of fire, in the likeness of burnished metal or of lustrous ware; clothed in garments opalescent, a riot of wondrous hues, a diffusion of brightness; like angelic spirits, constantly coming and going beside

the glorious wonderful Chariot. Amid all the noise of their progress sounds also the murmured intonation of blessings, and whenever they come round, they shout their holy hallelujahs.

The conflict between the ANGELS OF MERCY—Sandalphon's army—and Satan's host on Rosh Hashanah and Yom Kippur, the days of awe and judgment, is dramatically expressed in the *Hineni,* a prayer in which the cantor, leading the congregation, pleads with God that he "rebuke Satan and keep him from blocking the ascent of my prayers . . . and may all the angels who are assigned to prayers convey my prayer before the throne of your glory."

The Qedussah, the prayer of sanctification, is a vital part of every Jewish prayer service.

The Sanctus (Trisagion) of the Christian Mass continues the Qedussah and the unceasing glorification of God by the angels. In the New Testament, REVELATION 4:8 echoes the visionary experiences of Ezekiel and Isaiah: four many-eyed, winged "living creatures" circle God's throne "and day and night they never cease to sing, 'Holy, Holy, Holy, is the Lord God Almighty, who was and is and is to come!'"

Thus, both Jewish and Christian worship feature the participation of angels and the entire universe.

The songs of the church are the counterparts of heavenly songs, and, corresponding to the manner of participation in the heavenly song, the spiritual life of the church is incorporated in that of heaven. The Epistle to the Hebrews 12:22–23 declares that Christians approach the festive assembly in which countless angels, the citizens of the heavenly city, and the souls of just men made perfect take part. It was also assumed that the laity's song was of a lower order than that of the monks. ORIGEN said, "To man, the singing of psalms is appropriate; but the singing of hymns is for angels and those who lead a life like that of the angels."

Christian liturgists were conscious from the beginning of the heavenly hierarchy linking up with the church. In the first thousand years of monasticism, the orders of angels were believed to be literally augmented by priestly and monastic orders that resemble them. Thus their singing of the praises of God at the eight daily offices (matins at midnight, lauds at daybreak, terce, sext, and none during the working day, vespers at sunset, and finally compline before retiring) was in accompaniment of the angels. Monastic inner mental discipline included concentration on the song of praise of the angels, enabled by silence much of the time, broken only by song in some orders.

The Te Deum, an early Latin hymn used in the monastic office for Sundays and festivals, includes angels in the song praise of God, and it ends in the Sanctus:

Nineteenth-century songsheet (Reprinted courtesy of U.S. Library of Congress)

We praise you, O God; we acclaim you as the Lord.
Everlasting Father, all the world bows down before you.
All the angels sing your praise, the hosts of
heaven and all the angelic powers,
all the cherubim and seraphim call out to you in
unending song;
Holy, Holy, Holy, is the Lord God.

In the Eucharistic Liturgy, the Gloria is sung after intercessory prayers of angels are requested. The Gloria begins with the angels' proclamation to shepherds of the birth of Jesus. Originally, it was sung in Greek at Christmas Mass; Pope Symmachus (r. 498–514) extended its use to Sunday Mass and some feasts. The earliest Latin version of it is in the seventh-century Gregorian Sacramentary.

For a millennium the only music heard in the Christian churches, East and West, was vocal, specifically monophonic chant. Every community or individual church developed its own localized chant repertoire, which they passed on orally from generation to generation. Among more prominent versions were Byzantine, Celtic, Gallician (French), Mosarabic (Spanish), Benevental (lower Italian), Ambrosian (Milanese), and Gregorian for Rome. Earliest notation of the music dates from the eighth century.

By the ninth century the Mass liturgy was firmly established, and church composers began experimenting with ways to embellish it. Polyphony—music with two or more different yet related melodic parts—developed in the West because notation created written records of spontaneous or intentional embellishments of a given melody. By the 13th century hundreds of harmonic polyphonic liturgical pieces were on record, most of them in France. But polyphony created a conservative reaction, with Cistercian and Dominican orders forbidding it in services. In 1324 Pope John XXII issued a bull against it.

By then polyphony had crept into secular music, which featured the use of varied instruments and Eastern influences brought by the Crusades. By the 14th century, the Mass featured polyphonic choruses and solos. In the Renaissance, fully instrumented polyphonic pieces with female voices were established, and "classical" music was well launched, with Palestrina (ca. 1525–94) and Monteverdi (1567–1643) leading the way into Baroque. In late Renaissance England, Tavener, Tallis, and others developed polyphonic choral music for cathedral and university choirs. A great deal of composition into the 21st century continued to be liturgical, but the exclusive embodiment of the angelic connection in monophonic chant was over.

Music of the Spheres

The Hermetic tradition, rooted in ancient astronomy and particularly the mystic brotherhood of Pythagoras, codified all science, art, and law for its initiates under the principle of cosmic harmony. Plato demonstrated in the *Timaeus* that music and mathematics could be used to explain every terrestrial phenomenon. The notion of angelic INTELLIGENCES guiding the heavens resonates in the metaphor "the music of the spheres" stated by Plotinus:

If the stars pass a blessed existence in their vision of the life inherent in their souls, and if, by force of their souls' tendency to become one, and by the light they cast from themselves upon the entire heavens, they are like the strings of a lyre which, being struck in tune, sing a melody in some natural scale . . . if this is the way the heavens, as one, are moved, and the component parts in their relation to the whole, then the life of all things together is still more clearly an unbroken unity. (IV *Ennead* II, iv, 8)

Early Christian theologians such as Origen and Clement, steeped in Hermetic, Gnostic, and Platonic, lore, identified the celestial musical ratios of astral religion with the Word of God, arising from the ambiguity of the Greek word *logos*. "Theologia" in older Greek meant a poetic utterance about God, and thus could mean not merely science but also the *Logos*—especially the sublime integration of sound and sense—of the bards of yore. Clement conceived of JESUS as a song consummating the harmony of all things, "and on this many-voiced instrument of the universe He makes music to God, and sings to the human instrument." St. AUGUSTINE composed *De musica* in the fifth century, the first in a long line of scholarly theoretical treatments of the Pythagorean theme. St. THOMAS AQUINAS asserted that "everything that moves in nature is moved by the Ruler; the angels transmit the motion to the spheres." *The Liturgy of St. Mark* is one of many medieval musical tractates that begins with a reference to the music of the spheres. The concept was that the church's praise tunes in to the praises of the cosmos; the place of music in church worship accords with the sort of praise offered by sun, moon, and stars. The harmony of the spheres rings out, the angel sound resounds, and the liturgy of the church has found its voice.

Clement, bishop of Alexandria in the second century C.E., also described processions of ancient Egyptian priests singing magic hymns by Hermes (the Greek god who guides and brings messages to souls), and named Hermes Trismegistus as the author of the *Corpus Hermeticum* (Hermetica), a body of esoteric lore that included the invocation by music of all the angelic and demonic realms. St. Augustine affirms Hermes Trismegistus in *The City of God*: "As for morality, it stirred not in Egypt until Trismegistus's time, who was indeed long before the sages and philosophers of Greece." The Hermetica texts, popular in Europe during the Renaissance, are of doubtful Egyptian origin but probably were written as pseudepigrapha.

In 1460 Cosimo de Medici obtained an almost complete manuscript of the Hermetica and contracted the brilliant classicist Marsilio Ficino to translate it. Ficino occupies an essential position in the chain of musical philosophers, for he also translated the key works of Plato and the Neoplatonists. Ficino was a great believer in sympathetic magic, and he detailed principles of musical MAGIC, combining stars with corresponding celestial virtues. Ficino himself composed astrological music, which has not survived, based on the essential congruity between the music of the spheres, the music of the human organism, and ordinary music making, emphasizing the sympathetic relationship between the human soul and the cosmic spirit, reflected in the perfect proportions of instrumental music to which the human organism responds so profoundly. Ficino postulated that music concerts possess a living spirit analogous to the human soul and the cosmic spirit. Other Renaissance philosophers followed Ficino's lead, among them Giordano Bruno and Tommaso Campanella. However, Campanella believed that "if there is harmony in the heavens and in the angels, it is of a different order," that is, our instrumental music is in no way comparable; if the celestial music exists, we are incapable of hearing it.

Astronomer and mathematician Johannes Kepler (1571–1630) wrote the summa on this theme, the fifth book of *The Harmony of the Universe*. Kepler acknowledges Pythagoras and Plato as his conceptual masters, and he follows their idealistic schema of a universe ruled by perfect mathematical music. For Plato and Cicero and the Scholastics the music of the spheres consisted only of scales, but Kepler added the dimension of polyphony, with simultaneity as an essential component. Geneva-born Jesuit antiquarian Athanasius Kircher published *Musurgia universalis* in 1650, an encyclopedia of music applying the music of the spheres governed by seraphic INTELLIGENCES to a critique of music in his time, including the new Baroque musical styles and the opera as well as the older polyphonic music.

Sir Isaac Newtown was the first to use logarithms in musical calculations. Greek mythology formed an integral part of his natural philosophy. He used language similar to that of Pythagoras and Plato on the theme of the musical universe: "the soul of the world, which propels into movement this body of the universe visible to us, being constructed of ratios which created from themselves a musical concord, must of necessity produce musical sounds from the movement which it provides by its proper impulse, having found the origin of them in the craftsmanship of its own composition." Newton saw in the perfect order of music the most apt analogue of the orderly cosmos.

After Newton, the great theme vanishes until one last flowering in the Masonic movement of the 18th century, climaxed in Mozart's 1791 opera *Die Zauberflöte* (*The Magic Flute*). Johann Sebastian Bach also was familiar with the themes of the harmony of the spheres and incorporated them into his compositions.

Angelic Themes in Music

Almost every major composer has written sacred music. Mathematical purity and cosmic scope—the music of the spheres—are recurrent qualities of most great musical works. The Baroque "doctrine of the affections" held that the purpose of music was to illustrate or imitate various emotional of affective states. This was the basis of early opera and an influence on later composers such as Bach and George Frederic Handel. Spiritual tuning of "the human instrument" through mythology reached an apex in the 19th century in Richard Wagner's *Ring* cycle of operas, and also the several dozen musical treatments of Goethe's *Faust*, notably Gaetano Donizetti's *Fausta* (1832), Gounod's *Faust* (1859), once the world's most popular opera, and Louis-Hector Berlioz's *The Damnation of Faust*.

An angelic chorus occurs in the last movement of Gustav Mahler's Symphony #8 in E Flat ("Symphony of a Thousand"). The closing of Goethe's *Faust* is the text. The angelic chorus also finds its way into hundreds of Christmas carols and sacred works. The angel blows the trumpet of the last judgment in art, literature, instrumental works, spirituals, and sacred songs. The angelic orchestra was a popular Renaissance and Baroque theme.

Angelic motifs in popular music have been inspired by the renewal of interest in angels.

Artistic Inspiration and Angels

The connection between artistic inspiration and angels is embodied in the Muses of Greek mythology; the term "muse" suggests attunement with a divine source. Countless musicians, artists, and poets have described the experience of being seized by the muse and "shown" or "given" a work.

Wolfgang Amadeus Mozart did not identify his source of inspiration, but he did describe the characteristics of it in a letter:

Whence and how do they [the compositions] come? I do not know and I have nothing to do with it. Those which please me, I keep in my head and hum. . . . Once I have my theme, another melody comes linking itself to the first one, in accordance to the needs of the composition as a whole. Then my soul is on fire with inspiration, if, however, nothing occurs to distract my attention. . . . The work grows; I keep expanding in conceiving it more and more clearly until I have the entire composition finished in my head though it may be long. Then my mind seizes it as a glance of my eye a beautiful picture of a handsome youth. It does not come to me successively, with its various parts and worked out in detail, as they will be later on, but it is in its entirety that my imagination lets me hear it.

Today the same description given by an artist might easily be ascribed to angels.

FURTHER READING

Anderson, E. *The Letters of Mozart and His Family.* 3d ed. New York: Norton, 1990.

Gaster, Theodor H. *The Dead Sea Scriptures.* 3d ed. Garden City, N.Y.: Anchor/Doubleday, 1976.

James, Jamie. *The Music of the Spheres.* New York: Grove Press, 1993.

Lang, Judith. *The Angels of God: Understanding the Bible.* Hyde Park, N.Y.: New City Press, 1997.

Peterson, Eric. *The Angels and the Liturgy.* New York: Herder and Herder, 1964.

Raphael in the guise of a man with Tobias (Gustave Doré)

mysterious stranger

An angel who appears in the form of a human being to intervene in the affairs of mortals, usually those who are in distress. The mysterious stranger is one of the more common and more dramatic manifestations of angels.

Characteristics of angelic mysterious strangers vary, though there are common elements that occur in most episodes. Mysterious strangers can be male or female, and of any race. Most often they are male—usually a fresh-looking, cleancut youth. They are invariably well dressed, polite, and knowledgeable about the crisis at hand. Often they are calm but they can be forceful, and they know just what to do. They do speak, though they talk sparingly, and they will even take hold of the people in distress. They eat food. They are convincingly real as flesh-and-blood humans. However, once the problem has been solved, the mysterious stranger vanishes. It is that abrupt and strange disappearance that makes people question whether they have been aided by a mortal or an angel. Upon reflection, the arrival of the mysterious stranger—suddenly, out of nowhere, or in the nick of time—adds credence to the angel-as-stranger belief.

Perhaps the first notable mysterious strangers of record are the three angels, disguised as men, who visit ABRAHAM, as reported in Genesis 18. The angels have been dispatched by God to destroy the wicked cities of SODOM AND GOMORRAH. En route, they visit Abraham's tent on the plains of Mamre. He welcomes them and gives them water to wash their feet, the shade of a tree for rest, and food. He stands by while the angels eat a meal of curds, milk, cakes, and the meat of a calf. The angels tell Abraham, who is 99, that his 90-year-old wife, Sarah—who had been barren her entire life—will bear a child the following spring. Abraham and Sarah do not believe it, but Sarah does indeed conceive and bear a son, ISAAC. The moral of this tale is to always be kind to strangers, who may be disguised angels and emissaries of the Lord.

In the apocryphal book of TOBIT, probably written in the second century B.C.E., the archangel Raphael appears as a mysterious stranger to guide Tobias on a journey.

An example of a modern mysterious stranger and a medical rescue is the following story from *Angels of Mercy* by the author. The story concerns a woman who lives in California:

I was in a hospital suffering from some rare throat virus that caused me to cough so violently, I would begin to strangle. During one of those fits in the middle of the night, I called for a nurse. No one came right away, and I began to panic, for I couldn't breathe.

Suddenly the door flew open and a short, stocky nurse came bursting in, and with a voice of authority said, "Close your mouth and breathe through your nose." When I gestured that no air would come through my nose, she clamped her hand over my mouth and shouted, "Breathe!" And, breathe I did and I stopped choking. Her next words were, "Just can't understand why they haven't taught you that." And out she went.

Because I wanted to thank her, the next morning I asked the nurse who was it who was on night duty. When she asked me to describe her, she looked puzzled and said that description didn't fit anyone on their staff, but she would check on it.

Later, the head nurse came in and asked me to describe the nurse again. She said there was no one employed there who came close to my description. When I asked why they hadn't instructed me on what to do when I began to strangle, they said they had never heard of the method.

The doctor's response to the experience was interesting. He knew about the method, but why he hadn't told me,

I'll never know. But he whispered in my ear, "I think you met an angel." By then, I was convinced I had.

A frequent type of mysterious stranger intervention is the "roadside rescue," in which a mysterious stranger arrives to help a motorist stranded on a lonely road at night, or injured in an accident in an isolated spot.

Not all people who say they are aided by angels report mysterious strangers. Some hear clear but disembodied voices, feel invisible hands, or sense unseen presences. It is not known why angels manifest as humans in some cases and not in others. Modern angelologists hypothesize that the appearance of a mysterious stranger may in fact be the least unsettling form of angelic intervention. Many persons undergoing stress are more likely to respond to the aid of what appears to be a friendly fellow human being. Perhaps the shock of an obviously supernatural intervention would only serve to intensify the crisis.

FURTHER READING

Guiley, Rosemary Ellen. *Angels of Mercy.* New York: Pocket Books, 1994.

Howard, Jane M. *Commune with Angels.* Virginia Beach, Va.: A.R.E. Press, 1992.

Smith, Robert C. *In the Presence of Angels.* Virginia Beach, Va.: A.R.E. Press, 1993.

N

Naamah

In Kabbalistic lore, one of four angels of prostitution and a partner of Samael. The other three are Lilith, Agrat bat Mahlat, and Eisheth Zenunim. Naamah means "pleasing." Naamah is the mother of the great DEMON Asmodeus and other demons. She seduces men and spirits and, with Lilith, causes epilepsy in children.

Naaririel YHVH

In 3 ENOCH, a great PRINCE in the seventh HEAVEN. Naaririel bows down to Sasnigiel.

Naberius (Cerberus)

One of the FALLEN ANGELS and 72 spirits of SOLOMON. Naberius is a marquis who commands 19 legions. He appears as a crowing cock and flutters about the MAGIC circle. In a hoarse voice, he imparts skill in arts and sciences, especially rhetoric. He also restores lost dignities and honors. JOHANN WEYER said he procures the loss of dignities and prelacies.

Nag Hammadi literature See GNOSTICISM.

Nahaliel

Angel who governs running streams. Nahaliel means "valley of God" in Hebrew.

Nakir

In Islamic lore, one of two blue-eyed, black angels (the other is Munkar) who receives condemned souls from the angel Ruman and punishes them in HELL.

names

The identity of a person or being. Ancient esoteric lore holds that names convey and determine personality, power, essence, qualities, luck, destiny, and fate. The names of angels, DEMONS, and God are crucial to the success of MAGIC and spiritual practice. Names are used in meditation to attain higher states of consciousness; in prayer to invoke assistance; and inscribed on AMULETS to protect, heal, and bring good fortune.

Historical Background

The roots of the importance of angel and God names date to ancient Babylonia, Assyria, and Egypt, cultures which gave great importance to the power of names. Because names held the essence of a being, knowing the names of deities and spirits gave one the ability to invoke and command them. Great power could be unleashed simply by the vibration of speaking a name.

In magical rites these names were invoked with great precision and accurate pronunciation; anything less meant failure. Many beings had numerous names, any and all of which might be invoked in order to

273

cover all bases. For example, the god Marduk alone had 50 names.

Egyptian practice, which borrowed names and gods and spirits from other cultures, evolved into the use of barbarous and nonsensical names. If the original name and language were not understood, a similar-sounding word was substituted. The substitutes were held to carry the same force. Many incantations carried strings of names and name substitutes. The more corrupted the name, the greater power it was held to carry.

The use of multiple and barbarous names passed into Jewish, Hellenistic, Gnostic Essene, and Christian lore and magic. The importance of names is evidenced in the Old Testament. For example, when JACOB wrestles with the dark angel, he demands its name, but the angel does not give it, presumably because then Jacob could use the name to summon and command him. In the pseudepigraphon the Testament of Solomon, King SOLOMON learns the names of demons and their THWARTING ANGELS in order to have power over them.

The Essenes, a Jewish sect that existed at about the time of Jesus, had initiation rites in which the initiated swore never to reveal angel names, lest they be abused for evil purposes. The Gnostics also had rites of initiation that involved secret names of ARCHONS and AEONS.

The MERKABAH mysticism which preceded the KABBALAH (ca. 100 B.C.E.–1000 C.E.) emphasized the importance of names of power as a way of ascending through the layers of heavens to the throne-chariot of God. The names of angels and the secret names of God intermingle in the literature, and some names are not distinguished as referring specifically to one or the other.

By medieval times, names of power had acquired great importance, especially in Jewish mysticism. Texts such as the SEFER RAZIEL and the Sword of Moses underscored this importance and gave lists of names to use in incantations. Other secret names—held to have the most power—were transmitted orally.

The systems of GEMATRIA, notarikon, and temurah created sacred names of God and angels from the numerical values of letters and recombinations of letters. Words evolved into names. Other names were corrupted versions of mystical names inherited from other cultures.

In magical practice, the sacred names could be uttered only when the magician or practitioner had prepared and purified himself. Some taught that the names could not be said out loud at all, but could be meditated upon only within the heart. The powers ascribed to the names were limitless.

A typical incantation might open with 56 names of angels and contain names of angels and names of God lumped together. Pronunciations were open to interpretation.

Names of power passed into the writings of the "Western Kabbalah," a term often applied to the various magical texts or GRIMOIRES that flourished in Europe in the 17th–19th centuries, and which drew upon a variety of esoteric sources.

Names of Angels

Many angel names end in -el, a suffix meaning "of God" in Hebrew. Others end in -yah, meaning "Lord." The root of the name may be drawn from the function or duty of an angel. The name Nuriel, "fire of God," is based on the Aramaic word of fire, *nura*. Many angel names in the Merkabah seem to have no root meaning, and may be the products of glossolalia in trance—nonsensical names spontaneously created in the rhythmic repetition of hymns and prayers. (See METATRON.)

Each letter in a name shines a divine light that can be meditated upon and contemplated. Other names, such as those produced by letter recombinations, look impossible to pronounce, such as Zmrchd, created by combining the final Hebrew letters of the first five verses of Genesis.

Some angels have multiple names: Metatron, for example, has 70, a number that appears often in Jewish lore. There are 70 angels who protect against all sorts of dangers, and 70 attributes of God.

The angel names used most frequently are Michael, Gabriel, and Raphael, who are mentioned often in the Talmudic literature and are the only angels mentioned by name in the Catholic canon. Uriel/Phanuel and Metatron appear often in Jewish mystical literature.

Jewish literature and the writings in the APOCRYPHA AND PSEUDEPIGRAPHA TEXTS contain many angel names—especially the ENOCH books—but the Catholic Church does not permit the use of any proper names of angels other than Michael, Gabriel, and Raphael. All names from apocryphal writings were rejected by Pope Zachary in 745 C.E., and again by a synod at Aix-la-Chapelle, France, in 789. (See REPROBATED ANGELS.)

Names of God

The most powerful of all is the name of God. In Jewish lore, the greatest name of God, the "Ineffable Name," is the Tetragrammaton, the personal name of God in the Old Testament. It is given as YHVH, the Hebrew letters *yod, he, vau, he*. The numerical values assigned to these letters add up to 10, which in Hebrew numerology represents the basic organizing principle in the universe. So powerful is the Tetragrammaton that for centuries it was seldom spoken. As early as the time of JESUS, it was supposed to be whispered only on Yom Kippur by a high priest. The exact pronunciation of the Tetragrammaton is not known; the most accepted is "Yahweh." A common variation is "Jehovah." YHVH is sometimes appended to the names of the highest angels around God to denote their power and stature.

Since the name of God could not be uttered, other names of God were substituted. During Talmudic times, these names multiplied, all derived from the original four-letter Tetragrammaton. Secret 12-, 22-, and 72-letter names were taught to only the most worthy. These names were joined by many other names of other numerical values.

In the seventh century, Isadore of Seville compiled a list of 10 names of God used frequently: El, Eloe, Sabbaoth, Zelioz, Ramathel, Eyel, Adonay, Ya, Tetragrammaton, Saday, and Eloym. Another commonly used name was Ehyeh Asher Ahyeh ("I Am That I Am," which MOSES heard from the burning bush).

The 12-letter name of God was out of use by Talmudic times. The 22-letter name of God appeared in the Sefer Raziel, though probably it has much older origins. The Sefer Raziel offers no interpretation of it. Anaktam Pastam Paspasim Dionsim quickly was incorporated into charms and invocations, and it was added to the reading of the Priestly Benediction in the synagogue in the 17th century.

The 42-letter name of God may have been derived from an old prayer, though medieval mystics held that it came from the first 42 letters in the Bible.

The 72-letter name of God is divided into triadic syllables. According to the Sefer Raziel, it cannot be surpassed in power and no magic can be done without it. The name is derived from three verses in Exodus 14:19–21, each of which contains 72 letters. Different parts of the name have different uses. For example, the first part of the name will conquer evil and drive off evil spirits while the second part will protect against the evil eye and demons and help one acquire wisdom.

3 Enoch gives the following 70 names of God which may be expressed (some are repeated):

Hadririon YHVH of Hosts	Meromiron	Beroradin
Neuriron	Gebiriron	Kebiriron
Doriron	Sebiroron	Zehiroron
Hadidron	Webidriron	Wediriron
Peruriron	Hisiridon	Ledoriron
Tatbiron	Satriron	Adiriron
Dekiriron	Lediriron	Seririron
Tebiriron	Taptapiron	Apapiron
Sapsapiron	Sapsapiron	Gapgapiron
Raprapiron	Dapdapiron	Qapqapuron
Haphapiron	Wapwapiron	Pappapiron
Zapzapiron	Taptapiron	Apapiron

Mapmapiron	Sapsapiron	Napnapiron
Laplapiron	Wapwapiron	Kapkapiron
Haphapiron	Tabtabib	Ababib
Qabqabib	Sabsabib	Babbabib
Sabsabib	Gabgabib	Rabrabib
Harabrabib	Pabpabib	Habhabib
Ababib	Zabzabib	Sabsabib
Hashasib	Tabtabib	Wesisib
Mabmabib	Nupkabib	Mammambib
Nupnubib	Pastabib	Sassib

FURTHER READING

Charlesworth, James H., ed. *The Old Testament Pseudepigrapha*. Vols. 1 and 2. New York: Doubleday, 1983, 1985.

Scholem, Gershom, *Kabbalah*. New York: Dorset Press, 1974.

Trachtenberg, Joshua. *Jewish Magic and Superstition: A Study in Folk Religion*. New York: Berhman's Jewish Book House, 1939.

Nanael

Angel who belongs to the order of PRINCIPALITIES and who governs the great sciences, philosophy, and ecclesiastics. Nanael also is one of the 72 angels of the SCHEMHAMPHORAE.

Narcariel

In the LEMEGETON, the ruling angel of the eighth hour of the night, called Xymalim. Narcariel has 101,550 dukes and other servants divided into 12 orders to serve him.

Nasargiel (Nagrasagiel, Nasragiel)

Lion-headed good angel who rules HELL with Kipod and Nairyo Sangha. Nasargiel is the angel who shows MOSES the underworld on his heavenly journey.

Nathanael (Xathaniel, Zathael)

Angel who rules fire, vengeance, and hidden things. Nathanael means "gift of God." According to Jewish lore, Nathanael is the sixth angel created by God. In magical lore, he rules the sixth hour.

nature spirits

A type of being who dwells in the nature kingdom. Nature spirits are to earth what angels are to heaven and humans. They possess supernatural powers and watch over the well-being of all things in nature—animal, plant, and mineral.

Nature spirits come in countless types, shapes, sizes, and dispositions. Some are regarded as being benevolent toward humans, whereas others are mischievous or malevolent. Some are humanlike in appearance, whereas others assume the shapes of animals, half-human half-animals, or fabulous-looking beings.

Nature spirits tend to stay in one spot: They remain attached to a thing or place in nature, such as trees, rivers, plants, bogs, mountains, lakes, and so forth. (See GENII.)

Kabbalists assigned four angelic PRINCES to rule over the four winds and over the four quarters of the world. MICHAEL rules the east wind, RAPHAEL the west wind, GABRIEL the north wind, and ARIEL the south wind. According to FRANCIS BARRETT, a 19th-century English occultist, "every one of these spirits is a great prince, and has much power and freedom in the dominion of his own planets and signs, and in their times, years, months, days and hours; and in their elements, and parts of the world, and winds."

Barrett also observed that, in counterbalance to the heavenly angels, there are evil spirits who also rule the four winds and four quarters like kings: Urieus over the east, Anaymon over the south, Paymon over the west, and Egin over the north. (The Hebrew names are, respectively, Samael, Azazel, Azael, and Mahazuel.)

See DEVAS.

FURTHER READING
Barrett, Francis. *The Magus*. Secaucus, N.J.: The Citadel Press, 1967. First published 1801.

Naya'il

In Islamic lore, angel who tests the Sufi mystic Abu Yazid's devotion to God during his mystical ascent to HEAVEN. Naya'il offers the mystic a kingdom beyond description, but Abu Yazid ignores him, thus passing the test.

near-death experiences (NDEs)

A constellation of mystical-like phenomena experienced by individuals who come close to death, or who clinically die and then return to life. The near-death experience (NDE) often involves beings of bright light identified by some as angels.

The term "near-death experience" was coined by Dr. Raymond Moody, the first American physician to document and study the phenomenon. His initial research was published in 1975 in his book *Life after Life*. Moody found that few people would talk openly about an NDE out of fear of ridicule, and medical professionals tended to dismiss such episodes as hallucinations. Within two decades, NDEs were common in the media and were the subject of serious scientific inquiry. It is estimated that some 15 million people in the United States have had an NDE; children as well as adults report them.

Oft-reported characteristics of NDEs are:

- A sense of being out of body, looking down on one's self and others who try to resuscitate the body;
- Cessation of pain and a feeling of bliss or peacefulness;
- Traveling down a dark tunnel toward a brilliant light at the end;
- Meeting glowing beings who appear to be angels, JESUS, or other religious figures;
- Meeting dead friends and relatives;
- Seeing a life review;
- Seeing visions of the future;

Angel guiding the spirits' flight (Reprinted courtesy of U.S. Library of Congress)

- Undergoing a judgment of one's life that is not rendered by God, angels, or any being, but by one's self;
- Feeling reluctant to return to life.

Skeptics explain NDEs as hallucinations brought about by a lack of oxygen; the release of endorphins, the body's own painkillers; or increased levels of carbon dioxide in the blood. NDE researchers counter that drug-induced experiences can parallel an NDE but they lack the mystical, noetic quality of the NDE, which brings about profound life changes after return. NDErs often lose their fear of death and have a diminished interest in material pursuits; they begin leading more spiritual lives. Some change their careers. Some experience psychic openings and prophetic ability. Some feel evangelistic, and they want to impart to others the importance of love.

The beings of light seen in an NDE (which may or may not be identified as "angels"—cultural and religious conditioning appear to be influencing factors) often are seen initially as formless light that gradually takes on humanlike form made of brilliant light or clothed in brilliant white robes. The beings radiate an all-encompassing intense love that fills the person with joy and peace.

The beings function as both guide and gatekeeper. They take the person along on their after-death journey until they reach a threshold, such as an entrance or a bridge to a building or beautiful garden, or a place that the person intuitively knows marks the final boundary between life and death. The beings then tell their charges that they must go back because they have unfinished business. Sometimes the beings ask their charges if they wish to stay or return. Most people say they wish to stay, but usually a relationship such as a spouse or child pulls them back to the realm of the living.

In many instances, souls of the dead function as guide and gatekeeper, rather than angelic beings.

The NDE is thought by many experiencers and researchers to be a form of enlightenment or "gateway to a higher consciousness," which could have a transformative effect on humanity if enough people have similar experiences. It may not be necessary to come to the brink of physical death in order to have the experience.

Some researchers have proposed that the NDE may be a modern mechanism for the ongoing transmission of spiritual wisdom and truths and the maintenance of social order. From antiquity, the mythologies of the world have included stories of otherworld journeys by heroes, sages, and prophets. These visionary quests and journeys are laden with archetypal figures and symbols. The heroes are accompanied by guide figures (angels or beings comparable to angels), and they ascend to heaven or descend to the underworld. They encounter strange beings, have adventures, and learn the secrets of the cosmos. They are given laws, moral codes, and spiritual truths to deliver to others upon their return. This theme appears not only in mythology but in literature as well (see DANTE), and it is also documented in real-life NDEs from earlier times. (However, there is no historical evidence to indicate that such figures as MOSES, ISAIAH, EZEKIEL, or MUHAMMAD had their lives in jeopardy when they had their visionary experiences. Their experiences may have been spontaneous, or the result of intense prayer, meditation, and fasting, or produced by consciousness-altering techniques such as found in MERKABAH mysticism.)

In ages past, communities and social groups relied upon visionary figures as their intermediaries to other realms. The increase in NDEs into a wider pool of population, as well as the increased reporting of other kinds of "exceptional human experiences" (episodes of psi, out-of-body travel, mystical experience, and so forth) show a trend toward individuals becoming visionaries in their own right. Rather than obtain wisdom secondhand from a sage, the individual has his or her own direct experience of God. The NDE functions as one way in which the religious imagination mediates the search for ultimate truth in a scientific age.

NDE researcher Kenneth Ring has found numerous parallels between the NDE and the UFO encounter. In some UFO encounters, EXTRATERRESTRIALS, who arrive in brilliant light, take humans on cosmic trips and impart prophecies and wisdom to take back to earth. Some contactees consider the ETs to be angels, and some ufologists contend that ancient descriptions of angels and gods descending from the sky actually were visitations by ETs. However, most UFO episodes are negative; some involve abductions and unpleasant medical procedures. Seen from a mythological standpoint, the UFO encounter might be the demonic side of the NDE.

There also are similarities between the NDE and MARIAN APPARITIONS, or visions of the Blessed Virgin MARY. In Marian apparitions, formless light gradually assumes shapes interpreted as angels and Mary. Paranormal phenomena occur (such as the spinning sun at the Fatima apparitions in Portugal in 1917), and visionaries are imparted wisdom and given instructions for relaying information to others. They are told or shown visions of the future. The wisdom exhorts people to a more spiritual life, including prayer.

Many of the contemporary visions of the future seen in NDEs, UFO encounters, and Marian apparitions are apocalyptic, just as were the religious visions nearly two millennia ago: massive cataclysms, earth changes, economic woes, evil threats, wars, and upheavals in society. Some near-death experiencers say they do not see HEAVEN, however, but see terrifying fiery HELLS and demonic figures—just as did ancient visionaries. (See ENOCH; EZRA.) One of the major functions of angels is to usher in the "end times" and the day of judgment, to quell the forces of evil, and to separate the souls of the righteous and the sinners and escort them to their appropriate afterlife.

Philosopher Michael Grosso observes that the "end times" is an archetype deeply imbedded within humanity's collective unconscious and that history shows a pattern of a rise in apocalyptic experiences at major calendar milestones, such as the end of a century or millennium. These experiences, and the increased interest in angels as of the late 20th century, may be part of a broad psychic shift on a collective level, marking a new era of expanded consciousness, especially of a spiritual nature.

See ANGEL OF DEATH; APOCRYPHA AND PSEUDE-PIGRAPHA TEXTS; DEATHBED VISIONS; REVELATION.

FURTHER READING
Grosso, Michael. *The Final Choice*. Walpole, N.H.: Stillpoint, 1985.
Moody, Raymond A., Jr. *Life after Life*. Harrisburg, Pa.: Stackpole Books, 1976.
———. *The Light Beyond*. New York: Bantam Books, 1988.
Ring, Kenneth. *Heading toward Omega*. New York: William Morrow, 1984.
———. *The Omega Project*. New York: William Morrow, 1992.
Zaleski, Carol. *Otherworld Journeys: Accounts of Near-Death Experience in Medieval and Modern Times*. New York: Oxford University Press, 1987.

Nelchael

Angel who is both good and bad. Nelchael is one of the 72 angels of the SCHEMHAMPHORAE, but in other lore is a FALLEN ANGEL who teaches astronomy, geography, and mathematics to his fellow DEMONS in HELL.

Nephilim

A race of giants spawned by the cohabitation of angels (see WATCHERS) and human women. Nephilim means "fallen," "those who have fallen," or "those who were cast down." The Nephilim sometimes are called the SONS OF GOD, as are their FALLEN ANGEL parents. Helel is their chief. The Nephilim displeased God.

Genesis 6:4 implies that the Nephilim were already present upon the earth when the Sons of God began their relations with mortal women: "The Nephilim were upon the earth in those days, and also afterward, when the sons of god came into the daughters of men, and they bore children to them. These were the mighty men that were of old, the men of renown." The corruption brought by the mingling of angels and humans caused God to regret that he had made man upon the earth. He decides to blot out not only the human race but also every living thing on earth. He selects NOAH and his family to survive this disaster, the great Flood, and repopulate the earth.

Evidently not all the Nephilim perish, however, for a later reference in Numbers refers to the Anakim, the sons of the Nephilim: "and there we saw the Nephilim (the sons of Anak, who come from the Nephilim); and we seemed to ourselves like grasshoppers and so we seemed to them" (13:33). The Anakim are later destroyed.

1 ENOCH presents a more descriptive picture of the Nephilim as monstrous beings:

> And the women became pregnant and gave birth to great giants whose heights were 300 cubits. These (giants) consumed the produce of all the people until the people detested feeding them. So the giants turned against the (people) in order to eat them. And they began to sin against birds, wild beasts, reptiles and fish. And their flesh was devoured the one by the other, and they drank blood. And then the earth brought an accusation against the oppressors. (7:3–7)

Meanwhile, the Watchers spread more corruption by teaching people secret and magical arts they are not supposed to know. From the heavens above the angels Michael, Gabriel, and Surafal observe in horror the bloodshed and oppression upon the earth. They hear the prayers of the people begging for help. They petition God to intervene, saying that the giants have filled the entire earth with blood and oppression. God declares that he will punish these transgressions with complete destruction in the Flood. He tells Gabriel:

> Proceed against the bastards and the reprobates and the children of adultery; and destroy the children of adultery and expel the children of the Watchers from among the people and send them against one another (so that) they may be destroyed in the fight, for length of days have they not. They will beg you everything—for their fathers on behalf of themselves because they hope to live an eternal life. (They hope) that each one of them will live a period of 500 years. (10:9–11)

But evidently not all of the Nephilim are destroyed, for Enoch 15:8–9 says they shall be called "evil spirits upon the earth" who dwell both on the earth and in the earth, indicating that they become DEMONS.

The Nephilim also are the subject of a QUMRAN TEXT referred to as the Enochic Book of Giants (4Q532). The text tells that two Nephilim sons of Semyaza (leader of the Watchers), named Ahya and Ohya, have a shared DREAM vision in which they visit a world garden and see 200 trees being cut down by angels. They don't understand the dream and so they take it to the Nephilim council. The council appoints one of their members, Mahawai, to consult Enoch in Paradise and ask him what it means. Mahawai rises up into the air like the whirlwinds and flies with the help of his hands like an eagle until he reaches Enoch. Enoch says that the 200 trees symbolize the 200 Watchers who are going to be destroyed in the coming Flood.

Later in the text Mahawai transforms into a bird again to make another journey. He flies too close to the Sun and is threatened with incineration. He is saved by Enoch whose voice comes down from HEAVEN to tell him to turn back and not die prematurely.

FURTHER READING

Charlesworth, James H., ed. *The Old Testament Pseudepigrapha.* Vols. 1 and 2. New York: Doubleday, 1983, 1985.

Collins, Andrew. *From the Ashes of Angels: The Forbidden Legacy of a Fallen Race.* London: Signet Books, 1996.

Eisenman, Robert, and Michael Wise. *The Dead Sea Scrolls Uncovered.* London: Element Books Ltd., 1992.

Netzach See TREE OF LIFE.

Nike

The Greek winged goddess of victory and an early inspiration for the winged angel. The Greeks associated Nike with Athena, the queen of HEAVEN and the goddess of wisdom, skill, and warfare; Athena sometimes was worshiped as Athena Nike. In particular Nike embodied victory in athletics, music and especially battle. She appeared to the victorious on the battlefield, to whisper the favors of the gods. The Romans called her Victoria or VICTORY.

See IMAGES OF ANGELS.

Nisroc

Assyrian deity who became both a good and a FALLEN ANGEL. As a holy angel, Nisroc rules the order of PRINCIPALITIES. As a fallen angel, he rules cuisine in hell's House of PRINCES.

Noah

Patriarch who is chosen by God to repopulate the world after the destruction of the Flood. In the Old Testament, the story of Noah is told in Genesis 5:28–9:28. He is son of Lamech, grandson of Methuselah and the great-grandson of ENOCH. At his birth,

Lamech predicts, "Out of the ground which the Lord has cursed this one shall bring us relief from our work and the toil of our hands" (5:28–29).

When God becomes disgusted by the corruption wrought by the WATCHERS, he decides to destroy everything on earth with the Flood. But Noah, who is 600 years old, is righteous and blameless, and God elects to save him and his family—his wife, three sons, and their wives. God tells Noah about the coming Flood (in midrashim, Uriel is the messenger) and instructs him to build an ark of gopher wood. He and his family are to take aboard pairs of all living creatures and ride out the Flood. When the waters subside they will renew and repopulate the earth.

The waters rain for 40 days and 40 nights, and seven months pass before the waters abate enough for the ark to come to rest on the mountains of Ararat. God tells them to start anew and pledges that he will never again destroy every living creature. Noah becomes the first tiller (farmer). He dies at the age of 950. The descendants of his three sons, Shem, Ham, and Japheth, spread abroad on the earth.

Apocryphal texts imply that Noah was of supernatural, possibly angelic, origin. In 1 Enoch, the prophet Enoch describes Noah upon his birth:

> And his body was white as snow and as red as a rose; the hair of his head as white as wool and his *demdema* ["afro" hair] beautiful; and as for his eyes when he opened them the whole house glowed like the sun-(rather) the whole house glowed even more exceedingly. And when he arose from the hands of the midwife, he opened his mouth and spoke to the lord with righteousness. (106:2–4)

Lamech flees to Methuselah and says, "I have begotten a strange son. He is not like an (ordinary) human being, but he looks like the children of the angels of heaven to me; his form is different, and he is not like us. His eyes are like the rays of the sun, and his face is glorious. It does not seem to me that he is of me but of angels; and I fear that a wondrous phenomenon may take place upon the earth in his days" (106: 5–6). Lamech asks his father to find out the truth about his son from Enoch.

Enoch replies that angels have sinned by marrying women and begetting children with them. He foretells a great destruction upon the earth and a flood for one year. Noah has been born righteous and shall be left upon the earth, and his three sons shall spread his seed and multiply. Enoch says he know this because the Lord has revealed it to him and he has read it in the books of HEAVEN.

According to 1 Enoch, angels were involved in the building of Noah's ark.

In a Genesis aprocyphon, Lamech suspects his wife, Bat-Enosh, of having sexual relations with one of the fallen WATCHERS, but Bat-Enosh swears that Noah is Lamech's child.

The QUMRAN TEXT 4Q534–536 describes the birth of Noah. He weighs about seven pounds three ounces (350 shekels). The Holy Ones will teach him all the mysteries and he shall be great. At the age of two he will be able to discern one thing from another and in adulthood he will be wise and discrete. A vision will come to him while he is on his knees in prayer and he will know the secrets of mankind. He is the elect of God and his plans will endure forever.

FURTHER READING

Charlesworth, James H., ed. *The Old Testament Pseudepigrapha.* Vols. 1 and 2. New York: Doubleday, 1983, 1985.

Eisenman, Robert, and Michael Wise. *The Dead Sea Scrolls Uncovered.* London: Element Books Ltd., 1992.

notarikon See GEMATRIA.

numbers of angels See ANGELS.

Nuriel

Angel of hailstorms and spellbinding power who is invoked in MAGIC to protect against evil. Nuriel means "fire of God." Nuriel resides in the second HEAVEN, where he is attended by 50 myriads of angels who are made of fire and water. He manifests in the form of an eagle and sometimes is equated with Uriel. One of the tallest of angels, he measures 300 PARASANGS tall.

Obyzouth

Female DEMON whose principal acts of evil are to kill newborn infants and cause others to be stillborn. In the Testament of Solomon, Obyzouth appears with disheveled hair and arrogantly refuses to answer questions until King SOLOMON has purified himself by washing his hands and has sat on his throne. The king complies. Obyzouth describes how she travels about every night, visiting women as they give birth, and strangling their newborns. She is successful every night. She also injures eyes, condemns mouths, destroys minds, and makes bodies feel pain. She is thwarted by the archangel Raphael, and admits that she will flee to the "other world" (the realm of demons) if women who are in labor write her name on a piece of parchment.

The horrified king has Obyzouth bound by her hair and hung in front of the Temple of Jerusalem, so that everyone who passes through will glorify the God of Israel, who has given Solomon command over the demons.

Och

One of the seven ruling angels of the 196 Olympic provinces of HEAVEN, according to the Arbatel of Magic. As the fourth angel, Och rules the sun, 28 provinces, and 36,536 legions of spirits, each legion having 490 beings. Och is famous for his alchemical wisdom. He can transmute anything into gold and stones. He is invoked for longevity and can grant 600 years of perfect health.

Ohrmazd (Ahura Mazda)

The good God of ZOROASTRIANISM. Ohrmazd, originally known as Ahura Mazda, is the source of all being and all good. He is assisted by angel-like helpers, the AMARAHSPANDS and the YAZATAS, in the cosmic fight against his evil counterpart, Ahriman. Unlike the God of monotheism, Ohrmazd does not permit evil to exist; evil exists as a separate force that ultimately will be conquered by good.

Olympian spirits

In magical lore, angels or spirits of the air and interplanetary space, also called the Stewards of Heaven. The Olympian spirits rule the 196 provinces of the universe.

Omael

Angel who governs chemistry and the perpetuation of species and races. Omael is one of the 72 angels of the SCHEMHAMPHORAE, but he is also sometimes identified as a FALLEN ANGEL.

Onoel (Anael, Hamiel, Haniel, Oniel)
In GNOSTICISM, one of the seven great ARCHONS. According to ORIGEN, Onoel is a DEMON who appears in the form of an ass.

Onoskelis

In the Testament of Solomon, a female FALLEN ANGEL summoned by Beelzebub to the presence of King SOLOMON, and made to work on the king's Temple of Jerusalem. Onoskelis tells Solomon she lives in caves, cliffs, and ravines, and she perverts men and strangles them. She travels by the full moon. She is thwarted by the name of Yahweh (the "Holy One of Israel"). Solomon uses the name and his magical ring, and he forces Onoskelis to work day and night spinning hemp for ropes used in the temple construction.

Ophaniel (Ofaniel, Ofniel, Opanniel, Ophan, Yahriel)

PRINCE who heads the angelic order of the OPHANIM (THRONES)—from which he derives his name—and who is the "angel in charge of the disk (wheel) of the moon." He serves as one of the seven throne angels who executes the commands of the POWERS. He is sometimes equated with Sandalphon.

Ophaniel is described in 3 ENOCH 25: 2–4:

> He has 16 faces, four on each side, and 100 wings on each side. He has 8,766 eyes, corresponding to the number of hours in a year, 2,191 on each side. In each pair of eyes in each of his faces lightnings flash; from every eye torches blaze, and no one can look on them, for anyone who looks on them is at once consumed. The height of his body is a journey of 2,500 years; no eye can see it. No mouth can tell the mighty strength of his power, save only the King of kings of kings, the Holy One, blessed be he.

3 Enoch states that as prince of the ophanim, who are the order above the CHERUBIM, Ophaniel stands over them every day and tends them, beautifies them, praises them, arranges their running, polishes their platforms, adorns their compartments, makes their turnings smooth, and cleans their seats. His work increases their beauty, magnifies their majesty, and makes them swift in the praise of God.

Ophaniel has 88 angels who "make the moon's globe run 354,000 PARASANGS every night, whenever the moon stands in the east at its turning point," which is on the 15th of every night. (3 Enoch 17:5) In this lunar duty, Ophaniel ranks below Galgalliel, who is in charge of the sun, and above Rahatiel, who is in charge of the constellations.

FURTHER READING
Charlesworth, James H., ed. *The Old Testament Pseud-epigrapha.* Vols. 1 and 2. New York: Doubleday, 1983, 1985.

ophanim (aufanim, ofanim, ophannim)

In the MERKABAH, high-ranking celestial beings or angels who are "Many-Eyed Ones" and "WHEELS" by which God distinguishes the chaos. The ophanim are equated with THRONES and sometimes with CHERUBIM. In Jewish lore and in the Enochian books they are fiery beings. Their prince is given as Ophaniel, Raphael, and Ribkiel.

3 ENOCH 25:6–7 gives a description:

> All the ophanim are full of eyes and full of wings, eyes corresponding to wings and wings corresponding to eyes. From them light shines, like the light of the morning star. Seventy-two sapphire stones are set in their garments, on the left side of them, and four emeralds are set in each one's crown, the brightness of which shines in the four corners of 'Arabot, just as the brightness of the sun's orb shines into the four corners of the world. Pavilions of brilliance, pavilions of splendor, pavilions of light, sapphire, and emerald envelop them, so that no one should see the appearance of their eyes and faces.

According to the Sefer Yetzirah, God made fire from water and fashioned for himself a throne of Glory with ophanim, SERAPHIM, and cherubim as his MINISTERING ANGELS of fire, thus completing his dwelling. The ophanim exist in the universe of Asiyah (Making/Creation) and are the angelic order of Chokmah (Wisdom), the second sephirot of the Kabbalistic TREE OF LIFE, where they are under the rule of the archangel Ratziel.

A later name for the ophanim is GALGALLIM.

See EZEKIEL.

FURTHER READING
Charlesworth, James H., ed. *The Old Testament Pseud-epigrapha.* Vols. 1 and 2. New York: Doubleday, 1983, 1985.

Ophiel

One of the seven ruling angels of the 196 Olympic provinces of HEAVEN, according to the Arbatel of Magic. As the sixth angel, Ophiel governs all matters pertaining to Mercury, 14 provinces, and 100,000 legions of spirits, each legion having 490 beings. Ophiel can transmute quicksilver into a white stone. His name is sometimes invoked in necromantic rituals.

Opus Sanctorum Angelorum See DEVOTIONAL CULTS.

Oray See LERAJIE.

Orias

One of the FALLEN ANGELS and 72 spirits of SOLOMON. Orias is a marquis who has 30 legions of DEMONS. He appears as a lion with a serpent's tail that rides a horse and holds two huge, hissing snakes. He teaches the virtues of the planets and stars. He transforms men, grants dignities, prelacies, and confirmations, and gives the favor of friends and enemies.

Oriel

In the LEMEGETON, the ruling angel of the 10th hour of the day, called Lamarhon. Oriel rules 5,600 dukes and servants who are divided into 10 orders.

Orifiel (Orfiel, Orifel, Oriphiel, Orphiel)

One of the seven principal ARCHANGELS, a PRINCE of THRONES, ruler of the planet Saturn, and angel of the wilderness. According to the LEMEGETON, Orifiel serves under Anael as angel of the second hour of the day; he also is one of the ANGELS OF THE EARTH. Paracelsus described him as a TALISMAN that replaces one of the GENII of Egypt.

Origen (ca. 185–254)

Christian theologian, church father, and apologist in a time of intense religious turbulence. Origen wrote extensively about angels and their roles, influencing other theologians who came after him. His theology later was viewed as controversial, unorthodox, and heretical.

Life and Works

Origen was born in Alexandria, Egypt, and is recognized as the first of the church fathers who was born into a Christian family. His father Leonides reportedly was martyred in the persecution of Alexandria under Septimus Severus in 202. Tradition records that Origen's mother restrained her son from seeking the glory of martyrdom by hiding his clothes to keep him indoors. The oldest of seven children, Origen became a teacher of Greek to support his bereaved family and quickly achieved recognition and success within the church as an instructor of catechumens (adult converts in training for baptism).

Lore holds that Origen castrated himself in young manhood, an act of zeal not uncommon in the early church. Whether this is true or not, Origen retained a reputation for saintly asceticism, chastity, and an appetite for hard work that earned him the nickname Adamantius. In his later life he wrote a commentary on St. Matthew in which he deplores fanatics who take a literal interpretation of Matthew 19:12, which observes that some men make themselves eunuchs "for the sake of heaven."

Orifiel (Copyright 1995 by Robert M. Place; from *The Angels Tarot* by Rosemary Ellen Guiley and Robert M. Place)

One of Origen's admirers, Ambrosius, became the patron of his *Hexapla,* hiring for him seven scribes of the biblical text and seven transcribers of Origen's dictation. Origen was loved and revered in Palestine, Phoenicia, Greece, and Arabia. He traveled frequently to explain and defend Christian doctrine and teach educated prospective converts.

Origen's long productive years in Alexandria were ended with the hostility of the bishop Demetrius over Origen's having been ordained a presbyter during his travels in Palestine. Another persecution of Alexandria by Rome was also underway, this time by Caracalla. Thus Origen moved to Ceasarea in Palestine in 231 and continued there to teach, preach, and write.

Among his pupils were the great Eastern Orthodox church fathers St. Basil the Great and St. Gregory of Nyssa.

During the Decian persecution (249–250) Origen was imprisoned and tortured in an unsuccessful attempt to have him denounce his faith. His physical health may well have been broken by this suffering and he died shortly thereafter at Tyre (ca. 253–254). A marble monument marked his grave until the 13th century.

Origen's linguistic expertise was outstanding; he worked for 30 years on an authoritative edition of the Old Testament with his *Hexapla,* a huge set of documents that contained six parallel columns of the Hebrew and Greek textual versions.

He describes a complex ANGELOLOGY in *De Principiis* ("of first principles"). This work consists of a coherent system of Christian teaching about God and the cosmos to refute Gnostic dualism and a pioneer attempt to explain methods for attaining an accurate interpretation of the Bible. He was exploratory rather than dogmatic, and his speculations were later turned against him.

Only a fraction of his work survives in reliable texts. The *Hexapla* was lost and the original Greek *De Principiis* is available only in fragments. The latter was translated into Latin; in 398 Rufinus produced a version sanitized of heresy.

Angelology

The following are Origen's central concepts related to angels. Quotes are from *De Principiis* unless otherwise indicated.

COSMOLOGY

'Before the AEONS existed all spirits were pure; DEMONS, souls and angels alike all served God and did what he commanded them. The devil was one of them. He had free-will and wanted to set himself up against God, but God cast him down. All the other powers fell with him. The biggest sinners became demons, lesser ones angels, the least archangels. . . . Other souls were not sinful enough to be made demons but were too sinful to be made angels. These God punished by making the world, binding them to bodies and putting them into it. Although these spiritual creatures, then, all had the same nature, God made some of them demons, some angels, and some men. That does not mean that he is a respecter of persons. No, what he did was in keeping with their sins. If it were not so, and if the soul had no previous experience, how is it that we find men blind from birth, before they could possibly have sinned, and why do others go blind although they have done nothing wrong?'

This passage from Book II of *De Principiis* contains the basis of Origen's cosmology: The variety of beings and bodies issues from the use of free choice by all rational beings made *before* the creation of the world. One of Origen's most controversial tenets is his belief that even heavenly bodies, planets, and stars were once pure spiritual beings made material through their free choice toward evil. Two of these ideas were later considered heretical by some:

1. A pure, incorporeal plane which preceded the physical (a concept basic to Platonism and GNOSTICISM);
2. A system similar to the Eastern concept of karma: fate doled out to souls "in keeping with their sins" in past lives (suggesting reincarnation) or, according to Origen, previous planes of existence.

Origen believes God carefully planned the cosmos after the Fall to enable his free creatures to recover their original status by interacting with one another in all their diversity. Both ascent and descent are possible.

The whole of creation is divided into three main classes, corresponding to ST. PAUL:

1. The *coelestia* (angels, stars, and planets), closest to God with the tasks of helping to govern the systems and help their inferiors;
2. The *terrestria,* the human race, who are helped by the first class and are thus enabled to recover their lost happiness;
3. The wicked angels, who are incapable of being cured in this world, and who try to inhibit human souls in their upward progress.

These three classes are different degrees of the same downfall.

Origen believes Christ's incarnation and redemption made possible the return of all beings to their beginning: "Through the goodness of God, the unity of the Holy Spirit and surrender to Christ, they will all be brought to a single term, which will be like their beginning. . . . Because God's judgements are proportionate to the good and bad behavior of individuals and to their merits, some will receive the rank of angel in the world to come, some power or command over others, some a throne from which to rule over others, some dominion over servants. Those who have not fallen beyond redemption will be guided and helped by those just mentioned." The idea that some humans could ascend to angelic status shocked later thinkers.

Another controversial idea put forward by Origen is that devils can purify themselves and raise themselves to human rank and then back to angelic rank.

The soul is caught up in a test of will between good and evil spirits. Evil rests not in the body. Origen argues against Platonists and Gnostics who view the flesh as the seat of evil. Evil rests in the will; bodiliness is a consequence of the Fall. "We men acquired our bodies because of the sins we had committed, and the lights of the heavens were given their bodies for the same reason. Thus, some shine more and others less. Contrariwise, the demons were given aerial [made of ether] bodies because their sins were graver." One day, Origen asserts, corporeality will come to an end and there will be an *apocatastasis*, a return to a purely spiritual state.

God's overarching goal is to enable each soul to return to him under its own free will, and he has arranged everything to further that goal. The angels have postponed their personal enjoyment to assist those who are not so good. God will allow some to plunge deeper into evil; in Origen's image, the abscess must be allowed to burst. (In GNOSTICISM, a similar concept has been called a "homeopathetic" doctrine of salvation.) Some souls cannot be saved in this world; God defers these souls' acceptance of grace to another world but meanwhile uses them as a means of tempting the saints. Thus the roles of angels and their mission to govern humans, and also of demons and their permission to tempt humans, are part of the play of the divinely planned cosmos.

GENERAL DUTIES OF ANGELS AND DEMONS

Origen was well informed on Jewish angelology and the ENOCH books, and had looked carefully at angelic interventions in both Old and New Testaments. He rejects the Hellenistic and Gnostic idea that the angels created the cosmos, but he agrees that angels have hierarchical duties in running it. "There are angels in charge of everything, of earth, water, air and fire . . . used by the Logos as instruments to regulate the movements of the animals, the plants, the stars."

Elsewhere he mentions "the VIRTUES who preside over the earth and the seeding of trees, who see to it that springs and rivers do not run dry." In a response to a pagan philosopher, Celsus, he states that whereas the Greeks call the protectors that preside over nature DAIMONES, the Christians call them angels. Christians honor angels, but they do not worship them as pagans worship the daimones. The nature functions are governed by the lowest order of angels.

ANGELS OF NATIONS

Origen believes higher angels preside over human societies, citing Deuteronomy 32, which tells how God "assigned the nations their inheritance . . . in accordance with the number of the angels of God." Origen says that after the Tower of Babel people were "handed over to angels, who harried them in varying degrees,

according to the distance they had gone from the Orient [the true Light], and they were to remain under them until they had atoned for their folly." Each group was given a language and led to a dwelling place according to what they deserved.

The angels of nations are called PRINCES. Origen associates them with the occult sciences practiced in the various nations, mentioning Egyptian, Chaldean, Persian, Greek, and Hindu versions. He says that "in the prophet EZEKIEL the Prince of Tyre is obviously a spiritual power. These and the other Powers of this world have each some special science of their own, and they all teach their respective dogmas and opinions to men." These spirits do not intend to do harm, but they act on the belief that what they teach is true.

Every nation has two angels attached to it, one good and one ambiguous, a view that reflects biblical ambiguity. He considers that in the Enochian writings some of the angels turned traitor after their assignments were made. Origen does not reach a clear definition on the bad angels of the nations, but he says that bad angels were the instigators of idolatry because they urged people to worship them rather than God.

The power of angels over nations was withdrawn after Christ came. The good angels welcomed the change; they had toiled long in the pagan nations with little to show for their efforts. In the *Homily on Gospel of St. Luke,* Origen associates these with the shepherds on the night of Jesus' birth, who stand for "angels [of nations] to whose care men are entrusted. . . . It was to them that the [messenger] angel came and announced the . . . coming of the true Shepherd." There was a transition period before they were to be relieved of their duties in which great conversions to Christ were easily accomplished by the angels. Origen comments that this happened in Macedonia and in Egypt.

However, it was quite different for the bad angels, the "princes of the world." Conversion for them was not impossible—he uses the story of Jesus converting the centurion at Capharnum as an example—but most went against Christ. Origen quotes Paul in Ephesians 6:12: "It is not against flesh and blood that we enter the lists; we have to do with princedoms and powers, with the *cosmocratores.*" In Origen's own time the "princes and powers of idolatry" were still constantly challenging Christians on a life and death basis.

Israel was the one nation that went on worshiping the true God as it had done from the beginning. Origen believes the nation of Israel kept the original language of the world. They stayed where they were originally, but their subsequent slavery and banishment and eventual diaspora were the result of their sins.

GUARDIAN ANGELS

As soon as a person converts, renounces Satan, and gives himself to Christ, Christ hands the soul over to a GUARDIAN ANGEL. Origen teaches that "every one of the faithful, we are told, however insignificant he may be in the Church, is assisted by an angel, and Christ is our witness that these angels behold the Father's face continuously." He says that "every human soul has an angel who guides it like a brother." Origen uses this comforting concept constantly in guiding people in the spiritual life. When Christ came into the world, myriad angels descended to assist him in his work and became guardian angels.

Just like the nations, every individual has a good and a bad angel of their own, according to Origen. A battle is fought over every soul, and as long as humans worship idols, angels can do nothing. They cannot look freely upon the Father's face. But when a person becomes Christian, "no matter how insignificant I may be, my angel is free to look upon the Father's face. If I am outside the Church, he dare not do so."

Children gain spiritual direction from angels through good thoughts and desires (as Jesus indicated in Matthew 23:10), but maturing souls are capable of gaining instruction directly from Christ. Origen reminds the faithful: "God allows the opposing forces to fight against us, because he wants us to get the better of them. The function of bad angels is to tempt the just and put them to the test." Christ himself battled Satan many times, illustrating the struggle at the highest level.

Whatever progress angels instill in humans, their own degree of progress and bliss will increase. "Whether the angels look on God's face always, or never, or only sometimes, will depend on the merits of those whose angels they were," says Origen. The angels also collaborate with the apostles and the churches' shepherds, the bishops. Every church possesses both a visible bishop and an invisible angel. If the church goes badly, so it is with the angels. Origen stresses the identity of earthly and angelic authority: "The same functions are shared by an angel and a man and they are both perfectly good bishops."

Origen envisions an angel "encamped beside those who fear the Lord"; if many faithful were assembled so also would their angels. "Thus, when the saints are assembled, there will be two Churches, one of man and one of angels." Therefore, assembling for worship in a church brings great angelic forces together.

Origen also believes specific hierarchies of angels are present during practice of each of the sacraments. At the moment the priest immerses a child in baptismal water, the angels immerse the soul in the Holy Ghost. Higher echelons of angels are particularly involved in the sacramental life of the soul, with the Eucharist being a significant turning point.

Origen's broadminded views have earned him many admirers over the centuries, despite the official rejection of him as a heretic.

FURTHER READING

Crouzel, Henri. *Origen.* Translated by A. S. Worrall. San Francisco: Harper and Row, 1989.
Danielou, Jean. *Origen.* Translated by Walter Mitchell. New York: Sheed and Ward, 1955.
Scott, Alan. *Origen and the Life of the Stars.* Oxford: Clarendon Press, 1994.

origins

Celestial beings or a type of angel, mentioned in the Enochian writings. When ENOCH goes to the seventh HEAVEN, he sees origins, as well as THRONES, CHERUBIM, SERAPHIM, ARCHANGELS, AUTHORITIES, and DOMINIONS (2 Enoch 20:1).

orishas

Archetypal deities worshiped by followers of Santería and Candomblé. Closely related to DEVAS and other NATURE SPIRITS, orishas also are angels. Within Vodun, they are called the *loa*.

The orishas came to the New World with the West African slaves, principally from the Yoruban tribes along the Niger River. Forced to convert to Catholicism, the slaves worshiped their gods in secret, eventually seeing in them many characteristics of the Catholic saints and using the saints as covers for the African deities. Years later, the Spanish and Portuguese masters became fascinated with Yoruban magic and religion and embraced Santería (from *santo*, the Spanish word for saint), syncretizing it with their Catholic faith.

Like many other ancient and contemporary religions, particularly those practiced in the East, Santería and Candomblé acknowledge a Supreme, an Absolute, but find worship of such a distant, impersonal force too inaccessible. Instead, practitioners call on a pantheon of deities, each associated with a force of nature or ability to affect events and circumstances.

In Yoruban, *orisha* literally means "head-calabash," and is the term for "god." Each worshiper "chooses a head" or selects an orisha as spirit guide, a guardian angel who protects and promotes the interests of the petitioner. Selection is based on personality commonalities and the sense of energy one feels in a particular setting sacred to an orisha: the mountains, the ocean, the forests, the rivers. Occupations have patron orishas, as do those individuals involved in parenting, healing, or fortune-telling. Once a practitioner has chosen an orisha—or more exactly, the orisha has chosen his devotee—care is given to show deference to the orisha's desires, favorite colors and foods, special days, and worship preferences.

The orishas originate from a complicated cosmogony, wherein great tragedy and sexual passion explain their existence and temperament. One of the most popular orishas is Yemaya or Yemanja (Iemanja in Portuguese), the mother of many of the orishas and patron of the oceans and motherhood. Every year on January 1, thousands of Brazilians flock to the oceanside to ask Yemanja's blessing. A small boat decorated with candles, flowers, and statues of the saints is set adrift in the waves. If the boat sinks, then Yemanja has again accepted her devotees' offering.

Her son Chango (Xango) is the god of fire and thunder, and he supervises warfare and great sexual passion. Oshun (Oxum), Chango's sister and mistress, governs marriage, romantic love, and money. Ochosi (Oxossi) is the god of hunters, birds, and wild animals, and he dwells in the forests. Omolu (Omulu), the god of contagious diseases, has the power to begin and end epidemics. And Yansan (Iansa) controls wind, lightning, and storms.

Another important orisha is Eleggua, the god of entryways, doors, and roads, who permits the other orishas to come to earth. All homes keep an image of Eleggua behind the door to serve as gatekeeper. In Candomblé, worshipers pray to the Exus, similar in function to Eleggua but more like primal forces of nature who act as divine tricksters and messengers to the gods, a function of traditional angels. Eleggua has many manifestations, and some of them are called Eshus as well. The Eshus or Exus can be benign or malignant. King Exu often is identified with Lucifer, and works with Beelzebub and Astaroth to become Exu Mor (death) and Exu of the Crossroads. At his worst he is Exu of the Closed Paths, a wicked DEMON who closes off all paths to prosperity, love, success, and health.

FURTHER READING

Altman, Nathaniel. "The Orishas: Communing with Angels in the Candomble Tradition of Brazil." In *Angels & Mortals: Their Co-Creative Power,* compiled by Maria Parisen. Wheaton, Ill.: Quest Books, The Theosophical Publishing House, 1990.

Guiley, Rosemary Ellen. *Harper's Encyclopedia of Mystical and Paranormal Experience.* San Francisco: HarperSanFrancisco, 1991.

Ornias

One of the FALLEN ANGELS who is bested by King SOLOMON. According to the Testament of Solomon, Orniel is an annoying, vampirizing DEMON who lives in the constellation Aquarius. He has shapeshifting ability: he strangles men born under the sign of Aquarius because they have passion for women born under the sign of Virgo; he becomes a man who likes boys and causes them pain when he touches them; he turns into a heavenly, winged creature; and he can assume the form of a lion.

During the construction of Solomon's Temple of Jerusalem, Ornias comes at sunset and takes half the wages and food of the master workman's boy—Solomon's favorite—and sucks out his soul through his right thumb. The boy grows thin. Solomon asks him why he is losing weight, and the boy tells him about Ornias. Incensed, Solomon begs God for help, and he is given a magical ring by Michael that will give him power over demons.

Solomon gives the ring to the boy and instructs him to fling it at the demon's chest when he next appears and order him to go to Solomon. When Ornias next appears, as a flaming fire, the boy does so. Ornias screams and promises to give the boy all the gold and silver on earth if he will give the ring back to Solomon. But the boy binds the demon and delivers him to the king.

Solomon interrogates him and learns that Ornias is descended from an archangel, and he is thwarted by the archangel Uriel. Solomon sets Ornias to work cutting stone from the quarry. Terrified by iron, the demon begs for a measure of freedom, promising to call up other demons. Solomon summons Uriel, who helps him force Ornias to cut stones.

When that work is done, Solomon orders Ornias to fetch the Prince of Demons, and he returns with Beelzebub.

Ornias has the gift of prophecy, explaining to Solomon that demons fly up to HEAVEN, where they overhear God's plans. Those who are exhausted by doing so become FALLING STARS.

FURTHER READING

Charlesworth, James H., ed. *The Old Testament Pseudepigrapha.* Vols. 1 and 2. New York: Doubleday, 1983, 1985.

Orobas

One of the FALLEN ANGELS and 72 spirits of SOLOMON. Orobas is a PRINCE who appears first as a horse but then changes into a man. He causes the souls of the dead to appear and answer questions. He talks of divine virtue, the divinity, and creation. He gives true answers to questions about the past, present, and future. He gives dignities and prelacies and protects against temptation. Prior to his fall, Orobas was partly in the order of THRONES and partly in the order of ANGELS. Now he rules over 20 legions of DEMONS.

Oroiael

In GNOSTICISM, one of four great LUMINARIES who surround the self-begotten, the savior, or God. The other three are Harmozy, Daveithe, and Eleleth. St. Irenaeus equates Oroiael with Uriel or Raguel.

Orphamiel

Angel associated with the index finger of the right hand of God. Orphamiel, also known as "the great finger of the father," is well known in Coptic texts for rituals of power.

Ose

One of the FALLEN ANGELS and 72 spirits of SOLOMON. Ose is a president in HELL, who appears first as a leopard and then as a human. He teaches all liberal sciences, and he gives true answers to questions about divine and secret things. He can change people into any shape desired by the magician; the victims will not know they have been changed. According to JOHANN WEYER, Ose also will make people insane and delusional, so that they will believe they are kings and such. The delusions only last for an hour.

Osmadiel

In the LEMEGETON, the ruling angel of the eighth hour of the day, called Jafanym. Osmadiel rules 100 chief dukes and many lesser dukes.

Ouriel (Uriel)

According to the Testament of Solomon, an ARCHANGEL who assists SOLOMON in the commandeering of DEMONS. Ouriel thwarts the forces of Error.

See URIEL.

Padre Pio, St. See GUARDIAN ANGELS.

Paimon
One of the FALLEN ANGELS and 72 spirits of SOLOMON. Prior to his fall, Paimon was in the order of DOMINIONS. He was full of his own knowledge and remained obedient to Lucifer. In HELL he rules as a king. He appears as a crowned man seated on a camel, preceded by many musicians. He has a roaring voice. He teaches all arts, sciences, and secrets, subjugates people to the will of the magician, and gives good FAMILIARS. He is observed in the northwest.

Pahadron
Angel of terror who governs the month of Tishri (September–October).

palatinates
An order of angels equated with the POWERS. In magical lore, the palatinates are invoked to confer invisibility.

Pamyel
In the LEMEGETON, the ruling angel of the ninth hour of the night, called Zeschar. Pamyel rules 101,550 dukes and other servants who are divided into 12 orders.

parasangs
Persian units of measurement used often in Jewish literature such as the MERKABAH to describe the dimensions of the HEAVENS and the distances between them, and the heights of angels. One parasang equals approximately 3.88 miles.

Pathiel
Angel whose name means "the opener of God" and who is one of the 72 angels of the SCHEMHAMPHORAE. In MAGIC, Pathiel is invoked against forgetting and stupidity.

Paul, St.
Most important figure in the establishment of early Christianity. The Acts of the Apostles (generally ascribed to St. Luke, a close companion of Paul) and his own letters form two sources from which the facts and chronology of Paul's life can be constructed.

Life
Paul was born Saul in Tarsus about 10 C.E. to Jewish parents of the tribe of Benjamin, and was educated in Jerusalem in the school of the Pharisees. He vigorously opposed Christians and campaigned to imprison as many as possible. He is first mentioned in Acts 7, where he was present at the stoning of the martyr

Stephen. After Stephen's death, Saul participated in a great persecution of Christians in Jerusalem and the surrounding areas. Acts 8:3 says, "but Saul was ravaging the Church and entering house after house, he dragged off men and women and committed them to prison."

Around 34 C.E., Saul undertook a trip to Damascus to arrest Christians there and along the way. En route he had a transformational experience that led to his conversion, told in Acts 9:3–16. A vision of the risen JESUS told him he had been chosen as the apostle to the pagans:

> Now as he journeyed he approached Damascus and suddenly a light from heaven flashed about him. And he fell to the ground and heard a voice saying to him, "Saul, Saul, why do you persecute me?" And he said, "Who are you, Lord?" And he said, "I am Jesus whom you are persecuting; but rise and enter the city, and you will be told what you are to do." (9:3–6)

Paul was left blind for three days during which he neither ate nor drank. In a vision, God instructed a disciple in Damascus, a man named Ananias to go and heal Saul. Ananias was reluctant to do so because of who Saul was, but he obeyed God's directions. Ananias healed Saul in a laying on of hands and said to him

The conversion of St. Paul

"Brother Saul, the Lord Jesus who appeared to you on the road by which you came has sent me that you may regain your sight and be filled with the Holy Spirit" (9:17). Immediately something like scales fell from Saul's eyes and his vision was restored.

Once converted, Saul proselytized for Christianity as zealously as he had once campaigned against it. He took the name Paul. For the rest of his life, Paul dedicated himself to Christ, preaching and organizing. He traveled the eastern Mediterranean world from Jerusalem to Rome, throughout Greece and Asia Minor, preached, converted, established communities, and churches. When he could not revisit them or send another close disciple, he rendered them pastoral care through the Epistles.

Paul was arrested and imprisoned several times. In Philippi he and his helper, Silas, were beaten and jailed. Later, Paul was arrested in Jerusalem and then sent to Caesarea for trial. He spent two years waiting in prison and then was sent to Rome for trial. On the way, his ship was wrecked off the coast of Malta, but he and everyone on board escaped unharmed. In Rome he was kept under house arrest for more than two years, then was set free, probably after trial. Arrested again, Paul was martyred by beheading in Rome in 67 C.E. on the orders of Emperor Nero.

Epistles

Paul's Epistles, preserved in Greek, were not meant to be doctrinal treatises, but reflections on situations in the particular church to which Paul is writing. The Epistles reveal Paul's syntheses of Christian belief, philosophy, and practice as he himself understood it through his love of Christ kindled by his astounding conversion. He voiced his constant sense of Christ's leading him and urged the faithful to follow his degree of faith inwardly and outwardly to "new life" in spite of the Judaic, Hellenic, Roman, and other political, religious, and cultural realities of their time.

The Epistles became canonical and appear in Christian liturgy along with the Gospels. Their complexities have been studied and debated since by biblical scholars, some of whom dispute full authorship by Paul of several sections and whole epistles. Among the disputed material is the Epistle to the Hebrews, which most likely was not written by Paul himself; several of his close followers have been suggested as authors.

Angelology

Paul believed that human beings are influenced by spirits good, evil, and neutral. The source of his cosmology was the Judaism in which he was educated, which he built upon in the service of his theology of salvation.

GOOD AND NEUTRAL ANGELS

The good spirits are angels; once (1 Thessalonians 4:16) he refers to an archangel. God sends angels to earth on missions and as intermediaries in the giving of the law: "and it [the law] was ordained by angels through an intermediary" (Galatians 3:19). He also associates angels with the Second Coming and the final resurrection: "For the Lord himself will descend from heaven with a cry of command, with the archangel's call, and with the sound of the trumpet of God" (1 Thessalonians 4:16).

Though usually good, angels are sometimes neutral: "If I speak in the tongues of men and of angels" (1 Corinthians 13:1); and "For I think that God has exhibited us apostles as last of all, like men sentenced to death: because we have become a spectacle to the world, to angels and to men" (1 Corinthians 4:9).

However, angels should not be worshiped: "Let no one disqualify you, insisting on self-abasement and worship of angels" (Colossians 2:18).

Some of Paul's references to angels are ambiguous: "That is why the woman ought to have a veil on her head, because of the angels" (1 Corinthians 11:10), and "Do you not know we are to judge angels?" (1 Corinthians 6:3).

SATAN

Paul names Satan by name: "And to keep me from being too elated by the abundance of revelations, a thorn was given to me in the flesh, a messenger of Satan, to harass me, to keep me from being too elated" (2 Corinthians 12:7).

Other references to Satan and "the devil" (*ho satanas* and *ho diablos*) refer to the role of a satan as an accuser, tempter, and deceiver of men—but also as an enemy of God, an aspect not present in the original Jewish concept. These terms are often translated as a proper name:

> Do not refuse one another except perhaps by agreement for a season, that you may devote yourself to prayer; but then come back together again, lest Satan tempt you through lack of control. (1 Corinthians 7:5)

> What I have forgiven, if I have forgiven anything, has been for your sake in the presence of Christ, to keep Satan from gaining the advantage over us; for we are not ignorant of his designs. (2 Corinthians 2:10–11)

> for even Satan disguises himself as an angel of light. (2 Corinthians 11:14)

Satan is "the god of this world" who "has blinded the minds of the unbelievers, to keep them from seeing the light of the gospel of the glory of Christ" (2 Corinthians 4:4) and is the tempting serpent: "But I am afraid that as the serpent deceived Eve by his cunning, your thoughts will be led astray from a sincere and pure devotion to Christ" (2 Corinthians 11:3). He is the devil who ensnares men, especially recent converts (1 Timothy 3:6–7), and must be guarded against: "and give no opportunity to the devil" (Ephesians 4:27), and "Put on the whole armor of God, that you may be able to stand against the wiles of the devil" (Ephesians 6:11).

In 1 Thessalonians 2:18, Satan deliberately interferes with Paul's ability to reach disciples: "because we wanted to come to you—I, Paul, again and again—but Satan interfered with us."

In 2 Thessalonians 2:9, Satan abets the "lawless one": "The coming of the lawless one by the activity of Satan will be with all the power and with pretended signs and wonders." He does not clarify whether "lawless one" refers to a ruler, a supernatural power, Satan as the Antichrist, or some other person or agency.

In Romans 16:20, God prevails: "then the God of peace will soon crush Satan under your feet."

DEMONS AND EVIL OR DANGEROUS ANGELS

False pagan gods are represented as demons: "You cannot drink the cup of the Lord and the cup of demons" (1 Corinthians 10:21) lest God become jealous.

Angels can disguise evil: "But even if we, or an angel from heaven, should preach to you a gospel contrary to that which we preached to you, let him be accursed" (Galatians 1:8), and "And no wonder, for even Satan disguises himself as an angel of light" (2 Corinthians 11:14).

Angels are among the cosmic forces that can drive the faithful away from the love of God: "For I am sure that neither death, nor life, nor angels, nor principalities, nor things present, nor things to come, nor powers, nor height, nor depth, nor anything else in all creation, will ever be able to separate us from love of God in Christ Jesus our Lord" (Romans 8:38).

"POWERS" OF EARTH AND THE HEAVENS

Paul refers to "POWERS" under five names: archai ("rulers") eight times; EXOUSIAI ("AUTHORITIES") seven times; DYNAMEIS ("powers") three times; kyriotetes ("lordships") twice; and thronoi ("THRONES") once. These powers appear particularly in the Epistles of Paul's captivity, Colossians and Ephesians, communities that associated them with HEAVENLY BODIES. Their functions seem to be those of government. In the Old Testament and the apocryphal book of ENOCH, God's practice of entrusting nations to an angel was established.

For Paul some of these spirits appear to be mortal enemies. In 1 Corinthians 2:6–8, the "princes of this age" (*archontes tou aionos toutou*) have "crucified the Lord of Glory." The context of some of these references suggests heavenly powers, whereas others suggest human authorities manipulated by superior powers who influence the world.

Paul evidently shared the astrological idea of his place and time that the cosmos is ruled by celestial powers who operate from heaven as superior authorities over the human world, and are not like the angels who intervene through individual missions or who rule over particular atmospheric phenomena. They act through God's authority having been created by God in Christ: "for in him all things were created, in heaven and on earth, visible and invisible, whether thrones or dominions or principalities or authorities—all things were created through him and for him" (Colossians 1:16).

However, they have lost their original power and will cede it under the new regime set in motion by Christ's incarnation: "Yet among the mature we do impart wisdom, although it is not a wisdom of this age, or of the rulers of this age, who are doomed to pass away" (1 Corinthians 2:6), and "Then comes the end, when he delivers the kingdom to God the Father after destroying every rule and every authority and power" (1 Corinthians 15:24).

This evolution holds true of government and economy on earth, too. Prophecies, tongues (languages), knowledge, and all that is imperfect shall pass away (1 Corinthians 3:8–10).

This is not punishment but reordering. If the princes of this world crucified Jesus, it was because they knew not his true identity. The powers and principalities do not know everything; it is only now that they discover the mystery of salvation that was previously hidden from them.

Paul says that he especially—though he is "the very least of saints"—has been given the grace "to preach to the Gentiles the unsearchable riches of Christ, and to make all men see what is the plan of the mystery hidden for ages in God who created all things; that through the church the manifold wisdom of God might be made known to the principalities and powers in the heavenly places" (Ephesians 3:8–10).

FURTHER READING

Caird, G. B. *Principalities and Powers: A Study in Pauline Theology*. Oxford: Oxford University Press, 1966.
"Introduction to the Letters of St. Paul." In *The Jerusalem Bible*. Garden City, N.Y.: Doubleday and Company, 1966.
Knox, W. L. *St. Paul and the Church of the Gentiles*. Cambridge: Cambridge University Press, 1939.

Peliel (Pehel)

Angel who rules the order of VIRTUES and who is the PRECEPTOR of JACOB.

Penemuel (Penemue, Tamel, Tamuel, Tumael)

In the Enochian books, a FALLEN ANGEL who teaches humankind the corrupting art of how to write with ink and paper. Penemuel is invoked against stupidity in MAGIC.

Peniel

In Kabbalistic lore, angel who governs Friday and lives in the third HEAVEN. Peniel means "face of God." Peniel is sometimes identified as the dark figure who wrestles with JACOB in Genesis 32:24–30. After the all-night struggle, Jacob asks his adversary his name, but the other does not give it, only asking Jacob why he asks. Jacob then names the place where the struggle took place as Peniel, "For I have seen God face to face, and yet my life is preserved" (Genesis 32:30). The Zohar, however, names Samael as the adversary.

Perelandra

"Co-creative" garden and nature research center, similar in concept to FINDHORN, in which humans work in cooperation with the INTELLIGENCES of nature.

Perelandra was founded by Machaelle Small Wright and her partner, Clarence Wright, who moved to the land in 1973. In 1974, Machaelle Wright opened psychically, and, in 1976, she began communicating with overlighting intelligences in nature, who provide guidance for creating and cultivating the gardens.

The name Perelandra is taken from the science fiction novel by C. S. Lewis about Venus, which he called Perelandra, the planet of perfection. It is visited by two earth men, one good and the other evil. The good man moved within the harmony of Perelandra, while the evil man moved in destruction. Wright felt the name appropriate for their woodsy site, which still retained a spark of perfection despite the damage done to it by previous owners.

The site is located on about 22 acres near Jeffersonton, Virginia, about 60 miles southwest of Washington, D.C. Open houses are offered several times a year for the general public.

See GREEN HOPE FARM.

FURTHER READING

Atwater, P. M. H. "Perelandra: Cooperating Co-creatively with Nature." *New Realities* (May–June 1988): 17–20+.

Wright, Machaelle Small. "About Perelandra." URL: http://www.perelandra-ltd.com. Downloaded October 7, 2002.

———. *Behaving as if the God in All Life Mattered.* Jefferson-ton, Va.: Perelandra, 1987.

Pesagniyah

Angel who takes the prayers of those in grief and deep sorrow and kisses them and takes them to a higher place in HEAVEN. In the Zohar, Pesagniyah governs the south and the keys of the ethereal spaces.

Phaleg (Phalec)

One of the seven ruling angels of the 196 Olympic provinces of HEAVEN, according to the Arbatel of Magic. As the third angel, Phaleg is the war lord and rules over 35 provinces. Tuesday is the day when he is invoked in MAGIC.

Phanuel

Angel sometimes identified as being one of the four primary ARCHANGELS along with Michael, Gabriel, and Raphael. Phanuel is often equated with Uriel, as well as with Ramiel. In 3 Baruch, he an archangel, an angel of hosts, and an interpreter of revelations, who guides the scribe on his tour of the HEAVENS.

Phanuel appears in the Enochic Book of Parables. He governs repentance of those who aspire to eternal life, and he fends off "the satans," or the accusers. His name once was invoked as protection against evil spirits.

Pharzuph

Angel of fornication and lust. In occult lore, Pharzuph is one of the GENII of the fourth hour and is invoked in magical rites.

philangeli See DEVOTIONAL CULTS.

Philo (ca. 20 B.C.E.–ca. 50 C.E.)

Jewish philosopher who was a contemporary of Jesus and Paul. Philo's writings are important to an understanding of the Second Temple period of Hellenized Judaism and early Christianity.

Life

Little is known about the life of Philo. He was born to a prominent and wealthy family in Alexandria, home to the largest single Jewish community outside of Palestine at the time. Philo was well educated and was a leader within his Jewish community. He spent his entire life in Alexandria, although he is known to have visited the Temple in Jerusalem on one occasion.

Works

Philo's extensive writings are not as well known as those of his contemporary, the Jewish historian Josephus, perhaps because they were not translated into English until the Renaissance. He wrote in Greek and a few of his texts have survived in Armenian translations as well. His works were circulated in the early Christian communities, but in Jewish circles Philo sank into obscurity after his death until about the 16th century. This is perhaps due to his unique philosophy that was less orthodox and more a stream of Hellenistic Judaism. Only two complete English translations of Philo have been published.

Much of Philo's work are commentaries on the biblical texts of MOSES. Also important in his work are his views on the position of women and attitudes toward them by literate men during Second Temple Judaism and the early church, and his understanding of the Epistle to the Hebrews.

Philo relates angels to the invisible "powers" around the throne of God. In his discussion of the story of HAGAR in *On Flight and Finding,* Philo terms angels "the servants of God, and are considered actual gods by those who toil and slave" (212). Discussing Hagar again in *On Dreams—Book 1,* he confirms that God sometimes takes the form of angels, as well as men, and these appearances are like reflections of him that are required for humans to be able to perceive him:

> Why then do we any longer wonder, if God at times assumes the likeness of the angels, as he sometimes assumes even that of men, for the sake of assisting those who address their entreaties to him? so that when he says, "I am the God who was seen by thee in the place of God;" we must understand this, that he on that occasion took the place of an angel, as far as appearance went, without changing his own real nature, for the advantage of him who was not, as yet, able to bear the sight of the true God; for as those who are not able to look upon the sun itself, look upon the reflected rays of the sun as the sun itself, and upon the halo around the moon as if it were the moon itself; so also do those who are unable to bear the sight of God, look upon his image, his angel word, as himself. (XLI 238–239)

Angels can assume the forms of men, as evidenced by the WATCHERS who took mortal wives, and by the three angels who visit ABRAHAM. Of the latter, Philo says that the angels could not have condescended to appear as guests in a human habitation had they not known that their hosts were akin to them in service to

God. The angels only appeared to eat but did not actually eat because of their incorporeality. Their very presence blessed the household: "We must think indeed that at their entrance all the parts of the house became improved and advanced in goodness, being breathed upon with a certain breeze of most perfect virtue" (*On Abraham,* 116).

In *On the Cherubim,* Philo explains the two CHERUBIM who guard the gate of Eden as symbols of the powers of God's ruling authority and his goodness, and the flaming sword between them as reason. Additionally, one cherub represents the outermost circumference of heavens that contains the stars, and the other cherub represents the inner sphere that contains the planets. The continually turning sword of flame represents their "everlasting agitation of the entire heaven."

Philo describes the Logos as the "image of God," the "covenant of God," and "the seal of the universe." Some scholars have interpreted his views as referring to a second God, similar to the possible meanings of the ANGEL OF THE LORD. The "Existing One" has two primary powers: God, who creates the world and is beneficent, and Lord, who rules, commands, and punishes, and speaks from the ARK OF THE COVENANT. They are linked together by the cherubim.

See DREAMS AND VISIONS.

FURTHER READING

Barker, Margaret. *The Great Angel: A Study of Israel's Second God.* Louisville, Ky.: Westminster/John Knox Press, 1992.

The Works of Philo Complete and Unabridged. Translated by C. D. Yonge. Hendrickson, 1993.

Phoenix (Phenix, Phenix, Pheynix)

One of the FALLEN ANGELS and 72 spirits of SOLOMON. Phoenix reigns as a marquis in hell with 20 legions. He appears as a phoenix bird and sings sweetly in a child's voice. It is really a siren's voice, and so the magician must take precautions not to be seduced by it. Upon command Phoenix will assume a human shape, and then he will speak on all the sciences and deliver excellent poetry. He fulfills all commands well. Phoenix has the futile hope that he will return to the seventh throne in 1,200 years. He formerly was in the order of THRONES.

phoenixes

According to the book of ENOCH, a high order of angels along with the CHALKYDRI, and associated with CHERUBIM and SERAPHIM. The phoenixes are elements of the sun and attend its chariot.

In 2 Enoch, there are seven phoenixes in the sixth HEAVEN, which is full of radiant angels whose faces are like the sun, and who harmonize all earthly and heavenly activity. The phoenixes sing in unison with seven cherubim and seven "six-winged beings" (seraphim). Enoch says their song, which greets the rising sun, pleases God:

> The light-giver is coming,
> to give radiance to the whole world;
> and the morning watch appears,
> which is the sun's rays.
> And the sun comes out over the face of the earth,
> and retrieves his radiance,
> to give light to all the face of the earth.

In other mythologies, the phoenix is a bird that resurrects itself from its own ashes. According to Herodotus, it was associated with the Temple of the Sun in Heliopolis, Egypt.

The phoenix also is associated with the resurrection of Christ.

Phounebiel

In the Testament of SOLOMON, angel who thwarts Rhyx Nathotho, a disease-causing DEMON among the DECANS OF THE ZODIAC. The name may be a corruption of the Egyptian deity Ptah-Nun, father of Atum.

Phul (Phuel)

One of the seven ruling angels of the 196 Olympic provinces of HEAVEN, according to the Arbatel of Magic. As the seventh angel, Phul rules everything pertaining to the moon, and seven provinces. He is invoked on Monday, the day of the moon. Phul can transmute anything into silver and can cure dropsy. As supreme lord of the waters, he can destroy the evil spirits of water.

Pius XI (1857–1939)

Pope Pius XI (1922–39) publicly acknowledged his personal relationship with his GUARDIAN ANGEL during a time when angels were out of fashion in popular culture. He said he prayed to the angel every morning and evening—and throughout the day, if necessary.

As a young man, Achille Ratti was impressed by St. Bernard's assertion that it is humanity's duty to respect, love, and trust one's guardian angel. When Ratti became Pope Pius XI, he took the advice to heart, and his faith in his guardian angel came to play a role in all the good deeds he accomplished in life, he said.

Pius XI confided to Monsignor Angelo Roncalli, who later became JOHN XXIII, that angels helped him in his many delicate diplomatic dealings. Prior to a meeting with someone whom he needed to persuade, he would pray to his guardian angel, making his best case, and asking him to take it up with the guardian angel of the other person. Sometimes Pius XI would himself invoke the guardian angel of the other person, asking to be enlightened as to the other's viewpoint. Once the two angels had reached an understanding, he told Roncalli, the situation involving himself and the other person became smoother.

Pius XI was renowned for his diplomatic activity. He brought about the Lateran Treaty, signed in 1929. This concordat between the Holy See and Italy ended a dispute over papal sovereignty and created Vatican City as the new sovereign state. The treaty also recognized Roman Catholicism as the only state religion in Italy.

Pius XI actively opposed fascism, communism, and the Nazi party. He championed social reform and greater participation by the lay public in religion, as well as the rights of native cultures and "Oriental" Catholics.

Pius XI recommended to others that they pray to their guardian angels as well. He especially sought out people on the front lines: diplomats, teachers, missionaries, and the like. These individuals, who in turn influenced the lives of many others, were especially in need of angelic guidance, he said.

FURTHER READING
Huber, Georges. *My Angel Will Go before You.* Westminster, Md.: Christian Classics, 1983.

Pius XII (1876–1958)

Pope Pius XII (1939–1958) was a champion of angels, especially the GUARDIAN ANGEL. Yet unlike Pope PIUS XI and Pope JOHN XXIII, he did not reveal his own personal dealings with angels.

In an encyclical in 1950, Pius XII stated that it was a mistake to question whether angels are "real beings"—this was erroneous thinking that could undermine church doctrine. He urged people to renew their devotion to angels. On October 3, 1958, a few days before his death, he gave an address to a group of American tourists in which he reminded them of the existence of an invisible world populated with angels:

> Did Christ not say, speaking to little children, who were so loved by his pure and loving heart: "Their angels always behold the face of my Father who is in heaven." When children become adults, do their guardian angels abandon them? Not at all.
>
> The hymn at first vespers in yesterday's liturgy told us, "Let us sing to the guardian angels of men, heavenly companions, given to the Father by our frail nature, lest we succumb to the enemies who threaten us." This same

thinking is to be found time and time again in the writings of the Fathers of the Church.

> Everyone, no matter how humble he may be, has angels to watch over him. They are heavenly, pure and splendid, and yet they have been given to us to keep us company on our way: they have been given the task of keeping careful watch over you so that you do not become separated from Christ, their Lord.
>
> And not only do they want to protect you from the dangers which waylay you throughout their journey: they are actually by your side, helping your souls as you strive to go ever higher in your union with God through Christ.
>
> . . . We do not want to take leave of you . . . without exhorting you to awaken, to revive your sense of the invisible world which is all around us . . . and to have a certain familiarity with the angels, who are forever solicitous for your salvation and your sanctification. If

Guardian angel, from a Victorian postcard (Reprinted courtesy Jayne M. Howard-Feldman)

God wishes, you will spend a happy eternity with the angels: get to know them here, from now on.

FURTHER READING
Huber, Georges. *My Angel Will Go before You.* Westminster, Md.: Christian Classics, 1983.

planetary rulers
Seven angels who have the sole powers to thwart the demonic HEAVENLY BODIES of the world of darkness. The planetary rulers are:

1. Lamachiel, who thwarts Deception.
2. Baruchiel, who thwarts Strife.
3. Marmaroth, who thwarts Fate.
4. Balthioul, who thwarts Distress.
5. Uriel, who thwarts Error.
6. Asteraoth, who thwarts Power.

See ANGELS OF THE PLANETS; THWARTING ANGELS.

Planets See ANGELS OF THE PLANETS.

Plato See INTELLIGENCES.

Plotinus See INTELLIGENCES.

poetry and angels See LITERATURE AND ANGELS.

Poteh (Purah)
Angelic PRINCE of forgetting, invoked in magical rites.
See PURAH.

potentials See SERAPHIM.

potestates See POWERS.

powers (curetes, potestates)
In the pseudo-Dionysian hierarchy, the sixth highest order of angels. Powers fight against evil spirits who seek to wreak havoc through human beings. They protect the divine plans initiated by the DOMINIONS and carried out by the VIRTUES. They are sometimes equated with AUTHORITIES, DYNAMEIS, and EXOUSIAI.

St. PAUL alluded to their capability to be either good or evil: in Romans 8:38, he lists powers (as well as ANGELS and PRINCIPALITIES) as among obstacles that will not be able to separate man from the love of God in Jesus Christ. Pope Gregory the Great said powers presided over DEMONS. Their chief is said to be either

Power (From *The Hierarchie of the Blessed Angells* by Thomas Heywood [1635])

Samael or Camael, both angels of darkness. The Excerpt of Theodotus says that powers were the first created angels.

According to AGRIPPA, powers are equated with the Orphic curetes, of whom there are three, and who guard the king of gods, Jupiter (Zeus). They help men fight against "the enemies of this earthly tabernacle."

In Kabbalistic lore, powers—along with DOMINIONS and VIRTUES—form one of four triplicities of intelligible hierarchies.

In the Apocalypse of ADAM, a Gnostic text, the term "powers" refers to angels of the creator God who oppress humanity and try to rescue Gnostics.

Pravuil (Vretiel, Vrevoil)
Archangel who keeps all the records of HEAVEN. In 2 ENOCH 22:10–11, God summons Pravuil to present the records to ENOCH, and to instruct him in writing

down everything he saw and heard during his trip to heaven.

See DABRIEL; RADUERIEL; VRETIEL.

preceptor angels

Angels who are assigned to the great Jewish patriarchs to serve as special tutors and guides. The patriarchs and their preceptors are:

Adam–Raziel
Shem–Iofiel (Jophiel, Yophiel)
Noah–Zaphkiel
Abraham–Zidekiel (Zadkiel)
Isaac–Raphael
Joseph, Joshua, Daniel–Gabriel
Jacob–Peliel (Pehel)
Moses–Metatron
Elijah–Malashiel or Maltiel
Samson–Camael (Gamael)
David–Cerviel (Gerviel, Gernaiul)
Solomon–Michael

Prince of Darkness

Title given to Satan and Belial. In the Dead Sea Scrolls (see QUMRAN TEXTS), Belial is appointed by God to corrupt and to serve as "the PRINCE of the dominion of wickedness." He is followed by the children of falsehood. The Prince of Darkness also is the ANGEL OF DEATH.

Prince of Learning See PRINCE OF TORAH.

Prince of Peace

Title given to JESUS and in GNOSTICISM given to MELCHIZEDEK.

Prince of the Countenance

The chief angel of those angels who are privileged to look upon the face of God. Metatron in usually identified as the Prince of the Countenance.

Prince of the Divine Presence

The only angel who has the high privilege of serving in God's immediate presence inside the curtain (*pargod*) that surrounds him on his throne of Glory. 3 ENOCH identifies Metatron as the Prince of the Divine Presence. Another MERKABAH text, the Hekalot Rabbati, gives the office to Suryah.

Prince of the Face

Any of various high-ranking angels who have a special place in the presence of God. Among angels given the title of Prince of the Face are Sandalphon, Metatron, Michael, Phanuel, Uriel, Raziel, Akatriel, and Yefefiah.

Prince of the World

Angel who is in charge of the world as a whole. The Prince of the World appears in various rabbinic and MERKABAH texts, but he is not always specifically named. Metatron and Michael are the two angels most commonly identified with this office. In 3 ENOCH, the Prince of the World governs the PRINCES OF KINGDOMS and represents the world in the heavenly court of law. He also rules the HEAVENLY BODIES. Although 3 Enoch does not name the Prince of the World it implies that the role is filled by Metatron. Whenever the heavenly court is in session, the Prince of the World and the other great princes who are called Yahweh (who have YHVH as part of their name to denote their high office) are permitted to speak.

John 12:31 and 16:11 make reference to a prince or ruler of the world, but this is an evil figure and is distinctly different from the angelic Prince of the World in Merkabah literature.

Prince of Torah (Prince of Learning, Prince of Wisdom)

An angel who helps a person to understand the Torah and not forget what he has learned. In 3 ENOCH the Prince of Torah is Yepipyah, who assists MOSES in receiving and remembering the Law on Mount Sinai.

Prince of Wisdom See PRINCE OF TORAH.

princes

High-ranking angels who rule nations or major functions in the cosmos. Princes often are equated with ARCHONS and PRINCIPALITIES, as well as other high-ranking angels.

The belief that nations are assigned their own ruling deities was widespread in the ancient Near East. Although Deuteronomy 32:8–9 asserts that God alone rules Israel, the idea of ruling angelic princes entered the Old Testament and other Jewish writings. Joshua 5:14 refers to a man (probably an angel) who identifies himself as "the prince of the army of the Lord." The book of DANIEL makes multiple references to angelic princes of nations and calls Michael the prince of the Israelites.

1 Enoch 89:59 refers to 70 (also 72) shepherds, or angels/gods of nations. 3 ENOCH mentions 72 "princes of kingdoms" who correspond to the 72 nations of the

world, and who do not include the PRINCE OF THE WORLD, who is above them:

All of them are crowned with kingly crowns, clothed in regal dress, and decked with royal jewels. All of them ride on royal horses and grasp kingly scepters in their hands. Before each of them, when he travels through the Raqia, royal servants run, with great honor and much pomp, just as kings travel on earth in chariots attended by horsemen and great armies, in glory, greatness, praise, acclamation and splendor. (17:8)

Besides nations, princes govern other cosmic functions. 3 Enoch gives the names of the "princes who guide the world":

Gabriel, the angel of fire
Baradiel, the angel of hail
Ruhiel, the angel of wind
Baraqiel, the angel of lightning
Zaamiel, the angel of whirlwind
Ziqiel, the angel of comets
Ziiel, the angel of tremors
Zaapiel, the angel of hurricanes
Raamiel, the angel of thunder
Raasiel, the angel of earthquakes
Salgiel, the angel of snow
Matariel, the angel of rain
Simsiel, the angel of the day
Lailiel, the angel of the night
Galgalliel, the angel of the sun
Opanniel, the angel of the moon
Kokabiel, the angel of the stars
Rahatiel, the angel of the constellations

3 Enoch also names the princes of the seven HEAVENS.

Christ is called "the Prince of Angels." The Dead Sea Scrolls (see QUMRAN TEXTS) refer to the PRINCE OF LIGHT(S) who raises Aaron and MOSES, and who is followed by all children of righteousness.

Satan and Belial are called the PRINCE OF DARKNESS. Satan also is called "the prince of this world" in John 12:31 and "the prince of the air" in Ephesians 2:2 (a reference to the belief that all demons live in the air).

In magical lore some princes are evil spirits; however, Eleazar of Worms (see SEFER RAZIEL) believed princes to be angels, or MEMUNIM, who in MAGIC could be compelled to appear in the shape of their earthly charges.

Prince(s) of Light(s)

High-ranking angel of righteousness, identified as Michael, Melchizidek, or Uriel in the QUMRAN TEXT the

Testament of Amram (4Q Amram). In other fragments of the Dead Sea Scrolls, Michael is the Prince of Light(s) who is appointed by God to protect the faithful. All the children of righteousness follow him to walk in the ways of light. In ISQIII, the Prince of Light is also the ANGEL OF TRUTH, who, with the God of Israel, will succor the "sons of light."

princes of kingdoms

Angels who are assigned to each nation on earth as their angelic representatives in HEAVEN. The princes of kingdoms speak on behalf of nations on the heavenly court of law. 3 ENOCH refers to 72 princes of kingdoms, but names only three: Michael, the prince of Israel; Dubbiel, the prince of Persia; and Samael, the prince of Rome.

principalities (princedoms)

In the Pseudo-Dionysian CELESTIAL HIERARCHY, the seventh highest order of angels. Principalities possess, "princely powers" and watch over the actions of the earth's nations and cities—the visible world of humankind. Every nation has its own principality. They also govern and protect religion on this planet. Principalities can help humans call upon secret powers to subdue others and establish their own authority.

1 ENOCH 61:10 links principalities with other high-ranking angels, the CHERUBIM, SERAPHIM, OPHANIM, and "all the angels of power."

Principalities are linked to the element of air. They are sometimes equated with the ELOHIM. They rule Netzach (Victory), the seventh sephirot of the TREE OF LIFE. Their chiefs are Requel, Anael, Cerviel, and Nisroc.

St. AUGUSTINE said that while he acknowledged the existence of principalities, he did not know who they were specifically, or how they differed from seats (THRONES), DOMINIONS, and POWERS.

In the Old Testament, references to principalities or PRINCES (see ARCHAI and ARCHONS) refer to benevolent supernatural powers, such as in Daniel 10:20, which speaks of the "prince of Persia" and the "prince of Greece." But in the New Testament, it is not always clear whether the term is used for celestial or earthly powers, and sometimes the principalities are spoken of in a negative context. Meanings are shaded by how the original terms are translated. For example in Romans 8:38–39, St. PAUL is translated as naming principalities (as well as angels and powers) as among obstacles to God:

For I am sure that neither death, nor life, nor angels, nor principalities, nor things present, nor things to come,

Principate (From *The Hierarchie of the Blessed Angells* by Thomas Heywood [1635])

nor powers, nor height, nor depth, not anything else in all creation, will be able to separate us from the love of God in Jesus Christ our Lord.

Paul actually uses the Greek terms ARCHAI and DYNAMEIS, which have been translated into angels and principalities, respectively, and *hypsoma* and *bathos*, which have been translated as powers. However, Georg Luck translates archai and dynameis as "(supernatural) powers" and *hypsoma* and *bathos* as "(cosmic) forces above and below." Luck points out that *hypsoma* And *bathos* are astrological terms and may have referenced the influences of the stars, which were believed to possess semidivine powers.

In angel MAGIC there are "principalities of HELL."

FURTHER READING

Luck, Georg. *Arcana Mund: Magic and the Occult in Greek and Roman Worlds.* Baltimore, Md.: Johns Hopkins University Press, 1985.

van der Toorn, Karel, Bob Becking, and Pieter W. van der Horst, eds. *Dictionary of Deities and Demons in the Bible.* 2d ed. Grand Rapids, Mich.: William B. Eerdmans, 1999.

Procel (Crocell, Pucel)

One of the FALLEN ANGELS and 72 spirits of SOLOMON. Procel is a duke who appears in the form of an angel. He speaks mystically of hidden and secret things and teaches geometry and the liberal sciences. Upon command he will make a commotion and make waters roar. He also warms waters and tempers thermal springs baths. Before his fall he was in the order of POWERS. He rules over 48 legions.

Pronoia

In GNOSTICISM, an ARCHON who helps God to make ADAM by providing the nerve tissue. Pronoia is one of the PLANETARY RULERS and one of four angels sent by God to gather handfuls of dirt for the making of Adam.

The name "Pronoia" comes from the same Greek term, translated into Latin as Providentia (Providence). In Homer, "pronoia" referred to foreknowledge or anticipation. By the fifth century B.C.E., it was used to refer to planning for the care of family and for military planning. Divine providence—the ability and responsibility of God to care for the world—has been much debated and discussed by philosophers and theologians.

prophecy See DREAMS AND VISIONS.

Protestant Reformation

Split from the Catholic Church that led to the establishment of Protestant denominations within Christianity. The Protestant revolt began in the 16th century with Martin Luther's 95 Theses nailed on the door of Wittenberg Cathedral in 1517 and Henry VIII's 1534 Act of Supremacy, in which he declared himself the head of the Church of England. The founders of the various lines of Protestantism—Anglican, Lutheran, Calvinist—discarded some church dogma and much ecclesiastical law, and they modified practice for both clergy and laity, yet retained a great deal of both dogma and practice. Protestantism kept church dogmas on angels relatively intact.

The Roman Catholic Church had made an official statement on the subject of angels at the Fourth Lateran Council in 1215, about 50 years before St. THOMAS AQUINAS formulated his elaborate commentaries on angels. All the implications of the first sentence of the book of Genesis, expounded at great length by St. AUGUSTINE in Book XII of his *Confessions*, were made explicit in the statement of the council:

God is "creator of all things visible and invisible, spiritual and corporeal; who by his almighty power, together at the beginning of time, formed out of nothing the spiritual creature and the corporeal creature, that is, the angelic and the terrestrial; and then the human creature, composed of both body and spirit. For Satan and the other devils were created by God, and created good in nature; it is of themselves they have become evil." They "fell into sin of their own free will," and are "eternally damned."

The Council of Trent, held intermittently by the church between 1545 and 1563 in response to the Protestant Reformation, added to the last article above the following article of dogma: that "the first man, Adam, sinned at the devil's instigation . . . passed into the devil's powers, and with him the human race that was descended from him." This focus on Satan's strength and human susceptibility became a recurrent Protestant theme.

Martin Luther (1483–1546) led the Protestant theologians who made much of human corruption and the constant presence of Satan and the devils under his

Martin Luther triumphing over the monk's devil (Matthew Gnidius, *Dialogi*, 1521)

command. He wrote that "the acknowledgment of angels is needful in the church. Therefore godly preachers should teach them logically. First, they should show what angels are, namely, spiritual creatures without bodies. Secondly, what manner of spirits must be spoken of, not created evil by God, but made so by their rebellion against God, and their consequent fall; this hatred began in Paradise, and will continue and remain against Christ and his church to the world's end. . . . The devil is also near and about us, incessantly tracking our steps, in order to deprive us of our lives, our saving health, and salvation. But the holy angels defend us from him, insomuch that he is not able to work up to such mischief as willingly he would."

Luther, like St. PAUL, was concerned about idolatry. In *The Book of Concord*, still dogma of the modern Evangelical Lutheran Church, he says, "Although the angels in heaven pray for us (as Christ himself also does), and although saints on earth, and perhaps also in heaven, do likewise, it does not follow that we should invoke angels and saints, pray to them, keep fasts and vigils for them . . . serve them in still other ways, regard them as helpers in time of need, and attribute all sorts of help to them, assigning to each of them a special function, as the papists teach and practice. This is idolatry. Such honor belongs to God alone."

John Calvin (1509–64) reinforced the emphasis on the demonic and expressed skepticism about angels. In *The Institutes of Christian Religion,* he discusses "concise information concerning the nature of devils; that at their creation, they were originally angels of God, but by degenerating have ruined themselves, and become the instruments of perdition." Satan "can do nothing against God's will and consent" and "attempts those things which he thinks most opposed to God," but "God holds him tied and bound with the bridle of his power," so he can do "only those things which are divinely permitted."

Calvin's treatment of angels is limited to what he deduced from sacred Scripture, saying this is "what the Lord has been pleased for us to know concerning his angels." He begins to embody the conservative Protestant trend more explicitly when he enjoins us "not to speak, or think, or even desire to know, concerning obscure subjects, anything beyond the information given us in the Divine word." He cautions us, in reading Scripture, "to investigate and meditate upon things conducive to edification; not to indulge curiosity or the study of things unprofitable."

Calvin uses passages from Scripture to validate his assertions. For example, in *Institutes of the Christian Religion: The angels as protectors and Helpers of Believers*—he states, "Scripture strongly insists upon teaching us what could most effectively make for our consolation and the strengthening of our faith: namely, that angels are dispensers and administrators of God's beneficence toward us. For this reason, Scripture recalls that they keep vigil for our safety, take upon themselves our defense, direct our ways, and take care that some harm may not befall us." This is followed by citation and comments on no less than a dozen passages.

On the question of "whether individual angels have been assigned to individual believers for their protection," Calvin says that he "dare not affirm with confidence." In Matthew 18:10, although "Christ hints that there are certain angels to whom their safety [the children] has been committed . . . from this I do not know whether one ought to infer that each individual has the protection of his own angel. We ought to hold as a fact that the care of each one of us is not the task of one angel only, but all with one consent watch over our salvation." "If the fact that all the heavenly host are keeping watch for his safety will not satisfy a man, I do not see what benefit he could derive from knowing that one angel has been given to him as his especial guardian. Indeed, those who confine to one angel the care that God takes of each one of us are doing a great injustice both to themselves and to all the members of the church; as if it were an idle promise that we should fight more valiantly with these hosts supporting and protecting us round about!"

Calvin repudiates Aquinas's elaborate speculative treatment of angels, their number, form, and so on, arguing there is no scriptural evidence for any of it. Regarding the position of Aquinas that the number of angels vastly surpasses the number of material things, Calvin disagrees. "Let those who venture to determine the number of angels examine on what foundation their opinions rest." This question belongs to "that class of mysteries, the full revelation of which is deferred to the last day."

As far as the angelic hierarchy is concerned, Calvin considers PSEUDO-DIONYSIUS, Aquinas's chief source, unreliable, remarking "no man can deny that great subtlety and acuteness is discovered by Dionysius, whoever he was, in many parts of his treatise on the Celestial Hierarchy; but if any one enters into a critical examination of it, he will find the greatest part of it to be more babbling. . . . A reader of that book would suppose that the author was a man descended from heaven, giving an account of things that he had not learned from the information of others, but had seen with his own eyes. But Paul, who was 'caught up to the third heaven' [2 Corinthians 12:1] not only has told us no such things, but has even declared that it is not lawful for men to utter the sacred things which he had seen."

Calvin disputes Pseudo-Dionysius's claim to be the Areopagite who encountered Paul. The Protestant move-

ment, with its distaste for the kind of theoretical expertise demonstrated by Aquinas and others who wrote on angels, used this to discredit the Scholastics' pretense to being Christian, as well as systems showing the hierarchy of the angels as a prototype of the hierarchy of the church.

Karl Barth, a leading 20th-century follower of Calvin, comments that Aquinas's ANGELOLOGY "offers us a classic example of how not to proceed in this matter. . . . In the matter of angels it is better to look resolutely and exclusively in a different direction than to try to look at the Bible and other sources of knowledge at the same time." If we do that, "our philosophy will spoil our theology, and our theology our philosophy." "Holy Scripture gives us quite enough to think about regarding angels." In *Church Dogmatics,* he also agrees with Calvin's denunciation of Pseudo-Dionysius, dismissing him as "one of the greatest frauds in Church history," but he adds that "within its limits his work is one of those original and masterly ventures which do not often occur in the history of theology."

Calvin warns against the "superstition which frequently creeps in, to the effect that angels are ministers

The devil tempting Jesus (Gustave Doré)

and dispensers of all good things to us. . . . and what belongs to God and Christ alone is transferred to them." He discusses the difficulties Paul had with this worship of angels, a holdover from pagan philosophy and practice. "Farewell, then, to that Platonic philosophy of seeking access to God through angels, and of worshiping them with intent to render God more approachable to us. For that is what superstitious and curious men have tried to drag into our religion from the beginning and persevere in trying, even to this day."

Calvin dismisses the Sadducees and other fine-tuned thinkers who rejected the possibility angels were not real. Calvin held that scriptural evidence concerning the reality of angels required us to reject the notion that they were merely symbolic—visions or voices experienced by men. "So many testimonies of Scripture cry out against this nonsense that it is a wonder such crass ignorance could be borne with." The same "trifling philosophy" is refuted concerning devils.

The warfare of the Kingdom of God against the kingdom of Satan is a theme frequently presented by Calvin. "All that Scripture teaches concerning devils aims at arousing us to take precaution against their stratagems and contrivances, and also to equip ourselves with those weapons which are strong and powerful enough to vanquish these most powerful foes." Nevertheless, "we ought to accept as a fixed certainly the fact that he [Satan] can do nothing unless God wills and assents to it." The Christian elect, the true believers, are assured of victory in this holy war, according to Calvin. "God does not allow Satan to rule over the souls of believers, but gives over only the impious and unbelievers, whom he deigns not to regard as members of his own flock, to be governed by him." Satan "is said to blind all those who do not believe in the gospel [2 Corinthians 4:4]. Again, to carry our his 'work in the sons of disobedience' [Ephesians 2:2], and rightly, for all the impious are vessels of wrath. . . . as believers are recognized as the children of God because they wear his image, so are those rightly recognized to be the children of Satan from his image, into which they have degenerated."

The line of this branch of Protestantism gave birth to Puritanism, of which JOHN MILTON was a devout follower, and which was brought to North America in some strict versions by some of the first English settlers.

Two American Protestants who practiced Puritanism in 17th-century New England illustrate the ongoing metamorphosis of angelology set in motion by the Protestant revolt. Samuel Willard (1640–1707) was acting president of Harvard College for several years before his death and author of several books on divinity, among them *Compleat Body of Divinity*. He believed the human being was a unique creation who spans the cosmological divide between the visible, inconstant world of animals and the invisible, constant world of angels. The "most pure and subtle matter" of angelic beings is nonetheless matter; even though they are "perpetual and aeviternal," they are still creatures. "They are capable of torment; they are not a mere act, as God is, but have a protention; they are quantity and not infinite." The "rational soul" of human beings poses them at the juncture of earth and heaven, matter and spirit; with the body rooted in the inconstant world of terrestrial beings and the soul sharing with the angels the celestial sphere of constant natures, both are constitutive and both are "essential" to humanity.

Willard also believed there are a multitude of real demons, but he refers to them as if they were one being, the devil, or Satan, or "the god of the world," created by God but turned negative by the angelic revolt in the courts of heaven. In *Mercy Magnified*, Satan exercises power through "man's consent," which is derived mostly from the erroneous sense of "self-sovereignty" humans have that they can master life, and assisted by a "spy watching its season and advantage" within human concupiscence.

Edward Taylor (ca. 1642–1729), considered the first American poet, emigrated from England in 1668, graduated from Harvard College in 1671, and served as a minister on the western Massachusetts frontier until his death. Taylor's theology in most respects followed a straight enough Calvinist line. However, he extended the Protestant tendency to diminish the importance of angels to a belief, stated again and again, that humankind, partaking intimately of God's own being through Christ, must now stand even higher than angelic nature in the scale of creation, being "little lower than God." "Give place ye holy Angells of Light. Ye Sparkling Stars of the Morning. The Brightest Glory, the Highest Seate in the Kingdom of Glory . . . belong to my nature and not to yours. I cannot, I may not allow it You, without injury to Mine own Nature, and Indignity and Ingratitude to my Lord, that hath assumed it into a Personal Conjunction with his Divine Nature and seated it in the Trinity." In *The Experience* he states, "I'le Claim my right: Give place, ye Angells Bright./ Ye further from the Godhead stande than I. . . . Gods throne is first and mine is next: to you/ Onely the place of Waiting-men is due."

Taylor might have been influenced by a textual conflict. Whereas the King James Version translation of a line in Psalm 8 reads "a little lower than the angels," the Geneva Bible offered more support for the revised chain of being with its rendering: "a little lower than God." Modern commentators point out that the Hebrew ELOHIM translates in the plural as "gods," members of Yahweh's divine council. But the Hebrew words for angels, *malakh* and *elohim,* had a much wider range of application than can be pinned down by English.

Reformed theologians scorned Roman Catholic notions that heavenly messengers might act as intercessory agents or objects of prayer, and they had little incentive to inquire into benign, nonhuman mysteries of the invisible world. A few isolated works, such as Increase Mather's *Angelographia* (1696), discuss real, present influence of good angels in the lives of saints. But on the whole for Protestants, the angels' postbiblical functions paled before the importance to God of humanity's struggle against the devil to achieve divine identity as the elect of Christ.

FURTHER READING

Barth, Karl. *Church Dogmatics.* Edinburgh: T and T Clark, 1960.

Calvin, John. *Institutes of the Christian Religion.* Edited by John T. McNeill. Translated by Ford Lewis Battles. Philadelphia: Westminster Press, 1960.

Gatta, John J. "Little Lower than God: Super-Angelic Anthropology of Edward Taylor." *Harvard Theological Review* 75 (July 1982): 361–368.

Lowrie, Ernest B. *The Shape of the Puritan Mind: The Thought of Samuel Willard.* New Haven, Conn.: Yale University Press, 1974.

Luther, Martin. *Table Talk,* Vol. 54. Edited and Translated by Theodore C. Tappert. Philadelphia: Fortress Press, 1967.

———. *The Book of Concord: The Confessions of the Evangelical Lutheran Church.* Edited and Translated by Theodore C. Tappert. Philadelphia: Fortress Press, 1959.

pseudepigrapha See APOCRYPHA AND PSEUDEPIGRAPHA TEXTS.

The archangel Gabriel appearing to Mary

Pseudo-Dionysius

Pseudonymous early Greek writer who wrote extensively on Christian mysticism and on the CELESTIAL HIERARCHIES and nature of angels. Pseudo-Dionysius, also erroneously known as Dionysius the Areopagite (whom St. PAUL converted in Athens), may have been a Syrian clergyman, or many have been more than one person. The exact dates of his writings are unknown; they are believed to date to the fifth or sixth centuries C.E.

Pseudo-Dionysius's works include *The Celestial Hierarchy, The Mystical Theology, The Ecclesiastical Hierarchy,* and *The Divine Names.* These wielded a profound influence on medieval Christian thought, including St. THOMAS AQUINAS and St. John of the Cross, and on writers such as JOHN MILTON and DANTE.

St. John of the Cross perhaps most eloquently expressed Pseudo-Dionysian ideas, writing in his poetry that he pursued knowledge by unknowing. This is *agnosia,* "without knowing," the opposite of *gnosis,* and symbolizes a state of innocence. Pseudo-Dionysius believed that union with God is achieved when body and mind are "dead" and the spirit functions beyond time. Thus one attains "divine darkness," that is, to know God by knowing nothing.

Nature of Angels

Pseudo-Dionysius says that angels are nearer to God than are humans, "since their participation in him takes so many forms." In *The Celestial Hierarchy* he elaborates:

Their thinking processes imitate the divine. They look on the divine likeness with a transcendent eye. They model their intellects on him. Hence it is natural for them to enter into a more generous communion with the Deity, because they are forever marching towards the heights, because, as permitted, they are drawn to a concentration of an unfailing love for God, because they immaterially receive undiluted the original enlightenment, and because, ordered by such enlightenment, theirs is a life of total intelligence. They have the first and most diverse participation in the divine, and they, in turn, provide the first and most diverse revelations of the divine hiddenness. That is why they have a preeminent right to the title of angel or messenger, since it is they who first are granted the divine enlightenment and it is they who pass on to us these revelations which are so far beyond us. (180A–B)

Pseudo-Dionysius says that angels are only good and cannot be evil. They may seem evil only because of the punishment they deal out to sinners, which is also true of priests:

> The angel is an image of God. He is a manifestation of the hidden light. He is a mirror, pure, bright, untarnished, unspotted, receiving, if one may say so, the full loveliness of the divine goodness and purely enlightening within itself as far as possible the goodness of the silence in the inner sanctuaries. So, then, there is no evil in angels. (724B)

Not even devils are evil by nature because they have been created by God; they could not have fallen from goodness if they had always been essentially evil. Good is permanent and evil is impermanent. The evil of devils consists in the lack of angelic virtues.

Organization of Angels

Pseudo-Dionysius followed the Platonic and Neoplatonic pattern of the number three. He conceived of all reality in a hierarchy of triads. A hierarchy, says Pseudo-Dionysius in *The Celestial Hierarchy*, is "a sacred order, a state of understanding and an activity approximating as closely as possible to the divine;" its goal is "to enable beings to be as like as possible to God and to be at one with him." The hierarchy functions like a ladder, enabling humankind to ascend to God and God to descend into the realm of matter.

At the center of the angel kingdom is God, emitting rapid vibrations that slow as they move out from the source and become light, heat and finally matter. The nine orders of angels are divided into three realms, each of which contains three orders, each of which further is broken down into three levels of INTELLIGENCES.

The function of the first level is perfection or union; of the second level, it is illumination; and of the third level, it is purification. At any level, the higher angels possess all the powers of those lower, but not those of any higher level. The aim of each order is to imitate God so as to take on his form. The task of each is "to receive and to pass on undiluted purification, the divine light, and the understanding which brings perfection."

Dionysius named the orders according to biblical tradition; his names and ordering do not agree with other organizations found in Jewish mysticism. The upper triad is composed of SERAPHIM (love), CHERUBIM

(knowledge), and THRONES, all of whom are in direct contact with God. They receive "the primal theophanies and perfections," said Pseudo-Dionysius, which they pass on to the middle triad. These three levels are so close to God as to be perfect and utterly pure: "they are full of a superior light beyond any knowledge and . . . are filled with a transcendent and triply luminous contemplation of the one who is the cause and the source of all beauty." The hymns of these angels, who dance ceaselessly around God singing his praises, are transmitted to humans by prophets and visionaries.

The middle triad consists of DOMINIONS, POWERS, and VIRTUES, who are concerned with maintaining and administrating cosmic order. They in turn pass God's word to the last triad, which is home to PRINCIPALITIES, ARCHANGELS, and ANGELS.

The last triad of principalities, archangels, and angels is responsible for communicating God's word to humans.

Numbers of Angels

Pseudo-Dionysius reflects on the numbers of angels cited in the Bible (Daniel 7:10 and Revelation 5:11), "a thousand times a thousand and ten thousand times ten thousand" (similar phrasing is found in apocryphal texts). He is inclined not to take these numbers literally, but to interpret them as meaning simply that the true numbers of angels are innumerable and unknowable, surpassing the limits of human numbering.

Forms of Angels

It is no accident that angels are most often described in terms of flames, as being fiery, and constituting beings of fire or lightning, says Pseudo-Dionysius. Fire represents the Word of God: It passes undiluted through everything, lights up everything, and yet remains hidden at the same time. It cannot be looked upon; changes with its own activity; and bestows itself upon all who come near. It rises up and penetrates deeply.

Pseudo-Dionysius says it is also appropriate to give human descriptions to angels, for there is much in the human form that symbolizes the divine attributes of angels. For example, eyes symbolize the power to gaze up toward the light of God, and shoulders, arms and hands signify acting and achieving. That most angels depicted as humans are given adolescent vigor, Pseudo-Dionysius says shows the perennial vigor of living power.

Similarly, the clothing and accoutrements given angels also are laden with symbolism. Priestly raiments mean the capacity to guide others spiritually to the divine while sceptre shows the sovereignty and royal power with which angels guide. Spears show discriminating skills and sharpness of power. One need only use one's "discerning mind" to figure out all the symbolisms, Pseudo-Dionysius says.

It is also appropriate to describe angels as elements of nature, such as winds and clouds. Wind symbolizes the ability to move about freely and be anywhere quickly; clouds symbolize being filled in a transcendent way with hidden light. (Clouds and fire figure prominently in biblical descriptions of angels, the ANGEL OF THE LORD, and God himself.)

See IMAGES OF ANGELS.

FURTHER READING

Barnstone, Willis, ed. *The Other Bible*. San Francisco: HarperSanFrancisco, 1984.

Pseudo-Dionysius: The Complete Works. New York: Paulist Press, 1987.

psychopompoi

Angels and other spirits or gods who escort the souls of the newly dead to the afterlife. In angel lore, San-dalphon is the chief of the psychpompoi; Michael is one of the most prominent, as is Azrael. The term psychopomp (singular) means in Greek "leader" or "conductor." In Greek mythology, the primary psychopomp is the messenger god Hermes, with whom Michael shares characteristics.

See ANGEL OF DEATH.

Purah (Poteh, Puta)

Angel of forgetfulness and lord of oblivion. In Jewish lore, Purah is invoked in necromantic rites (the conjuring of the dead) at the close of the Sabbath.

Puriel (Puruel, Pusiel)

One of the ANGELS OF PUNISHMENT. Puriel means "the fire of God." In the Testament of ABRAHAM, Puriel is a pitiless angel who scrutinizes souls. Puriel is sometimes identified with Uriel.

Purson (Curson)

One of the FALLEN ANGELS and spirits of SOLOMON. Purson was once in the order of VIRTUES and partly in the order of THRONES. In HELL he is a great king. He appears as a lion-headed man, riding on a bear, and carrying a viper. He is preceded by many trumpeters. Purson hides and reveals treasure, discerns the past, present and future, provides good FAMILIARS, and gives true answers about things both human and divine.

putti

Secular child figures with wings. Putti appeared in early Renaissance Christian art along with winged adult angels. Putti also are called "cherubs," a term not to be confused with the mighty CHERUBIM named in Scripture.

Putti became popular in idyllic scenes from the New Testament, especially the Nativity and the childhood of Christ. Essentially they represent innocence and purity. Usually they are depicted in pairs, or in happy flocks that form an entourage for Christ. Like the Italian *amorini*, they often are shown dancing and making music.

Putti were inspired both by EROS, the god of love, and by the Roman EROTES, funerary winged boys. Although putti are not angels, their use in Christian art increasingly identified them with angels, and they contributed to the overall decline in the importance of the angel in theological thought.

FURTHER READING

Berefelt, Gunnar. *A Study on the Winged Angel: The Origin of a Motif*. Stockholm: Almquist and Wiksell, 1968.

Three putti with shield and helmet (Albrecht Dürer, c. 1500)

qaddisin (kadashim, kadishim)
A class of angels who reside in the sixth or seventh HEAVEN and who have a higher rank than MERKABAH angels. Qaddisin means "holy ones." According to rabbinic lore the chief of the order is made of hail and is so tall it would take 500 years to walk his height. The qaddisin are charged with singing unceasing hymns of praise and adoration to God. They serve on the seat of judgment along with the IRIN. When MOSES travels to heaven he sees the qaddisin and the irin together.

Qaspiel (Qafsiel, Qaphsiel, Quaphsiel)
Angel who rules the moon and who is invoked in MAGIC to drive away enemies. In 3 ENOCH, Qaspiel is the leader of the GUARDIANS OF THE DOORS of the seventh heavenly hall.

Qedussah (Kedushah)
The song of praise and devotion to God sung by the angels in HEAVEN. Qedussah means "sanctification," and it consists of the words given in ISAIAH 6:3: "Holy, holy, holy is the Lord of Hosts; the whole earth is full of his glory." Most of the hymns and songs recited by MERKABAH mystics on their ascents to the throne of Glory end with the Qedussah.

According to 3 ENOCH the Qedussah is one of the more important duties of the angels. It must be per-

formed correctly in order to avoid God's wrath. The singing of the "Holy" causes the very heavens and the earth to shake. The constellations and the stars are alarmed; the Sun and the Moon hurry in flight and seek to fling themselves from heaven. But the PRINCE OF THE WORLD soothes them and bids them to stay in their places. However, all the sacred NAMES that have been engraved with a pen of flame on the throne of glory fly off like eagles with 16 wings and surround God on the four sides of the abode of his SHEKINAH.

When the Qedussah is performed in its proper order, the angels rejoice with great joy. Each of the ministers of the throne has a thousand thousand and myriads and myriads of starry crowns that they put on the heads of the MINISTERING ANGELS and the great PRINCES. When the angels recite the "Holy" in its proper order they receive three crowns.

But if mistakes are made God becomes angry, and a devouring fire goes out from his little finger and splits into 496,000 myriads of parts the camps of angels and devours them in a single stroke. Then God opens his mouth and with one word creates new angels to take their place. Each of them recites the "Holy" as it is instructed to be given.

Of the angels who are destroyed, they become fiery coals in the RIVER OF FIRE, but their spirits and souls stand behind the Shekinah surrounded by walls of fire. They have the faces of angels and wings of birds.

See MUSIC AND ANGELS.

FURTHER READING

Charlesworth, James H., ed. *The Old Testament Pseudepigrapha*. Vols. 1 and 2. New York: Doubleday, 1983, 1985.

Scholem, Gershom. *Kabbalah*. New York: Dorset Press, 1987. First published 1974.

Qemuel (Camael, Kemuel)

Angel destroyed by either God or MOSES. Qemuel objected to the deliverance of the Torah to Moses and led 12,000 angels in opposition to it. He was punished by his destruction.

See KEMUEL.

Quabriel

In the LEMEGETON, the ruling angel of the ninth hour of the day, called Karron. Quabriel rules 66 chief dukes and many lesser dukes, who have hundreds and thousands of servants.

Qumran texts (Dead Sea Scrolls)

A body of Jewish-Christian texts and fragments first discovered in caves near the Dead Sea at Qumran in 1947. The literature reflects the messianic movement in Palestine and was associated with the Essenes, a Jewish sect that withdrew into the desert at Wadi Qumran. Written in Hebrew and Aramaic, the texts span the first century B.C.E. to the first century C.E., and contain a rich lore of angels and MAGIC.

The first scrolls were discovered in a cave in 1947 by a Bedouin boy who was searching for a lost goat. After tossing a rock into a cave the boy unexpectedly heard a vase break. Investigating, he discovered the jars containing the scrolls. In 1954 another important cache was discovered in a fourth cave. For years scholars and governments struggled over access to the scrolls; few were translated and published prior to 1991.

According to some scholars, the Qumran texts are associated with the Essenes. This idea is dismissed by others, who view them as representative of a messianic elite who practiced withdrawal into the wilderness to purify themselves to meet angels and prepare for the apocalyptic battle with evil. The texts also shed light on the beginnings of Christian liturgy.

The texts include messianic and visionary recitals; prophecies; biblical interpretations; testaments; laws; hymns, songs, and mysteries (reminiscent of literature in the MERKABAH and KABBALAH); and procedures for divination and magic.

FURTHER READING

Eisenman, Robert, and Michael Wise. *The Dead Sea Scrolls Uncovered*. London: Element Books, 1992.

Gaster, Theodor H. *The Dead Sea Scriptures*. 3d ed. Garden City, N.Y.: Anchor/Doubleday, 1976.

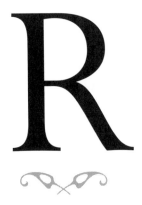

Rachiel

Angel in the order of OPHANIM, a ruler of Venus and governor of human sexuality. In magical lore, Rachiel is one of three angels who rule Friday, along with Anael and Sachiel.

Rachmiel

In rabbinic lore, one of the ANGELS OF MERCY. Rachmiel means "mercy." Rachmiel also is one of the CHILDBIRTH ANGELS.

Radueriel (Radweriel)

Angel in charge of heavenly archives, who has the unusual power to create other angels. In 3 ENOCH 27:1–3, Radueriel is described as ranking above the SERAPHIM as a prince exalted above all other PRINCES and more wonderful than all ministers:

> He takes out the scroll box in which the book of records is kept and brings it into the presence of the Holy One, blessed be he. He breaks the seals of the scroll box, opens it, takes out the scrolls and puts them in the hand of the Holy One, blessed be he. The Holy One receives them from his hand and places them before the scribes, so that they might read them out to the Great Court which is in the height of the heaven of Arabot, in the presence of the heavenly household.

Radueriel is so named because every utterance from his mouth creates an angel that joins in the songs of the MINISTERING ANGELS and recites the song before the Holy One when the time comes to say "Holy."

Radueriel also is the angel of poetry and the muses. He is one of eight great judgment angels who rank above Metatron.

See QEDUSSAH; RECORDING ANGELS; PRAVUIL.

Raguel (Akrasiel, Raguhel, Rasuil, Rufael, Suryan)

Archangel assigned to watch over the good behavior of other angels. Raguel means "friend of God."

In the ENOCH books, Raguel is the archangel who transports Enoch to the HEAVENS—a task also attributed to the angel Anafiel. 1 Enoch describes him as one of four great archangels who watch, along with Michael, Raphael, and Suriel, and one of the holy angels "who take vengeance for the world and for the luminaries." Enoch calls Raguel the Angel of the Earth. He also is a guardian of the second heaven, ruled by the archangel Raphael, which is a penal colony where fallen angels await judgment. There, Raguel is instrumental in meting out justice to erring angels.

The Revelation of John tells of God calling upon the services of Raguel in the Judgment, after the separation of the sheep from the goats: "Then shall He send the angel Raguel saying: go sound the trumpet for the angels of cold and snow and ice and bring them together every kind of wrath upon them that stand on the left."

In 745, Pope Zachary, at a church council, reprobated Raguel, Uriel, Tubuel, Inias, Sabaoc, and Simiel. Pope Zachary termed Raguel as a DEMON "who passed himself off as a saint," a curious sentence to give an angel whose job it is to make sure other angels do not fall from grace. Raguel was thrown out of the saints' calendar.

Rahab

An ANGEL OF DEATH and destruction, sometimes synonymous with Behemoth and Leviathan. Rahab (the name means "violence") is the demon of insolence and pride.

He also rules over the primordial sea and is not always malevolent. Rahab's name can be invoked through MAGIC to obtain the assistance of the sea. Jewish mystical tales tell of Rahab obligingly offering up treasures and possessions lost in shipwrecks, in response to incantations invoking his holy NAME. In one story he retrieves an evil amulet that was sunk in the seas, which a rabbi then uses to exorcise the curse of a witch.

Jewish lore tells that God destroyed Rahab for refusing to part the upper and lower waters at creation. Apparently he was resurrected, for God destroys him again for chasing the Israelites across the parted Red Sea. In a benevolent act, Rahab rescues the SEFER RAZIEL, containing all knowledge and mystical secrets, after the other angels have cast it into the sea to prevent it from being used by humans.

FURTHER READING
Schwartz, Howard. *Gabriel's Palace: Jewish Mystical Tales.*
    New York: Oxford University Press, 1993.

Rahatiel (Rahtiel)

Angel who is PRINCE of the constellations. Rahatiel, whose name means "to run," ranks beneath Ophaniel, who is in charge of the OPHANIM and the workings of the moon. According to 3 ENOCH 17:6, Rahatiel's name is derived from his duty of making the constellations run 339,000 PARASANGS in their cycles and orbits every night. Assisting him are 72 great and honored angels. Under him is Kokabiel, who is in charge of the stars.

Rahmiel (Rachmiel, Rahamael, Rhamiel)

Angel of mercy and love who in MAGIC is invoked against the evil eye.

rainbow

Symbol of God's covenant. In Genesis 9:11–17, God sets a rainbow in the HEAVENS after the Flood has receded, as a sign to NOAH that God shall never again destroy the earth. Whenever the rainbow appears, it shall remind both God and people of this promise.

In 3 ENOCH, the arches of the rainbow rest upon Arabot, the seventh heaven. The arches are 1,000 and a myriad of myriads of measures high and encircle the throne of Glory. They are fairer and brighter than the whiteness of the sun at summer solstice and whiter than blazing fire. The wheels of the OPHANIM rest upon them, 1,001 myriad of myriads high.

In art, the wings of angels—a symbol of the connection between heaven and earth—are often painted in rainbow colors.

In mythologies around the world, the rainbow is a universal symbol of the bridge to the realm of the gods. The rainbow is the path along which walk the souls of the dead as they cross over into the afterlife; it is the road walked by deities and the enlightened to the higher planes of consciousness.

Rainbow People

Beings who exist in the high ethereal realms of timelessness and spacelessness.

Members of the Rainbow People revealed themselves in the 1980s in INSTRUMENTAL TRANSCOMMUNICATION (ITC), which is two-way communication with the dead and beings in higher planes via high technology. According to the Rainbow People, their existence of Light is beyond the comprehension of humans. They are like angels in that they are close to God. They have great wisdom and goodness, and their entire being is illuminated by understanding and forgiveness.

When they move down to the lower planes, such as the astral plane, the Rainbow People have the appearance of brilliant gold-white light or a shimmering rainbow.

Ramiel (Jeremiel, Ramael, Remiel, Phanuel, Uriel, Yerahmeel)

Angel who oversees true visions and the souls of the dead on their day of judgment. Ramiel appears in apocryphal texts. In the Enochian writings, he is described as both a FALLEN ANGEL and one of the seven angels who stand before God. In the Sybylline Oracles he is one of five angels who lead souls to judgment; the others are Uriel, Arakiel, Samiel, and Aziel.

In 2 Baruch, Ramiel is the angel who presides over true visions and interprets the apocalyptic vision of BARUCH, and he gives the prophet the vision of victory over the army of Sennacherib. In the Apocalypse of

Baruch he is the angel who actually destroys the army (Michael, Gabriel, Remiel, Uriel, and other angels also are credited with this act). Ramiel describes the messiah to Baruch as "bright lightning."

Ramiel presides over thunder, as do Remiel and Uriel.

FURTHER READING

Barnstone, Willis, ed. *The Other Bible.* San Francisco: HarperSanFrancisco, 1984.

Raphael

One of the principal angels in Judeo-Christian angelologies, accorded the rank of archangel. Raphael's name originates from the Hebrew *rapha*, which means healer or doctor; thus Raphael is "the shining one who heals;" also "the medicine of God." He is often connected with the symbol of healing, the serpent. He is entrusted with the physical well-being of the earth and its human inhabitants, and, in Christian lore, he is regarded as one of the friendliest of the angels. He is one of four principal archangels—together with Michael, Gabriel, and Uriel—who are sometimes aspects of the ANGEL OF THE LORD.

Raphael is not mentioned by name in Scripture; he is best known as the angel guide and teacher in the apocryphal book of TOBIT. In that, Raphael teaches the arts of both healing and exorcism. He acts as a guide and companion on a journey, thus making him the angel of travelers and safety. He imparts the message that God is always with his people and sends his angels to aid them.

Raphael has numerous titles and duties. He is counted among the seven angels who stand before God mentioned in REVELATION, and is part of five orders of angels: SERAPHIM, ARCHANGELS, CHERUBIM, DOMINIONS, and POWERS. He is the angel of the evening winds, guardian of the TREE OF LIFE, and the angel of joy, light, and love. He is sometimes identified as an aspect of the ANGEL OF GREAT COUNSEL; the ANGEL OF PEACE; the ANGEL OF PRAYER; the ANGEL OF REPENTANCE; an ANGEL OF THE EARTH; and an ANGEL OF THE PLANETS.

Raphael, from Eastern Orthodox Church, Romania (Author's collection)

Tobias and the Angel (Andrea del Verrocchio, c. 1480; reprinted courtesy of the National Gallery, London)

In Kabbalistic lore, Raphael is charged with healing the earth. He is one of the 10 sephirot of the TREE OF LIFE. He is believed to be one of the three angels who visits ABRAHAM, though he is not named as such in Genesis. He is credited with healing Abraham of the pain of his circumcision, and JACOB of his wounded thigh due to the fight with the dark adversary.

According to several rabbinic sources, a pearl hung on Noah's ark, which indicated when day and night were at hand. Others say this light came from a sacred book NOAH was given by the archangel Raphael, bound in sapphires and containing all knowledge of the stars, the art of healing, and the mastery of DEMONS. Noah bequeathed this to Shem, who passed it by Abraham to Jacob, Levi, Moses, Joshua, and Solomon. (See SEFER RAZIEL.)

In 1 ENOCH, Raphael is one of the holy WATCHERS who punish the FALLEN ANGELS. In the Testament of Solomon, Raphael thwarts the birth demon Obyzouth.

Catholic devotional lore contains numerous stories about the deeds of Raphael, a saint whose feast day is September 29. St. Cyriaca (also called Dominica), who was martyred under the Emperor Maximilian in the fourth century, was addressed by Raphael during her tortures. The angel, identifying himself by name, said he had heard her prayers and congratulated her on her courage. Because of her suffering, she would glorify the Lord. Sister Mary Francis of the Third Order of St. Francis, who lived during the late 18th century, was frequently ill and was told on one occasion by the angel that he would heal her—and he did. She and others were witness to a smell of sweet perfume, which she attributed to the presence of Raphael. The angel also is credited with healing others of various afflictions, including epilepsy, and of providing protection during journeys.

Raphael is the patron saint of the blind, happy meetings, nurses, physicians, and travelers.

FURTHER READING

Charlesworth, James H., ed. *The Old Testament Pseudepigrapha*. Vols. 1 and 2. New York: Doubleday, 1983, 1985.

Giudici, Maria Pia. *The Angels: Spiritual and Exegetical Notes*. New York: Alba House, 1993.

Lang, Judith. *The Angels of God: Understanding the Bible*. Hyde Park, N.Y.: New City Press, 1997.

O'Sullivan, Fr. Paul. *All about the Angels*. Rockford, Ill.: Tan Books and Publishers, 1990. First published 1945.

Rathanael

Angel of the third HEAVEN. In the Testament of SOLOMON, Rathanael is the angel who thwarts the two-headed female DEMON Enepsigos.

Raum (Raym)

One of the FALLEN ANGELS and 72 spirits of SOLOMON. Raum is an earl who appears as a crow but will shift to human form when commanded to do so. He steals treasure, even from kings, and carries it anywhere. He destroys cities and dignities. Raum also discerns the past, present, and future, and he makes friends and enemies love each other. He governs 30 legions. Before his fall, he was in the order of THRONES.

Raziel (Akrasiel, Gallizur, Rasiel, Ratziel, Reziel, Saraquel, Suriel)

Angel of the secret regions, chief of the THRONES, and chief of the Supreme Mysteries, who is charged with guarding the secrets of the universe. The name "Raziel" means "secret of God" or "angel of mysteries." Raziel is important in Kabbalistic and rabbinic lore, and in apocryphal writings, especially the book of ENOCH.

Raziel is best known as the keeper of the SEFER RAZIEL, or the Book of the Angel Raziel, a text of angel MAGIC and MERKABAH mysticism said to hold all the secrets of the cosmos—even things unknown to other angels.

In the KABBALAH, Raziel is an archangel assigned to guard the second sephirah, Chokmah (Wisdom) on the TREE OF LIFE. He is one of the archangels in the world of Briah, the second of the four worlds of creation.

MAIMONIDES names Raziel as chief of the ERELIM, the herald of God and the preceptor of ADAM.

recording angels

Angels who are charged with keeping track of all celestial and earthly events. The information is presented to God and is used in judgment.

The idea that humans learn secret lore and powers from heavenly writings is ancient. In Babylonian lore, the recording deity is Nabu or Nebo; in Arabic mythology, it is Moakkibat. The Egyptians had Thoth as the scribe God; the Greeks had Hermes as the swift in wisdom messenger god. In the Enochian writings, Pravuil, Radueriel, Vretiel, and ENOCH are the wise keepers of heavenly records. In Kabbalistic lore, the angel Raziel can be called a recording angel, as keeper of the book containing all the celestial secrets.

In Islam every believer is attended by two angels, called the *Kiramu'l katibin*, "Guardians and Noble Scribes" (Surah 82.10–11). One on the right contemplates and dictates; the other on the left records. The closing of the Muslim daily prayer ritual, the *Salat*, acknowledges their presence. The angels constantly watch and record each person's good and bad actions.

Upon death, the life's record is given to Azrael, the ANGEL OF DEATH.

See DAIMONES; HERMAS.

Remiel (Jeremiel, Phanuel, Ramiel, Rumael, Uriel, Yerahmeel)

Angel charged with leading souls to judgment. Remiel means "mercy of God." Remiel also is called the "Lord of Souls awaiting Resurrection." He presides over thunder, as do Ramiel and Uriel.

Remiel appears in apocryphal texts. In the ENOCH books, he is identified both as one of the seven ARCHANGELS who stand before God and also as one of the FALLEN ANGELS. As an archangel, he is set over "those who rise" and is charged with spreading the instructions of all seven archangels. In 4 EZRA he is equated with Jeremiel and Uriel, and in the Apocalypse of Baruch he destroys the army of Sennacherib.

reprobated angels

Seven angels condemned in a trial conducted by a church council in Rome in 745 during the pontificate of Pope Zachary. The trial was undertaken because church officials were alarmed at the rise in veneration of angels and feared idol worship. The seven condemned angels were Adimus, Inias, Raguel, Sabaoc, Simiel, Tubual, and Uriel. Bishops Adalbert and Clement, who had advocated veneration of these angels, were convicted of heresy and excommunicated. The church forbade the veneration or invocation of any angels other than those named in the Bible: Michael, Gabriel, and Raphael.

Revelation (The Apocalypse)

The final book of the New Testament, which foretells the second coming of Christ, the end of the world, the last judgment, Armageddon, and the establishment of a new heaven and new earth. The authorship is not certain; tradition attributes the book to the apostle John. Even if John is the author, a different person may have written the Epistles of John. There are many stylistic and linguistic differences among the five Johannine writings but there are striking similarities as well.

Revelation describes in graphic images the final confrontation between good and evil. Sinners shall be punished and the righteous shall be rewarded in a new heavenly city. The contemporaries of the author of Revelation were familiar with the symbolic Jewish, Greek, and Roman allegory and imagery in which the book was written; today the symbology is more difficult to understand. Its angels, however, are consistent with the cosmology of the times.

The crowned Virgin in the heavens (Gustave Doré)

In 1:1, God sends his angel to make it known to his servant John to bear witness to the word of God and the testimony of JESUS Christ. In 1:12, John sees seven gold lamps that are the seven churches, and seven stars are their heavenly counterparts (angels). In 1:20, the angels of the seven churches accord with the Jewish belief Exodus 23:20) that individuals, nations, and communities have angels who are responsible for them. (See ORIGEN.)

John addresses his letters not to the bishops but to the angels, and he holds them responsible for the faults of the communities they represent. In John's world HEAVEN and earth are equally parts of the physical universe that God created; they belong inseparably together, and everything on earth, including its evil, has its counterpart in heaven. When the old order is finally destroyed, John sees a new heaven and a new earth, for the former heaven and earth together, along with their contaminating evil, have been removed.

In chapter 4, John has a vision of the heavens. There are seven flaming lamps burning and seven spirits of God; the number seven suggests completion. A

RAINBOW surrounds the throne of emerald, and a presence sits upon the throne, attended by 24 elders. Four many-eyed, four-faced "living creatures" like those in the vision of EZEKIEL ceaselessly sing praises. (See QEDUSSAH.) The creatures may be the four angels responsible for directing the physical world; four symbolizes the physical world. Their many eyes symbolize God's omniscience and providence. They give unceasing glory to God for his creation. Their figures of lion, bull, man, and eagle suggest all that is noblest, strongest, wisest, swiftest, in the created world. Since the early Christian theologian Irenaeus, these four creatures have been associated with the four evangelists.

In 5:11–12, "myriads and myriads and thousands of thousands" of angels around the throne shout praises of the Lamb. The redeemed are singled out in 7:1–3: "Next I saw four angels, standing at the four corners of the earth, holding back the four winds of the earth, that no wind might blow on earth or sea against any tree. Then I saw another angel ascend from the rising of the sun, with the seal of the living God, and he called in a loud voice to the four angels who had been given the power to harm earth and sea: 'Do not harm the earth or the sea or the trees, til we have sealed the foreheads of the servants of our God upon their foreheads.'"

In 8:2–5: "Next I saw seven trumpets being given to the seven angels who stand in the presence of God. Another angel, who had a golden censer . . . filled it with the fire from the altar, which he then threw down on to the earth; immediately there came peals of thunder and flashes of lightning, and the earth shook. Verses 8:6–12 state that the seven angels that had the seven trumpets now made ready to sound them. The first brings hail and fire; a third of the earth is burnt up. The second drops a great mountain, all on fire into the sea, which turned into blood. The third trumpet causes a huge star to fall from the sky, burning rivers and springs. This was the star called Wormwood; the water turned bitter. The fourth trumpet blasts a third of the sun and a third of the moon and a third of the stars. Verses 9:1–11 state, "Then the fifth angel blew his trumpet, and I saw a star [one of the FALLEN ANGELS] that had fallen from heaven onto the earth, and he was given the keys to the shaft leading down to the Abyss" [where the fallen angels were imprisoned pending their ultimate punishment] . . . the smoke from the Abyss darkened the sun and out of the smoke dropped locusts who attacked any man who was without God's SEAL on their foreheads. . . . Their tails were like scorpions', with stings, and it was with them that they were able to injure people for five months. Their emperor was the Angel of the Abyss, whose name in Hebrew is Abaddon, or Apollyon in Greek (Destruction, or Ruin)."

In 9:13–19, the sixth angel blows his trumpet and a voice speaks to the sixth angel to "release the four angels that are chained up at the great river Euphrates." They are released to destroy a third of the human race. Their horses have lions' heads from which issue fire, smoke, and sulphur. In 10:1–7, a powerful angel comes down and in his hand is a scroll; he announces that when the seventh angel blows his trumpet, God's secret intention will be fulfilled.

Verses 11:1–12 refer to two martyred prophets, often interpreted as ELIJAH and MOSES, but interpreted by many early church fathers as ENOCH and Elijah. The prophets are resurrected by God and they go up to heaven. Earthquakes kill their foes. God's temple in heaven opens, and the ARK OF THE COVENANT is visible within his temple.

Chapter 12 opens with a vision of a pregnant woman clothed with the sun with the moon under her feet, and wearing on her head a crown of 12 stars. A

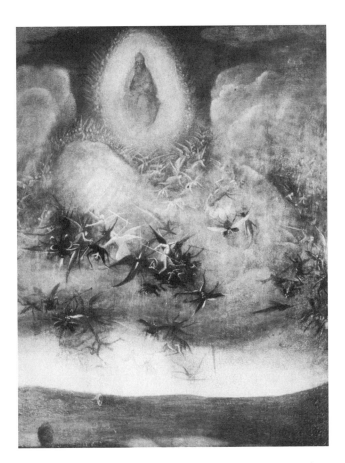

Heavenly war between good and evil angels (Gustave Doré)

great red dragon with seven heads and 10 horns and seven diadems on each head appears, and his tail sweeps a third of the stars in heaven down to the earth. (This recalls the reference in ISAIAH to the fall of the morning star, LUCIFER.)

Verses 12:7–17 describes the war in heaven between the forces of good and evil. Michael and his angels attack the dragon, the primeval serpent, known as Satan, who fights back with his angels, but they are defeated and driven out of heaven. Satan is "hurled down to earth and his angels were hurled down with him."

In 14:6–11, another angel flies overhead to announce the gospel of eternity to all who live on the earth and to announce the last judgment. A second angel follows, announcing that Babylon has fallen. A third angel says those who followed the beast will be tortured in the presence of the Lamb and his holy angels, and the smoke of their torture will go on for ever and ever. In 14:14–20, four angels with sickles gather in the harvest.

Chapters 15–16 tell that seven angels bring the seven plagues that were the last "because they exhaust the anger of God." They all have harps, and they sing the hymn of Moses and the Lamb. One of the four animals gives the seven angels seven golden bowls filled with the anger of God. The last seven plagues are sores; death of the sea creatures; rivers turning to blood; sun scorching people with flames; the throne of the beast turned to darkness and people cursing with pain; beasts coming from the Euphrates for the battle of Armageddon; and a violent earthquake and falling hail destroying everything.

Chapters 17–18 tell that angels explain to John the famous prostitute, the beast yet to come, and the fall of Babylon. In 19:17–21, John sees an angel standing in the sun who announces to the birds, "come and get ready to eat the flesh of kings, heroes, generals, horse and riders." Then is fought the first battle of the end: the rider Faithful and True conquers the beast and his army, and the birds gorge on their flesh.

The monster and whore are titanic forms of evil in the world. The monster is associated by John with the Roman Empire of his own day, but each has a much longer history. The monster has characteristics of all four empires of Daniel's vision (Daniel 13:1–2); the whore is Babylon the great but also bears the allegorical names of Sodom and Egypt and the character of Jerusalem. Each has in its own way the power to delude the whole world, apart from those who are protected from such delusion by the seal of God. The essence of evil is deceit and counterfeit. Satan is the deceiver of the whole world who misleads men by telling lies about God. The beast is the Antichrist, the false Messiah, who makes blasphemous claims to deity.

In 20:1–15, an angel (assumed to be Michael) throws the beast into the Abyss and chains him up for a thousand years. After a thousand years, Satan will come again to rally forces, Gog and Magog, for another great war against the saints. But fire will come down and consume them. The devil will be thrown into the lake of fire and sulphur, where the beast and false prophet are, and their torture will never stop. Anyone whose name is not found in the book of life will be thrown into the burning lake.

Chapters 21–22 tell that a new heaven and new earth are now shown to John by angels. The bride is shown in the holy city with 12 gates, each guarded by an angel. An angel measures the city and gates and walls with a gold measuring rod. An angel shows John the river of life flowing crystal clear down the middle of the street. Finally the angel says that all John has written is sure and will come true, and happy are those who treasure the prophecy of this book. He reminds John that he, too, is a servant. The epilogue in 22:16 states: "I, Jesus, have sent my angel to make these revelations to you for the sake of the churches."

FURTHER READING
Bowman, J. W. "Book of Revelation." In *The Interpreter's Dictionary of the Bible*. New York: Abingdon Press, 1962.
Caird, G. B. *A Commentary on the Revelation of St. John the Divine*. New York: Harper and Row, 1966.
Glasson, C. F. *The Revelation of John*. Cambridge: Cambridge University Press, 1965.

Rhamiel (Rahmiel)

The angelic name of St. FRANCIS OF ASSISI in his aspect as one of the ANGELS OF MERCY.

Rikbiel YHVH

One of seven ruling angels of the order of GALGALLIM, PRINCE of judgment and angel concerned with the divine chariot. Rikbiel is also identified as chief of the WHEELS. In 3 ENOCH, he is a high prince of the seventh HEAVEN, standing above Soperiel.

Rimmon

Aramaen deity and Syrian idol who became an inferior fallen archangel. Rimmon means in Hebrew "exalted" or "roarer." In Babylonian and Semite lore, Rimmon is the god of thunder and storms. As a DEMON, he is infernal ambassador to Russia.

rishis

In Vedic lore, seven or 10 spirits from whom humankind descended. The rishis are comparable to the ANGELS OF THE PRESENCE and also to the AMA-RAHSPANDS of ZOROASTRIANISM.

River of Fire

River that flows beneath the throne of the glory of God in the seventh HEAVEN. Various Jewish texts refer to either one river, four rivers, or seven rivers of fire. In 3 ENOCH, the angels who attend God bathe or baptize themselves in the River of Fire and restore themselves 365 times. They take fire from the river and cleanse their lips and their tongues. When the QEDUSSAH is sung by the MINISTERING ANGELS, the River of Fire rises and its fires increase in strength a thousand thousand and myriads and myriads of times.

Rizoel

In the Testament of SOLOMON, angel who has the power to thwart Soubelti, one of the DEMONS who is among the DECANS OF THE ZODIAC.

Rogziel

One of the ANGELS OF PUNISHMENT. Rogziel means "the wrath of God."

Ronobe (Roneve, Ronove)

One of the FALLEN ANGELS and 72 spirits of SOLOMON. Ronobe is an earl and marquis who appears as a monster. He teaches rhetoric and art as well as knowledge and understanding of languages. He gives the favor of friends and enemies. He has 19 legions.

Ruax

In the Testament of SOLOMON, a headache DEMON and the first of the 36 HEAVENLY BODIES. Ruax is imprisoned by Michael.

rulers

An order of angels equated with the DOMINIONS or PRINCIPALITIES.

Ruman

In Islamic lore, angel who screens souls consigned to HELL. Ruman requires the souls to write down all the evil deeds that led to their condemnation. He then delivers the souls to Munkar (Monker) and Nakir.

Sabaoc

One of the seven REPROBATED ANGELS in a church council trial in 745 in Rome.

Sabaoth (Ibraoth, Tsabaoth)

One of the seven ANGELS OF THE PRESENCE; in GNOSTICISM, one of the seven ARCHONS. Sabaoth is invoked as a divine name in MAGIC.

Sabathiel (Sabbathi)

Angelic PRINCE who stands continually before God, and an INTELLIGENCE of the planet Saturn. Sabathiel communicates divine light to those in his dominion.

Sablo (Samlo)

Angelic being of graciousness and protection named frequently in the Nag Hammadi and other Gnostic literature. Sablo is a great AEON who brings the elect into HEAVEN. He usually is part of a trinity of angels including Abraxas and Gamaliel.

Sabnack (Salmac)

One of the FALLEN ANGELS and 72 spirits of SOLOMON. Sabnack is a marquis who appears as an armed soldier with a lion's head, riding on a pale horse. He builds and fortifies towers, camps, and cities. Upon command he torments people with wounds and maggot-filled, putrid sores. He also gives good FAMILIARS. He rules 29 legions.

Sabrael (Sabriel)

One of the seven ARCHANGELS and ruler of the order of TARSHISHIM, a duty shared with Tarshiel. Sabrael guards the first HEAVEN and thwarts Sphendonael, the DEMON of disease.

Sabrathan

In the LEMEGETON, the ruling angel of the first hour of the night, called Omalharien. Sabrathan rules 1,540 dukes and other servants divided into 10 orders.

Sachiel (Zadkiel)

Angel who belongs to the order of HASHMALLIM and who is a ruler of Jupiter. Sachiel means "covering of God." Sachiel lives in the first HEAVEN.

Sagnessagiel (Sagansagel, Sasniel, Sasnigel)

Chief of the angelic guards of the fourth hall of the seventh HEAVEN and a PRINCE of wisdom. In 3 ENOCH, Sagnessagiel is one of the many names of Metatron.

Sahaqiel

In 3 ENOCH, prince of the fourth HEAVEN.

St. Michael's Mount See MICHAEL.

Salathiel (Salatheel, Sealthiel, Sealtiel)

In the Book of ADAM AND EVE, angel who rescues Adam and Eve from the mountaintop where Satan had taken them. Salathiel takes them to the cave of treasures. Salathiel is one of seven ministering archangels and rules the movements of the spheres.

Saleos

One of the FALLEN ANGELS and 72 spirits of SOLOMON. Saleos is a duke who appears as a soldier wearing a duke's crown and riding on a crocodile. He promotes love between men and women and speaks authoritatively about the creation of the world.

Samael (Sammael)

A Gnostic god and, in Judaism, the evil angel who comes to be identified with Satan. Samael actually is the name of a kingdom of the Aramaens, in the area of Syria in the second millennium B.C.E.

Some mythologists have associated this name with "Dread God," a Semitic version of the Asiatic Sama, Samana, or Samavurti, the "Leveller." The Sama Veda called him a storm god, clothed in black clouds.

Samael is a name that arises several times within GNOSTICISM. In one Gnostic text, Sophia (originally a high angel, or AEON) confronts her imperfect son Ialdabaoth, who in another reading is her "shadowed" creation (an abortion of her wish to create on her own), who has subsequently created angels to create this world. Ruling them, he thinks he is the ruler of all, sufficient unto himself. Sophia tells him: "You are wrong, Samael."

The name Samael means "the blind god." Blindness is a theme that runs through Gnosticism, for which ignorance, not willful sin, is the seat of evil. In another Gnostic text Ialdabaoth casts ADAM AND EVE, and the serpent who tempted them, out of Paradise after they have eaten of the tree of Gnosis (Knowledge of Good and Evil). The serpent then uses the angels begotten upon Eve by the planetary powers to bring into existence six sons. These sons, along with himself, become seven earthly DEMONS; the serpent is called Michael or Sammael. The concept of seven evil demons is an old one in the East, and a demonic connotation lingers around this name.

In Jewish demonology, the name Samael first appears in the story of the fall of the angels in the Ethiopic Book of ENOCH. Samael also is identified as the ANGEL OF DEATH, the head of all devils, and the chief of all tempters. He leads the rebel armies of angels in heaven.

Prior to the fall, Samael is higher than the mighty SERAPHIM. He has 12 wings. His duties include being in charge of all nations, except Israel, over which he shall have power only on the Day of Atonement. Then he will war with the archangel Michael, the guardian of Israel. The war will last until the end of days, when Samael will be handed over to Israel in shackles.

Samael is described as flying through the air, with one long hair streaming from his navel. As long as the hair remains intact, he will reign. Samael, however, does not know the way to the Tree of Life. He is the angel who governs the planet Mars.

He has three brides, Lilith, a night demon, and Namaah and Agrat bat Mahlat, angels of prostitution.

FURTHER READING
Scholem, Gershom. *Kabbalah*. New York: Dorset Press, 1987. First published 1974.

Samkiel

In 3 ENOCH, one of the ANGELS OF DESTRUCTION who sits in the heavenly court of law and is in charge of purifying souls of their sin in SHEOL.

Samuel

In the LEMEGETON, the ruling angel of the first hour of the day. Samuel has numerous dukes and servants under his command.

Sandalphon (Sandalfon)

A giant angel who in rabbinic lore is a weaver of prayers, and the twin brother of the mighty Metatron. The name Sandalphon means "co-brother."

In rabbinic lore, Sandalphon is so big that his size strikes fear into the heart of MOSES when the prophet is taken into heaven to receive the Torah. There he finds the angel weaving garlands out of the prayers of Israel, which place themselves on the head of God upon completion. In addition he fights Samael (Satan) endlessly, a job he shares with the archangel Michael. He also determines the sex of the unborn.

Sandalphon's abode is placed variously in the third, sixth and seventh HEAVENS in rabbinic literature, and in the fourth heaven in Islamic lore.

Saniel

In the LEMEGETON, the ruling angel of the sixth hour of the day, called Genapherim. Saniel rules 10 chief dukes and 1,000 lesser dukes and their servants.

Santería See ORISHAS.

Sarakiel (Saraqael)
Angel who rules the MINISTERING ANGELS and presides over their judgment councils. Sarakiel also rules the sign of Aries with Sataaran. In 1 ENOCH, he is one of the holy seven angels and is charged with watching over the children of sinners.

Sarandiel
In the LEMEGETON, the ruling angel of the 12th hour of the night, called Xephan. Sarandiel has many dukes and servants.

S(a)raosha See AMARAHSPANDS.

Sarasael (Sarea, Saraqael, Sarga)
Seraph sent by God to NOAH to advise him on replanting the Tree of Life involved in the fall of ADAM AND EVE. Sarasael also is one of the five angels who recorded the 204 books dictated by EZRA. He has jurisdiction over those who sin in the spirit.

Sariel (Sarakiel, Saraqael, Saraqel, Suruquel, Suriel, Uriel, Zerachiel)
Good and FALLEN ANGEL. In the Enochian writings, Sariel is Saraqel, not the same as Uriel. Sariel rules Aries and is one of the nine angels who preside over the summer solstice. As a fallen angel, he teaches the course of the moon.

In the War of the Sons of Light and the Sons of Darkness (also known as the Triumph of God), one of the QUMRAN TEXTS, Sariel is one of the four leaders of the forces of good. The human warriors are given exact instructions on who is to fight where, with weapons described carefully. There are four subdivisions (towers) and each is to have the name of their archangel inscribed on their shield. Sariel is on the third tower.

In the Ladder of JACOB, the Qumran fragments of the book of ENOCH, and in the Neofiti Targum, Sariel is the angel who is in charge of dreams and their interpretation.

See DREAMS AND VISIONS.

sarim
In 3 ENOCH, an angelic order of PRINCES of the Song-Uttering Choirs led by Tagas.

Saru See ZOROASTRIANISM.

Sasnigiel YHVH
In 3 ENOCH, one of the PRINCES OF THE WORLD, one of the SERAPHIM, and one of the ANGELS (princes) OF THE PRESENCE. Sasnigiel bows down to Zazriel. Sasnigiel also in one of the many names of Metatron.

Sasquiel
In the LEMEGETON, the ruling angel of the fifth hour of the day, called Fealech. Sasquiel rules 10 chief dukes and 100 lesser dukes and their servants.

Satan
In Christianity, a FALLEN ANGEL who is the PRINCE and embodiment of all evil, and who is committed to tempting humanity into sin and thus condemning them into everlasting hell. Satan means "adversary," "opponent," or "obstacle" in Hebrew.

Originally, among the Hebrews, Satan was not so thoroughly evil. He was not even any one angel in particular. Rather, the term *satan,* with a lowercase "s," was a common noun applied to an obstacle or adversary. The Israelites, who were engaged in constant struggles, demonized their enemies in the forms of monstrous beasts. But as time went on the term *satan* became applied to enemies, with an increasingly malevolent tint.

Storytellers as early as the sixth century B.C.E. used a supernatural character called a *satan,* by which they meant any of God's angels—the BENE HA-ELOHIM ("SONS OF GOD")—whom God dispatched to block or obstruct human activity. Sometimes the blocking was a good idea, if the human characters were following a sinful path.

In the Bible, the term *satan* appears for the first time in Numbers 22:23–35. God sends an ANGEL OF THE LORD to act as a satan to block the journey of BALAAM, who has displeased God. When Balaam's ass sees the satan standing in the road, she balks, causing Balaam to strike her three times. The angel of the Lord reveals himself, and Balaam promises to do what God tells him through his emissary, the satan.

In the book of Job a character named Satan, who seems to have the job of roaming the earth and keeping an eye on humans, torments JOB to test his faith. This Satan is described as one of God's loyal servants.

At about this same time in history—about 550 B.C.E.—the term *satan* described internal strife among the Israelites. In 1 Chronicles 21, a satan convinces King David to number his people against the wishes of God, causing God to send a destroying angel to kill 70,000 Israelites by means of the plague (despite the fact that David repents).

ZECHARIAH uses *satan* to describe internal conflicts among the Jews. He also shows Satan as being hostile in his opposition to Joshua (Zechariah 3:1–2).

Radical dissenters among the Israelites began to use *satan* more and more to characterize their own Jewish opponents, whom they viewed as obstacles to their objectives. They also used other terms including the names of wicked angels. All of these became associated with evil enemies: Satan, Beelzebub, Semyaza, Mastema, Azazel, and Belial. The name Satan was applied more than any other. Stories about angels who sinned and fell from heaven were applied to Jewish opponents. Satan as a figure became increasingly prominent as a personality, one of evil.

Satan became identified with the FALLEN ANGELS called WATCHERS who cohabited with women and thus were cast into a pit of darkness. The leaders of the Watchers are Semyaza and Azazel. The Enochian writings tell of God sending the four archangels Raphael,

Satan (Gustave Doré)

Gabriel, Uriel and Michael to slay the giant offspring of the Watchers (the NEPHILIM) and attack the Watchers themselves. Raphael binds Azazel and casts him into a pit. The book of JUBILEES says that one-tenth of the Watchers were spared by God so that they might be subject before Satan, their leader, on earth. (Jubilees also castigates Jews who do not keep themselves separate from Gentiles; the conflicts that arose were attributed to Satan, Belial, or Mastema, all of whom represented the enemy within.)

The story of the Watchers underwent many transformations and was influential among the Christians. The casting out of sinful angels, who became the demons of hell under a prince of evil, formed a crucial part of Christian theology. Satan became identified with Lucifer primarily from a passage in Isaiah 14:12–15: "How you have fallen from heaven, bright morning star." "Bright morning star," or more literally "bright son of the morning," was translated into Latin as Lucifer.

Christian thought also was influenced by the Essenes, a Jewish sect that coexisted briefly with Christianity. The Essenes saw themselves as "sons of light" who battled the "sons of darkness." Both forces were ruled by princes. However the Essenes did not personify these princes, but instead they saw them as universal principles.

The writers of the Gospels portrayed Satan as having been cast out of heaven for sin (in Luke 10:18 he falls like lightning), a being of evil who opposes God and Jesus. Jews who did not follow Jesus were cast in the role of agents of Satan (later, any gentiles who opposed Christians fell into the same camp). Jesus was cast as the focal point in the war between God's forces of Good and Satan's forces of Evil. His resurrection is a victory over Satan; thus those who follow Christ cannot lose in the great cosmic battle for souls.

Throughout the New Testament, the name of Satan is associated only with evil. He is called: "accuser of the brethren" in Revelation 12:10; "adversary" in 1 Peter 5:8; "Beelzebub" in Matthew 12:24; "the Devil" in Matthew 4:1; "the enemy" in Matthew 13:39; "the evil one" in 1 John 5:19; "the father of lies and a murderer" in John 8:44; "the god of this age" (i.e., of false cults) in 2 Corinthians 4:4; "a roaring lion" (in terms of destructiveness) in 1 Peter 5:8–9; a "tempter" in Matthew 4:3; and a "serpent" in Revelation 12:9.

Among his evil acts described in the New Testament are: tempting believers into sin (Ephesians 2:1–3; 1 Thessalonians 3:5); tempting believers to lie (Acts 5:3); tempting believers to commit sexually immoral acts (1 Corinthians 7:5); accusing and slandering believers (Revelation 12:10); hindering the work of believers in any way possible (1 Thessalonians 2:18);

waging war against believers (Ephesians 6:11–12); inciting persecutions against believers (Revelation 2:10); opposing Christians with the ferociousness of a hungry lion (1 Peter 5:8); and fostering spiritual pride (1 Timothy 3:6).

The role of Satan as the agent of evil became magnified over time. By the Middle Ages, Satan, as the devil, was believed in as a real, potent being who possessed terrible supernatural powers and was intent upon destroying man by undermining his morals. In this pursuit he was aided by his army of evil demons. Satan's machinations were a driving force behind the Inquisition, which persecuted any enemy of the Christian church—moral, political, ethnic, social, or religious—as being one of Satan's disciples.

Modern views of Satan vary. Fundamentalists view him as a real being of pure evil, whose trickster tactics will trip up the unwary. His avowed purpose is to thwart the plan of God by any means possible. He fosters false prophets, teachers, Christs, and apostles.

Others believe in Satan more in terms of the Essenes' idea of a cosmic principle, the shadow aspect of light. According to the Catholic Church, the devil's objective is to ruin the church. He is given special powers by God to try people, in order that they may have an opportunity to be cleansed. By keeping the Ten Commandments and steering clean of all sin, one stays out of the devil's reach. God also permits evil spirits to possess people who have sinned.

FURTHER READING

Pagels, Elaine. *The Origin of Satan.* New York: Random House, 1995.

Russell, Jeffrey Burton. *The Devil: Perceptions of Evil from Antiquity to Primitive Christianity.* Ithaca, N.Y.: Cornell University Press, 1977.

———. *Lucifer: The Devil in the Middle Ages.* Ithaca, N.Y.: Cornell University Press, 1984.

Satanail

In 2 ENOCH, former ARCHANGEL and the leader of the WATCHERS, imprisoned in the fifth HEAVEN. Satanail is a name for Satan.

Enoch relates the creation story as revealed to him by God, and how Satanail is cast from heaven on the second day, the day in which he creates all angels from a great fire he cuts off from the rock (foundation) of the heavens:

> But one under the order of the archangels deviated, together with the division that was under his authority. He thought up the impossible idea that he might place his throne higher in the clouds which are above the earth, and that he might become equal to my power.

> And I hurled him from out of the height, together with his angels. And he was flying around in the air, ceaselessly, above the Bottomless. (29:4–5)

Satanail is imprisoned in the fifth heaven along with the Watchers and NEPHILIM.

FURTHER READING

Charlesworth, James H., ed. *The Old Testament Pseudepigrapha.* Vols. 1 and 2. New York: Doubleday, 1983, 1985.

Satqiel

In 3 ENOCH, PRINCE of the fifth HEAVEN.

Savatri (Savitar, Savitri)

In Vedic lore, one of the seven or twelve ADITYAS or "infinite ones" who are comparable to angels. Savatri is a son god or goddess with golden eyes who is identified with Prajapati, the Creator.

Scepter

In the Testament of Solomon, DEMON who appears in the form of a gigantic dog and who causes quartan fever. Scepter tells SOLOMON he has accomplished many unlawful deeds in the world and is so strong that he restrains the stars of heaven. He deceives men who follow his star closely and leads them into stupidity. He also subdues the hearts (thoughts) of men through their throats and destroys them. Solomon asks Scepter why he is so prosperous. The demon tells him to turn over his manservant, whom he will spirit off to a place in the mountains where he will be shown an emerald stone. The stone will adorn Solomon's temple.

Solomon does this, but he gives his servant his magical ring with which he can quell the demon. The servant retrieves the emerald, which is shaped like a leek and binds Scepter. Solomon extracts 200 shekels from the stone and locks it up. He commands Scepter and the headless demon Murder to cut marble for the temple.

Scepter is thwarted by the angel Briathos.

Schemhamphorae

Seventy-two angels who bear the Names of God, which are given in Hebrew Scripture and expressed at the end of every verse. The verses are used in invocation and in magic. The Schemhamphorae function as NAMES of power.

The Schemhamphorae and their verses are:

1. Vehujah: Thou, O Lord, art my guardian, and exaltest my head.

The Cabula.

Shewing at one View the Seventy-two Angels bearing the name of God Shemhamphoræ.

Caliel	Loviah	Hakamiah	Hariel	Mebahel	Ielael	Hahiah	Lauviah	Aladiah	Haziel	Cahethel	Akaiah	Lelahel	Mahasiah	Elemiah	Sitael	Ieliel	Vehuiah
Monadel	Chavakiah	Lehahiah	Iehuiah	Vasariah	Lecabel	Omael	Reiil	Sehiah	Ierathel	Haaiah	Nithhaiah	Hahuiah	Melchael	Ieiaiel	Nelchael	Pahaliah	Leuuiah
Nithael	Nanael	Imamiah	Hahaziah	Daniel	Vehuel	Mihael	Asaliah	Ariel	Saaliah	Ielahiah	Vevaliah	Michael	Hahahel	Ihiarel	Rehael	Haamiah	Aniel
Nevamaih	Haiaiel	Ibamiah	Rochel	Habuiah	Eiael	Menkl	Damabiah	Mochael	Annauel	Iahhel	Umabel	Mizrael	Harahel	Ieilael	Nemamaih	Poiel	Mebahiah

Table showing the 72 angels bearing the name of God (From *The Magus* by Francis Barrett)

2. Ieliel: Do not remove Thy help from me, O Lord, and look to my defense.

3. Sirael: I shall say so to the Lord, Thou art my guardian, my God is my refuge, and I shall hope in Him.

4. Elemijel: Turn, O Lord, and deliver my soul, and save me for Thy mercy's sake.

5. Lelahel: Let him who lives in Zion sing unto the Lord, and proclaim His goodwill among the peoples.

6. Achajah: The Lord is merciful and compassionate, long-suffering and of great goodness.

7. Mahasiah: I called upon the Lord and he heard me and delivered me from all my tribulations.

8. Cahatel: O come let us adore and fall down before God who bore us.

9. Haziel: Remember Thy mercies, O Lord, and Thy mercies which have been forever.

10. Aladiah: Perform Thy mercies upon us, for we have hoped in Thee.

11. Laviah: The Lord liveth, blessed is my God, and let the God of my salvation be exalted.

12. Hahajah: Why hast Thou departed, O Lord, so long from us perishing in the times of tribulation.

13. Jezalel: Rejoice in the Lord, all ye lands, sing, exult, and play upon a stringed instrument.

14. Mebahel: The Lord is a refuge, and my God the help of my hope.

15. Hariel: The Lord is a refuge for me and my God the help of my hope.

16. Hakamiah: O Lord, God of my salvation, by day have I called to Thee, and sought Thy presence by night.

17. Leviah: O Lord our Lord, How wonderful is Thy name in all the world.

18. Caliel: Judge me, O Lord, according to Thy loving kindness, and let not them be joyful over me, O Lord.

19. Luviah: I waited in hope for the Lord, and He turned to me.

20. Pahaliah: I shall call upon the name of the Lord, O Lord free my soul.

21. Nelakhel: In Thee also have I hoped, O Lord, and said, Thou art my God.

22. Jajajel: The Lord keep thee, the Lord be thy protection on thy right hand.

23. Melahel: The Lord keep thine incoming and thine outgoing from this time forth for evermore.

24. Hahajah: The Lord is well pleased with those that fear Him and hope upon His mercy.

25. Haajah: I have called unto Thee with all my heart and shall tell forth all Thy wonders.

26. Nithhaja: I shall acknowledge Thee, O Lord, with all my heart, hear me, O Lord, and I shall seek my justification.

27. Jerathel: Save me, O Lord, from the evil man and deliver me from the wicked doer.

28. Sehijah: Let not God depart from me, look to my help, O God.

29. Rejajel: Behold, God is my helper, and the Lord is the guardian of my soul.

30. Omael: For Thou are my strength, O Lord. O Lord, Thou art my hope from my youth.

31. Lecabel: I shall enter into the power of the Lord, my God, I shall be mindful of Thy justice only.

32. Vasariah: For the word of the Lord is upright, and all His works faithful.

33. Jehuvajah: The Lord knows the thoughts of men, for they are in vain.

34. Lehahiah: Let Israel hope in the Lord from this time forth and for evermore.

35. Chavakiah: I am joyful, for the Lord hears the voice of my prayer.

36. Manadel: I have delighted in the beauty of Thy house, O Lord, and in the place of the habitation of Thy glory.

37. Aniel: O Lord God, turn Thy power toward us, and show us Thy face and we shall be saved.

38. Haamiah: For Thou art my hope, O Lord, and Thou has been my deepest refuge.

39. Rehael: The Lord has heard me and pitied me and the Lord is my helper.

40. Jejazel: Why drivest Thou away my soul, O Lord, and turnest Thy face from me?

41. Hahahel: O Lord, deliver my soul from wicked lips and a deceitful tongue.

42. Michael: The Lord protects thee from all evil and will protect thy soul.

43. Vevaliah: I have cried unto Thee, O Lord, and let my prayer come unto Thee.

44. Jelabiah: Make my wishes pleasing unto Thee, O Lord, and teach me Thy judgments.

45. Sealiah: If I say that my foot is moved, Thou wilt help me of Thy mercy.

46. Ariel: The Lord is pleasant to all the world and His mercies are over all His works.

47. Asaliah: How wonderful are Thy works, O Lord, and how deep Thy thoughts.

48. Michael: The Lord hath made thy salvation known in the sight of the peoples and will reveal His justice.

49. Vehael: Great is the Lord and worthy to be praised, and there is no end to His greatness.

50. Daniel: The Lord is pitiful and merciful, long-suffering and of great goodness.

51. Hahasiah: Let the Lord be in glory for ever and the Lord will rejoice in His works.

52. Imamiah: I shall make known the Lord, according to His justice, and sing hymns to the name of the Lord, the greatest.

53. Nanael: I have known Thee, O Lord, for Thy judgments are just, and in Thy truth have I abased myself.
54. Nithael: The Lord hath prepared His seat in heaven and His rule shall be over all.
55. Mebahiah: Thou remainest for ever, O Lord, and Thy memorial is from generation to generation.
56. Polial: The Lord raiseth up all who fall and setteth up the broken.
57. Nemamiah: They who fear the Lord have hoped in the Lord, He is their helper and their protector.
58. Jejalel: My soul is greatly troubled, but Thou, O Lord are here also.
59. Harahel: From the rising of the Sun to the going down of the same, the word of the Lord is worthy to be praised.
60. Mizrael: The Lord is just in all His ways and blessed in all His works.
61. Umbael: Let the name of the Lord be blessed from this time for evermore.
62. Iahael: See, O Lord, how I have delighted in Thy commandments according to Thy life-giving mercy.
63. Anaviel: Serve ye the Lord with gladness and enter into His sight with exultation.
64. Mehikiel: Behold the eyes of the Lord are upon those that fear Him and hope in His loving kindness.
65. Damabiah: Turn, O Lord, even here also, and be pleased with Thy servants.
66. Meniel: Neither leave me, Lord, nor depart from me.
67. Ejael: Delight in the Lord and He will give thee petitions of thy heart.
68. Habujah: Confess to the Lord, for He is God, and His mercy is for ever.
69. Roehel: The Lord is my inheritance and my cup and it is Thou who restorest mine inheritance.
70. Jabamiah: In the beginning God created the heaven and the earth.
71. Hajael: I shall confess to the Lord with my mouth and praise Him in the midst of the multitude.
72. Mumijah: Return to thy rest, my soul, for the Lord doeth thee good.

FURTHER READING

McLean, Adam, ed. *A Treatise on Angel Magic*. Grand Rapids, Mich.: Phanes Press, 1990.
Scholem, Gershom. *Kabbalah*. New York: Dorset Press, 1987. First published 1974.

scribes

In 3 ENOCH, a high order of angels who record all the deeds of all people and read the books of judgment at the celestial court.

seals

Symbols representing the names or essences of angels, INTELLIGENCES and spirits, including those of the planetary and celestial bodies. Seals are used in MAGIC in the invocation of a desired entity. They also are important in the mystical practices of the MERKABAH, in which the mystic must use the proper seal to gain entry to each level of HEAVEN and the seven halls within the highest heaven.

seasons   See ANGELS OF THE SEASONS.

seats

An order of angels equated with THRONES. ST. AUGUSTINE mentions seats in his *City of God.*

sebalim

In 3 ENOCH, an order of angels in the order of Song-Uttering Choirs led by the angel Tagas.

sedim

In Assyrian lore, GUARDIAN SPIRITS created by the angels Azza and Azael with the angel of prostitution, Naamah.

Seere

One of the FALLEN ANGELS and 72 spirits of SOLOMON. Seere is a PRINCE under Amaymon, the King of the East. He appears as a beautiful man riding a strong, winged horse. He makes things happen instantly, transports anywhere instantly, and discovers all thefts. Seere will follow commands and is indifferent to good or bad.

Sefer Raziel (Sefer ha-Raziel, Sefer Reziel, Sepher Rezial Hemelach, Raziel ha-Malach)

According to lore, the first book ever written, containing the secrets of the cosmos—secrets and mysteries of creation, even things that angels do not know—given by God via the angel Raziel to ADAM and his lineage. The Sefer Raziel is made of sapphire.

The origin and date of the text are not known, but it was in existence in the 13th century. The Sword of Moses, a GRIMOIRE, makes reference to it. The Sefer Raziel appears to be a collection authored by different people. Some sources credit authorship to either Eleazar of Worms of Isaac the Blind; Eleazar of Worms, who lived from 1160 to 1237, may have authored at least part of it. Most likely, it was compiled in the 13th century. It was so highly revered that it was believed mere possession of it would prevent fire. By the 19th century, there were 25 editions of it. In 2000 the first

Angelic script in the Sefer Raziel

English translation was published of the entire text of a Hebrew edition published in Amsterdam in 1701.

According to legend, the book originates in heaven. When God expels Adam from Paradise, he takes pity on him and tells Raziel to give him the book so that he can gaze into the mirror of all existence and see the face of God, and himself as an image of God. Adam and his lineage are visited constantly by the archangel Michael and other angels for instruction and consolation.

The book passes down to NOAH, who uses it for making the ark, and to SOLOMON, who is shown the book by Raziel in a DREAM and uses it for learning his great magical wisdom and power. ENOCH consulted the book.

According to the Zohar, Raziel gives Adam the book while he is still in Paradise. It contains the secret wisdom of the 72 letters of the name of God and its esoteric 670 mysteries, and 1,500 keys, which had not been given even to angels. As Adam reads the book, angels gather around him and learn the knowledge of Chokmah (wisdom). (See TREE OF LIFE.) The angel Hadraniel sends one of his subordinates to Adam, who tells him to guard the book well and not disclose its contents to anyone. Adam obeys, keeping

it secret. But when he is expelled from Eden, the book mysteriously disappears, causing Adam such distress that he immerses himself up to his neck in the Gihon River. When his body becomes covered with sores, God sends Raphael to give the book back to him. Adam acquires full occult knowledge, and he passes the book to his son Seth when he dies. Seth bequeaths it, and it eventually comes into the possession of ABRAHAM.

In other lore, the angels are jealous at being left out of the cosmic secrets and steal the book from Adam and throw it into the sea. God orders Rahab, the Angel of the Sea, to retrieve it and return it to Adam. It later is passed to ENOCH, where much of it is incorporated into the books of Enoch.

Although the keys in the book are not understood by any other angel, Raziel nonetheless is said to stand on the peak of Mt. Horeb every day and proclaim the secrets to humankind.

The 1701 edition includes five manuscripts, all of which seem to have been written at different times.

Important material deals with the 22-fold, 42-fold, and 72-fold NAMES of God; the five names of the human soul (*Neshemah*, breath of life; *Nephesh*, the soul itself; *Ruoch*, spirit or mind; *Cheyah*, life or vitality of the spirit; and *Yechideh*, the unity or uniqueness of the spirit); the seven hells (*Gihenam*, hell itself; *Sha'arimath*, gates of hell; *Tzalemoth*, shadow of death; *Baraschecath*, the pit of destruction; *Tithihoz*, clay of death; *Abbadon*, perdition; and *Shahol*, the highest hell); the divisions of the Garden of Eden; and the types of angels and spirits who have dominion over various things in creation. The book also gives angelic scripts, ANGEL LANGUAGES, long lists of magical incantations for directing the MEMUNIM (deputy angels), and magical instructions for rituals and the making of TALISMANS and AMULETS.

FURTHER READING

Godwin, Malcolm. *Angels: An Endangered Species.* New York: Simon and Schuster, 1990.

Savedow, Steve. *Sepher Rezial Hemelach: The Book of the Angel Rezial.* York Beach, Maine: Samuel Weiser, 2000.

Trachtenberg, Joshua. *Jewish Magic and Superstition: A Study in Folk Religion.* New York: Berhman's Jewish Book House, 1939.

Sefer Yetzirah See KABBALAH.

Semyaza (Semiaza, Shemhazi, Shamayza, Shemyaza) A leader of the FALLEN ANGELS, one of the Sons of God who cohabits with women. (See WATCHERS.) Semyaza probably means "meaning the name of Azza" or Uzza, which in turn mean "strength."

According to the Zohar, Semyaza cohabits with one of Eve's daughters and produces two sons, Hiwa and Hiya, who eat every day a thousand each of camels, horses, and oxen. As punishment for his sins, he hangs upside down in the constellation Orion, suspended between heaven and earth.

In 1 ENOCH, he is identified as the leader of the Watchers, and he is warned of their punishment by Michael.

Separ See VEPAR.

sephirot See TREE OF LIFE.

Seraphiel (Serapiel)
One of the angels named as chief of the SERAPHIM; one of eight judgment throne angels and a PRINCE of the MERKABAH. In 3 ENOCH, Seraphiel is described as an enormous, brilliant angel as tall as the seven HEAVENS with a face like the face of angels and the body like the body of eagles. He is beautiful like lightning and the light of the morning star. His body is full of eyes like the limitless stars of heaven and each eye is like the morning star. He wears on his head a sapphire stone as big as the entire world. His radiant crown is the height of a journey of 502 years. As chief of the seraphim he is committed to their care and teaches them the songs to sing for the glorification of God.

In magical lore, Seraphiel is one of the rulers of Tuesday and also the planet Mercury. He is invoked from the north.

seraphim
In the pseudo-Dionysian hierarchy of angels, the highest and closest angels to God. The name "seraphim" is thought to be derived from the Hebrew verb *saraf,* which means to "burn," "incinerate," or "destroy," and probably refers to the ability of seraphim to destroy by burning. The seraphim may have evolved from the uraeus, the gold serpent (specifically a cobra) worn by Egyptian pharaohs on their foreheads. Uraei without wings and with two or four wings were depicted in iconography throughout the Near East. They protected by spitting their poison, or fire. The seraphim who became angels in lore perhaps originally had serpent forms with human characteristics.

In the Hebrew Bible, the term *saraf* is applied to fiery serpents. Numbers 21:6–8 refers to fiery serpents sent by the Lord to bite and kill sinning

Seraph (From *The Hierarchie of the Blessed Angells* by Thomas Heywood [1635])

Israelites. After Moses prays for forgiveness, he is instructed to set a fiery serpent atop a pole. Whoever was bitten by it, when he looked upon it, would live. Moses makes a bronze serpent. Deuteronomy 8:15 refers to the "fiery serpents" and scorpions in the land of Egypt.

The prophet ISAIAH described more humanlike seraphim in a vision (Isaiah 6:2–3). He sees the Lord on his throne with six-winged seraphim standing above him. Two wings covered the face and two the feet—probably to protect them from the intense brilliance of the Lord—and the other two wings were used for flying. The seraphim call out to each other, "Holy, holy, holy is the Lord of hosts; and the whole earth is full of his glory." One seraphim takes a burning coal and touches it to Isaiah's lips, proclaiming that his guilt is taken away and his sin forgiven.

According to 3 ENOCH there are four seraphim who correspond to the four winds of the world. Each has six wings that correspond to the six days of creation;

each wing is as big as the fullness of a HEAVEN. Each has 16 faces, four facing in each direction, and each face is like the rising sun, the light of which is so bright that even the HAYYOTH, OPHANIM, and CHERUBIM cannot look upon it.

The text goes on to say that the seraphim are so named because they burn the tablets of Satan. Every day Satan sits down with Sammael, prince of Rome, and Dubbiel, prince of Persia, to write down the sins of Israel on tablets. Satan gives the tablets to the seraphim to take to God so that God will destroy Israel. But the seraphim know that God does not wish to do so, and so they take the tablets and burn them.

The Sefer Yetzirah says seraphim are the highest order of angels, and they exist in the Universe of Beriyah, where Binah, which is represented by fire, dominates. Beriyah is the world of the Throne that Isaiah sees in his vision. Some Kabbalists call the seraphim POWERS, forces, or potentials rather than angels.

Seraphim are mentioned in Jewish literature and pseudepigrapha, sometimes without specific description, but as part of the high heavenly host. According to the Testament of Adam, the seraphim stand before God and serve his inner chamber, and, like the cherubim, sing the hourly "holy, holy, holy." 2 Enoch describes them as having four faces and six wings. 3 Enoch says there are four seraphim, corresponding to the four winds of the world.

Seraphim are not mentioned by name in the New Testament.

In other lore, seraphim are the created representations of divine love, the fire of which consumes them and keeps them close to the throne of God. They are the only angels to stand above the throne. They establish the vibration of love, which in turn creates the field of life. They purify all and dispel the shadows of darkness. They are of such subtlety that they rarely are perceived by human consciousness. Rulers of the seraphim are Seraphiel, Jahoel, Metatron, Michael, and Satan prior to his fall from heaven.

According to AGRIPPA, seraphim help humans perfect the flame of love.

The seraphim are sometimes equated with the Hayyoth. In the KABBALAH, they govern Geburah (Strength), the fifth sephirah of the TREE OF LIFE.

FURTHER READING

Kaplan, Aryeh. *Sefer Yetzirah: The Book of Creation.* Rev. ed. York Beach, Maine: Samuel Weiser, 1997.

van der Toorn, Karel, Bob Becking, and Pieter W. van der Horst, eds. *Dictionary of Deities and Demons in the Bible.* 2d ed. Grand Rapids, Mich.: William B. Eerdmans, 1999.

Serguanich

In the LEMEGETON, the ruling angel of the third hour of the night, called Quabrion. Serguanich commands 101,550 dukes and servants who are divided into 12 orders.

Seven, the

A group of seven angels or higher ethereal beings assigned to the earth who participate in INSTRUMENTAL TRANSCOMMUNICATION (ITC).

In communications with ITC researchers, the Seven have described themselves as genderless and not human, animal, Light being, or God. They have their own individual natures but exist as a group fused together out of a common bond. The Seven have no names; their technical expert calls himself TECHNICIAN. The Seven are part of the RAINBOW PEOPLE.

The Seven are assigned as a "Gatekeeper between Heaven and Earth, between time and space." They have stayed in this assignment for thousands of years. Their purpose is to provide assistance, guidance, and protection to earth. They have been especially close to the planet during seven periods of climactic growth; the present constitutes the seventh period. They liken their role to a popular Victorian print of an angel guiding two children across a bridge, though without wings.

According to the Seven, the fusion in a group is discretionary. Many highly evolved beings who have incarnated in earth, including JESUS, MUHAMMAD, and Gautama Buddha, return after death to this ethereal realm of clusters.

Deceased people who are part of ITC reportedly have communicated that when they have the opportunity to go up to the level of the Seven, they perceive brilliant beings like "banks of supercomputers exchanging oceans of information at lightning speed."

FURTHER READING

Macy, Mark H. *Miracles in the Storm: Talking to the Other Side with the New Technology of Spiritual Contact.* New York: New American Library, 2001.

shaitans (mazikeen, shedeem, shedim, sheytans)

In Hebrew and Arabic mythology, evil spirits who have cock's feet.

Shamsiel

Angel who is both good and fallen. Shamsiel means "light of day" or "mighty son of god." As a good angel, Shamsiel is a PRINCE of paradise, guardian of Eden, and ruler of the fourth HEAVEN. According to the Zohar, he is chief of 365 legions of angels and is one of two aids to Uriel in battle. He crowns prayers and takes them to the fifth heaven. Shamsiel served as guide to MOSES when he visited Paradise in the flesh.

As a FALLEN ANGEL, Shamsiel is identified as one of the WATCHERS in the book of JUBILEES. In 1 ENOCH he is fallen angel who teaches the signs of the sun.

Shax (Chax, Scox)

One of the FALLEN ANGELS and 72 spirits of SOLOMON. Shax is a marquis who comes in the form of a stork and speaks with a hoarse voice. He destroys the eyesight, hearing, and understanding of any person upon command. He steals money from kings and then returns it in 1,200 years. After he is commanded into the magician's triangle, Shax will transport anything; otherwise, he will be deceptive. Upon command he will steal horses. He will find all hidden things unless they are being kept by evil spirits. He gives good FAMILIARS. He commands 30 legions.

Shekinah (Sekinah)

In Jewish mysticism, the divine presence of God on earth. Shekinah—regarded in a feminine light—absorbed Gnostic ideas of the divine spark exiled in the physical world. Originally, it was a name for that aspect of God, but it later became a hypostasis of God and was distinguished from him. (See WISDOM.)

In the Garden of Eden, Shekinah resides on a cherub. It is luminous and has protective and restorative powers. In 3 ENOCH, ADAM AND EVE gaze at:

> the bright image of the Shekinah, or the brilliance of the Shekinah radiated from one end of the world to the other, 365,000 times more brightly than the sun; anyone who gazed at the brightness of the Shekinah was not troubled by flies or gnats, by sickness or pain; malicious demons were not able to harm him, and even the angels had no power over him. (5:4–5)

God sends Shekinah to reside on the earth. But when wickedness and idolatry begin in the generation of Enosh (son of Seth and grandson of Adam), the MINISTERING ANGELS complain to God, and he withdraws Shekinah. The ministering angels surround it, blow their trumpets, and send it back up to heaven.

In the MERKABAH tradition, the withdrawal of Shekinah is final and accounts for the transcendence of God, but in some rabbinic lore the Shekinah returns to earth on other occasions.

In heaven Shekinah is guarded and attended by four camps of ministering angels who are ruled by four PRINCES. The Masseket Hekalot gives them as Michael on the right, Gabriel on the left, Uriel in front, and Raphael behind. 3 Enoch states that all angels, even the highest princes in heaven, must attend to the need of Shekinah while standing, which contradicts rabbinic lore that angels cannot or do not sit. (See SOPERIEL.) Four chariots of Shekinah stand in the seven palaces of the seventh heaven, and before each of them stand four camps of Shekinah. A RIVER OF FIRE flows between each camp. Between each river are circles of bright clouds, pillars of sulphur, and circles of fiery wheels.

In the KABBALAH, Shekinah is the tenth or last sephira (Malkuth) of the TREE OF LIFE, and acts as the opening or gateway to higher consciousness. Shekinah is symbolized by the Tree of Knowledge of Good and Evil in the Garden of Eden. Adam's sin causes Shekinah to split off from the higher sephirot, thus divorcing her from her husband, the sephira Tifereth on the Tree of Life. This disruption in the unity of the cosmos results in the withdrawal of Shekinah, who is driven from the Garden of Eden along with Adam and Eve. They all wander in exile.

In the Zohar, Shekinah expresses the fullness of divine speech and spells out all the letters of the Hebrew alphabet, from aleph to tav. "Et" is kabbalistic code for the Shekinah. Once Et is cast out of the Garden, language is corrupted and remains so until MOSES receives his revelation at Mt. Sinai.

Shekinah has been interpreted as the Holy Spirit, though this comparison is not explicit in Kabbalistic texts.

See SOPHIA.

FURTHER READING

Charlesworth, James H., ed. *The Old Testament Pseudepigrapha*. Vols. 1 and 2. New York: Doubleday, 1983, 1985.

Scholem, Gershom. *Kabbalah*. New York: Dorset Press, 1987. First published 1974.

Zohar: The Book of Enlightenment. Translated by Daniel Chanan Matt. Ramsey, N.J.: Paulist Press, 1983.

Shelley, Percy Bysshe See LITERATURE AND ANGELS.

Sheol

In Judaism, a shadowy place under the earth where souls continue their existence in the afterlife. The equivalent Greek term for the Hebrew Sheol is "Hades," a place after death, not as a place of punishment. Daniel 12:2, which concerns the coming of the messianic kingdom, expresses the conviction that God will not abandon souls in Sheol: "And many of those who sleep in the dust of the earth shall awake, some to everlasting life, and some to shame and contempt."

Nearly all souls go initially to Sheol; select righteous souls are taken by God straight to heaven. In 3 ENOCH, two ANGELS OF DESTRUCTION, Zaapiel and Samkiel, escort "intermediate" souls (those equally good and bad) and wicked souls to Sheol. The intermediate souls are purified in fire in order to be fitting for God's presence. They have spiritual forms that are human faces with eagle bodies. The faces are green because of the taint of their sin, and they will remain so until they are purified. The wicked souls, whose faces are as black as the bottoms of pots because of their sins, are taken by Zaapiel to Gehenna (HELL) for punishment with rods of burning coal.

Shepherd

Angel known as the ANGEL OF REPENTANCE who appears to HERMAS.

shinanim

In 3 ENOCH, a high class of angels made of fire who descend from heaven to be present on Mt. Sinai when the Torah is revealed to MOSES. The shinanim are equated with the order of OPHANIM. According to the Zohar, myriads of thousands of them are on the chariot of God. The shinanim are led by either Zadkiel or Sidqiel.

Shoftiel

One of the ANGELS OF PUNISHMENT. Shoftiel means "the judge of God."

Sidqiel (Sidquiel)

In 3 ENOCH, PRINCE of the OPHANIM or SHINANIM and ruler of Venus.

Sidriel

PRINCE of the first HEAVEN, according to 3 ENOCH.

Simiel (Chamuel, Semibel)

Archangel who was one of seven REPROBATED ANGELS condemned by a church council in Rome in 745.

Sizouze

In Persian lore, the ANGEL OF PRAYER.

Smith, Joseph, Jr. See MORMONISM; MORONI.

Sodom and Gomorrah

In the Old Testament, two cities destroyed by angels because of the evil ways of their inhabitants.

In Genesis 18, the prophet ABRAHAM, visited by three angels, learns after their departure for Sodom that God intends to destroy the cities of Sodom and Gomorrah because "their sin is very grave" (18:20). Abraham asks if God will destroy the righteous along with the wicked. He asks God if the cities would be spared if 50 righteous people could be found within them. God agrees. Abraham then bargains God down to 45, then 30, and finally 10 righteous people. But no such 10 can be found.

Two of the angels who visited Abraham (one is often identified as Gabriel) arrive in Sodom in the evening and are met by Lot, Abraham's nephew, who offers them food and shelter. They say they prefer to spend the night in the street. He entreats them, and they enter his house and partake of a feast of food (by some accounts, it only appears to Lot that the visitors eat). Lot's hospitality is not as generous as that of Abraham. He serves the angels unleavened bread, and he is not as attentive as his uncle.

The men of Sodom surround the house and demand that Lot produce the two visitors; it is implied that their intent is to sexually abuse the visitors. Lot offers them his daughters instead. The men attempt to break down the door. The angels hold the door fast, and they strike the intruders blind.

The angels then inform Lot that Sodom is about to be destroyed because of the wickedness of its inhabitants, and that he should gather his family and flee. Lot attempts to warn the two men who are about to marry his two daughters, but they think he is joking.

At dawn, the angels tell Lot to take his wife and two daughters and flee, and to not look back lest they be destroyed along with the city. Lot fears for his safety, and begs the angels to spare a small city called Zoar, where he decides to go. The angels agree.

During their flight, Lot's wife looks behind her and is turned into a pillar of salt. The rest of the party is safe. Then God rains down fire and brimstone upon Sodom and Gomorrah: "the smoke of the land went up like the smoke of a furnace" (19:28).

Christian and Jewish theologians have disagreed over whether Lot was addressed by God or two angels; the question of what happened to the third angel also has been debated. Three angels visit Abraham but only two are said in Genesis to depart for Sodom. The third party sometimes is identified as the Lord.

See ANGELS OF DESTRUCTION.

FURTHER READING

The New Oxford Annotated Bible with the Apocrypha. New York: Oxford University Press, 1977.

Mays, James L., ed. *Harper's Bible Commentary.* San Francisco: HarperSanFrancisco, 1988.

Solas (Stolas)

One of the FALLEN ANGELS and 72 spirits of SOLOMON. Solas is a powerful PRINCE who appears first as a raven and then as a man. He teaches astronomy and the virtues of herbs and precious stones.

Solomon (10th ca. B.C.E.)

King of the Israelites, son of David, builder of the Temple of Jerusalem, and commander of an army of DEMONS or DJINN.

Solomon is one of the most important figures of the Old Testament. He is granted great wisdom and understanding by God, far surpassing the wisdom of any other man. He knows the lore of plants, animals, and everything in the natural world. Men from far away seek him out for his counsel.

In 1 Kings, Solomon takes the throne upon his father David's death. The Lord comes to him in a dream and says, "Ask what I shall give you" (3:5).

King Solomon (Gustave Doré)

Solomon replies that he wishes to be given an understanding mind for governing and for discernment between good and evil. Pleased that he has not asked for riches, God says, "Behold, I give you a wise and discerning mind, so that none like you has been before you and none like you shall arise after you" (3:12). God also grants him incomparable riches. Thus does Solomon become famed for his wisdom.

In the fourth year of his reign, Solomon builds his famed temple of Jerusalem and his palace and administrative complex. In the temple, he places two gilded olivewood CHERUBIM in the innermost part of the sanctuary. He positions them so that a wing of one touches one wall and the wing of the other touches the other wall, and their other wing touches the wing of the other cherub in the middle of the house. When the temple is dedicated, priests place the Ark of the Covenant, containing the two stone tablets of MOSES upon which are written the Ten Commandments, underneath the wings of the cherubim.

Solomon has another vision, in which the Lord promises that his house will prosper as long as the commandments are kept and no other gods are worshiped. If there are any transgressions, God will bring ruination to the kingdom.

For most of the 40 years of his reign, Solomon prospers: "Thus King Solomon excelled all the kings of earth in riches and in wisdom. And the whole earth sought the presence of Solomon to hear his wisdom, which God had put into his mind" (10: 23–24). He rules over the natural world as well as people.

By his later years, he has acquired 700 wives, princesses, and 300 concubines. Some of his wives convince him to turn away from God and worship pagan deities, especially the goddess Ashtoreth. Angry, God sends adversaries against him. In the end, God decides not to wrest his kingdom away from Solomon, but instead to take it away from all but one of his sons.

Other texts expand upon Solomon's wisdom; he becomes the greatest of magicians, a ruler over the realm of nature, able to summon angels and command demons. Such details are found in the apocryphal Testament of Solomon, Odes of Solomon, Psalms of Solomon, and in the Wisdom of Solomon. Josephus's *Antiquities* credits Solomon with writing 1,500 books of odes and songs and 3,000 books of parables and similitudes. The SEFER RAZIEL, a magical text, says that Solomon was heir to the famed book (also called the Book of Mysteries), which enabled him to become the source of all wisdom.

From the time of ORIGEN, Solomon becomes more prominent in Christian lore than in Jewish lore, appearing on AMULETS, TALISMANS, and lintels, and in numerous incantations for protection against and removal of demons. His magical SEAL is a pentagram or hexagram.

In Islamic lore, Solomon becomes the greatest of world rulers, a true apostle and messenger of Allah, and the prototype of MUHAMMAD. His magical powers against demons, the djinn, are famous.

Numerous magical handbooks, or GRIMOIRES, attributed to the authorship of Solomon arose even in the early centuries of Christianity. By the 12th century, at least 49 texts were in existence. The most famous was the Greater Key of Solomon, quoted often in the magical books of the 17th to 19th centuries. Another grimoire attributed to Solomon is the LEMEGETON, or The Lesser Key of Solomon.

Testament of Solomon

The Testament of Solomon, a pseudepigraphon written between the first and third centuries C.E., is a legendary tale about how Solomon built the Temple of Jerusalem by commanding demons. The text is rich in demonology, angelology, and lore about medicine, astrology, and MAGIC. The author is unknown, but he may have been a Greek-speaking Christian who was familiar with the Babylonian Talmud. The magical lore related to demons, which dominates the text, shows Babylonian influences.

The demons are described as FALLEN ANGELS or the offspring of fallen angels and human women, and they live in stars and constellations. They can shapeshift into beasts and forces of nature. They lurk in deserts and haunt tombs, and they dedicate themselves to leading people astray. They are ruled by Beelzeboul (Beelzebub), the Prince of Demons.

The stellar bodies themselves are viewed as demonic, wielding destructive power over the affairs of humanity. The 36 decans, or 10-degree portions of the zodiac, are called "HEAVENLY BODIES" and likewise are ruled by demons, who cause mental and physical illnesses. There are seven "world rulers" who are equated with the vices of deception, strife, fate, distress, error, power, and "the worst," each of whom is thwarted by a particular angel (with the exception of "the worst").

The testament considers angels as God's messengers, but it does not describe their origin or hierarchy. The main purpose of angels is to thwart demons and render them powerless. Each angel is responsible for thwarting specific demons. Humans must call upon the right angel by name in order to defeat a demon; otherwise, demons are worshiped as gods. Among the angels named are the archangels Michael, Raphael, Gabriel, and Uriel.

When the demon Ornias vampirizes his favorite boy by sucking out his soul through his thumb, Solomon begs God for power over the demon. While he prays, Michael appears and gives Solomon a ring with a seal engraved upon a precious stone. Michael tells Solomon this magical ring will give him power over all demons, male and female, and that they will help him build the temple. The demons are subdued when the ring is thrown at their chests with the command, "Solomon summons you!" Solomon interviews the demons and demands from them the names of their THWARTING ANGELS. When they are subdued, they are made to construct his temple.

Michael imprisons Ruax, a headache demon and first of the 36 heavenly bodies. Uriel thwarts Ornias and Error and imprisons Artosael. Raphael thwarts Asmodeus and Obyzouth and imprisons Oropel. Gabriel imprisons Barsafel.

The testament provides a significant contribution to the legends of Solomon's magical powers and the magical handbooks attributed to Solomon.

FURTHER READING

Charlesworth, James H., ed. *The Old Testament Pseudepigrapha.* Vols. 1 and 2. New York: Doubleday, 1983, 1985.

Sons of God

Term in the Bible referring to angels. Job 38:7 mentions the "sons of God" shouting for joy when the morning stars sing. More often, the term is associated with FALLEN ANGELS also known as the WATCHERS. Genesis 6:1–4 tells of "the sons of God, looking at the daughters of men, saw they were pleasing, so they married as many as they chose." The cohabitation produces a race of giants called NEPHILIM (also sometimes called the "Sons of God") and leads to great corruption among humans. Yahweh is not pleased at the mixture of his spirit with flesh and casts the offending angels out of HEAVEN. The corruption leads to God's decision to destroy life on the earth with the Flood.

The title "Son of God" also appears elsewhere in the Old Testament and in the New Testament and refers to an intimate relationship between God and his creature. The title is given to the Chosen People (Exodus 4:22; Wisdom 18:33), to individual Israelites (Deuteronomy 14:1; Hosiah 2:1), and to their leaders (Psalms 82:6). The title was applied to the Messiah (1 Chronicles 17:13; Psalms 2:7) and in the New Testament to Jesus (Mark 15:39; Luke 23:47; Matthew 21:37, 22:42–46, and 24:36) to denote his heavenly rank and status above all angels.

FURTHER READING

Godwin, Malcolm. *Angels: An Endangered Species.* New York: Simon and Schuster, 1990.

Graves, Robert, and Raphael Patai. *Hebrew Myths*. New York: Doubleday Anchor, 1964.

Introductions and Notes. *The Jerusalem Bible*. Garden City, N.Y.: Doubleday, 1966.

Soperiel YHVH (Soperiel Mehayye and Soperiel Memeth)

In 3 ENOCH and the Zohar, two PRINCES in the seventh HEAVEN who keep the records of the names of all the living and the dead. In 3 Enoch, they are both referred to as Soperiel. They are clothed in royal robes and cloaks of majesty, and they wear kingly crowns. They are tall—the height of the seven heavens—and splendorous and have eyes like the sun. Their tongues are blazing torches and fire and lightning issue forth from their mouths; their sweat kindles fire. On their heads are sapphires (one each) and on their shoulders are wheels of swift cherubs. In their hands are pens of flame 3,000 PARASANGS tall and burning scrolls 3,000 myriads of parasangs long. Each letter they write is 365 parasangs tall. Though angels cannot or do not sit according to rabbinic lore, the Soperiel angels sit to write by standing upon the wheels of storms.

Above Soperiel in stature is Rikbiel.

Sophia

In GNOSTICISM, the youngest of the AEONS and one of the most important of them, who plays a key role in the creation of this world and early human history. Sophia is also associated with the figure of Divine WISDOM (Sophia means "wisdom" in Greek) in Judaism and Christianity and is important in contemporary feminist spirituality.

The Gnostic Sophia

The Gnostic Sophia has a strong association with the Egyptian goddess Isis. Both undergo tearful wanderings: Isis in search of Osiris, with their ultimate reunification and transformation, and Sophia seeking "the Father" (the Unknown God), with her ultimate reunification with Logos (Christ, the Father's son). Like Isis, Sophia encompasses opposites: virgin and mother, father and mother, prostitute and virgin, male and female, whole and part, self and other.

Nag Hammadi documents—a collection of Gnostic Coptic Christian texts discovered in Egypt in 1945—reveal a decline in the prestige of personified Sophia from the earlier non-Christian documents (that is, with a pagan or Jewish bias) to the later Christianized Gnostic documents. For example, in the early Jewish-Gnostic Apocalypse of Adam, the life-giving principle of salvation is given to Adam by Eve. In a late Christian tractate the male spirit is presented as the necessary agent of the feminine soul's salvation. Non-Christian Gnostic texts such as the Apocryphon of John, the Second Stele of Seth, and the Second Treatise of the Great Seth portray Sophia as the preeminent female aeon in the divine realm. In On the Origin of the World, the mythological presentation is almost entirely set within feminine imagery, from the formation of the world by Pistis Sophia and the creation of Eve before Adam to the destruction of the world by the mindless fury of an unnamed goddess.

In the pagan letter Eugnostos the Blessed, Sophia appears as Agape (Love), and Aletheia (Truth), as Genetress, as Syzygos (Consort), as Mother of the Universe, and as Sige (Silence). In both extant versions of this document Sophia is described as part of the androgyne Sophia/Immortal Anthropos. Both female and male aspects are necessary for creation to take place. Their union produces another male-female being, Savior/Pistis Sophia, and, from their union, six androgynous spiritual beings are generated. The unions of these 12 entities create 72 powers, and the resultant 360 powers are regarded as the 360 days of the year.

The Sophia of Jesus Christ, a text parallel to Eugnostos the Blessed, follows the elaborate cosmology and naming in Eugnostos and adds material from another myth about Sophia as a fallen feminine deity in need of the male spirit of Christ for her salvation.

The most significant body of work is the Pistis Sophia ("Faith Wisdom"), a series of books dating to the first and second centuries C.E. They comprise a teaching given to the disciples of Jesus after his resurrection. The Pistis Sophia describes a complex universe, the central figure of which is the fallen Sophia. Her return to the Christ restores the cosmic matrix.

Sophia and Wisdom

In Jewish mysticism, the attributes of Sophia are taken by Wisdom (Divine Wisdom), an intermediary force by which God creates the world and then takes up residence in it.

Sophia in Christian Scripture

New Testament texts associate Jesus with Sophia, sometimes translated as Spirit. In 1 Corinthians St. PAUL says:

> But we still have a Sophia to offer to those who have reached maturity; not a philosophy of our age, it is true, still less of the masters of our age, which are coming to an end. The hidden Sophia of God which we teach in our mysteries is the Sophia that God predestined to be for our glory before the ages began. She is a Sophia that none of the masters of this age have ever known. (2:6–8)

The portrait of Jesus in the Gospel of John is fully understood only in the context of Wisdom/Sophia. For example, in John 1:1–3, "In the beginning was the Word . . .," the meaning of Word corresponds to the meaning of Wisdom in the Hebrew Scriptures. Jesus's declarations of who he is ("You are of this world; I am not of this world" (John 8:23–24) and "I, the light, have come into the world, so that whoever believes in me need not stay in the dark any more" (John 12:44–48) are similar to Wisdom's remarks about herself in Sirach 24: "Wisdom speaks her own praises, in the midst of her people she glories in herself." The model of the self-proclaiming teacher does not exist in the Hebrew Scriptures outside of Wisdom.

Other Gospels contain references that depend on an understanding of Wisdom/Sophia, such as Matthew 11:19, "Yet wisdom is justified by her deeds" and Luke 7:35, "Yet wisdom is justified by all her children." There is a parallel between Matthew 11:28–30, in which Jesus says, "Come to me . . . shoulder my yoke and learn from me," and Sirach 51:26: "Put your necks under her yoke, and let your souls receive instruction" and Sirach 6: "Give your shoulder to her yoke."

Gnosticism was a serious rival of Christianity, and it is not surprising that the presence of Wisdom/Sophia is downplayed in the New Testament. As the early Christians were compiling the documents for the New Testament, the Gnostics were embracing the Jesus-Sophia identification, emphasizing that "gnosis" saved humanity rather than Jesus' suffering and death. Though knowledge of Sophia is necessary to Christology, the Gnostic connection has interfered.

Eastern Orthodoxy adored Sophia and erected in Constantinople her greatest shrine in the sixth century C.E. It was one of the wonders of the world: the Church of Holy Sophia (Hagia Sophia). The Roman church was embarrassed by this magnificent monument and created a saint named Sophia, whose tenuous story lacked even a date. Some Catholic scholars now say that the Church of Hagia Sophia was never dedicated to the Great Mother in any form, not even that of a female saint. They say its name (which in Greek means "Holy Female Wisdom") really means "Christ, the Word of God."

Sophia in Arts and Philosophy

A great female figure appeared in Europe in the late 18th century that threw her shadow over several generations of artists. Her power is especially apparent in GOETHE's *Faust,* where he conflates qualities of Isis, Mary, Sophia, and Helen of Troy. The final words of the poem are "the eternal feminine leads us upward." The goddess Isis and Egyptian mysteries found their way into Masonic rituals; it has been suggested those rituals are derived from some of the literary works in question. The mysteries of Isis were the inspiration for Mozart's *The Magic Flute* and so interested Goethe that he wrote *The Second Part of the Magic Flute* in 1798.

In the philosophy of JAKOB BOHME (1575–1624), a major influence on WILLIAM BLAKE, Sophia represented not only Wisdom, the mystical spouse, half of the androgynous Adam, but also the Virgin of Light, identified with Logos. After the death of his fiancée, Novalis (1772–1801) recorded in his journal "Christ and Sophia." His sensuous *Hymns to the Night* (1800) represent the triumph of the nocturnal and feminine side of the being.

Sophia and Feminist Spirituality

Sophia holds a significant attraction to Western women exploring their spiritual and mythical power and roots. Jewish, Christian, and pagan feminists alike find inspiration in the myths, the texts, the motifs, and the compelling presence of Sophia, the Wisdom-Woman goddess. In the Pistis Sophia alone, the female disciples of Jesus—Mary his mother, Mary Magdalene, Martha, and Salome—play far greater and more authoritative roles collectively than do the male disciples, who are given such prominence in orthodox Christianity, thus documenting the importance of women in humanity's relationship to the divine.

FURTHER READING

Arthur, Ruth Horman. *The Wisdom Goddess: Feminine Motifs in Eight Nag Hammadi Documents.* Lanham, Md.: University Press of America, 1984.

Cady, Susan, Marian Ronan, and Hal Taussig. *Sophia: The Future of Feminist Spirituality.* San Francisco: Harper and Row, 1986.

Frymer-Kensy, Tivka. *In The Wake of the Goddess: Women, Culture and the Biblical Transformation of Pagan Myth.* New York: Fawcett Columbine Books, 1992.

Good, Deirdre J. *Reconstructing the Tradition of Sophia in Gnostic Literature.* Atlanta: Scholars Press, 1987.

Hurtak, J. J. *Pistis Sophia: A Coptic Gnostic Text with Commentary.* Los Gatos, Calif.: The Academy for Future Science, 1999.

King, Karen, ed. *Images of the Feminine in Gnosticism.* Philadelphia: Fortress Press, 1988.

Legge, Francis. *Forerunners and Rivals of Christianity.* New Hyde Park, N.Y.: University Books, 1964.

Soqedhozi YHVH (Shoqed Chozi, Soqed Hozi, Skd Huzi)

In 3 ENOCH a PRINCE of the heavenly law court in the seventh HEAVEN who keeps the divine balances and weighs the merits of men in the presence of God.

Soqedhozi is one of four angels appointed by God to the sword of MOSES. He bows down to Zehanpuryu.

Sorath

In MAGIC, angel who is the spirit of the sun and whose number is 666. RUDOLF STEINER considered Sorath to be a great evil power.

Sorush

In Persian lore, angel equated with Gabriel who punishes souls on Judgment Day. Sorush and the angel Mihr stand on a bridge called *al Sirat*. Souls found worthy are passed to Paradise by Mihr. Condemned souls are thrown into hell by Sorush, who represents divine justice.

Soterasiel YHVH (Sother, Sother Ashiel)

In 3 ENOCH, a great PRINCE of the seventh HEAVEN who prosecutes divine judgment in the heavenly court of law. The name Soterasiel means "who stirs up the fire of God." Soterasiel is 70,000 PARASANGS tall. He serves in the divine presence over the four heads of the RIVER OF FIRE and is the keeper of their SEALS. He determines who will have permission to enter before the SHEKINAH, and he enters and leaves the presence of the Shekinah himself to explain the records of the inhabitants of earth. Soterasiel bows down before Soqedhozi.

In GNOSTICISM, Sother is a name for God. He marries SOPHIA.

Spangler, David See FINDHORN.

Spenser, Edmund See LITERATURE AND ANGELS.

spirit guides

Nonphysical beings who function as guides and protectors, and who provide inspiration. Spirit guides include angels, the dead, semidivine entities, and animal totems.

It is widely believed that one or more primary spirit guides appear at birth. These remain close during a person's life, and they assist in the transition at death (compare to GUARDIAN ANGELS and GUARDIAN SPIRITS). In addition to primary spirit guides, secondary spirit guides may appear on the scene for temporary periods.

Spirit guides also can appear at any time in life, especially if mediumistic abilities open suddenly. Such spirit guides, usually souls of the dead, communicate with the medium to relay information to others. The primary spirit guide to a medium is called a "control,"

A "spiritual guide" (Reprinted courtesy of U.S. Library of Congress)

who monitors the access of other entities to the medium.

Like angels, spirit guides can manifest in physical form, appear in dreams, and communicate via the inner voice.

See DAIMONES; DREAMS AND VISIONS.

FURTHER READING

Myers, Frederic W. H. *Human Personality and Its Survival of Bodily Death*, Vols. 1 and 2. New ed. New York: Longmans, Green, 1954. First published 1903.

spirit of understanding

The gift of understanding granted to SOLOMON and DANIEL and others. The spirit of understanding is linked to ANGEL OF THE LORD, and it is promised as a divine gift to the royal line of David, (Isaiah 11:1–3).

Solomon is given the spirit of understanding (or a "wise and discerning mind") in a dream vision in which the Lord appears to him and Solomon asks for an "understanding mind." (1 Kings 3:5–11) God gives Daniel "understanding in all visions and dreams" (Daniel 1:17).

In the Testament of the Twelve Patriarchs, the spirit of understanding shows LEVI how all of mankind persists in sin, deceit, and injustice. The revelation leads to a profound dream vision in which Levi ascends to heaven to receive his charge as the founder of the priestly line of Israel (2–3).

See DREAMS AND VISIONS.

spirits of form See Rudolf STEINER.

Sraosha (Serosh, Sirush, Srosh)
In Persian lore, angel who sets the world in motion. In ZOROASTRIANISM, Sraosha is either one of the AMA-RAHSPANDS or one of the YAZATAS; his chief duty is to carry souls to HEAVEN after death. In Manichean lore he is the angel who judges the dead.

See PSYCHOPOMPOI.

star of Bethlehem
The bright star that guided the three Magi to the Christ child, as told in the New Testament. The star of Bethlehem is sometimes interpreted as an angel rather than a star.

The Gospel of Matthew tells of the star seen by the Magi in the east, which went before them as a beacon and guided them to the infant JESUS in Bethlehem. The light moves about in a fashion uncharacteristic of a star

but in keeping with other biblical descriptions of guiding angels as being lights, lightning, stars, and flames.

The book of Judges tells how stars played a role in a victory by Israel, and the book of Job speaks of the morning stars singing together. The book of ISAIAH mentions the angel Lucifer, whose name means "bearer of light" or "son of the morning." REVELATION describes angels as being stars. The apocryphal book of ENOCH describes angels of fire, with eyes like burning lights. SERAPHIM, the angels closest to God, are "fire-makers." Such burning lights appearing in the sky could have been described by the ancients as stars. Angels are associated or equated with stars in various philosophical writings.

See BOEHME, JAKOB; JESUS; ORIGEN.

Steiner, Rudolf (1861–1925)
Philosopher, artist, scientist, and educator whose "spiritual science" called Anthroposophy blends many strands of occult lore into an esoteric Christian frame. Rudolph Steiner's teachings about higher beings, INTELLIGENCES, angels, and the four major archangels—Michael, Gabriel, Raphael, and Uriel—are extensive.

Life
Steiner was born to Austrian parents on February 27, 1861, in Kraljevic, Hungary. His father, a railway clerk, hoped Rudolf would become a railway civil engineer, but an early manifestation of psychic gifts set him on a different path. Steiner began to experience clairvoyance at the age of eight. At 19 he was initiated by an adept whose identity was never revealed. In 1886 he was hired by the Specht family to tutor four boys, one of whom was autistic. His exceptional tutoring enabled the boy to finish school and become a medical doctor. Later one wing of Steiner's activity was developing the Waldorf schools—the first was in Stuttgart in 1919—now the largest nonsectarian system of education in the world. The Waldorf system also addresses the needs of retarded children.

Steiner found rapport with the Theosophical Society, becoming the secretary of the German branch in 1902. However, he withdrew about 10 years later, after becoming disillusioned with what he termed the "triviality and dilettantism" of many members. He questioned Annie Besant's cultist championship of Jiddu Krishnamurti as the next Messiah, believed cofounder Helena P. Blavatsky had distorted occult truths, and ultimately concluded it was not possible to build a spiritual science on Eastern mysticism.

In 1913 Steiner formed the Anthroposophical Society, taking some members with him from the Theosophists. He described his path as one leading to

Star of Bethlehem shining over angel heralding the birth of Jesus, from a 19th-century Bible (Author's collection)

spiritual growth on four levels of human nature: the senses, imagination, inspiration, and intuition. In Dornach, near Basel, Switzerland, he established the Goetheanum, a school for esoteric research, where he intended to produce Goethe's dramas and his own mystery plays. The building burned down in 1920 but was rebuilt in 1922, and it now serves as the international headquarters for the organization.

In the 25 years before his death in 1925, Steiner traveled around continental Europe and Great Britain giving more than 6,000 lectures. His published works include more than 350 titles, most of which are collections of lectures. His key works outlining his occult philosophy are *Knowledge of the Higher Worlds and Its Attainment* (1904–05), *Theosophy: An Introduction to the Supersensible Knowledge of the World and the Destination of Man* (1904), and *An Outline of Occult Science* (1909).

Spiritual Science and Philosophy

The intent of Steiner's philosophy is the transformation of the individual, and thereby the culture. Significant influences were the scientific works and ideas of JOHANN WOLFGANG VON GOETHE (which Steiner edited in his university years) and Johann Gottlieb Fichte (on whose scientific teaching Steiner wrote his doctoral dissertation). Steiner's first two philosophical works, *Truth and Knowledge* (1892) and *Philosophy of Freedom* (1894) hold that original thinking can and must be developed as a liberating activity. The ills of the world are caused by human failure to achieve a "free" or "spiritual" mode of thinking that combines both heart and will. In *Knowledge of the Higher Worlds and Its Attainment*, Steiner says that every individual can develop a spiritual, transformed consciousness:

> There slumber in every human being faculties by means of which one can acquire for oneself a knowledge of higher worlds. Mystics, Gnostics, Theosophists—all speak of a world of soul and spirit which for them is just as real as the world we see with our physical eyes and touch with our physical hands. At every moment the listener may say to himself: that, of which they speak, I too can learn if I develop within myself certain powers which today still slumber within me.

At 40, Steiner felt he was ready to speak publicly about his spiritual philosophy, his clairvoyant experiences, and what he learned from them. By this time he had gained much experience in the nonphysical realms through profound meditation. Steiner claimed to have access to the Akashic Records, from which he learned the true history of human evolution. He said that at one time humankind was more spiritual and possessed supersensible capabilities but lost them on the descent

to the material plane. At the nadir of human descent, Christ arrived and provided the opportunity to reascend to higher spiritual levels. For Steiner the life, death, and resurrection of Christ were the most important events in the history of humankind and the cosmos. However, the Gospels did not contain the complete story.

Higher Beings and the Millennium

According to Steiner, since the mystery of Golgotha Christ has become the Spirit of the earth, and yet he comes from regions beyond the earth. If we are only stirred by what belongs to the earth, we can never develop our Spirit Self. We lay the first seeds for this when we Christianize science, for it is Christ who brings the forces we need from outside the earth. "Progressive Angels" in whom the power of Christ is working will teach that the substance of the world, even to the minutest particle, is permeated with the spirit of Christ, and he will be found working in the very laws of chemistry and physics. Two new impulses are arising, moral love and confidence in one another. Pure love, stronger than ever before, will have to be given wings within us. We must meet the other person as an ever-changing riddle, who evokes confidence in an individual way from the very depths of our soul.

The initiate comes to know the spiritual Beings active behind phenomena, both the divine Hierarchies who are already preparing spiritually that which will later descend to become physical events, and the powers which oppose them. In addition, there are elemental beings who are the earthly servants of these higher beings, both in nature and in humans. The initiate can see what they are doing and discovers that the truly creative Gods have their workplace within the human skin, in the inner organs, and that what permeates these will develop the form of the future. The initiate sees how past phases in the evolution of humanity will emerge again in metamorphosed form during the involution, the respiritualization of the earth, and how we already work with these germinal forces during the depths of sleep, preparing not only our own next incarnation but also the future of the earth—though only that which is great and cosmic, not the details.

In *Planetary Spheres and Their Influence on Man's Life on Earth* and in *Spiritual Values* Steiner states that

> of all that the Spirit has to accomplish on Earth through man, by far the greater part is accomplished during sleep. . . . While we are asleep, lofty Spiritual Beings work upon the human soul, with the object of bringing man to his full and complete evolution in Earth existence. . . . [E]very night man grows out into the Cosmos. Just as here on Earth we are connected with the plants,

with the minerals, with the air, so are we connected in the night with the constellations of the fixed stars. From the moment we fall asleep, the starry heavens become our world, even as the Earth is our world when we are awake.

DREAMS carry the experience of the Cosmos through the threshold of the astral into the physical body, gathering images and feelings that vibrate with cosmic residue.

The Elohim: The Spirits of Form

In Steiner's spiritual perspective of human evolution, the original divine forces under the rulership of the Being known as Jehovah, one of the ELOHIM or Spirits of Form, lost control in the course of the 19th century. But Christ brought to earth at the time of Golgotha the forces of the other six Elohim, who together with Jehovah had created man in their own image and breathed into him the living soul. The first of these forces for the future starts to become active in those who receive the new Christ impulse mediated by spiritual science. The events of the present are part of a greater battle behind the scenes between Wisdom/SOPHIA—all the forces of the past which have created us under the guidance of Jehovah, and Love—the great forces of the other six Elohim, which work creatively into the future. Only through the rhythmic swing of the pendulum between Wisdom and Love, not through sleepy rest, will the future be rightly formed. The Hierarchies intend for us only that to which we contribute from now on in full consciousness. In order to act in full consciousness, we have to go through inner and outer soul battles that make us strong.

Michael: The Spirit of the Age

During the 19th century, the consciousness of humankind unconsciously crossed the threshold that separates the outer world of senses from the spiritual world that manifests within the human soul. In consequence, human thinking, feeling, and willing are no longer fully coordinated. This shows itself in many ways, for example, in increased incidence of mental illness and the development of psychiatric techniques to handle it, drug addiction and drug trafficking, and heartless terrorism. However, since 1879 we have come under the guidance of Michael as Spirit of the Age. As ruler of the Cosmic Intelligence, he helps the enlightened understand what is happening, and he inspires them to act in the spirit of cosmopolitanism, which will characterize the new millennium.

In those who progress to active thinking, it will be possible to make Inspiration the determining element of soul. This is what rulership by Michael really means.

Michael does not work so much for the initiate as for those who wish to understand spiritual investigations. Michael stands cosmically behind man, while within man there is an etheric image that wages the real battle through which we can become free. Because Michael won the battle over the dragon in 1879, the spiritual will lay hold of humanity more and more, and spiritual truth will take root among men, although it will not become the general conviction. Steiner predicted that before the end of the 21st century, buildings would arise all over Europe dedicated to spiritual aims.

Angelic Assistance

While science and technology "can only apprehend the corpse of reality" at this time, the old Christian spirituality is falling apart and cannot be repaired. The possibility of help from spiritual beings is now dependent on the cooperation of the individuals. The beings will help, but only if we do not act as puppets. Furthermore, Luciferic and Ahrimanic beings constantly challenge angelic forces in human thought, sense, and will,

Rudolph Steiner (Used by permission of the Anthroposophic Press, Hudson, N.Y. 12534)

thus making it crucial to learn a discerning spiritual science.

In a lecture given on October 9, 1918 (*The Work of the Angels in Man's Astral Body*). Steiner described how the angels were seeking to implant three impulses in people before 2000 C.E., and how these impulses would turn to harm if they were not properly assimilated.

First, the angels brought a strong impulse toward brotherhood, based on a deep interest in others and the inability to be happy so long as another is unhappy. The negative side of this impulse was misuse of sexuality and terrorism. Second, angels brought recognition of the hidden divinity in each other person, so that every meeting became a sacred rite; the sharing of ideas became a communion without need of church. The negative of this was cultishness and addictions to drugs and materialism. Third, angels facilitated spiritual insight through thinking. The negative side was egoism, selfish acts and policies, and "cut-throat" business practices.

Steiner remarked in a lecture on April 4, 1912, that without new spiritual impulses, technology will not only dominate outer life but also will overpower and numb humanity. It will drive out the religious, philosophical, artistic, and ethical interests, and it will turn people into "living automata." Many people today, even highly professional ones, are already unwitting slaves of outer material conditions, he said. Fallen spirits belonging to the hierarchy of angels—active in the information and computer technologies and economic networks—spread evil over the earth through racism and nationalism, though their approach is so subtle and intimate that people think they are not influenced by them.

Luciferic and Ahrimanic Beings

Some beings encourage the advancement of humankind's spiritual consciousness, but others encourage destruction through vices. Steiner labeled the latter as Luciferic spirits. Still other spirits wish people to remain mired in a materialistic, mechanistic world. These last spirits Steiner called "Ahrimanic" beings, after the Persian personification of evil. He linked Lucifer with air and warmth and Ahriman with earth and cold. The changes of seasons reveal the eternal struggle between the two forces.

Steiner faced serious inner battles with evil forces, and he felt that his ultimate victory over them was his immersion in the esoteric mysteries of Christ. He warned that the spiritual path to higher consciousness entails such battles. He noted that people strongly resist taking responsibility to fight on the inner plane, preferring to project the battle out onto imagined enemies. Every thousand years as a new millennium approaches,

Luciferic and Ahrimanic beings make particularly strong attacks on human progress. Our fear and projections make us increasingly susceptible to spiritual debasement, mental slavery, and mass hysteria.

Like CARL G. JUNG, Steiner thought that the most profound challenge of our age is to understand the polarity between Lucifer and Ahriman (see ABRAXAS). Modern consciousness understands the polarity between God and the devil and HEAVEN and HELL. We need to understand that to strive toward Paradise is just as bad as the opposite. We must recognize that our true nature can be expressed only in dynamic equilibrium.

Chaos, in which Luciferic and Ahrimanic forces participate, is necessary for human evolution, but it is highly antisocial. Steiner's commitment to "higher civility" spurred his reappraisal of human relations. At Dornach a sculpture shows the Representative of Man standing between Lucifer and Ahriman. We will achieve this balance by paying attention to those who have educated, befriended, and even injured us. Steiner said on October 10, 1916, that as a rule we do not encounter anyone we have not met in previous incarnations. Likes and dislikes are great enemies of real social relations. Condemning a person obliterates a karmic relationship entirely, postponing it to a next incarnation, and no progress can be made.

Steiner explains that Ahrimanic beings are highly intelligent, extraordinarily clever, and wise. They act behind the veil of nature and work to destroy the human physical organism. When we enter their world, destruction, hatred, or the like arise within us. Sensuous urges and impulses are enhanced. They move us to destroy others without any benefit to ourselves. They replace thinking by all kinds of lower organism powers, especially the impulse to lie.

The Luciferic beings do everything to foster egoism within us, and they instill in us a passion for creating, bringing things into existence. Steiner insists that future evolution will be endangered if the Luciferic and Ahrimanic beings are not recognized and counteracted by spiritual science.

Sorath

Steiner saw other beings beginning to generate evil with a far mightier force than Lucifer and Ahriman. One is Sorath, the Sun-Demon of Revelation. Steiner predicted that toward the millennium spiritual people would be able to see the Sun-Genius, the etheric vision of Christ. In response, Sorath will foment opposition through men who are possessed by him, who have strong natures, raving tongues, destructive fury in their emotions, and faces which look outwardly animalized. They will mock that which is of a spiritual nature. In the mystery of 666, or Sorath, is hidden the secret of black MAGIC. The power by which the Sun-Genius overcomes Sorath is Michael, who has the key to the abyss and the chain in his hand.

The Four Seasons and the Archangels

In October 1923 Steiner gave five lectures at Dornach later published separately as *The Four Seasons and the Archangels: Experience in the Course of the Year in Four Cosmic Imaginations.* This material is a symphonylike treatment of the divine continuity in the four movements of the seasons for earth, higher beings, elemental beings, human consciousness and spiritual skills and lessons, alchemy with its minerals and colors, Christian liturgy, mythology, Goethe's poetry, and Steiner's own iconography. He describes each season in the context of a mystery play and the esoteric meanings of his choices of colors and images. His lectures were illustrated with his own colored chalk drawings.

AUTUMN: MICHAEL

Steiner starts with autumn, Michaelmas (feast day September 29). Michael Imagination, like Michael, wields a sword of iron, which symbolizes iron in the blood and strength in the spirit. Michaelmas celebrates the sulphurizing and meteorizing processes in man—everything that opposes anxiety and love of ease, and encourages the unfolding of inner initiative and free, strong, courageous will. Michaelmas is the festival of strong will and the renewal of the soul of humankind.

Michael wears a gold and silver raiment made of rays of silver streaming up from the earth and gold rays flowing down from the sun. As autumn approaches, the silver given by the earth to the cosmos returns as gold, and the power of this transmuted silver is the source of what happens in the earth during winter.

In the spring Michael is below working through the earth from the other hemisphere, coming to meet mankind with his positive gaze, showing the way into the world, and glad to draw the eyes of men in the same direction as he stands close to mankind, the complement of Raphael in spring.

WINTER: GABRIEL

Gabriel—the angel most closely connected with MARY and the birth of new consciousness—is the angel of the Christmas Imagination or the Mary Imagination, a blending of the senses, imagination, inspiration, and intuition, and used imaging, poetry, and all the arts to express his teachings.

In the depths of winter the earth becomes self-enclosed earth, with a concentrated earth-nature. When earth is most herself, the Redeemer comes from

The archangel Michael: the Spirit of the Age (Reprinted courtesy of U.S. Library of Congress)

its juncture with heaven, and Gabriel announces it to humankind surrounded by the heavenly host. The Redeemer connects the cosmos with the birth-forces of the earth, represented as the Madonna and Child: formed out of the clouds, endowed with the forces of the earth, with the moon-forces below, with the sun-forces in the middle, and above, toward the head, with the forces of the stars. This picture of Mary with the Child arises out of the cosmos itself. Gabriel's is a mild and loving gaze and a gesture of blessing.

SPRING: RAPHAEL

Easter Imagination brings Raphael, the Physician Angel who transmutes healing forces. Easter celebrates the death and resurrection of the Redeemer. Raphael is the Hermes-like mediator with a fiery serpent staff who arouses in us the rightful approach, through reverence and worship, to the essence of the Easter Imagination.

Spring activates both Luciferic and Ahrimanic powers; the former try to take up the etheric into their own being, the latter try to ensoul the earth with astrality.

The risen Christ stands triumphant between reddish Ahriman under his feet and the Luciferic blue/yellow power hovering above that seeks to draw the upper part of man away from the earth. Raphael takes on a Hermetic/Healer stance with a mercurial staff; sulphur and phosphorous are both present for combustion. The Easter Imagination celebrates transformation for healing through the world-therapy that lives in the Christ principle.

In autumn Raphael brings to humans the healing forces, which he has first kindled in the cosmos. Raphael, with deep wisdom in his gaze, leans on the staff of Mercury, supported by the inner forces of earth.

SUMMER: URIEL

The St. John (the Baptist) Imagination of high summer, with creative, admonishing Uriel presiding, is a festival of radiant Intelligence, sulphur yellow and fire red, of consolidated Imagination of Cosmic Understanding. At the height of summer, the elemental spirits soar upward and weave themselves into Uriel's realm, the shinning *intelligence* above.

Uriel, the representative of the weaving cosmic forces, embodies himself in light. His intelligence arises from the working together of the planetary forces and the fixed stars of the zodiac. At midsummer the Trinity reveals itself out of the midst of cosmic life and activity. Steiner says, "it comes forth with inwardly convincing power if . . . one has first penetrated into the mysteries of Uriel."

TRINITY OF HEAVEN, EARTH, AND CHRIST

Steiner's Trinity is not of Father, Son, and Holy Ghost. He says that at midsummer "we behold the outcome of the working together of Spirit Father and Earth Mother, bearing so beautifully within itself the harmony of the earthly silver and the gold of the heights. Between the Father and the Mother we behold the Son. Thus arises the Trinity Imagination, which is really the St. John Imagination. The background is Uriel, the creative, admonishing Uriel."

INTERPLAY OF THE ARCHANGELS

In order to understand man's circumstances in the world, we must first understand the secret interworkings of the angels and other beings. From Michael, Gabriel, Raphael and Uriel stream out therapeutic forces: Gabriel's are forces for nourishing, Raphael's are forces for healing, Uriel's are forces of thought, and Michael's are forces of movement.

Whatever is permeated by Ahrimanic influences during one season is transformed into healing powers at another season. Thus the archangels and Imagina-

tions of one season are the "medicine" of another, as shown below:

> Winter: Gabriel above, Uriel below.
> Spring: Raphael above, Michael below.
> Summer: Uriel above, Gabriel below, with man.
> Autumn: Michael above, Raphael below, with man.

Steiner was influenced by Goethe's *Faust* (which borrows from a much older source), which describes angels ascending and descending—much like the ladder dreamed by JACOB—and develops the theme of the archangels passing to each other their "golden vessel" containing their special healing powers. For example, Raphael passes to Uriel, whereby the healing forces are made into the forces of thought. Michael receives from Uriel the thought-forces, and through the power of cosmic iron, out of which his sword is formed, transforms these thought forces into the forces of will, which become in man the forces of movement.

Steiner's voluminous talents as artist, philosopher, spiritual teacher, and "scientist of the invisible" have only been introduced here. He presents a sweeping mystical visionary system that ties into the anxieties of our time, showing how the angelic realms are intertwined with our inner and outer lives.

FURTHER READING

McDermott, Robert A., ed. *The Essential Steiner.* San Francisco: Harper and Row, 1984.

Sheperd, A. P. *Rudolf Steiner: Scientist of the Invisible.* Rochester, Vt.: Inner Traditions International, 1954, 1983.

Steiner, Rudolf. *An Autobiography.* Blauvelt, N.Y.: Rudolf Steiner Publications, 1977.

———. *The Four Seasons and the Archangels.* Bristol, England: Rudolf Steiner Press, 1992.

———. *Planetary Spheres and Their Influence on Man's Life on Earth and in the Spiritual Worlds.* London: Rudolf Steiner Press, 1982.

Suriel (Sariel, Sauriel, Suriyel, Suruel, Surufel, Surya) A PRINCE OF THE PRESENCE, angel of healing and ANGEL OF DEATH. Suriel means "God's command." Suriel is sometimes identified with Ariel, Metatron, Uriel, and Saraqael. In 1 ENOCH, he is one of the four holy archangels who is "of eternity and of trembling." In Kabbalistic lore he is one of seven ANGELS OF THE EARTH. ORIGEN identified Suriel as one of seven angels who are primordial powers. In Jewish lore, MOSES learns all of his knowledge from Suriel, who comes as the angel of death at the end of Moses's life. In GNOSTICISM, Suriel is invoked for this protective powers.

Swedenborg, Emanuel (1688–1772)

Scientist and mystic who communicated with God and his angels and traveled into HEAVEN and HELL in visions. Emanuel Swedenborg described in great detail the structure and hierarchy of both heaven and hell and the transitional place spirits go after death before choosing their eventual home. He stressed that mankind is totally free to select either heaven or hell, and that only through man's humanity can God truly be revealed.

Swedenborg's books on his revelations met with derision and rejection during his lifetime, yet they influenced the works of philosophers and theologians from the 19th century on.

Life

Swedenborg was born in Stockholm on January 29, 1688, the second son of the Lutheran bishop of Skara. The family name was then Swedberg; the father changed it to Swedenborg when they became part of the nobility in 1719. The elder Swedenborg served for many years as a professor at the University of Uppsala, and Emanuel studied Latin, Greek, other European and Oriental languages, astronomy, geology, metallurgy, anatomy, mathematics, economics, and other sciences there from age 11 to 21. After graduation he traveled to the Netherlands, Germany, and England, where he met the astronomers Edmund Halley and John Flamsteed. By the time of his return to Sweden in 1716, his reputation brought him to the attention of King Charles XII, who named him a special assessor to the Royal College of Mines. Fascinated by the mining industry, Swedenborg turned down the opportunity to teach at Uppsala.

Although Swedenborg attempted to marry twice, neither woman accepted him, and he devoted himself to work instead. In 1718 he invented a device to carry boats overland for a distance of 14 miles. He worked on designs for submarines and air-guns, which could fire 60 or 70 rounds without reloading, and he even dabbled in flying machines. In 1734, he wrote the *Opera Philosophica et Mineralia*, in which he described his theory of "nebular hypothesis" as the basis for planet formation—ideas often erroneously attributed to Emmanuel Kant. For the next 10 years, Swedenborg wrote various treatises on animals, mineralogy, geology, creation, and anatomy. But not until the publication of *Worship and the Love of God* in 1745 did he turn his attention completely to the study of religion and God's revelations.

In childhood Swedenborg discovered during prayer that regulating his breathing by minimizing it produced deep and intense states of meditation. He used these techniques throughout his life to focus his concentration. Breath reduction is used in MERKABAH, Eastern mysticism and the hesychasm of Eastern Orthodoxy. Swedenborg was aware of the similarity of his own methods to these other practices.

Swedenborg began having ecstatic visions in 1743. Up to that time he had not given much thought to spiritual matters, although he had argued that the soul existed. Suddenly he was overcome with revelations about heaven and hell, the work of angels and spirits, the true meaning of Scripture, and the order of the universe.

Although Swedenborg maintained he was fully conscious during the visions, he could remain in a trance for up to three days. During these times, his breathing would be severely reduced and he would be insensible, but his mental activity remained sharp. He once likened his trances to what happens when a person dies and is resuscitated—what is now called the NEAR-DEATH EXPERIENCE.

He also had the unusual ability to remain for prolonged periods in the borderland state between sleep and wakefulness, either as he was going to sleep or as he was awakening. In this twilight state of consciousness, one is immersed in vivid images and voices, and it is possible to interact with these in ways that are more difficult in the dream state. Swedenborg called this visionary travel as being "in the spirit," and he knew that he was out of his body.

He believed that angels cause our dreams and that dream imagery corresponds to the thoughts and feelings of angels. (See DREAMS AND VISIONS.)

In 1744 and 1745, he had visions that had a profound effect on him and greatly opened his spiritual senses. He later was able to exist simultaneously in the material world and the spiritual realms.

Swedenborg was so convinced that God had selected him to be his spiritual emissary that he quit his post as assessor in 1747 at age 59, and went on half-pension to devote himself fully to his visionary work.

In his later years he moved to England, a country that captivated him when he first visited it as a young man. He died there at age 84 and is buried in London.

Swedenborg exerted tremendous influence on later 19th-century thinkers, especially Ralph Waldo Emerson and WILLIAM BLAKE. Emerson greatly admired Swedenborg but found heaven and hell as Swedenborg described them to be deadly dull. Emerson also chafed under the premise that once a human had made his choice for heaven or hell there was no turning back, no atonement nor redemption. Blake initially embraced Swedenborgianism but eventually rejected it along with other examples of the Age of Reason. His "The Marriage of Heaven and Hell" satirized Swedenborg's

Heaven and Hell as a means of direct revelation, yet the idea of a clearly defined other world continued to influence Blake's art and writing.

After his death in 1772, some of Swedenborg's followers established various churches and societies to study and put forth the mystic's theories. The Church of the New Jerusalem was founded in England in 1778 and in the United States in 1792. The New Church did not see itself as a separate religion but as a help to further enlightenment. The Swedenborg Society was established in 1810 to publish translations of Swedenborg's books, create libraries, and sponsor study and lecture. Spiritualists embraced Swedenborg's concept of the spirit's survival after death and the possibility of communication with the spirits. Like Swedenborg, they rejected reincarnation.

Works

Swedenborg recorded his visionary experiences with a scientist's detachment and attention to detail. He realized that few would accept his visions as true revelations but would instead accuse him of blasphemy or insanity. But he did not care, asserting that he had heard, seen, and spoken to God's heavenly representatives. He composed 30 volumes in Latin.

Arcana Coelestia ("Heavenly Secrets") is a 12-volume work published between 1749 and 1756. It delves into the symbolism in the books of Genesis and Exodus, presents Swedenborg's ideas on the law of correspondences, and gives extensive descriptions of the afterlife. *Apocalypse Revealed* (1766) discusses the symbolism in the book of Revelation, and the New Church or New Jerusalem. It also contains many visions of the spiritual world. *Conjugial Love* (1768) explains the sacred nature of love and marriage as they relate to wisdom and truth. Many conversations with angels discuss the state of marital love and sex in the spiritual world. *Heaven and Hell* (1758) describes how souls go to the spiritual world and chose the realm with which they resonate in terms of their earthly interests. It describes societies, cities, life, work, children and other topics. *The True Christian Religion* (1771) is a two-volume work that discusses the universal theology and doctrine of the New Church, illustrated by Swedenborg's visits to the spiritual world.

Other notable works are *Divine Love and Wisdom, Divine Providence, Spiritual Diary,* and *Five Memorable Relations* (published posthumously).

THE FIRST STATES OF THE AFTERLIFE

Swedenborg's theology centers on two main points: that it is only through the eyes of mankind that God is truly revealed (although at no time did Swedenborg presume that God had exhausted all his revelations); and that man, through free will, creates his life and eventual choice of heaven or hell. Men and women are completely at liberty to pursue lives devoted either to love of the divine and charity toward their neighbor or to glorify self-love and evil. By so doing, they make their own heaven or hell. Choices are final.

Immediately after death, the soul goes to an intermediary state called the spiritual world or world of the spirits, halfway between earth and heaven and hell. The spiritual world and the material world are separate and distinct, but they mirror each other through the law of correspondences. The soul awakens to find himself in an environment similar to the one he left behind. This "first state" lasts for a few days. Angels, friends, and relatives come to greet the newcomer. If a spouse has preceded the newly arrived soul, they may reunite.

The first state is followed by a second state in which the soul enters an interior contemplation and judges its true character, which is impossible to hide. One's secret thoughts and intentions in life are more important than actions, for the soul may have acted falsely or to impress others or curry favors for itself. This self-examination prepares the soul to move into its permanent home in heaven or hell. In the first state, evil and good souls are together, but they separate in the second state.

Evil souls go on to hell at the end of the second state. Good souls go through a "vastation," or a purification of spiritual impurities. They then enter the third state, in which they receive instruction for becoming angels in heaven.

HEAVEN

Heaven for Swedenborg little resembled the sylvan paradise usually found in religious literature. Heaven remains in a state of perpetual spring daylight, with no shadows. The sun stays suspended halfway up in the sky and never sets or rises. The angels who live in heaven—all of them former humans, not separately created beings—lived much as they had on earth. They have faces, arms and legs, eyes, ears, noses, and hair; they live in houses similar to their earthly domiciles, grouped into communities, towns, and cities; they wear clothing; they speak and write; they eat food; they marry; never idle, they organize into different governments and perform useful occupations; they play, listen to music, and generally live no different from "natural," as opposed to spiritual, man. They have no sense of time, however, only of varying states of faith, intelligence, love, and wisdom. Heavenly food is love, wisdom, and usefulness.

The angels communicate in an ANGEL LANGUAGE understood by all which expresses their interior wisdom and love. Angels can say in one word what mortals must say in 1,000 words. Swedenborg conversed with angels in their own language.

As the angels progress into higher states they appear to grow older but tend to remain as young adults once the Lord's love and wisdom have been accepted. Spatial relativity is unknown as defined on earth. Those in similar states are near to each other and those of dissimilar states are farther apart.

Angels of the inmost heaven exist solely as expressions of divine will and love, taking no credit for any thought or action separate from the Lord. No matter which way they turn, they always face east, the direction of the rising sun and thereby the light of the divine. They hear, speak, and see more keenly, for as spiritual beings they understand so much more than humans, especially the universal language of all angels. Such complete life in the Lord yields immeasurable bliss and joy, often expressed as completely innocent delight.

All children are admitted to heaven, no matter whether they were baptized or not. Baptism does not signify salvation but merely the need to be reborn in the divine. In fact, all people, not just Christians, are accepted into heaven if they have lived lives of love and charity. Once in heaven, the angels instruct them in the ways of the Lord. Even the rich, often thought excluded at the expense of the poor and meek, are welcome if the intent of their lives has been divinely inspired.

Perhaps lonely in his bachelorhood, Swedenborg gave special emphasis to the state of married love in heaven. He explained that true marriage love is the total bonding of two minds into one, the blending of discernment and intent, the expression of the good and the true. To the extent that such a complete bond exists, that couple becomes one angel, for an angel represents the good and the true together. And since each angel is a heaven in miniature, with all the angels constituting all the heavens, married love is itself heaven.

Marital sexual love exists in heaven, but not in the manner it exists on earth. It is a purer love which joins man and woman in marriage of goodness, truth, love, and wisdom. Spiritual children can arise from this union.

Hell

Swedenborgian hell differs greatly from the eternal fire of damnation propounded by preachers of his day. It is quite a modern place, peopled by those who choose self-love and evil rather than divine love and truth. The Lord casts no one into hell but instead works steadfastly through his angels to save that soul. During life, angels try to replace evil thoughts and intentions with good ones. But those who still embrace evil and falsehood make their own hell after death.

Hell's denizens continue their earthly lives and habits, much as angels do, but with the continual threat of punishment if they exceed acceptable levels of vice and corruption. Retribution is the only restraint on their evil natures. There is no fallen Lucifer or Satan leading this gang of rogues. "Lucifer" and "Satan" themselves mean hell, and there is no devil in charge for all the spirits in hell are former human beings. Because they have chosen malice and darkness, their faces are distorted into monstrous, repulsive shapes. They live in gloom yet appear burned by the fire of their own hatred. They speak with anger and vengefulness, they crave each other's company, and they shrink back in loathing and pain from the approach of an angel. The constant clash of their falsehoods and senses produces a sound like the gnashing of teeth. The openings, or "gates," of hell are numerous and everywhere but only visible to those spirits who have chosen that path. Inside, hell resembles cavernous, bestial liars, with tumbledowm homes and cities, brothels, filth, and excrement. Others hells may be barren deserts.

Swedenborg had conversations with evil spirits. Once, a man and a woman were given permission to come up to heaven from hell. The woman was a siren who served as the man's concubine. That man said that in his hell nature was their God, and religion was only a toy for the lower class. He dismissed angels and heaven as having no significance. On another occasion, Swedenborg was told by devils that they cannot help bothering people, and they become enraged when they see angels.

In any of these afterlife worlds, time does not exist as it does on earth. It is measured by changes of one's interior state. Space also is different; spirits of like mind are "near" each other whatever their actual "location."

Swedenborg places responsibility for the permanent state of the soul squarely upon the individual and not on a judging God or a redeeming savior. The road to heaven or hell begins in early life with thoughts and intentions. Ultimately, each soul is true to its own nature.

FURTHER READING

Bergquist, Lars. *Swedenborg's Dream Diary*. West Chester, Pa.: Swedenborg Foundation Publishers, 2001.

Fox, Leonard, and Donald L. Rose, eds. *Conversations with Angels: What Swedenborg Heard in Heaven*. Translated by David Gladish and Jonathan Rose. West Chester, Pa.: Chrysalis Books, 1996.

Kirven, Robert H. *Angels in Action: What Swedenborg Saw and Heard.* West Chester, Pa.: Chrysalis Books, 1994.

Lachman, Gary. "Heavens and Hells: The Inner Worlds of Emanuel Swedenborg," *Gnosis,* no. 36 (Summer 1995): 44–49.

Stanley, Michael, ed. "Angelic Nature: From Works of Emanuel Swedenborg." In *Angels & Mortals: Their Co-creative Power.* Compiled by Maria Parisen. Wheaton, Ill.: Quest Books, Theosophical Publishing House, 1990.

Swedenborg, Emanuel. *Heaven and Hell.* Translated by George F. Dole. New York: Swedenborg Foundation, 1976.

Sytry

One of the FALLEN ANGELS and 72 spirits of SOLOMON. Sytry is a PRINCE who appears as a man with a leopard's head and griffin wings, but he will change to a beautiful man when commanded to do so. He causes love between men and women, and he makes women show themselves naked.

Taap See GAAP.

Tagas

In 3 ENOCH, angelic PRINCE who governs all the choirs of singing angels. Tagas bows down to Barattiel.

talismans

Objects, drawings, inscriptions, or symbols endowed with supernatural or magical power, which confer their power upon their possessors. Talismans attract good luck, success, fortune, health, fecundity, virility, love, and power.

Talismans are active objects—they are transformers and manifestors. Like AMULETS, they also protect. An example of a talisman is the magic hat, which renders the wearer invisible or transports him wherever he wishes in the blink of an eye.

Talismans can be wands, tools, stones, jewelry, and virtually any other object. They are inscribed with the NAMES of God and angels, which the magician uses to command angelic and demonic forces. SEALS, sigils, symbols, and inscriptions in ANGEL ALPHABETS engraved on metal, stone, parchment, or wax also are talismans.

In angel MAGIC, a talisman is a physical object believed to be energized by an angel, which then carries the energy of that angel. There are two types of angelic talismans: protective and practical. Protective talismans keep the magician safe when conjuring powerful angels who are difficult to control or are potentially dangerous. Practical talismans are like batteries, in that they store an angel's psychic energy so that it can be used magically at a later time.

Talismans acquire their power in three primary ways: (1) they are endowed by nature; (2) they are endowed by God, angels or supernatural agencies; and (3) they are endowed ritually by a magician who follows specific instructions in a magical text such as a GRIMOIRE.

See AGRIPPA; DEE, JOHN.

FURTHER READING

James, Geoffrey. *Angel Magic: The Ancient Art of Summoning and Communicating with Angelic Beings.* St. Paul, Minn.: Llewellyn Publications, 1999.

Three Books of Occult Philosophy Written by Henry Cornelius Agrippa of Nettesheim. Translated by James Freake. Edited and annotated by Donald Tyson. St. Paul, Minn.: Llewellyn Publications, 1995.

Tall Angel

Angel with 70,000 heads seen by MOSES in the third HEAVEN. The identity of the Tall Angel is not certain.

tapsarim

A high order of angel, mentioned in 3 ENOCH 14:1–3. The PRINCES of the tapsarim, along with the princes of the ERELIM and ELIM, pay homage to Metatron. The Maseket Hekalot refers to tapsarim as angels. Tapsarim appears twice in the Bible, but references rank: in Jeremiah 51:27 it is "officer" and in Nahum 3:17 it is "scribe."

tarshisim

In Jewish lore, an order of angels whose name means "brilliant ones." One of the angelic visitors to DANIEL is a tarshis:

> I lifted up my eyes and looked, and behold, a man clothed in linen, whose loins were girded with gold of Uphaz. His body was like beryl, his face like the appearance of lightning, his eyes like flaming torches, his arms and legs like the gleam of burnished bronze, and the sound of his words like the noise of a multitude. (Daniel 10:5–6)

The tarshisim are one of the angelic orders of Netzach (Victory), the seventh sephiroth of the TREE OF LIFE in the KABBALAH. They are sometimes equated with VIRTUES.

Tartys

In the LEMEGETON, the ruling angel of the second hour of the night, called Panezur. Tartys rules 101,550 dukes and servants who are divided into 12 orders.

Tatrasiel YHVH

According to 3 ENOCH, a great angelic PRINCE. Tatrasiel bows down to Atrugiel.

Technician

Angel-like being who is part of THE SEVEN, and whose duty it is to facilitate technological communication between humans and the spiritual realms, a field of research known as INSTRUMENTAL TRANSCOMMUNICATION (ITC).

Technician made himself known in 1986 to Jules Fischbach and Maggy Harsh-Fischbach of Luxembourg, a couple experimenting in communicating with the spirit world. Inspired by the work of American engineers George Meek and Bill O'Neill, the couple tried to capture spirit voices on tape. Initially anonymous, Technician manifested as a strong, high-pitched voice that opened and closed every session. The voice also displayed a vast knowledge of earth's history, religions, sciences, mathematics, and other subjects. Technician also provided instructions in creating a receiving station for ITC.

Technician described himself as a being who has never had a physical form and who is part of a fused group called the Seven, who exist in ethereal realms of timelessness and spacelessness, and who are assigned to help the earth. Names are not important to the group, he said, and so he could be called by his job, technician.

FURTHER READING

Macy, Mark H. *Miracles in the Storm: Talking to the Other Side with the New Technology of Spiritual Contact.* New York: New American Library, 2001.

Temperance, the angel of time, balance, and patience (Copyright 1995 by Robert M. Place; from *The Angels Tarot* by Rosemary Ellen Guiley and Robert M. Place)

Temeluch (Abtelmoluchos, Tartaruchus, Temeluchus, Temleyakos)

One of the CARETAKING ANGELS who protects newborns and children. Temeluch also is an angel of fire in HELL who rules torment.

Temperance

In Kabbalistic lore, angel who pours the elixir of life from one chalice into another. Temperance has the sign of the sun on his forehead and the square and triangle of the septenary on his breast. Temperance is the 16th major arcanum in the Tarot and symbolizes patience and balance.

temurah See GEMATRIA.

Teresa of Avila, St. (1515–1582)

One of the great Christian mystics and the founder of the Discalced Carmelite Order, whose authoritative works on prayer remain classics. Teresa of Avila also had astounding experiences involving angels. Her books are *Life,* her autobiography (1565); *The Way of Perfection* (1573), about the life of prayer; and *The Interior Castle* (1577), her best-known work, in which she presents a spiritual doctrine using a castle as the symbol of the interior life.

She was born Teresa de Cepeda y Ahumada to a noble family on March 28, 1515, in or near Avila in Castile. Her mother died when she was 15, which upset her so much that her father sent her to an Augustinian convent in Avila. Her exposure to the monastic life convinced her that she wanted to become a nun, but her father forbade it as long as he was living. At about age 20 or 21 she left home and secretly entered the Incarnation of the Carmelite nuns in Avila. Her father dropped his opposition.

In 1538, soon after taking the habit, Teresa began to suffer from ill health, which she attributed to the change in her life and diet. It was through her chronic and severe afflictions that Teresa discovered the power of prayer, which enabled her to heal herself and which then became the focus of her spiritual life and her writings.

In her autobiography, *Life,* Teresa comments on her "many ailments" during her first year in the convent, including increasingly frequent fainting fits and heart pains so severe that others became alarmed. She was often semiconscious or unconscious altogether. She opined that these problems were sent by God, who was offended at her innate "wickedness." Rather, she may have suffered from malaria.

Teresa's health failed to the point where a grave was dug for her at her convent. She astonished everyone by recovering on her deathbed. She remained bed-ridden for eight months, and spent the next three years regaining her health. It was not until she reached the age of 40 that the principal symptoms of her illness finally disappeared. Later, she credited the power of prayer and the intercession of St. Joseph with her recovery.

Throughout her monastic life, Teresa was blessed with numerous ecstatic experiences. She did not seek them out, but considered them a divine blessing. She spent long periods in the prayer of quiet and the prayer of union, during which she often fell into a trance and at times entered into mystical flights in which she felt as if her soul was being lifted out of her body. She likened ecstasy to a "delectable death," saying that the soul becomes awake to God as never before when the faculties and senses are "dead."

Teresa often came out of deep prayer states to find herself drenched in tears. These were tears of joy, she attested. Mystics in modern times also experience this.

She made such rapid progress in her prayer that she was concerned that she was being deceived by the devil, because she could neither resist the favors when they came nor summon them. Rather, they came spontaneously. Since she considered herself to be a weak and wicked person, she feared she was vulnerable to the influence of the infernal.

Teresa sought out spiritual counsel in an attempt to allay her fears. Some of her advisers agreed that such favors could be experienced by a weak woman, and they fueled her fears of devilish interference. One, more objective adviser told her to put the matter before God by reciting the hymn "Veni, Creator" as a prayer. This she did for the better part of a day, at which point a rapture came over her so strong that it nearly carried her away. She said, in her autobiography, *Life:*

> This was the first time that the Lord had granted me this grace of ecstasy, and I heard these words: "I want you to converse now not with men but with angels." This absolutely amazed me, for my soul was greatly moved and these words were spoken to me in the depths of the spirit. They made me afraid therefore, though on the other hand they brought me much comfort, after the fear—which seems to have been caused by the novelty of the experience—had departed.

Her greatest experience with an angel occurred in 1559 and is known as "the transverberation of St. Teresa." "Transverberation" means "to strike through"; the mystical episode involved an angel piercing her heart with an arrow of love. In *Life,* Teresa says:

> Beside me, on the left hand, appeared an angel in bodily form, such as I am not in the habit of seeing except very

rarely. Though I often have visions of angels, I do not see them. They come to me only after the manner [of intellectual vision]. But it was our Lord's will that I should see the angel in the following way. He was not tall but short, and very beautiful; and his face was so aflame that he appeared to be one of the highest rank of angels, who seem to be all on fire. They must be of the kind called cherubim, but they do not tell me their names. I know very well that there is a great difference between some angels and others, and between these and others still, but I could not possibly explain it. In his hands I saw a great golden spear, and at the iron point there appeared to be a point of fire. This he plunged into my heart several times so that it penetrated to my entrails. When he pulled it out, I felt that he took them with it, and left me utterly consumed with the great love of God. The pain was so severe that it made me utter several moans. The sweetness caused by this intense pain is so extreme that one cannot possibly wish it to cease, nor is one's soul then content with anything but God. This is not a physical, but a spiritual pain, though the body has some share in it—even a considerable share. So gentle is this wooing which takes place between God and the soul that if anyone thinks I am lying, I pray God, in His goodness, to grant him some experience of it.

Teresa was so affected by this experience that she vowed to do everything in a manner that would be perfect and pleasing to God.

In 1562 Teresa founded a convent in Avila with stricter rules than those that prevailed at Carmelite monasteries. Her aim was to establish a small community that would follow the Carmelite contemplative life, especially its unceasing prayer. She was met with great opposition, but in 1567 she was permitted to establish other convents. She dedicated herself to reforming the Carmelite order. At the age of 53 she met the 26-year-old John Yepes (later known as St. John of the Cross), who became one of her allies and worked to reform the male Carmelite monasteries. After a period of turbulence within the Carmelites from 1575 to 1580, the Discalced Reform was recognized as separate.

By 1582, Teresa had founded her 17th monastery, at Burgos. Her health was now broken, and she decided to return to Avila. The rough journey proved to be too much, and upon arriving at the convent Teresa went straight to her deathbed. Three days later, on October 4, 1582, she died. The next day the Gregorian calendar went into effect, dropping 10 days and putting her death on October 14. Her feast day is October 15. Teresa was canonized in 1662 by Pope Gregory XV, and she was declared a Doctor of the Church—the first woman to be so honored—in 1970 by Pope Paul VI.

FURTHER READING
The Life of St. Teresa of Avila by Herself. Translated by J. M. Cohen. London: Penguin Books, 1987.

Tetragrammaton See NAMES.

Theliel
In magical lore the PRINCE of love. Theliel is invoked to procure the love of women.

theophany See ANGELOPHANY.

Theosophy See DEVA.

Theliel (Copyright 1995 by Robert M. Place; from *The Angels Tarot* by Rosemary Ellen Guiley and Robert M. Place)

Thomas Aquinas, St. (1225–1274)

Great medieval scholar, theologian, and Doctor of the Church. Often called the "Angelic Doctor," Thomas Aquinas is still considered the chief synthesizer of philosophy and theology for the Catholic Church. At a phenomenal rate, Aquinas synthesized in a system of *sacra doctrina* (God's truths revealed in Scripture) all knowledge available in the West at the time, coupled with a strong method of ordering, reason, and argument. In addition, Thomistic angelology became that of the Catholic Church.

Life and Works

Aquinas was born Tomasso Aquino into the central Italian local gentry in Roccasecca near Aquino. At the age of six he was sent to study at the famous Benedictine monastery at Montecassino. When he was 14 he entered the University of Naples, known for being innovative and one of the first conduits of Aristotle's complete works, which had only recently entered the Western world via Arabic translations. At 18 Aquinas decided to join the Dominicans, a new order of mendicant monks committed to study, teaching, and preaching. His family attempted to foil this decision by detaining him for almost two years, but they failed to deter him.

He rejoined his Dominican brethren and soon was sent to Paris, where he transcribed the lectures of the Dominican scholar Albert (St. Albert the Great) on Dionysius the Areopagite (see PSEUDO-DIONYSIUS); the latter exerted a strong influence on Aquinas's angelology. From 1248 to 1252 Thomas lived at the priory of the Holy Cross in Cologne, studying with Albert the works of Aristotle and impressing his teachers and superiors. Tradition says he was called "the dumb ox" because he was physically heavy and had a silent, reserved manner. Albert reportedly told his classmates: "We call this lad a dumb ox, but I tell you that the whole world is going to hear his bellowing!"

After completing his study at Holy Cross, Aquinas was sent back to Paris to prepare to teach Dominicans. He received a license to teach in 1256 and first worked as an apprentice professor lecturing on Scripture. Next he was promoted to teach on the official university textbook for theological instruction, the *Sentences* of Peter Lombard. Throughout his years of official teaching and writing, Aquinas worked on a line by line commentary on Aristotle's texts.

In 1257 he was made a professor of theology, and for the next few years he lectured on the Bible and worked on a series of discussions based on classroom debates. The *Disputed Questions* became some of his earliest written works. *On Spiritual Creatures* was his earliest comment on angels. From 1258 to 1269 Aquinas taught in various cities in Italy: Naples as Dominican preacher general; Orvieto in the curia of Pope Urban IV; and Viterbo with Pope Clement IV. In 1269 he returned to Paris to resume his teaching post, and he wrote volumes. In addition to his incessant work, he was devoted to prayer and to the life of his religious order.

Aquinas's complete writings include biblical commentaries, a series on Aristotle, and polemical tracts. His most famous works are two enormous treatises covering the whole range of Christian doctrine and its philosophical background: the *Summa Contra Gentiles* ("on the truth of the Catholic faith against the unbelievers," commissioned as an aid to Dominican missionaries); and the *Summa Theologica,* a massive work ranging over God, creation, angels, human nature and happiness, grace, virtues, Christ, and the sacraments. Begun in 1266, it remained unfinished at his death. The *Summa Theologica* amazed Aquinas's own and subsequent generations with its orderly system, unflagging intellectual eagerness, and sustained clarity. He acquired a reputation for supernormal mental capacity. One report said he dictated to more than one secretary on different subjects at the same time; another insists that he composed even in his sleep.

In December 1273 he suddenly abandoned his usual routine and neither wrote nor dictated anything else again. According to lore, this sudden change was due to disillusionment, but more likely he suffered a stroke or breakdown from nervous exhaustion caused by overwork. Soon he was called to attend the Second Council of Lyons as Dominican theologian. He set out in late December and became ill on the way. He lodged with his niece in Maenza, but, after two months, he requested to go to a religious house. He was taken to a nearby Cistercian monastery, where he died in a guest room on March 7, 1274.

Protests were lodged at his canonization proceedings that few miracles were attributed to him, but Pope John XXII declared that every proposition he wrote was a miracle. He was canonized in 1323, named *Doctor Angelicus* of the church by Piux X in 1567, and declared patron saint of Catholic schools by Leo XIII in 1880.

Thomistic Method

It struck Aquinas in his early study of Aristotle that philosophers had arrived at truths about God that are equivalent to some revealed truths. The first question that Aquinas takes up in *Summa Theologica* is: What need is there for any science other than those that make up philosophy? The answer is: We cannot arrive at the revealed content of Christian faith merely by philosophical argument. Philosophical argument, however, is the most convincing way to present all truths.

Aquinas's treatment of angels is a synthesis of *sacra doctrina*, what can be assumed true from Scripture as revealed by God (theology) and what can be assumed true on the basis of common experience of the world (philosophy). He applies to angels the same grid he applies to God, creation, the soul, and so forth, involving language and distinctions common to philosophic discourse: cause and effect, general and principle causes, matter and form, essence and being.

Existence of Angels

Aquinas believed and proved that the world, including matter itself, was created by God. Angels are creatures whose existence can be demonstrated. In certain exceptional cases they have even been seen, which Scripture attests. To disregard them destroys the balance of the universe considered as a whole. God's principal end in creation is the supreme good constituted by assimilation to God. God produces a continuous hierarchy of creatures by intelligence and will. The perfection of the universe demands the existence of intellectual creatures that do not have bodies.

Angels are pure forms, unmixed with matter. Every angel is a complete species of being in itself, a single pure form that actualizes in its own individuality the full perfection of a whole species. Since it can so exist, it does not need to be repeated over and over in matter in order to fill out a specific degree of perfection.

By contrast the human soul is incomplete; it is a form but not a species. It becomes a species through matter (the body), involving repetition and multiplicity. Human intelligence issues from its senses, which are lodged in the body. Creatures below humans are living beings without intellect.

The imperfect in any genus always points to the more perfect in that genus, and ultimately to the absolutely perfect. Therefore it is impossible to believe that the human intellect, the most imperfect conceivable, should be the only intellect, or even the only created intellect. Intellect and matter are the opposite poles of being, and if, as in humanity, intellect is found united with matter, then most surely it exists also separate from matter. Consequently, the existence of angels is perfectly credible on grounds of natural reason alone.

Nature of Angels

The attributes of angels are consistent with their being pure spirits and immaterial intelligence. The angels are more numerous than all material things. They are incorruptible and pure spirits, and they cannot die, decay, break up, or be substantially changed. They can assume bodies as instruments through angelic power, as when the archangel Raphael accompanies Tobias,

but they do not have the true functions of a bodily life. An angel is not in a place but rather contains a place, somewhat similar to sunlight being both in a room and beyond it. An angel cannot be in several places at once nor can two angels be in the same place at the same time because there cannot be more than one complete cause of the same effect. Angels do not have to move through space to get from one place to another; they exercise their power to be in one place and are instantly there.

Humans have an active and passive intellect, whereby they process their sense experience, but angels have their knowledge directly from God at creation; thus, they need not learn nor work anything out. However, they can have knowledge of the material things that human beings know by the senses. The degrees of knowledge of angels follows a hierarchy. Each receives what is fitting depending on their status and service. Aquinas compares these degrees of knowledge to light (God's knowledge) passing through successive panes of glass.

Angels cannot know future events—only God knows the future—but they have a type of knowledge of the future in terms of creating causes for effects willed by God. An angel cannot know the secret thoughts or will of humans or another angel. They must be "spoken to" by both humans and other angels.

Angels do not know the workings of divine grace, but higher angels impart their knowledge of such mysteries to the lower angels. The angelic mind is like a clear mirror that takes in the full meaning of what it turns upon. Angels also know how humans go about composing, dividing, and reasoning, though they do not do so themselves.

A good angel knows no falsehood nor errs; the FALLEN ANGELS are totally divorced from divine wisdom, so they are prone to err in things supernatural. Angels have free will and exercise it more perfectly than humans, since they have no outside influences from senses.

Where there is will, there is love; therefore the angels have love. Angelic love is knowledge of an intellectual order and involves not only inclination but choice. Angels love themselves both by natural tendency and by choice. Since angels are all of the same nature, they love one another, and they love God more than they love themselves.

God alone exists from eternity. It is most likely that angels and the bodily world were created at the same time, not the angels first. Angels were created in heaven, with happiness *de natura*, but not in glory, the possession of the beatific vision. Angels were created with sanctifying grace, leaving them free to choose love of God, but they were not confirmed in that choice because some angels fell. Those who chose God gained the beatific vision and enjoy it according to their status in the hierarchy. Beatified angels cannot sin. There is no evolution in their degree of beatitude, since a capacity that is perfectly filled up cannot be made more full.

The sinning angels are guilty of all sins in that they lead men to commit every kind of sin, but they have no tendency to fleshly sins themselves. They commit only two sins: pride and envy. Lucifer wanted to be as God, a prideful sin because he knew equality with the creator was impossible (self-deception is impossible for angels, even Lucifer). He wanted to be like God in a way not suited to his nature. The evil angels are not naturally evil nor created in wickedness. But they sinned immediately after creation, rejecting the good that was meant for them. Lucifer was probably highest of the angels before his fall. He attracted the others who fell by bad example, and to this extent was the cause of their sin.

There are more good angels than fallen angels because sin is contrary to the natural order. The fallen angels did not lose their natural knowledge nor their angelic intellect by their fall. They are unrepentant and inflexibly determined in sin, since a being of immaterial spirit is necessarily final and unchanging. There is sorrow in them, though not repentance, in knowing they cannot attain beatitude, though humans may get to HEAVEN. The fallen angels are engaged in battling against human salvation and in torturing lost souls in HELL. Wherever they are they endure the pains of hell.

The Divine Government

God directly preserves and orders all that he created; otherwise, it would fall back into nothingness. He does not delegate. He is in all conserving forces like air, light, and warmth. He does not annihilate anything, since that would be contrary to divine wisdom. God works in all things in such a way as it suits the operation natural of each thing. A miracle is an effect produced in the bodily universe outside the natural order of creation.

Superior angels can enlighten inferior angels but cannot influence their will. The higher the angel, the more it partakes in the divine good, and the more it gives. Higher angels remain superior even when they give all their knowledge, for the lower angels have less capacity than the superior.

Angelic speech has nothing to do with sounds or words and is not impeded by time or distance. An angel speaks by directing its thought to another angel. Angels "speak" to God by consulting his divine will and contemplating him. (See ANGEL LANGUAGE.)

Just as there is human hierarchy there is angelic hierarchy according to three grades of angelic knowledge. Each hierarchy has three orders. In all there are nine orders of angels. The fallen angels have hierarchy insofar as some subjugate others. Fallen angels have speech like beatified angels, but they do not enlighten the inferiors. The nearer creatures are to God, the greater is their rule over other creatures. Therefore, the good angels rule and control the DEMONS.

Angels, Guardian Angels, and Demons

Superior rules inferior; therefore, angels rule the bodily world in the sense that they can stir bodily agencies to change. They cannot work miracles of their own volition, which is God's proper work, but they do serve as ministers or instruments in working miracles. Angels are superior to humans and thus can act upon the human intellect in strengthening awareness and understanding. They cannot influence human will, but both good and bad angels can indirectly affect human will by stirring up images in the human imagination. Angels also can work upon the human senses, either outwardly by assuming some visible form or inwardly by disturbing the sense functions, for example, making one see what is not there.

God sends angels to minister to his purposes in the bodily world. Only five of the nine orders of angels are sent for the external ministry; the superior angels are never sent. Aquinas agrees with St. Jerome's comment on Matthew 18:10 that each human soul has a GUARDIAN ANGEL.

This guardian office is taken by the ninth and lowest order, the angels. The guardian angel comes at the moment of birth, not at the moment of baptism. In hell, each fallen human soul has a fallen angel to punish him. Angel companions different from guardian angels are given to the humans who gain heaven. Guardian angels never fail or forsake their charges. Humans cannot teach or enlighten angels, but, through speech or prayer, they can make known to angels their thoughts and wishes, which the angels would not otherwise know. The guardian angels do not will the sin that humans commit nor do they will their punishment. They do will the fulfillment of divine justice, which requires free will. All angels are in perfect accord with the divine will as it is revealed to them, but there may arise conflict among them because their revelations of the divine will differ. This explains Daniel 10:13, in which Daniel's guardian angel resists the archangel Gabriel.

God gives humans sufficient aid to resist the temptations of demons. He permits sin and turns it into human benefit and opportunity. The devil plans all the campaigns and assaults on mankind. In a strict sense, humans can sin on their own from their weakness and inordinate appetites, without temptation of a demon. After an assault, God's mercy provides a breathing space because the demon cannot return at once to strike again. However, demons can do astonishing things and cause real havoc.

The Celestial Hierarchy

Aquinas closely follows the PSEUDO-DIONYSIUS system of organizing angels into three tiers of nine orders. The names and features have appeared in many cultures with many forms, some of which differ from Aquinas's scheme.

Quality equals simplicity; the lower the nature of intelligence, the more numerous its means of knowing. The angels closest to God have superiority over the others below. God's total fullness in knowledge is contained in one point, his Essence. The closer a creature is to his Essence, the less differentiated will be the intelligence. The first triad know intelligible essences as preceding from the first principle. The second triad know intelligibles as subjected to the most universal created causes. The third triad know intelligibles as applied to singular beings and dependent upon particular causes.

The following are some of Aquinas's comments from *Summa Theologica* on the various orders, from the highest to the lowest:

SERAPHIM
FIRST HIERARCHY, FIRST ORDER

"Those who see most clearly are called SERAPHIM, the ardent and burning ones, because to be designated in terms of fire associates one with the depth of love or of longing, and love and loving are directed toward the ultimate role. Therefore Dionysius the Areopagite says that this name indicates both their ardent immutability in regard to the Divine and their versatility in guiding those below them to God as the ultimate goal."

The seraphim (fiery ones) are at the highest end of the universe, which is the goodness of God. They are aglow, on fire with love for this object which they know with an exceedingly perfect love.

CHERUBIM
FIRST HIERARCHY, SECOND ORDER

"The second rank fully acknowledge the ground of providence in the essential form of the Divine itself. They are called CHERUBIM, which may be interpreted as 'fullness of knowledge,' in other words, knowledge is fulfilled through the essential form of the knowable. Therefore Dionysius says that this designation means that they are observers of the primal creative power of divine beauty."

The cherubim contemplate the divine goodness not directly and in itself but as Providence. They are the fulness of science because they see clearly the first operative virtue of the divine model of things.

THRONES
FIRST HIERARCHY, THIRD ORDER

"Those of the third rank contemplate the enactment of divine justice. They are called THRONES, for the power of judgment is shown by the throne. Hence Dionysius says that this designation means that they are bearers of God and wholly capable of undertaking all that is divine."

DOMINATIONS
SECOND HIERARCHY, FOURTH ORDER

"For providence is enacted through many agents; through the order of Dominations (see DOMINIONS). It is the concern of those who exercise dominion to command what others should do. Hence Dionysius says that the name 'Domination' indicates leadership in one's own right, removed from all serfdom and subjection."

The second hierarchy does not know the reasons of things in God Himself, as in a sole object, but in the plurality of universal causes.

VIRTUES
SECOND HIERARCHY, FIFTH ORDER

"Second, the enactment of providence . . . is extended through many agencies, and through the power of VIRTUES. This order, as Dionysius says, indicates courage and maturity in all godly action, that no godly movement may languish in inertia. Clearly the primal ground of comprehensive action belongs to this order of angels. Therefore it would seem that this order is entrusted with the movement of the heavenly bodies. From them as from inclusive causes there derive the particular operations of nature; hence they are also known as the 'heavenly powers,' meaning that the celestial powers will be shaken (Luke 21:26). . . . [A]nything else that is inclusive and primary among the divine tasks . . . falls by rights to the lot of this order of angels."

The general directives issued by dominations are received by virtues, who multiply them and channel them according to the various effects to be produced.

POWERS
SECOND HIERARCHY, SIXTH ORDER

"Third, the general order of providence, once it has taken effect, is unerringly preserved, and whatever could disturb that order is prevented. This is the concern of POWERS. Hence Dionysius says that the name

'Powers' means well-ordered and precise enactment of what has been received from God."

PRINCIPALITIES
THIRD HIERARCHY, SEVENTH ORDER

"In human affairs there is a general good which is the welfare of the state or nation. That would seem to be the concern of the order of PRINCIPALITIES. Hence Dionysius says that the name 'Prince' indicates rule together with holy order. . . . Hence the order of kingdoms and the transitions from one tribe to another must be part of the work of this order of angels. It would also seem to be the office of this order to instruct those who are among men about all that concerns the exercise of rule."

The third hierarchy is placed directly over the affairs of humanity.

ARCHANGELS
THIRD HIERARCHY, EIGHTH ORDER

"There is also a human good which is not located in the community but concerns the individual man in

The Archangel Gabriel (Masolino da Panicale, c. 1420–30; reprinted courtesy National Gallery of Art, Washington, D.C., Samuel H. Kress Collection)

himself, but which is nevertheless of use not merely to one but to many men, as for instance that which is to be believed and followed by all as well as the individual; i.e., the worship of God. . . . That is the concern of the ARCHANGELS who, Gregory says, announce the highest things. Hence we call Gabriel the Archangel because he announced the incarnation of the only-begotten Word, in whom all men must believe."

ANGELS
THIRD HIERARCHY, NINTH ORDER

"But other matters have more to do with the individual. They are the concern of the order of ANGELS. Gregory says that they have to impart lesser things. They are also known as the guardians of men, in accordance with Scripture: 'For he has charged his angels to guard you wherever you go" (Psalm 91:11).

See CELESTIAL HIERARCHIES.

FURTHER READING

Clark, Mary T. *An Aquinas Reader.* New York: Fordham University Press, 1988.

Davies, Brian. *The Thought of Thomas Aquinas.* Oxford: Clarendon Press, 1992.

McInerny, Ralph M. *A First Glance at St. Thomas Aquinas.* Notre Dame, Ind.: Notre Dame University Press, 1990.

Thomas Aquinas. *Summa Theologiae.* Edited by Timothy McDermott. Allen, Tex.: Christian Classics, 1989.

thrones

In the Pseudo-Dionysian celestial hierarchy, the third highest order of angels. The term "throne" generally refers to a symbol of majesty and the seat of God and God's glory, and as such it is not a spirit being. Thrones are personified in Jewish mystical literature. The Bible has only one reference to thrones as heavenly beings or angels: Colossians 1:16, which says of Jesus, "for in him all things were created, in heaven and on earth, visible and invisible, whether thrones or DOMINIONS or PRINCIPALITIES or AUTHORITIES—all things were created through him and for him."

Thrones as personified heavenly beings are mentioned in texts such as the Testament of LEVI, the Life of ADAM AND EVE, the Apocalypse of ELIJAH, and the Enochian writings, among others. (See ENOCH.)

In lore thrones are the "many-eyed ones." They serve as the chariots of God and are driven by the cherubs (derived from the description in the visions of EZEKIEL). They are characterized by peace and submission; God rests upon them. Thrones are depicted as great wheels containing many eyes and reside in the area of the cosmos where material form begins to take shape. From where they reside in the fourth HEAVEN, they chant glorias to God and remain forever in his presence. They mete out divine justice and maintain the cosmic harmony of all universal laws. AGRIPPA says that through thrones humanity is knit together and collected into itself." Their ruling prince is given as Oriphiel, Zabkiel, or Zaphkiel.

ST. AUGUSTINE called thrones "seats." Thrones are sometimes equated with OPHANIM and GALGALLIM.

FURTHER READING
Van der Toorn, Karel, Bob Becking, and Pieter W. van der Horst, eds. *Dictionary of Deities and Demons in the Bible.* 2d ed. Grand Rapids, Mich.: William B. Eerdmans, 1999.

thwarting angels

Angels who are charged with nullifying the powers of specific DEMONS. All diseases, bad weather, and other misfortunes are caused by certain demons. Each demon has a counterpoint thwarting angel who can be summoned in prayer and MAGIC to stop or cancel out the demon's mischief. For example, Ruax is the demon who causes headaches; he is thwarted by Michael. Knowing the appropriate thwarting angel is important magical knowledge in order to invoke the fastest and best help.

See AMULETS; MAGIC; PLANETARY RULERS; SOLOMON.

Tipareth   See TREE OF LIFE.

Tobit

Apocryphal story establishing the healing ministry of angels. Tobit tells how the archangel Raphael, whose name means "the shining one who heals," provides magical formulae for healing. The story underscores the concept that angels do not act on their own but are emissaries of God, and that they have no physical form

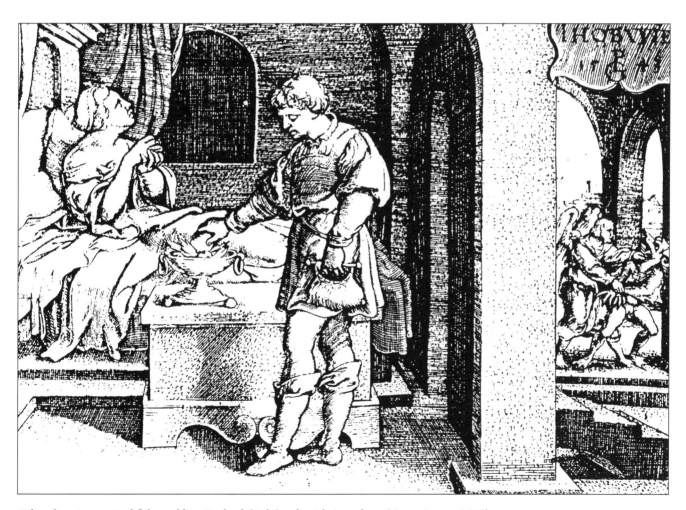

Tobias burning magical fish, enabling Raphael (right) to banish Asmodeus (Georg Pencz, 1540)

but can create the appearance of form for the benefit of humans.

The book of Tobit was originally written in Hebrew or Aramaic, probably in the second century B.C.E. The story concerns a pious man named Tobit and his son, Tobias. It takes place in the late eighth century B.C.E. in the Assyrian capital of Nineveh, where the people of Northern Israel have been taken captive. The story-teller is Tobit himself, who is instructed by Raphael to write an account of the events that happen to him, his son, and others.

By his own description, Tobit is a model of piety, walking "in the ways of truth and righteousness." He gives money, food, and clothing to the poor. He defies Sennacherib the king by burying his fellow Israeli dead, whose bodies were left in the open by their captors.

On one occasion Tobit, who is 50 years old, is sitting down to dinner when he learns of another corpse in need of burying. He leaves his meal and attends to the body. He is defiled from handling the corpse and so does not return home that night, but sleeps by the wall of the courtyard with his face uncovered.

Unbeknownst to Tobit, sparrows are perched on the wall, and their droppings fall into his eyes, rendering him blind. He seeks the help of various physicians, to no avail. His wife is forced to work to earn money.

After eight years, Tobit, depressed and in despair, begs God to let him die. In preparation for death he calls in his only son and tells him to journey to Media, where he has left money in trust with another man. He instructs Tobias to find a man to accompany him on the journey, whom he will pay for his time and trouble.

While this drama unfolds in Nineveh, another is taking place in Media. There, a young woman named Sarah is possessed by the demon Asmodeus, "the destroyer." Sarah has been given to seven men in wedlock, but the demon has killed them all on their wedding night, before the marriages could be consummated. Sarah's parents, Raguel and Edna, fear that they will never marry off their only daughter.

God hears the prayers of both Tobit and Raguel and dispatches Raphael to heal Tobit's blindness and exorcise the demons from Sarah.

Tobit looks for a man to accompany him on the trip to Media and finds Raphael, who appears as a human and introduces himself as Azarius, the son of one of Tobit's relatives. They strike a deal for wages and depart.

The first evening they camp along the Tigris River. Tobias goes down to the river to wash, and a giant fish jumps up and threatens to swallow him. Raphael tells him to catch it, which he does with his hands, and throw it up on the bank. Raphael says, "Cut open the

Throne (From *The Hierarchie of the Blessed Angels* by Thomas Heywood [1635])

fish and take the heart and liver and gall and put them away safely." Tobias does this. They roast and eat the rest of the fish.

Tobias asks the angel of what use are the saved parts. Raphael replies, "As for the heart and the liver, if a demon or evil spirit gives trouble to any one, you make a smoke from these before the man or woman, and that person will never be troubled again. And as for the gall, anoint with it a man who has white films in his eyes, and he will be cured."

As they near their destination, Raphael tells Tobias that they will stay in the house of Raguel, and that he should take Sarah as his wife. Tobias is not pleased to learn that seven prospective husbands have all died at the hands of the demon. But the angel assures him, "When you enter the bridal chamber, you shall take live ashes of incense and lay upon them some of the heart and liver of the fish so as to make a smoke. Then the demon will smell it and flee away, and will never again return. And when you approach her, rise up, both of you, and cry out to the merciful God, and he will save you and have mercy on you. Do not be afraid, for she was destined for you from eternity. You will save her, and she will go with you, and I suppose you will have children by her."

The events come to pass as the angel predicts. Tobias is offered the hand of Sarah in marriage, and a contract is drawn up immediately. In the bridal chamber, Tobias follows Raphael's instructions for exorcising Asmodeus. The demon flees to "the remotest parts of Egypt" (the traditional home of MAGIC and witchcraft), where Raphael binds him up.

After a 14-day wedding feast, Tobias, his bride, and Raphael return home to Tobit. Tobias anoints his father's eyes with the gall of the fish, and Tobit's sight is restored. In gratitude, he and Tobias offer Raphael half of the monies that Tobias retrieved from Media.

The angel reveals his true self to the men. "I am Raphael, one of the seven holy angels who present the prayers of the saints and enter in the presence of the glory of the Holy One," he says. He tells Tobit that he has been ever-present with him, and has taken his prayers for healing to God. He urges the men to praise and thank God, and to lead righteous lives.

Tobit and Tobias are alarmed to be in the presence of an archangel, and fall to the ground in fear. But Raphael assures them that no harm will befall them. "For I did not come as a favor on my part, but by the will of our God," he says. "Therefore praise Him forever. All these days I merely appeared to you and did not eat or drink, but you were seeing a vision. And now give thanks to God, for I am ascending to him who sent me. Write in a book everything that has happened." Raphael vanishes.

The book of Tobit remains one of the most popular books in the apocrypha, illustrating the Jewish values of prayer and piety, and the moral vibrancy of its folklore as well.

FURTHER READING

Guiley, Rosemary Ellen. *Angels of Mercy.* New York: Pocket Books, 1994.

May, Herbert G., and Bruce M. Metzger, eds. *The New Oxford Annotated Bible with the Apocrypha.* New York: Oxford University Press, 1977.

Tree of Life

In the KABBALAH, a two-dimensional symbol of the schematic organization of the cosmos. The symbol is a ladder array of 10 sephirot, a term derived from the Hebrew word for sapphire. The sephirot are vessels for the emanations of Ain Soph ("not ending") or God, who has no name or form and cannot be compre-

hended. Ain Soph created the cosmos through the sephirot, sending energy down and then back up again.

The sephirot channel streams of divine energy, which becomes denser and coarser as it reaches the material plane. Each sephirah has its own color, titles that express its divine qualities, divine NAMES by which one can attempt to contemplate Ain Soph, and its own assigned ruling angels, angelic orders, archdemons, and demonic orders. The sephirot are linked to each other by pathways on which divine light flows both up to God and down to the material world.

In spiritual study, the Tree of Life ladder is used to achieve altered states of consciousness toward union with God. Sin disrupts the upward flow of divine energy.

Organization of the Tree

Each sephirah is a state of consciousness and a level of attainment in knowledge: mystical steps to unity with God. The 10 sephirot are arranged in different groups, which facilitate the understanding of their meanings. The first sephirah, Kether (Crown), is the closest to Ain Soph and is the source of all life and the highest object of prayer. Malkuth (Kingdom) penetrates the physical realm and is the only sephirah in direct contact with it. The lower seven sephirot are associated with the seven days of creation. Another division splits them into two groups of five, the upper ones representing hidden powers and the lower five representing manifest powers. In another division, the top three—Kether, Chockmah (Wisdom), and Binah (Intelligence)—are associated with the intellect; the middle three—Chesed (Love), Geburah (Strength), and Tipareth (Beauty)—are associated with the soul; and the lower three—Netzach (Victory), Hod (Splendor), and Yesod (Foundation)—are associated with nature.

The sephirot also are split into three pillars. The Right Pillar, masculine, represents Mercy and includes Chockmah, Chesed, and Netzach. The Left Pillar, feminine, represents Severity and includes Binah, Geburah, and Hod. The Middle Pillar represents Mildness or Moderation and includes Kether, Tipareth, Yesod, and Malkuth. The Middle Pillar alone also is called the Tree of Knowledge.

Sometimes an 11th sephirah is included, Daath (Knowledge), located on the Middle Pillar below Chockmah and Binah, and it mediates the influences of the two; it is also considered to be an external aspect of Kether. Daath made its appearance in the 13th century. When represented on the Tree, it is depicted as a sort of shadow sphere. Daath cannot be a true sephirah, for the Sefer Yetzirah, the key text of Kabbalistic philosophy, states that there can be only 10 sephirot, no more, no less.

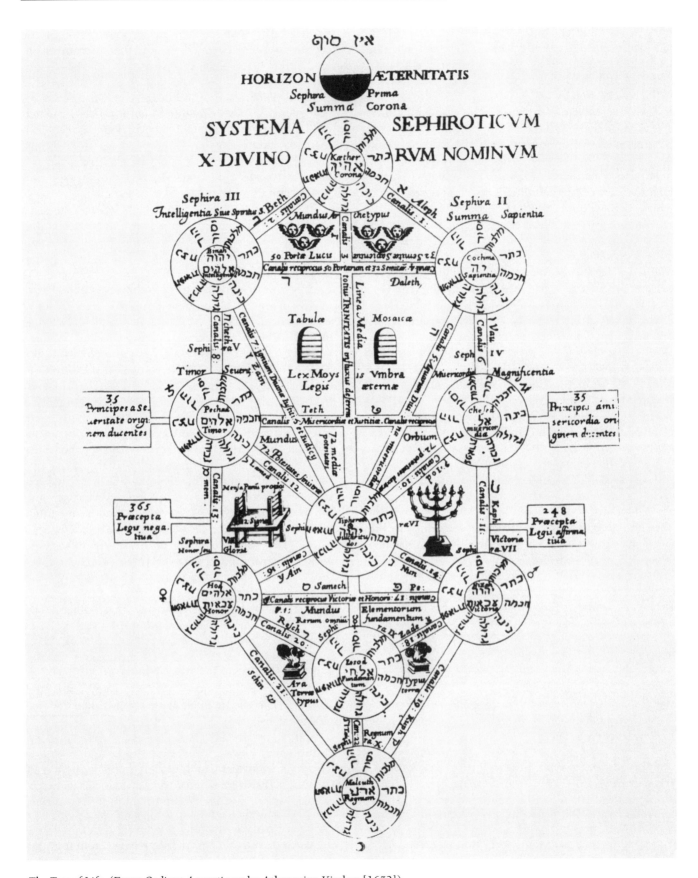

The Tree of Life (From *Oedipus Aegyptiacus* by Athanasius Kircher [1652])

The 10 sephirot each have an unholy counterpart, who are emanations from the left side of God.

The pathways linking the sephirot have become more complex over time. Illustrations in the early 16th century, for example, depict only 16 pathways. By the 17th century, there were 22 pathways, each of which was assigned a letter of the Hebrew alphabet. Thus, God's creation is made through the essences of numbers and letters.

Together the sephiroth of the Tree of Life comprise a unity and create a five-dimensional continuum: the three dimensions of the physical world, plus time, plus the spiritual realm. Like the Akashic Records, they serve as a permanent record of everything that has ever taken place and ever will take place—the memory of God. The sephirot also serve as a means of communication with the unknowable God. The totality of the sephirot is expressed in the Tetragrammaton, the sacred and unspeakable name of God, given as YHVH (Yahweh), or "the Lord."

Applications of the Tree of Life

The sephirot are ineffable and cannot be understood verbally, so descriptions of them cannot begin to approach their true essence. They can be reached only through the second sephirah, Chockmah (Wisdom), which is nonverbal consciousness. Binah (Intelligence) is verbal consciousness. The Kabbalist learns to oscillate between Chockmah and Binah states of consciousness in order to grasp the sephirot.

Consciousness is altered by using the Tree of Life as a ladder for ascent in contemplation, prayer, and meditation. Mantras of arrays of Hebrew letters, having specific numerical properties, are employed. Only the most stable and ethical, who have first purified their bodies, minds, and spirits, are permitted to approach the Tree of Life.

The sephirot are contemplated by visualizing them vibrating with color (which represent various qualities), together with images of their corresponding Hebrew letters of the divine names of God, and the planets, angels, metals, parts of the body, and energy centers. Breath and sound also are utilized to raise consciousness.

The Tree of Life is a central part of the Western magical tradition.

Following are the names and associations of the sephirot, as given in Agrippa's *Occult Philosophy,* edited and annotated by Donald Tyson:

KETHER

Number: One
Titles: The Crown; The Ancient One; The Aged; The Most Holy Ancient One; The Ancient of the Ancient Ones; The Ancient of Days; The Concealed of the Concealed; The Primordial Point; The Smooth Point; The White Head; The Inscrutable Height; The Vast Countenance (Macroprosopus); The Heavenly Man
Divine Name: Eheieh (I Am)
Archangel: Metatron
Angelic Order: Hayyoth (The Holy Living Creatures)
Archdemons: Satan, Moloch
Demonic Order: Thamiel (The Two Contenders)
Heavenly Sphere: Primum Mobile
Part of Man: Head

CHOCKMAH

Number: Two
Titles: Wisdom; Divine Father; The Supernal Father
Divine Names: Jah; Jehovah (The Lord); Yod Jehovah (given by Agrippa)
Archangel: Raziel
Angelic Order: Ophanim (The Wheels)
Archdemon: Beelzebub
Demonic Order: Ghogiel (The Hinderers)
Heavenly Sphere: Zodiac
Part of Man: Brain

BINAH

Number: Three
Titles: Intelligence; The Mother; The Great Productive Mother
Divine Names: Elohim (Lord); Jehovah Elohim (The Lord God)
Archangel: Tzaphkiel
Angelic Order: Aralim (The Thrones)
Archdemon: Lucifuge
Demonic Order: Ghogiel (The Concealers)
Heavenly Sphere: Saturn
Part of Man: Heart

CHESED

Number: Four
Titles: Love; Greatness
Divine Name: El (The Mighty One)
Archangel: Tzadkiel
Angelic Order: Hasmallim (The Shining Ones)
Archdemon: Ashtaroth
Demonic Order: Agshekeloh (The Smiters or Breakers)
Heavenly Sphere: Jupiter
Part of Man: Right arm

GEBURAH

Number: Five
Titles: Strength; Judgment or Severity; Fear
Divine Names: Eloh (The Almighty); Elohim Gabor (God of Battles)
Archangel: Camael

Angelic Order: Seraphim (The Fiery Serpents)
Archdemon: Asmodeus
Demonic Order: Golohab (The Burners or Flaming Ones)
Heavenly Sphere: Mars
Part of Man: Left arm

TIPHARETH

Number: Six
Titles: Beauty; Compassion; The King; The Lesser Countenance (Microprosopus)
Divine Names: Eloah Va-Daath (God Manifest); Elohim (God)
Archangel: Raphael
Angelic Order: Malachim (Kings or Multitudes)
Archdemon: Belphegor
Demonic Order: Tagiriron (The Disputers)
Heavenly Sphere: Sun
Part of Man: Chest

NETZACH

Number: Seven
Titles: Firmness; Victory
Divine Name: Jehovah Sabaoth (Lord of Hosts)
Archangel: Haniel
Angelic Order: Elohim (Gods)
Archdemon: Baal
Demonic Order: Nogah (The Raveners)
Heavenly Sphere: Venus
Part of Man: Right leg

HOD

Number: Eight
Titles: Splendor
Divine Name: Elohim Sabaoth (God of Hosts)
Archangel: Michael
Angelic Order: Bene Elohim (Sons of Gods)
Archdemon: Adrammelech
Demonic Order: Samael (The False Accusers)
Heavenly Sphere: Mercury
Part of Man: Left leg

YESOD

Number: Nine
Titles: The Foundation; Eternal Foundation of the World
Divine Names: Shaddai (The Almighty); El Chai (Mighty Living One)
Archangel: Gabriel
Angelic Order: Cherubim (The Strong)
Archdemon: Lilith (The Seducer)
Demonic Order: Gamaliel (The Obscene Ones)
Heavenly Sphere: Moon
Part of Man: Genitals

MALKUTH

Number: Ten
Titles: The Kingdom; The Diadem; The Manifest Glory of God; The Bride (of Microposopus); The Queen
Divine Names: Adonai (Lord); Adonai Malekh (Lord and King); Adonai he-Aretz (Lord of Earth)
Archangel: Metatron in manifest aspect; also Sandalphon
Angelic Order: Issim (Souls of Flame)
Archdemon: Nahema (The Strangler of Children)
Demonic Order: Nahemoth (The Dolorous Ones)
Heavenly Sphere: Elements
Part of Man: Whole body

FURTHER READING

Kaplan, Aryeh. *Sefer Yetzirah: The Book of Creation.* Rev. ed. York Beach, Maine: Samuel Weiser, 1997.
Scholem, Gershom. *Kabbalah.* New York: New American Library, 1974.
Three Books of Occult Philosophy Written by Henry Cornelius Agrippa of Nettesheim. Translated by James Freake. Edited and annotated by Donald Tyson. St. Paul, Minn.: Llewellyn Publications, 1995.

Trithemius, Johannes (1462–1519)

German abbot, alchemist, magician, and historian. Johannes Trithemius authored numerous works on occult philosophy that influenced writers and artists, among them AGRIPPA.

Trithemius was born in Trittenheim near Trier to the von Heidenberg family. His father died when he was one year old. He later took as his last name the place where he was born, a custom of the day.

An unhappy childhood with an abusive stepfather propelled him into deep study at an early age; he was fascinated by mysticism and the occult arts. Later, he said that an angel had appeared to him in childhood and offered him two tablets with letters written upon them. After he chose one, the angel promised to fulfill his prayers and then vanished. After that, he had an insatiable desire to study and learn. He taught himself how to read German, and he engaged in secret lessons at night to learn Latin.

Trithemius left Trittenheim for Heidelberg—a center of alchemy and occultism—where he became the student of an unknown teacher. He went to Trier and entered the university there.

In 1482, an incident altered the course of his life. While traveling back to Trittenheim, he was forced by a blizzard to seek shelter at the Benedictine monastery of St. Martin at Spanheim. He was so taken by the life of the monks that he entered the order, and within two years—at age 23—he was named abbot. One of his passions was building up the monastery's library from a mere 48 books to more than 2,000. He took on students, one of whom was Henry Cornelius Agrippa von Nettesheim.

Trithemius's knowledge eventually led to accusations that he was a sorcerer, and stories of his conjurations arose. He is said to have enabled Emperor Maximilian to see a vision of his dead wife, Mary of Burgundy.

Trithemius resigned his post in 1506, but soon he was named abbot at another Benedictine monastery, St. Jakob at Wurzburg. He remained their for the rest of his life.

He wrote some 70 works, among them *Stenoganographia,* on his original shorthand method for conjuring spirits; *Polygraphia,* on ciphers and magical alphabets; *De septem secundeis,* on the planetary angels who rule the cycle of ages; and *Veterum sophorum sigilla et imagines magicae,* descriptions of TALISMANS and magical images.

Agrippa wrote his first version of his monumental work, *Occult Philosophy,* while studying with Trithemius, and he dedicated the work to him.

FURTHER READING

Melton, J. Gordon, ed. *Encyclopedia of Occultism & Parapsychology.* 5th ed. Detroit: Gale Group, 2001.

Seligmann, Kurt. *The Mirror of Magic.* New York: Pantheon Books, 1948.

Three Books of Occult Philosophy Written by Henry Cornelius Agrippa of Nettesheim. Translated by James Freake. Edited and annotated by Donald Tyson. St. Paul, Minn.: Llewellyn Publications, 1995.

Tubiel

Angel who governs summer and who is invoked in MAGIC for the return of small birds to their owners.

Tubuas (Tubuel)

One of seven REPROBATED ANGELS condemned by a church council in Rome in 745.

tutelary spirits See ANGELS; GUARDIAN SPIRITS; INTELLIGENCES.

Tzadkiel (Azza, Tsadkiel, Tzidkiel, Zadkiel)

Angel of justice and guard of the gates of the East Wind. Tzadkiel is also the INTELLIGENCE of the planet Jupiter and the PRECEPTOR of ABRAHAM.

Ubaviel

Angel who governs the sign of Capricorn.

Umabel

Angel who governs physics and astronomy and is one of the 72 angels of the SCHEMHAMPHORAE.

Uriel

One of the most important angels, described as an archangel, seraph, and cherub. Uriel probably means "fire of God" or "God is my light." Uriel is often identified as one of the four primary angels, along with Michael, Gabriel, and Raphael, possibly aspects of the ANGEL OF THE LORD. He is not part of the official Catholic canon, but he is prominent in Jewish texts and apocryphal writings.

Uriel is among the angels identified as the ANGEL OF DEATH; ANGEL OF GREAT COUNSEL; ANGEL OF PEACE; ANGEL OF TRUTH; and as one of the ANGELS OF THE EARTH; ANGELS OF THE PRESENCE; ANGELS OVER THE CONSUMMATION and one of the ANGELS OF DESTRUCTION sent to destroy SODOM AND GOMORRAH. He is an angel of September, summer, and Libra and Aquarius.

In 1 Enoch Uriel (Suriel) is identified as a guide to ENOCH on his trip through the layers of heavens; he is the angel who "watches over thunder and terror." As a cherub, Uriel is said to guard the Gate of Eden with a fiery sword in hand. He also appears as a "benign angel" who attacks MOSES for not observing the circumcision rite of his son, a role also credited to Gabriel. In the Testament of SOLOMON, Uriel thwarts Error, who leads men astray. He is one of the seven PLANETARY RULERS. (See THWARTING ANGELS.)

Uriel is portrayed as a stern and punishing angel. Enoch said he is head of the seven archangels, and he presides over Tartarus or HELL, where he pursues punishment of sinners. According to the Apocalypse of St. Peter, this punishment consists of burning sinners in everlasting fire and hanging blasphemers by their tongues over unquenchable fires. On the day of judgment, he will break the brazen gates of Hades and assemble all the souls before the judgment seat.

Uriel is among the angels identified as the dark angel who wrestles with JACOB. In the Prayer of Joseph, Uriel states, "I have come down to earth to make my dwelling among men, and I am called Jacob by name." The exact meaning of this statement is not clear, but it suggests that Uriel might have become Jacob, thus making him the first angel of record to become a mortal.

Various Jewish sources relate the story that when Cain kills Abel and tries to bury the corpse, earth spews it up again and cries, "I will receive no other body until the clay that was fashioned into Adam has been restored to me!" At this Cain flees, and Michael,

Gabriel, Uriel, and Raphael place the corpse upon a rock, where it remains many years without corrupting. When Adam dies, these same archangels bury both bodies at Hebron side by side, in the very field from which God had taken Adam's dust.

According to midrashim and 1 Enoch, the FALLEN ANGELS Azael and Semyaza (see WATCHERS) cause such wickedness on earth that the archangels tell God. He sends Raphael to bind Azael hand and foot, heaping jagged rocks over him in the dark Cave of Dudael, where he now abides until the last days. Gabriel destroys the Fallen Ones by inciting them to civil war. Michael chains Semyaza and his

Uriel (From *The Angels Tarot* by Rosemary Ellen Guiley and Robert Michael Place. Reprinted courtesy of HarperSanFrancisco)

fellows in other dark caves for 70 generations. Uriel becomes the messenger of salvation who visits NOAH. Dispatched by Metatron, he warns Noah about the coming Flood.

Like Metatron, Uriel also is credited with giving the gift of the KABBALAH to humanity. He is said to have led Abraham out of Ur and to have interpreted prophecies for the benefit of humanity. In 4 Ezra, Uriel reveals heavenly mysteries to EZRA and answers weighty questions about evil and justice. He serves as a guide of the luminaries.

Uriel appears in QUMRAN TEXTS, such as the Gospel of Barnabas.

Uriel was condemned as one of the REPROBATED ANGELS in 745 C.E. by a church council, but he was later reinstated. He is often portrayed as holding a flame in his open hand.

FURTHER READING
Gaster, Theodor H. *The Dead Sea Scriptures*. 3d ed. Garden City, N.Y.: Anchor/Doubleday, 1976.
Godwin, Malcolm. *Angels: An Endangered Species*. New York: Simon and Schuster, 1990.
Margolies, Morris B. *A Gathering of Angels*. New York: Ballantine Books, 1994.

Usiel (Uziel, Uzziel)

Angel who is both good and fallen. In the SEFER RAZIEL, Usiel is a good angel who is among the seven who stand before the throne of God and the nine who are set over the four winds. In Kabbalistic lore, he is a FALLEN ANGEL who married women and begat giants.

Uzza (Ouza, Semyaza, Uzzah)

FALLEN ANGEL. Uzza means "strength." In 3 ENOCH, Uzza is named as one of three primary MINISTERING ANGELS with Azael and Azza, who live in the seventh (highest) HEAVEN (probably prior to their fall). The three object to the elevation of the prophet ENOCH into the great angel Metatron. Uzza also is a tutelary spirit of Egypt.

See SEMYAZA.

Uzziel (Usiel)

Angel in the order of CHERUBIM and sometimes identified as the ruler of the order of MALACHIM, who are equated with VIRTUES. Uzziel means "strength of God." In 3 ENOCH, Uzziel is an ANGEL OF MERCY under the direction of Metatron. In the SEFER RAZIEL, Uzziel is a good angel who is among the seven who stand before the throne of God and the nine who are set over the four winds.

Vahuman See AMARAHSPANDS.

Valac
One of the FALLEN ANGELS and 72 spirits of SOLOMON. Valac is a president who appears as a small boy with angel wings riding on a two-headed dragon. He gives true answers about hidden treasures. He reveals where serpents can be seen, and delivers them harmless to the magician.

Valefor (Malaphar, Malephar)
One of the FALLEN ANGELS and 72 spirits of SOLOMON. Valefor is a duke who rules 10 legions. He appears either as a many-headed lion or as a lion with the head of a human thief. He leads people into thievery and leaves them at the gallows.

Vapula
One of the FALLEN ANGELS and 72 spirits of SOLOMON. In HELL Vapula is a duke with 36 legions. He appears as a lion with griffin wings. He gives skill in handicrafts, philosophy, and all science contained in books.

Varhmiel
In the LEMEGETON, the ruling angel of the fourth hour of the day, called Elechym. Varhmiel rules 10 chief dukes and 100 lesser dukes and their servants.

Vassago
One of the FALLEN ANGELS and 72 spirits of SOLOMON. Vassago is a PRINCE who discerns past, present, and future. He discovers all things lost or hidden. Good natured, he is invoked in divination rituals.

Vepar (Separ)
One of the FALLEN ANGELS and 72 spirits of SOLOMON. In HELL Vepar is a duke with 29 legions. He appears as a mermaid and has jurisdiction over certain things pertaining to the sea: he guides the waters and battleships and causes the sea to seem full of ships. When commanded, he will raise storms at sea. He can cause a person to die in three days of wounds that putrefy and become filled with maggots. According to JOHANN WEYER, a person so afflicted can be healed "with diligence."

Vequaniel
In the LEMEGETON, the ruling angel of the third hour of the day, called Dansor. Verquaniel has 20 chief dukes and 200 lesser dukes and their servants under his command.

Verchiel (Zerachiel)
Angel who is one of the rulers of the order of POWERS, and who rules the month of July and the sign of Leo.

Victory

The winged Roman goddess of victory, adopted from the similar Greek deity, NIKE, served as a model for the winged angel of Christian art.

Victory symbolizes invincibility. In mythology she is the daughter of Pallas and Styx. The Romans used her as a symbol of the invincibility of their own empire, and she became the protector of the Roman city and state. But as emperors and others converted to Christianity, Victory kept her place alongside Christian imagery. Like angels, Victory acted as a messenger of the gods, especially bestowing news of victory in battle.

In art, Victory is shown as a female figure with prominent breasts. Usually, one breast is exposed from the flowing tunic; sometimes she is portrayed naked with a mantle. She is crowned with laurel. She holds medallions and palm branches, which Christian artists borrowed for their angels. Her image appears in funerary art, ceremonial and triumphal art, statuary, and on coins.

While Victory joined winged angels in art of the Roman Empire beginning in the fourth century, she never became confused with angels, nor became an angel. She was always distinguished from them by her female form. It was not until the Renaissance that Christian artists began to portray angels as feminine in appearance.

See IMAGES OF ANGELS.

village-angel See HINDUISM.

Vine

One of the FALLEN ANGELS and 72 spirits of SOLOMON. In HELL Vine is a king and earl. He appears either as a monster or as a lion seated on a black horse, holding a viper. When commanded, he assumes human form. Vine discerns hidden things, reveals witches, and knows the past, present, and future. Upon command he will build towers, demolish walls, and make seas stormy.

virtues

In the Pseudo-Dionysian hierarchy, the fifth highest order of angels, whose name means "powers," especially in relation to performance of miracles and MAGIC. The primary tasks of virtues are to execute miracles on earth and provide courage, grace, and valor. According to PSEUDO-DIONYSIUS, virtues are one of the 10 orders of the blessed. They carry out the instructions of the DOMINIONS. Through virtues, God governs the seasons, elements, and heavens, though lower orders of angels have direct responsibility for those tasks. The angels of the ascension are virtues. According to the Life of ADAM AND EVE, two virtues (EXCELLENCIES) and 12 other angels helped Eve to prepare for the birth of Cain. Angels who rule the order of virtues are Barbiel, Michael, Peliel, Raphael, and Uzziel, and Satan prior to his fall.

AGRIPPA says that humans receive power from virtues that strengthens them and enables them to constantly fight the enemies of truth.

Virtues are equated with MALACHIM and TARSHISIM in Hebrew lore, and they are sometimes referred to as "the shining ones" or the "brilliant ones."

In Kabbalistic lore, virtues—along with dominions and POWERS—form one of four triplicities of intelligible hierarchies.

See DYNAMEIS.

visions See DREAMS AND VISIONS.

Virtue (From *The Hierarchie of the Blessed Angells* by Thomas Heywood [1635])

Vodun   See ORISHAS.

voices

In GNOSTICISM, seven angels who reside in the Treasury of Light. The alchemist Robert Fludd identified voices as one of three primary orders along with ACCLAMATIONS and APPARITIONS.

Vretiel   (Pravuil, Vrevoil)

Archangel who records all of God's deeds and who is "swifter in wisdom than the other archangels." The etymology of "Vretiel" is unknown and unexplained. As an archangel, he resembles Uriel, but as a scribe he is probably derived from Thoth, the Egyptian god of writing and MAGIC and scribe to the god Osiris (and the equivalent of the Greek Hermes).

Vretiel is mentioned in 2 ENOCH. In 22:10–11 God instructs him to bring out the books from God's storehouses and a pen for "speed-writing" and give them to Enoch. Vretiel hurries away to do God's bidding and returns with the books and pen so that Enoch can record what God wishes him to. Vretiel instructs Enoch for 30 days and 30 nights without ceasing his talking. Enoch writes it down in 366 books.

Vretiel is sometimes identified as the "man clothed in linen, with a writing case at his side" in Ezekiel 9:2.

See RADUERIEL; RECORDING ANGELS.

Vual

One of the FALLEN ANGELS and 72 spirits of SOLOMON. Once a member of the order of POWERS, Vual is a duke in HELL. He appears first as an enormous dromedary camel, then changes into human form and speaks in Egyptian. He procures the love of women, knows the past, present, and future, and makes enemies become friends.

Watchers

Angels who cohabited with human women and fell from God's grace. The term Watchers also describes angels who do not fall but who are close to the throne of God, thus causing some confusion. Watchers are also referred to as SONS OF GOD. Their monstrous offspring, the NEPHILIM, and the corruption the Watchers created on earth so revolted God that he decided to send the great Flood to destroy all life on earth. The cohabitation of the sons of god and the daughters of men is briefly described in Genesis 6:1–4.

The term Watcher meaning an angel appears in the book of DANIEL. King Nebuchadnezzar, referring to his dreams, mentions "watchers" and "holy ones" three times:

> "I saw in the visions of my head as I lay in bed, and behold, a watcher, a holy one, came down from heaven." (4:13)

> The sentence is by the decree of the watchers, the decision by the word of the holy ones, to the end that the living may know that the most high rules the kingdom of men and gives it to whom he will, and sets over it the lowliest of men. (4:17)

> And whereas the king saw a watcher, a holy one, coming down from heaven and saying "hew down the tree and destroy it but leave the stump of its roots in the earth. (4:23)

These references in Daniel are the only places that the term "watcher" (translated from the word *ir*) is used in connection with angels.

1 ENOCH tells in detail the story of the Watchers and their fall. The Watchers, described as angels who are "the children of HEAVEN," see the beautiful daughters of men and desire them. They decide to take them as wives. But their leader, Semyaza, expresses the fear that he alone will be held accountable for this great sin. The angels, who are 200 in number, swear an oath binding them all together. Their chiefs (called "chiefs of tens") who serve under Semyaza are Arakeb, Rameel, Tamel, Ramel, Danel, Ezeqel, Baraqyal, Asel, Armaros, Batrel, Ananel, Zaqeel, Sasomaspweel, Kestarel, Turel, Yamayol, and Arazyal.

The Watchers descend to earth and take the women. Many of them committed adultery against their new wives. Their offspring, the giant Nephilim, turn against the people, cannibalize them, and drink their blood.

The Watchers teach people secret arts such as magical medicine, incantations, and knowledge of plants and herbs. Azazel teaches the art of making weapons of war, jewelry and cosmetics, and dye making and alchemy. Amasras teachers plant lore and how to perform MAGIC.

Baraqiyal teaches astrology; Kokarerel teaches the zodiac; Tamel teaches about the stars; Asderel teaches about the moon and the deception of man.

Later in the text, 1 Enoch gives the names of 21 chiefs of the fallen (some angels are named more than once):

Semyaza	Aristaqis
Armen	Kokbael
Turel	Rumyal
Danyul	Neqael
Baraqel	Azazel
Armaros	Betryal
Besasel	Hananel
Turel	Sipwesel
Yeterel	Tumael
Turel	Rumel
Azazel	

Other fallen angel names and their activities are:

- Yeqon, who misleads all the children of the angels, brings them down upon the earth, and perverts them by the daughters of the people;
- Asbel, who gives the children of the holy angels and misleads them so that they will defile their bodies by the daughters of the people;
- Gaderel, who shows the children of the people all the blows of death, who misleads Eve, who shows the children of the people how to make weapons and all other instruments of war and death;
- Pinene, who demonstrates to people the bitter and the sweet, reveals to them all the secrets of their wisdom, and teaches them the secret of writing with ink and paper, thus causing them to err from eternity to eternity;
- Kasadya, who reveals the flagellations of all evil including the flagellation of the souls and the demons, the smashing of the embryo in the womb so that it may be crushed, and the flagellation of the soul, snake bites, sun strokes, and the son of the serpent whose name is Tabata.

Sin, corruption, and oppression spread across the earth. Horrified, the angels Michael, Surafel (Suriel/Uriel), and Gabriel petition God to take action, for the people on earth are suffering. God declares that he will wipe out the wicked and all life on earth in a great flood. He instructs Raphael to bind Azazel hand and foot and to throw him into darkness. Raphael makes a hole in the desert, casts Azazel into it, and covers him with sharp rocks. God tells Gabriel to destroy the children of the Watchers. He tells Michael to inform Semyaza that they will die together with their wives and children in their defilement. He is to bind them for 70 generations beneath rocks until the day of judgment. They will be led into the bottom of fire where they will be locked up in prison and in torment forever. All those who collaborated with the Watchers will be similarly punished. Finally, Michael is to eradicate injustice from the face of the earth.

The Watchers call to the prophet Enoch for help, and he hears them in a DREAM vision. Upon awakening, he tells Azazel there will be no peace for him, for a grave judgment has come upon him. Enoch then speaks to all the Watchers, who are frightened and full of fear and trembling. They beg him to write a prayer of forgiveness for them. Enoch records their prayers and petitions and then reads them until he falls asleep. He has another dream vision in which he sees plagues. When he awakens, he goes to the Watchers and reprimands them for their sins, and he tells them their petitions will not be heard.

Enoch nonetheless tries to intercede on behalf of the Watchers but is refused by God. God says that their giant offspring shall be called evil spirits upon the earth, for they will dwell on the earth and in the earth. He tells Enoch to inform the Watchers that because they have rejected heaven they shall have no peace.

1 Enoch also gives the names of "the holy angels who watch," implying that the term Watchers was given to angels in heaven, not just the fallen ones. The holy angels are:

Suruel—angel of eternity and trembling
Raphael—angel of the spirits of man
Raguel—angel who takes vengeance for the world and for the luminaries
Michael—angel who is obedient in his benevolence over the people and the nations
Saraqael—angel who is over the spirits of mankind and who is in the spirit
Gabriel—angel who oversees the garden of Eden, the serpents, and the CHERUBIM.

In 2 Enoch, Enoch sees the "innumerable armies" of the Watchers and Nephilim imprisoned in the fifth heaven. They are dejected and silent. Enoch—who unsuccessfully tries to intercede on their behalf with God—urges them to sing a liturgy to God so that God will not be enraged against them "to the limit." They do so, singing in a piteous and touching way.

3 Enoch describes the Watchers as holy angels. According to the text, four great PRINCES called

"Watchers and holy ones" (the terms used in Daniel) reside in the seventh heaven opposite the throne of glory facing God. They are called Watchers and holy ones because on the third day of judgment (after death), they sanctify the body and soul with lashes of fire (a reference to preparing the soul for God's presence).

Each Watcher has 70 names corresponding to the 70 languages of the world and all of them are based on the name of God. Each name is written with a pen of flame on God's crown. Such sparks and lightning shoot forth from them that no angels, not even the SERAPHIM, can look upon them.

The Watchers are praised with the praise of the SHEKINAH, and God does nothing without taking their counsel. They function as officers in the heavenly court and debate and close each case that comes up for judgment. They announce the verdicts, proclaim the sentences, and sometimes come down to earth to carry out the sentences.

A QUMRAN TEXT called the Testament of Amran (Q543, 545–548), which exists only in several fragments and manuscripts, concerns the Watchers. In Manuscript B Fragment 1, the anonymous author describes a dream vision in which two Watchers are fighting over him. He asks, "Who are you that you are thus empowered over me?" They tell him that they have been empowered to rule over all mankind and they ask him to choose which of them he would choose as a ruler. One of them has a terrifying appearance, like a serpent wearing a dark cloak of many colors. He has a "visage like a viper."

Fragment 2 identifies Belial as one of the Watchers. He has three titles, Belial, Prince of Darkness, and King of Evil, and he is empowered over all darkness and his every way and every work are darkness. Fragment 3 mentions the "sons of Light" who are ruled by a being who identifies himself with three names: Michael, Prince of Light, and King of Righteousness.

Another fragment says that all the sons of Darkness will be destroyed because of their foolishness and evil and the sons of Light will have eternal joy and rejoicing for all peace and truth will be made Light.

The term "watchers" is sometimes used to refer to the RECORDING ANGELS of Islam.

FURTHER READING

Charlesworth, James H., ed. *The Old Testament Pseudepigrapha.* Vols. 1 and 2. New York: Doubleday, 1983, 1985.

Collins, Andrew. *From the Ashes of Angels: The Forbidden Legacy of a Fallen Race.* London: Signet Books, 1996.

Eisenman, Robert, and Michael Wise. *The Dead Sea Scrolls Uncovered.* London: Element Books Ltd., 1992.

Weyer, Johann (1515–1588)

German physician who opposed the torture and execution of accused witches during the Inquisition, and who catalogued the DEMONS of HELL.

Johann Weyer was born to a noble Protestant family in Brabant. He studied medicine in Paris, and he became a physician, serving as a court physician to the duke of Cleves in the Netherlands. His witch sympathies were influenced by one of his teachers, the famous occultist Agrippa von Nettesheim, who had successfully defended an accused witch only to suffer personally for it.

Weyer believed in the devil and his legions of demons, but he did not believe that witches were empowered by the devil to harm humankind. Nor did he believe stories of witches flying through the air and attendance at sabbats in which the devil was worshiped and babies were eaten. He thought that belief in witchcraft was caused by the devil, and that the

Johann Weyer

Catholic Church served the cause of the devil by promoting belief in the evil power of witches.

In his book, *De praestigiis daemonum* (1563), Weyer gave a rational analysis of reports of alleged witch activity, and he concluded that most witches were deluded and mentally disturbed old women, the outcasts of society who were fools, not heretics. Some might wish harm on their neighbors but could not carry it out. If harm occurred coincidentally, they believed in their delusion that they had brought it about. He did believe that some witches served Satan and did harm people, but not through supernatural means. He urged the church to forgive those who repented, or at most, to levy fines upon them.

Weyer successfully discouraged witchhunting in much of the Netherlands for a time, but he was forced out by the Catholic governor, the duke of Alba. His book had almost the opposite effect he intended. He was savagely denounced by critics such as Jean Bodin and King James I, both of whom advocated the extermination of witches. James's authorship of his anti-witch treatise *Daemonologie* served as a direct response to Weyer and another witch sympathizer, Reginald Scot. Bodin urged that copies of Weyer's book be burned. Others wrote books refuting Weyer, and these tracts helped to stimulate more witch hunts. Weyer himself was accused of being a witch.

Weyer then turned his attention to cataloging the realms of hell, just as theologians had cataloged the realms of HEAVEN. In 1568, he published the *Pseudo-Monarchy of Demons,* an inventory and description of Satan's legions. He cited 7,405,926 devils and demons organized in 1,111 divisions of 6,666 each, ruled over by 72 princes. Later, the Lutheran Church thought his estimate too low, and raised the census of the demonic population to 2,665,866,746,664, or roughly 2.6 trillion.

FURTHER READING

Ankarloo, Bengt, and Gustav Henningsen, eds. *Early Modern European Witchcraft: Centres and Peripheries.* Oxford: Clarendon Press, 1990.

Russell, Jeffrey B. *A History of Witchcraft.* London: Thames and Hudson, 1980.

wheels

Order of "many-eyed" angels, equated with the OPHANIM or THRONES, or grouped with the CHERUBIM and SERAPHIM. The chief of the wheels is Rikbiel.

Winged Dragon

A FALLEN ANGEL and one of the 72 spirits of King SOLOMON. Winged Dragon has the form of the limbs of a dragon, wings on its back, and the face and feet of a man. His activity is to copulate with certain beautiful women through their buttocks. He tells Solomon that one woman he attacked bore a child that became Eros. The woman was killed by others. While he is speaking, the DEMON breathes out fire that burns the forest of Lebanon and all the wood intended for the construction of the Temple of God. Solomon learns that the Winged Dragon is thwarted by the angel Bazazath. He invokes this angel and then condemns the demon to cut marble for the building of the temple.

Wisdom (Divine Wisdom)

God's feminine attribute and companion. The scriptural roots of Wisdom are Job 28 and Proverbs 1–9. Wisdom also appears in apocryphal works, such as the book of ENOCH, the Wisdom of SOLOMON, and Sirach.

Job 28 poses the questions, "where shall wisdom be found?" And "where is the place of understanding?" Man does not know the way to wisdom. It is not in the earth, in gold, gems, or the land; it is hidden from the eyes of all living things. Abbadon (the ANGEL OF DEATH) and Death says they have only "heard a rumor of it with our ears" (28:22). But God understands wisdom and knows its place. He tells man, "Behold, the fear of the Lord, that is wisdom; and to depart from evil is to understand" (28:28).

Proverbs encompasses Wisdom from the cosmic to the virtues of a capable wife. She is brought forth at the very beginning of God's creation and speaks as a prophetess to proclaim her worth (Proverbs 8); she witnesses and has knowledge of all matters. She is God's eternal companion. She is a lover, ceaselessly seeking men, builds a house, prepares a feast, and sends maids to invite all to "walk in the way of understanding" (9:6). Wisdom, beloved of man, is also the beloved of God who mediates the gulf between humanity and God. By loving Wisdom, an attachment to the cosmic world is formed.

In 2 Enoch, God orders Wisdom on the sixth day of creation to make man out of seven substances.

In the Wisdom of Solomon, Wisdom is personified:

For she is a breath of the power of God, and a pure emanation of the glory of the Almighty; therefore nothing defiled gains entry into her.

For she is a reflection of eternal light, a spotless mirror of the working of God, and an image of his goodness.

Though she is but one, she can do all things, and while remaining in herself, she renews all things; in every generation she passes into holy souls and makes them friends of God, and prophets; for God loves nothing so much as the man who lives with wisdom.

For she is more beautiful than the sun, and excels every constellation of the stars.

Compared with the light she is found to be superior, for it is succeeded by the night, but against wisdom evil does not prevail.

She reaches mightily from one end of the earth to the other, and she orders all things well. (7:25–8:1)

Chapters 10 and 11 tell the sacred history of the Hebrew people from Wisdom's point of view. In this version of the stories of ADAM AND EVE, Cain and Abel, NOAH, ABRAHAM and Lot, JACOB, Joseph, and MOSES, Wisdom takes the place of man as the designer and controller of history.

Sirach (known as Ecclesiasticus—"The Church Book"—in the Latin Christian Church) was written around 180 B.C.E. It is the last great Wisdom text as exemplified by Proverbs and the first of the form of Judaism that developed in the rabbinical schools of the Pharisees and Sadducees. Sirach opens with the declaration, "All wisdom comes from the Lord and is with him for ever" (1:1) and goes on, "The Lord himself created wisdom; he saw her and apportioned her, he poured her out upon all his works. She dwells with all flesh according to his gift, and he supplied her to those who love him (1:9–10).

In Sirach 24, Wisdom describes her creation:

Wisdom will praise herself, and will glory in the midst of her people.

In the assembly of the Most High she will open her mouth, and in the presence of his host she will glory:

"I came forth from the mouth of the Most High, and covered the earth like a mist.

I dwelt in high places, and my throne was in a pillar of cloud.

Alone I have made the circuit of the vault of heaven and have walked in the depths of the abyss.

In the waves of the sea, in the whole earth, and in every people and nation I have gotten a possession.

Among all these I sought a resting place; I sought in whose territory I might lodge.

Then the Creator of all things gave me a commandment, and the one who created me assigned a place for my tent.

And he said, "Make you dwelling in Jacob, and in Israel receive your inheritance."

From eternity, in the beginning, he created me, and for eternity I shall not cease to exist.

In the holy tabernacle I ministered before him, and so I was established in Zion.

In the beloved city likewise he gave me a resting place, and in Jerusalem was my dominion.

So I took root in an honored people, in the portion of the Lord, who is their inheritance." (1–12)

Wisdom is also identified with the Hebrew law (chapters 23–25).

Men devoted themselves to the service of Wisdom, abandoning family ties. Rabbinic Judaism identified Wisdom with Torah, and made sacred study its form of seeking women. But Judaism made the search for Wisdom a communal affair (within the community of men) and avoided individual celibate devotion, quite a different spiritual path than that of Christians in love with God.

Biblical scholars agree that the Wisdom literature was a late entry into the Scriptures, but they can find no direct source. Possible explanations are that Wisdom was an invention of Hebrew theologians; she was the product of a long-suppressed female role in the Hebrew religion; or that she was the product of philosophers in the court of a monarch. However, during the probable time of the composition of The Wisdom of Solomon there was no king in Israel; nor does the material speak to the concerns of such an elite. The fact that a good part of the Wisdom literature exists only in the Greek language attests to a strong influence on Jewish scholars by the Greek devotion to philosophy (philosophy equals love of learning/Sophia), and Greek culture did not lack female figures of stature comparable to SOPHIA.

See SHEKINAH.

FURTHER READING

Cady, Susan, Marian Ronan, and Hal Taussig. *Sophia: The Future of Feminist Spirituality.* San Francisco: Harper and Row, 1986.

Scholem, Gershom. *Kabbalah.* New York: Dorset Press, 1987. First published 1974.

witches See DEMONS.

Wormwood

According to the book of REVELATION, the name of a FALLEN ANGEL who will bring plagues upon the earth during the end times. The name *Wormwood* means "bitterness," and it is derived from the Latin term *absinthium*.

Revelation tells of the end times of the world. It says that God sits on his throne, holding a huge book fastened by seven seals. When Christ breaks the seals, each releases a disaster upon the earth. The seventh and last seal brings seven disasters, each ushered in by the trumpet blast of an angel.

Wormwood is a star (angel) that falls from HEAVEN at the trumpet blast of the third angel, and it poisons many waters of the earth, causing multitudes to die. Revelation 8:10–11 states:

> The third angel blew his trumpet and a great star fell from heaven, blazing like a torch, and it fell on a third of the rivers and on the fountains of water. The name of the star is Wormwood. A third of the waters became wormwood, and many men died of the water, because it was made bitter.

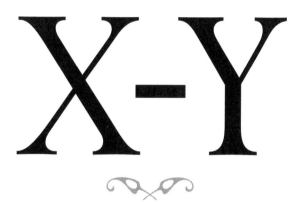

Xaphan (Zephon)
Apostate angel who attempted to set fire to HEAVEN and was cast to the bottom of the abyss. As a DEMON, Xaphan fires the fires of HELL.

Xathanael (Nathanael)
In the Gospel of Bartholomew, the sixth angel created by God.

Yabbashael
One of the seven ANGELS OF THE EARTH. Yabbashael is derived from Yabbashah, which means "the mainland."

Yarhiel (Yarheil, Yehra, Zachariel)
In the SEFER RAZIEL, angel who rules the moon.

yazatas
In ZOROASTRIANISM, angel-like beings who are legion and serve in either the heavenly (spiritual) or earthly (material) realms. Yazatas means "adorable beings." They also can be compared to celestial INTELLIGENCES and the daemons of water, air, fire, and earth.

The yazatas work for the AMARAHSPANDS, who are comparable to ARCHANGELS.

Yefefiah (Iofiel, Jefefiyah, Yofiel)
One of seven great ARCHANGELS and an angelic PRINCE of the Torah who taught the KABBALAH to MOSES. Yefefiah is sometimes identified with Metatron.

Yehudiah (Yehudiam)
A benevolent ANGEL OF DEATH who is attended by myriads of angels. Yehudiah is mentioned in the Zohar.
    See PSYCHOPOMPOI.

Yerachmiel
One of seven angels who rule the earth along with Uriel, Raphael, Michael, Gabriel, Suriel, and Raguel.

Yeshamiel
Angel who rules the sign of Libra.

Yesod See TREE OF LIFE.

YHVH (YHWH, Yahweh)
In Jewish mysticism, the Tetragrammaton, the most sacred name of God. YHVH is composed of the Hebrew letters yod-he-vau-he. It is sometimes

appended to the names of the highest angels around God to denote their power and stature. For example, in 3 ENOCH the great PRINCES of HEAVEN all have YHVH after their names.

See NAMES.

Yofiel (Iofiel, Jofiel, Yefefiah, Youfiel)

Angelic PRINCE OF TORAH who commands 53 legions of angels. Yofiel is the PRECEPTOR of the patriarch Shem, one of the three sons of NOAH, and also is a spirit of the planet Jupiter.

Z

Zaapiel (Za'afiel)

In 3 ENOCH, one of the ANGELS OF DESTRUCTION who sits in the heavenly court of law and is in charge of punishing the souls of the wicked with burning rods of coal in Gehenna (HELL).

Zaazenach

In the LEMEGETON, the ruling angel of the sixth hour of the night, called Thaazaron. Zaazenach rules 101,550 dukes and servants, who are divided into 12 orders.

Zabkiel

A ruler of the order of THRONES.

Zachariel

Angel who rules Jupiter.

Zachriel

Angel who governs memory.

Zadkiel (Tzadkiel, Zadakiel, Zedekiel, Zidekiel)

One of the nine rulers of HEAVEN, one of the seven ARCHANGELS who stand in the presence of God, chief of the order of DOMINIONS and cochief with Gabriel of the order of SHINANIM. Zadkiel means "righteousness of God." Zadkiel is said to be the angel sent by God to stop ABRAHAM from slaying ISAAC. He is sometimes identified as the ruler of the planet Jupiter. In the Zohar, Zadkiel is a chieftain along with Zophiel who assists Michael in the bearing of his standard in battle.

Zadkiel is the angel of benevolence, along with Hasdiel, and is also one of the ANGELS OF MERCY and memory.

Zagan

One of the FALLEN ANGELS and 72 spirits of SOLOMON. Zagan is a president and king who appears first as a bull with griffin wings and then as a man. He makes men clever and witty. He turns water into wine, blood into oil and oil into water, and wine into water or blood. Zagan can turn any metal into money and can make fools wise. He commands 33 legions.

Zagzagel (Zagzagael, Zagnzagiel, Zamzagiel)

PRINCE OF TORAH and Wisdom who instructs MOSES in the mystery of the Ineffable Name. Zagzagel means "divine splendor." Zagzagel is a PRINCE of the presence and a teacher of angels who speaks 70 languages. He resides in the seventh HEAVEN but guards the fourth heaven. He is identified as the angel of the burning bush. With the angels Michael and Gabriel he accompanies God who descends from heaven to take the soul of MOSES upon his death.

Zakzakiel YHVH

In 3 ENOCH, a great PRINCE of the seventh HEAVEN who is appointed to record all the merits (good deeds) of Israel upon the throne of Glory. Zakzakiel means "merit-God." Zakzakiel bows down to Anapiel.

Zaphiel (Iofiel, Zophiel)

A ruler of the order of CHERUBIM, PRINCE of the planet Saturn, and PRECEPTOR of NOAH. Zaphiel is sometimes identified as the chief of the order of THRONES.

Zaphkiel (Zaphchial, Zaphiel, Zophiel)

One of the nine ruling angels of HEAVEN, one of the seven ARCHANGELS, chief of the order of THRONES, and ruler of the planet Saturn. Zaphkiel means "knowledge of God." The alchemist Robert Fludd identified Zaphkiel as ruler of the order of CHERUBIM.

Zarall

Cherub who, with his twin Jael, guards the ARK OF THE COVENANT.

Zarika   See ZOROASTRIANISM.

Zazel

Spirit of the planet Saturn. In MAGIC Zazel is invoked in love spells and also against sudden death.

Zazriel YHVH

In 3 ENOCH, one of the PRINCES who guards the seventh hall of the seventh HEAVEN. Zazriel means "strength of God." Zazriel is the angel of divine strength and power. He bows down to Geburatiel.

Zechariah

Jewish prophet whose vision is guided and explained by an angel. Zechariah was born during the Jewish exile in Babylon. His prophecies date from 520 to 518 B.C.E. and concern a call to repentance, encouragement to the Jews who had returned from exile, prophecy of a rebuilt temple of Jerusalem, and the coming of the messianic age. His experiences are described in the book of Zechariah, part of the Old Testament. The book actually has two distinct parts: chapters 1–8 recount Zechariah's initial visions, and chapters 9–14 comprise two oracles, which probably were added in the fourth and third centuries B.C.E. by anonymous authors.

Zechariah writes that God is angry with the people for their evil deeds. In a night dream vision, Zechariah

beholds a man riding upon a red horse. The figure is an angel and he stands among myrtle trees in a glen. Behind him are red, sorrel, and white horses. The angel says that the horses have been sent by God to patrol the earth. He tells Zechariah that God is very angry with the nations. He has returned to Jerusalem in compassion and his house shall be built in it. The city shall overflow again with prosperity.

Zechariah sees four horns, which symbolize the powerful nations of the world. The angel says the horns are the forces that have scattered Judah. Zechariah then sees a man—probably another angel—who has a measuring line. Zechariah is told he will measure Jerusalem. Another angel comes forward and says that the Lord will build a wall of fire around Jerusalem and will be the glory within the city.

Zechariah is shown the high priest Joshua standing before the ANGEL OF THE LORD with Satan, in the role of the accuser, standing at his right. Joshua is dressed in filthy clothing, a symbol of the sins of the people. The Lord says he has chosen Jerusalem to rebuke Satan. The angel tells Joshua to remove his dirty clothing and he will be given new and rich garments. A clean turban

Zechariah's vision of four angels who go forth from the presence of the Lord (Gustave Doré)

is placed on Joshua's head. The Angel of the Lord tells Joshua to walk in the ways of the Lord, for which he will be rewarded and the guilt of the land will be removed.

Zechariah's angel comes again and wakes him "like a man that is wakened out of his sleep." He asks Zechariah what he sees and the prophet replies that he sees a golden lampstand with seven lamps flanked by two olive trees, probably a symbol of the unified community or God's presence on the whole earth. The angel says that the lamps are the eyes of the Lord and the olive trees represent the anointed ones who stand by the Lord. Zechariah then sees a flying scroll that measures 20 cubits in length and 10 cubits in width. The angel says the scroll is the curse that goes out over the land against everyone who sins.

The angel then shows Zechariah a woman sitting in an ephah (a container that holds approximately six gallons). Her name is Wickedness. The angel pushes her into the ephah and places a leaden weight on top of it. Two winged women, whose wings are like those of a stork, come forward and lift up the ephah between earth and HEAVEN. The angel says they will take Wickedness to the land of Shinar (Babylonia), where they will build a temple for her.

Zechariah sees four chariots pulled by red, black, white, and dappled grey horses, which are being sent out by the Lord to patrol the earth.

The rest of the vision deals with God's admonitions to the people of Jerusalem to lead proper lives, and the promise that if they obey, all things in the vision shall come to pass.

In the second part of the book of Zechariah, oracles discuss the defeat of Israel's enemies in preparation for the messianic era. Zerubbabel (a leader of exiles who returned from Babylon to Judah in 537 B.C.E.) is championed. Tyrants will fall and the dispersed Israelites will come together. God alone controls nature and history. In the coming great day of the Lord, he shall cleanse Jerusalem of sin, reestablish his covenant, and reign over all the earth. Jerusalem will lament her sin and be purged of idolatry. The enemies of Israel will be smitten by plagues.

See DREAMS AND VISIONS.

FURTHER READING
May, Herbert G., and Bruce M. Metzger, eds. *The Oxford Annotated Bible with the Apocrypha*, Revised standard version. New York: Oxford University Press, 1965.

Zehanpuryu YHVH

In 3 ENOCH, angelic PRINCE in the seventh HEAVEN who ranks higher than Metratron. Zehanpuryu means "this one sets free." Zehanpuryu is a guardian of the seventh hall of the seventh heaven, and he is a member of the heavenly court of law. According to Metatron in 3 Enoch, the angel is so named because "he is angry at the RIVER OF FIRE and quenches it in its place" (18:21). Zehanpuryu bows down to Azbogah. He also is one of the ANGELS OF MERCY.

Zepar

One of the FALLEN ANGELS and 72 spirits of SOLOMON. Zepar is a duke who appears wearing red clothing and armed like a soldier. He makes women love men and can transform them into other shapes until they have been enjoyed by their lovers. Alternately, he makes women barren.

Zephaniah

In apocalyptic literature, prophet who is escorted to HEAVEN by angels and shown the rewards of the righteous and the punishment of sinners. Zephaniah is a biblical figure, an important priest probably of royal descent. The book of Zephaniah in the Old Testament places him in the reign of Josiah (640–609 B.C.E.). In it the prophet condemns corruption and religious syncretism, and he prophesies doom, ruin, and divine judgment. In 2 Kings 25:18, he is the second-in-command priest of Jerusalem who is executed, along with other Jewish captives, by King Nebuchadnezzer of Babylon. According to 2 Chronicles 6:36, Zephaniah's son is among those named by King David to oversee the service of song in the temple.

It is unlikely that Zephaniah is the author of the Apocalypse of Zephaniah, which describes his visionary journey. Authorship is attributed to an unknown Jewish writer who probably lived in Egypt, and who borrowed Zephaniah's name in order to give weight to the testimony. The text was written in Greek between the first century B.C.E. and first century C.E. Only about one-fourth of it survives in fragments, including a quote in St. Clement of Alexandria's *Stromata*. It is not known whether or not the quote actually is part of the apocalypse.

Though preserved by Christian monks, the Apocalypse of Zephaniah contains few distinctive Christian elements. Its central theme deals with the judgment and righteousness of God that faces every person, and the mercy that God extends to those who repent. Angels record all of everyone's deeds, both good and bad, for the final accounting. The beastlike appearances of some of the angels run counter to the tradition that all angels are beautiful and brilliant.

Zephaniah goes with the ANGEL OF THE LORD, who takes him up over the city and into the heavenly spheres. He sees souls in torment and cries out to God to have compassion upon them. The angel takes him to the place of righteousness, Mount Seir (often associated with Mount Sinai). He is told by his guide that the souls of the righteous always exist in light.

The angel explains that angels sit at the gate of heaven and watch everyone. The angels of the Lord Almighty write down all of a person's good deeds and take them to the Angel of the Lord, who writes down the names of the righteous in the Book of Living. If there are no righteous deeds to record, the angels weep and pray on behalf of those souls. Angels of the accuser, who is upon the earth, write down the sins of everyone and give them to the accuser, so that he can accuse the souls when they die and come into the heavenly spheres. The accuser, who is not named, is not fallen or demonic; there are no evil spirits who seek to lead humans astray. Rather, humankind is free to make choices, and angels carry out the consequences of those choices.

After seeing the RECORDING ANGELS, Zephaniah is taken to a place where he sees thousands of thousands and myriads of myriads of angels. They are ugly, with faces like leopards and teeth like wild boars. They have eyes mixed with blood and long hair worn loose like a woman's hair. They carry scourges. Zephaniah is afraid. He is told by his angel guide that these angels are the "servants of all creation who come to the souls of ungodly men and bring them and leave them in this place" (4:6–7). When they collect the souls, they "go around with them in the air" for three days and then leave them in the place of eternal punishment. The guide assures Zephaniah that he is pure and will not be subject to the ugly angels. The ugly angels run from Zephaniah.

The guide takes Zephaniah to bronze gates and opens them to a beautiful city. The angel transforms himself. Zephaniah turns and sees a great sea that at first he thinks is water and then realizes it is a "sea of flame like a slime which casts for much flame and whose waves burn sulfur and bitumen" (6:2). The waves come closer to him.

Zephaniah then thinks that the Lord Almighty has appeared before him, and he falls down on his face and begs to be saved from distress. The figure is not that of the Lord, but of a great angel who has a body like a serpent, hair like a lioness, and teeth like a bear. Zephaniah collapses on his face in fear and prays again to the Lord to be saved.

When he rises, he sees a great angel standing before him with a perfect face shining like the glorious rays of the sun, feet like bronze, which is melted in fire, and wearing a gold girdle. Zephaniah again thinks that it is the Lord, but the angel introduces himself as "the great angel Eremiel" who watches over and cares for the

souls trapped in Hades since the end of the Flood. Eremiel identifies the beastlike angel with the serpent's body as the accuser, who accuses men in the presence of the Lord.

Eremiel shows Zephaniah two manuscripts. The first documents all of his sins and shortcomings throughout his entire life. Listed were such transgressions as failing to fast or pray at appropriate times, not visiting the sick, and so on. Zephaniah is afraid of being punished and begs God for mercy. The angel assures him he is among the righteous.

The text of the second manuscript is missing, but probably documents Zephaniah's good deeds.

Zephaniah is placed on a boat so that he can make the "crossing of the crossing place," that is, the river that separates Hades. Thousands of thousands and myriads of myriads of angels sing praises of Zephaniah, and he puts on an angelic garment and understands their language (see ANGEL LANGUAGE). Zephaniah proclaims that "this is the trial, because it is necessary that the good and the evil be weighed in balance" (8:5).

A great angel (not named) blows a golden trumpet and tells Zephaniah his name is recorded in the Book of the Living. Zephaniah tries to embrace the angel in joy, but he cannot because the angel's glory is too great. The angel goes to the righteous ones, ABRAHAM, ISAAC, JACOB, ENOCH, ELIJAH, and DAVID.

The angel then blows the trumpet again toward heaven, and it opens wide. Zephaniah sees the sea of Hades and its waves coming up to the clouds. He has visions of the souls who are sinking in the sea. He is told their sins. Those whose hands and feet are bound to their necks were bribed with gold and silver until souls of men were led astray. Those covered with mats of fire were moneylenders who collected interest. Those who are blind were catechumens who were not perfected by the word of God that they studied.

Zephaniah then sees multitudes of the righteous, who are summoned every day by trumpet sounds in heaven and on earth to pray for those who are in torment.

The last surviving chapter of Zephaniah describes the great angel blowing his trumpet again and describing how God in his wrath will destroy the earth and the heavens.

FURTHER READING

Charlesworth, James H., ed. *The Old Testament Pseudepigrapha.* Vols. 1 and 2. New York: Doubleday, 1983, 1985.

Zerachiel (Saraqael, Suriel, Verchiel)
Angel of the sun and the month of July and ruler of Leo. Zerachiel is described as one of the seven angels who "keep watch" in 1 ENOCH and 4 EZRA.

zodiac See ANGELS OF THE ZODIAC.

Zohar See KABBALAH.

Zophiel (Zaphiel)

A chieftain who assists the archangel Michael when he bears his standard in battle. Zophiel means "God's spy."

Zoroastrianism

Religion of ancient Persia based on the teachings of the prophet Zarasthustra (Zoroaster in Greek). Zoroastrianism influenced the development of Western angelologies.

Zarasthustra may have been born as early as 650 B.C.E. Historical documentation of his life is fragmentary, and documents attributed to him have been dated hundreds of years apart. RUDOLPH STEINER maintained that the first prophet named Zarasthustra lived quite earlier than recorded history and that subsequent followers were named for him. It may never be known for certain whether the original prophet or one of the followers composed the gathas, songs, or odes of the

The Three Wise Men, probably Zoroastrian priests, following the Star of Bethlehem, from a 19th-century Bible (Author's collection)

sacred book of Zoroastrianism, the *Avesta,* the religion's central doctrines.

Central Concepts

Zoroastrianism shares some common origins with polytheistic Hinduism and borrows some of its deities, but it differs from it in significant ways. Its cosmology is dualistic, and the conflict between the forces of good and evil is played out on a hierarchical scale of spiritual and material spheres. Some Hindu demigods named in the *Yashts,* a document similar to the song-cycle of the earliest Indo-Aryans, the *Rig-Veda,* are turned into angels. As Zoroastrianism was reformed, the gods and demigods called DEVAS in the *Veda* were demonized, and the class of deity called *ahura* by Iranians and *asura* by the Indians were eliminated. The exception is Ahura Mazda (later called Ohrmazd), who was elevated to the status of the one true God from whom all other divinities proceed.

Evil is a separate principle and substance standing against the good God and threatening to destroy him. Against the God stands Angra Mainyu (in Hinduism Aryaman), later Ahriman, the Destructive Spirit. The duration of this conflict is limited; Ohrmazd will defeat Ahriman. God needs man's help in his battle with the "Lie," as the principle of evil is frequently called in the ancient documents. Evil is not identified with matter. The material world is the handiwork of God, a weapon fashioned by the Deity with which to smite the Evil One. The world is the trap God sets for the devil, and in the end Ohrmazd will deal Ahriman the death blow.

According to the *Bundahishn,* or Book of the Primal Creation, the two antagonists had always existed in time, but when Ohrmazd first chants the *Ahunvar* (True Speech), the key prayer of Zoroastrianism (similar to "in the beginning was the Word" opening the Gospel of John), it reveals to Ahriman that his annihilation is certain. Assaulted by this truth, Ahriman falls unconscious for 3,000 years. Ohrmazd creates the universe, the two worlds (spiritual and material) as a weapon with which to defeat Ahriman. An unorthodox document called the *Zurvan* indicates that early creation myths varied or were altered, for in the Zervanite version, Ahriman creates first the Lying Word (the exact opposite of the *Ahunvar*) and then Akoman, the Evil Mind, which he could not do if he were unconscious.

The human soul is a spiritual being called FRAVASHI or *fravahr,* a concept that encompasses not only individual human souls and GUARDIAN ANGELS but also local GENII.

Both human body and its *fravashi* are creatures of Ohrmazd and his wife/daughter Spandarmat, the earth. The soul preexists the human body but is not eternally preexistent as in many Eastern religions. Humankind belongs to Ohrmazd and will return to him. The first Primal Man mates with Ahriman's "Demon Whore." Each individual is free to choose good or evil, but evil is an unnatural act.

Life on earth is a battle between Ohrmazd and his attendant powers on one hand and Ahriman and his demonic hordes on the other. For Zarasthustra it was a very real battle, since deva worshipers were still adherents of the traditional religion; he identified these with all that is evil.

Heavenly Helpers

The orders of Zoroastrian creation, with interplaying spheres of beings and their adversaries are full of ARCHETYPES and are similar to those in GNOSTICISM and the myths surrounding Sophia.

Ohrmazd is helped by the six AMARAHSPANDS (or Amesha Spenta), the Bounteous Immortals who are comparable to ARCHANGELS and serve as Ohrmazd's ministers. After Ohrmazd adopts Man, each of the amarahspands adopts one of the material creations. Their names are personifications of abstract concepts or virtues:

Vahuman—Good Thought, Good Mind
Artvahisht—Best Righteousness, Truth
Shahrevar—Choice Kingdom, Material Sovereignty
Spandarmat—Bounteous Rightmindedness,
   Wisdom in Piety; also identified with the earth
Hurdat—Health, Wholeness, Salvation
Amurdat—Life, Immortality

Beneath the Amarahspands are the YAZATAS ("adorable beings") who are legion and are divided into heavenly (spiritual) and earthly (material) subcategories. Ohrmazd himself leads the spiritual Yazatas, and Zarasthustra the material Yazatas. They have assignments similar to the celestial INTELLIGENCES and the daemons of water, air, fire, and earth.

Forces of Evil

Ahriman is served by a host of DEMONS, most of which are personified vices like concupiscence, anger, sloth, and heresy. There are six archdemons who oppose the amarahspands and try to destroy their good work. According to the *Bundahishn*, they are assisted by "furies in great multitude" who are "demons of ruin, pain, and growing old, producers of vexation and vile, revivers of grief, the progeny of gloom, and vileness, who are many, very numerous, and very notorious."

The six archdemons are:

Akoman, the Evil Mind, who opposes Vahuman
Andra, who opposes Artvahisht
Saru, the Tyrant, who opposes Shahrevar
Naoghatya, Arrogance, who opposes Spandarmat
Taru, Evil Hunger, who opposes Hurdat
Zarika, Evil Thirst, who opposes Amurdat

Zoroastrianism in Practice

Zoroastrians consider that their role in this world is to cooperate with nature and to lead a virtuous life; they oppose all forms of asceticism and monasticism. Their duty is to marry and rear children, for human life on earth is a sheer necessity if Ahriman is to be defeated. Agriculture is honored for making the earth fruitful, strong, and abundant in order to resist the Enemy, who is the author of disease and death.

There is a rigid dogmatism preserving the purity of the body, the care of useful animals, agricultural practice, and strict ritual observance. Celibacy is both unnatural and wicked.

On the moral plane all the emphasis is on righteousness or truth and on doing good works, for deeds are the criterion by which alone one is judged after parting this life on the "Bridge of the Requiter," the bridge of Rashn the Righteous, who impartially weighs each soul's good and evil deeds. If there is a preponderance of good, the soul proceeds to heaven, but if evil, it is dragged off to hell. If good and evil deeds are exactly equal, the soul goes to the "place of the mixed," where it experiences mild correction, and the only pains suffered are those of heat and cold. Zoroastrian hell is like the Christian purgatory in that the punishment is only temporary. The final purgation from sin takes place at the Last Judgment at the end of time. The stain left by sin is purged from all souls, and from this all without exception emerge spotless. None are punished eternally for sins committed in time.

Sin is viewed as perversity; it is a failure to recognize who is your friend and who is your enemy. Ohrmazd is one's friend and Ahriman is the enemy, from whom all evil and suffering proceed. Unlike the Western God, Ohrmazd does not permit evil, for such would give him characteristics of Ahriman. Monotheists have been deceived in this way and this represents a genuine triumph for Ahriman, for besides being the Destroyer, he is also the Deceiver, the Liar, and his deception takes the form of persuading men that evil proceeds from God. But his triumph is shortlived, for in the end all human souls, reunited with their bodies, return to Ohrmazd, who is their creator and father.

The Islamic conquest of Iran in the seventh century sent all Zoroastrian sects into disarray. Many Zoroastrians went east to India, where they are called Parsis. In present times there are only about 150,000 followers, of whom most live in and around Bombay, India.

FURTHER READING
Dhalla, Maneckji Nusservanji. *History of Zoroastrianism.* New York: Oxford University Press, 1938. Reprint AMS Press, 1977.

Zaehner, R. C. *The Dawn and Twilight of Zoroastrianism.* New York: Putnam, 1961.

Zuriel

Ruler of the order of PRINCIPALITIES and the sign of Libra. Zuriel means "my rock is God." Zuriel is one of 70 angels who protect newborn infants. (See CHILDBIRTH ANGELS.) In MAGIC he is invoked against stupidity. Zuriel is sometimes equated with Uriel and in that aspect governs the month of September.

BIBLIOGRAPHY

Adler, Mortimer J. *The Angels and Us.* New York: Collier Books/Macmillan, 1982.

Allison, Alexander W., et al. *The Norton Anthology of Poetry.* 3d ed. New York: W. W. Norton, 1983.

Altman, Nathaniel. "The Orishas: Communing with Angels in the Candomble Tradition of Brazil." In *Angel & Mortals: Their Co-creative Power.* Compiled by Maria Parisen. Wheaton, Ill.: Quest Books, Theosophical Publishing House, 1990.

Anderson, E. *The Letters of Mozart and His Family.* 3d ed. New York: Norton, 1990.

Ankarloo, Bengt, and Gustav Hennings, eds. *Early Modern European Witchcraft: Centers and Peripheries.* Oxford: Clarendon Press, 1990.

Arbel, Ilil. *Maimonides: A Spiritual Legacy.* New York: Crossroad/Herder and Herder, 2001.

Arintero, Juan. *Mystical Evolution in the Development and Vitality of the Church.* Vol. I. St. Louis: B. Herder, 1949.

Arthos, John. *Dante, Michaelangelo and Milton.* London: Routledge and Kegan Paul, 1963.

Arthur, Ruth Horman. *The Wisdom Goddess: Feminine Motifs in Eight Nag Hammadi Documents.* Lanham, Md.: University Press of America, 1984.

Attwater, Donald. *The Penguin Book of Saints.* Baltimore: Penguin Books, 1965.

———. *A Dictionary of Mary.* New York: P. J. Kennedy, 1960.

Atwater, P. M. H. "Perelandra: Cooperating Co-creatively with Nature." *New Realities* (May–June 1988): 17–20+.

Augustine. *Confessions.* Translated by F. J. Sheed. New York: Sheed and Ward, 1943, 1970.

———. *The City of God.* Translated by Marcus Dods, George Wilson, and J. J. Smith. Introduction by Thomas Merton. New York: Modern Library, 1950.

Azam, Umar. *Dreams in Islam.* Pittsburgh: Dorrance Publishing Co., 1992.

Barker, Margaret. *The Great Angel: A Study of Israel's Second God.* Louisville, Ky.: Westminster/John Knox Press, 1992.

Barnstone, Willis, ed. *The Other Bible.* San Francisco: HarperSanFrancisco, 1984.

Barrett, Francis. *The Magus.* Secaucus, N.J.: Citadel Press, 1967. First published 1801.

Barrett, William. *Death-Bed Visions: The Psychical Experiences of the Dying.* Wellingborough, England: Aquarian Press, 1986. First published 1926.

Barth, Karl. *Church Dogmatics.* Edinburgh: T and T Clark, 1960.

Battenhouse, Roy W., ed. *A Companion to the Study of St. Augustine.* New York: Oxford University Press, 1955.

Beasley-Murray, G. R. "The Interpretation of Daniel 7." *The Catholic Biblical Quarterly* 45, no. 1 (January 1985).

Bell, Rudolph. *Holy Anorexia.* Chicago: University of Chicago Press, 1985.

Berefelt, Gunnar. *A Study on the Winged Angel: The Origin of a Motif.* Stockholm: Almquist and Wiksell, 1968.

Bergquist, Lars. *Swedenborg's Dream Diary.* West Chester, Pa.: Swedenborg Foundation Publishers, 2001.

Bishop, Eric F. F. "Angelology in Judaism, Islam and Christianity." *Anglican Theological Review* 40 (January 1964).

Blavatsky, H. P. *The Secret Doctrine.* Pasadena, Calif.: Theosophical University Press, 1977. First published 1888.

Blofeld, John. *The Tantric Mysticism of Tibet.* New York: E. P. Dutton, 1970.

Blumenthal, David R. "Maimonides on Angel Names." *Hellenica and Judaica.* Edited by A. Caquot. Paris: Editions Peeters, 1986.

Bonnefoy, Yves, comp. *Mythologies.* Chicago: University of Chicago Press, 1991.

The Book of Enoch the Prophet. Translated by Richard Laurence. San Diego: Wizards Bookshelf, 1976.

The Book of Mormon: An Account Written by the Hand of Mormon upon Plates taken from the Plates of Nephi. Translated by Joseph Smith Jr. First published 1830. Salt Lake City: The Church of Christ of Latter Day Saints, 1981.

Bourke, Vernon J. *Wisdom from St. Augustine.* St. Thomas, Tex.: Center for Thomistic Studies, 1984.

Bowman, J. W. "Book of Revelation." In *The Interpreter's Dictionary of the Bible.* New York: Abingdon Press, 1962.

Bramley, William. *The Gods of Eden.* San Jose: Dahlin Family Press, 1989.

Brooke, John L. *The Refiner's Fire: The Making of Mormon Cosmology, 1644–1844.* Cambridge: Cambridge University Press, 1994.

Brown, Peter. *Augustine of Hippo.* Berkeley: University of California Press, 1967.

Budge, E. A. Wallis. *Amulets and Superstitions.* New York: Dover Publications, 1978. First published 1930.

Burckhardt, Titus. *Alchemy: Science of the Cosmos, Science of the Soul.* London: Stuart and Watkins, 1967.

Bush, Douglas, ed. *The Portable Milton.* New York: Viking Press, 1949.

Bushman, Richard L. *Joseph Smith and the Beginnings of Mormonism.* Urbana: University of Illinois Press, 1984.

Cady, Susan, Marian Ronan, and Hal Taussig. *Sophia: The Future of Feminist Spirituality.* San Francisco: Harper and Row, 1986.

Caird, G. B. *Principalities and Powers: A Study in Pauline Theology.* Oxford: Oxford University Press, 1966.

———. *A Commentary on the Revelation of St. John the Divine.* New York: Harper and Row, 1966.

Calvin, John. *Institutes of the Christian Religion.* Edited by John T. McNeill. Translated by Fred Lewis Battles. Philadelphia: Westminster Press, 1960.

Carter, George William. *Zoroastrianism and Judaism.* New York: AMS Press, 1970.

The Catechism Explained. Rockford, Ill.: Tan Books and Publishers, 1921.

Cavendish, Richard. *The Black Arts.* New York: Perigee Books, 1967.

———. *Visions of Heaven and Hell.* London: Orbis Publishing, 1970.

Cavendish, Richard, ed. *Man Myth & Magic: The Illustrated Encyclopedia of Mythology, Religion and the Unknown.* Vol. 11. New York: Marshall Cavendish, 1985.

Cellini, Benvenuto. *Autobiography.* New York: P. F. Collier, ca. 1910.

Chadwick, Henry. *Early Christian Thought and the Classical Tradition.* New York: Oxford University Press, 1966.

Charlesworth, James H., ed. *The Old Testament Pseudepigrapha.* Vols. 1 and 2. New York: Doubleday, 1983, 1985.

Chessman, Harriett Scott, ed. *Literary Angels.* New York: Fawcett Columbine, 1994.

Christian, William A. Jr. *Apparitions in Late Medieval and Renaissance Spain.* Princeton, N.J.: Princeton University Press, 1981.

Cicciari, Massimo. *The Necessary Angel.* Albany: State University of New York Press, 1994.

Clark, Mary T. *An Aquinas Reader.* New York: Fordham University Press, 1988.

Collins, Andrew. *From the Ashes of Angels: The Forbidden Legacy of a Fallen Race.* London: Signet Books, 1996.

Corbin, Henry. *History of Islamic Philosophy.* Translated by Liadain Sherrard. London: Kegan Paul International, 1993.

———. *Avicenna and the Visionary Recital.* Translated by William R. Trask. Bollingen Series 46. Princeton, N.J.: Princeton University Press, 1960, 1988.

———. *Creative Imagination in the Sufism of Ibn 'Arabi.* Translated by Ralph Manheim. Bollingen Series 91. Princeton, N.J.: Princeton University Press, 1969.

Crim, Keith, ed. *Abingdon Dictionary of Living Religions.* Nashville: Abingdon Press, 1981.

Cross, F. L. *The Early Christian Fathers.* London: Gerald Duckworth, 1960.

Crouzel, Henri. *Origen.* Translated by A. S. Worrall. San Francisco: Harper and Row, 1989.

Cruz, Joan Carroll. *Mysteries, Marvels, Miracles in the Lives of the Saints.* Rockford, Ill.: TAN Books, 1997.

Danielou, Jean. *Origen.* Translated by Walter Mitchell. New York: Sheed and Ward, 1955.

Dante Alighieri. *La Vita Nuova.* Translated by Barbara Reynolds. Harmondsworth, England: Penguin Books, 1969.

———. *The Divine Comedy.* Translated by John Ciardi. New York: W. W. Norton, 1961.

Davidson, Gustav. *A Dictionary of Angels.* New York: Free Press, 1967.

Davies, Brian. *The Thought of Thomas Aquinas.* Oxford: Clarendon Press, 1992.

Dermenghem, Emile. *Muhammad and the Islamic Tradition.* Woodstock, N.Y.: Overlook Press, 1981. First published 1955.

Dhalla, Maneckji Nusservanji. *History of Zoroastrianism.* Oxford: Oxford University Press, 1938. Reprint AMS Press, 1977.

Downing, Barry H. *The Bible & Flying Saucers.* New York: Lippincott, 1968.

Eisenman, Robert, and Michael Wise. *The Dead Sea Scrolls Uncovered.* London: Element Books, 1992.

Eliade, Mircea. *The Myth of the Eternal Return.* Princeton, N.J.: Princeton University Press, 1971. First published 1954.

———. *Shamanism.* Princeton, N.J.: Princeton University Press, 1964.

———. *Images and Symbols.* Princeton, N.J.: Princeton University Press, 1991. First published 1952.

Elledge, Scott, ed. *John Milton: Paradise Lost. An Authoritative Text*. New York: W. W. Norton, 1975.

Evans, Hilary. *Gods, Spirits, Cosmic Guardians: A Comparative Study of the Encounter Experience*. Wellingborough, England: The Aquarian Press, 1987.

Every, George. *Christian Mythology*. London: The Hamlyn Publishing Group, 1970.

Field, M. J. *Angels and Ministers of Grace: An Ethno-Psychiatrist's Contribution to Biblical Criticism*. New York: Hill and Wang, 1971.

Findhorn Community. *The Findhorn Garden*. New York: Harper and Row Perennial Library, 1975.

Flint, Valerie I. J. *The Rise of Magic in Early Medieval Europe*. Princeton, N.J.: Princeton University Press, 1991.

Fowler, Raymond. *The Watchers*. New York: Bantam Books, 1990.

Fox, Leonard, and Donald L. Rose, eds. *Conversations with Angels: What Swedenborg Heard in Heaven*. Translated by David Gladish and Jonathan Rose. West Chester, Pa.: Chrysalis Books, 1996.

Fox, Robin Lane. *Pagans and Christians*. San Francisco: Harper and Row, 1986.

Frazer, James G. *The Golden Bough*. New York: Avenel Books, 1981. First published in 1890.

———. *Folklore in the Old Testament*. New York: Avenel Books, 1988. Abridged ed.

Frymer-Kensy, Tivka. *In The Wake of the Goddess: Womens Culture and the Biblical Transformation of Pagan Myth*. New York: Fawcett Columbine Books, 1992.

Gaster, Theodor H. *The Dead Sea Scriptures*. 3d ed. Garden City, N.Y.: Anchor/Doubleday, 1976.

Gatta, John J. "Little Lower than God: Super-Angelic Anthropology of Edward Taylor." *Harvard Theological Review* 75 (July 1982): 361–368.

Gilchrist, Cherry. "Dr. Dee and the Spirits." *Gnosis*, no. 35 (Summer 1995): 33–39.

Gilson, Etienne. *The Philosophy of St. Bonaventure*. London: Sheed and Ward, 1940.

Giudici, Maria Pia. *The Angels: Spiritual and Exegetical Notes*. New York: Alba House, 1993.

Glasson, C. F. *The Revelation of John*. Cambridge: Cambridge University Press, 1965.

Goddard, David. *The Sacred Magic of Angels*. York Beach, Maine: Samuel Weiser, 1996.

Godwin, Malcom. *Angels: An Endangered Species*. New York: Simon and Schuster, 1990.

Goethe, Johann Wolfgang von. *The Autobiography of Johann Wolfgang von Goethe*. Vols. 1 and 2. Chicago: University of Chicago Press, 1976.

———. *Faust*. Edited by Cyrus Hamlin. Translated by Walter Arendt. New York: Norton, 1976.

Good, Deirdre J. *Reconstructing the Tradition of Sophia in Gnostic Literature*. Atlanta: Scholars Press, 1987.

Goodman, Lenn Evan. *Avicenna*. London: Routledge, 1992.

Graham, Billy. *Angels: God's Secret Agents*. New York: Doubleday, 1975.

Grant, Robert. "Gnostic Spirituality." In *Christian Spirituality I: Origins to 12th Century*. Edited by Bernard McGinn and John Meyendor. New York: Crossroad, 1987.

Grant, Robert J. *Are We Listening to the Angels?* Virginia Beach, Va.: A.R.E. Press, 1994.

Graves, Robert, and Raphael Patai. *Hebrew Myths*. New York: Doubleday Anchor Books, 1964.

Greene, Thomas. *The Descent from Heaven: A Study of Epic Continuity*. New Haven, Conn.: Yale University Press, 1963.

Grillot de Givry, Emile. *Witchcraft, Magic and Alchemy*. New York: Dover Publications, 1971. First published 1931.

Grosso, Michael. *The Final Choice*. Walpole, N.H.: Stillpoint, 1985.

———. "UFOs and the Myth of the New Age." *ReVision* 11, no. 3 (Winter 1989): 5–13.

———. "The Cult of the Guardian Angel." In *Angels and Mortals: Their Co-creative Power*. Compiled by Maria Parisen. Wheaton, Ill.: Quest Books, Theosophical Publishing House, 1990.

———. *The Millennium Myth: Love and Death at the End of Time*. Wheaton, Ill.: Quest Books, 1995.

Guiley, Rosemary Ellen. *The Encyclopedia of Saints*. New York: Facts On File, 2001.

———. *Dreamwork for the Soul*. New York: Berkeley Books, 1998.

———. *The Miracle of Prayer: True Stories of Blessed Healings*. New York: Pocket Books, 1995.

———. *Harper's Encyclopedia of Mystical and Paranormal Experience*. San Francisco: HarperSanFrancisco, 1991.

———. *Angels of Mercy*. New York: Pocket Books, 1994.

———. *The Encyclopedia of Witches and Witchcraft*. 2d ed. New York: Facts On File, 1999.

Guthrie, W. K. C. *The Greeks and Their Gods*. Boston: Beacon Press, 1950.

Halewood, William H. *Angels: Messengers of the Gods*. London: Thames and Hudson, 1980, 1994.

———. *Six Subjects of Reformation Art*. Toronto: University of Toronto Press, 1982.

Harkness, Deborah E. *John Dee's Conversations with Angels*. Cambridge: Cambridge University Press, 1999.

Harner, Michael. *The Way of the Shaman*. New York: Bantam Books, 1986.

Hawken, Paul. *The Magic of Findhorn*. New York: Bantam Books, 1976.

Hawthorne, G. F., and Merrill Tenney, eds. *Patristic Interpretation*. Grand Rapids: Erdman, 1975.

Heick, O. W. *A History of Christian Thought*. Philadelphia: Fortress Press, 1965.

Henson, Michael, ed. *Lemegeton: The Complete Lesser Key of Solomon*. Jacksonville, Fla.: Metatron Books, 1999.

Highet, Gilbert. "An Iconography of Heavenly Beings." *Horizon*, 3, no. 2 (November 1960): 26–49.

Hillman, James. *Archetypal Psychology.* Dallas, Tex.: Spring Publications, 1983.

Hodson, Geoffrey. *The Kingdom of the Gods.* Adyar, Madras, India: Theosophical Publishing House, 1972.

———. *The Brotherhood of Angels and Men.* Wheaton, Ill.: Theosophical Publishing House, 1982.

Hoeller, Stephan A. *The Gnostic Jung and The Seven Sermons of the Dead.* Wheaton, Ill.: Quest Books, 1982.

Howard, Jane M. *Commune with Angels.* Virginia Beach, Va.: A.R.E. Press, 1992.

Huber, Georges. *My Angel Will Go before You.* Westminster, Md.: Christian Classics, 1983.

Hultkrantz, Ake. *The Religions of the American Indians.* Berkeley: University of California Press, 1979. First published 1967.

Humann, Harvey. *The Many Faces of Angels.* Marina del Rey, Calif.: DeVorss Publications, 1991.

Hurtak, J. J. *The Scrolls of Adam and Eve: A Study of Prophetic Regenesis.* Los Gatos, Calif.: The Academy for Future Science, 1989.

———. *Pistis Sophia: A Coptic Gnostic Text with Commentary.* Los Gatos, Calif.: The Academy for Future Science, 1999.

Hyatt, Victoria, and Joseph W. Charles. *The Book of Demons.* New York: Fireside, 1974.

"Introduction to the Letters of St. Paul." *The Jerusalem Bible.* Garden City, N.Y.: Doubleday, 1966.

James, Geoffrey. *Angel Magic: The Ancient Art of Summoning and Communicating with Angelic Beings.* St. Paul, Minn.: Llewellyn Publications, 1999.

James, Jamie. *The Music of the Spheres.* New York: Grove Press, 1993.

Jonas, Hans. *The Gnostic Religion.* 2d ed. Boston: Beacon Press, 1963.

Jung, Carl G. *Collected Works.* Edited by Sir Herbert Read. Translated by R. F. C. Hull. Bollingen Series 20. Vols. 1–20. Princeton, N.J.: Princeton University Press, 1958.

———. *The Archetypes and the Collective Unconscious.* 2d ed. Bollingen Series 20. Princeton, N.J.: Princeton University Press, 1968.

———. *Memories, Dreams, Reflections.* Edited by Aniela Jaffe. Translated by Richard and Clara Winston. New York: Pantheon, 1961.

Kaplan, Aryeh. *Sefer Yetzirah: The Book of Creation.* Rev. ed. York Beach, Maine: Samuel Weiser, 1997.

King, Karen, ed. *Images of the Feminine in Gnosticism.* Philadelphia: Fortress Press, 1988.

Kirven, Robert H. *Angels in Action: What Swedenborg Saw and Heard.* West Chester, Pa.: Chrysalis Books, 1994.

Knox, W. L. *St. Paul and the Church of the Gentiles.* Cambridge: Cambridge University Press, 1939.

Koester, Helmut, ed. *Shepherd of Hermas: A Commentary.* Carolyn Osiek, commentaries. Minneapolis: Augsburg Fortress Publications, 1999.

Kramer, Heinrich, and James Sprenger. *The Malleus Maleficarum.* London: John Rodker, 1928.

Kubis, Pat, and Mark Macy. *Conversations beyond the Light: Communicating with Departed Friends & Colleagues by Electronic Means.* Boulder, Colo.: Griffin Publishing and Continuing Life Research, 1995.

Laccarriere, Jacques. *The Gnostics.* Translated by Nina Rootes. New York: City Lights, 1989.

Lachman, Gary. "Heavens and Hells: The Inner Worlds of Emanuel Swedenborg." *Gnosis,* no. 36 (Summer 1995): 44–49.

Lang, Judith. *The Angels of God: Understanding the Bible.* Hyde Park, N.Y.: New City Press, 1997.

Leaman, Oliver. *Moses Maimonides.* London: Routledge, 1990.

Legge, Francis. *Forerunners and Rivals of Christianity.* New Hyde Park, N.Y.: University Books, 1964.

Levinson, Ronald B., ed. *A Plato Reader.* Translated by B. Jowett. Boston: Houghton Mifflin, 1967.

The Life of St. Teresa of Avila by Herself. Translated by J. M. Cohen. London: Penguin Books, 1987.

Lindbergh, Charles. *The Spirit of St. Louis.* New York: Charles Scribner's Sons, 1953.

Lippman, Thomas W. *Understanding Islam: An Introduction to the Moslem World.* New York: New American Library, 1982.

Little, Gregory L. *People of the Web.* Memphis: White Buffalo Books, 1990.

Lowrie, Ernest B. *The Shape of the Puritan Mind: The Thought of Samuel Willard.* New Haven, Conn.: Yale University Press, 1974.

Luck, Georg. *Arcana Mundi: Magic and the Occult in the Greek and Roman Worlds.* Baltimore: Johns Hopkins University Press, 1985.

Lukacs, Georg. *Goethe and His Age.* New York: Grosset and Dunlap, 1969.

Luther, Martin. *The Book of Concord: The Confessions of the Evangelical Lutheran Church.* Edited and Translated by Theodore C. Tappert. Philadelphia: Fortress Press, 1959.

———. *Luther's Works.* St. Louis: Concordia, 1971.

———. *Table Talk.* Vol. 54. Edited and Translated by Theodore C. Tappert. Philadelphia: Fortress Press, 1967.

MacDonald, William Graham. "Christology and 'The Angel of the Lord.'" In *Current Issues in Biblical Patristic Interpretation.* Edited by G. F. Hawthorne and Merrill Tenney. Grand Rapids, Mich.: Eerdmans, 1975.

MacGregor, Geddes. *Angels: Ministers of Grace.* New York: Paragon House, 1988.

MacKenzie, Donald A. *Indian Myth and Legend.* Boston: Longwood Press, 1978.

Maclean, Dorothy. *To Hear the Angels Sing.* Hudson, N.Y.: Lindisfarne Press, 1990. First published by Lorian Press, 1980. 2d ed. by Morningtown Press, 1988.

Macy, Mark H. *Miracles in the Storm: Talking to the Other Side with the New Technology of Spiritual Contact.* New York: New American Library, 2001.

Maimonides. *Guide of the Perplexed.* Vols. 1 and 2. Translated by Shlomo Pines. Chicago: University of Chicago Press, 1974.

Maimonides. *Mishne Torah.* Edited by J. Cohen. Jerusalem: Mossad Harav Kook, 1964.

Margolies, Morris B. *A Gathering of Angels.* New York: Ballantine Books, 1994.

May, Herbert G., and Bruce M. Metzger, eds. *The Oxford Annotated Bible with the Apocrypha.* Revised Standard Version. New York: Oxford University Press, 1965.

———. *The New Oxford Annotated Bible with the Apocrypha.* New York: Oxford University Press, 1977.

Mays, James L., ed. *Harpers Bible Commentary.* San Francisco: HarperSanFrancisco, 1988.

McClure, Kevin. *The Evidence for Visions of the Virgin Mary.* Wellingborough, England: Aquarian Press, 1983.

———. *Visions of Bowmen and Angels: Mons 1914.* St. Austell, England: The Wild Places, ca. 1992.

McDermott, Robert A., ed. *The Essential Steiner.* San Francisco: Harper and Row, 1984.

McInerny, Ralph M. *A First Glance at St. Thomas Aquinas.* Notre Dame, Ind.: Notre Dame University Press, 1990.

McLean, Adam, ed. *A Treatise on Angel Magic.* Grand Rapids, Mich.: Phanes Press, 1990.

Mellor, Anne Kostelanetz. *Blake's Human Form Divine.* Berkeley: University of California Press, 1974.

Melton, J. Gordon, ed. *Encyclopedia of Occultism & Parapsychology.* 5th ed. Detroit: Gale Group, 2001.

Mercantante, Anthony S. *An Encyclopedia of World Mythology and Legend.* Frenchs Forest, Australia: Child and Associates Publishing, 1988.

Moody, Raymond A. *The Light Beyond.* New York: Bantam Books, 1988.

———. *Reflections on Life after Life.* Harrisburg, Pa.: Stackpole Books, 1977.

———. *Life after Life.* Georgia: Mockingbird Books, 1975.

Morewedge, Parvis. *The Mystical Philosophy of Avicenna.* Binghamton: Global Publications at State University of New York at Binghamton, 2001.

Morley, Henry. *The Life of Henry Cornelius Agrippa.* London: Chapman and Hall, 1856.

Moore, R. Laurence. "The Occult Connection? Mormonism, Christian Science and Spiritualism." In *The Occult in America.* Edited by John Godwin. New York: Doubleday, 1982.

Murphy, Michael, and Rhea A. White. *The Psychic Side of Sports.* Reading, Mass.: Addison-Wesley, 1978.

Myers, Frederic W. H. *Human Personality and Its Survival of Bodily Death.* Vols. 1 and 2. New ed. New York: Longmans, Green, 1954. First published 1903.

Nasr, Seyyed Hossein. *An Introduction to Islamic Cosmological Doctrines.* Boulder, Colo.: Shambhala, 1978.

Nasr, Seyyed Hossein, and Oliver Leaman, eds. *History of Islamic Philosophy.* London: Routledge, 1996.

Nigg, Walter. *Warriors of God: The Great Religious Orders and Their Founders.* Translated by Mary Ilford. New York: Alfred Knopf, 1959.

Oliphant, Mrs. *Francis of Assisi.* London: Macmillan, 1898.

Osis, Karlis. *Deathbed Observations by Physicians and Nurses.* Monograph No. 3. New York: Parapsychology Foundation, 1961.

One Hundred Saints. Boston: Little, Brown, 1993.

Osis, Karlis, and Erlendur Haraldsson. *At the Hour of Death.* Rev. ed. New York: Hastings House, 1986.

O'Sullivan, Fr. Paul. *All about the Angels.* Rockford, Ill.: Tan Books and Publishers, 1990. First published 1945.

Pagels, Elaine. *The Gnostic Gospels.* New York: Random House, 1979.

———. *The Origin of Satan.* New York: Random House, 1995.

Parente, Fr. Pascal P. *The Angels: The Catholic Teaching on the Angels.* Rockford, Ill.: Tan Books and Publishers, 1973. First published 1961.

Parisen, Maria, comp. *Angels & Their Co-creative Power.* Wheaton, Ill.: Quest Books, 1990.

Parish, James Robert. *Ghosts and Angels in Hollywood Films.* Jefferson, N.C.: McFarland, 1994.

Patai, Raphael. *The Jewish Alchemists.* Princeton, N.J.: Princeton University Press, 1994.

Paul, Erich Robert. *Science, Religion, and Mormon Cosmology.* Urbana: University of Illinois Press, 1992.

Peers, Glenn. *Subtle Bodies: Representing Angels in Byzantium.* Berkeley, Calif.: University of California Press, 2001.

Pernoud, Regine. *Joan of Arc: By Herself and Her Witnesses.* New York: Dorset, 1964. First published 1962.

Peters, F. E. *Muhammad and the Origins of Islam.* Albany: State University of New York Press, 1994.

Peterson, Eric. *The Angels and the Liturgy.* New York: Herder and Herder, 1964.

Pseudo-Dionysius: The Complete Works. New York: Paulist Press, 1987.

Randolph, Vance. *Ozark Magic and Folklore.* New York: Dover Publications, 1964. First published 1947.

Rawson, Philip. *Sacred Tibet.* London: Thames and Hudson, 1991.

Remy, Nicolas. *Demonolatry.* Secaucus, N.J.: University Books, 1974. First published 1595.

Ring, Kenneth. *Heading toward Omega.* New York: William Morrow, 1984.

———. *The Omega Project.* New York: William Morrow, 1992.

———. *Life at Death.* New York: Coward, McCann and Geoghegan, 1980.

Robinson, James M., ed. *The Nag Hammadi Library in English.* San Francisco: Harper and Row, 1977.

Rogerson, John. "Wrestling with the Angel: A Study in Historical and Literary Interpretation." In *Hermeneutics, the*

Bible, and Literary Criticism. Edited by Ann Loades and Michael McLain. New York: St. Martin's Press, 1992.

Rorem, Paul. "The Uplifting Spirituality of Pseudo-Dionysius." In *Christian Spirituality.* Vol. I. Edited by Eivert Cousins. New York: Crossroads, 1985.

Russell, Jeffrey Burton. *The Devil: Perceptions of Evil from Antiquity to Primitive Christianity.* Ithaca, N.Y.: Cornell University Press, 1977.

———. *Lucifer: The Devil in the Middle Ages.* Ithaca, N.Y.: Cornell University Press, 1984.

———. *A History of Witchcraft.* London: Thames and Hudson, 1980.

Savedow, Steve. *Sepher Rezial Hemelach: The Book of the Angel Rezial.* York Beach, Maine: Samuel Weiser, 2000.

Scholem, Gershom. *Kabbalah.* New York: Dorset Press, 1987. First published 1974.

Schroff, Lois. *The Archangel Michael.* Herndon, Va.: Newlight Books, 1990.

Schwartz, Howard. *Gabriel's Palace: Jewish Mystical Tales.* New York: Oxford University Press, 1993.

Scott, Alan. *Origin and the Life of the Stars.* Oxford: Clarendon Press, 1994.

Seligmann, Kurt. *The Mirror of Magic.* New York: Pantheon Books, 1948.

Shearer, Alistair. *The Hindu Vision.* London: Thames and Hudson, 1993.

Sheperd, A. P. *Rudolf Steiner: Scientist of the Invisible.* Rochester, Vt.: Inner Traditions International, 1954, 1983.

Shipps, Jan. *Mormonism: The Story of a New Religious Tradition.* Urbana: University of Illinois Press, 1985.

Singer, June. *Seeing through the Visible World: Jung, Gnosis, and Chaos.* San Francisco: Harper and Row, 1990.

Snugg, Richard P., ed. *Jungian Literary Criticism.* Evanston, Ill.: Northwestern University Press, 1992.

Sogyal, Rimpoche. *The Tibetan Book of Living and Dying.* Edited by Patrick Gaffney and Andrew Harvey. New York: HarperSanFrancisco, 1992.

Spangler, David. *Revelation: The Birth of a New Age.* Elgin, Ill.: The Lorian Press, 1976.

Stanley, Michael, ed. "Angelic Nature: From Works of Emanuel Swedenborg." In *Angels & Mortals: Their Cocreative Power.* Compiled by Maria Parisen. Wheaton, Ill.: Quest Books, Theosophical Publishing House, 1990.

Steiner, Rudolf. *Planetary Spheres and Their Influence on Man's Life on Earth and in the Spiritual Worlds.* London: Rudolf Steiner Press, 1982.

———. *The Four Seasons and the Archangels.* Bristol, England: Rudolf Steiner Press, 1992.

———. *An Autobiography.* New translation. Blauvelt, N.Y.: Rudolf Steiner Publications, 1977.

Steinmetz, Dov, M. D. "Moses's Revelation on Mount Horeb as a Near-Death Experience." *Journal of Near-Death Studies* 11, no. 4 (Summer 1993): 199–203.

Stoudt, John Joseph. *Jacob Boehme: His Life and Thought.* New York: Seabury Press, 1968.

Sugrue, Thomas. *There Is a River: The Story of Edgar Cayce.* New York: Holt, Rhinehart and Winston, 1942.

Suster, Gerald. *John Dee: Essential Readings.* London: Crucible, 1986.

Swedenborg, Emanuel. *Heaven and Hell.* Translated by George F. Dole. New York: Swedenborg Foundation, 1976.

Teague, Raymond. *Reel Spirit: A Guide to Movies That Inspire, Explore and Empower.* Lee's Summit, Mo.: Unity House, 2000.

Thomas Aquinas. *Summa Theologiae.* Edited by Timothy McDermott. Allen, Tex.: Christian Classics, 1989.

Thomas, Keith. *Religion and the Decline of Magic.* New York: Charles Scribner's Sons, 1971.

Thompson, C. J. S. *The Lure and Romance of Alchemy.* New York: Bell Publishing, 1990. First published 1932.

Three Books of Occult Philosophy Written by Henry Cornelius Agrippa of Nettesheim. Edited and annotated by Donald Tyson. Translated by James Freake. St. Paul, Minn.: Llewellyn Publications, 1995.

Trachtenberg, Joshua. *Jewish Magic and Superstition: A Study in Folk Religion.* New York: Berhman's Jewish Book House, 1939.

Turnbull, Grace H., ed. *The Essence of Plotinus.* Translated by Stephen MacKenna. New York: Oxford University Press, 1948.

Turner, Alice K. *The History of Hell.* New York: Harcourt Brace, 1993.

van der Toorn, Karel, Bob Becking, and Pieter W. van der Horst, eds. *Dictionary of Deities and Demons in the Bible.* 2d ed. Grand Rapids, Mich.: William B. Eerdmans, 1999.

Waite, Arthur Edward. *The Book of Black Magic and of Pacts.* York Beach, Maine: Samuel Weiser, 1972.

Walsh, Michael, ed. *Butler's Lives of the Saints.* Concise Edition. San Francisco: Harper and Row, 1985.

Walshe, M., ed. *Meister Eckhardt.* London: Watkins, 1981.

Weeks, Andrew. *Boehme: An Intellectual Biography.* Binghamton: State University of New York at Binghamton Press, 1991.

Wilson, Ian. *Stigmata: An Investigation into the Mysterious Appearance of Christ's Wounds in Hundreds of People from Medieval Italy to Modern America.* San Francisco: Harper and Row, 1989.

Wilson, Peter Lamborn. *Angels.* New York: Pantheon Books, 1980.

Winn, Kenneth H. *Exiles in a Land of Liberty: Mormons in America 1830–1846.* Chapel Hill: University of North Carolina Press, 1991.

The Works of Philo Complete and Unabridged. Translated by C. D. Yonge. Hendrickson, 1993.

Wright, Machaelle Small. *Behaving as If the God in All Life Mattered.* Jeffersonton, Va.: Perelandra, 1987.

Zaehner, R. C. *The Dawn and Twilight of Zoroastrianism.* New York: Putnam, 1961.

Zaleski, Carol. *Otherworld Journeys: Accounts of Near-Death Experience in Medieval and Modern Times.* New York: Oxford University Press, 1987.

Zimdars-Swartz, Sandra L. *Encountering Mary.* Princeton, N.J.: Princeton University Press, 1991.

Zimmer, Heinrich. *Myths and Symbols in Indian Art and Civilization.* Princeton, N.J.: Princeton University Press, 1946.

Zohar: The Book of Enlightenment. Translated by Daniel Chanan Matt. Ramsey, N.J.: Paulist Press, 1983.

Zumkeller, Adolar. *Augustine's Ideal of the Religious Life.* Translated by Edmund Colledge. New York: Fordham University Press, 1986.

INDEX

Page numbers in **bold** indicate main entries; page numbers followed by *f* indicate illustrations.

7500